PHILIP FRENEAU

Champion of Democracy

PHILIP FRENEAU

CHAMPION OF DEMOCRACY

By Jacob Axelrad

UNIVERSITY OF TEXAS PRESS, AUSTIN & LONDON

Title page portrait of Philip Freneau by courtesy of the
New York Public Library

Library of Congress Catalog Card No. 66-15699
Copyright © 1967 Jacob Axelrad
All rights reserved
Printed by The University of Texas Printing Division, Austin
Bound by Universal Bookbindery, Inc., San Antonio

To
my wife
KATE

PREFACE

No book is an island, entire of itself. This paraphrase of the poet John Donne will be disputed by no writer, certainly by none who has ever attempted to portray the soul and spirit of another human being. An old Chinese proverb has it that no man can be truly judged until the last nail shall have been driven into his coffin, for only then, if then, is it at all possible to assess what has happened to him, how it has happened, and above all, why it has happened. A true appraisal of a man is scarcely possible without an understanding of his work, his hopes and ambitions, his friends, and his enemies; these and all other witnesses who may give testimony about the man must be heard, their evidence weighed, and a conclusion derived as far as possible that shall at the very least approximate the truth about him. The goal should, of course, be the whole truth; and to achieve this as nearly as possible I have gone to many places, examined many documents, read many books.

Philip Freneau, an essentially simple man, was also a poet, and no poet, however simple, could avoid the complexities of the revolutionary era in which he lived. By force of circumstance the poet also became a soldier, a sailor, a philosopher and teacher, a journalist and pamphleteer, a politician and a revolutionist. Such a man was sometimes too difficult to understand. His Princeton classmate James Madison understood him, and so did Thomas Jefferson. The patriots who froze at Valley Forge and in far-flung camps of the Revolutionary War—they also understood him as they sang his songs and read his poems, often written so that they could not possibly misunderstand his meaning.

Others were outraged by what they considered sheer propaganda in an unworthy cause by an irresponsible newsmonger, by one who often indulged in senseless slander to achieve not his own ambition, but the ambitions of others, of the democratic upstarts who demanded revolutionary changes after a long and bloody war. Perhaps it was not strange that Washington should refer to the first American poet as "that rascal Freneau," or that John Adams (and his good wife Abigail) or Alexander Hamilton should find many reasons for impeaching the poet's honesty and integrity. In reality, while Thomas Paine had appealed to the common man of America in a time that tried men's souls, Philip Freneau was equally busy urging that common man to reveal that he did indeed have a soul.

I must acknowledge my great indebtedness to all who have been so helpful to me in the long and laborious task which, after many interruptions and diversions, I have at last completed. Especially and most important of all I wish to record my profound gratitude to Professor Lewis Leary of Columbus University without whose scholarly work, *That Rascal Freneau*, this biography would have been much more difficult to accomplish. More than this, Dr. Leary gave me every help and encouragement as I proceeded to its conclusion. I also wish to thank Dr. Irving Brant for his help and suggestions about material on James Madison; to Dr. Philip Marsh I am grateful for his many courtesies in responding to my appeals for information about Freneau garnered by him over many years of research; to Dr. Broadus Mitchell, an authority on Alexander Hamilton and the author of a perceptive biography of that statesman, I extend my sincere appreciation. Finally, I wish to thank Miss Doris Cook, curator of the Connecticut Historical Society, for her work in verifying for me the material by Hamilton on Freneau. The debt which I owe to librarians and assistants—in particular to the staffs of the Congressional Library; the Rutgers University Library; the Princeton University Library; the Pennsylvania Historical Society; the Monmouth County Historical Association; the Public Library of the Municipality of St. Thomas and St. John, Virgin Islands; the New York Public Library; and the New York University Library—is acknowledged with sincere thanks.

The portrait which appears as a frontispiece to this volume was obtained from the Picture Collection of the New York Public Library. It is the one used in Freneau's *Poems Relating to the American Revolution, with a Memoir by E. A. Duyckinck*, published in 1865. According to Duyckinck (p. xxxi) this portrait (engraved by F. Halpin) was "sketched by an artist at the suggestion and dictates of several members of the poet's family . . . It was pronounced by them a fair representation." His daughter, his grandson, and his adopted son "were among those who pronounced it a satisfactory likeness." The same portrait appears in *A Library of American Literature* (edited by H. C. Stedman and Ellen Mackay Hutchinson), Vol. 3, p. 445, as well as in S. G. W. Benjamin, "Notable Editors between 1776 and 1800," in *Magazine of American History,* XVII (January–June 1887), 121. See also Edwin Salter and G. C. Beckman, *Old Times in Old Monmouth,* pp. 110–111.

The Utopian society which Philip Freneau envisioned for his country was something quite new in the thought and literature of his time. In some of the finest poems and prose works of his day, with almost clairvoyant power and uncanny accuracy, he prophesied the development of the new world. He saw clearly the broad democratic vistas that stretched from revolutionary fervor to great social and political goals. In his life, as in his work, he sought only the enhancement of the rights of man, and according to his strength he carried the everlasting hope, voiced a century later by Abraham Lincoln, that America was and would always remain the last best hope of man—forever striving for, if never achieving, the great society.

JACOB AXELRAD

CONTENTS

PHILIP FRENEAU
Champion of Democracy

"Be steadfast in the covenant, and be conversant therein,
and grow old in the work of thy commandments."
Ecclesiasticus

"Of liberty and life; sweet liberty,
Without whose aid the noblest genius fails."
Philip Freneau

1. IN THE BEGINNING

PIERRE FRESNEAU, wine merchant, farmer, lumberman, and land speculator, died at his home in Mount Pleasant, Monmouth County, New Jersey, on October 17, 1767. As he was laid in his grave in Trinity Churchyard in New York, his elder son, Philip, noted the sad event in his father's letterbook. "Here ends," he wrote, "a Book of Vexation, Disappointments, Loss and Plagues, that sunk the Author to his grave short of 50 years."[1] Many years later the same words might have been written of Philip himself by *his* son—if he had had one. As his life span had been greater, his vexations were more frequent. As his nature was more combative, his disappointments were greater. He also knew many losses and passed through many plagues. Suffering, common to all men, was no stranger to the Fresneaus. One thing more they all had in common. They were all rebels.

Pierre Fresneau, born in New York in 1718,[2] had only a legendary knowledge of the persecutions to which his forebears had been subjected in their native France. As Huguenots, they had been suffered to worship God in a manner not approved by the Catholic Church, and the Edict of Nantes was a compromise, which, like all compromise, solved nothing save for the moment. For the moment only, it had solved the problem of Huguenot heresy. Safe for a while from religious persecution, they had turned to the business of making a living.

The Fresneaus had a long history of sober and industrious pursuits on the small island of Oléron[3] in the Bay of Biscay, not far from La

[1] Pierre Fresneau's Letter Book, final page, in Freneau Collection (Rutgers).

[2] Huguenot Society of America Collection, Register of Births, Marriages and Deaths of the Eglise Française à la New York, I, 122 ff.

[3] Hammell Notes, Mss.; and Lewis Leary, *That Rascal Freneau*, pp. 4, 365 n.

Rochelle, a city that was already ancient in the year 1590, when Pierre's ancestor, Philip P. Fresneau, may have sought there some diversions not to be found in his remote and secluded island of Oléron. But that history did not save them from persecution. For heresy there was no defense; and industry, or sobriety, was no shield for rebels. Philip Fresneau's grandson, Jean, like his father and grandfather before him, also learned this lesson, and in learning it, he also learned one other lesson. To be a rebel, to indulge in the fantasy of freedom, was a dangerous proceeding, fraught with the most tragic possibilities. Jean, attempting to elude the long arm of the Church, was captured off the coast of Brittany. The rest of his years were spent in a dark cell, behind high walls, with no other record of his end than the meager word of a son who survived him.[4] André, the son, was perhaps content to remain in Oléron, to marry, to enjoy without contention his little round of life, but his own son, named André after him, was not content. When the revocation of the Edict of Nantes was proclaimed in 1685, André, the son, was certain that no compromise of conscience could long endure, and attached himself to the exodus of Huguenots from the province of Aunis and the coast of Saintogne to the free city of London across the channel.[5] Here, though they possessed nothing— not even the language—they were safe from hanging. At home, if they had even been caught in public worship, they would have been subject to the extreme penalty. They were no martyrs, and if they were nonconformists, dissenters, and rebels, it was life, not death, that they sought in abandoning the past and fleeing to the future. The future, more than the past, was the special concern of young André himself, for whom the slums of London, though free, had little more appeal than the prison house of France from which he had escaped. A man needs more than liberty—if liberty is defined as little else than poverty and bleakness. Men may even give up their freedom for a change of prospect, for a lure beyond the horizon that beckons with the siren song of safety. Others will venture not for safety alone, but for serenity above all other things, for an inward composure that is the safest haven of all. At thirty-seven, André, with neither safety nor serenity in any part of his past, considered well the future, and saw it in the new

---

[4] Leary, *That Rascal Freneau*, p. 4.

[5] David C. A. Agnew, *Protestant Exiles from France in the Reign of Louis XIV*, pp. 32, 43–69. See also final chapter of O. I. A. Roche, *The Days of the Upright: A History of the Huguenots;* and Albert F. Koehler, *The Huguenots or Early French in New Jersey*, p. 9.

world beyond the seas, equally far from the persecutions of his old home and the poverty of his new one. With little more than the one possession which he prized above all others—the old family Bible on whose flyleaf was carefully noted the genealogy of his family from the year 1590— he sailed for America. In 1709 he reached the small, somnolent seaport of New York.[6]

André did not know it, but scarcely three years earlier the religious liberty he was now seeking in America had been denied in this city to almost all but communicants of the English Church. The founder of the Presbyterian Church in America, Francis Mackenzie, had been jailed in 1706 for presuming to preach without a license. Lord Cornbury, one of the worst of provincial governors, had been replaced in 1708 by Lord Lovelace, who was scarcely better. Soon after André's arrival, General Robert Hunter, one of the best governors, was installed in New York, which became, with his accession, a refuge not only of Huguenots, but of all the persecuted of whatever faith. Hunter himself brought over from England nearly three thousand Palatines, wards of Queen Anne, who were fugitives from the religious fury of Louis XIV of France. Louis, seeking to hunt out heretical Huguenots in Germany, trampled on heretical Lutherans as well. Under Governor Hunter, there would be no persecutions, no arrests for preaching; his own experiences as a prisoner of France, his friendship with men like Dean Swift, Addison, and Steele, his keen intellect and broad sympathies would not suffer the oppression of the mind or conscience of any man. Other oppressions he was powerless to prevent. The practice of slavery was accepted in the new world. At the foot of Wall Street a slave market would soon flourish, while sailing vessels with such strange names as *Good Prophet* brought in cargoes of bewildered and shackled Negroes in one of the most lucrative traffics of the time. Not conscience but color was still in fetters.[7]

The stalwart immigrant who had come to America to make his fortune would seek it elsewhere than on the auction block of liberty. His people had always been merchants of the things men needed— not of men themselves. André, joining with other Huguenots likeminded for opportunity in the land of promise, managed to acquire

[6] Freneau Family Bible; M. S. Austin, *Philip Freneau,* pp. 48–49; and Leary, *That Rascal Freneau,* p. 365 n.

[7] Ann Maury, *Memoirs of a Huguenot Family,* p. 112; M. J. R. Lamb, *History of the City of New York,* Vol. 3, p. 419; Albert Ullman, *A Landmark History of New York,* p. 67.

some tracts of land in northern New Jersey at the same time that he
engaged in the West Indian trade in wine and sugar. It was not long
before he achieved the status of a freeman of the city of New York,
and became the owner of a warehouse on the waterfront in which
he stored his increasing imports of sugar, rum, indigo, and snuff. He
needed only a house of his own, and a wife to adorn it, to make him
one of the substantial citizens of New York. The house, close by
Bowling Green, was soon bought, and Marie Morin, seventeen and
comely, the daughter of Pierre Morin, a Huguenot immigrant like
André himself, was very willingly installed in it as his wife on June
17, 1710.[8]

Nor was that all. André, alert to his own affairs, did not forget those
of his community either. As the star of his fortunes rose higher in the
heavens, his fellow townsmen took notice of him with mounting interest. They honored him with positions of high trust as a legal peti-
tioner and administrator; they chose him as an elder of the important
Church of Esprit, and elected him assessor from the East Ward of
New York. As his honors grew, so did his business prosper. More
tracts of land were added to those already held in Jersey, this time in
Middlesex and Monmouth Counties, and other acres were obtained
also in New York. André became a shareholder in a copper mine in
Simsbury, Connecticut, while his trade with the West Indies grew to
really respectable proportions. As was quite proper for a man in his
position, he acquired a "negro woman slave" to help about the house.
Nothing seemed to be lacking to his happiness—not even the children,
who were provided with the greatest contentment by his devoted
Marie.[9]

But the fortunes of men—like men themselves—are unpredictable.
In the case of André they were destined to a precipitous fall. The death
of his beloved Marie in 1721 was a blow from which André, who
was a practical man, would soon recover, and the five children who
survived her would help him over the short span of his grief. Esther,
the new wife, who was probably the sister of the deceased Marie,

---

[8] New York City, Roll of Freemen, in New York Historical Society Collections, 1885, XVIII, p. 9. See also Huguenot Society Collection, Register, I,
122 ff.; John J. Latting, Collection of Freneau Papers, January 1, 1710. On the
Marriage of "Andries Freneau" and Marie Morin, see Leary, *That Rascal
Freneau*, p. 366 n.

[9] New York City, *Minutes of the Common Council of the City of New York,
1675–1776*, pp. 181, 210.

would soon replace the love he had lost. Some losses it was more difficult to replace. The copper mine yielded almost no profit at all. A cargo of snuff which was adjudged contraband led to interminable litigations, and the Connecticut properties were sold to pay clamoring creditors. The load of adversity that piled up on the defeated André was too heavy for him to carry. In the immemorial manner of men, he dumped it all when, on August 7, 1725, he departed this life, leaving his widow and children in such financial straits that they were compelled to move from New York to "their dwelling house at New Hanover in Symsbury."[10]

His sons, as time would show, fared no better than he, and one of them, Andrew, the oldest, would fare even worse. After a checkered career as merchant and speculator, he disappeared altogether for nearly ten years, to be discovered at last in the debtor's prison in New York, a hopeless bankrupt. Francis, the youngest of the boys, essaying the same route to affluence, went the same way to bankruptcy. He did not land in a debtor's prison, however. He succeeded in escaping to Madeira, and at his death on the island of Surinam in 1744 it fell to the lot of Pierre, the last surviving of André's three sons, to settle his tangled affairs. Pierre, who had settled in Madeira some time before, was considered—and considered himself—a very successful businessman. All the Freneaus were businessmen. And all of them failed in business. Pierre would be no exception.[11]

Like his father and grandfather before him, Pierre was a wine factor, a dealer in sundry merchandise from beeswax to Indian corn, and a purveyor of codfish. He too had encountered good times and bad, the bad always seemingly more frequent than the good. Despite his appeals for help to relatives, to friends, to some of the great names in New York with whom he had a financial or social acquaintance— men like Abraham Van Courtlandt, Samuel Livingston, Abram de Peyster, and Anthony Rutgers—his affairs went unsteadily from bad to worse until it was clear even to him that his business was irretrievably lost, his prospects for the future destroyed beyond the hope of resurrection. Even his redoubled efforts at recoupment by long and hazardous journeys on horseback through the American Colonies, after quitting Madeira in 1758, availed him nothing. Neither Philadelphia, nor the "western parts," nor the Carolinas, in which he labored for a

[10] James Alexander Papers, Mss., Box III; also *Decree in the Case of Solomon de Midina etc. against Rene Het etc.*, 1728.

[11] Pierre Fresneau's Letter Book, June 16, 1749.

new trial with fortune, offered any promise more substantial than the false one he had forsaken in Madeira.[12]

One thing did happen which Pierre considered of good omen. In his travels though New Jersey he met the young and buxom daughter of a thriving Scotch yeoman from Monmouth County. Agnes Watson, at twenty-three, was more than a desirable match for a man who had little more than honesty, perseverance, and a succession of failures to offer her. On March 12, 1750, the day he married Agnes Watson, in addition to a thrifty and practical wife, Pierre also acquired her prosperous and close-knit family. Her father, her brothers, her uncles, all of them sturdy and independent planters, accepted Pierre as one of themselves, a son and a brother—as a friend and an equal.[13]

Pierre, more confident of the future than ever before, still thinking of great ventures in business and of fortunes far removed from mere tilling of the soil, returned to New York, the beckoning gateway to fortune. He installed his bride in a small home on Frankfort Street, certain that the future would be as fair as the lady who was soon to present him with a child.[14]

When the child was born, on January 2, 1752 (O.S.), he was well content. It was a boy, whom he named Philip Morin Fresneau.[15]

[12] *Ibid.*
[13] State of New Jersey, *Marriage Records, 1665–1800,* F29.
[14] Leary, *That Rascal Freneau,* p. 366 n.
[15] Freneau Family Bible; Hammell Notes, Mss.; Huguenot Society Collection, Register, I, 122 ff.

2. FATHER AND SON

THE SUN, once more slowly rising on the fortunes of Pierre Fresneau, was intermittently clouded during the decade that followed the birth of his son. There was always the warmth of the Watsons to replace its diminished heat if not its light. When the smallpox epidemic struck the City of New York during the spring of 1752, Pierre could escape its murderous threat to his first-born by retreating to New Jersey, to the pest-free and sweet-smelling air of the Monmouth countryside, where he already owned a house of his own, built on land given by the Watsons. It was neither a large house nor a fine one, yet it did answer a deep yearning in Pierre, as in all men, for a piece of the good earth, a refuge in time of need from the compulsions of mundane realities. Moreover, the roving spirit that was still strong in him was by ever so little allayed by the wide-reaching horizons, the nearness of the sea, and the gently rolling hills that mantled Locust Grove, the Jersey home.[1]

The name which Pierre had given to his "estate" was no more fanciful than that of the secluded hamlet in which it was set. Mount Pleasant was not even a hamlet, but it did rest on a rise of ground and was nestled in wooded lands that reached all the way to Middletown Point, close by the edge of the sea.[2] Pierre's estate of some hundred acres, "more or less," was only a pinpoint in all that vast expanse of field and forest, but to the west lay the far greater tracts of the devout and hard-working farmers of Dutch, Scotch-Irish, and English stock, who cultivated their fields of corn and wheat with a single-minded devotion to duty; while to the south, if one looked out from the eminence of the Navesink hills, the jagged contours of the coast were

[1] Rhea and Wickoff, Mss. Ledger A, pp. 41–42; Freneau Family Bible.
[2] W. J. Mills, *Historic Houses of New Jersey*, p. 164.

plainly to be seen, and on the blue-green waters some sails were always billowing before the wind. The vessels moved slowly by until they were lost below the rim of the sea, and Pierre, watching them go, often wished that he could follow them with more than his eyes. He had "become quite a farmer," as he informed his friends in Madeira, but then he hastened to reassure them. "But despair not (if God assists me) to be concerned once more with my favorite isle."[3]

He *was* concerned. Not long after the birth of Philip, he set sail again for Madeira, though he stayed there only for a short time. He could pick up none of the threads of his ravelled wine trade, and this time he resolved never to try again. It was, moreover, no easy matter to leave a young and blooming wife for months at a time, to say nothing of an infant son who needed a father's guidance and affection. If the "estate" afforded him no living, and the wine trade was too sour for salvage, there was doubtless other merchandise that might do better. The Watsons, of course, would help him. They built for Pierre a sufficient but modest warehouse "near a convenient landing," where dry goods and nonperishable produce could be stored for shipment to other ports.[4] What he needed even more than a warehouse, even as much as dry goods or produce, was cash, the solvent of most troubles, those of business no less than others. But cash was something the Watsons had little of. Their substance was in the earth, in lands richly burdened with heavy stands of timber, in fields furrowed and sowed with seed. Cash was a "very scarce article" with men who lived on the soil or labored with their hands.[5] Pierre had never done either of these, yet he too had no hard currency. The new venture like the old ones also failed, though he did succeed in adding to his modest landholdings still other acres, and to his small family still other children. With the passage of time, Agnes gave birth to a daughter, Mary, to another son, Peter, and to a fourth child, Margaret. As the household grew so grew the acres also. From his brother-in-law, David Watson, Pierre acquired some hundred acres in East New Jersey for five pounds and "love and affection";[6] another hundred or more he bought

[3] Pierre Fresneau's Letter Book, May 13, 1756, in Freneau Collection (Rutgers).

[4] *Ibid.*, July 9, 1754.

[5] Lewis Leary, "Philip Freneau's Father," *The Rutgers University Library Journal*, II (June 1939), 46–52.

[6] Freneau Family Bible; Freneau, *The Poems of Philip Freneau* (ed. F. L. Pattee), Vol. 1, p. xv; M. S. Austin, *Philip Freneau*, p. 65; and Monmouth County Deeds and Mortgages, Mss., K.60.

at Boles Mills, and still other tracts with a sawmill on the creek close
by. Most of the land was leased to tenants for a stipulated rental—
but the rentals were rarely paid. When Pierre objected that this was
entirely unbusinesslike, he was on sure ground, both morally and
legally. When, in addition, he lost his temper, he was still on sure
ground morally, but no longer legally. For his pains, he was arrested
for "making a commotion."[7] Neither the rents nor the paltry profits
from the Simsbury mines provided sufficient provender, in any event,
for the growing family at Locust Grove. The sawmill did return a
meager income, and the produce from his farm and grain field a little
more. Assisted by occasional fees for translating from the French
into English some legal documents such as the will of Henry Gerbeau,
Pierre was able to support his brood in a manner that was accounted
adequate if not luxurious. Of equal importance, in the New York
circles where his business often took him, he was highly thought of
and respectfully referred to as "Peter Fresneau, Gent."[8]

It was a good and simple environment in which the little lad, Philip,
was reared. Both Agnes and Pierre were devout people, while Pierre
loved to read books that were not confined to the words of God alone.
He had a well-stocked library of his own, and Shakespeare held an
honored place on its shelves. He was partial also to *The Spectator,* if
no less interested in the works of the Reverend Isaac Watts.[9] The boy
as he grew older was even more enamored of the printed word, especially of those words that were written with rhythm and ended in
rhyme. He tried to write some of them himself, as a childish warning
to those who might be tempted to purloin a treasured volume. He admonished anyone who weakened not to

. . . steal this Book my
Honest Friend
For fear the Gallows will
be your end.[10]

---

[7] Lewis Leary, *That Rascal Freneau,* p. 14.

[8] Pierre Fresneau, Executor of Francis Fresneau, New York Historical Society Collections, 1897, XXX, pp. 417, 418, 448; James Alexander Papers,
Mss., Box III.

[9] Pierre Fresneau's Letter Book. The cultural aspects of the household are
evident in the books which were in the library of Pierre and later of Philip.
These volumes are now among the Freneau items in the Monmouth Historical
Association and in the Freneau Collection (Rutgers).

[10] In Freneau's handwriting on a copy of *The Spectator,* in the Freneau Collection (Rutgers).

The wages of sin were well-known to the lad, carefully explained perhaps by Agnes, or by Pierre himself. More likely Pierre had inspired the early trials at versification, for he was given to "scribbling verse" in moments when he was not pursuing the phantoms of business. He would stir the boy's imagination with tales of his voyage to lands far removed from Mount Pleasant and glamorous beyond the dreams of Locust Grove. He could tell him of the sunny and exotic islands that brooded endlessly on the bosom of the sea, lovely green oases on the vast desert of water, where the chill blasts of a Jersey winter never froze the marrow in one's bones, and nature was eternally warm and festive. These pictures, doubly enchanting for the nostalgia with which Pierre informed them, affected the boy with the same recurring wanderlust, and he was moved by the same deep longing as once had moved Pierre himself and all his people to travel across wide seas, to seek strange adventures in remote and alien lands.[11]

As Philip slowly learned the rudiments of language and the principles of arithmetic from his mother, and listened wide-eyed to the more engrossing tales of his father, he lived an inner, a secret, life, to which both Agnes and Pierre were strangers. It was a life of unspoken, scarcely known joys, daydreams that enriched the uneventful hours in the backwoods of the lonely, isolated clearing in Monmouth County. He was a shy, sensitive child, small for his age, who might wander off by himself, alone with his thoughts, to roam the countryside, tramp through the woods, or climb on stout legs to the summit of the highlands, to stand there and gaze through dark-grey eyes upon the calm or heaving sea. The stories of Pierre took on added meaning in the highlands, and in frequent walks about the country they may have achieved a measure of reality—not of the truth, but of his yearning for the truth. Sometime—someday—they could be true for him too.[12]

That was all still a dream, the wistful revery of a lad who must first learn about the world of realities. The years at a New York school may have helped to teach him some of these, though it was at the Mattisonia Grammar School in Manalapan, New Jersey, fifteen miles distant from Mount Pleasant, that those realities began to shape into some clear pattern for the future.[13] Pierre, no longer indulging his son in stories about the remembered past, had given deep thought to

[11] Pierre's stories of his travels are reflected in Philip Freneau's own works. Later, of course, he had access to the Letter Book.

[12] Austin, *Philip Freneau*, p. 71.

[13] Hammell Notes, Mss., p. 3.

that future. For him, quite simply, it had assumed the soft and beguiling features of a religious career, the best possible one for a young
man who was quiet and retiring, always concerned with books more
than with games, with reading more than with playing, a thoughtful
and brooding child who was usually silent and always impractical.
Pierre had made up his mind. The ideal life for his first-born was that
of a clergyman. Under the guidance of Alexander Mitchell, a young
graduate of Nassau Hall at Princeton and the Reverend William Tennent, its acting president, the boy of fifteen, reading into the night by
the flame of sputtering candles, became familiar with the Greek and
Latin classics, equally proficient in Horace and Cicero, the Greek Testament and Xenophon.[14]

Pierre was well pleased with his son, and he needed this comfort,
for there were few others that remained to him. Neither the help of the
Watsons nor his own strivings had availed to bring him the security
which he had so long labored to win and which, alas, seemed to elude
him completely. Cash was still a "very scarce article" with him, and
the income from his properties barely sufficed to meet his own needs,
to say nothing of those of his creditors, who were becoming "very
urgent for their money." Their insistence was almost more than he
could cope with—and if he could get no help from others, the results
"must inevitably have fatal consequences."[15] He had tried to appease
his creditors by selling his timber, by raising some money on a mortgage of his lands in New York, by borrowing wherever he could.
Nothing seemed to stem the flood of their demands. The load became
too heavy for the harassed Pierre any longer to endure. On October
17, 1767, he collapsed beneath it, leaving his family some scattered
tracts in Westchester, Orange, and Albany counties in New York,
his heavily mortgaged holdings in Monmouth County, New Jersey,
and his profitless shares in the Simsbury mines of Connecticut. Besides
all this, he left them a debt of thirteen hundred pounds.[16]

As Pierre was laid away, Philip sadly put a finis to the letter book
of his father. The boy, who understood his loss, restrained his tears.
He was now the man of the house.

[14] *Ibid.;* Old Tennent Church Records, Monmouth County Historical Association, II, 36–37; W. S. Horner, *This Old Monmouth of Ours,* p. 187.

[15] Pierre Fresneau's Letter Book, July 1767; Leary, *That Rascal Freneau,*
p. 15.

[16] Freneau Family Bible; Pierre Fresneau, Will of Pierre Fresneau. Secretary
of State, Trenton, New Jersey, K161.

3. A POET AT PRINCETON

THE REVEREND Mr. Alexander Mitchell must have been an excellent teacher as well as a good scholar. And Philip, it appears, was an apt pupil. Within two years of his entry at the Mattisonia School, he was considered ready for Princeton, not as a first-year student but as a member of the sophomore class. When he was admitted on November 7, 1768, a new world of life and letters, revealing and also disturbing, lay before him.[1]

Princeton, save for the college community, was not too different from Mount Pleasant. The village, indeed, was a metropolis by comparison with the tiny hamlet he had left behind, but the countryside was the same: quiet and remote from the trade and bustle he had known in New York. No noise of commerce disturbed the hush of Nassau Hall, unless it was the students themselves, who disturbed it not with commerce but with the frolics or debates common to all youth. These were tempered by a strict regimen which was new to the young man from Locust Grove, and often irksome as well. Under the benevolent if sometimes severe discipline of President John Witherspoon, a certain routine, regulated by the stern demands for scholarship, was enforced, and accepted, not always cheerfully, but always with a good grace befitting the high and noble purposes of students and teachers alike. The boys were permitted their own pleasures, discreet ones, it was hoped, free from rigorous supervision, though hedged about by commandments and commitments for self-control and impeccable conduct. The 150 students who lived together in Nassau Hall were expected to foster a love of learning in others as well as possess it

[1] Hammell Notes, Mss., pp. 7–8.

themselves, and in their habits and experience to be devout, unblem-
ished exemplars of the moral and intellectual life of their time. The
Reverend Mr. Witherspoon was such a man himself, and he ruled his
domain with a firm if gentle hand. He was proud of the grey stone
building that stood, full four stories high, on the crest of a slope, its
belfry tower, ornate and aloof above the brick chimneys, visible from
afar against the blue curtain of the sky. Nassau Hall was a monument
—one of the few in the new world—to learning and piety; and should
anyone be inclined to doubt it, there, at the main entrance, stood the
bust of Homer to reduce that doubt to dust and mingle it with the
dust that blew into the college yard from the adjoining highway. No
doubt was possible about what transpired within those walls.[2]

Philip, like all the students, must be up at the five o'clock bell.
Clean and polished, his "shoes and stockings tight," he was required
to be punctual at morning prayers in the chapel, and equally assiduous
in study between prayers and breakfast, which was served at eight.
By nine o'clock all classes were in session. If the round of learning
allowed, the lax moments of the day were given over to the study of
orations by those who needed the knowledge and the practice of persuasion.[3] The budding lawyers, the lads who would one day teach
the word of God, the future purveyors of knowledge to other lads,
would fill the quiet purlieus of Nassau with the most strange decla-
mations, some of them so strange indeed that one of their number,
who rarely participated save as a spectator, was moved to burlesque
them in stinging satires, which he could write with scarcely any trouble
at all.[4] It is a phenomenon which Nature must have supplied as a
warning to the loquacious, that those who speak more rarely should
have the power to lampoon the others. Philip, who was no speaker,
wrote his orations, and they were such as usually pinned the bearers
of platitudes to the wall, and often dressed the boys that spoke them
in the motley of clowns. These were sometimes only the occasions for
pure fun, for the others as well as for Philip, when those who spoke
and those who listened might momentarily relax the rigors of Nassau
discipline despite even the frowning presence of the Reverend (and
respected) Mr. John Witherspoon. He was a tolerant, understanding
man, as well as a learned and godly one. Moreover, the students were

[2] John MacLean, *History of the College of New Jersey,* Vol. 1, pp. 300 ff;
George R. Wallace, *Princeton Sketches: The Story of Nassau Hall,* pp. 54–57.
[3] Wallace, *Princeton Sketches,* p. 18.
[4] P. V. Fithian, *Journal and Letters,* pp. 7–9.

no mere automatons. They were allowed a certain freedom, for freedom was something that John Witherspoon cared about greatly.[5] He
may have been amused himself when the students, putting aside solemnity in a moment of exuberance, exercised the prerogatives of youth
in such lusty songs as "Pauvre Madelon," "Jersey Blue," or "Cupid
Triumphant," as a few of them played the accompaniments on the
flute, the guitar, or the violin.[6] Their less tuneful japeries were always
indulged when the President was *not* around. He would have severely
punished such antics as "strowing the entries in the night with greasy
feathers, freezing the Bell . . . [or] making squibs and other frightful
compositions with gunpowder and lighting them in the rooms of
timorous boys and newcomers."[7]

Such escapades were perhaps not conducive to the moral and intellectual growth of young men, nor were those others that transpired
after the evening meal had been despatched with all haste and no relish
at all. Simple and severe as the Hall and its appointments, the food
dispensed there was intended not to pamper but to nourish. If the
boys craved some tidbit, in food (or in friend), they would more
likely look to the tavern in the village, where the atmosphere was truly
convivial and the restraint of tutor or president completely absent.
Here, if there were orations, there could also be brawls. If a stimulant
was required beyond the natural one of youth, it could be had here,
with neither stealth nor concealment. A game of dice or of cards could
be played without censure or discovery, and the stakes could be high
or low without fear of dismissal. Such pleasures were properly frowned
on by the masters of the College, and perhaps by the young poet
who penned its satires. He was never involved in the brawls, since
he shrank from violence and preferred to express his antipathies in
words rather than in deeds. Like all sensitive and retiring souls, he
was readier with his pen than with his fists, and as one destined for
the Church, he could be subtly pugnacious without being openly violent. He too may have enjoyed the liquid stimulants obtainable only
at the tavern, for wine had been the trade and commerce of his family
and the ancient need of his race.[8]

But he had little money to expend on this or any of the other re-
freshments offered to the students of Princeton. Many of the others

[5] John Witherspoon, *Works*, Vol. 3, pp. 321 ff.
[6] Thomas Boyd, *Light-Horse Harry Lee*, p. 4.
[7] *Ibid.;* see also Fithian, *Journal and Letters, passim.*
[8] MacLean, *History of the College,* Vol. 1, p. 32.

were from homes where the father was still the head of the house and provided for the needs of the son in ample measure. What Philip knew of his home back in Mount Pleasant, of the bankrupt estate bequeathed to the family by his father, did not permit of any careless indulgence in luxury, in loose spending, or in light indulgence. The youth with the habitually pensive expression was capable of fun, but the dark-grey eyes, set deep in their sockets beneath a shock of brown hair, saw deeply beneath the surface of the present, and already peered steadily into the future. The prospect envisioned for him by Pierre was far from alluring. Was he to be a clergyman? Was that the destiny that implacably awaited him? The tavern was no place for thoughts like these, and besides, it was time to return to Nassau Hall, for by nine each man must be inside the looming walls of Princeton.[9]

Philip Freneau (he had dropped the old spelling after his father's death) was not too greatly irked by the rule and regimentation of the College. A studious young man, he preferred the fellowship of those less given to the lighter things of life and more concerned with the enduring ones of the mind and the spirit. He loved the fling of good comradeship, and if there was an occasion for it, he could exhibit some of the vivacious spirit of his Gallic heritage. Usually, however, he was too busy—even in his leisure moments—writing, always writing, some lines of verse, some bit of doggerel, or perhaps a subtler piece of satire; in more serious vein, he would compose a few cantos on the meaning and fragility of life. Since his father's untimely death, he seemed preoccupied with the transience of all living things, the brevity of all that is born, has its being, and is fleeting as the breath that sustains it. His study of religion, like his belief in immortality, was neither profound nor spiritually satisfying. The lectures of the Reverend Mr. Witherspoon, his own earlier teaching, were not quite forgotten as he delved deeper into the writings of Horace and Alexander Pope, not alone to glean from them the secret of prosody, but also, along the way, to imbibe their pervasive sense of skepticism. He underscored many passages in his two-volume edition of Pope's works, and one passage in particular which was in close harmony with his own belief that "a true relish of the beauties of nature is the most easy preparation and gentlest transition to an enjoyment of those of heaven."[10] Such sentiments might even be helpful for a budding

---

[9] *Ibid.;* Wallace, *Princeton Sketches,* p. 21.
[10] Marginalia in Pope's *Works,* in Freneau Collection (Rutgers).

clergyman, in spite of the frequent proofs in the "Essay on Man" of the irony, the satire, and the humanistic fervor of the "heav'nly Pope." Nor was Philip content with studying only Pope. He wrote out his views on the works of Horace, he analyzed them according to their length and meter, and commented with youthful presumption on their quality and intent. The translations of the Odes by others— by Creech, by Francis, by Pope himself—he copied out carefully for future reference, learning from Horace the two great truths treasured by all the lovers of poetry: the poet is above the practical affairs of the world, and poetry, if not that alone, is truly immortal.[11]

The young novitiate would rarely swerve too far from these two precepts, though time and circumstances would temper them, as all truths are often tempered. For neither poets nor their poems could be altogether objective in the face of compulsions that deflected them from their course and involved not only the man but also the poet, who must deal with the fragile and ephemeral as with the strong and eternal; in a world that is ever-changing, always becoming, nothing is everlasting. Man is man before he is poet, and while he is poet, and in all the cracks and crannies of his nature; as in all of nature about him, in what he utters, what he writes, what he thinks—in his trochees and his dactyls, in his odes and his elegies, in his satires and his epics— are fashioned the facets of the man who is so many things besides a poet. His verse may be immortal; he himself is not, unless the words, the thoughts, their truth, and their beauty, persist beyond the time of their creator. The creator himself will not persist.

These were strange thoughts for a youth of sixteen, for one who was preparing for the ministry even as he hoped to excel as a poet. He gave his ideas a poetic but not a clerical form in the five cantos of "The Poetical History of the Prophet Jonah" which he composed at this time.

> Enjoy thy gifts while yet the seasons run
> True to their months, and social with the sun.
> When to the dust my mandate bids thee fall,
> All these are lost, for death conceals them all—
> No more the sun illumes the sprightly day,
> The seasons vanish and the stars decay:
> The trees, the flowers, no more thy sense delight.
> Death shades them all in ever-enduring night.[12]

[11] Freneau Collection (Rutgers).
[12] Freneau, *The Poems of Philip Freneau* (ed. F. L. Pattee), Vol. 1, p. 14.

Philip did not always write such doleful and depressing lines during his leisure moments at Princeton. He would vary them with others on a subject that increasingly caught his interest: tyranny in the world and his belief in its inevitable defeat. In "The Pyramids of Egypt"—his first blank verse effort on the theme—he portrayed the powerful pharoahs of antiquity and the false façade of their temporal might. In a lighter mood he might practice a few sharp rapier thrusts of satire, during which, without either malice or spleen, he also indulged a broad grin at the foibles of some of his schoolmates. Nor did he omit the usual poems of the romantic adolescent, verses in which he looked at life with all its suffering and its joys, its tender moments and ultimate disillusion—the verses all, the serious and the comic, derived from his masters of the eighteenth century—while at the same time he sought, with but small success, to express his own vision of a future dedicated to poetry, the poetry of the new world, the young and adolescent America, which had almost no poems of its own, and no true poet to write them.[13]

Of this America—to the young man unknown beyond the tiny hamlet of Mount Pleasant, yet already stirring to a strange maturity both in him and in the peculiar events about him—he became increasingly aware. Others, his fellow classmates and students from other parts of the country, from provinces far removed from his, had opened up new vistas of the land before him, and brought him pictures of places he had never seen, and new ideas that germinated in the hills and valleys of America. They brought, no less, some serious, studious minds that stimulated his own, and offered a friendship that would persist throughout the years. Like him, they too had their visions of greatness, and they also put into words the visions that moved them. Young Henry Lee, whose strength and integrity were but poorly concealed behind a dandified front of frills and powder, might choose other means than words, but Hugh Brackenridge, who came from the frontier of Western Pennsylvania, would use words as well.[14]

More than these, a sickly young man from Virginia, small, shy, with light hair and a bridgeless nose, a weak chin and a weaker tongue, James Madison presented a rather undistinguished appearance despite the Negro boy who always attended him. In many ways his appearance belied his real strength. In the privacy of his mind he was neither shy

---

[13] *Ibid.;* and Freneau's Note Book, in Lea and Febiger Collection.
[14] H. C. Cameron, *History of the American Whig Society,* pp. 42 ff.

nor sickly. One day his strength would become public, when he—and his country—needed it most.[15]

The poor young man of Monmouth, and the scion of Virginia aristocracy, were roommates, and soon became fast friends. The future of America was also their future. Both of them would mold and fashion it, each in his own way, with words and with deeds, according to their power and the power they achieved.

[15] Madison to Thos. Martin, August 10, 1769, in James Madison, *Papers,* Vol. 1, pp. 42–43; Madison to Father, July 23, 1770, and Madison to J. Boyle, May 17, 1771, in *ibid.,* Vol. 1, p. 60.

4. ECHOES IN THE WIND

CHILDHOOD FRIENDSHIPS are not the most lasting. As the shape of one's nose, the contour of one's face, the color of one's eyes alter with time, so too the sense and sensibilities of children are transmuted by the years until they are finally formed, settled, hardened (or softened) by the understanding and experience of maturity. The subtle play of personality, the interplay of thought and action, the trauma of joy or sorrow, these will dissolve the old ties that once seemed eternal, while the new ones, if they are truly joined, may be more rare but also deeper. In the absence of powerful deterrents they will be for life.

The childhood of Philip Freneau had been uneventful, and little different from that of any other lad of his time and circumstances. The countryside about Mount Pleasant, far removed from the busy center of commerce, provided for him as for other boys a happy if torpid youth, with occasional forays into the hills beyond his home—but not too far away where Indians not too friendly to the white invaders of their lands were said to live. It was not as far as that to Middletown Point, a few miles to the north, which was a port of Northern Monmouth, where the boy, his father's son in this as in many other respects, could watch the sloops, loaded with home-grown produce, raise anchor and set sail for the metropolis of New York, in reality but a thriving village across the bay. In those moments which he snatched from school and surveillance, he loved to watch the tall masts in the harbor and the white sails filling in the wind, as sloop and brig and barquentine steered courses for distant lands, some of them with strange names which a boy of wandering mind could invest with high adventure and surpassing loveliness. In the port of New York itself, where Philip knew almost every quayside, he had roamed to lands never spoken of in the grammar school at home, even in the pages of Cicero and Horace, of Xenophon or the Greek Testament.[1]

The lad's daydreams were often disturbed by distant cries of anger and revolt, and in the year 1766 by alarms and tumults that emanated from faraway Williamsburg in Virginia, where a firebrand called Patrick Henry had made a speech against the Stamp Act of England. The speech was heard the whole length of the Atlantic seaboard and it echoed in the rocky fastness of the Alleghenies.[2] Remote Monmouth had been shaken too in its accustomed quiet, but the tumult and the danger had passed with the repeal of the Act. The Colonies had seethed with incipient rebellion, while Philip, who was in New York during the riotous events that stirred the city before the repeal, must have been a witness to the passions that swirled and eddied about him. At Old Slip Market, at the City Tavern, the crowds were gathered to air their hostile views on the British Ministry. The cries of protest against the impositions of the mother country were more dignified at the Merchant's Coffee House near Wall Street, where even the respectable burghers wore mourning for the death of liberty and covered with crêpe their boxes of dice and backgammon. The vessels riding at anchor in the harbor lowered their colors in "lamentation and woe," as two thousand citizens stood guard at the Battery to prevent the smuggling of any of the offending stamps.[3]

The Sugar Act of 1764 had been bad enough, despite its lowering of imposts on the imports from the West Indies. The Stamp Act filled to overflowing the cup of bitterness against the Parliament that sat three thousand miles away and made ruinous levies on honest men who were saddled without their consent and had no recourse but to futile protest. If the British had some measure of justice in their demands, the methods they pursued to enforce them were intolerable to free men. The Sons of Liberty would show them how intolerable they were by hanging—but only in effigy—his Majesty's governor of New York, the able if conservative Cadwallader Colden. He was wise to beat a hasty retreat to the shelter of the *Coventry*, which was an-

---

[1] Freneau's love of the sea was perhaps also induced by the books in his library; see H. H. Clark, "The Literary Influences of Philip Freneau," *Studies in Philology*, XXII, 1 (January 1929), 1.

[2] Jacob Axelrad, *Patrick Henry: The Voice of Freedom*, pp. 42–44.

[3] T. J. Wertenbaker, *Father Knickerbocker Rebels*, p. 336 (quote from Montresor's Journal).

chored at a safe distance in the harbor, as angry mobs with lighted torches swarmed over the Common in search of Tory enemies. They found few of them, but their torches would not spare what they did find. The home of Major James, close by King's College, could not escape the fire nor his office the cleansing of Tory sentiment. Ripped mattresses, smashed china, broken furniture, his library, maps, papers —everything within reach of the Sons of Liberty—they all made an excellent bonfire, while the Major's cellar yielded up its stock of rare wines and liquors to lend a really festive air to the destruction of the Major's goods and chattels. Isaac Sears and John Lamb, the leaders of the Sons, were in no mood to restrain the shopkeepers, the laborers, the teamsters, the carpenters—a few of the "better classes" too—who kept the City of New York in a tumult of rebellion.[4]

The boy Philip perhaps understood little of all this. His mother, busy with domestic matters alien to such iniquities, could not enlighten him, and Pierre, who was struggling to avoid the "fatal consequences" of his debts, soon succumbed to them altogether. The youth's education in this as in so many other matters was delayed until he reached the one place where education was to be found. At the College of New Jersey, in Nassau Hall, in addition to the prescribed curriculum of the humanities, he would learn a few things that were still strange to humanity. From the swift current of events as it swept from England to America, from Williamsburg to Boston, New York, and Philadelphia, from the seats of commerce to the seats of learning, Philip could catch bits and pieces of fact and fancy that flowed by the yard of Princeton. And from friends he made there he would learn a great deal more.

Jemmy Madison, born into a society where slavery was an old and established institution, had grown up in a family that owned many slaves who served the needs of the vast plantation that belonged to his father. The home at Montpellier, in Orange County, Virginia, was something of a self-contained village in itself, with many cattle, hogs, sheep, and horses, and hundreds of fruit trees, besides an assortment of workshops where the Negroes built and repaired, tooled and hammered for the house and the plantation—and for other Negroes as well, those who labored in the fields of tobacco and corn and wheat, in the cleared tracts cultivated between dense forests. The blue-eyed

[4] *Ibid.*

Jemmy, suffering from a species of epilepsy which further weakened his short, slight body, was spared all physical effort. He preferred the library to the outdoors, and the view of the distant Blue Ridge Mountains was inspiring from any point of vantage. He did like to ramble through the woods near his home, and he was interested far more in the calls and songs of the birds who were there, than in the fields and their crops. He could distinguish the calls no less than the trees of the forest, the oak and the poplar, the hickory and the dogwood, the gum and the chestnut. He did not wander too far, for reports of the defeat of Braddock by the French and Indians near Fort Duquesne had reached Montpellier, though such things were beyond the clear comprehension of a child of five. The fear which the news aroused throughout the countryside was something a child could share without understanding it. His own people, like all the settlers in the Piedmont, were always on guard against surprise attack in the Shenandoah Valley, a danger that happily ended with the end of the French and Indian War, in 1763. Other dangers, not French and Indian, but British, soon replaced them.[5]

Slightly younger than his classmate, James Madison had many things in common with Philip Freneau. Despite the difference in their social stations, James, like Philip, had received his early education from his mother, and had access in his father's library to some similar volumes, among which the Holy Bible and Addison's *Spectator* were well read and well thumbed. Jemmy's formal schooling, begun at eleven under Donald Robertson, was later continued with the Reverend Mr. Thomas Martin, who taught him Latin, Greek, and English literature. At fifteen he was able to write with a certain authority on "Logic or Dialectick," with impressive references to Socrates, Plato, Euclid, and Locke, and to descant, with more assurance than accuracy, on the Copernican solar system.[6] He knew French well enough not to be understood by any Frenchman. "I might as well," he explained, "have been talking Kickapoo."[7]

In Virginia, as in New York, Boston, and elsewhere, there had been riots and harangues against the Stamp Act. It was in Virginia

[5] Irving Brant, *James Madison,* Vol. I, *The Virginia Revolutionist,* pp. 60–64.

[6] "Notes on Brief System of Logick," in James Madison, *Papers,* Vol. 1, pp. 32–41.

[7] Brant, *James Madison,* Vol. 1, p. 64.

that the spark had been set which caused the conflagration to spread throughout the colonies. There was no record of Pierre Fresneau's reaction to the Act; but James Madison, Sr., like his close friend and client, Edmund Pendleton, one of the leaders in the Virginia House of Burgesses, while opposed to the new impost, would not go so far as Patrick Henry and the other radicals in defying the powers of the King and Parliament. He would have preferred to circumvent them without straining too greatly his oath of office as a justice of the peace. The climate of opinion in the Old Dominion was not favorable to the practice of taxation without representation, but there, as in most of the other provinces, that climate was frequently affected by the possessions and political preferments of the people themselves. Yet even the wealthy, the high placed, and the well born would veer with the wind of circumstance, and everywhere the wind was blowing with some hot gusts of revolutionary warning. In Virginia it was howling through Gloucester Street in Williamsburg from the capitol at one end to William and Mary College at the other, and its echoes were being heard, its lash was being felt, in all of the thirteen colonies.[8]

James Madison, the classmate of Philip Freneau, must have heard and felt it too. That he was in Princeton at all was proof that in this, if in no other respect, he was aware of the temper of the times. It was astonishing for a Virginian to choose the College of New Jersey over the College of William and Mary, but at Nassau Hall there was a fresher breath of freedom—of freedom of religion, in any event. William and Mary was a bulwark of the Established Church, while the College of New Jersey enforced its dictums and dogmas on no one. Indeed, the highly satirical pamphlet by President Witherspoon, *Ecclesiastical Characteristics,* struck out boldly against all church authority. There was an added reason for the choice of a Northern college. Jemmy was a puny, ailing lad, for whom the "sickly season" of the tidewater country held special terrors. And in Jersey as in Virginia, he would have the care and company of his ever-faithful "Sawney." Usually attended by the Negro slave, he soon became one of a small group of friends who were as studious and as book-loving as he, and as curious-minded about the strange events, the contrary winds, the political ferments, which so often swept across the pleasant quietude of Princeton. In Philip Freneau he recognized a kindred spirit; and

[8] Axelrad, *Patrick Henry,* pp. 44–45.

later there would also be William Bradford, the son of the Pennsylvania newspaper publisher who had once been the friend of Philip's
father. Now, another friend of Philip's became also the friend of
James Madison.[9]

Hugh Henry Brackenridge, a few years older than either James or
Philip, unlike them was foreign born. When he was brought by his
poverty-stricken parents from Campbelltown, in Scotland, to the frontier village of York City in Pennsylvania, he was scarcely five years
old. His formal studies did not begin until he was twelve, but he knew
enough of the classics by the age of fifteen to take charge of a small
school at Gunpowder Falls, across the Pennsylvania line in Maryland.
That was both a pleasant and necessary task if he was ever to get
enough money to pay for his tuition at the College of New Jersey.
Even as a student there, he would have to teach at the grammar school
in Princeton to make both ends meet. Possessing a ready tongue, a fine
voice, a sharp wit, and a keen mind that understood the meaning of
liberty as it was practiced on the open frontier, he was an ideal companion for the two lads whose poor power of speech and natural reti-
cence needed such qualities as his. Brackenridge was also fond of the
written word, and could use it as well as they. He and Philip Freneau
were not the equal of James Madison as students, but neither did they
apply themselves as furiously as Jemmy to the work assigned them.
Madison, because he would not, or could not, sleep, rarely wasted more
than three, never more than five, of his precious hours in bed. It was
no wonder that he succeeded in doing two years work in one, while no
less than his friends, he also spent much of his leisure time debating
the pressing problems of government and the more abstruse ones of
human conduct.[10]

None of the young men were wholly absorbed by the more serious
aspects of the life about them, nor altogether devoted to a solution of
the political puzzles that increasingly occupied their time. They could
break out, separately or together, in a humorous bit of light verse, and
vent some individual or collective spleen in satire, but it was Brackenridge who would join Freneau in literary escapades for which the
more literal-minded Madison had small relish or capacity. More often
he was busy composing stiff, formal letters to his father, long-winded

[9] Brant, *James Madison,* Vol. 1, pp. 71, 74, 83; H. C. Cameron, *History of
the American Whig Society,* pp. 6, 21, 46.

[10] Brant, *James Madison,* Vol. 1, p. 78; C. M. Newlin, *Life and Writings of
Hugh H. Brackenridge,* pp. 6–11.

epistles replete with details about the College and the events that transpired there. Madison Senior might be interested to know that at commencement honorary degrees—the first ever granted in America—were bestowed on John Dickinson the eminent farmer, and on Joseph Galloway, the speaker of the Pennsylvania Assembly. They would earn still other honors later, more substantial ones than these, and the young man who now regaled his father with this important news would some day achieve a few himself. He was diligently preparing for them even now, while his friends Philip Freneau and Hugh Brackenridge wasted their precious hours in compositions that were too fanciful for him.[11]

Not that he failed to enjoy their first serious collaboration, "Father Bombo's Pilgrimage to Mecca in Arabia," which they completed in October 1770. A highly imaginative prose tale which in some measure derived from Swift and Cervantes, the work contained some special contributions by Freneau alone. Among them were a lusty lyric in praise of love and the beauty of nature, and, more solemnly, an entire "Essay on Luxury," which was far from relevant to the story. Poor in the world's goods and never too far from a condition of penury, the young scholar was giving as much thought to his own private problems as to those of a less pressing nature. He did not, indeed, neglect the life of the spirit, a real, almost tangible, experience to him. Finished with Father Bombo, he composed "The Power of Fancy," whose Miltonic lines anticipated by almost half a century a more mature and polished work by John Keats on a similar theme.

> Wakeful, vagrant, restless thing,
> Ever wandering on the wing,
> Who thy wondrous course can find,
> Fancy, regent of the mind.[12]

Here was the fledgling's first flight into the sun, a tentative escape from the mundane realities of his life at Princeton. More than a need to seek for greener pastures than any he had known before, Philip Freneau was also expressing an inchoate desire for a bolder, braver

[11] Madison to Father, September 30, 1769, and July 23, 1770, in Madison, *Papers,* Vol. 1, pp. 49–50, 60. Madison kept his father informed on all that transpired at Princeton.

[12] Freneau, *The Poems of Philip Freneau* (ed. F. L. Pattee), Vol. 1, p. xvii; see also Newlin, *Life of Brackenridge,* pp. xi, 15–21. The original manuscript of "Father Bombo's Pilgrimage" is in the Historical Society of Pennsylvania.

search of the eternal verities, as well as a loosening of the accustomed ties, in thought and in deed, to the ancient conformities. America was still bound to the cultural and political stakes of the past; in "The Power of Fancy," a new call was sounded and a theme was heard—a call to adventure in untried paths, and a theme of independence for the mind and spirit. Above all, this was Freneau's initial attempt to excel in the use of the word, and to adorn it with his often faltering pen.[13]

His father had chosen for him one career. He was already dedicated to another, the difficult and dubious one of poetry.

[13] Freneau, *Poems* (Pattee), Vol. i, p. 34.

5. THE LAW OF NATURE

NASSAU HALL, under the benign if somewhat dictatorial reign of President Witherspoon, was no exception to the extracurricular propensities of undergraduates everywhere. The campus was not so tightly sealed against outside alarums but that the students themselves were moved by events that troubled their elders in places far removed from the quiet environs of Princeton. They could not long remain quiet as news of the Stamp Act, its repeal, the imposition of new taxes, and the properly propagandized Boston Massacre filtered into the College. The incident of March 3, 1770, was far from a massacre, though blood had been shed. Indeed, it had been so named not by the participants in either the British or Colonial camps, but by the silversmith patriot, Paul Revere, who was a man of many parts, equally able to ride a horse or engrave a picture. It was his cartoon, done in an imaginative and inflammatory broadside, that described the clash between the red coats and the citizens as wanton butchery of Americans. With the astute help of Sam Adams, the palsied son of a Boston brewer, who was a fierce partisan of freedom and a firebrand of liberty, the news had been broadcast of the wanton murder of innocent men and the horrendous outrages on a peace-loving people by the despised soldiery and officials of the Crown. Young men, coming from provinces involved in skirmishes with royal officials, took up the quarrels as their own, and soon formed their lines for or against the British authority.[1]

President Witherspoon might confidently assert that even those

[1] R. A. Billington, B. L. Lowenberg, and S. H. Brockunier, *The United States: American Democracy in World Perspective*, p. 52; Jacob Axelrad, *Patrick Henry: The Voice of Freedom*, pp. 66–67.

who were against the usurpations of England did not lack in "loyalty
to our Most excellent Sovereign," yet his sympathies were with the
opposition. Few if any went so far as to denounce the ties between the
mother country and the Colonies, but John Witherspoon himself, like
many of his students, looked on the British provocations with suspicion
or downright antipathy. Soon he would declare his belief in the unity
of the Colonies for self-defense, "to assure the people of Great Britain
that we will not submit voluntarily, and convince them that it would
be either impossible or unprofitable for them to compel us by open
violence." The College campus, seething with rumors of violence
against patriots in Boston, had become the spawning ground of a
"mischievous kind of knowledge."[2]

Philip Freneau, his friends Hugh Brackenridge and William Bradford, and a few others like Samuel Smith—in later years to become
the president of Nassau Hall—were determined that the knowledge
of the campus should be enlightening as well as mischievous. They
started a movement to establish at Princetown a club which would replace the one suppressed by the College a few years earlier. Not one,
but two student organizations had been banned when the acrimony
of their debates and the disturbances which frequently attended their
rivalries resulted in brawls considerably more heated than enlightening.
The old Plain Dealing Society, less conservative than the rival Well
Meaning Society, was like it at least in one respect. Both of them were
intended primarily as forums for the discussion of literature. And in
both of them the discussions were often colored by political predilec-
tions far removed from academic objectivity. Those who would never
be guilty of splitting an infinitive, were apt to indulge in splitting a
hair.[3]

On June 24, 1769, the new club, plainly labelled as the "American
Whig Society," gathered to its roster the young men who were opposed
to the English encroachments on American liberty. It was really the
old Plain Dealing Society in a new garb, and boasted as its motto
"Litterae, Amicitia, Mores"—nothing which portended any trouble
of a political nature. Perhaps the young men who formed it preferred
to wait on events to reveal its other purposes. James Madison, temperamentally less impatient than Freneau and Brackenridge, was not one

[2] John Witherspoon, Works, Vol. 3, p. 321; see also Thomas Boyd, Light-
Horse Harry Lee, pp. 6 ff. Witherspoon, recently from Scotland, signed the
Declaration of Independence.

[3] H. C. Cameron, History of the American Whig Society, pp. 6–23, 46 ff.

of the founders. But he too soon joined his friends in the new society
where literature was to be honored above all things. Honored, that is
to say, until other matters, more important than literature, demanded
the attention of its members.[4]

Soon enough they intruded into the decorous meetings of the Whig
men. Before the year was up, the old and defunct Well Meaning
Society was also revived, this time with the highly academic title of
"Clio-Sophic Society," whose members, by tradition no less than inclination, were the rivals of the Whig Club. The Clios were not uni-
formly sympathetic to the British, but it pleased the Whigs to think
so, and frequently to say so. They called them, quite simply, Tories,
the greatest insult they could think of. The war—the campus war—
was on.

In such a war, Philip Freneau, the poet and patriot, must take a
leading part. His friends, Madison and Brackenridge, would also be
in it, but in this battle of words—of literature leavened by politics—
they recognized his leadership. Brackenridge acknowledged his
friend's poetic powers in a soliloquy which he put into the mouth of
one of the Clios:

> ... in his turn Freneau
> Will send me headlong to the school below.
> I hear his muse proclaiming from afar
> The thund'ring prologue to the burning war.[5]

Madison, like Brackenridge, considered his roommate to be a poet of
promise. Philip's romantic verses, which he tossed off with apparent
ease, already included such impressive subjects as "The Citizen's Resolve" and "Columbus to Ferdinand," in which young Freneau assumed not only the mantle of the muse but that of a prophet as well.
In these verses the future of America is pictured for the students who
are so intensely interested in discovering it. If any of them doubt
that America will ever be free of the tyranny of kings and auto-
crats, the poet-prophet hastens to inform them, in the blank verses of
"The Pyramids of Egypt," that history has always proven the con-

---

[4] *Ibid.* A fire in Nassau Hall, March 6, 1802, destroyed many of the records.
The work of the founders of the American Whig Society are preserved, however, in the manuscript, "Satires against the Tories," in the Historical Society
of Pennsylvania.

[5] "Satires against the Tories," Mss., pp. 23–24. Also C. M. Newlin, *Life and
Writings of Hugh H. Brackenridge*, pp. 11–14.

trary. What has become of the rulers and masters of other lands, of the despots who strutted their brief hour upon the stage of history in tinsel glory and in mock immortality?

> . . . all, all are gone,
> And like the phantom snow of a May morning
> Left not a vestige to discover them.[6]

James Madison was so impressed with his friend's poetic gifts that he used his poems for the instruction of his own brothers and sisters in the "first rudiments of literature." Some of the poems he could not use. In the war of words against the "Tories" of the Clio-Sophic Society, Freneau employed a saber more often than a scalpel in satires which revealed more wrath than scorn.

> Rage gives me wings and boldly prompts me on
> To conquer brutes the world would blush to own.
> No peace, no quarter to these dogs we lend.
> Death and destruction in each line I send.

The poet, in reality more violent in words than in deeds, nevertheless proclaims:

> A Patriot's flame can meet with no control,
> It swells my breast and sends forth half my soul.[7]

This patriot flame, so uncontrollable in his sophomoric verse, was real enough to him and to his friends. They saw nothing to criticize in his salute to the Tories with

> Hail worthy sages, sprung from dust and dirt,
> With scandal clothed, besides a lousy shirt.[8]

Madison, inspired with equal fervor, paid his own respects to Samuel Sprung, later to be known as an eminent clergyman but now the poet laureate of the Clios. Jemmy Madison, so rarely given to unseemly abuse, admonished the correct and inoffensive Samuel:

> —disdain these sons of screech-owls, monkeys
>   and baboons,

---

[6] "Pyramids of Egypt," in Freneau, *The Poems of Philip Freneau* (ed. F. L. Pattee), Vol. 1, p. 25.

[7] "Satires against the Tories," Mss., Satire II, ll. 7–16; Satire III, ll. 9–14.

[8] *Ibid.*

who,

> skulk within their dens together
> Where each one's stench will kill his brother.[9]

The Pennsylvania lad with the fine voice, Hugh Brackenridge, contributed his own bit of poison gas to the war between the clubs, and it was he, rather than the weak-voiced Madison or the reserved Freneau, who probably read the lucubrations of all three in the Princeton Prayer Hall before the assembled students of the College. Carefully written out in Philip's notebook, the "Satires against the Tories" announced on its title page the information that in this wordy war between the Whigs and the Clios, "the former obtained a complete victory." How could it be otherwise? Freneau had lambasted the Clios with utmost abandon, aspersing their presumptions as poets, while conceding the enemy's right to defend himself in any medium best suited to his talents. Poetry, however, is not the one he should have chosen. Still,

> His very braying saves the Ass.

Does the enemy resent the slur, and seek further combat? Let him beware!

> We never gave you what you wanted yet,
> It was but play to what you now shall get.

In satire after satire the Clios continued as targets of attack. In "Cliosophians Bewitched," in "Dialogues in Verse," in "Soliloquies," and in "Satires," Philip carries the war into the camp of the Clios, with a rare assist from Brackenridge and Madison. Brackenridge, in "The Origin of the Tories," traces their strange ancestry back to the very dawn of creation:

> In wretched Cain the wicked race began.[10]

Madison, in a moment of unleashed temper, discovered the origin of the Clios elsewhere than in the Bible. A Clio himself divulges his source of inspiration. The

> . . . ever grateful muse,
> Sprinkled my head with healing dews,

---

[9] Irving Brant, *James Madison*, Vol. 1, *The Virginia Revolutionist*, p. 86.
[10] Newlin, *Life of Brackenridge*, pp. 11–14, shows that Brackenridge contributed ten "pastorals."

> Then took me to her private room
> And straight an Eunuch out I came.[11]

Some of these literary effusions, too broad and salty for the sensitive and scholastic ears of the tutors, were suppressed. In this paper war between the factions there was more than a little spitefulness on both sides, and less controversy than appeared on the surface. Among the combatants there were many whose ideas were closer together than their verses would indicate.

When news reached the College of the steadily mounting trouble between the British and the Americans, most of the students in both societies expressed views that were unimpeachable and patriotic. Loyal to Britain, they were also partial to the Colonies in their opposition to the Townshend Acts, which infringed alike on liberty and on their oath of fidelity to the motto: *"Omnes Homines, Jure Naturae, Liberi sunt."* The law of nature, already proclaimed by Patrick Henry, made all men free. The students, like all Colonists, were British subjects, not British slaves. For many of them, the nonimportation agreement of the Colonies was "a notable exertion of self-denial and public spirit," whose virtues they believed in as fully as did their elders.[12] Their contempt for those who tried to flout the agreement was equally strong. When some New York merchants dispatched a letter to their colleagues in Philadelphia exhorting them to ignore the nonimportation resolutions, it was intercepted and publicly burned by Whigs and Clios alike in the College yard. They voted on a resolution of their own, as Madison was quick to inform his father on July 23, 1770. After presiding at the incineration of the offensive letter, the Seniors, "all of them appearing in their black gowns and the bell tolling," agreed in solemn conclave to appear at commencement in clothes of American manufacture alone.[13] More than anyone else, Philip Freneau had contributed to the general unrest at Princeton, as he was the first to admit:

[11] "Satires against the Tories," Mss., signed "J. Maddison."

[12] Brant, *James Madison,* Vol. 1, p. 94.

[13] Madison to Father, July 23, 1770, in James Madison, *Papers,* Vol. 1, pp. 49–50. The germ of revolution was planted at home in the fireside talks of the Madisons and Thomas Martin (Brant, *James Madison,* Vol. 1, p. 67). See also Madison to Thos. Martin, June 23, 1770, in *ibid.,* pp. 82–83; and J. F. Hageman, *History of Princeton and Its Institutions,* Vol. 1, pp. 101–102.

> I long have strove to be a poet.
> Besides this sin, alas, God knows,
> I've wrote some dirty things in prose.[14]

In poetry or prose, in play or in good earnest, he had written only what he believed against the usurpations of England and for the rights— the natural rights—of America.

The days of student pranks and wars were over. The time for serious appraisal was close at hand. Graduation was only a few months off, and the students were involved more deeply in their country's plight. Philip, devoting less time to his studies, was now spending most of his leisure hours writing, always writing, a poem that had less to do with culture and more with his country. With some slight help from Brackenridge, who knew so much more about the frontier outposts of America than he did, Freneau completed a work which revealed not only a native poet of promise, but an imaginative power unique in the new world.

"The Rising Glory Of America" foreshadowed his own glory too.[15]

[14] "Satires against the Tories," Mss., signed "P. F."
[15] Freneau, *Poems* (Pattee), Vol. 1, p. 49.

6. THE MUSE OF LIBERTY

THE CHAPEL at Nassau Hall was crowded on Wednesday, September 25, 1771, Commencement Day, with underclassmen as well as friends and relatives of the graduates. There were only twelve of these, among them James Madison and Hugh Brackenridge; but Philip Freneau, who was not only a graduate but the most conspicuous contributor to the impressive ceremonies, was absent. Junior honors had been distributed the day before, when William Bradford, a devoted member of the Whig Society, had received a prize in oratory and Aaron Burr, a member of the Clios, had won an award for spelling.[1]

On the gala occasion of the graduation exercises. Philip, though "necessarily absent," was present poetically in a twofold manner. His contribution to the debate on the question, "Does Ancient Poetry Excel the Modern," in which his love of the classics and his preoccupation with poetry were eloquently set forth, was read by another student.[2] It was not, however, with the Ancients that he was concerned in his principal contribution to the program. In the poem read for him by Brackenridge, it was the future not the past which Freneau considered, the Moderns not the Ancients to whom he appealed for a new and native pattern in American poetry. Brackenridge, adding his fine voice to the lines he had helped in some measure to fashion, gave them a passionate urgency that enthralled the hearers and moved them to "great applause." They recognized the poem as the work of an au-

---

[1] Irving Brant, *James Madison,* Vol. 1, *The Virginia Revolutionist,* p. 96; John MacLean, *History of the College of New Jersey,* Vol. 1, pp. 312, 313.

[2] MacLean, *History of the College,* Vol. 1, pp. 312–313; Freneau, *The Poems of Philip Freneau* (ed. F. L. Pattee), Vol. 1, p. xx.

thentic poet; a work to which Brackenridge readily admitted that his own part "was a task of labor, while the verse of his associate flowed spontaneously."[3] Brackenridge was more interested in prose, a medium he had tried before and was to use again later, far more effectively, in his novel *Modern Chivalry*.

What he had failed to supply in the verse he was now reciting for his absent friend, he more than amply provided in the quality of his delivery. As the tall, slender youth applied his power of speech to the poetic dialogue on which Freneau had lavished his love of poesy equally with his love of liberty, "The Rising Glory of America" was transformed from a poem of prophecy to a grand vision of the future land of great expanses that would one day be as free as it was great. The vision was not altogether a new one. John Trumbull, a Connecticut lad, only the year before had composed "The Prospect of the Future Glory of America," for his commencement poem at Yale. More deeply searching than Trumbull's poem, Philip Freneau's hewed closely to the theme of liberty, which inspired him as profoundly as it did the heroes who march so proudly through its many stanzas.[4]

In the poem, too, there is a subtle plea for independence, a novel idea that is not yet either widely held or often broached. Freneau's heroes are still English, though later, when nothing British is heroic, he would make a thorough revision in which new heroes, all American, would replace them. Sufficient unto the time was the present vision of a glory that was rising but had not yet risen. Freneau was now concerned with faith as much as prophecy, with liberty more than with independence. His ancestors were French, not English, but he was American, and America was the offspring of the British. The climate of opinion in the Colonies was the same as that in Princeton, where John Witherspoon, though he also believed in freedom, fostered careful thought of American problems without intruding the less hospitable one of complete separation from Britain.

"The Rising Glory of America" was not without its praise of "Brittania's warlike troops, choice spirits of her isle." When Freneau later revised his work the warlike troops had been used against his own people; no longer "choice spirits of her isle," they became the

[3] Hugh H. Brackenridge, *Modern Chivalry*, p. xi. This novel, of course, was published much later. See also Madison to Father, September 30, 1769, in James Madison, *Papers*, Vol. 1, p. 45.

[4] A comparison with Trumbull's poem reveals the differences in views of the two young poets.

wanton destroyers of liberty, no different from their hired mercenaries, the Hessians, who were bought and paid for to do their bidding. The egg of Revolution was still in the nest of time, and "The Rising Glory of America" would keep it warm for the ultimate hatching. America was a land

> Of liberty and life; sweet liberty!
> Without whose aid the noblest genius fails.

For such a land the poet could prophesy a sure future:

> —I see, I see
> Freedom's established reign; cities and men,
> Numerous as the sands upon the ocean shore,
> And Empires rising where the Sun descends!
> The Ohio soon shall glide by many a town
> Of note; and where the Mississippi stream,
> By forests shaded, now runs sweeping on,
> Nations shall grow, and states not less in fame
> Than Greece and Rome of old![5]

Walt Whitman would sing of the hope of America, of its future, in more arresting rhythm, in more muscular measures, but he would have a long perspective of the years to guide and inform him. Freneau, with no such guide, was more clairvoyant. He saw not alone the future greatness of his country, he conjured up the poets who would sing that greatness—poets, perhaps, like the sage of Camden himself:

> I see a Homer and a Milton rise
> In all the pomp and majesty of song.[6]

By this final fling at Princeton Freneau established himself, not only for his friends Brackenridge and Madison, but for a much wider audience outside the walls of Nassau, as a poet of mark. The publication of "The Rising Glory of America," flattering enough as a proof of his genius, persuaded many others, himself not least among them, that his true vocation was that of the written word, and of poetry more than of prose. It was equally apparent that, whatever the forms might be, the theme of his work would be always the same. Liberty, and America, were the substance of its fabric, however he might color it with variations, sentimental or somber, of love or nature, or of death and the fragility of life, its transient moment and its ineluctable dis-

---

[5] Freneau, *Poems* (Pattee), Vol. i, p. 49.
[6] *Ibid.*

solution. In the great romantic tradition of England but with the authentic voice of America, he would write his music for the new world, borrowing sometimes the style, often the ideas, of the old, yet never omitting the ideals that moved him beyond all others, the ideals of freedom and justice in the land that was struggling to achieve them.[7]

The struggle for these ideals had scarcely begun. The conflict, still limited to words, would soon burgeon in bloodshed. The young graduate of Princeton would probe deeply the basis of royal prerogative, and damn with assured confidence if not always with assured craftsmanship all prerogatives that flowed from any source but that of the people.[8] The rights of man—of the common man—included many things, many dimly perceived and not clearly understood. Philip Freneau, though he perceived them, did not understand them either. At the moment, more pressing problems for a man, or a poet, called for immediate solution.

At twenty, a young man is already old enough to take his place in the world. In the world of Philip Freneau, an embryo poet of some learning and no money was under the necessity of using his learning and putting aside his poetry for the more prosaic business of earning a living. His widowed mother, with the wreckage of Pierre's fortunes cleared away, was having a difficult time supporting the three children at home. Creditors were still pressing for payment, and some more of Pierre's holdings were sold to satisfy them. The widow, for these reasons, and because, in addition, a woman who was still young and comely could not long relish the single state, had considered the proposal of marriage which Major James Kearney had made to her. Major Kearney, a landowner and neighbor with five children of his own by his late wife, was no attractive match for Philip's mother; yet Agnes thought the union might offer some compensations for the burdens which patently it would impose. For her son, just returned from Princeton, her marriage on June 5, 1771, settled at least one question about his immediate future.[9]

---

[7] H. H. Clark, "What Made Freneau the Father of American Poetry?" in *Studies in Philology*, XXII, 1 (January 1929), 1–22, is a perceptive treatment of the development of Freneau as a poet of the Revolution.

[8] H. H. Clark, "What Made Freneau the Father of American Prose?" in *Transactions of the Wisconsin Academy of Sciences, Arts, and Letters*, XXV (1930), 39–50, is also extremely interesting for this aspect of Freneau's work.

[9] Marriage Agreement dated June 5, 1771, in State of New Jersey, *Marriage Records, 1665–1800*, K364.

For a person of his sensitive temperament, the thought of a crowded home and complete dependence on the bounty of a virtual stranger was not inviting. The Major also appeared to be a hard-headed, even a close-fisted, man, a parched soul who would give up nothing to which he could possibly hold on. In a prenuptial agreement he had provided that his wife should have no claim on any part of his property, an exceedingly wise precaution, since within less than two years of his marriage to Agnes he left her a widow once more, with little else of him for her to remember but an annual "income" of three loads of salt grass.[10]

Pierre had been as explicit as possible about his son's future; and Agnes, anxious for her own sake as well, was of her sainted Pierre's mind that Philip must be a preacher. The prospect was never an alluring one for the lad whose head was filled with other hopes and ambitions, nor could he, even if he were so inclined, afford the expense which further studies entailed. He could loaf a while at Nassau Hall, and then try to resolve his problem in a manner that was far less rewarding than the solution of his parents. Fitted by his studies for nothing in particular, he decided on a career not infrequently chosen by many who are fitted for nothing in particular. He would try the profession of the Law.[11]

It is probable that Philip went to Philadelphia, to read there for the Bar. What he actually did there, for how long he did it, and whether he devoted his time solely to Coke and to Blackstone, are questions whose answers are closely veiled in the obscurity of time. It is certain that his forthright nature and his love of the Muse could find few sympathetic responses in the querulous ambiguities of codes and contracts. The City of Brotherly Love boasted of better things than these —and of men of equal stature to Coke and Blackstone and Littleton, men like the eminent Benjamin Franklin, who had achieved an intellectual ferment greater than any other man in America. In Philadelphia, the spirit and substance of learning were not neglected. Anthony Benezet had already written his "Historical Account of Guinea." Dr. Benjamin Rush was busy with his works on hygiene. Both of these men were active in antislavery movements, something in which the young Philip Freneau was also interested, if as yet only mildly. Not until later would he join a society for the abolition of slavery. In

[10] *Ibid.*
[11] Freneau's Theology Note Book, in Freneau Collection (Rutgers).

Philadelphia, too, there were men like Francis Hopkinson, a poetaster who aspired to laurels as a musician and artist in addition to a career as lawyer and satirical essayist. There was David Rittenhouse, the astronomer, of whom Thomas Jefferson was later to say that "he approached nearer" the maker of the world "than any man who has lived from the creation to this day." And in Philadelphia, where the young man must have realized that he possessed neither the gift of speech necessary to a successful career in the Law nor the adjustable mind for its shifting definitions of right and wrong, he found a prospect that pleased him infinitely more—a printer for his slender, twenty-four-page pamhplet of poems in which "The Rising Glory of America" symbolized his own discreet and plodding ascent to glory as an American poet.[12]

The great event did not, however, solve the pressing problem of a living. Poets never hoped to live on their writings, and in the time of Philip Freneau, no poet would have been considered worthy of respect if he did. Though Philadelphia's trade and commerce were, like its cultural life, first among all the Colonies, there was no place for the young man in that city. He had already cast about elsewhere for the sustenance which poets, even more than most men, have always had great difficulty in obtaining.

Philip thought he had found it when he was offered a position as tutor in a school in the Flatbush Section of Long Island. The work was no more suited to him than the Law, and his pupils were so difficult that after only thirteen days of quiet desperation, he incontinently ran off, deserted both school and pupils alike, without the formality of any release or resignation. In a letter to Madison, written on November 22, 1772, the short-lived teacher poured out his heart to one of the few friends who would understand his troubles.

"Those who employed me," he said, "were some of the gentlemen from New York; some of them are bullies, some merchants, others scoundrels. They sent me eight children, the eldest of whom was ten years old. Some could read, others spell, and a few stammer over a chapter of the Bible—these were my pupils and over these I was to preside." After his escape from this dungeon "they proscribed me

---

[12] C. and J. Bridenbaugh, *Rebels and Gentlemen,* pp. 258, 345; S. E. Forman, "The Political Activities of Philip Freneau," in *Johns Hopkins University Studies,* Vol. 20, Nos. 9–10 (1902), pp. 1–105; and Thomas Jefferson, *Notes on Virginia.*

for four days and swore if I was caught in New York they would either Trounce or Maim me . . ."[13]

The brief and trying experience was soon most scathingly portrayed in his sketch of "The Miserable Life of a Pedagogue," which eloquently satirized the desperate lot of needy young men driven to despair by undisciplined children.[14] At the moment, he was less in need of a satirical outlet than a shelter that was free from "bullies, merchants and other scoundrels." Princeton, where his friend Brackenridge was now the master of a school while pursuing his own studies for the Ministry at Nassau Hall, and where he himself, free of any expense for tuition, might do the same, was the most promising haven of all. Perhaps Agnes was still prodding him to fulfill the wishes of Pierre, yet Philip had little more stomach for a clerical future than for the others he had already abandoned. With or without the prescribed curriculum of Dr. Witherspoon, he consumed as much of his time as possible in work that was more important to him than anything else. He was writing some unusual poems concerned with the American scene, poems as original as they were striking, which soon found a printer in New York. This time, the event of publication was more decisive for his future than the writing itself. On the title-page, for the first time in his life, appeared the name of the author— Philip Freneau. He hastened to give the details of his work to James Madison, the one confidant in all his personal affairs. "As to the main poem [The American Village] it is damned by all good and judicious judges." Even so, Philip was proud of his work, and of his name on the volume, though "this is called vanity by some." Pride was often the only coin in which poets were paid.[15]

"The American Village," in part imitative of Virgil and Milton, of Pope and Thomson, and echoing some sentiments of Goldsmith's "Deserted Village" is nevertheless completely American in its theme and flavor. Goldsmith's Auburn, "where wealth accumulates and men decay," was the victim of a suffocating industrialism, but Freneau's sleepy little village is still unspoiled. In America the creeping poison of private enterprise has not yet polluted the sweet springs of life, and

[13] Freneau to Madison, November 22, 1772, in Madison, *Papers,* Vol. 1, p. 77; also R. W. Griswold, *The Poets and Poetry of America,* p. 31.

[14] Freneau, *Poems* (Pattee), Vol. 1, p. xxii.

[15] Freneau to Madison, November 22, 1772, in Madison, *Papers,* Vol. 1, p. 77; see also Madison to Bradford, November 9, 1772, in *ibid.,* Vol. 1, pp. 74–76, in which he asks for Freneau's *Poems* for his brothers and sisters.

the poet, concerned for the unhappy threat to its continued peace, fervently hopes that it may always remain a haven of lovely lassitude and untrammelled beauty. The poem expressed, with a certain skill and the evocation of an abiding charm, his deep affection for the simple solitudes, the wide horizons, the lifting hopes when

> . . . Each one lab'ring in his own employ,
> Comes weary home at night, but comes with joy.

Here, too, in the earliest American poem that does adequate justice to the Indians, the children of Nature whose virtues he extols, Freneau explores the nature of the land he loves so well, the land that is as fair and free as Nature itself. The country is unspoiled by greed such as wrought the ruin of ancient Rome and Carthage, a grasping self-concern which now threatens to engulf the British themselves, as once the barbarians engulfed the civilization of another time. Unless curbed and restrained, Britain may succumb to the same

> Strange fate, but yet to evr'y country known,
> To love all other riches but its own.

If America, the last best hope of man, shall also fall

> . . . by this decay,
> The world itself must fall as well as she.
> No other regions latent yet remain,
> This glorious globe has been researched in vain.[16]

More mature, and of far greater importance in the development of his poetic powers, is "Discovery," a poem in which he again envisions a great America whose one dominant passion is liberty. When Freneau considers the old conquistadors and their subjugation of weaker peoples to their wills, he pours out his wrath and scorn on all warriors, modern or ancient, whose strength was used to tear down and desecrate the soul of man—martial adventurers who, like

> . . . fierce Pizarro stock'd a world with graves,
> [and] Montezuma left a race of slaves.
> . . .
> What are all wars, where'er the works you trace,
> But the sad records of our world's disgrace?[17]

[16] "The American Village," in Freneau, *Poems* (Pattee), Vol. 1, p. 16, reprinted from a facsimile copy in the John Carter Brown Library, Brown University.

[17] "Discovery," in Freneau, *Poems* (Pattee), Vol. 1, p. 85.

Warriors were not the only ones responsible for this destruction.

> Howe'er the groves, howe'er the gardens bloom,
> A monarch and a priest is still their doom!

The naming of priests as partners in desolation was a bad augury for the piety of one who had contemplated wearing the clerical robe. And the inclusion of monarchs in his makers of war, foretold the change in his former opinion about "Brittania's warlike troops, choice spirits of her isle."[18]

The year 1772, soon to close on Philip's twentieth year, had been a difficult one. Grown to manhood, he had nothing to show for all the years that had gone before—nothing but some slender verses which he himself did not regard too highly, since he revised many of them again and again before their inclusion in later editions, while omitting others as unworthy of any revision. His fame was still an exceedingly muted one, and his earnings were nil. Perhaps the "judicious judges" were right when they "damned" his poetic offspring. These were not, indeed, wholly his own, yet scarcely another's. The form, often the substance, of some of his poems were derivative, yet greatly modified to his own uses; and the content of many of them was entirely original. For the most part they were native to the soil and life of America. Moreover, they struck a new and unusual note in American poetry, with an idiom at once strange and inspiring.

For the first time in the country's history, the poems of Freneau provided the metrical music of an upsurging love of liberty, and sounded the first clear call for democracy in the new world. Unlike the earlier poets of Puritan vintage, Philip Freneau was more concerned with the future of a young country than the past of an old tradition. Anne Bradstreet, Michael Wigglesworth, Edward Taylor—for them the world was a chimera, and heaven the sole reality; the truth was spun from the silken threads of a smile and the salt tears of suffering. The good place was not here, but hereafter.[19]

For Freneau, the world, the little, scarce-known world of America, with its dreams and hopes and aspirations, was the one reality above all others. Heaven, if it was to be found at all, must be sought for here on the earth.[20]

---

[18] *Ibid.*

[19] V. L. Parrington, *Main Currents in American Thought: The Colonial Mind,* pp. 85 ff; see also J. L. Onderdonk, *History of American Verse, passim.*

[20] N. F. Adkins, *Philip Freneau and the Cosmic Enigma, passim.*

7. THE STUDY OF NOTHING

MAN CANNOT LIVE on vanity alone. The vanity of Philip Freneau, so modestly titillated by the sight of his name on a book of verses, could scarcely satisfy his more pressing need for money. The last line of "Bombo's Pilgrimage," which proclaimed the need of men—and of poets—for food, while far from poetic, was nevertheless true. They had to eat.

In the fall of 1772 he could, with somewhat greater urgency, have said the same thing. He did say it, in his letter of November 22, 1772, to James Madison. "The old hag Necessity," he wrote him, has "a prodigious gripe of me." All that year he had "met with a variety of rebuffs," among which the worst was the unhappy experience of the Flatbush school. Now, he must go back to the same kind of work again, not indeed to Flatbush, where he had so barely escaped a trouncing, but to Princess Anne in Maryland, where his friend Hugh Brackenridge was the master of Somerset Academy at Back Creek. His mood, sufficiently bad as it was, became further depressed by the journey to Back Creek. In Annapolis there were difficulties of which he tells us—and Madison—nothing beyond the fact that "I got clear very handsomely." When he finally reached the school, he was "destitute even of a brass farthing." Even so, "this is the last time I shall enter into such a business; it worries me to death and by no means suits my giddy, wandering brain."[1] He had left Nassau Hall and the study of divinity to make his own way in the world, but the road of pedagogy was a *via dolorosa* for him. Reducing his antipathies to verse, he explained why.

[1] Freneau to Madison, November 22, 1772, in James Madison, *Writings*. Also Freneau's Note Book, in Freneau Collection (Rutgers); and William Hall, *Philip Freneau*.

> A plague I say on such employment,
> Where's neither pleasure nor enjoyment,
> Whoe'er to such a life is ty'd,
> Was born the day he should have dy'd.[2]

The new school at Back Creek is larger than the one from which he decamped. Its fifteen trustees are "gentlemen of the first reputation" and, apparently, only the children of gentlemen can afford the charge of thirteen pounds a year for board, in addition to the five pounds a year for tuition. Nevertheless, the students are much the same as those in Flatbush. All thirty of them "prey upon me like Leeches." Not yet twenty-one, Freneau "already feel[s] stiff with age." His hair is like a mop upon his head, while on his chin he carries "a huge tuft of beard." But he eats—at least he eats—and he also finds some time to write poetry, about four hundred lines of it about his adventures on the journey to Maryland. Teaching, studying, writing—"these three take up all my time." Occasionally he dips, ever so lightly, into the mysteries of medicine, but medicine, no more than Law or religion, can hold his interest for long. One thing alone absorbs him completely:

> Deep to the woods I sing a Shepherd's care,
> Deep to the woods, Cyllenus calls me there,
> The last retreat of love and verse I go,
> Verse made me mad at first and—will keep me so.[3]

Of the verses that he wrote we know a good deal more than of the love he suggests. He rarely says more than this, here or hereafter, about the amatory adventures which befall him, and which, indeed, may have occurred only in his poetic imagination as beguiling material for some romantic verses. Was there any feminine involvement in the life of the young man? Was the retreat in the woods only for verse and not for that of which poets, like other men, perhaps more than most men, have need as they have need for poetry? Was the trouble in Annapolis the result of some "affair" from which he got clear so "handsomely"? At Princeton there had been plenty of high times with the girls, but if Philip or his friends ever tasted of the succulent fruit, they had managed to keep the occasion a close secret from the pryings

---

[2] Freneau, *The Poems of Philip Freneau* (ed. F. L. Pattee), Vol. i, p. xxi; Lewis Leary, *That Rascal Freneau*, p. 43.

[3] Freneau to Madison, November 22, 1772, in Madison, *Writings;* see also Leary, *That Rascal Freneau*, p. 46.

of posterity. Philip was more reticent than others, even when he sang like a troubadour about some lady who had moved him. In a sparsely settled country where marriage occurred early and was enjoined by economic and social stringencies unknown in older lands, he remained a bachelor until many years later. It was a total lack of money, a failure to find a place for himself, and a deep-seated restlessness that were the transparent reasons for his celibacy. More likely it was the Gallic spirit of impatience with the multiple ties of body and soul, and his own refusal to accept the disciplined labor which they entailed. To write was no burden for him, however difficult the task of creation. Let the hag of need ride ever so hard, he was still the master, his own master, if only a nobly pathetic one like Don Quixote. He too had his dreams, and the fragments which fell from the anvil of disillusion. He would often be reduced to borrowing money—when he visited his mother some time later, he borrowed a pound from Samuel Forman, an old neighbor at Middletown Point, who would never miss the money. Samuel Forman, a friend of the family, looked on the young man with a certain affection and favor, though he could not possibly foresee the close ties that would bind them together in the future. The man who now borrowed the pound would later, much later, also take his daughter, Eleanor, to wife. Eleanor, sweet and saucy, was still only a child, too young to know anything about either money or marriage.[4]

At Somerset the round of duties, despite the "leeches," allowed Philip a little time to pry into mysteries which were even less rewarding than those of Medicine. He had not entirely given up the notion—not his, but Pierre's—of making a career of Religion. Of all the honorable professions it was still the only one in which a man was always assured of his bed and board. There was no adventure in it, of course, unless a pallid one of a purely spiritual nature; but it might have some modest compensations for a descendant of Huguenot ancestors for whom the life of the spirit was considered precious above all others. To Philip's forebears religion had been as a stout fortress. What kind of security could it offer to him?[5]

[4] Samuel Forman, *Narrative of a Journey Down the Ohio and Mississippi.* The friendship between the Formans and the Freneaus appears to have been of long duration. The amatory problems of Philip, because of the paucity or total lack of reliable data, are purely conjectural. See also Samuel Forman Papers, Mss.

[5] Freneau's Theology Note Book, in Freneau Collection (Rutgers); N. F. Adkins, *Philip Freneau and the Cosmic Enigma;* and Leary *That Rascal Freneau,* p. 45.

In the months that he spent at Somerset, he pondered the question until some answer, definite and conclusive, might resolve it. At the same time, in the fleeting moments snatched from the "leeches," other enterprises, equally absorbing, left him little leisure to meditate on events which transpired outside the woodland fastness of Back Creek. What was happening in the struggle between the Colonies and the mother country made hardly a ripple in the sheltered harbor of his seclusion, though that struggle was fast assuming the forbidding aspects of a continental quarrel. It had already burst the bonds of provincial displeasure. The alarms were louder, the roll of martial thunder was greater, the portents of rebellion became more sinister.

In Virginia Governor Dunmore's high-handed proceedings under the guise of royal authority had led the Burgesses to enact resolutions for the appointment of a Committee of Correspondence and Inquiry, "whose business it shall be to obtain the most early and authentic intelligence of all such acts and resolutions of the British Parliament, or proceedings of the Administration, as may relate to or affect the British Colonies in America." The Burgesses went even further. To ensure unity of action, they provided that the Committee "Keep up and maintain a correspondence and communication with our Sister Colonies, respecting these important considerations . . . and request them to appoint some person or persons of their respective bodies to communicate from time to time with the said committee."[6] There was a pressing need for this action by the Burgesses of Virginia. To prevent a recurrence of the Rhode Island incident in which the British ship *Gaspee* had been destroyed when it attempted to stop and search vessels suspected of smuggling, Parliament had decreed that anyone who should damage or destroy any British property in the future, though it were only "the button of a mariner's coat," was to be transported to England for trial. On conviction, the penalty was to be— death. This was justice with a vengeance. Under such a law there could never be peace. And the committees of correspondence, in Virginia, in all the Colonies, would be on strictest guard to defeat it.

Did the young teacher, poet, and theologian at Somerset know about the Committee of Correspondence and what it forboded? It is doubtful that he had any time for such matters, what with all his other duties, to which he added still one more, in reality a pleasure rather than a duty. He had begun composing a new poem, greater in scope and vastly more

[6] Jacob Axelrad, *Patrick Henry: The Voice of Freedom,* pp. 72–74.

ambitious than any he had attempted before. The work progressed slowly, and no one—not even his friend Madison—was informed of its subject matter. In the pressure of closer concerns, it was not likely that Freneau would have learned of the turmoil in New Hampshire, where a mob of men raided Fort William and Mary, and took all the small arms for use against England. Later, another exploit of even greater magnitude erupted, when the patriots assaulted the government treasury and made off with two thousand pounds in cash.[7]

Lord North, Prime Minister of England, was too astute not to take notice of the yeasty ferment in the Colonies. Perhaps it could be subdued without a show of force, with some innocuous concession to the sensibilities of the proud Americans. Lord North hoped that his new decree of April 1773 would cajole the recalcitrant Colonies into accepting, not many taxes, just one tax, a tax on tea, so slight and unimportant that it would add nothing to the cost of the beverage; on the contrary, they would get it for less than they had ever hoped. But the principle of taxation by a Parliament where the Colonies had no voice or power would remain; it might even be accepted by the radical incendiaries of Massachusetts.[8]

Philip Freneau, whether he knew of the events that preceded it or not, learned with interest about the Boston Tea Party, in which not oil but tea was spread on the troubled waters of Boston Harbor. His reaction had reached no further than the writing of a satirical dialogue in which, though he strikes a soft blow at those who still use the hated brew, he also indicates his concern for the virtues of the "Yankees." At the same time, he does not fail to see the dangers that loom for the future of his country.

> Englishmen, of all mankind,
> Are the bravest and most blind.[9]

In the remote environs of Back Creek the hot words of Sam Adams, urging his countrymen to violence, may not have penetrated, nor the

[7] P. Davidson, *Propaganda and the American Revolution*, pp. 227 ff. See also R. A. Billington, B. L. Lowenberg, and S. H. Brockunier, *The United States: American Democracy in World Perspective*, pp. 53–54. The rumblings of rebellion had been heard long before in Freneau's country of Monmouth (Davidson, *Propaganda*, p. 34; C. H. Van Tyne, *The Causes of the War of Independence*, p. 14).

[8] G. M. Trevelyan, *History of England*, p. 550.

[9] *The True American*, July 27, 1822; see also Leary, *That Rascal Freneau*, p. 53.

news of the appointment of General Gage as the new governor of the
Bay Colony, to put down the rabble of Boston, by arms if necessary.
The poet, removed in space and circumstance from involvement in
these political problems, was not therefore alien to them.

Only mildly concerned with the events that were soon to erupt on
Lexington Green and on Concord bridge, Philip Freneau was not
alone in shrugging off the echoes of distant shouts and tumults. Most
of his countrymen were equally loath to face the inevitability of armed
conflict. In England, only the men charged with power saw the danger
of a conflagration in the sparks of British intransigence on the tinder
of American pride and patriotism. The Earl of Chatham protested
against the "mad and cruel measures" of the mother country, whose
one purpose was "to crush the spirit of liberty among the Americans."[10]

The teacher of Somerset is deeply interested in this matter of
liberty, as he proves in his new poem, "The Pictures of Columbus,"
which he has just completed. In addition to portraying the trials of
Columbus, the misadventures of his voyage, and the final tragedy of
his chains, Philip Freneau considers the entire question of freedom in
America, and comes to the only conclusion which his ignorance of the
most recent events would seem to permit.

> . . . No tyrant Kings
> Enact hard laws to crush fair freedom here;
> No gloomy jails to shut up wretched men;
> All, all are free—here God and nature reign.

With the poet's instinct for the eternal at the heart of the transitory,
Freneau, in this, his finest work thus far, considers the timeless future
of America,

> When Empires rise where lovely forests grew,
> Where Freedom shall her generous plans pursue.[11]

As in his earlier poems, the theme of liberty obsesses him in this one.
It is more than an impersonal abstraction, an ideal to be achieved or
maintained for his country's sake alone. He yearns for it himself, and

---

[10] Trevelyan, *History of England,* pp. 549 ff. For his far-seeing policies of accommodation with America, the elder Pitt was called a "Trumpet of Sedition"
by George III. For the measure of his prophetic warnings to this country see
Dictionary of National Biography, XV, 1249.

[11] Freneau, *Poems* (Pattee), Vol. 1, p. 89.

hopes to retrieve it some day, when at long last he shall escape the "leeches" of Somerset and the depressing atmosphere of seclusion at Back Creek.

> Yet, in this joyless gloom while I repose,
> Some comfort will attend my pensive shade,
> When memory paints, and golden fancy shows
> My toils rewarded, and my woes repaid.[12]

Neither his memory nor his fancy are of any present help in the quest for freedom. Uncertain of his plans for the future, he still wrestles with the problem of Religion as a career, probing the pages of Bucani and Turettino's "Theological Institutions," Burnet's "Exposition of the Thirty-Nine Articles," and Pearson's "Exposition of the Creed." Carefully he considers what he has read and the numerous notes he has made. He has, at long last, come to some definite conclusions, the most important of which is: "It was a vain notion that a Parson's occupation was the high road to wealth and independency in Life." More directly, he addresses himself: "You have collected a considerable variety of extracts and hints but it was lost labour; it never answered the trouble." And finally: "Farewell to the study of Divinity—which is, in fact, the Study of Nothing!—and the profession of a priest is little better than that of a slothful Blockhead."[13]

The "study of nothing" had nevertheless yielded a few "Themes for Sermons" in the remote possibility that they might some day be useful. They would indeed serve a purpose in his future prose and poetic work, when he would enlarge on such questions as "Where is Hell?" and find the answer in "the conscience of a wicked man." In life alone lay the punishment and reward of man, for "Death leaves the body a useless, shameful, and putrefying thing." Pleasure and pain are here, now, on earth; not in heaven or in hell. The truth could not be dodged. Let man's faith keep pace with man's hope, and his hope keep step with the realities of the world. "Pain," the poet of Somerset knows too well, "is no stranger in this world, for in this world every day the sun looks down on thousands of miserable creatures who groan in agonies of pain—"[14]

Was there any hope in such a world? The student of theology, though rarely free from the accumulating shadows of doubt, had

[12] *Ibid.,* Vol. I, p. 122.
[13] Freneau's Theology Note Book.
[14] *Ibid.*

once had a few moments of certainty. As he delved deeper into the mysteries of Religion and confronted its dogmas with the realities of his own life, he gradually reached the position of the Deists. There was a God, no man could deny it—but men were still doomed to live, to suffer, and to die. That was the substance of all history, the fate of all men. In America, perhaps, that fate could be softened, sweetened, made more palatable than ever known to recorded history. America's slate was almost clean—what would the future write upon it? Here, Philip Freneau believed, they might at least "look forward to a better country," and a finer life than was possible anywhere else.[15]

His hopes, his doubts, his labors with the "leeches" and his fumblings with the certainties led to no certain resolution for the future. All were sunk in the common pool of frustration. A man of complete integrity, he could not accommodate himself to the mere urgencies of the moment. The easiest way, the path of least resistance, the quickest compromise, would lead to a future of false, if certain, security. To one who was incurious and contented, such a prospect might seem a valid consummation of his life. Would it not also be drawing close the curtains of night against the emptiness of the earth and sky? Philip would have some occasions to draw the curtains, but more often he would open them wide to let in the light. That was the secret at the heart of all his doubts, his hopes, and his feeble efforts to chart a course that would not end in a blank wall but in the free spaces of the soul.

Philip Freneau decided to give up all further thoughts of the Church as a career. He was also forever done with teaching. If his life was to have any meaning at all, he must find it in the freedom of choice that he demanded for himself, and in his work, where for good or for ill he would try to express the freedom that he also wanted for his country. Poetry? It was not a good time for words strung together in meter or in rhyme, as William Bradford had informed James Madison.[16] If Philip could write such words, who was there to read them? Who, in all conscience, would pay to read them? On a continent, in a world that was threatened by many fires, soon to burst into many conflagrations, who cared about words, even fine words, when deeds, and only great deeds, could quench the flames.

The flames were rising higher and higher in the Colonies, and more fires were being set by incendiaries of New England and Virginia. The

[15] *Ibid.* Adkins, in *Philip Freneau and the Cosmic Enigma,* proves beyond any question that Freneau was a Deist.

[16] Letter of October 15, 1774, in William Bradford Papers, Mss.

"Intolerable Acts," the "Quebec Act," all were passed by the British Parliament to quench the spreading conflagration. They failed even to quench the ardor of patriots for freedom. In Philadelphia, the First Continental Congress was already meeting to consider united action by the Colonies against the enveloping danger to all of them. Patrick Henry had electrified the delegates by declaring that "the distinctions between Virginians, Pennsylvanians, New Yorkers, and New Englanders are no more. I am not a Virginian, but an American." He warned his countrymen of imminent hostilities and the need to prepare for them. Tories were to be watched as enemies of the people. Freneau's friend, the mild-mannered Madison, back home in Virginia, advocated forceful measures, not only against the Tories, but against their clerical supporters as well. He was certain that even a parson could be brought to book quickly, "should his insolence not abate," by the simple expedient of dressing him up "in a coat of tar and surplice of feathers." As the year 1775 began its fateful and tortuous march across the page of history, the Second Continental Congress was preparing to meet in Philadelphia and the Virginia Convention at Richmond.[17]

Philip Freneau, having no business with either of them—having indeed no business at all—had quit Somerset and gone home for a short visit with his mother. In the early spring of 1775 he appeared in New York.

[17] Billington, et al., United States, p. 55; Axelrad, Patrick Henry, pp. 80 n., 90–91, 93 n., 99.

8. REVOLT INTO REVOLUTION

AT BACK CREEK, deep in the Maryland woods, little had seeped through of the drama that was unfolding on the stage of Revolution. Philip learned more about it in New York. The port of Boston was closed and the city itself was occupied by Gage, General of the British Army and the city's military governor. He was, in addition, preparing a coup that would deprive the citizens of the Bay Colony of the powder—and the power—which they needed to defend themselves. But the patriots of Boston were ready to resist him to the end, as the patriots of Virginia were rallying to Patrick Henry's cry of "Liberty or Death," ready to resist the royal authority in the Old Dominion.[1]

In New York, where the cry was also heard, the cause of Boston, of Richmond, of all the Colonies, became the cause of the men whom Philip Freneau watched as they set a liberty pole, "upwards of eighty feet in height, including its topmast." He did not see the "gang of the disaffected to the American cause" who "approached the unguarded Pole at midnight," to hack it down and cut it into "thirteen different portions." He was certain, however, that the miscreants, if discovered, "would have fared badly." When a new pole was erected to replace the one destroyed, Philip prepared a poem fitting for the occasion which was "read to the surrounding multitude," and "printed in a hand-bill, and circulated in all directions, and carried thro' every street, and thrown into every door in the city."[2] New York, a Tory stronghold,

[1] R. A. Billington, B. L. Lowenberg, and S. H. Brockunier, *The United States: American Democracy in World Perspective*, pp. 54–55.

[2] "Recollections of Past Times and Events," Nos. II and IV, in *The True American*, July 27, 1822, and August 17, 1822; also T. J. Wertenbaker,

needed such propaganda, even the propaganda of a poet, as much as it needed the more vigorous action of its patriots. The poet, at last moved by events within the province of his own knowledge, had dashed off what was desperately demanded, not a poem full of fancies for the future, but a ringing challenge to all who took the present lightly. He called it "The New Liberty Pole—*Take Care.*"

> Seized from the woods, this honored Tree,
> We dedicate to Liberty;
> Here may it stand while time remains,
> Or Liberty, with reason reigns.
>
>   . . .
>
> Let them advance, by night or day,
> Let them attempt a new affray,
> And speedy vengeance will ensue,
> —At least their hides beat black and blue.[3]

For one who shrank from violence himself, these were strong words indeed. Even so, they were far less violent than those used by Madison, his equally peace-loving friend down in Virginia.[4] The poet might not have approved so drastic a remedy as tar and feathers for those who questioned the opposition to England. In common with most people, Freneau still harbored the hope of conciliation. Britain was a stern parent, but at times also a helpful one. It was true, as John Adams, the level headed cousin of Sam Adams, declared, that the Navigation Laws compelled the Colonies to buy in the dearest market and sell in the cheapest. But did they not also grant a virtual monopoly to Colonial staples in the domestic trade, to say nothing of some generous bounties to stimulate the native production of certain specialties? Did not Colonial ships enjoy equal favors with the British, and equal protection from the Royal Navy? Yet the restrictions, the imposts, the callous hand of authority and the monstrous injustice of taxation without any representation had all conspired to fray the bonds that held the two

---

Father Knickerbocker Rebels, pp. 41, 44–45, and Lewis Leary, *That Rascal Freneau,* pp. 54–55.

[3] "Recollections of Past Times and Events," No. IV, in *The True American,* August 17, 1822. Also, P. Davidson, *Propaganda and the American Revolution,* pp. 15 ff. *Letters from an American Farmer,* by J. H. St. John Crèvecoeur, added fuel to the fire of propaganda—a Virginia edition of the *Letters* was prepared by Richard Henry Lee.

[4] Madison to Bradford, July 28, 1775, in James Madison, *Papers,* Vol. I, p. 159; Jacob Axelrad, *Patrick Henry: The Voice of Freedom,* p. 99.

countries together. The bonds were still strong, and if they were to be severed, it seemed certain that nothing but the sword would cut them asunder. The patriots themselves scarcely envisioned such an end to the ancient and honorable traditions rooted in a language, a culture, a history that was common to both lands. One of their toasts, uttered as a prayer and supplication even when accompanied by angry scowls and mounting passions, was the hope, sincere and deeply felt, that "the sword of the parent" would "never be stained with the blood of her children."[5] And Philip Freneau, while single-minded on the subject of liberty, also yearned for the time when "Britannia [ruled] our hearts again."[6]

It became evident to most men as to Freneau that such a possibility was no longer in the realm of reason when news reached New York of the fighting at Lexington and Concord. On April 19, 1775, it appeared as if Samuel Johnson, the London wit, was speaking more than his own mind when he told Boswell that Americans were "a race of convicts and ought to be thankful for anything we allow them short of a hanging."[7] There was to be no hanging on that day, for Paul Revere had broken the silence of the dark night with his news of a British force that was marching from Boston to take the rebel leaders Sam Adams and John Hancock prisoners. The redcoats lost their men and a hanging, but they had other business too, and this they did not lose. Major Pitcairn's well-armed soldiers were after the guns and powder of the patriots at Concord. When the poorly clad rebels tried to stop the British at Lexington, they were shot down; when their comrades tried to halt the redcoats at Concord, they were put to the sword, their guns and powder captured or destroyed. The rebels were not daunted. They fought bravely and with strange effect. The British, for the first if not the last time, met their match. The untrained, uncouth minutemen of New England, hiding behind trees and shrubs and walls along the route of returning redcoats, picked them off one by one, turning defeat into victory, and despair into hope.

Blood had been shed; the sword of the parent had been stained with the blood of the children. More fighting had occurred at Ticonderoga,

[5] Axelrad, *Patrick Henry,* p. 97.

[6] Freneau, "A Voyage to Boston," in Freneau, *The Poems of Philip Freneau* (ed. F. L. Pattee), Vol. 1, p. 158. It is true that colonial staples enjoyed a monopoly in the home market and colonial ships shared the same favors granted to English vessels. But Freneau was a propagandist now.

[7] James Boswell, *Life of Samuel Johnson,* p. 239.

in which the Americans under Ethan Allen and Benedict Arnold had
won a victory at the cost of more blood. And now there was also the
tragedy of Bunker Hill, where brave men on both sides were slaugh-
tered without mercy, with no further qualms about the ancient ties of
language, or commerce, or culture. The sword had sundered them all.
Bunker Hill was no mere skirmish, no inflated "massacre," no small
rebellion. This was war! This meant Revolution!

America was getting ready to try the issue of liberty and democracy
in the new world. On June 15, 1775, the Second Continental Congress
made George Washington its unanimous choice as commander-in-
chief of "the forces raised, or to be raised, in defense of American
liberty." In that defense, young Philip Freneau enlisted with full poetic vigor. In this same month of June he published a poem "Libera
Nos, Domine," in which the plea for independence, still a muted one,
is made more definite, as he prays that God may free his country.

> From the valiant Dunmore, with his crew of banditti,
> Who plunder Virginians at Williamsburg City,
> From hot-headed Montague, mighty to swear,
> The little fatman with his pretty white hair.
>
> From the Caitiff, Lord North, who would bind us in chains,
> From a royal King Log, with his toothfull of brains,
> Who dreams, and is certain, (when taking a nap)
> He had conquered our lands, as they lay on his map.
>
> From a Kingdom that bullies, and hectors, and swears,
> We send up to heaven our wishes and prayers
> That we, disunited, may freemen be still,
> And Britain go on—to be damned if she will.[8]

Like his lines on "The New Liberty Pole," these were less poetry
than propaganda, more incitement than inspiration. As often in the
future if the occasion required it, so now, he stooped to conquer, and
he stooped too much. A poet's laurels were flattering to the spirit, but
liberty was necessary for the soul. The bitterness reflected in Freneau's prayer was matched only by the provocations which induced it.
If Lexington and Concord, Boston and Bunker Hill, were not enough,

---

[8] Freneau, *Poems Written and Published during the American Revolutionary
War*, Vol. 1, p. 161; see also V. L. Parrington, *Main Currents of American
Thought: The Colonial Mind*, pp. 372–373; and S. E. Forman, "The Political
Activities of Philip Freneau," *Johns Hopkins University Studies*, Vol. 20,
Nos. 9–10 (1902), p. 17.

George III was urging Guy Johnson, his American agent, to stop at
nothing to induce the Indians to "take up the hatchet against the
Colonists."[9]

Yet many of the Colonists persisted in the hope that the ties between parent and child might somehow be salvaged, the break healed,
the umbilical cord not entirely severed. They were not quite ready for
the final step that would separate them forever from the flow of economic, cultural, and political blood that had strengthened and sustained them for so many, many years, and might still nourish them in
the years to come. Their laws, their customs, their memories, all were
English; their institutions, their lives, and the lives of generations yet
unborn were all built upon their English heritage.

To Philip Freneau himself it was no small thing that his beloved
masters of prosody were also Englishmen. To him as to all sensitive
men, the memories of Britain, scarred as they were by unseemly exactions and compulsions, were powerful enough to temper the outrage
of bloodletting. Thomas Jefferson, soon to fashion the instrument of
independence, was not yet ready to do so. Like most Americans, he was
averse to complete independence. "There is not in the British Empire a
man who more cordially loves a union with Great Britain than I do,"
he said.[10] Glossing over the bloody events of the recent past, he maintained that necessity had not yet driven the people to that desperate
measure. Philip Freneau probably thought so too, despite his broadside
against England and its addle-brained monarch. He was far removed
from any of the actual fighting and only knew by hearsay of the sanguinary conflicts in remote Boston and the sinister threats in distant
Virginia. In New York, not a few incidents were likely to explode at
any moment into full-fledged rebellion, but in New York too, perhaps
more than elsewhere, the hope for conciliation was strong and vocal,
as the Tory sentiment there was more widespread and powerful.

Agitators like John Lamb and Isaac Sears, leading their followers in
raids and riots against royal authority, might find a good fund of sympathy in some of the wealthy citizens of New York, men of "superior
condition" like Lewis Morris and Philip Livingston, John Jay and
Philip Schuyler, who joined the general clamor against the New York

[9] Carl Van Doren, *The Secret History of the American Revolution*, pp. 121–
122. Congress appointed (July 1775) a committee, consisting of Patrick Henry,
Benjamin Franklin, and James Wilson, "to treat with the Indians."

[10] "A Summary View," in Thomas Jefferson, *Writings* (ed. P. L. Ford),
Vol. 1, pp. 421–432. See also Frank Donovan, *The Jefferson Papers*, p. 74.

Assembly when it refused to send delegates to the Second Continental
Congress. But such men, with more at stake than the common man,
were more restrained in their views. For the most part it was the common people, the "rabble" with no great risks in property or position,
who were most active in their opposition to Britain. They had little
political or economic power, and their strength lay only in their numbers. While New York was mostly Tory at the top, the common people
supplied the energy and the drive of organizations like the Sons of Liberty, who, as one visitor from London had discovered, were passionately engaged in such enterprises as "rubbing of arms, enlisting, exer-
cising," taking their orders, not from authorities as the New York Assembly, or Lieutenant Governor Colden, or even Governor Tryon or
other officials, but from their own selected assemblies and authorities
—the Committee of Fifty-One, the Committee of Sixty, the Committee
of One Hundred. All of them were busy as bees against the imminent
prospect of war, at the same time ordering everybody to "perfect themselves in the military art."[11]

That, many citizens were doing with a rare gusto. Already in April,
"with drums beating and colors flying," they had broken into the City
Hall stores, taken hundreds of bayonets, muskets, and cartridge balls,
and executed a swift assault on the Freshwater Powder-House. After
a march on the Custom House, the Sons of Liberty had compelled the
Collector to hand over his keys. If some Tories forgot that discretion
was the better part of valor, they were quickly taught the lesson with
more vigor than charity. Dragged to the liberty pole, their smart
clothes torn from their backs, they were forced to kneel before the
new symbol of freedom. For others, more recalcitrant than these, tar
and feathers provided a more lasting proof of the virtues of liberty. If
the editors of conservative newspapers were careless or critical, they
were apt to receive the same treatment. James Rivington, whose *New
York Gazette* was frequently filled with hateful propaganda against
the patriots, fled from the wrath of an outraged mob to the safety of
the British warship *Kingfisher*, just in time to save his skin, but his
press was destroyed. The New York rebels, lacking any official power,
nevertheless succeeded in preventing the *James* and the *Beulah* from
discharging their heavy cargoes of arms and matériel so desperately
needed by General Gage. New York, so long dependable as a port of
entry for the British, was no longer a sure source of supply for the

11 Wertenbaker, *Father Knickerbocker Rebels,* pp. 41 ff.

redcoats in Boston. It would not be long before the Royal Governor himself would be forced to flee to the shelter of the *Halifax* in the harbor—just as Governor Dunmore of Virginia fled to the safety of the *Fowey* at Yorktown. Many of the "better" classes were already leaving for England or the West Indies, to save their wealth or their persons from the mounting orgy of lawlessness and violence; they were completely out of sympathy with the vagaries and vulgarities of the freedommongers who had nothing themselves and had no respect for the property or position of others. Some of them would stay on, and fight for the mother country here, in New York or elsewhere in the Colonies, loyal Englishmen and Tories to the end. For them the growing rebellion was no less than a civil war. No matter what America might do, or its people attempt, this was England, now and forever, and they were Englishmen. They too would defend their homes—and their liberties—and pay, if compelled to pay, the penalty exacted by patriots who defined a Tory as "a thing whose head is in England and its body in America, and its neck ought to be stretched."[12]

There were still others, the great amorphous mass of yeomen, small tradesmen, skilled workmen, laborers, immigrants, and refugees from foreign tyrannies. For them there was no other home but the one they had toilsomely built in the new land, no other haven of hope but the one they had found in America. The memories of many of them were derived from indentured servants and other immigrant ancestors who had come to the new world to seek a new life, as Philip Freneau's own people had come. For these, as for millions more later, America was a land of opportunity, fabulous in its promise if not always in the product. Their stake in the country was the ineffable one of the wanderer in far places and the seeker after new horizons. They had wandered thus far, and the horizon stretched beyond their utmost seeking. Not now, but another time, they would seek still further, after they had acquired for their children—and themselves—freedom and independence. They knew what they wanted, if they were as yet untutored in all the ways to achieve it.

The thoughts of Philip Freneau could match theirs in all they had left behind and all that they sought in America. A poet, and a fighter only in the manner of poets, he would write the words, the poems, the songs, to incite and encourage, to inspire and uplift the hearts and the

[12] *Ibid.*, pp. 56–57; see also E. B. Greene, *The Revolutionary Generation,* p. 131.

hopes of the masses in the vast struggle which was fast approaching a climax—which was already a revolt and would soon flare into a revolution. What he gave in song and in doggerel, in verses of high beauty and lines of low satire, was of worth equal to, perhaps of value greater than, the fighting, the bleeding, and the dying of his compatriots in uniform. He too would wear a uniform when that seemed the better way—and he too would suffer, as he never ceased to suffer, with it or without. For him the business of soldiering was not yet, nor the way of violence his way. As the great conflict began, Philip Freneau would wield no sword, bear no gun, and even absent himself altogether from the fight.

As poets before him have often been the inspiration of revolution— so was he. As they were the chroniclers of vast and bloody events, so he too would set them down, as a man and as a poet. As other men were true soldiers for the right as they saw it, so Philip Freneau, gentle and intolerant by turns, comic or tragic as the occasion required, with an abiding love of freedom and an everlasting hatred of oppression, dipped his quill both in beauty and in bile, in love and in loathing, but always for America, the promise and fulfillment, its first poet in its first trial for liberty.[13]

[13] Freneau, *Poems Relating to the American Revolution, with a Memoir by E. A. Duyckinck.* All these poems, with few exceptions, expound the theme of freedom from England.

9. WHAT IS A REBEL?

ON JULY 6, 1775, there appeared an advertisement in Holt's *New York Journal,* "humbly addressed to all true lovers of this once flourishing country, whether they shine as soldiers or statesmen," announcing the sale, at John Anderson's bookstore on Beekman's Slip, of a poem by Philip Freneau. "American Liberty" was his first loud blast against the British, addressed not only to the men who stood fast against the stronger armament of General Gage's troops in Boston, but to patriots everywhere who still wavered before the implications of the emerging struggle.

> What breast but kindles at the martial sound?
> What heart but bleeds to feel its country's wound?
> For thee, blest freedom, to protect thy sway,
> We rush undaunted to the bloody fray;
> For thee, each province arms its vig'rous host,
> Content to die, ere freedom shall be lost.[1]

What the lines lacked in the suave and classic dignity of the English masters, they did possess in poetic appeal to plain and often unlettered men. The poet himself did not "rush undaunted to the bloody fray," though he was doubtless "content to die e'er freedom shall be lost." But the place to die was in far-off Boston, where a war was waging, not in New York, where a few raids and riots had sent some men of power and property scurrying for safety. A poet's task, in such a case, was clear—if also safe. Philip Freneau is as yet content to be the story-

[1] Freneau, *The Poems of Philip Freneau* (ed. F. L .Pattee), Vol. 1, p. 142; the original poem with Freneau's autograph corrections is in the Brown University Library.

teller, the chronicler of events, the inciter to action, the trumpeter of passions that must be inflamed to douse the flames of tyranny.

> Oh, see with grief fair Massachusett's plains,
> The seat of war, and death's terrific scenes;
> Where darling peace with smiling aspect stood,
> Lo! the grim soldier stalks in quest of blood.[2]

"American Liberty" is more than an appeal to passion, more than a call to action. The poet stoops to conquer, but he also rises on soaring wings, uplifted by surging lines that inspire with courage and with hope like that of the Puritan fathers who crossed wide seas and wrestled with a barren, savage-infested land to sow the seed of liberty —at least a love of liberty. What they had suffered then, men must suffer now. Do any hold back?

> Perish the thought, nor may one wretch remain,
> Who dares not fight and in our cause be slain;
> Great souls grow bolder in their country's cause,
> Detest enslavers, and despise their laws.

The struggle must be united and potent, the whole country must be galvanized into action, and money and supplies must flow in a steady stream from a central source. What source?

> O Congress fam'd, accept this humble lay,
> The little tribute that the muse can pay;
> On you depends Columbia's future fate,
> A free asylum or a wretched state.

The use of "Columbia" by Freneau imbedded in the language a term until then only loosely employed for the rare concept of a union of all the Colonies.

At the same time that he urges Congress to provide the sinews of war, he appeals also to the minutemen to fight to the end.

> O if that day, which Heaven avert, must come,
> And Fathers, Husbands, Children, meet their doom,
> Let one brave onset yet that doom precede,
> To shew the world America can bleed.
> One thund'ring raise the midnight cry,
> And one last flame send Boston to the sky.

But the end will not, cannot be one last flame. A city may be ruined,

[2] Freneau, *The Poems of Philip Freneau* (ed. F. L. Pattee), Vol. 1, p. 142.

men may die—America will survive and prosper. The poet-prophet foretells its future greatness.

> The time shall come when strangers rule no more,
> Nor cruel mandates vex from Britain's shore;
> When one vast cultivated region teems,
> From ocean's edge to Mississippi's streams.

This was a voice as new as it was clairvoyant. No other in America had ever spoken like this, or with equal authority. The old romantic twaddle was for old, deluded souls—in a people and in a country. The classic conformities had no place in a people or a country that was young and virile and on the march to liberty.[3]

While he is thus addressing the patriots of Boston and America, he is composing a message to the man who champions their oppressors. The broadside, which he calls "General Gage's Soliloquy" is a rather obvious satire on the British general who had once boasted that four regiments were sufficient to "Prevent any disturbances" in Boston. Gage was lampooned as the feckless instigator of all the trouble and the stupid hero of his own malevolence.

> A life like mine is of such mighty worth,
> I'll wrong my King if I should sally forth.
> A random bullet from a rifle sent
> Might pierce my heart, and ruin North's intent.[4]

All this was not quite just to the Royal Governor of Massachusetts. General Gage was only doing the job he was ordered to do—as an Englishman loyal to his country and his oath. He was no coward—nor was his critic the man to say so. The young poet, safe at home, was wielding a bloody pen instead of a sharp sword, firing from an inkwell instead of a musket. If he finds some solace of conscience for himself, he has a little for the general too.

> Ye souls of fire, who burn for chief command,
> Come! take my place in this disastrous land;
> To wars like these I bid a long good-night—
> Let North and George themselves such battles fight.[5]

Gage was, indeed, recalled within a few months, when Major General

[3] *Ibid.*
[4] Freneau, *Poems of Philip Freneau Written Chiefly during the Late War,* pp. 66–71.
[5] *Ibid.*

Howe was sent to replace him. It was not because of any softening on the part of England toward the rebels that he was withdrawn. He was considered too incompetent to cope with the rising tide of sanguinary opposition.

As that tide slowly yet inexorably reached its greatest flow, as patriot leaders everywhere were massing their forces for the inevitable confrontation with the troops that were pouring in from Britain, as the tension increased and the ragged recruits of Washington were feverishly being whipped into some semblance of an army, the man who wrote their poems apparently forgot all about them. Nor was it surprising. Fighting seemingly had ceased and there was little violence anywhere in the country, as both sides prepared for a major struggle. The lull in the fighting, conspicuously reflected in the calm and quiet of New York, provided no stimulus to the poet's pen. Not here, but elsewhere, he might find it again.

It is a poet's privilege to do as he pleases, and all experience is grist to his mill. Time and again the young man's fancy led him far afield from the boredom of inaction and the muted alarms of warfare. That he returned to the scene of action and the vortex of violence when the prod of conscience and the danger to liberty moved him as a man and a poet, was less a contradiction of a nature that was essentially pacific than the resumption of a task set aside briefly but never forsaken—a task in which his greatest, strongest, deepest emotions were engaged. In his own fashion, according to his own powers, Philip Freneau was dedicated to the struggle for freedom, and his occasional flights from the field were never desertions of the goal he held precious above all others in the world. Mindful of his revulsion against violence and his distaste for action, he masked his weakness, his unadmitted fears perhaps, in attacks on the weakness of others. With more understanding than charity he exposed their spiritual failures in a time of crisis. In "The Expedition of Timothy Taurus," he castigates the self-seeking, mean-minded merchants, the insensitive lawyers and ignorant judges, the grasping doctors, and the flesh-pot clergy.[6]

Like a disgruntled Daumier with a bad spleen, Philip Freneau caricatures the so-called leaders, the elite of society, whose one concern is, now as always, with themselves, their own pleasures and profits. They were like tinsel frames whose ornate surface enclosed little of

[6] Freneau, *Poems Written and Published during the American Revolutionary War*, Vol. i, pp. 167–178; Freneau, *Poems* (Pattee), Vol. i, p. 123.

either truth or beauty. He does not like these people with their shams and pretenses, their puny lies and false verities, yet he was himself a subject for caricature. He is spared—and spares himself—because there is no guile in him. He makes no pretense, affects no pose. He betrays no one, and will never betray himself.[7]

Turning from the depressing frivolities of the passing scene, Freneau casts an appraising eye on the new dictum by General Gage, who is still in Boston. Gage has threatened to shoot as rebels all of Washington's militiamen captured by his troops. Rebels? the poet asks in "Reflections on Gage's Letter to General Washington." What is a rebel? What is rebellion?

> If to control the cunning of a knave,
> Our freedom love, and scorn the name of slave;
> If to protest against a tyrant's laws,
> And arm for battle in a righteous cause,
> Be deem'd rebellion—'tis a harmless thing.
> This bug-bear name, like death, has lost its sting.

And Freneau, in the heat of wordy battle, sounds the trumpet call for action:

> To arms, to arms, and let the trusty sword,
> Decide who best deserves the hangman's cord.[8]

That all this is no mere rhetoric, the poet proceeds, a short while later, to prove in "A Voyage to Boston," the best of all his satires of this period of seething calm and turbulent quiet. Though not involved in any far-off dangers, he is never aloof from them in spirit or in feeling. Like most of his satirical writing, "A Voyage to Boston" is poetry only in the most restricted sense, with little of the beauty or the winged wonder of true prosody. A time of crisis was no time for pure poetry. Perhaps there would never be any future time for poetry in America. For liberty there was, there must be, a future. Without it nothing was possible to the spirit of man. Poetry was the luxury of a few, and Freneau was now writing for the many, for the common people, for all those to whom the sentiments of liberty, the rollicking and astringent humor of the simple verses, and their deadly serious appeal for a final rupture with Britain, were more exciting than the

---

[7] Freneau, *Poems* (Pattee), Vol. i, p. 123.
[8] Freneau, *Poems Written and Published during the American Revolutionary War,* Vol. i, pp. 201–205.

soaring strophes of which, in other times, he was equally capable. No wonder that "A Voyage to Boston" ran to several editions in Philadelphia alone, and was widely distributed in pamphlet form to fighting men who needed its heady draught for their sagging morale. As he makes his imaginary journey through Boston, safely concealed by the magic vest which renders him invisible, he eavesdrops on the midnight talks of Burgoyne and Gage, of Percy and Howe, of others too, all of them drawn with an acid pen as their imagined speech alternates between admiration for the enemy and censure for their own failures. Freneau offers a few generous words to England's soldiers; they, at least, are doing their country's work. But what of those others, not Englishmen but Americans, who were also engaged in Britain's bloody chores. Freneau flays the American Tory and inquires with appropriate venom,

> What is a Tory? Heavens and earth reveal!
> What strange blind monster does that name conceal?[9]

The question, of course, is only rhetorical, and he proceeds to answer it by laying the monster's "heart and inmost entrails bare." His portrait of the Tory, his commentary on the struggle for liberty, his discussion of the virtues of the patriots and the vices of the enemy, his increasing insistence on independence—all set forth in rousing couplets that stirred the heart and strengthened the resolve of revolution—were a necessary tonic to the hungry, the wretched, the wavering forces of freedom.[10]

When General Gage, the victim of these and other barbs, was finally recalled to England, Freneau fired a parting shot at the disgraced leader. In "General Gage's Confession," a satirical poem issued in a pamphlet of eight pages, not only Gage, but the Church that gave him aid and comfort, are arraigned before the bar of justice and found guilty of high crimes against humanity. The enormity of a crime cannot be measured by the degree of its punishment, but the scathing satire of the relentless poet was not only effective propaganda for the cause of liberty, but also a penetrating criticism and analysis of the events of the day as they were flashed upon the screen of the Revolution. The power of the British is portrayed as augmented by the power of the Church; the erstwhile student of religion considers them equally as foes to liberty—and to America. From his earliest "Satires against the Tories,"

[9] Freneau, "A Voyage to Boston," in Freneau, *Poems* (Pattee), Vol. 1, p. 158.
[10] *Ibid.*

written when he was still a student at Princeton, his purpose and design were woven into the simple fabric of his belief in America, in its high destiny as a free nation, and in the democratic process which he believed was the only way to achieve it. As the contending forces were preparing for the inevitable storm that must follow the portentous calm, the prospects appeared encouraging for the ultimate triumph of Philip Freneau's belief. The British, while seeking to starve the patriots of Boston into submission, had themselves been starved into defeat. The besiegers were in effect the besieged. Gage had been unable to subdue Boston. Soon Howe would abandon it altogether.[11]

In New York there was neither siege nor submission. The Tories were still there—and so were the rebels. The quarrels between partisans continued unabated; they were savage without being bloody, verbal rather than violent. The tumult persisted, and the distemper of the city troubled many who were not yet rebels, though far from friendly toward Britain. Like Freneau's own cousin John Morin Scott, a prominent lawyer of New York, they were of the "better" classes, prosperous citizens who were no less affronted by British infringements on American liberty than by English assaults on American profits. To them, to such as Scott, it was becoming clearer each day that the people of New York must "be prepared for the worst." According to Scott, "who can prize life without liberty? It is a bauble only fit to be thrown away," a sentiment with which many of his friends agreed, still hoping for the best while not neglecting to prepare for the worst. Freneau, less practical than they if equally concerned, had nothing else to do but prepare his satires. They may have had almost no persuasive power over George III and Lord North; on the minds and tempers of the King's pious and political defenders in New York they did have a rasping, grating effect. To the Tories, the satires were not poetry at all, but frothy effusions without pretense to any literary merit, offensive only to their sensitive and cultivated souls.[12]

It was not Freneau's poetry which they really despised; the cause for which he wrote was their prime target. He was mocked at by the eloquent dialectic of the ablest Tories, men of learning like Myles Cooper, president of King's College, for whom the words of the poet, like the actions of the Whigs, were a clear abasement of virtue and

[11] Lewis Leary, *That Rascal Freneau*, p. 60.

[12] M. S. Austin, *Philip Freneau*, p. 96; quoted also in E. F. De Lancey, "Philip Freneau, The Huguenot Patriot," *Proceedings of the Huguenot Society of America*, II, 2 (1891), 1-21.

a profound shame to honest minds and true gentlemen. The idealism of the dissenters from British rule was trampled on by the rough-shod rhetoric of men like these, who were bolder in New York than elsewhere in the Colonies, and whose perverse logic further inflamed the partisan passions of the rebels.[13]

The critical barbs which they hurled at young Freneau found their mark. They lacerated the pride of one who was vulnerable because, as criticisms of his verse, the attacks were essentially valid. Recalling that once before his work had been "damned by all good and judicious judges," he suffered as much from his wounded pride as from the fear that the wound was merited. An author may survive controversy; often he will thrive upon it, if his honesty and craftsmanship are unimpugned. To a sensitive soul the critical cut is the worst one of all. The body will heal sooner than the spirit, a man more quickly than a poet.

Philip Freneau did not know who made these attacks and cast these insults upon him, for anonymity was the rule more than the exception. His reactions to them soon became apparent. In this war of words, where paper and ink took the place of arms and blood, the weight of intellect and authority was heavily balanced against the rebels. The shining battalions were on the side of the Tories. The truth, so it seemed to Freneau, was perverted by scholars like Myles Cooper, and by churchmen like Samuel Seabury, the rector of St. Peter's in Westchester, and Charles Inglis, of Trinity, in New York. It was to be expected that few of the clergy would support the rebel cause. Not many survived in the pages of history as the champions of revolution. Some had seen the light of reason, and among men of learning it was assumed there were those who also possessed that light.[14]

Myles Cooper, it appeared, was not one of them. One of "the most thoroughly hated men in America," Cooper considered the Sons of Liberty to be the "Sons of licentiousness, faction and confusion." In addition to all their other crimes, they had committed the capital one of burning his pamphlet, *The American Querist*, which maintained, with a curious logic, the injustice of the patriot cause. His acute sense of outrage was understandably further inflamed by the rabble's attempt to beat him, and his undignified escape from a drubbing by jumping the back fence of his home and hiding in a strange house at the edge

[13] T. J. Wertenbaker, *Father Knickerbocker Rebels*, p. 55; W. C. Abbott, *New York in the American Revolution*, pp. 129 ff.

[14] Wertenbaker, *Father Knickerbocker Rebels*, p. 55; Abbott, *New York in the American Revolution*, pp. 144–145.

of the North River. Finally, he too was compelled to seek the safety of the *Kingfisher* in the harbor.[15]

The writings of Philip Freneau were not the only reason for Loyalist attacks, nor any reason at all for the countermeasures of the rebels. His poems might arouse them to action, but the action to which they were incited had nothing to do with the poet or his poetry. That was outside their province. There had been paper wars before, and until they reached the stage of violence, the writers were the only ones who fought them. Violence, when it occurred, was the job of others. At Princeton the war of words had been fought by Madison, by Brackenridge, by Bradford; Freneau had received their support when he needed it. Now he also needed the help of others, of men like himself, of men with words, and there were none to help him. In Princeton the war had been in good part make-believe; not entirely sham, but goodhumored in the spirit of student rivalry as much as the deeper one of principle. Now it was in deadly earnest, without humor or pleasantry, without sham or make-believe. The stakes were too high for trifling.

Honest men could differ about the merits of the struggle that was being waged with words and violence. Decent men could compromise in a war between radicals and conservatives, the left and the right. Such men were of the center, deploring the power of the British while rejecting the rebel extremes to subdue it. Slow to conviction, they remained aloof in the tumult that soon would erupt into open warfare, always hoping for the reconciliation that should quell that tumult without bloodshed. They were everywhere, in all the provinces, and among all classes and professions, and a few of them could write, and some of them were poets. Still tentative in their loyalties, not yet clear about their sympathies, they remained uncertain and hesitant as other loyalties, other sympathies, erupted into violence in New York and in Boston.

In Connecticut the poets, like the learned and devout whose feelings toward the Revolution were cool if not entirely hostile, were of a social station far removed from that of the struggling satirist of New York. They were young men with brilliant careers before them, the product of refined and cultivated environments whose social and political prejudices they could hardly escape. Joel Barlow was perhaps too young to take more than a platonic interest in the plight of his country, though he would approve the displeasure of older men than himself, the men

---

[15] Abbott, *New York in the American Revolution,* p. 129.

of fine family and promising futures like John Trumbull and Timothy Dwight. Trained in the use of language that was correct in spirit as in syntax, such superior souls had no sympathy with the vulgarities of Philip Freneau, nor with his passionate support of patriots who were really revolutionaries. Passion of any kind was in bad taste and violence, physically or spiritually, in bad odor. Any extreme conduct was contrary to the Greek concept of "nothing too much," and a poet like Freneau had forgotten—if indeed he had ever known— about this or any other concept of the classics. Learned young men like John Trumbull and Timothy Dwight and Joel Barlow were less volatile than the Princeton upstart, who patently lacked their intellectual and literary capacity.[16]

John Trumbull was a patriot, as much a patriot perhaps as Philip Freneau, as would become known when he soon published the first part of his satirical poem "M'Fingal," a caricature of a species of Tory who is, at the same time, the hero of the work. M'Fingal is far less obnoxious than the Tories portrayed by most patriots and the poem is in the best of taste, in reality a burlesque that tickled the risibilities and made more people laugh than fight. It offered little comfort for those who saw nothing at all to laugh at in the usurpations of British power.[17]

Timothy Dwight, the grandson of Jonathan Edwards, was more definite in his antipathies for rebel antics. These two did not love the Tories more but the radicals less. Equally they were disturbed by the pretensions of the masses, and looked on the democratic mobs with ill-concealed aversion. Only Joel Barlow, the youngest of the Connecticut poets, would one day break through the shell of indifference which imprisoned him; but now they were all superior to the grime and litter of the emerging revolt and concerned only with their own sheltered world of polite letters.[18] They had none of Freneau's bitterness and paid no attention to his work. He stood alone.

Hurling his stinging satires like some puny David at the British Goliath, Philip Freneau was answered with more venomous attacks on his personal honesty; and his poems were again assailed as illiterate tales told by an idiot signifying nothing. Was his poetry really so bad? Was the ambition so deeply held, so long cherished, to make a career of

[16] Leon Howard, *The Connecticut Wits:* on Trumbull, pp. 70–77; on Dwight, pp. 180 ff; on Barrow, pp. 20, 138–140.

[17] *Ibid.,* pp. 70–77.

[18] *Ibid.,* pp. 20, 138–140, 180 ff.

poesy doomed to failure? True, only his enemies said so—but his
friends said nothing. He himself could scarcely defend his integrity or
his work. Was it enough that his cause was just and his motives pure?
Was it answer enough for now and forever that his only reward was
poverty and his only purpose freedom? The future would give its
answer—for the present he must meet the slanders and the insults
without any help from his friends who were also busy adding fuel
to the fires of revolution.

> Alone I stand to meet the foul-mouth'd train,
> Assisted by no poets of the plain.[19]

In "A Satire—In Answer to a Hostile Attack," a less jocose version
of his earlier "Satires against the Tories," he makes an effective reply
not only to those who impugn his honesty, but to the bigots, the royal-
ists, the wealthy and powerful, the learned, and the godly, who have
maligned him. With more pride than humility, he proclaims:

> Great Jove in wrath a spark of genius gave,
> And bade me drink the mad Pierian wave,
> Hence came these rhimes, with truth ascribed to me,
> That swell thy little soul to jealousy.[20]

But jealousy is not the real motive for the attack on him. The men
who hate him—men who are thinly disguised as the MacSwiggen of
his poem—revile him for the cause he defends, and for no other reason
at all. It is the Revolution which they despise, and their own prejudices
and privileges which they treasure. Sincere or sycophants, they are the
purveyors of betrayal, and the betrayal of others is first of all the betrayal of oneself. Freneau wants to make all this clear to his detractors,
who will surely read his answer though few others will take the trouble
to do so.

> I interfere not with your vast design.
> Pursue your studies, and I'll follow mine,
> Pursue, well-pleas'd, your theologic schemes,
> Attend professors, and correct your themes.
> Still some dull nonsense, low-bred wit invent,
> Or prove from Scripture what is never meant,
> Or far through Law, that land of scoundrels, stray,
> And truth disguise through all your mazy way.[21]

[19] Freneau, *Poems* (Pattee), Vol. i, p. 209.
[20] *Ibid.*
[21] *Ibid.*

Was this intended for the poets who remained silent as well as for those who slandered him? John Trumbull was as ambitious for the Law as for the Muse; he had already served an apprenticeship in the office of John Adams. Timothy Dwight, ambitious in quite another way, might rival his grandfather as a minister of the Gospel.

There were no poets of the plain. Those who tried the wings of Pegasus had their eyes fixed on Parnassus. They were above the battle or sheathed in a thick armor of righteous invulnerability, spirits alien to the herd that clamored for freedom and the poets who abetted their unseemly demands. The people themselves often seemed alien to the poets who sang for them. Living from hand to mouth on the petty earnings from his broadsides and pamphlets, Philip Freneau was spiritually isolated from those who should have been his allies. Frequently, he was physically isolated as well, when he was forced to retire to Monmouth for the sheer creature necessities that Agnes was always glad to share with him. The meager income from the farm rarely provided any surplus which she could spare for her quixotic son. With no assured income, and with barely any prospect of achieving one, Freneau's spirits were further depressed by the blows to his pride. A poet could scarcely hope for either a livelihood or an honorable esteem in the City of New York; at best he might expect only the crumbs from other tables, crumbs that were hardly less bitter because some of them came from the table at Mount Pleasant. In Monmouth, at least, there was a pervasive peace that was good for the soul, an aura of content that the bustling City of New York failed to achieve, despite the lull in the fighting. Riots were not yet revolution, and raids were not yet rebellion. The big trouble seemed to have spluttered, and died down altogether.

In New York especially there were few for whom it had really begun. The idea of liberty was not yet converted into an ideal of spiritual substance. Sporadic violence was always followed by a new hope of settlement. The "gentlemen" of the city, many of the "rabble" as well, were more interested in horse races, bowling matches, cock-fighting, target shooting, card playing, billiard and backgammon contests, than in the imminent danger of a full-blown war. The Inns were as crowded as ever; the King's Arms, the Merchant's Coffee House, the Three Pigeons, were filled with citizens who wanted to forget the rantings of the radicals, and who had the money and leisure to buy a respite from the hustings. There were many ways for men to amuse themselves, but for a young man who had no amusement save in the privacy of his pen and whose pride forbade the fellowship of "gentle-men" who might have helped him to a more rewarding life—men like his cousin Scott—there was no place in the turbulent City of New York. Old comrades like Brackenridge and Madison, friends who might have helped him, were in places far removed from New York, busy with matters more important than poetry.[22]

And poetry was still his great love—as she was his first one, too. He had lost her in the seething city, and where would he find her again? Freneau had never forgotten the golden tales told him by his father of enchanting islands beyond the sea, far from the city, far from all cities, islands which he had already discovered so many times for himself, if only in fancy, through the rigging of ships in the harbor, at the wharves by the battery, and from the heights of the Navesink hills. Now he thought of them again, when the earth was noisy with the tread of volunteers who were being drilled with inadequate arms and fed with inadequate food. For what? For more fights that would only result in more compromises, succeeded by new hopes for new settlements that settled nothing since liberty could never be compromised or settled. For Freneau there was no future in the fights or settlements—there was only insult and beggary, and for ends like these he was "averse to enter the army and be knocked on the head." Nor was he one to volunteer for the killing of men or for the specific purpose of learning how it could best be done. Each man gave what he could, with a pen or with a sword.[23]

Freneau was not the only patriot who was "averse to enter the army." Other citizens of America were not eager to enter it either. Appraising the leaders in the First Congress, John Adams thought that most of them were "trimmers and time-servers"; in his opinion Congress indulged in its "nibbling and scribbling as usual." After four months as commander-in-chief, Washington himself believed that "such a dearth of public spirit and want of virtue, such stock-jobbing and fertility in all the low arts to obtain advantages of one kind or another . . . I never saw before."[24] This was perhaps too pessimistic a

[22] W. E. Woodward, *The Way Our People Lived;* and Wertenbaker, *Father Knickerbocker Rebels,* pp. 126–129.

[23] Alexander Anderson, Diary for 1794, Mss., p. 101. In view of the date this sounds somewhat apocryphal.

[24] Washington to Reed, November 28, 1775, in George Washington, *Writings* (ed. W. C. Ford), Vol. 3, p. 246; also Rupert Hughes, *George Washington,* Vol. 2, p. 280.

view of the American response to the crisis, and it was in part refuted by the sacrifices of the common soldier and his officers. The army was indeed weak, its morale was bad, but the vacillating purposes of the Revolution were as much at fault as the petty interests of the people themselves. The one clear purpose of the struggle would soon be blazoned across the skies of the Atlantic seaboard—Independence; nothing less than this would end forever the cry for conciliation, the hope of compromise, and give final direction to the raids and riots, the struggles and sacrifices of the people of America. Or justify them.[25]

In New York, as elsewhere, the conciliators were still plying their trade with a logic that appeared irrefutable. There was no army to withstand the British should they attempt to take the city. For the time being, the gateway from the North had been closed by the capture of Ticonderoga, but that point was not invulnerable. The way was still open from the East—by sea from Boston. In addition, the *Asia* was anchored close by the *Kingfisher* in the East River, threatening the city with guns which could pound it to rubble almost at will. The Provincial Congress was too feeble, too dilatory to protect New York, an indubitable fact clear beyond cavil by September 1775, when nearly a third of the inhabitants had moved from their homes into tents and huts beyond the zone of danger. Royal power, in the person of Governor Tryon, was only partly affected by his escape to the *Halifax* on October 19. Sears and his men might assume an authority that was not really theirs, arrest those who were a menace to their cause, including Samuel Seabury himself, the loyalist divine who spoke for the British in the name of God. By the end of 1775 the rebel cause needed more assurance than this, and greater precautions for its success. The hope of conciliation was at long last finished. New York must prepare for war with whatever strength it possessed. Trenches must be dug, redoubts must be built, cannons must be placed, barricades must be thrown across Broad Street and Cortlandt Street and Wall Street, and batteries must be set up before the Battery and behind Trinity Church. In the early days of 1776, heaving, sweating, freezing men were laboring in the streets of the city for their homes, their lives, and their phantom liberties.[26]

Philip Freneau had no home. He had no ties to bind him to the city,

[25] John Adams' Diary, September 8, 1774, in John Adams, *Diary and Autobiography,* Vol. 1, p. 150.

[26] Wertenbaker, *Father Knickerbocker Rebels,* pp. 55–57; J. E. Jameson, *The American Revolution Considered as a Social Movement,* pp. 16–20.

and he had little capacity for the labors which others employed to secure them. Liberty was an ideal to which he had given what he had —now he would seek a little of its savor in those distant isles which Pierre had so lovingly portrayed and for which he had so often yearned. If it were at all possible, he would leave New York and go

> As far as winds can blow,
> As ships can travel, or as waves can flow,
> To some lone island beyond the Southern pole,
> Or lands round which pacific waters roll,
> There shall oblivion stop the heaving sigh,
> There shall I live at last with liberty.

There, at any rate, he might live in peace with himself and with others, free to do the work for which he was fitted.

> In distant isles some happier scene I'll choose,
> And court in softer shades the unwilling Muse.[27]

What Pierre had omitted to tell him of those isles was supplied by another who knew much more about them. John Napier, his mother's cousin, was both a good businessman and an eloquent teller of tales. On a visit to Mount Pleasant, his wonderful stories of the West Indies quickly convinced the young poet that his resolution to travel was a good one. Napier had his home in Santa Cruz (St. Croix in the Virgin Islands), a fabulous island of the Caribbean, lovely beyond the dreams of any poet. Only one small obstacle could prevent anyone from getting there—money for the passage—and Philip had little difficulty surmounting it. He needed no money. He could work his passage across if any shipowner was willing to take him on. John Napier may have taken the young man to Captain Hanson, the master of a vessel being loaded with a cargo for Santa Cruz and owner of a large and profitable island plantation. Captain Hanson must have been taken with the slender, soft-spoken youth with the deep-set eyes and fine features whose quick intelligence and infectious eagerness were more persuasive than his slender frame and slight physique. He agreed to take him along not only free of passage but as his guest in Santa Cruz. If, at the same time, Philip could learn something about the mysteries of the sea and the sailing of a ship he might be useful some day if his help was ever needed. To encourage Philip's industry as well as his usefulness, his uncle David Watson presented him with a copy of the *Mariner's*

---

[27] "MacSwiggen," in Freneau, *Poems* (Pattee), Vol. i, p. 211.

Manual. Before they were out of sight of land, the apprentice seaman was already deeply engrossed in it.[28]

As the American Revolution slowly became a reality; while other men who also loved liberty were preparing to fight—and die—for it, the poet-turned-mariner settled down to a pleasant voyage far away from it all. With a clear mind if not a clear conscience, he studied his manual diligently. So well did he learn the pages of maritime lore that he was soon able to replace the ship's mate who had died before the sun-drenched sea of the Caribs was reached. Captain Hanson was perhaps as much mate as master, but the poet was sufficiently absorbed in the science of sailing to make himself then, or later, a master mariner in his own right. In the days ahead the knowledge would serve him well.[29]

Freneau's decision to leave his country was not arrived at without a profound wrenching of his deepest convictions. However he rationalized them, the conflicts persisted. He never ceased to be burdened with the sense, if not the certainty, of guilt. Even before he sailed away to safety and ease he had written out a rough draft of a strangely macabre poem which he called "The House of Night," a tentative examination of his doubts and scruples, set aside for closer contemplation in the silence of the sea. If poetry was truly the recollection of emotion in tranquillity, then he would find the time to perfect the verses in the first major romantic work in American literature in which he would attempt to exorcise the implacable foe of all that lives and must one day succumb to the inexorable demand for dissolution. The fear of death was a tawdry, childish fear, and in the poem it is vanquished by its own futility—by the death of death itself. If everything is of the moment, fleeting and transitory, in the great flux of time and circumstance, nothing is immortal, not even death itself.

> What is death, ye deep read Sophists, Say?—
> Death is no more than one unceasing change;
> New forms arise, while other forms decay,
> Yet all is Life throughout creation's range.

Once bedevilled by his fears, now he could reason with them, face them, vanquish and perhaps abolish them entirely.

[28] Lewis Leary, "Philip Freneau's Captain Hanson," in *American Notes and Queries,* II, 4 (July 1942), 51–53; and Freneau's copy of Robertson, *Elements of Navigation,* in Freneau Collection (Rutgers).
[29] *Ibid.*

Enough—when God and nature give the word,
I'll tempt the dusky shore and narrow sea:
Content to die, just as it be decreed,
At four score years, or now at twenty-three.[30]

As the green hills and the flowering plains of Santa Cruz hove into sight, he could not know how long it would be before the dusky shore of his stricken land would reclaim him. He had no way of knowing how dusky it was already, how black with the smoke of many fires, how strewn with the bodies of many dead. Amid an opulence of colors instead of alarms, in a setting of peace more profound than any he had ever known before, such knowledge never obtruded.

America with its blood and carnage was nothing like this. It was not at all like Santa Cruz—sunny and smiling—which he gazed on with an ill-restrained rapture, and found to be "inexpressibly beautiful."[31]

[30] Freneau, *Poems* (Pattee), Vol. I, p. 212; *The United States Magazine,* August 1779.
[31] "Account of the Island of Santa Cruz," in *The United States Magazine,* February 1779.

10. THE MASK OF BEAUTY

THE SMOOTH SURFACE of the sea reveals none of the racing tides and currents beneath it. The beauty of a landscape masks the toil and travail that lurk behind it. The silence across pathless water, like that of Santa Cruz's trackless jungles, was greater than the turmoil of New York and shut it out completely. Yet in both, the ceaseless, bloody struggles of nature were the same, while behind the multicolored panorama of Captain Hanson's island, so fair to look upon, was hidden the endless inhumanity of man to man. Here as elsewhere liberty was less real than apparent; it was not even apparent when one pried behind the mask of indescribable beauty. Nature offered the poet some new and ravishing colors for his palette, colors that would enrich his poems as few others of his time were enriched. In the shallows by the shore as in the depths beyond it, in the ebb and in the flood, the fancies of his verse reflected the surpassingly lovely angel-fish which glowed "with all the lustre of the most brilliant diamonds"; the fantastic sponges and the seaweeds; the water itself, "blue and bottomless," from whose depths the headlands rose and fell away to "enchanting plains" teeming with groves of orange and of mango. Enchanting at any time, the island was breathtaking in the grandeur of those fleeting moments when an overpowering tropical sunset was charged with a supernal beauty, and appeared to float in the luminous clarity of the circumambient element.[1]

Captain Hanson's estate, nestling at the shore line of Bassend, has

[1] "Account of the Island of Santa Cruz," in *The United States Magazine,* February 1779.

a "beautiful little bay of its own," while back of it, rising in majestic splendor, the mountains keep vigil over the wooden huts and stone houses that repose beneath them. The mountain top, beyond which lie the "vales of Paradise displayed in their primal beauty," reminds the poet of John Milton's lines about

> Mountains on whose barren breast,
> The laboring clouds do often rest.[2]

The plains spreading on all sides are clear enough to reveal the groves of orange and mango, and rarely do the clouds enmist the far-reaching rectangles of sugar and cotton plantations, to one of which Captain Hanson may lay a modest claim. If he was the son of that James (or Jens) Hansen who had once been the governor of the Danish West India and Guinea Company, he had inherited some choice lands which gave him access also to the harbor, a necessary convenience for those whose crops were useless if they could not be quickly moved to markets. A planter's business, his home, the fields themselves, were orderly and thriving, as was natural to a place like Santa Cruz, where "the sky is ever serene" and where "too much cannot be said of the happy climate." How different from the icy streets of New York, or the windy valleys of the Hudson on whose banks nothing was ever heard but "the sound of woe." Even when the hurricane blows at Santa Cruz, "a continual solitude and silence reigns," and "the noise and tumult of the world" are hushed—if only figuratively, if only by the use of poetic license.[3]

Was it really as idyllic as all that? Did no clouds of war, no clash of arms, disturb the sweet serenity of Santa Cruz? As he searched farther afield Freneau discovered some disquieting aspects in this beguiling paradise of his. Every paradise had its own species of serpent, and slavery was the venomous reptile of Santa Cruz. Philip was no stranger to the ugly fact of human bondage, not alone from the revelations of Benezet and Rush, or the visible black men who served their masters in places where he had lived. He owned a copy of the published address of Benjamin Rush "To the inhabitants of the British Settlement in America upon Slave-Keeping" and its indictments had forti-

---

[2] *Ibid.*

[3] *Ibid.,* and *The United States Magazine,* August 1779. See also Danish Government, Virgin Island Records, Mss.; *St. Croix Packet Companies;* and J. A. Jarvis, *Brief History of the Virgin Islands.*

fied his hatred of the enslavement of human beings.[4] His father, his stepfather, even his mother, owned some slaves. In Monmouth, in New York, in the North as in the South, slaves were held, though in the North only a few held them. The economy of the North needed no slave labor, and those who owned them considered their Negroes as unfortunate rather than subhuman. Slowly they were being emancipated in the North, though Philip's own father had never freed his slaves, and his mother had inherited them with the land. Without them, the land itself, so poor in any event, would have yielded nothing. As state after state outlawed the "peculiar institution," Philip's own state of New Jersey lagged far behind the rest in effecting complete freedom. Long before that happened, the few slaves that he himself would inherit were manumitted.[5]

In the paradise which he now examined with careful scrutiny there was almost no talk at all of present or future freedom for the black man. Indeed, to ensure against any repetition of an uprising and to thwart any hope of insurrection, the most stringent laws had been enacted and continually strengthened since the revolt of 1733. The utmost brutality was sanctioned by law for any infraction of the slave status, and at the time that Philip Freneau examined that status on the island of Santa Cruz there were laws that might have turned the stomach of anyone with far tougher sensibilities than his. From lesser to greater crimes the punishments progressed with rare abandon. A slave discovered with a knife or firearm on his person would receive 100 lashes—"without any expense to the owner." Gaming in the streets, riding horseback, walking abroad after eight, were all punishable with 150 lashes—similarly with no expense to the owners. Older laws already provided the penalty for runaway slaves; if caught, they might be deprived of one leg, unless the owner could be softened in his wrath. In such an event, he might exact only one ear, after inflicting 150 lashes. The quality of mercy was finely strained on the island of Santa Cruz. In their daily life, the plight of the Negroes was less forbidding, though Freneau, seeing them on the fields and plantations,

[4] E. B. Greene, *The Revolutionary Generation,* pp. 25–26. A copy of Rush's "Address" is in the Freneau Collection (Princeton).

[5] R. A. Billington, B. L. Lowenberg, and S. H. Brockunier, *The United States: American Democracy in World Perspective,* p. 62; Benjamin Quarles, *The Negro in the American Revolution*; and F. Ellis, *History of Monmouth County, passim.*

was outraged by what he saw. In a population of perhaps twenty-six thousand, all but two thousand were slaves. To control them, to keep them subservient. to hold them on leash, was a task no poet could properly envisage; and methods were used which no liberty-loving youth could forgive, or ever forget.[6]

In the West Indies, the black man was a beast of burden and nothing more. He had no more status in Bassend (or Bassin), also known as Christiansted, the capital of the islands, than in the deep interior where outlanders rarely penetrated. The world only touched the hem of Bassend, exchanged its goods with Santa Cruz, and sometimes brushed it with some of the new ideals of freedom that were blown from afar. The white men were scarcely affected, and the black men remained without the most elementary rights save those a kindly master might graciously bestow. The business of the island was built on servile labor and the rule of business was a strong and jealous power. What the curious young man had seen of slavery elsewhere had not prepared him for the awful spectacle that he witnessed on this island that was so "inexpressibly beautiful." The condition of the slave was a vast, obscene blot on the lovely landscape where "no class of mankind in the known world undergoes so complete a servitude." The cruelty, the degradation, suffered by these forgotten souls left him "melancholy and disconsolate, convinced that there is no pleasure in this world without its share of pain," that perhaps the keenest of all pleasures was the release from pain.[7]

This was no new discovery for Freneau, though never before so poignantly impressed on his sensitive nature. He was no stranger to pain at the heart of pleasure, to the dialectic balance of nature in its smiling and scowling aspects, to evil in the womb of good. Had he not noted as much in his father's letter book, it seemed so long, so long ago? He had known some of the peaks as well as the valleys of human existence, and he had learned that the peaks were few and the valleys were many. The troubles with Britain, the struggle between right and wrong, justice and injustice, liberty and oppression—he knew about these, and when he had turned from them to seek some respite here, he found in this never-never land of enchantment what he had never

---

[6] Jarvis, *Brief History of the Virgin Islands,* p. 44; *St. Croix Packet Companies,* pp. 12–17 .

[7] "Account of the Island of Santa Cruz," in *The United States Magazine,* February 1779.

known before. No trouble was like this trouble, no wrong as great as this one, no injustice so inhuman, no cruelty so bestial. This was not tyranny to man—it was man denied, for whom there is not even tyranny. Here, at the heart of peace, there beat the eternal tom-tom of utter despair and everlasting hopelessness.

A poet and a rebel, seeing all this, was involved in it too. The times needed not sentiment but action, or the words that would inspire action. A poet's duty was to wield a weapon for freedom even if that weapon was only a pen, for the contemplation of beauty was not enough, nor its portrayal much of a remedy for hurts too deep for assuagement. Freneau did not feel entirely guiltless either. He had escaped defilement at home for his soul's sake, yet here was defilement also. In a world he never made there was no refuge from the sinister serpent of power.

And thus the Earth [he wrote], which were it not for the lust of pride and dominion, might be an earthly paradise, is by the ambition and over-bearing nature of mankind, rendered an eternal scene of desolation, woe and horror; the weak goes to the wall, while the strong prevails, and after an ambitious phrenzy has turned the world upside down, we are contented with a narrow spot, and leave our follies and cruelties to be acted over again by every succeeding generation.

As in America many men were being killed and maimed by "the lust of pride and dominion," so here the black men were suffering for reasons, for purposes, that were very much the same.[8]

Would it ever be different? Despite history, despite the ever changing, ever recurring eras of oppression, the skeptical observer was permitted to hope. In his poem on "The Pyramids of Egypt," Freneau considers the ancient tyrannies and concludes that all tyrannies, like those, must inevitably be destroyed by the canker at their hearts. Oppression held the seed of its own dissolution. It was like the stone of Sisyphus, forever pushed to the summit for enthronement, and forever rolling down to defeat. Liberty, on guard at the peak, must remain on watch to the end of time. As other tyrannies have fallen, so this one of slavery would also fall.

> O come the time and haste the day,
> When man shall man no longer crush;
> When reason shall enforce her sway,

[8] *Ibid.*

> Nor these fair regions raise one blush,
> Where still the African complains,
> And mourns his yet unbroken chains.[9]

To acquaint his own countrymen with the conditions which he saw in Santa Cruz, Freneau sent a report of them to *The United States Magazine,* published by his friend Brackenridge in Philadelphia. Prefacing his observations on slavery under the Danish occupation of Santa Cruz with lines from *Julius Caesar,* he warns his readers: "If you have tears, prepare to shed them now." He refuses to detail the horrors and cruelties to which Negroes are subjected, nor does he dwell on past insurrections which have accomplished some slight restraints on ancient tortures. The Dutch, the English, the Spanish, the French—all races have had their part in the exploitation of Santa Cruz, not least among them the French Huguenots who owned some of the greatest plantations on the island. To seek freedom and opportunity for oneself and deny them to another was not the only paradox of human nature, nor did its bitter irony escape the seeker after sweetness and light. His own people, who had come to America—or to Santa Cruz—as refugees from tyranny, were among the worst offenders against the liberty of others. In "The Hermit of Saba," Freneau cried out: "Perdition on those fiends from Europe, whose bloody malice or whose thirst for gold . . . lays the world in ruins." Everywhere the tale was the same, a tale told not by an idiot signifying nothing, but by shrewd and designing men whose conscience and humanity were submerged by "the lust and pride of dominion."[10]

It was in "The Jamaica Funeral" that Freneau expanded on the "bloody malice" and the "thirst for gold" which he found in the West Indies. In this poem we are witness to some strange obsequies and an even stranger interment. The poet's bile is sweetened only by his levity, his despair is lightened only by his skepticism. The immense villainy of the world is no illuson, but neither is the death that cancels it out completely. Why must we make a mountain out of an anthill? Evil is eternal—so be it! Let us at least enjoy the lighter moments we can snatch from life to forget it.

> A few short years, at best, will bound our span,
> Wretched and few, the Hebrew exile said;

[9] Freneau, *The Poems of Philip Freneau* (ed. F. L. Pattee), Vol. 2, p. 25.
[10] "Account of the Island of Santa Cruz," in *The United States Magazine,* February 1779; and Freneau, *Poems* (Pattee), Vol. 2, p. 359.

> Live while you may, be jovial while you can;
> Death as a debt to nature must be paid.
>
> Like insects busy, in a summer's day,
> We toil and squabble, to increase our pain,
> Night comes at last, and, weary of the fray,
> To dust and darkness all return again.
>
> Mere glow-worms are we all, a moment shine;
> I, like the rest, in giddy circles run,
> And grief shall say, when I this life resign,
> His glass is empty, and his frolics done.

But what bitter skepticism or poignant irony is enough to blot out the picture of men who are not even glow-worms?

> See yonder slave that slowly bends this way
> With years, and pain, and ceaseless toil opprest;
> Though no complaining words his woes betray,
> The eye dejected proves the heart distrest,
> Perhaps in chains he left his native shore,
> Perhaps he left a helpless offspring there,
> Perhaps a wife, that he must see no more,
> Perhaps a father, who his love did share.
> Curs'd be the ship that brought him o'er the main,
> And curs'd the hands who from his country tore,
> May she be stranded, ne'er to float again,
> May they be shipwreck'd on some hostile shore.[11]

The poet must take a holiday, if only a brief one, from the seamier aspects of his island retreat. For him as for all men, there can be some interludes of enchantment, when the siren song of youth will lure the spirit from the ugly face of civilization. In "The Beauties of Santa Cruz," he sings a paeon of praise for the seductive, sensual delights of the Caribbean world.

> Betwixt old Cancer and the midway line,
> In happiest climate lies this envied isle.
> Trees bloom throughout the year, streams ever flow,
> And fragrant Flora wears a lasting Smile.

In flowing pentameters Freneau pictures the lush vegetation, the exotic fruits, the flora and fauna, the colors, the sounds and smells, which become vivid and palpable realities for us; we hear, we see, we breathe,

---

[11] Freneau, *Poems* (Pattee), Vol. I, p. 239.

we embrace, the fabulous and abundant life he spreads before us in rich and festive stanzas unique in the poetry of his time. And he concludes:

> Such were the vales which youthful Eden saw,
> Ere crossing fates destroy'd her golden reign—
> Reflect upon the loss, unhappy man,
> And seek the vales of Paradise again.

Where shall it be sought? The man who revels in the beauties of Santa Cruz cannot entirely forget its iniquities, while they, in turn, remind him of something that was never long absent from his mind. Where he is, often recalls where he came from. The fate of freedom shackled in Santa Cruz, prods his conscience about liberty threatened in America.

> Far o'er the waste of yonder surgy field,
> My native climes in fancied prospect lie,
> Now hid in shades, and now by clouds conceal'd,
> And now by tempests ravish'd from my eye.
> There, triumphs to enjoy, are, Britain, thine,
> There, thy proud navy awes the pillaged shore,
> Nor sees the day when nations shall combine,
> That pride to humble and our right restore.[12]

There is no doubt that his deepest feelings were engaged as much in what he fled from in America as in what he saw in Santa Cruz. What he saw was more affecting, but only because the war was only something he heard about, read about, and had never really seen at all. If the news of the full-scale revolution now raging in the homeland reached him at all, it was muffled by distance and tempered by time. He knew nothing of the fury of events that broke in the Colonies of America, in the North and in the South, as the conflict grew ever more venomous between the redcoats and the rebels. He did not know that the early months of 1776 were bitter ones for the patriots, and for their commander who was desperately striving to weld an army out of a mass of untrained, undisciplined men. The matériels of war were lacking, and Congress, though it had voted for ships and munitions, had no power to provide the money for them. Washington, so many times desperate before, was now beside himself with fear—fear of an imminent and final defeat. "I know the unhappy predicament I stand in," he said. "I know that much is expected from me. I know that with-

---

[12] *Ibid.,* Vol. i, p. 249.

out men, without arms, without ammunition, without anything fit for the accommodation of a soldier, little is to be done." In a wrenching cry of despair, he added: "I know that I cannot stand justified to the world."[13]

Who could stand justified? The poets, at home—or abroad? The leaders, who were not yet persuaded that the war, already begun, was inevitable? Only the radicals of Massachusetts, of New York, of Virginia, were convinced, but the men "of superior condition" still held aloof. They had not given up hoping that everything might still be settled amicably. Lord Dartmouth believed the storm was likely to blow over, for he reassured Cadwallader Colden, the lieutenant governor of New York, that the substantial citizens "would not be likely to advise or support rash and violent measures." But violent measures had already been taken, not perhaps by the substantial citizens of New York, though in other colonies even by some of them, as Hugh Brackenridge was dramatizing in the two plays he had just written. One of these plays was "The Battle of Bunker Hill," and the other "The Death of General Montgomery," in which the patriot cause was portrayed as the cause of all honest and substantial citizens, who would stand justified before the world.[14] The time was one of sheer desperation for America, so powerfully pictured by Thomas Paine. *Common Sense,* the greatest summons to patriot action yet written, was also the clearest call for complete independence from Britain.

While Philip Freneau enjoyed the hospitality of Captain Hanson, helping him perhaps at odd jobs on his plantation or his ship; while he was composing his poems on the beauties and the horrors of Santa Cruz, the war he had left behind was seething in barracks and encampments, in conventions and in Congress. The last, irrevocable step was taken on July 4, with a Declaration of Independence which made it clear to all the world that America was no longer subject to Britain. For time and eternity it was a free country, though the proof must still be provided on the fields of battle and in the hearts of its people.

The battle of Long Island, ending in a defeat for the patriots, failed to supply that proof. By August, Clinton and Cornwallis were in New York. The Provisional Congress had moved swiftly to Harlem, to Fort Washington, to White Plains, to Philipse Manor, to Poughkeepsie, to Fishkill, to Kingston. New York itself was laid in ashes.

[13] Washington to Jos. Reed, February 10, 1776, in George Washington, *Writings* (ed. W. C. Ford), Vol. 3, p. 411.
[14] C. M. Newlin, *Life and Writings of Hugh H. Brackenridge,* pp. 35–36.

Washington, presiding at the collapse of a great dream, was almost ready to throw in his hand. He was "wearied almost to death with the retrograde Motion of things," he wrote to his brother. The game appeared to be nearly up.[15]

The game seemed to go better when he gave the country a victory at Trenton. The Hessians under Colonel Rall were defeated, but it was only one heartening interlude in a long succession of reverses. The winter of 1777 at Morristown, the defeat at Brandywine and German-town, the frightfulness of Valley Forge—the game did seem worse, not better; almost all the proof pointed the other way. Men were deserting in droves, so many of them, indeed, that Washington was sure that the end had come. The army, he lamented to the Continental Congress, was "upon the eve of its political dissolution."[16] The men who had deserted were no traitors. They were wretched beyond all limits of human endurance in this war for independence, but far more wretched than they and even more miserable victims of that war were the wives and the children they had left behind them. Their fields were as barren as their apparently hopeless fight for freedom. The men had little food and less clothing against the cold blasts of a harsh winter, and their sufferings were like open wounds into which the salt of the tragic letters from home was rubbed with excruciating pain. Their families are "without bread, and cannot get any. The children will starve, or if they do not, they must freeze; we have no wood, neither can we get any."[17] The women pleaded: "Pray come home." Further north, at Ticonderoga, Anthony Wayne was crying out to all who would listen about "the miserable state of this country."[18]

There were some brighter pages than these in the current history of the war for liberty. At Bennington Colonel Stark had cut down the Hessians under Baume; at Saratoga Burgoyne was defeated by Gates and Arnold. The game was not altogether up. At home and abroad, those who had thought so, began to change their minds. The clouds were lifting, the sun was coming through, and the light of liberty was commencing to shine with a new and warming splendor.

---

[15] Washington to Brother, November 19, 1776, in Washington, *Writings* (Ford), Vol. 1, p. 246; see also T. J. Wertenbaker, *Father Knickerbocker Rebels*, p. 69.

[16] Washington to Congress, October 1776, in Washington, *Writings* (Ford), Vol. 1, p. 152.

[17] John H. Preston, *Revolution—1776*, pp. 157–158.

[18] Billington *et al., United States*, p. 56.

During these crucial days in America, Philip Freneau was still idling in the Caribbean. As the patriots at home were rejoicing in the splendid victories that came to them at last, he was having some splendid times of his own. He was adventuring out to sea on the sloop *Liberty,* either Captain Hanson's or another's, working or only loafing. He was discovering new vales of paradise on the island of St. James, where they took on a cargo of coral rock, tinted like the sunset. More lovely than St. James is Demerara, south of the Orinoco, and the island of Curassoe, (Curaçao) of the Lesser Antilles. Ravishing beyond the words of any poetic license is Comana (Cumaná, Venezuela) on the mainland, and Maracaybo (Maracaibo, Venezuela) in the Gulf of Mexico, and Puerto Cavallo in Honduras. The island of Bermuda is the best of all. There, the traveler finds a flower surpassing all he has ever seen before, a bloom more lovely than any he ever hopes to find again; and there he returns once again, in April 1778, to study and admire it a great deal more. For the first time in his life, Freneau appears to be interested in women—in one woman above all the others.[19]

The British colony of Bermuda, presided over by Governor George James Breure, was a strange place for a poet with any notions of liberty to visit. It was, indeed, less a colony than an independent autonomous government over which Governor Breure ruled, bound to Britain more by ancient ties of language, commerce, and tradition than by political need. At the very beginning of the Revolution, Washington had asked for, and received from its ample magazines, the gunpowder he badly needed to fight the British. That was in 1775; in 1778 there was still no firm sentiment in Bermuda against the American struggle for independence. The satirical vaporings of a little-known poet had probably never reached the island where the Governor, in aloof contemplation of that struggle, lived with those of his fourteen children who still remained under the paternal roof. Two of his sons were not there. They had volunteered in the army of General Gage—and one of them had already lost his life at Bunker Hill. One of the Governor's daughters, the wife of Captain Pendock Neale, a British privateer, was no friend of the patriot cause either. Her sister Frances, the eldest of the girls, was married to Henry Tucker, an avowed sympathizer of the

---

[19] *Pub. Ovidii Nasonis Opera Omnia* (London: Cornelius Schrevello, 1662), Vol. III end papers, Monmouth County Historical Association; see also Lewis Leary, *That Rascal Freneau,* p. 376, n. 24.

rebel cause. One other daughter, whom our poet calls Amanda, appears to have been entirely neutral. She was the rare bloom, surpassing all others, for whom Philip Freneau reveals a passion he has never shown before.[20]

Love, until he declared it in the fervent lines addressed to this lady, was an emotion strangely absent from the young man's life. Cupid has either ignored him as an unlikely target or loosed against him only blunted barbs. For what had the restless, foot-loose lad to offer to any lady besides a doubtful flair for poetry and a decided propensity for poverty. During his brief stay as a guest of the Governor, it became apparent that he was little more than an engaging roustabout, little better than a beachcomber, who had no roots in the past and no branches in the future. His prolonged odyssey had brought him no new prospects of fortune, and the old ones, it appeared, were equally without promise. Amanda seems to have been as neutral toward him as toward his country.

If Amanda was the flame of a new interest, bright enough to pale those he had left behind, Philip was again destined to disappointment. In the first of his poems to her, "On a Lady's Singing Bird," he appeals for her favor in the manner of a love-lorn youth who has already had his first rebuff.

> Fair Amanda! Pity me,
> Pity him who sings for thee.

We do not know whether she made him any answer, or if she ever considered the need for one. He courted her; like a timid boy he ached for her; and finally, like a man of wisdom he renounced her. He

> —Sighed, and said—I am not for you.

In words, only in words, like his love for liberty, he poured out his love for Amanda. Long after he had left the island her image pursued him with profound nostalgia, for the

> —Charming shade,
> Where once, Amanda, once with you I strayed,

[20] "Amanda Poems," in Freneau, *Poems Written and Published during the American Revolutionary War,* Vol. 1, pp. 235–240. See also J. R. Williams, *Bermudiana, passim,* and Freneau, *Poems* (Pattee), Vol. 2, pp. 319 ("Florio to Amanda"), 326 ("Amanda in a Consumption"), 392 ("Amanda's Complaint").

> And fondly talked, and counted every tree,
> And minutes, ages, when removed from thee—[21]

Removed forever, not only in time and space, but for eternity itself, for the lovely flower of Bermuda was also a frail one. Thomas Burnet, whose pages in *The Theory of the Earth,* Freneau has carefully studied, says that people live longer in Bermuda than elsewhere, but it is not true. According to the bereaved lover, it is "contrary to fact." In this paradise as everywhere else in the world, the young, the fair, the strong, also die young. Amanda, stricken with consumption, is cut off in her youth. For the poet, there remains only a poignant memory of Amanda, and a last farewell to the flower—

> Her whole duration but an hour.

The face, the features, the fragrance, of Amanda will linger on for a long, long time. So also will the memory of the "lovely green hills" of Bermuda, as he sets sail for home on May 24, 1778. With Amanda lost there is nothing else to look for in the wonderland of the West Indies.[22]

[21] *Ibid.*
[22] *Ibid.*

11. SOLDIER AND SEAMAN

THE FIRST NEWS that greeted the returning wanderer when he landed at Shrewsbury, New Jersey, on July 9, had nothing in common with green valleys or the lovely memory of Amanda. He had no premonition of what to expect, even when his ship was boarded off the Carolina coast by an English privateer. As a noncombatant, he was soon released. His momentary fears were quickly dispelled, with no indignity to his person or threat to his liberty.[1]

What he heard, what he saw, at Shrewsbury, was something quite different. The cruelties he had witnessed, and the stark reality he had discovered behind the beauty of the Caribbean, were as nothing to the death and destruction which he found in his own country, among his own people. Monmouth had just been overrun by the British. In the five-mile journey from Shrewsbury to Mount Pleasant, what Freneau saw was no mere matter of hearsay like the battles of Lexington and Concord or the bloody struggle of Bunker Hill. For the first time, with his own eyes, he looked on the incarnation of his "House of Night." Here was no figment of his imagination, no license of the poet, but an appalling picture which even he, in all his satires on the British, had never conjured up against them. Beyond a visitation from the enemy, his mother, his brother, his sisters, had escaped unharmed—but the whole countryside was an awful shambles. Fields were in ruins; buildings were in ashes; homes had been looted and cattle stolen; the dead

[1] Freneau's copy of Robertson, *Elements of Navigation,* in Freneau Collection (Rutgers).

and the wounded were everywhere; while terror-stricken women and children wandered helpless in the rubble of a great catastrophe.[2]

All this was the work of an enemy who had vented his wrath on helpless civilians. The battle of Monmouth Court House had given neither side a victory—and each side had barely escaped a defeat. General Charles Lee's grudging attack on the rear guard of the British line, his inexplicable retreat despite the strictest orders to hold, his strange and senseless maneuvers which almost lost the battle (and the war) for Washington and upset his plans in a confusion of cross purposes, might have been blamed on the exhausting heat, the overwhelming dust, the cries of the dying, and the stench of the dead. Each side shared in these disasters equally. If there were still other reasons for the near collapse of American arms they would wait until the trial of General Lee later, when this more pressing trial of Monmouth was finished. Now only a miracle could save the day, and Washington, beside himself with anger and frustration, was the only man to conjure more than defeat from the field of battle. In a desperate attempt to rally his confused and wavering troops and transform impending chaos into some semblance of order, the Commander-in-Chief rode from one sector to another, from one command to another, from volunteers to conscripts—swearing, sweating, rushing, raging, from one end of the line to the other. Lee was sent to the second line in the center, under the watchful eye of General Knox; Wayne joined forces with Steward and Ramsay, his light infantry cutting deeply into the ranks of the Royal Fusiliers; while Knox, now bravely supported by Lee himself, hammered at the British cavalry with heavy guns from the heights of Comb's Hill. Von Steuben, who had impatiently waited for this moment, attacked with the stalwart men he had drilled so long and so well at Valley Forge. While the Negro conscripts from Massachusetts harried Lord Cornwallis and his smart troops, the sharpshooters of Nathanael Greene, with calm and deadly purpose, picked off the Queen's Rangers, cream of the British crop. What had seemed like a rout of American troops had suddenly become an exhilarating onslaught on the enemy as Washington, still racing back and forth along

[2] Lewis Leary, "Philip Freneau and Monmouth County," *Monmouth County Historical Association Bulletin,* Vol. I, No. 2 (July 1948), pp. 59–81; State of New Jersey, *Archives,* 2nd Series, Vol. II, pp. 233–234; Freneau's poem, American Independence," in *Poems of Philip Freneau Written Chiefly during the Late War,* pp. 153–165.

the entire line, shouted his orders, encouraged his men, and fought to a finish even as they were fighting. The Marquis de Lafayette voiced the judgment of soldiers and officers alike when he declared: "I never beheld so superb a man." As darkness fell on the field of Monmouth, Sir Henry Clinton drew back his forces, without a defeat, but also without a victory. As the British moved across the countryside, they proceeded to carry out the orders of their leaders. Like a swarm of locusts they ruined whatever lay in their path. Every man, woman, and child, every home, every field, was to be destroyed. This was war—and war was a stranger to mercy. This was war—and what could not be subdued must be annihilated.[3]

The poet of Monmouth, looking on the carnage, at last decided to do his own part to annihilate the enemy: not with words this time, but with deeds; not with a pen, but with a musket. On July 15, 1778, he enlisted in the First Regiment of the New Jersey Militia under Colonel Asher Holmes, for duty in the company commanded by Captain Barrent Smock. Stationed as a "Scout and guard along the shore" between South Amboy and Long Branch, he patrolled the coast "day and night," and engaged "in several skirmishes" with the British. For company he had his dog Sancho with him. He needed company, for since the red tide had swept over Monmouth, the duties of a guard were not too exacting, nor the adventure too exciting. With everything destroyed there was precious little to protect. Freneau, with the stripes of a sergeant, was proud to have received them, but this was no time for pride, any more than the bullet wound in his knee was a cause for quitting.[4] The man who had once been afraid to get "knocked in the head," was afraid no longer. If there was so little to do as a soldier, there was perhaps more that he could do as a poet. No longer the romantic escapist of the lovely isles, he became the realistic interpreter of the American Revolution. His irony, once bitter and amusing, became vitriolic and humorless. He had courted the Muse in the land of "inexpressible beauty"—now he was devoted only to Mars. The invaders must be fought with any weapons still left in the arsenal of liberty.

Philip Freneau's earlier work had been an important contribution

---

[3] *Ibid.*; and John H. Preston, *Revolution—1776*, pp. 224–226.

[4] General Administration Services, Case #23069: Pension Records of Philip Freneau, Mss.; and New Jersey, *Official Register of the Officers and Men of New Jersey in the Revolutionary War*, p. 465.

to American poetry; it was also the authentic first page in the history
of a native literature in prosody. His use of the Miltonic blank verse,
followed by the more dramatic couplet of Pope, was often only rhetorical and didactic. Sometimes he stooped to doggerel and pure invective.
He never forgot the higher purposes of poetry, yet his own purpose
was deflected by the exigencies of the times. Now they were more
pressing than they had ever been before his long absence from the
country, and while he was still the poet he was also the soldier of revolution. What he wrote was for fighting men more than for critics,
meant to inform and inspire, to encourage and arouse, to instruct and
reflect on events that transpired, and to prophesy the things to come.
Some of them he foresaw with an almost mysterious power.

In "American Independence"—printed in Philadelphia by Robert
Bell, the publisher of *Common Sense*—Freneau was less concerned
with the momentous declaration of 1776 than with the dangers that
threatened its realization in 1778. Did Britain think it could defeat the
intent of Providence itself?

> When God from chaos gave this world to be,
> Man then he form'd, and form'd it to be free,
> In his own image stampt the favorite race—
> How darest thou, tyrant, the fair stamp deface!

Britain and her mercenary Hessians were engaged in the business of
plain murder for the perpetuation of power.

> Cursed be that wretch who murder makes his trade,
> Cursed be all wars that e'er ambition made.

Let the enemy be warned—America does not stand alone in this struggle for freedom. Not mercenaries, but friends, will help her. France is
an ally, not yet fully committed, but fast approaching the status of
equal partner in the Revolution.

> At last to arrest your lawless hand,
> Rises the genius of a generous land.

The help of France, the fatherland of his own people, was the one ray
of hope in a time of infinite darkness. It was still only a ray, too weak to
light up the fields where men despaired and died, not knowing when
more help would come, or if it would ever come at all. The world
would never forget, nor history fail to record, the wrongs that were
heaped on the struggling, suffering defenders of their homeland.

> Pests of mankind! remembrance shall recall
> And paint these horrors to the view of all.

In the meantime, with or without the help of others, the tragic task of avenging the horrors of the British is for his countrymen alone. In some of the strongest, most inspiring lines ever written as a challenge to free men anywhere, in any time, Philip Freneau sounds the trumpet of liberty.

> Americans! revenge your country's wrongs;
> To you the honor of this deed belongs.[5]

The wrongs were no longer those suffered by strangers in some distant city. The scourge of war was now a personal affront beside which the affront to his pride as a poet was but a scratch on the surface of granite. He could praise the heroism of men in the face of insuperable odds—of leaders like Captain Nicholas Biddle, who sailed his frigate against the belching guns of the *Yarmouth*, and John Paul Jones, with his quixotic sallies against the mighty navy of England. Freneau's stirring call for volunteers in the puny navy of America were more than poetic translations of his own great love of the sea. He is truly involved in this great struggle against despotism, yet some small part of him is not yet engaged. The individual is not wholly submerged in the universal; he has seen outrage—he has not yet suffered it. He is a poet as well as a soldier.[6]

And now he is also a seaman. The dull routine of a guard is lackluster and without interest—and it is without profit. He could be of greater benefit to his country and to himself if he answered the call for volunteers for sea duty. As a member of the militia it was also possible to be a sailor; with his knowledge of ships he might even become a master.

On October 25, 1778, Freneau, having relinquished his musket, has become the captain of the *Indian Delaware,* with sailing orders of public and private importance.[7] Moving down the Shrewsbury River,

---

[5] Freneau, *The Poems of Philip Freneau* (ed. F. L. Pattee), Vol. 1, p. 27 (poem formerly called "American Independence").

[6] "Capt. Jones Invitation," in Freneau, *Poems of Philip Freneau Written Chiefly during the Late War,* pp. 169–171; "The Death of Capt. Biddle," in Lewis Leary, *That Rascal Freneau,* p. 75; "Barney's Victory over Gen'l Monk," in *ibid.,* p. 96; and "The Memorable Victory of Paul Jones" (called by Pattee one of the glories of American literature), in Freneau, *Poems* (Pattee), Vol. 1, p. 279.

[7] Freneau's copy of Robertson, *Elements of Navigation.*

his craft is heading for Philadelphia, to take on supplies for the run to St. Eustacia (St. Eustatius) in the Caribbean. For four months he will ply the dangerous waters of the Atlantic, shuttling back and forth from one port to another, to bring back the supplies badly needed at home. Without a single interception by the enemy, he pursues his commerce until he is recalled for shore duty again. After a short turn as soldier once more, he returns to the sea in July 1779, this time as master of the sloop *John Couster* for another run from Philadelphia to the West Indies.[8] In September, he ships as supercargo on the brig *Rebecca,* under Captain Chatham, this time bound for the Azores. While his work is now limited to the commercial aspects of the voyage, there are many moments of danger and excitement when the vessel is twice nearly captured before it reaches the safety of the tiny port of Santa Cruz, on the island of Teneriffe, off the West Coast of Africa. This was not the island of "inexpressible beauty," though it too had "a handsome appearance at a small distance."[9]

More exciting—and far more profitable—was the capture of the brig *Brittania* by Freneau and his comrades of the Monmouth Militia on December 30, 1779. Caught in a howling gale off the Jersey Coast near Middletown Point, the British privateer, filled with all manner of merchandise, was trapped in the ice-pack, a helpless victim of the boarding party which braved the high winds and the thick snow to possess her. The British, with all their strength in men and armament, found the task of keeping their lengthening supply lines open made increasingly difficult by the courage and alertness of patriot volunteers who guarded the Jersey coast. American whaleboats were quick to prey on British ships, even on the smaller gunboats that tried to run the gantlet of the shore patrol, while their shallow draft, their pointed ends, their leather-muffled oars, often saved them from capture or destruction. Manned by militiamen of experience at sea and of proven courage, armed with pistols, duck-guns, and cutlasses, the deadliest of weapons at close range, these American boats were a silent and continuous threat to enemy supplies—the valor of the intrepid seamen perhaps fortified by the booty in which all of them shared.[10]

Philip Freneau shared in the booty from the *Britannia* together with all the others. The foodstuffs—the Irish beef, the bread, coffee, and

[8] *Ibid.*

[9] Freneau's Log Book, in Freneau Collection (Rutgers).

[10] Asher Holmes Papers, Mss. Also Decision of Court of Admiralty, February 2, 1780, and *Asher Holmes* vs. *Brig Brittania,* in Brig Brittania Papers, Mss.

sugar—were always distributed among the country folk who needed them most. The sails, the rigging, the copper from the ship's bottom, were sold for cash, together with the "Blunder Busses, muskets and pistols, cutlasses and fire arrows," plundered from the vessel. The poet's portion came to the considerable sum of eight hundred dollars, a fortune greater than he had ever possessed—if, indeed, he possessed it even now. It was all in Continental paper, whose value fluctuated with the fortunes of war, and often fell from day to day, almost from hour to hour. The purchase of a sorely needed pair of shoes reduced Freneau's fortune by one hundred and twenty dollars, and his remaining wealth melted so rapidly in the heat of swiftly rising prices that a bookseller refused to sell him a copy of Beccaria's *Essay on Crime and Punishment* for anything but hard money. Paper currency, he was told, "'was not worth a straw." The shoes—and little else besides—were to be the sole remuneration for all his services in the American Revolution.[11]

For one who rarely had any money, the problem of a depreciated currency presented no matter for great concern. To have nothing when one has little is no tragedy. For a poet there could be greater misfortunes than this. The nightmare of war was the greatest one of all, but this too did not alter the fact that as a poet, as a writer, his work was equally unfortunate. Once it had been judged as mediocre. Later it had been reviled as dishonest. Now it was not even read, and no man could suffer a calamity approaching this one. For years Freneau had written the poems of freedom; in Santa Cruz, in St. James, in Bermuda, he had written other poems as well, some of them achieving a high order of beauty. In addition, he had seen such outrages on liberty in those islands as needed to be told to others who were fighting for liberty. Would his poems, or the outrages, ever be known to others?

It seemed likely that some, if not all of them, would be made known by the honest Hugh Brackenridge, who had quit the Somerset School and the profession of teaching, and was now publishing *The United States Magazine* in Philadelphia. In a city that was larger than any other in America—larger indeed than New York and Boston combined —where culture was blooming as nowhere else on the continent, and where money, to judge by the Quaker City's prosperous citizens with their fine houses, gay clothes, and ornate coaches, seemed so plentiful,

---

[11] General Administration Services, Case #23069: Pension Records of Philip Freneau, Mss.; and see Freneau's account on Beccaria's *Essay on Crime and Punishment,* in Freneau Collection (Rutgers).

a paper such as *The United States Magazine* would doubtless prosper. It offered not only domestic news and foreign intelligence, but for the elite, some literary samplings as well. Brackenridge and his partner Francis Bailey, the well-known printer, were certain that the project could not fail. They were equally certain that the poems and essays of Philip Freneau would appeal to many whose love of liberty had no other outlet save support of those who wrote its songs and inspired its victories.[12]

In the year of 1779, some poem, some essay, from the hand of the Monmouth militiaman appeared in each issue of the paper. "The House of Night," revised for added relevancy to the times, was printed together with other pieces which gave a certain literary flavor and cultural dignity to its columns. The journal was well edited, its treatment of controversial matters both intelligent and restrained. Yet it did not prosper. The people of Philadelphia were strangely unmoved either by its publisher or its poet. The Loyalists, of whom there were many in "Phillie," were less concerned with the vagaries of literature or liberty than with their own interests of a more practical nature. Profound as was their hatred for the Revolution, they could scarcely be expected to give any aid or comfort to an enterprise that was tainted with anti-British propaganda. Freneau attacked them bitterly, even as he baited some patriots too—most of all he deplored the effete, disengaged writers of Philadelphia, the custodians of its culture and the purveyors of its morals, especially the soft and sentimental poets whose music had no relevancy at all to the "times that tried men's souls," the

> Sylvan Bards who deal in flow'ry themes,
> Who sing the meadows and the purling streams.[13]

While "'blood and murder" are sapping the strength of the fighters for liberty, these poets turn their eyes from the pain and suffering of their countrymen to more mellow scenes, indulging their gift of language for purposes less hazardous than revolution. They are above the battle. Freneau had never been above it even in far-off Santa Cruz or Bermuda, but only at a distance, removed for the time from its violence, while he examined still other aspects of tyranny. Now he saw it at closer range at home. It was the part of poets, he was convinced, to see it in the raw, for "the world is undone by looking at things at a distance." The shock that spurs to action comes through

[12] *The United States Magazine,* January 1779.
[13] "The Loyalists," in *The United States Magazine,* July 1779.

the eyes, and the ears, indeed, from the viscera, as well as the mind.[14]

In his poems for *The United States Magazine,* Freneau looks at things more closely. Discarding both "Flowry themes" and the niceties of language, he discards the leaven of literature and writes more propaganda than poetry. His purpose is to make the reader understand clearly what is transpiring in America and what is at stake in this war against Britain.[15]

And the readers? Hugh Brackenridge had been too optimistic about them. Caught in the cross-currents of political and social upheaval, his magazine was being wrecked by both malice and indifference. Neither the vaunted culture of Philadelphia nor the zeal of its patriots was sufficient to keep it afloat. With the twelfth issue, it went down altogether. "Too many people," the editor complained, "inhabit the region of stupidity." Though they suffered many trials, "reading to them is the worst of all torments." They would suffer almost anything but enlightenment, and no torment was equal to that of learning. If they survived their stupidity, it was because survival was the first law of nature—and learning the last. Hugh Brackenridge would also survive this failure, and try in fields less hostile than this one to build a future. At Annapolis the study of the law under Samuel Chase would open up a new career, more promising than this. One day he would emerge as a powerful political figure in the frontier village of Pittsburgh.

It was not entirely true, as Brackenridge had said, that the failure of his paper was due to stupidity and the torment of reading. Other torments, worse ones than this, afflicted the patriots themselves, many of them potential readers of *The United States Magazine.* The whole atmosphere of Philadelphia was poisoned with suspicion and incipient treachery since the evacuation of the city by the British and the installation of Benedict Arnold as its military governor. The Conway cabal, which had sought to displace Washington with Gates, was but a sullen memory of ambitious connivance, but the long stalemate after Monmouth had done little to encourage the hope of victory for the Revolution. The French alliance had not yet shown any signs of adequate fulfillment to justify an ample optimism, while the withdrawal of the enemy from the Quaker City had left it little more than a shell of its former self. Under the British it had been a place of gay and

[14] *Ibid.*

[15] *The United States Magazine,* various issues in 1779. See also Freneau, *Poems Written and Published During the American Revolutionary War.*

festive abandon, which the British were not the only ones to enjoy. The American Tories had been in high feather, and not a few of the patriots themselves had been glad to collect some of the crumbs from the table of Dives. Gay assemblies, concerts, and similar pleasures had made them believe that the war was really a capital joke, a sentiment shared by the Hessian Jaegers who were stationed there. Carnivals, regattas, festivals amused the conquerors, and the conquered were also often amused. *The Meschianza,* staged by the brilliant and charming Major André, was a fabulous affair; and fabulous too was the buxom beauty of his friend, Peggy Shippen, the daughter of Judge Edward Shippen, one of the most prominent of Loyalists in the city. Most of the Loyalists had left with the British troops, but many had remained in Philadelphia to tend their financial and social gardens when the patriots moved in. Not a few of them were punished for their temerity, but others, even those who had refused to recognize the validity of the Test Acts and to foreswear their allegiance to George III, escaped with a watered-down parole which scarcely touched a single nerve of their accustomed way of life. The people, the common people of Philadelphia, were little better off under the new masters than under the old. With paper money almost valueless, they appeared worse off than they had ever been before. The gaiety of the British was gone, the circuses were at an end, and they had none of the bread either, which, in some measure, they had once obtained. Yet it seemed abundant enough for the same people as before. Luxury and gross indulgence were still prevalent among them, as always, and as usual, too, there was no lack of exotic dishes and sumptuous tables. Washington, enjoying a brief respite from the rigors of the camp, was disturbed by the opulence he saw in high places, and wrote to his friend Benjamin Harrison late in 1778: "'If I was to be called upon to draw a picture of the times, and of men, from what I have seen, heard, and in part know, I should in one word say that idleness, dissipation and extravagance seem to have laid fast hold of most of them." Nor was the Congress doing anything to change the picture, which it, too, observed at close range. Like the Commander-in-Chief, it appeared helpless to change anything.[16]

[16] M. Jensen, *The New Nation,* pp. 181, 186, 224; Washington to Benj. Harrison, December 18, 1778, in George Washington, *Writings* (ed. J. C. Fitzpatrick), Vol. 13, p. 42; C. H. Van Tyne, *The Causes of the War of Independence,* pp. 133, 137–138; and E. C. Burnett (ed.), *Letters of Members of the Continental Congress,* Vol. 1, pp. 418, 468, 470, 473.

It was no wonder that angry mobs wandered through the streets of the city that prided itself on its reputation for brotherly love; that riots raged, with such pauper patriots as Thomas Paine to lead them. Less surprising, perhaps, was the accusation that wealthy men like Robert Morris were reaping fabulous profits from the necessities of the people, than that the city's supreme guardian, the newly appointed governor, Benedict Arnold, should be seen openly employing the military wagons and material of the government for his private use. As if that was not bad enough, Arnold, in an exalted and sensitive position of trust, was taking to wife the daughter of the Loyalist Edward Shippen, a beautiful young lady who had been the steady partner of the British Major André during the entire occupation. Whatever people suspected or knew, they did not know that already, in May or June of 1779, Governor Arnold was in correspondence with Sir Henry Clinton for the betrayal of West Point, and that his pretty Peggy was arranging the details of his treason with her charming Major André. They only knew that Arnold owned the fine mansion which he called Mount Pleasant (a far different home from the one of the same name in Monmouth, New Jersey), and that their own lives were devoid of anything like the luxuries acquired by their military governor. The atmosphere of Philadelphia was fetid with fear, suspicion, and hatred, and the torments of most men were such as to move the eminent and embittered Silas Deane to write that "There are few unhappier cities on the globe than Philadelphia . . . It is a melancholy reflection to think that whilst our common enemy is wasting our sea coasts and laying our fairest and most peaceable towns in ashes, we are quarreling among ourselves and can scarcely be contained from plunging our swords in each other's bosoms."[17] In such a city, in such a climate, who was interested in the rhetorical blandishments of Hugh Brackenridge or the lengthy indictments of Philip Freneau?

In New York, where the British were firmly entrenched, there was no lack of readers for *The Royal Gazette,* still confidently published by the redoubtable Rivington. Many of the patriots also read it, perhaps for the appeals of Clinton to the misguided who were promised a full pardon if they returned to the bosom of the mother. *The Gazette* provided as well the pungent satires of the greatest Tory poet of the day,

[17] Silas Deane to Simeon Dean, July 27, 1779, in Silas Deane, *Papers, 1774–1790: Collection of the New York Historical Society, 1887–1890,* XXII, 22–24; see also W. E. Woodward, *The Way Our People Lived,* pp. 139–155; Moses Coit Tyler, *The Literary History of the American Revolution,* Vol. 2, p. 109.

Jonathan Odell, who blasted the Revolution with a carefully contrived mixture of truth and fiction, spiced with a measure of vituperation that pleased the palates of many who were not Tories. Odell, like
Freneau a graduate of the College of New Jersey, had forsaken the
practice of Medicine for the Church, and both for the literary laurels
of the Loyalists. Implicated in the treachery of Benedict Arnold, he
was safe from the vengeance of the patriots in the City of New York,
where he wrote his scathing satires against their cause which he described as a witch's brew of

> Treason's rank flowers, ambition's swelling fruits,
> Hypocrisy in seeds, and Fraud in roots,
> Bundles of Lies fresh gathered in the prime,
> And stalks of Calumny grown stale with time.[18]

Nor was he alone in saying so, or in saying it so well. Joseph Stansbury,
a Tory writer with a greater regard for the truth, also poured out his
verses for the cause of Britain. Such writers would not be safe in Philadelphia, but neither could writers like Brackenridge or Freneau ever
prosper there, when their words fell on ears deafened by despair or
muffled with malice. They must look for employment elsewhere.

After the experience of *The United States Magazine* it was clear to
the militiaman of Monmouth that there was as little to be gained
from writing as from soldiering. The dull duties of a guardsman in a
war that seemed equally dull had no appeal for him. The people of
the South were suffering as his own people had suffered in the North,
but the South was a long way off, while the North provided nothing
more exciting than the watchful waiting of Washington as he agonized
over the scourging, which, as Silas Deane said, was taking place on the
seacoasts and "laying our fairest and most peaceable towns in ashes."
The Scots officer James Murray, writing to his beloved Bessie in
Britain, could pleasantly inform her: "We have been a little employed
of late in burning and destroying and we are in hopes that the fashion
may take root, which perhaps might prove as speedy a means of finish-
ing the Rebellion as what has hitherto been adopted."[19]

As the year 1778 came to a close, it appeared quite likely that the
Rebellion was indeed about to expire. A British fleet had landed an
army on the Georgia coast; Savannah was already in the hands of the
enemy. Charleston would soon suffer a similar fate. General Lincoln,

[18] M. J. R. Lamb, *History of the City of New York*, Vol. 3, pp. 686 ff.
[19] James Murray, *Letters from America, 1773–1780,* October 24, 1778, p. 61.

surrendering to Clinton, would also surrender over five thousand men, hundreds of guns, and numerous muskets, all desperately needed, and all of them irreplaceable. Horatio Gates would fare even worse. Running away from Cornwallis at Camden, South Carolina, Gates would leave behind him several thousand troops, dead, wounded, or missing, without having made the least firm stand to rally the men who still could fight. Horace Walpole was justified in his appraisal of the staggering Revolution. Despite the victory of Anthony Wayne at Stony Point, and the fantastic exploits of John Paul Jones in distant waters, Walpole could confidently claim: "We look on America as at our feet." James Madison, a member of the Continental Congress, had read the mind of the British command correctly when he declared that they knew the Americans would never be beaten save by the Southern route. In 1780 it became certain that the British planned to destroy them in their most vulnerable parts as Lord Cornwallis and Banastre Tarleton prepared for a grand assault on the southland.[20]

Philip Freneau, completing his term of enlistment, decided to quit the Militia. He was not finished with the war, but if he fought he would fight at sea. After his experience with the *Brittania,* the sea seemed safe enough—in any event a ship was more exciting than any land patrol. There was little more profit in one than in the other, but profit was something that had always eluded him anyway.

At sea as on land it would still elude him, yet he might find the action, the motion, the sense of purpose that was so patently missing on the barren shores of Jersey. And he would see more of the war than he had ever seen before. More, indeed, than he wanted or expected to see when he decided to become a sailor.[21]

[20] Jacob Axelrad, *Patrick Henry: The Voice of Freedom,* pp. 200, 204, 207.

[21] Freneau's love of the sea, already noted, was to be sorely tested by his experiences as a seaman rather than as a tourist. See Philip M. Marsh, "Philip Freneau: Our Sailor Poet," in *American Neptune, VI* (April 1946), 115–120.

12. A PRISONER OF THE BRITISH

IN HIS EXPERIENCES with the Revolution Philip Freneau had suffered, directly and physically, only a bullet wound in the knee.[1] It scarcely bothered him, for he was never incapacitated and the pellet, which he said was never removed, does not appear to have hindered his duties on land or at sea. He was almost a total stranger to fleshly pain and consuming danger; his own extinction was as remote as the aloof anxiety of one who closely scans the obituaries of others, seeking, while deploring, the name of some friend who may have passed on. The shock of recognition is softened by the relief of survival.

Freneau's involvement in the war was deep and depressing; his escape from violence, only temporary. When he had returned from his beautiful isles, its evidence was there, on his very doorstep. He had been spared the demonic hate, the bloody fury of war, and had seen their awful fruits only after the event. Though its ravages were plain enough to see, the war was many steps removed from him; like his own future it was shrouded in the heavy mist of uncertainty. At twenty-eight, plainly he had no future. As a poet or a soldier he had found no solutions to the problems of making either a life or a living. On land he had succeeded at nothing. Perhaps the sea would yield something more.

From the day he had sailed with Captain Hanson, Freneau had studied the problems of navigation in Robertson's volume; he returned to it often for a better understanding of the science which was in many respects also an art. There was much that he did not know even after

[1] "Application," in General Administration Services, Case #23069: Pension Records of Philip Freneau, Mss.

his service on both brig and sloop, and on his retirement from the
Militia in 1780 he was still confused in the computations of latitude
and longitude, "which," he noted in his log book, "I find to be
wrong." Yet he persisted. This was absorbing work, exhilarating and
agreeable far more than the education of "leeches," the shouldering
of a musket, or perhaps the writing of verses that no one bothered
to read. The study of the sea brought with it the tang of fresh air, the
promise of foreign lands, and a sense of life and liberty no landlubber
could ever know.[2]

A ship was like a dog, faithful and obedient, honest and dependable; it responded to kindness and understanding; it was a friend
whose moods were wholesome and whose virtues—even whose vices—
were robust and unaffected, yet delicately responsive. On a crest or in
a trough, when it heaved or rolled, if it were but gently guided, it
would answer to the helm of an honest mariner always. As one
sailed into the future, beyond one horizon lay still another. There
might be a landfall one day that was safe and free; God-willing, it
would be worth a poet's dreams.

On May 25, 1780, a ship like this one sailed from Philadelphia.
The *Aurora*, a Pennsylvania privateer, carried twenty guns and was
filled with a cargo of tobacco, bound for St. Eustacia. Besides his chest
of clothes Freneau brought with him nothing else but Robertson's
Navigation, for he was to be the *Aurora*'s third mate; there must be no
mistakes now in his reckonings of the ship's position. Not only did
the voyage promise another sight of his beautiful island of Santa
Cruz but, equally important, he would make a little money while doing his patriotic duty. Any British vessel that crossed their path would
be fair spoils for the entire crew of the *Aurora*—always assuming they
could capture and hold the prize. The prospects for profits and patriotism seemed fairly alluring. For one who, unhappily, failed to consider the troublesome alternatives of other prospects, the enterprise
was more promising than the snaring of the *Brittania*.[3]

The prospects were still good when the *Aurora*, at the very outset of

[2] Freneau's Log Book, in Freneau Collection (Rutgers); and Philip M.
Marsh, "Philip Freneau: Our Sailor Poet," *American Neptune*, VI (April
1946), 115–120.

[3] Freneau, *Some Account of the Capture of the Ship "Aurora"*; see also S. E.
Forman, "The Political Activities of Philip Freneau," *Johns Hopkins Univer-
sity Studies*, Vol. 20, Nos. 9–10 (1902), pp. 24, 25; and "Some Account of the
Capture of the Ship Aurora," in Freneau Collection (Rutgers).

the voyage, was "hindered from standing out to Sea." The delay could portend trouble with their plans, but at the moment it meant trouble only for the British, since the *Aurora* had no other immediate task than that of overtaking a small sloop loaded with corn. By the time Freneau and the rest of the *Aurora* men had finished "putting the pilot on board the sloop, handcuffing the prisoners, and sending the prize to Cape May," the night was gone, the wind had died, and the sea outside the sheltered waters of Delaware Bay was as calm as a corpse. The air was hot, still, and sultry. The sails hung limp and lifeless over the bemused hulk of the *Aurora*.[4]

At three in the afternoon the lookout on the foretop espies what seems like a spot on the horizon. As it grows larger, he is alarmed to recognize the spot as a ship—not one ship but three, all of them now clearly visible in his glass. Looming in the distance are two brigs and, in addition, a "pretty large" vessel that turns out to be a British frigate. The news electrifies the whole crew. There are sharp orders by Captain Sutton to set all sails, to tack, to turn as fast as the lifeless wind and unwilling tides make possible back to the shelter of the bay. Plainly, the enemy is "in chase of us." The pursuers have become the pursued. Unless the *Aurora* can elude the British and get back to the safety of the bay, it is in danger, indeed, in mortal danger, of capture itself. Before the voyage is fairly begun, it appears doomed never to be a voyage at all. The prospects of Philip Freneau, as of the rest of the crew, are at low ebb unless a fight on the open sea can be avoided.[5]

That, at least, is the opinion of Captain Sutton, master of the *Aurora*, though Philip Freneau has a few ideas of his own. Nobody pays much attention to what he thinks anyway, but to him it seems far better "to stand for Egg Harbor or any port of the Jersey shore and run the ship on the flats, rather than be taken."[6]

As the *Aurora* attempts to "stand in" for Cape Henlopen, the sun has begun to set. Still pursuing, the hunter draws closer, always closer, as the quarry, becalmed and helpless, is turned and twisted by the heavy ebb tide off the Cape. The looming frigate grows larger, its name almost plainly readable. It carries no less than thirty-six guns, perhaps more, for not all of them are unmasked. At its stern, bobbing in mock humility, ride two brigs—American brigs—taken at sea. Soon, soon, there will be a third, for the *Aurora* has no chance now to avoid

[4] Freneau, "Some Account of the Capture of the Ship Aurora."
[5] *Ibid.*
[6] *Ibid.*

capture. It cannot even maneuver for a run to shore, or try to escape according to the plan so artfully conceived by its third mate, Philip Freneau. The coast is only three hundred yards away, yet it might as well be three hundred miles distant. The *Aurora*, held fast in the dead calm of the sea, can only wait for the inevitable salvo from the gaping guns of the *Iris*.[7]

In another moment the air is split wide open with the burst of its battery. At the same instant the hull of the helpless *Aurora* is also split, a misfortune "which made the ship to leak amazingly." A futile blast from its own four-pounder barely scratches the frigate, which remains equally untouched by the nine-pounder let loose by Sutton from his cabin window. A more furious attack is the only answer of the *Iris*, with a demand for immediate surrender. The demand seems inescapable as Captain Laboyteaux is caught in the right thigh, and his belly is laid open by a nine-pounder. As Laboyteaux is buried hastily at sea; as the sea itself sweeps into the hold of the *Aurora* and over the wounded and the dying on its decks, no one can doubt that the fight is finished. Before the final broadside is fired that shall hasten the swift completion of the conflict, the colors of the battered vessel are struck.[8]

The hopeless battle between unequals is over. The poet's part in it is a tale yet to be told. His employment was at an end; his chance to earn some needed dollars was wrecked; but only for a while. There would be other times, other ships, for profit as well as adventure. Freneau really believed all this as he naively explained his presence to the prize master who boarded the *Aurora*. He was no combatant; he was a civilian now as he had been before, when another ship had been taken in South Carolina waters. No one had doubted him then. This time there appeared to be a doubt. The British officers would make a careful investigation before releasing anybody, even a poet. For the time being everyone was a prisoner; everyone, including the poet, was taken to the *Iris*. He was not permitted to take his belongings with him. Herded between decks with more than a hundred other men, the intense heat, the overpowering stench, "made it a pretty just representation of the infernal region." Bad enough for a poet, it was even worse to be handcuffed like all the others, though he loudly maintained that he was no privateer, had committed no act of war, was no

---

[7] *Ibid.*
[8] *Ibid.*

member of the crew; he had paid his passage and had never fired a gun. He was finally spared the shackles—but only because Hugh Ray, an officer of the frigate who recognized the young man, could truthfully attest that he knew him only as a poet. Besides, the ship's papers were not too clear. Perhaps there was some truth in his protestations of innocence. If he was indeed innocent, he was entitled to be treated as a "gentleman."[9]

His innocence remained unproven, however, and as an ordinary prisoner he was treated with no regard at all for the meanest creature comforts. Save for a few minutes during the entire day he was kept below deck. His chest of clothes was never returned to him. When the *Iris* reached Sandy Hook he was still a prisoner; when anchor was finally cast in the North River several days later he had not ceased to hope for a quick release. It was no longer possible to delude himself with the hope of freedom when the bail proffered by his friends was refused. Whether he had paid for his passage or not, there was no denial that he was enrolled as a third mate and gunner on the *Aurora*. On June 1 he was transferred to the prison-ship *Scorpion*, idling at anchor in the Hudson River.[10]

And here he spent his first night sleeping on a chest, "almost suffocated with the heat and stench" of three hundred other prisoners. The *Iris* had been insufferable. This was inhuman. "I expected to die before morning, but human nature can bear more than one would at first suppose." It could bear the brutalities of the steward Gauzoo, the filth and stink of men herded together like cattle, the cramp and the crush, the oaths and the curses, the disease and the hunger. It could bear the stampede of desperate men, trapped like animals, when the bilge washed in and the *Scorpion* listed as if it were about to capsize. The cruel beatings by the Hessian guard with swords and marquets made the fear-crazed men more frantic for freedom. Only point-blank shots from pistols could drive them back, while the final, futile break for liberty was won only by the dead, and by the wounded who were soon to die. They alone were spared from further agony. Philip Freneau, neither dead nor wounded, was spared nothing. He had never known such things before, had never lived the life that might have

[9] *Ibid.*

[10] "The British Prison Ship," in Freneau, *The Poems of Philip Freneau* (ed. F. L. Pattee), Vol. 2, p. 18; General Administration Services, Case #23069: Pension Records of Philip Freneau, Mss.; and Freneau, "Some Account of the Capture of the Ship Aurora."

known them. After three weeks of such a life, he was "taken with a fever," transferred to the hospital ship *Hunter,* lying in the East River, to live or to die according to the fortunes of war.[11]

Now the poet must drink the cup of despair to the dregs. The *Hunter* was not only insufferable and inhuman; it was bestial. "Dirty and cluttered," her decks leaked so badly "that the sick were deluged with showers of rain." Exhausted from "putrid and bilious fevers," they wandered weakly between decks "in the agonies of death." Many of them died, still others lay in a stupor, "totally insensible, and yielding their last breath in all the horrors of light-headed frenzy." As they died, they were despatched like offal, transported to shallow graves on the Long Island shore, while those who unhappily survived were left untended for days on end by the indifferent Hessian doctor. The fortunate few who could eat were fed with vile meat, "generally heads and shanks" of beef crawling with vermin, a little bread, and some spruce beer. By July 6 or 7, "in spite of all the remedies" he had tried, Freneau's fever mounted. On July 12, after six weeks of unremitting torture, he was released. His friends had succeeded in rescuing the shadow of a man, "with such pains in my joints I could scarcely walk."[12]

He walked, nevertheless, the two long, endless miles from Elizabethtown Point to Elizabethtown, where he was picked up for the short ride to Molly Budleigh's home. There he rested for the night before continuing the slow and wrenching struggle to reach home. In two days more he was at Mount Pleasant. "For fear of terrifying" the neighbors "with my ghastly looks," Philip plods a path through the woods.[13] On July 14, scarcely recognizable, with eyes sunken in their sockets, his face gray and cadaverous, and in a condition of utter exhaustion, he is home at last, no prodigal returning to the parental roof but the bitter wreck of a man who has seen the world close up and "not from a distance." Penniless, his meager possessions all gone, he has seen war and has known its barbarism, not in theory, not by hearsay, not alone by the evidence of others; more than all that, he has felt the bloody hands of the British laid wantonly on his own person, obscenely laid on his own soul.[14]

[11] *Ibid.*
[12] *Ibid.*
[13] Freneau, "Some Account of the Capture of the Ship Aurora."
[14] "The British Prison Ship," in Freneau, *Poems* (Pattee), Vol. 2, p. 18; General Administration Services, Case #23069: Pension Records of Philip

The errant feelings of other days for the culture, the traditions, of Britain, were gone. Deep and envenomed hatred, no longer general and diffuse but personal and profound, for all things British, festered in the man who slowly grew whole again in the sheltered solitude and lavish love of Mount Pleasant. As he regained his strength, so also did he recover his poetic powers, now put to the one task that was important above all others. To expose the brutality, the abysmal cruelty, the inhumanity, of his captors became the first, the only, purpose of his life, to which he dedicated all his troubled days and haunted nights. The future—his future—was no longer in doubt. The British had provided him with a career. His countrymen must be made to see the enemy as he saw them, know them as he knew them, merciless and monstrous in their means as in their ends. He had always believed it; at Monmouth he had seen what he had believed. If further proof were needed, then he was the final proof himself.[15]

Did Americans handle their prisoners more gently? Had not Patrick Henry, the governor of Virginia, found it necessary to warn Colonel Charles Lewis and George Rogers Clark about harsh treatment of British prisoners taken at Saratoga? The dictates of "humanity" must not be outraged—yet they frequently were in American as well as in British camps. Was it true, as Rivington's *Royal Gazette* reported, that Loyalists were chained and driven for hundreds of miles into exile, though they were guilty of no overt act of hostility?[16] Was war a game for gentlemen, played with the rules of sportsmen? There was no civilized warfare. Tyrants never paused before humanitarian roadblocks, and liberty was not for the squeamish.[17]

Philip Frencau knew all this, though what he knew was in the realm of feeling rather than reason. For a poet there is more of truth in feeling than in reason, and Freneau's feelings colored what he wrote into the poem of his capture and imprisonment. His songs, his satires, printed in many broadsides and read in many encampments, had given some hope and courage to soldiers desperate with cold and

Freneau, Mss.; and Freneau, "Some Account of the Capture of the Ship Aurora."

[15] Freneau's work, in poetry and prose, was henceforth unrelentingly bitter and uncompromising.

[16] Jacob Axelrad, *Patrick Henry: The Voice of Freedom,* pp. 186, 188, 189, quoting Patrick Henry to Col. Charles Lewis, December 1778.

[17] Freneau, "Some Account of the Capture of the Ship Aurora"; see also E. B. Green, *The Revolutionary Generation,* p. 217.

hunger; but more than that, they had often suggested, though faintly as the struggle continued, the possibility of peace between the mother and her children. After Monmouth he had little faith and less hope for any compromise. In "The British Prison Ship" he at last called for implacable and unremitting war. The struggle was now one to the death, for a complete break with the past, with the culture and traditions of Britain no less than with its power and privilege. Independence, spiritual as well as political, total and everlasting, was America's only salvation.

"The British Prison Ship" was one of the greatest, most venomous, indictments of England yet drawn in the history of America. Beyond further doubt Freneau was the poet of the American Revolution, seeking as never before to arouse the faltering patriots to every last ounce of their energy, to incite them to every last bit of their feeling, to instill in them his own vast hatred so they might fight with utmost abandon as they had never fought before.

> Weak as I am, I'll try my strength to-day,
> And my best arrows at these hell-hounds play.
> To future years one scene of death prolong,
> And hang them up in infamy, in song.

In lines strung taut with passion, he did hang them up in infamy. He drew a monstrous picture of the villainies of England and the cruelties of the "base-born" Hessians, of the

> Stewards and mates that hostile Britain bore,
> Cut from the gallows on their native shore.

The prison ship was unspeakably horrible; the hospital, "a slaughterhouse" where

> Along the decks the dying captives lay,
> Some struck with madness, some with scurvy pain'd,
> But still of putrid fevers most complain'd!

The counts in his indictment are many and of mounting intensity. The heartless crimes of Britain must be punished with equal ferocity.

> *Americans!* a just resentment shew,
> And glut revenge on this detested foe.
>
> . . .
>
> Can you forget the greedy Briton's ire,
> Your fields in ruins and your homes on fire,

> No age, no sex from lust and murder free,
> And, black as night, the hell-born refugee!

If punishment is to fit the crime—

> Rouse from your sleep, and crush the thievish band,
> Defeat, destroy, and sweep them from the land.[18]

The British and their hirelings were not the only culprits. Americans were also among them. The Tories, the Loyalists, were known; the stockjobbers and speculators, the pimps and profiteers, all the scum that floats on the surface of every war, these too were known. But there were many who were not known, who remained invisible from the watchful eyes and swift vengeance of the patriots. They were the traitors and sappers who worked in mysterious ways their villainies to perform. One of them had just been discovered, too late for punishment. Benedict Arnold, the brave and brilliant soldier of Saratoga and Quebec, of Ticonderoga and Fort Stanwix, was deep in the mire of treason. Peggy, his lovely wife, was in it too, and both of them had escaped any penalty for their crimes. Arnold had fled to the safety of the British lines, the buxom Peggy to the hearts of gullible Americans as a betrayed and deserted woman. Not until she also was safe from retribution was it discovered how gullible they had been, and what payment in good English coin she had received for her part in the treachery. Only Major André, the British spy, as gallant as he was unfortunate, was hanged for the crime.[19] In "The British Prison Ship" Freneau did not forget to pay his compliments to the Benedict Arnolds of all degrees,

> Traitors, lost to every sense of shame,
> Unjust supporters of a tyrant's claim.

Brooding on the tragedy of treason, he also hoped to compose a drama of the Arnold episode as it was revealed in the testimony before the military court.

---

[18] "The British Prison Ship," in Freneau, *Poems* (Pattee), Vol. 2, p. 18; Philip M. Marsh and M. Ellis, "Broadside of Freneau's British Prison Ship," *American Literature,* X, 4 (January 1939), 476–480. Thus, Philip Freneau, who once had shuddered at the thought of killing a chicken for his dinner, was losing his inhibitions about bloodshed, even of humans (see M. S. Austin, *Philip Freneau,* p. 131).

[19] John H. Preston, *Revolution—1776,* pp. 158, 262, 263; E. P. Oberholzer, *Philadelphia: A History of the City and Its People,* Ch. 2; Irvine Haines, "Peggy Shippen," *New York Times,* January 31, 1932.

The evidence did not yet include the part of Peggy nor any word of the bribe of 350 pounds which she received "for her services which were meritorious." The man who was enticed to his ruin as much by her "beautiful bosom" as by lusts of a more substantial nature, would not be content with the plan—happily frustrated—to deliver West Point and Washington himself to the British. He had failed in this— he would not fail again. As a British officer his descent on Virginia to burn and devastate the granary of the revolution would not be frustrated.[20]

Freneau knew enough of the depravity of which men were capable to portray it in all its nakedness in his drama, "The Spy." In verse and in prose, he wanted to paint the whole tragic story of a soul's debasement and the profound pathos of its self-inflicted penalty, reserving his genuine feeling of compassion for the youthful André, a British patriot who possessed a true courage and nobility to the end. Nobility in any man was a precious, priceless attribute, and wherever found, in a foe as in a friend, it was a treasure beyond the reach of hatred—even the hatred of Philip Freneau. "The Spy" was never quite completed; only a few of the speeches of those who played their brief parts in one of the greatest tragedies of the American Revolution remain to remind us of the poet's spiritual understanding of evil in the midst of his own turbulent emotions.[21]

Slowly recovering his strength at Mount Pleasant Philip began to think once more of the future. In his unhappy scheme of life the problem of a living remained as pressing as ever. He had literally crawled home when there was no other place to go to, no one else to turn to but his mother. He could not stay there, a burden added to all the others which Agnes must bear. He was a grown man whom they all loved and cherished, but he must make his own way in the world, to succeed or to fail, a man among men, if not a poet among poets.

Where would he go? New York was in the hands of the enemy. He knew nothing of Boston save as a subject for the poem he had once written. There remained only Philadelphia. In the Quaker City, Francis Bailey, once the partner of Hugh Brackenridge, was in business again after the ill-fated venture of *The United States Magazine.* He was publishing a new paper, *The Freeman's Journal,* and a writer

[20] J. T. Flexner, *The Traitor and the Spy,* pp. 275, 394–404.
[21] Philip M. Marsh, "Philip Freneau's Ms. of the Spy," *The Rutgers University Library Journal,* IX, 1 (December 1945), 23–27. The manuscript is in the Freneau Collection (Rutgers). See also Freneau, *Poems* (Pattee), Vol. 2, p. 39.

like Philip Freneau might be an asset to its frankly partisan policy of revolutionary appeal.[22] A career at sea seemed finished—perhaps forever, surely for the war's duration. A career as a writer was never finished. It could be put on and taken off like a coat. Whatever the condition of one's fortunes, it was still worth while if it offered a little —even a little—warmth and comfort to a man who had no other. Perhaps it was less a career than a makeshift, less a makeshift than a momentary refuge—it was all he could do. After a fashion, it *was* a living.

As the winter loosed its frozen grip on the Monmouth countryside and the sun softened the icy roadways leading to the South, Freneau packed his meager belongings and set off again from Locust Grove to seek his doubtful fortune in the wide, wide world. Spring was in the air and his spirits were lighter than they had been for a long time. With the passage of time his misfortunes had come to seem less tragic, his wounds less painful. In the springtime a young man does not find it hard to hope, for without hope there is no prospect of a resurrection. On the front page of his book on navigation, Philip Freneau had noted as much himself. *"Il faut bien l'espérer,"* he wrote, *"car sans cette consolation il n'y aurait qu'à mourir."* He was not yet ready to die.[23]

In April 1781 Francis Bailey announced in *The Freeman's Journal* that a new writer, "a young philosopher and Bel Esprit," would contribute to its columns.[24] This was meant to describe the young poet who had just arrived from Monmouth.

He was, perhaps, a philosopher in spite of himself. Surely he was no *bel-esprit*. He was in reality nothing but a poor poet, an ex-prisoner of the British, whose past scarcely justified Francis Bailey's flattering intimations for the future.

[22] *The Freeman's Journal,* April 25, 1781, according to General Administration Services, Case #23069: Pension Records of Philip Freneau, Mss.

[23] Freneau's copy of Robertson, *Elements of Navigation,* in Freneau Collection (Rutgers).

[24] *The Freeman's Journal,* April 25, 1781.

13. GOD-ATTENDING STAR

PHILADELPHIA, in the springtime of 1781, was noted for many things. For one thing, however, the City of Brotherly Love was not noted. Love, in its less romantic sense, was conspicuously absent as a catalyst of the political and social life in the largest city of America. Politics of a local rather than a national character simmered and boiled over in fighting factions while the Continental Congress was immersed in more pressing problems of the country's survival. Financial and economic problems of a personal nature often animated the politicos who were always alert to all the implications of their own power and profit in the city and the state. Yet the power of the entire country was at stake, and the profit of a whole people was in the balance. For here as elsewhere not only the people, the army itself and the whole course of the Revolution were affected by political maneuvers which barely masked the purpose of a few against the many.[1]

Congress had not failed to pass appropriate resolutions condemning "the spirit of sharping and extortion, and the rapid rise of every commodity." Resolutions alone could condemn but they could not curb such a spirit, which was far from unique to the Quaker City or the state of Pennsylvania. It was rife in all the Colonies, and Congress was powerless to stem the rising tide of greed. By the end of 1779, prices were at the rate of twenty to one, in terms of paper money. Soon, they increased to sixty to one. A pound of beef was five dollars—then it rose to eight dollars. Black markets thrived.[2]

Edmund Randolph thought that paper money was "viler than rags,"

---

[1] Allan Nevins, *The American States during and after the Revolution*, p. 261.
[2] Jacob Axelrad, *Patrick Henry: The Voice of Freedom*, pp. 187, 189, 199.

while Washington, lacking the strength to engage the enemy, confided to Benjamin Harrison that if his recommendations to Congress were "much longer neglected, I shall not scruple to add, that our affairs are irretrievably lost." The despair of the Commander-in-Chief had reached inordinate bounds and the future seemed all but ruined. "Party disputes and personal quarrels," he declared, "are the great business of the day, whilst the momentous concerns of an empire, a great and accumulated debt, ruined finances, depreciated money, and want of credit (which in its consequences is the want of everything) are but secondary considerations."[3]

This was the situation at the end of 1779; in 1780 and in the spring of 1781 it was still the same. Patriots were themselves deeply involved in the business of mounting prices and high profits. In the City of Brotherly Love, Robert Morris was charged with extorting huge gains from the poor, while riots, staged by radicals who failed to understand the immutable law of supply and demand, or the even more abstruse one of Gresham which operated with cruel rectitude in the realm of money, were an almost daily occurrence. In 1780 martial law, superceding all other laws but these, had been declared, followed by a mutiny in the Pennsylvania line at Morristown. In the spring of 1781 rumors were rife of the huge waste and graft and outright theft of public funds by those who were solemnly appointed to guard them. Philadelphia, the nesting-place of neutrals and the sanctuary of Loyalists, was a hotbed of political fevers and a cauldron of economic chicane when Philip Freneau arrived to become the editor of *The Freeman's Journal or North American Intelligencer* for Francis Bailey.[4]

The man who had seen something of the fury of violent men on the British side was now to learn more of the violence of furious men on the American side. The scene which Freneau surveyed was a confused and depressing one, hardly calculated to release that *bel-esprit* with which Bailey had endowed him or enhance the philosophical objectivity which the occasion might demand. He also knew of other

[3] Washington to Benj. Harrison, May 7, 1779, in George Washington, *Writings* (ed. J. C. Fitzpatrick), Vol. 15, p. 5; Nevins, *The American States,* pp. 259 ff.; and E. C. Burnett (ed.), *Letters of Members of the Continental Congress,* Vol. 2, p. 51.

[4] Nevins, *The American States,* pp. 261, 266; see also C. H. Van Tyne, *The Loyalists in the American Revolution,* pp. 113–117. *Rivington's Royal Gazette,* May 29, 1779, portrays the situation in New York; see also J. G. Wilson, *The Memorial History of the City of New York.*

scenes, enacted in other places, where honest, dedicated men suffered and died without any thought of profit save the profit that was the essence of freedom.

Washington's criticism was perhaps too stringent as his responsibility was too great. There were patriots everywhere—even in Philadelphia—whose integrity was beyond reproach, whose sacrifices were beyond censure. Men—women too—gave unstintingly of themselves and their substance where the need was great and the danger imminent. The crises of war were met heroically on the battlefield by common soldier and officer alike; in the market places of America by the common man and his leaders equally. Hope was not completely gone. It blossomed anew with each rumor of help at home and abroad, and help, in the dwindling fortunes of the Revolution, was desperately needed. The North had felt the heavy hand of war, but the South had felt scarcely more than its velvet glove. Now it was to know the bare fist, and the spiked boot as well.[5]

The legislature of the Old Dominion was already fleeing for its life from Richmond to Charlottesville closely pursued by Cornwallis, and from Charlottesville to Staunton before entrapment by Tarleton. Benedict Arnold was in the South also, in command of massive British plunder and destruction of public stores which no one had the means or the power to defend. Fire and fury had come to the southland, and James Madison, who was there, described what he saw in a letter to his friend Philip Mazzei. Madison had little to do with any fighting, less indeed than his classmate Philip Freneau. His talents lay rather in the forum, in the places where law was made, where he would help to make it. What he wrote to Mazzei was like an echo of the words Freneau had written after Monmouth. "No description," he informed Mazzei, "can give you an adequate idea of the barbarity with which the enemy have conducted the war in the Southern States. Every outrage which humanity could suffer has been committed by them. They have acted more like desperate robbers or buccaneers than like a nation making war for dominion." And he concluded: "They are a daily lesson to the people of the United States of the necessity for perseverance in the contest."[6]

[5] H. C. Hockett, *Growth of the American People,* pp. 231–234; Douglas Southall Freeman, *George Washington,* Vol. 5, Ch. 22; Axelrad, *Patrick Henry,* Ch. VI.

[6] Madison to Mazzei, July 7, 1781, in Irving Brant, *James Madison,* Vol. 1; *The Virginia Revolutionist,* p. 159.

Could they persevere? Greene had retreated through North Carolina; Muhlenberg was defeated at Petersburg on the Appomattox; the Virginia navy was captured on the James. Writing to Clinton on March 7, 1781, Lord Germain was confident of "the speedy suppression of the Rebellion."[7] Suspicion tore at the minds of honest men; doubt was like a canker in the hearts of simple men; passion supplanted reason; and the end, the tragic and inglorious end, of the Revolution seemed close at hand. The speedy suppression of the rebellion was about to liquidate the final hope of liberty.

In the everlasting struggle for freedom, many battles may be lost—the war itself goes on. Burned, ruined, desolated—the Revolution persevered, and hope was again rekindled when Greene met Cornwallis at Guilford Court House in North Carolina. On March 15, one week after Germain's note to Clinton, Lord Cornwallis lost a full third of his forces. The end was not yet. The French, as Freneau had prophesied, had sent Rochambeau to help Washington with men and money to save the Revolution. The two men were already perfecting their plans while Congress, taking heart at the new turn of events, was shaping some plans of its own in Philadelphia. Philip Freneau, the new editor of *The Freeman's Journal*, with an access of his recently discovered *bel-esprit*, commenced a campaign of incitement and vengeance that would implement the perserverance of all America.[8]

He was already discreetly known in Philadelphia, where "The British Prison Ship" had been printed as a pamphlet and sold on the streets.[9] Now he again dipped his pen in the bitter bile of his own experiences to warn and to incite his countrymen. These were the days for a poet to teach men the meaning of despotism, to use his pen like a naked sword, like a spiked bludgeon, like a thundering cannon against the ruthless enemy. The editor would report the news, of course—all properly spiced with patriotic propaganda to give it bite

[7] Axelrad, *Patrick Henry*, p. 205. Lord Germain was perhaps responsible for the débâcle of the British at Saratoga, an event that gave impetus to the resolve of France to rescue the American Revolution.

[8] Freneau's personal file of *The Freeman's Journal*, from April 25, 1781, to February 9, 1785, is at the New Jersey Historical Society. In these are contained his earlier poems and prose, pieces later included in *The Miscellaneous Works of Philip Freneau*, published by Bailey in 1788. See Philip M. Marsh, "Philip Freneau's Personal File of *The Freeman's Journal*," *Proceedings of New Jersey Historical Society*, LVII, 3 (July 1939), 163–170 .

[9] Philip M. Marsh and M. Ellis, "Broadside of Freneau's British Prison Ship," *American Literature*, X, 4 (January 1939), 476–480.

and flavor—to bolster the flagging morale of America in verse and in prose for the certain triumph of liberty.

The first issue of *The Freeman's Journal* emphasized what was patent to only a few.

At no period of time [Freneau wrote], in no era of important events from the first establishment of social government, have the liberties of man, have the rights of human nature, been more deeply interested than at the time in which we presume to address you. While Liberty, the noblest ornament of society, without which no community can well be organized, seemed to pine and sicken under the trammels of despotic restraint in every one of the ancient nations of the earth, it fairly promises to resume its pristine majesty here.

The policy of the paper, Freneau informs his readers, is to acquaint freemen "with the real state of their affairs, and that the characters of their public servants, both individually and collectively, be made manifest, is our object." To this end he promises "a Free Press, universally free to every citizen indiscriminately, whose principles coincide with those of the Revolution and whose object is confessedly known to point at public or private good."[10]

He gives no quarter to anyone whose principles are contrary to his own; if it suits his purpose he uses the old weapons of scathing satire or unabashed vituperation. For more considered judgments he reverts to the more sober essay form. In a series of articles supposedly written by a "Pilgrim," he analyzes the issue of the bloody struggle with a trenchant simplicity that any man, however illiterate, can easily understand, adding some occasional piece of lighter fare to amuse his readers. According to the custom of the day, most of his work is printed anonymously or under a variety of pseudonyms like "Pylades" or "Orestes" or "Hermes." Together with grim reminders of disastrous defeats suffered by patriot forces, he exults over the victories they have won. If there is only bad news, he supplies something to offset it, to soften it, some bit of humor that is discerning as well as amusing. In the midst of trouble, any trouble, men can still be seduced by a momentary glimpse at the lovelier aspects of life. It is of the first importance for them to browse for a little while in pastures not green but white—perhaps the lovely, ample bosoms of the ladies who expose them more than the editor of *The Freeman's Journal* can approve. Not that he finds any fault with those who seek to help nature in its

10 *The Freeman's Journal,* April 25, 1781.

laudable purpose of stimulating the stronger sex. Freneau grudgingly approves the simple diversions of the weaker sex, their "plumy head-dress, with all its gay streamers, towers and battlements, the rustling silk with its flounces and furbelows, the diminutive foot shrouded in damask, or the neck veiled by the half-concealing lawn." It was right that women should attract men who might otherwise escape them. As for their bosoms, why not display them altogether, so that "these charms, which while partially concealed are so fatal to the eye of sensibility, by common view, like the face and arms, become incapable of kindling the fire of love."[11]

This kind of literary indulgence by one who has sedulously avoided speaking, save in his verses to Amanda, of the "fire of love," is a strange excursion indeed. In the Amanda poems he is less singed than slightly warmed by the flames of passion, an ethereal more than an ardent observer of either bosom or feet, or the lady's neck, half-concealed in lawn. He appears somewhat impervious to charms like these, and but for a random line, seems likely to remain so forever. No faint whisper of gossip or of slander ever gives any hint of a romantic involvement; it does not exist or he quite successfully curtains it from the public gaze.

His time is otherwise too fully occupied and there are few occasions for levity. Only rarely is his bitterness, his disillusionment, tempered by a fling of fellowship and fun. For the first time in his life he has a real and satisfying employment, poor in pay but richly rewarding to him as a writer, as a laborer in the vineyard of liberty; for him it is a labor of love as much as of hate, a supremely serious and tragically important work for the American Revolution. For a moment, but only for a moment, he might indulge himself in the sunnier sentiments of the male animal, and then rarely beyond the point of the strictest propriety. A man of high principle and almost puritanical precepts, he would wait for a less burdensome occasion to translate the demands of his other nature into more than words written with tongue in cheek and the pen in his heart.

Freneau's work on *The Freeman's Journal* afforded few opportunities for anything like light satire. The war went badly despite the victories—most of them at sea, too few of them on land. John Paul Jones, against insuperable odds, had won a fantastic victory over the British. The poet played it up in verses to make it plain that victory was more

---

[11] *Ibid.,* May 8, 1782.

a matter of will than of strength. With a will to win America could hold out until the promised help of France would turn the tide and sweep all invaders off the soil of freedom.

> Bend to the *Stars* that flaming rise
> In Western, not in Eastern skies,
> Fair Freedom's reign restor'd.
> So when the Magi, come from far,
> Beheld the God-Attending Star.
> They trembled and adored.[12]

The God-Attending Star was at long last rising in the heavens. The French were coming—they were already here—to give their full measure of help to the courageous men who needed it now more desperately than ever. The prostrate South was a scene of carnage; one more vicious assault by the British, and it would become the grave of the Revolution. But the French had come. In Philadelphia, on August 31, 1781, Rochambeau and Washington were digging another grave, and sewing the cerements, in which alien ambitions and foreign tyranny would be buried instead. For them and for their soldiers Freneau was writing the words to move the hearts and raise the hopes of all who fought and died for liberty.[13]

> What men, like you, our warfare could command,
> And bring us safely to the promised land?
> Not swol'n with pride, with victory elate,
> 'Tis in misfortune you are doubly great.
>
>   .   .   .
>
> O! May you live to hail that glorious day
> When Britain homeward shall pursue her way—
> That race subdued, who filled the world with slain,
> And rode tyrannic o'er the subject main!
> What few presumed, you boldly have achieved,
> A tyrant humbled, and a world relieved.[14]

His prophecy was soon justified by events. Money—six million livres in gold—was sent to America by France. From his own scanty stores, Rochambeau advanced another twenty thousand dollars. Men, ships, arms, arrived. De Grasse was sailing from Haiti with twenty-eight vessels crowded with thousands of soldiers to reinforce Lafayette,

[12] *Ibid.*, August 8, 1782.
[13] *Ibid.*, August 28, 1782.
[14] "To His Excellency, General Washington," in *Ibid.*, September 5, 1781.

who was waiting for him at Williamsburg. Destouches had despatched a strong contingent of men under Baron de Viomesnil, while Rochambeau, in close conjunction with Washington, was moving swiftly, softly, secretly, to Yorktown with a shattering army of nine thousand troops. Wayne was meeting with Lafayette; Steuben had replaced Muhlenberg; and Nelson, the governor of Virginia, was waiting at the James. With three thousand militia from the Old Dominion, he was helping to close the trap at Yorktown.[15]

In September, in October, the plans of Washington and Rochambeau became clear, the improbable gave way to the possible, the fantastic to the inevitable, and the truth to fiction (fiction, as everyone knew, must be more persuasive than the truth). It soon became apparent that the fortunes of war were indeed incalculable, the errors of man were as beneficent for some as his wisdom was for others. To reduce Virginia and subdue the South, Cornwallis had unaccountably moved to Yorktown, to the strip of land that jutted into the sea between the James and the York. He was in a trap, one of his own devising, and the plans to spring it were providentially perfected in the penultimate hour of decision. By sea De Grasse was waiting. In the bay Barras was watching. Lynn Haven was shut tight against any escape by water. On land Lauzun and Choisy were chasing Tarleton out of Gloucester Point as Washington and Rochambeau made ready for the kill. Before Clinton could bring on his men from New York to avert a defeat, the British were already beaten.[16]

On October 8 Freneau, carefully studying the moves on the chessboard of the maneuver, was sure the British were trapped. In an address "To Lord Cornwallis," he informed him that the end was near.

> Woulds't thou at last with Washington engage,
> Sad object of his pity not his rage?
> See round thy posts now horribly advance
> The chiefs, the soldiers, and the fleets of France![17]

On October 19, 1781, the posts were taken. Cornwallis surrendered. The God-Attending Star was at the zenith.

[15] S. Bonsal, *When the French Were Here,* pp. 67–68, 79–81, 128–130, 142.
[16] *Ibid.,* Ch. 9.
[17] *Ibid.;* and *The Freeman's Journal,* October 8, 1781.

14. THE FRUITS OF VICTORY

WHEN THE NEWS of the British collapse reached Philadelphia the people, as reported by *The Freeman's Journal,* rejoiced with wild abandon as guns roared their salvos and fireworks turned the night into day. Philip Freneau, scorning any pity for the invader, composed a poem for the occasion that was savage beyond most of those he had ever written before. Recalling the whole tragic past, he was less generous than Washington himself. The military courtesies were not for him. If those who had shown so little mercy in the bloody years since 1775 were entirely extirpated, he would have had no scruples. More than any other man, their commander Lord Cornwallis was responsible for all of them.

> What pen can write, what human tongue can tell
> The endless murders of this man from hell!
> Nature in him disgraced the form divine,
> Nature mistook, she meant him for a—swine.[1]

The men who followed his orders are not spared either. The ruin they spread, the plundering they practiced, the havoc they wreaked, their cruelty and barbarism, these debasements of the human spirit have sapped the compassion of the man who had so little violence in himself. He demands a stark and swift justice for all these crimes— nothing less. To forgive would be monstrous; mere revenge was beneath the dignity of the cause of freedom. What justice will be done to those who sent

> . . . their slaves their project to fulfill,
> To wrest our freedom, or our blood to spill:

[1] *The Freeman's Journal,* November 7, 1781.

> Such to forgive, is virtue too sublime,
> For even compassion has been found a crime.[2]

For deeds like these "the halter" or "the knife" is the only punishment to fit the crime. Despots who seek to enslave a whole people are beyond the call of pity, as their deeds are beyond the voice of humanity. They must be trapped, and they must be destroyed.

If the poet's spleen spilled over in his wrath at the British, his gentler emotions were equally engaged for the sacrifice and suffering of his own country. His tribute "To the Memory of the Brave Americans" who fell at Eutaw Springs in South Carolina was a deep and anguished sorrow for the victims of British cruelty, voiced in lines of quiet dignity and profound pathos. The battle at Eutaw Springs had been only a pyrrhic victory for the enemy, and for the patriots only a momentary defeat. For Freneau, however, it was one of the high moments of the war, a proof of the American will to win and the dauntless courage that conquers over all. Shorter than most of his poems, this was also the simple and touching tribute of his homage to the spirit of man in his ageless quest for freedom.

> At Eutaw Springs the valiant died;
> Their limbs with dust are covered o'er—
> Weep on, ye Springs, your tearful tide,
> How many heroes are no more!
>
> If in this wreck of ruin, they
> Can yet be thought to claim a tear,
> O smite your gentle breast; and say
> The friends of freedom slumber here.
>
> . . .
>
> They saw their injured country's woe,
> The flaming town, the wasted field;
> They rushed to meet the insulting foe,
> They took the spear—but left the shield.[3]

On the wings of compassion a poet may rise above the hatreds of men. Tears are more potent than blood to wash away anger. The poem made a deep impression on readers at home and abroad. Walter Scott thought it one of the greatest in the English language. He paid it

---

[2] *Ibid.*

[3] *Ibid.*, September 8, 1781; Lewis Leary, *That Rascal Freneau*, p. 42; and Nathanael Greene, "General Greene's Report of the Battle of Eutaw Springs," *The Magazine of History, with Notes and Queries*, Extra #139.

the added compliment of borrowing a line for use in his own "Marmion."[4] Nor was that the only time when Freneau would "lend" a
line to others.[5] In this war there were still many lines to be written,
for the Revolution was not yet finished. As it became increasingly clear
that the British would fight on, Freneau continued his own relentless
attack on them; as his countrymen pursued them for the final blow,
he too pursued them with unabated vigor. The issue was not yet settled even though many Americans and their French friends believed
there was nothing left to settle. Greene had not delivered Georgia.
The Carolinas were still occupied by the enemy. Clinton was firmly
entrenched in New York.

The Paris crowds could rejoice that the war was over—their generous greetings to Benjamin Franklin at Passy proved that the rebels
had won. Was not Lafayette making last moment preparations to leave
for home and his pretty wife? Indeed, he had just notified the French
Prime Minister, the Comte de Maurepas that "the play is over, the
fifth act has just finished." The fifth act was finished, but a few more
waited to be done in this long drama of American independence.[6]

The actors were tired. They were ready to relax and go home. Their
leaders, even Congress, considered Yorktown as the end for Britain.
Washington, wiser than most of them, saw the danger of diminished
vigilance and wrote to Greene that his "greatest fear is that Congress,
viewing this stroke in too important a light, may think our work too
nearly closed, and will fall into a state of languor and relaxation."
Not only Congress—the army itself was infected with the lassitude of
over-confidence and the poison of a false optimism. Soldiers wanted
to go home and were clamoring for their pay. The states were demanding an end of Federal encroachments and the return of their "un-
alienable rights," relinquished only for the duration of the war. The
people, sick of all the suffering, were expecting a quick peace—but
where was that peace now? Some of the disgruntled ones were con-
spiring with the malcontents; plots were fomenting that had the hideous aspects of treason and sedition. Cornwallis had surrendered at
Yorktown but the tumult of war persisted.[7]

---

[4] In Introduction to the 3rd Canto of "Marmion," 4th line; see also E. A. and
G. L. Duyckinck, *Cyclopoedia of American Literature*, Vol. 1, p. 335.

[5] Thomas Campbell, in his poem, "O'Conor's Child," used a line from Freneau's "Lines on Visiting an Old Burying Ground."

[6] S. Bonsal, *When the French Were Here*, Ch. 9.

[7] Washington to Greene, November 16, 1781, in George Washington, *Writ-*

De Grasse, fresh from one victory, had suffered an almost shattering defeat at the hands of the British Admiral Rodney in the West Indies; the *Ville de Paris,* his flagship, had been sunk, and thousands of his men were dead. Encouraged by the news, Lord North and the King himself were demanding of Parliament that the struggle against America continue. The people of Britain were sick of war, and they were ready to prove it with riots in the streets of London. Did Lord North still hang on to the illusion of victory after Wayne had captured Savannah and Greene had taken Charleston? Lord North would be driven from power, the Whigs would supplant him, and the universal cry for peace would prevail as Greene, tenacious in his strategy of retreat and attack and withdrawal, cleared the entire Southland and the invaders were driven into the sea. They held on for a while longer in the North, where Clinton still held New York, but soon he too would move out, and peace, peace at last, would come to a war-weary people on both sides of the Atlantic. When Washington, on January 2, 1782, was feted in Philadelphia for his supreme courage and brilliant leadership, he was greeted with the poetic accolade of the editor of *The Freeman's Journal:*

> Illustrious hero may you live to see
> These new republics, powerful, great, and free;
> Peace, heaven-born peace, o'er spacious regions spread,
> While discord sinking veils her ghostly head.[8]

The man who inspired these lines was indeed an illustrious hero. With never more than ten thousand effectives in the field he had inspired them to victory in the face of almost certain defeat. But for his tenacity, the French would have come too late—or not at all—and the errors of Sir William Howe, of Clinton and Cornwallis, availed nothing in the final liberation. And now, the big-boned man with the large nose, high cheekbones, and pockmarked face would need the same heroic qualities to cope with the shadows that were falling on his own countrymen.

To divert the passions of discord among Americans into channels of hatred for the British, Freneau, forsaking the verse form entirely, launched a series of essays in which satire was lightly mixed with propaganda of a more forthright nature and seasoned with a homely

ings (ed. J. C. Fitzpatrick), Vol. 23, pp. 346–347; and Douglas Southall Freeman, *George Washington,* Vol. 5, p. 404.

[8] Freneau, *The Poems of Philip Freneau* (ed. F. L. Pattee), Vol. 2, p. 109.

philosophy of reason readily digested by the average citizen. The "Pilgrim" papers, intermittently appearing in the columns of *The Freeman's Journal*, were the intellectual probings of Freneau's mind into the problems of the day, problems that were of more than immediate importance to the welfare of a country slowly emerging from the morass of a long war. The best of these essays, later collected and issued under the title of *The Philosopher of the Forest,* were the first serious and sustained treatment of American themes in this medium.[9]

Many of the essays have a purpose more immediate, as the need for action is more pressing. The danger from the enemy is still a potent one since the war is not yet finished, and peace not yet truly won. In the issue of November 28, 1781, the editor of *The Freeman's Journal* warns his readers,

that native, wanton and inherent cruelty is nowhere so conspicuous as in the inhabitants of Britain . . . Even the brute and bird creation, as well as the human in this island, are almost wholly destitute of that mildness, good nature, and familiarity that we observe in the animals of other countries . . . Thousands of unfortunate wretches are annually hurried out of the world for trifling thefts and other petty crimes.[10]

The picture is overdrawn, oversimplified, for his more gullible readers, while the truth is exaggerated for its dramatic effect. With as much heat and equal truth he could have attacked the harsh treatment of petty offenders in his own country, in Philadelphia itself, where civil debtors and criminals of doubtful depravity were punished with medieval cruelty. In New York sixteen assorted crimes were still punishable by death; in Delaware the number was even higher. In Virginia the extreme penalty was imposed where the crime itself was frequently less than extreme. In Pennsylvania many infractions of the law were strictly defined as meriting execution, though often they were less strictly enforced than by a sentence of death. The inhuman reprisals once permitted by law—branding, ear-cropping, heavy flogging—had been stopped years before; but variations of these still persisted in many of the Colonies, while pauper debtors were considered as worthy of nothing less than imprisonment and the deprivation of the most elementary rights of human beings. *The Pennsylvania Packet*

[9] "The Pilgrim Papers" and "Philosopher of the Forest," in Freneau, *The Miscellaneous Works of Philip Freneau,* pp. 281–288, 305–311, 311–313, 320–325, 360–367, 375–380.

[10] *The Freeman's Journal,* November 28, 1781.

still carried appeals by some of these unhappy souls for rescue before they succumbed to a fate of slow extinction. Prison conditions in the City of Brotherly Love were horrible beyond description, and an unfortunate though "Estimable debtor" might be thrown into a cell with some "disgusting object of popular contempt besmeared with filth from the pillory; the unhappy victim of the lash, streaming with blood from the whipping post; the half-naked vagrant, the loathesome drunkard."[11]

The political propagandist of *The Freeman's Journal* omitted to write about these: his only purpose was to damn the enemy and leave to others—and to other times—the crying need for reforms at home. He did not neglect them entirely, yet neither did he dilute his hatred for the enemy abroad with his contempt for the enemy at home. He would rather expand on the great beneficence of nature and on her finest product—"a just, distinterested, benevolent, upright, and honest man"—in one issue, and in the next set forth his opinion of the English "as lovers of discord, tyrannical, cruel, and the enemies to peace and harmony; there are also more gluttons and drunkards in that nation than I ever beheld in any other."[12] For the most part this was plain propaganda in the cause of American independence, for Philip Freneau had never seen any Englishman, drunk or sober, anywhere in Britain. He had never even been there. This was a species of poetic license that did not include the poets of England, all of them beloved and most of them dead.

Freneau often varied his envenomed attacks on Englishmen with some philosophic flights on the condition of *homo sapiens;* man, he said, is "at the head of all sublunary excellence. His eye is fixt upon the celestial canopy: he reasons upon the design and nature of his own existence: his breast glows with noble and exalted ideas: he measures the distance of the stars from each other." Dispassionate in his objective appraisal of man, he challenges the pessimists of the race to "make a more perfect creature if you can."[13]

The mellow mood is only a temporary one. A philosopher must also take account of war, and the inhumanity of man in both war and peace is not to be glossed over. So many men are not perfect creatures.

[11] Allan Nevins, *The American States during and after the Revolution,* pp. 453 n., 457–459.

[12] *The Freeman's Journal,* December 19, 1781; Freneau, *The Miscellaneous Works,* pp. 292–294.

[13] Freneau, *The Miscellaneous Works,* pp. 297–298.

"One was a thief; another was a bully and a wrangler; a third was a dunce; a fourth an idiot; a fifth a monster of avarice and envy; a sixth a sycophant." Yet evil can be banished among men by the simple expedient of implanting in society "the principle of Honour, which will in some degree compensate for the want of inner rectitude of heart." This, with "severe and perpetual labour," will keep men in the way of decency, without the need for either onerous penalties or religious homilies. The honest man was possible in America—but what of the Englishman? Freneau was back again to the prime business of propaganda.

Amongst all the authors of antiquity, even those most famed for candor, I do not remember one who, in making mention of Britain, did not describe the inhabitants in an unfavorable light; barbarous, cruel, inhospitable . . . After a criminal is suspended to a gibbet, no nation but this takes him down when half-dead, rips up his bowels, tears out his heart, and throws it, reeking with blood, into his face!

Was he still suffering the outrage of his own treatment in the prison and hospital ships?

Other nations, [he continues], when the fate of war has thrown a number of unfortunate captives into their hands, generally behold them afterwards with an eye of pity and compassion and strive to render their captivity as light as possible; but Britain, remorseless Britain, dooms them to experience every species of misery while in her possession. I infer from the histories and annals of the English nation, that had it not pleased the Almighty to check them frequently in their career of cruelty, ambition and tyranny, they would, long before this day, as the monster nation of the universe, have subjected and enslaved all before them.[14]

Forgetting the struggles of the English themselves for that liberty which he is now defending with truths, half-truths, and gross exaggerations, he seeks to arouse the people to far greater efforts in the final push to hurl the British from the shores of America. The English language itself comes under his condemnation. He is "sorry to say" that it is "the prevailing tongue in these United States," and justifies his absurdities because English is the language of poltroons as well as poets. It is the tongue of James Rivington, the New York Tory and printer of *The Royal Gazette,* foremost organ of the British from the beginning of the Revolution. Rivington, with an easy conscience, had

[14] *The Freeman's Journal,* February 2, 1782.

played the Tory game according to Tory strength at any given moment. When the star of the patriots was ascendant, James Rivington was not averse to acting as a spy for them. Freneau, watching his game from distant Philadelphia, hurled some of his most bitter shafts at him, while not neglecting another New York printer, Hugh Gaine, whose moral scruples and political philandering were also continually accommodated to the stronger side in the shifting fortunes of the war.[15] With the British still in possession of New York in 1782, it appeared that men like these would never be dislodged, save by the intercession of death itself. Reverting to satirical verse once more, Freneau prepared "Rivington's Last Will and Testament," in which the man who changed his politics with the wind of warfare provided:

> Imprimis, my carcase I give and devise,
> To be made into cakes of a moderate size,
> To nourish those Tories whose spirits may droop,
> And serve the King's army with potable soup.[16]

The editor of *The Freeman's Journal* understood the need for more than a negative propaganda against the British. What the people knew about enemy warfare and the cruelties of civilized barbarism was not the whole picture of American suffering. Freneau himself, in his utmost fictions, could scarcely dream up the atrocities that occurred to isolated communities, in lonely outposts, no dreams but nightmares of the tragic truth about savageries not yet known to simpler civilizations. To inform his countrymen about them, Freneau enlisted the help of Hugh Brackenridge, who supplied the stories of frontier warfare as fought by Indian marauders with the blessing of British Christians and the inspiration of British money.[17]

The struggle dragged on interminably. Men still died for freedom. The Revolution was not yet won. It needed more blood and more tears —and it needed, too, more songs to lift the sinking hearts of patriots. Philip Freneau wrote them also. In the columns of his paper the stored-up ammunition of fact and fancy was poured out with the deadliest intent. In pamphlets and broadsides he printed the songs that went to camp and bivouac, to soldiers and civilians, who often preferred them to his more serious work. The "Song on Captain Barney's Victory," set to the tune of the "Tempest or Hosier's Ghost," served his purpose

[15] *Ibid.*, May 29, 1782.
[16] *Ibid.*, February 27, 1782.
[17] *Ibid.*, April 30, 1783.

as well as any satire. It spread his modest fame as the poet of the American Revolution.[18]

As the negotiations for peace moved slowly to a conclusion, and the war receded from the field to the forum, Freneau considered the value of the impending peace and its cost in men and treasure. In the first of his Pilgrim essays he had descanted on what he saw and heard in his imaginary travels about the world. As the series progressed he delved more deeply beneath the surface of appearance and ran the gamut of all questions affecting the human race. The Philosopher of the Forest now considered the war which was almost done and the peace it had almost achieved, and he came to the conclusion that violence was no answer to man's problems nor pride a solution for his spiritual malaise. He had urged violence when it seemed the only way to freedom, yet he abhorred it in theory as in practice; pride, except for some momentary aberrations, had never moved him to any action which reason could not approve. A child of the Enlightenment, he had written often, and in stirring lines, on the need, the beneficence, of force in the defense of liberty and against the enslavement of the body or the spirit of man. Reason might persuade without violence—though whose reason, was a question the poet answered too glibly. He believed in the kind which men accepted who were cultivated in "the heavenly arts of music and poetry." Such men would never tolerate "the grunting of swine and the croaking of ravens." In addition to music and poetry, did they understand that a small pinch of love on the tail of reason might catch and hold it even for the swine and the ravens? Man was also like a poem. And like music, he was composed of many parts, some of them harsh as a trumpet or dull as a drumbeat, as delicate as a flute or plaintive as a cello or sad as an oboe.[19]

[18] Freneau, *Poems* (Pattee), Vol. 2, pp. 149–150. It should be clear that Freneau in almost all his prose works and poems in *The Freeman's Journal* touched on every phase of the human condition. No mere philosopher of the forest could have pried so deeply or known so much about the profoundly spiritual elements of which man is composed.

[19] Freneau, *The Miscellaneous Works*, pp. 338–414. It is interesting to note how Freneau, for the moment relenting on the British, descants on the entire spectrum of human events from the subject of higher education to women's bosoms (Pilgrim Papers 12 and 14, in *The Freeman's Journal*, February 12 and and May 18, 1782). He uses a number of pseudonyms in these as in other writings, and does not neglect the more serious business of man's relation to God and the possibility of a future life. See also *The Freeman's Journal*, April 9, 1783, where he discusses Milton's *Paradise Lost* .

In the small circles of his knowledge, at home or abroad, Freneau had seen but few of the delicate and desirable aspects of human nature. In the little world of Philadelphia, there was much that was unreasonable and ugly. In the City of Brotherly Love, where the gentler instincts of man were "little more than" names, love "was understood in a very limited sense. Hospitality was sold for ready money; sheriffs and constables were as busy and brutal as in Europe, landlords as oppressive." Yet he looked for reason, for beauty, to temper the oppression and brutality of men. He wanted to compel some allegiance to these, so that man might one day renounce the violence that flourished in war and left its sinister shadow even on peace. As Pilgrim and Philosopher, he tried to teach men that the natural rights of all men were precious for each of them, and only at the peril of war, in one's self as in one's country, could they be denied. Domestic slavery was no better than alien tyranny.[20]

Perhaps the tender virtues were possible only where nature intended that man should live on the soil and by his own labor. Jean Jacques Rousseau was close to the truth when he saw society as the product of men who were unfettered by greed and ambition, if only they possessed intelligence and dignity. But how were they to acquire intelligence without education or dignity without labor? Freneau did not believe in the sumptuous learning of the rich, who used it as a mantle for display, but in the simple rules of wisdom and reason gleaned from the ages for the enrichment of life. Learning like this was the right of all men who could profit from it spiritually and morally, the poor as much as the rich, the common man equally with the well-born.[21] Here was no system of philosophy which he expounded, but his own modest insights into the human comedy that too often was played with such tragic results. Man, the most perfect creature of nature, is made unendurably despicable through the unnatural devices of lust and greed, of pride and power, Freneau had denounced these evils in the time of war. With the advent of peace he would still attack them.

In his satire "The Island of Snatchaway," Freneau contrasts the rulers of the island with the "brave, generous, and humane" "Ficklelanders," who are the helpless objects of their abuse.[22] Philip Freneau is no Dean Swift, and his satire possesses little of the subtlety of *Gulli-*

---

[20] Freneau, *The Miscellaneous Works*, p. 349.

[21] An excellent summary of Freneau's position on education is given in Leary, *That Rascal Freneau*, pp. 106–107.

[22] Freneau, *The Miscellaneous Works*, pp. 314 ff.

ver's Travels. He is not writing for the elite or for the intellectually alert. He is aiming at the poor and middle-class reader who was stirred by his wartime poems and might now be moved to consider the special implications, social and economic, of the peace. These were important enough to clarify and emphasize for the masses who had suffered so greatly for a noble cause, and were still suffering after that cause was won.

In Pennsylvania, where politics were again localized in the eternal quest for power, the old struggle over the state constitution was renewed with unaccustomed vigor and great personal rancor. The constitution which Benjamin Franklin had done so much to formulate, and which he had so proudly exhibited to Turgot, to La Rochefoucauld, and to Condorcet in the early days of the Revolution, provided for a single chamber with "supreme legislative power," and a President and Council of Censors which, to many, created a political structure not only ill-balanced, but far from democratic as well. The old struggle between the friends and foes of the constitution flared again in the year 1782, with the issues, already confused by old wrangles, becoming still further involved in the personalities and ambitions of warring political leaders. George Bryan, spearhead of the radical party, was opposed to a change which would add a second, an upper, chamber to the lawmaking body. For him, as for the mass of his followers, such a chamber would be nothing more than the tool of a rich and powerful minority, the banks and their mercantile retainers.[23]

The Freeman's Journal spoke for the radicals. For the conservatives, *The Pennsylvania Packet* and *The Pennsylvania Gazette* opened their columns to debates that discussed the more abstruse problems of state government. The conflicting arguments soon deteriorated into a slugging match in which the conservative papers observed the greater decorum, while *The Freeman's Journal,* currying favor with its less sophisticated readers, was soon in the trough of yellow journalism. What might have been an enlightened discussion, conducted on a high plane with dispassionate logic and calm reason, became a mud-slinging campaign of slander and invective, with the editor of *The Freeman's Journal* up to his knees in the mud.

For Freneau, the meaning of a select chamber of the elite, with power equal to that of the people's representatives, was clear and unmistakable. An upper chamber was always suspect as the rendezvous

---

[23] Nevins, *The American States,* pp. 151–152.

of the politically powerful minority. The welfare of the people was at stake in this combined assault on democracy by financial and commercial interests under the leadership of the conservative patriot John Dickinson, widely known for his perceptive and influential *Letters of a Pennslyvania Farmer*. Dickinson's fame and fortune had appreciably increased since Freneau's days at Princeton. The broad basis of government for which the war had been fought, and the people's sovereignty for which the peace had been won, were threatened by a new autocracy. Liberty was doomed at the source if democracy failed to nourish it.[24]

Whatever the virtues or the vices of the old constitution, the attacks on it by those identified with the Bank of North America and the Bank of Pennsylvania were met with suspicion and heated defense by the radicals. Was the government of Pennsylvania an anachronism in a country that was slowly emerging into nationhood? Was its constitution unresponsive to the needs, and offensive to the rights, of all classes of citizens? Was the majority sacrosanct and democracy valid only if the minority was bereft of a forum? What, exactly, was the essence of democracy, and what its quintessential virtue? These questions, legitimate enough for calm consideration, were to be asked, and answered, not alone in Pennsylvania but in all the Colonies, in the nation itself before it achieved the status of a nation—and forever after, in all the years of its trials and travail. Better minds than Philip Freneau's would seek to solve them, and it was possible they would never be solved. More heat than light would inform their future debates, even as it informed them now in the paper battles between the conservatives and radicals. Dusty answers, not the clean and polished ones which reflected the truth as in a mirror, would lead to others equally blurred. And the answers would depend not so much on the honesty and rectitude of those who gave them as on their political bias and the economic interests they subserved.[25]

The Freeman's Journal was dedicated to the simple proposition that the people—all the people—were the beneficiaries of the Revolution. For them—for all of them—independence had been achieved and liberty secured. Unless they were the equal masters in their own house, nothing had been won, and everything had been lost. Because he believed all this and passionately maintained it, Philip Freneau,

[24] *Ibid.,* pp. 185–186.
[25] *Ibid.*

more than ever before the mouthpiece of the masses, was the same target of contumely as of old. At him more than at anyone else the slanders of hostile critics were launched with bitter invective. When to the attacks on his political sagacity were added some stinging aspersions on his intellectual honesty and literary integrity, he lost whatever judgment remained to him. Issues were forgotten; personalities became the butt of his counterattack and the subject of his scathing satire. Colonel Eleazer Oswald, the object of his most venomous thrusts, was an able journalist and editor of the conservative *Independent Gazetteer,* whose courage in this bloodless battle was equal to that he had shown at Quebec and Monmouth. When Colonel Oswald accused the poet of plagiarism, of trying

> To shine in *borrowed plumes*

Freneau replied:

> Scribbler retire—what madness would it be
> To point a cannon at a mite like thee!
> Such noxious vermin crawling from the shell,
> By squibs and crackers might be kill'd as well.

The doughty Colonel caught the spear in mid-air, and was prepared to hurl it back doubly envenomed,

> When men will prostitute the power of rhime,
> Their dirt and malice jingling out of time;
> When men the sacred shrine of truth forsake,
> And deal in slander just for slander's sake.[26]

The editor of *The Freeman's Journal* was equal to any attack; and he was ready to exchange any insult.

> Such an odour atmosphered your song,
> I held my nose, and quickly passed along,
> Grieved for the wretch who could such filth display,
> His maw disgorging in the public way.[27]

It was not strange that the paper which printed these lines was referred to by its enemies as "Bailey's Chamber Pot." The jibe was a

---

[26] *The Freeman's Journal,* September 4, 1782; *The Independent Gazetteer,* August 31, 1782; and Leary, *That Rascal Freneau,* p. 113.

[27] Freneau, *Poems* (Pattee), Vol. 2, p. 180; *The Freeman's Journal,* September 11, 1782.

vicious one, and it deeply wounded the man who believed himself to be writing in the public interest when he stooped to conquer. In a final fling at Colonel Oswald and his "Scribblers" of *The Gazetteer,* Freneau wrote finis to the political and personal combat which was as distasteful to him as it was humiliating to his friends.

> Long may they write unquestion'd and unhurt,
> And all their rage discharge, and all their dirt:
> Night owls must screech by heaven's severe decree,
> And wolves must howl, or wolves they would not be.[28]

The issue of December 18, 1782, in which these lines appeared, was the last one under his editorial guidance. The man who had never hurt anyone but in a cause he considered just was too depressed by the low estate of politics in the Quaker City to take any further interest in it. For him, the cause of justice was too deeply affronted by the new alignment of wealth and privilege in America. The Revolution had vanquished one tyranny only to be threatened by another. Everywhere, not alone in Pennsylvania, the same struggle was being waged, openly or beneath the surface, for government by the few, or control by the many. Congress was weak—must it also remain powerless? The republic was a delusion—was then a monarchy the only rule to replace it? The country, split into many factions, needed a firm hand to guide and to lead it; who could do it better than the man—the one man—who had shown the way out of the dilemma of disunity? Washington was the one person who could cope with the new troubles as he had with the old, and no rabble must be allowed to hinder him now as they had almost hindered him then. Make the leader king; give him the power to enforce order; an end to the festering evils of freedom![29]

Were such cures the true remedies for a people's victory? Was so much blood spilled for such a peace? Were personal power and private profit the sole fruits of a long and exhausting war? Freneau had never sought for fruits like these, and never, in any of his writings, had he pleaded for anything but the common good. His pleadings were not always in the best of taste nor his verses in the best tradition of the art of poesy. If, like Shakespeare, he often wondered

[28] *The Freeman's Journal,* December 18, 1782.
[29] Max Savelle, "Nationalism and Other Loyalties in the American Revolution," *American Historical Review,* LXVII, 4 (July 1962), 901–923.

>   Why is my verse so barren of new pride?

like Shelley he could answer

>   Our sweetest songs are those that tell of saddest thought.

More and more his thoughts were not sad but angry, wrought by hatred, not by compassion, and anger was seldom sweetened with pride. At such times he was concerned less with justice than with rhyme, meter, and metaphor as weapons with which to destroy, and not as measures of music to inspire. As so many times before, his only reward was slander, his only recompense poverty.

To escape from one, he had relinquished his post as editor of *The Freeman's Journal.* To avoid the other, he accepted an appointment as clerk in the Post Office of Philadelphia.[30]

[30] F. L. Pattee, "Philip Freneau as a Postal Clerk," *American Literature,* IV, 1 (March 1932), 61–62.

15. THE POET AS POSTAL CLERK

THE UNITED STATES was little more than a geographical abstraction when Philip Freneau entered the service of its general Post Office in Philadelphia. The pay was small, and since there was no Federal government, the duties of a clerk were circumscribed by a few amorphous regulations. The work itself was far from exacting. The country was not yet free of the British incubus, and other matters of greater importance than the mail were not yet resolved. There was no longer war—and there was not yet peace.[1]

As the year 1783 began New York was still in British hands. From the time the House of Commons had voted to end the war on February 28, 1782, negotiations dragged on endlessly; a year later they had not been finished. The one haven of refuge for Tories and Loyalists was New York, to which all of them flocked from cities in the South, from Savannah and from Charleston, as quickly as the British pulled out. Soon they would be forced to flee again, in any available transport, to Nova Scotia, to the Bahamas, to tropical Jamaica or frigid Fort Frontenac. When Washington pressed Carleton to evacuate the City of New York, and when the treaty of peace was signed at last, the stampede of frightened men became a frenzy of flight from the vengeance of patriots.[2]

In the turmoil and confusion of fear-ridden thousands, the tragedy of war was doubly shared and suffered by the victims of peace. The

[1] R. A. Billington, B. L. Lowenberg, and S. H. Blockunier, *The United States: American Democracy in World Perspective,* pp. 61 ff. Dr. Rush was clairvoyant when he said that "the American war is over, but that is far from being the case of the American Revolution" (*ibid.,* p. 102).

[2] T. J. Wertenbaker, *Father Knickerbocker Rebels,* pp. 230–231, 258 ff.

echoes of their cries, no less than the jubilations of the conquerors, reached the ears of the clerk in his postmaster's cubicle at Philadelphia. Sheltered from the political confusions of Pennsylvania and the tumult of New York, yet he heard the echoes of distress as he stamped the packets of mail which lacked the proper postage or completed the stint of sealing papers that must make a long, slow journey from one city, one state, to another. It was only by chance that he found and acknowledged the payment of postal charges by John Paul Jones, one of the citizens who used the central system of which Philadelphia was the first branch. The work of the new postal clerk, which was of little interest and less pay, was almost entirely a matter of chance. The Department of the Post Office was neither fully prepared for its duties nor particularly efficient in their accomplishment. The service, changing slowly from a Colonial to a national status, was growing, not yet grown; and while it provided only a paltry living for the new clerk, it assured him a degree of leisure more important to him than the money. He could continue his writing—the kind of work that was closer to his heart than any other. His main business, no matter what other business might intervene, was still the cause of the plain people, the struggling yeoman, the common soldier, the poor artisan, the small tradesman, the little man of America.[3]

No great ability was needed to stamp papers or signs receipts, but Freneau's chief, Postmaster General Ebenezer Hazard, thought it took considerable talent to write the poems which his young assistant was composing in his leisure time. Even the Reverend Jeremy Belknap, who read some of them, admitted that the poet had "a good, practical genius," adding, however, "he plays rather too freely with the Scriptures."[4] The Reverend Belknap himself gave a good deal less time to Scripture than to work of a purely historical nature. Thick-set and corpulent, possessed of a keen mind and alert intelligence, he was better known as a historian than a preacher. His three-volume *History of New Hampshire* and his researches into early Americana were only a small portion of his extraclerical labors. His judgment on the postal clerk's "practical genius" was both flattering and important, far different from that of another writer more widely known than either of them.

[3] F. L. Pattee, "Philip Freneau as a Postal Clerk," *American Literature,* IV, 1 (March 1932), 61–62.

[4] Hazard to Belknap, February 12, 1783, Belknap to Hazard, March 17, 1783, in Timothy Pickering Papers, Mss., Ser. V, Vol. II, pp. 186, 198–199.

Francis Hopkinson's judgment on the young poet was perhaps not altogether unbiased. He was one of the leaders of conservative Anti-Constitutionalists in Pennsylvania, and, unlike Freneau, he was universally respected as a stout pillar of society. A signer of the Declaration of Independence and a writer of verse and prose that never stooped to inelegancies of language or the display of passion of which the man whom he called the "scapegrace" was guilty, Hopkinson was a patriot whose eminent good taste was beyond all question. His refined sensibilities were offended by the literary vulgarities as well as by the radical sentiments of Philip Freneau, and he forgot, or chose to ignore, his other works, his other lines, which sang their way into men's hearts, which healed the bruised spirits of men with their sympathy and compassion, and buoyed up their faltering hopes in the ultimate victory of reason over passion, of good over evil, of freedom over the awesome manifestations of tyranny. Francis Hopkinson had little regard for Freneau or for his political and social views, however they were expressed in verse or in prose. It was nothing to him that Freneau was truly the poet of the people, applauded even by the most caustic critics of his abandoned moments. When other moments in public affairs recalled him to the higher purpose of prosody, he was not unequal to the event. What the common men felt and could not express, Philip Freneau also felt, and he expressed it for them too.[5]

When Washington, freed at last from public service by the evacuation of New York, passed through Philadelphia on his way to Annapolis to relinquish his command to Congress, Freneau, no less than the people of the Quaker City, was prepared to give him a welcome that was of the heart as well as the pen. This man had given eight years of his life to a cause that was often hopeless and always desperate. His courage and sacrifice had inspired the country; his humility and greatness had transformed defeat into victory. In *The Freeman's Journal* Philip Freneau paid tribute to the man because of whom

> Freedom's bright stars more radiant rise,
> New charms she adds to every scene,
> Her brighter sun illumes our skies,
> Remotest realms admiring stand,
> And hail the *Hero* of our land.[6]

[5] Philip M. Marsh, "Philip Freneau and Francis Hopkinson," *Proceedings of New Jersey Historical Society,* LXIII, 3 (July 1945), 141–148; E. B. Greene, *The Revolutionary Generation,* p. 394.

[6] *The Freeman's Journal,* December 8, 1783.

At the same time the poet could not forget the price which had been paid for all of this. So that his fellows would not forget it either, he translated the *New Travels through North America* of the Abbé Claude Robin, military chaplain of Rochambeau, from the French into English. The campaigns in the northern and middle states were described in the Abbé's book with all the details of marches and countermarches, battles and bloodshed, including also the gentler aspects of the struggle, the simple habits of the people and the scenic beauties of the country. The volume had a small sale, without any profit to the translator or his publisher, Robert Bell, a friend of many poets, "a truly philanthropic bookseller," who had earlier brought out Thomas Paine's *Common Sense* and Freneau's own "American Independence."[7]

It was the friendship of men like Francis Bailey and Robert Bell that sustained the struggling poet-clerk in the city where he had long since discovered that the boast of brotherly love was a vain and empty one. With men like these, and with Peter Markoe, another poet of Huguenot descent, Philip Freneau felt most free and untrammelled. Possessing a common taste for convivial friendship stimulated by the inevitable bottle of wine, they all loved books, and for all of them literature was a way of life. Indeed, Peter Markoe, an ebullient young man of generous if intemperate habits, had forsaken the Law for the pen, to his complete satisfaction if not that of his family, who referred to him with diminishing esteem as "Peter the Poet." Born in Santa Cruz, Markoe loved the beautiful island even as his friend Freneau loved it, and he loved his friend sufficiently to pay him the warmest tribute in "The Storm," one of the many poems that he wrote. Like Freneau, too, he was a dissenter and radical who attacked with bitter satire the political and social evils of the day, nowhere so keenly as in "The Times," a poem that was highly praised by Colonel John Parke, the first translator of Horace in America. Soon, he would also publish "The Reconciliation: or The Triumph of Nature," the first comic opera written in the New World.[8] The fat bookseller Robert

[7] The *New Travels* was less popular, perhaps, than it deserved to be, for it was a creditable job of translation and, in some instances, of correction. It did convey an accurate picture of a country still wild and beautiful, almost unspoiled in its pristine vastness. See Greene, *The Revolutionary Generation*, p. 135.

[8] M. C. Diebels, *Peter Markoe;* and Freneau, *The Poems of Philip Freneau* (ed. F. L. Pattee), Vol. 2, p. 260 n.

Bell discovered in Markoe, as well as in Philip Freneau, the promise of a high talent that merited his support—and he gave it in a generous if discreet manner. Bell's own resources were limited, for few books sold well and poetry scarcely at all. Even his circulating library, the first to be established in the Quaker City, brought little profit. Only by the device of auction sales, to which the canny bookseller enticed prospective customers with amusing anecdotes about his authors and with his no less entertaining, if somewhat bibulous, capers with an enormous beer-jug, could the bookman hope to eke out an indifferent living from the precarious pursuit of literature. He was a hearty and an honest man whose memory, when he died a short while later, Freneau saluted in sad and simple lines as one

> Bound to no sect, no systems to defend,
> He loved his jest, a female, and his friend.[9]

The loss of Robert Bell, a rare friend among the few he had ever known, was unfortunate. But Francis Bailey, of *The Freeman's Journal*, still remained, to publish the contributions of the postal clerk, as often as not, with no remuneration at all. A translation of some French articles, a new satire on Rivington, a deeply-felt romantic poem, "The Dying Indian"—these and others were published by Bailey after Freneau had ceased to edit the paper. "The Dying Indian" more than any other suggested his own somber mood and low estate, reflected in his own condition as in that of the redman who was the victim of a civilization he scarcely understood and never accepted. In lines of the most tranquil beauty and quiet majesty the dying warrior, soon to depart for the happy hunting grounds, bids his comrades

> Prepare the hollow tomb, and place me low,
> My trusty bow and arrows at my side,
> The cheerful bottle and the venison store;
> For long the journey is that I must go,
> Without a partner, and without a guide.[10]

These occasional pieces in *The Freeman's Journal* became fewer and appeared at lengthening intervals as the year 1784 reached its climactic moment in the city of Philadelphia. In May the joyful tidings of a final peace with Britain were celebrated with all the fervor and abandon possible after the unconscionable wrangling and delay over terms.

[9] Freneau, *Poems* (Pattee), Vol. 2, p. 260.
[10] *The Freeman's Journal*, March 17, 1784.

At last the deed was done. Peace was a monumental reality. The United States was free and independent. In his final contribution to *The Freeman's Journal,* Freneau, despite his plaguing doubts for the future— his country's and his own—mingled his joy with that of America at the realization of its dream and voiced his hopes for the republic, risen like the Phoenix, from the rubble of war.

> Born to protect and guard our native land,
> Victorious virtue! still preserve us free;
> Plenty, gay child of peace, thy horn expand,
> And, Concord, teach us to agree!
> May every virtue that adorns the soul
> Be here advanc'd to heights unknown before.[11]

His work at the Post Office was of short duration, the wage entirely inadequate for a living. He was forever in a state of insecurity, always in a condition of penury; and the city had nothing further to offer him when the alarms of war gave way to the tantrums of peace. To write was for him a necessity; to make a living from his writing seemed hopeless. The problem had vexed him all his life; and though he was still young, he frequently felt that he was young no longer. His burdens were rarely lightened; his spirits were rarely uplifted; his temper too often was churlish. In the past it had been possible for him to win some respite from the tumult of the world by escaping to the sea. There he could stretch his mind as well as his body, and breathe in deeply that freedom which was no mere luxury but a pressing necessity. What else could he do besides write some poetry which a few commended and many denounced? For which, also, no one paid.

He could sail a ship, but where would he find one and who would employ him? He had vowed never again to board a vessel after his painful experiences on the *Scorpion* and the *Hunter;* but the war was over, the seas were free; there was nothing to fear but the wind and the weather. Freneau did not fear them. What he could do, he must do soon, as the little money he still had would only keep him in a state near beggary. When it was gone, he would indeed be a beggar.

Peter Freneau, Philip's younger brother, was aware of the poet's plight. More practical than Philip, Peter was the business brains of the family. By the time he was twenty he had already amassed sufficient money to help his friend John Mott with a loan of fifteen pounds—in

---

[11] *Ibid.,* May 19, 1784. The Treaty of Paris, of course, had been signed much earlier—on September 13, 1780.

hard specie.[12] He was a prosperous businessman in Charleston, South Carolina, sufficiently well-off to contribute to the support of his mother and sisters at Mount Pleasant. Philip was another problem. Peter loved and respected the quixotic poet who was always fighting someone—or something—and was always impoverished for his pains. Peter also had ideals, he also was a patriot, but he always had kept his eyes wide open for some of the more substantial rewards in life. He wanted to help his brother, but there was nothing he could suggest except the one thing that Philip really knew anything about—printing, writing, journalism. In Charleston, in 1784, there seemed to be as little use for any of these as in Philadelphia. Perhaps later—[13]

Philip, waiting for definite word from Peter, could wait no longer. Neither could he camp at Mount Pleasant, another mouth to feed, another burden added to those which Agnes must bear. Restless and despondent, he could only linger a short while at Monmouth to see his mother and sisters, and then move on. But where? To what end? He had no answer save the old one that cancelled out the questions themselves. He would see once more his "lovely isles," the Caribbean paradise which he had never forgotten and which he could now, with nothing at all to restrain him, revisit again. After the hectic years in Philadelphia, Jamaica beckoned like the promised land. On June 24, 1784, he left Middletown Point on the brig *Dromelly*, whether as passenger or as seaman is not known.[14]

[12] Peter Freneau to John Mott, August 1, 1781, in Philip and Peter Freneau, Letters, Mss. On the back of this letter is a receipt date August 1, 1784, for nine pounds, to "John Mott," and another for six pounds to the same, dated December 11, ?, and signed by Agnes Kearny.

[13] R. B. Davis and M. B. Siegler, "Peter Freneau," *Journal of Southern History*, XIII, 3 (August 1947), 395–405; and see Lewis Leary, "Philip Freneau in Charleston," *South Carolina Historical and Genealogical Magazine*, XLII, 3 (July 1941), 89–98.

[14] *Pub. Ovidii Nasonis Opera Omnia* (London: Cornelius Schrevello, 1662), Vol. III flyleaf, Monmouth County Historical Association, cited in Lewis Leary, *That Rascal Freneau*, p. 416; Philip M. Marsh, "Philip Freneau: Our Sailor Poet," *American Neptune*, VI (April 1946), 115–120.

16. CAPTAIN PHILIP FRENEAU

ALL ESCAPE IS ILLUSION, and all men seek it. Poets, more than peasants, are susceptible to its allure, for poets are more the victims of their dreams. Fertile in imagination, they conjure up the good places, the better times, the prospect that is closer to the heart's desire. The West Indies, with its opulent memories of a gracious climate and seductive beauty, still had its other side, its sinister aspects curtained by the colors of its hills and valleys. Slavery still flourished there, and Freneau could never forget the hell he had once discovered when he reached that distant paradise. There was no danger now from a dead-calm sea, but what if the sea was not calm? He had no fear of the wind and weather, but what did he know about them? The beauty of an illusion is a fragile thing—and escape may be just another trap, for poets no less than for peasants.

In all his time at sea, the sailor-poet had never experienced any exceptionally foul weather. High winds and heavy seas were normal in all waters, but he had never known the fury of a hurricane. After five uneventful weeks at sea, he knew it as it had not been known by anyone for nearly forty years. When the full force of the storm broke on the *Dromelly* on July 30 it seemed as if the world was coming to an end—the world and the brig and the poet himself. "Such a conflict of elements I never saw before," he explained, as the vessel, helpless in the swirling waters off Kingston, miraculously avoided the coral reefs and shoals which would have been its graveyard. The noise of toppling structures could be heard above the tempest, while uprooted trees floated through the cloud-tumbling air as if the whole island was being swept to sea. The sea itself heaved from its dark depths as from a universal nausea, and spewed up the black waters in waves like mountains upon the puny vessel and all who were in it. Terror-stricken, they waited for destruction. And the poet, no less terror-stricken than the rest, was certain that this was the end. Yet the brig was spared, though it was clear that she would never sail again. Of 150 ships moored in the harbors of Kingston and Port Royal, only 8 would ever sail again.[1]

To Freneau, happily saved from this threat of doom, the hurricane was only an added proof of the transitory state of man and all his works. There was little room here for any comforting illusion. The ruin of the devastated island became more apparent as he set foot on shore at Kingston. The scene was one of utter desolation. The entire island was sunk in a morass of depair, unrelieved by the harshness of masters who ruled the ruins as if they, themselves, were indestructible. Moving slowly from place to place, from Kingston to Port Royal, while waiting for a ship to carry him back to the States, Freneau was by turns saddened and enraged by the wickedness of which men were capable.[2] Hurricanes, like plagues and pestilence—like the earthquakes which once had wiped out three thousand souls in three minutes at old Port Royal—were among the cruelties of insensate nature. But what of the cruelties of sensate man? Here were British residents who refused fresh water to these refugees from the sea. Here were the black slaves who were still whipped and branded like cattle by their owners, for whom hurricanes were only an inconvenience and not a tragic reminder of their own poor humanity. Helpless to aid the unfortunate among whom he was thrown, the poet could at least voice his protest against this evil so that others too might know of it, be aroused to abolish it.

> If there exists a hell—the case is clear
> Sir Toby's slaves enjoy that portion here:
>
> . . .
>
> Here whips on whips excite perpetual fears,
> And mingled howlings vibrate on my ears:

Compared to horrors like these the hurricane is almost a pleasant interlude. The agony of a natural catastrophe lasts but a moment of time—the brutality of slaveowners goes on forever.

> One, with a gibbet wakes his negroe's fears,
> One to the windmill nails him by the ears,

[1] Freneau's "The Hurricane," "Cape Hatteras," and "Lines Written at Sea," in *The Freeman's Journal*, August 20, 1788; and Freneau, *The Poems of Philip Freneau* (ed. F. L. Pattee), Vol. 2, p. 250.

[2] *Ibid.*; and Peter Marsden, *An Account of the Island of Jamaica*, pp. 13 ff.

One keeps his slave in darkened dens, unfed,
One puts the wretch in pickle e're he's dead:

. . .

O'er yond' rough hills a tribe of females go,
Each with her gourd, her infant, and her hoe;
Scorched by a sun that has no mercy here,
Driven by a devil whom men call overseer—
In chains, twelve wretches to their labors haste;
Twice twelve I saw, with iron collars graced![3]

So the poet details the items of barbaric cruelty, one by one. In "The Island Field Hand" (later called "To Sir Toby") he asks the age-old question posed by poets everywhere, the rending, universal, eternal question about man's colossal inhumanity to man. With rhymes, with rhythms, that recall those of Burns and Goldsmith (far greater poets than he though not more greatly outraged by the enslavement of the poor and defenseless), Freneau exposes the tragedy of man's fate as they exposed it. They, at least, had a milieu, a tradition, a history of literature from which to draw the inspiration for their work. America had little to offer of any such history until Philip Freneau began to write its first bitter pages. What he saw, what he heard, he put into those pages if they concerned the human comedy, the human tragedy, of his time. He tried to write them as truly, as clearly, as the events themselves permitted, even at the expense of any "literary" quality which they might lose in the telling. If that served his purpose he was not above the practice of a poetic license for added emphasis: it was the sole purpose of his indictment to convey a message comprehensible to the ordinary man, a message of the depravity of other men.[4]

In *The Freeman's Journal* of April 9, 1783, he had written a criticism of Milton's *Paradise Lost* in which he said: "Poetry ought to paint what is within the reach of human comprehension, or can be rationally admitted or supported." Milton, he added, "was a bold and daring genius," but "the insipid harangues, long conversations, tedious narrations," the religious vagaries and "flagrant contradictions" of the poem seemed like poetic sins scarcely justified by poetic license. Homer was guiltless of these, and so were Virgil and Tasso, all of them greater poets, he thought, than Milton. Even a genius must speak to men in a

[3] "To Sir Toby," in Freneau, *Poems* (Pattee), Vol. 2, p. 258.
[4] *Ibid.,* and various issues of *The Freeman's Journal* for the West Indies poems.

tongue they understood. In any age the private symbols of a poet were of little worth to the public need for help and inspiration.[5]

Freneau had some justice on his side. The unintelligible, like the irrational, was no help when only the best energies of men, applied to their pressing problems, could fashion a new world out of the political, social, and cultural débris of the old. Not his clarity nor his message was at fault in the verses which flowed from his pen. They had their uses, and they were of timely importance. It was his weakness as a poet that he stooped too low to conquer the readers to whom he addressed his poems, for whom they were intended, and who were only momentarily moved by them. Too often he pointed with the finger, with his whole hand, and while his finest lines carried their full freight of meaning, much of his work was heavy-laden with homily or entangled with passion, sometimes too obvious for humor or too subtle for the shock of recognition.[6]

Save for events that involved him deeply, he scarcely touched on the facets of his own life, dwelling rather on the life of his time. The thoughts, the deeds, that affected the welfare of America were more important for him because they were more important for his country, which was fighting for an idea barely broached in other lands and was still struggling to achieve it. He was only an instrument in the hands of inscrutable fate, anxious to help in that fight as well as he could. America, not Freneau, was the theme of his work, and it remained the only theme, in all its variations, during the strange vicissitudes of his life. To America, after the ruin of the *Dromelly*, he returned on the brig *Mars*, which sailed from Kingston on September 23 and reached Philadelphia on November 4, 1784.[7]

In *The Freeman's Journal* of December 15 appeared the first installment of his "Sketches of American History," a series of poems that portrayed the story of the struggle for freedom from Roger Williams to the Revolution. For Freneau this story was the richest heritage of

[5] *The Freeman's Journal,* April 9, 1783; see also Rica Brenner, chapter on Freneau in *Twelve American Poets before 1900;* and H. H. Clark "What Made Freneau the Father of American Poetry?" *Studies in Philology,* XXVI, 1 (January 1929), 1–22.

[6] *Ibid.;* N. F. Adkins, *Philip Freneau and the Cosmic Enigma, passim;* also Freneau, *A Collection of Poems on American Affairs.*

[7] Freneau's copy of Robertson, *Elements of Navigation,* in Freneau Collection (Rutgers); and Lewis Leary, *That Rascal Freneau,* p. 131.

his country, precious beyond all others. In fast-flowing quatrains the
drama of civilization in the new world was unfolded with a deep pride
for its many conquests and a sad rebuke for those who

> ... never perceived that in Nature's wide plan,
> There must be that whimsical creature called Man,
> Far short of the rank he affects to attain,
> Yet a link in its place, in creation's vast chain.[8]

Man was forever striving onward and upward. He climbed with
heartbreaking labor, fell back, and climbed again. In America, of all
places, he might reach the highest pinnacle of achievement. But could
he? In Philadelphia the "whimsical creature called Man" was busy
with many devices that were making America something quite different from the kind of country the poet had hoped for. The Revolution
had ended with independence from Britain; peace had replaced war.
Yet war was still being waged, this time between Americans themselves, for selfish interests and not for the common good. Each state
thought of itself as the special beneficiary of the long and bloody struggle, and there was an almost complete absence of cooperation among
the states. New York levied duties on firewood from Connecticut and
on cabbage from New Jersey. Connecticut paid annual tribute that covered nearly a third of New York's expenses. Pennsylvania enacted a
stringent protective tariff which effectively hampered the trade of the
other states. New Jersey, which had no tariff, suffered greatly from
the multiple restrictions of the others. Where duties had once been
levied for the sole purpose of easing the burden of taxation, they were
now imposed to discourage competition. Of the Southern states, only
Virginia enacted similar laws, but these were on a few commodities
and of moderate extent. Charleston was the funnel for imports from
the lower South, Baltimore and Philadelphia the channels of the upper
South, while the markets of the middle states and New England were
tapped through Philadelphia, New York, Boston, and Providence.
Heavy imposts for shipments through these ports were sharp thorns in
the side of business—and business was profoundly pained by the exactions. Fisher Ames, a foremost champion of business, summarized
the entire problem when he said that "The King of New York levied
imports on New Jersey and Connecticut, and the nobles of Virginia
bore with impatience their tributary dependence upon Baltimore and

---

[8] *The Freeman's Journal*, December 15, 1784; "Philosopher of the Forest,"
No. 10, in Freneau, *The Miscellaneous Works of Philip Freneau*, p. 351.

Philadelphia. Our discontents," he added, "were fermenting into Civil War."[9] Congress, powerless to intercede, was little more than a precarious balance wheel of the union whose cogs were the creaking Articles of Confederation. It would take more than a revolution, perhaps some new threat to the hard-won freedom so terribly achieved, to waken the warring states to the new danger from within. Only in times of crisis, it appeared, could men be welded into a common front for a common purpose.[10] The evocation of old memories might induce a real attempt to avoid old dangers. The dangers, patent enough to Philip Freneau, he was powerless to avoid.

His friend James Madison, more politically minded than he, was keenly aware of the tragic risks inherent in a loose confederation of the states. Freneau wanted the strength of union without knowing how to achieve it. Madison, casting a backward glance at the precious sovereignty of his own Virginia, was thinking more fruitfully of the greater good of the nation. There was little ambiguity in his objections to the position of Henry Laurens, the American agent in the peace negotiations of 1782, when Laurens maintained that he was acting as a native of South Carolina and not "as a citizen of the United States." This, Madison protested, "was a denial of the sovereignty of the country which he was appointed to represent," and inadmissible in any dealings with a foreign power. Like many of the leaders whose hearts were still with their states, he believed in the unity of all the states and the pre-eminence of the Republic over any of its parts.[11] One day the dilemma of state and national sovereignty would be solved—and Madison would help to fashion the instruments of unity.

As yet there was no unity. Congress, the sole source and symbol of concerted action, was too weak in power, too diffuse in its elements, too hobbled by the old Articles of Confederation, to enforce or command any respect for its mandates. There were thirteen Americas, not one. As the rivalry among them continued unabated, and selfish interests continued to spark the danger of new explosions, Congress, the only central body that might stop them, had no power to prevent them. Few men took it seriously; fewer considered it superior to any state sovereignty. Indeed, as Francis Hopkinson observed to Thomas Jeffer-

[9] Allan Nevins, *The American States during and after the Revolution*, pp. 556–560.

[10] *Ibid.*

[11] Irving Brant, *James Madison*, Vol. 2, *Madison the Nationalist, 1780–1787*, p. 394. See also Nevins, *The American States*, pp. 556–560.

son, "The name of Congress is almost forgotten." What was more important, Hopkinson added, was that "For every person that will mention that respectable body, a hundred will talk of the Air Balloon." Literally and figuratively the people were up in the air with newfangled contraptions like a gas-bag, forgetting, in the playthings of the moment, the more mundane problems that were so difficult to solve, and that must be solved at the peril of all they had ever fought for.[12]

Freneau, never business-minded, was not greatly interested in the competitive struggle for markets, nor was he too familiar with the machinations of merchants. He said little about the Congress that was floundering in debate on the Articles of Confederation, hoping to find some solid footing in these, if nowhere else. What was happening up in the skies intrigued Freneau too, for a new marvel had appeared through the clouds, and he, like everybody else in the Quaker City, was excited about the possibilities suggested in the experiments of Jean de Roseier, Corallo, and the brothers Montgolfier with lighter-than-air balloons. Not only in Philadelphia but in other cities as well the contagion of the miraculous ascent of man to the heavens was spreading. Professional and amateur scientists were writing serious articles on machines "Proper to Be Navigated through the Air"—on balloons that went up, and on those that fell down again. The possibilities presented by air travel thrilled the masses, who had few other novelties to excite them. Daedalus and Icarus were the progenitors of a novel varition on the ancient theme of bread and circuses.[13]

There were some who saw in the first cross-channel flight of Dr. John Jeffries and Jean Pierre Blanchard the shadow of more sinister events to come. Jefferson perceived the possibility of "the destruction of fortified works unless they can be closed from above, the destruction of fleets and what not." Benjamin Franklin, on the other hand, was more taken with the idea that he might be carried through the air with the greatest of ease, and so spared the anguish of his gout when crossing the cobblestone streets of Philadelphia. Both of them recognized the employment of such a contrivance in war as well as in peace, while Francis Hopkinson went so far as to sketch some feasible plans for a balloon driven, not by a caprice of the wind but by more de-

[12] Hopkinson to Jefferson, March 31, 1784, in Thomas Jefferson Papers, Mss., X, 1656; see also Leary, *That Rascal Freneau*, p. 133.
[13] Lewis Leary, "Phaeton in Philadelphia," *Pennsylvania Magazine of History and Biography,* Vol. 67 (January 1943), pp. 49–50.

pendable propellors.[14] Philip Freneau, contributing his own brand of fantasy, wrote for *The Freeman's Journal* "The Progress of Balloons," in which he prophesied that

> The man who at Boston sets out with the sun,
> If the wind should be fair, may be with us at one,
> Gunpowder Ferry drink whiskey at three,
> At six be in Edentown, ready for tea.

He foresaw more practical results, too, from this new conquest of the air:

> If Britain should ever disturb us again,
> (As they threaten to do in next George's reign)
> No doubt they will play us a new set of tunes,
> And pepper us well from their fighting balloons.[15]

He had a special grievance against England in 1785, when he published in *The Pennsylvaia Gazette* a scathing satire on the British boycott of Ramsay's *History of the Revolution*. England had not yet accepted the United States as an equal, and was careful to keep from its people the truth about the war which had cost it the lost dominion.[16]

Britain was the only enemy that might use the frightening weapon imagined by the poet, who ended his poem on a note that has echoed in all the corridors of the world from his time to the moment of Hiroshima and Nagasaki. His prophecies, terrible as they are, have yet to be proven in the expendable catastrophies of fission and of fusion.

> Such wonders as these from balloons shall arise—
> And the giants of old, that assaulted the skies
> With their Ossa on Pelion, shall freely confess
> That all they attempted was nothing like this.[17]

Previsions of the future were of less immediate importance, however, than his own problems which demanded some solution. Fugitive pieces in *The Freeman's Journal* or elsewhere, like the rhymed broadsides which held the general fancy for a brief moment—though they were reprinted or pirated in other papers—provided little sustenance for one who had no steady income or the remote prospect of obtaining

---

[14] *Ibid.;* Carl Van Doren, *Benjamin Franklin*, p. 741.

[15] *The Freeman's Journal,* December 22, 1785.

[16] *Ibid.,* October 11, 1786.

[17] *Ibid.;* S. W. Patterson, *The Spirit of the American Revolution as Revealed in the Poetry of the Period, passim.*

any. Freneau's thoughts turned to Charleston again as a possible source of help. It would be well, in addition, to avoid the approaching winter of the North with its cold and sunless weather. At the Pacolet Springs near Spartansburg he might find the tonic for his physical and mental malaise. Late that summer, with nothing better to do, he decided to visit Peter and leave behind him the ill-starred fortunes of Philadelphia.[18]

But he did not leave them for long. In Charleston besides a cordial welcome from his brother he also found a controversy that had distressed him once before and now threatened to embroil him again. The proximity of the poet was a signal for renewed attacks on his poetry by critics who took the occasion to assault him with all their potshots. These critics were the same kind of conservatives who had depreciated his work in Philadelphia, and they saw an opportunity to strike at him, and through him at Peter, whose views were almost as offensive. The Huguenots of Charleston were an important segment of the population, and Peter Freneau was a respected citizen whose opinions were less offensive to the mechanics and small tradesmen of the city than to the planters and merchants who controlled the state of South Carolina. It was not surprising that only the progressive *Columbian Herald* carried the views of Freneau's friends as well as his enemies, giving space also to one writer who had kept aloof from polemics and politics alike. Dr. Joseph Brown Ladd, a young physician who aspired to some modest poetic laurels himself, greeted the disconsolate visitor from the North with a tribute that was as generous as it was rare.

> Hark! *Freneau's* voice attunes the solemn air,
> He sings to freedom, and he sings of war;
> With noble warmth shows man created free,
> When God, from chaos, gave this world to be.[19]

The poetry of Dr. Ladd was less important than the sentiments it expressed about the known enemy of slavery, in a society based on a slave economy. Freneau might even discover some devastating parallels between the city of Charleston and the island of Jamaica, between the state of South Carolina and the West Indies. The city was clearly

---

[18] Lewis Leary, "Philip Freneau in Charleston," *South Carolina Historical and Genealogical Magazine,* XLII, 3 (July 1941), 89–98.

[19] *Ibid.,* Joseph B. Ladd, *The Prospects of America: The Literary Remains of J. B. Ladd,* pp. 34–35.

hostile to the man who had come there for warmth and friendship, and the kindness of Dr. Ladd, the hospitality of Peter, provided cold comfort where his work was maligned and his search for a living was thwarted.[20]

Long ago Freneau had complained that "Barbers cannot possibly exist as such among a people who have neither hair nor beards." If it was an exaggeration of the truth, it still seemed essentially true that the career of letters was a futile and a thankless one, usually leading to nothing but failure and penury. Perhaps he was sensitive to the point of hysteria, a victim of his own feeling of inadequacy as much as the belief of others in his lack of talent. Though he professed to scorn them, it was these others who affected him most deeply. Those who attacked his poetry were not critics in any real sense, for these were no literary scholars passionately concerned with the form and substance, the insight and beauty, of creative writing. Good taste alone was a poor guide for judgment, and good taste itself was confused by preconceptions and attitudes hardly amenable to objective opinion. The people for whom Freneau primarily wrote were kinder to him; they were moved by his emotions and understood his message; with simple approbation they accepted his indictment of spurious leadership and selfish purpose. But a poet also needs the understanding and applause of other poets, of the men who can judge and perhaps grant him the laurels they so niggardly dispense. Few men can ignore the real or fancied insults to a brainchild—and Freneau was not one of these. He would not ignore them. He would try to avoid them. A job, not here in Charleston, not in Philadelphia, but far from the guns of all his enemies, was the only solution to his troubles.[21]

The dilemma of making a living without being abused in the process was solved not by Philip but by Peter. Peter, more practical than his brother, was a rising businessman, who remembered that Philip, while a poet, was also a seaman. There was nothing he could do in Charleston —but he could sail a ship, and this was work in which there was a future no poetry could ever assure. Peter decided to buy the sloop *Monmouth* which was moored at Middletown Point, and offer his brother the

---

[20] *Ibid.;* Peter had encouraged Philip to follow the printer's trade in Charleston, as shown in a letter of December 2, 1782, in the possession of Edmund Freneau, a descendant. I must acknowledge the kindness and helpful suggestions of Mr. Freneau.

[21] Freneau, *Poems* (Pattee), Vol. 1, p. xl; Philip M. Marsh, "Philip Freneau: Our Sailor Poet," *American Neptune,* VI (April 1946), 115–120.

equal part of any profits earned in the coastal and cargo trade. Philip, naturally, was to be the captain, the master of the ship that would sail "to any port of the State of Georgia" or "to any free port in the West Indies."[22] He could still write as he pleased, and, save for a storm, he might be at peace with the world and with himself.

On November 24, 1785, Captain Freneau turned the helm of the forty-ton *Monmouth* southward from Middletown Point. A fortnight later he sailed into Charleston harbor, ready to begin his new business. He did not altogether forsake his old one either; waiting for a cargo, he contributed some pieces to *The Columbian Herald* under the pseudonym "K," determined to fire a few parting salvos at those who had attacked him. As the *Monmouth* slowly filled with merchandise for the run to Sunbury, Georgia, the Captain was content at last to have a prospect more alluring than any he had ever had before. When he sailed with a fair cargo on January 21, 1786, the sun shone brightly in Charleston—and equally in Philadelphia. For there, too, some tangible and equally gratifying rewards were preparing for him. His old friend Bailey, the printer of Philadelphia, was putting together a volume of his better poems for publication, in the hope that "they will afford a high degree of satisfaction to the lovers of poetical wit and elegance of expression." So great was the response to this volume that Francis Bailey was soon trying to collect subscriptions for a second one.[23]

Bailey was too optimistic, however. It was true that the public had approved the poet and practically bought out the small edition of the first volume. But who, among the literati, the wits, the men of influence and distinction, even deigned to notice it? Only Colonel Parke, barely known as a poet at all, bothered to bestow any praise that was more than "an empty smile." In *The Freeman's Journal* of June 21, 1786, Parke offered the lines:

> Your name to bright honor, the spirits shall lift,
> That glow'd in the bosoms of Churchill and Swift.
> And when you are numbered, alas! with the dead,
> Your works by true wits will forever be read,

[22] Marsh, "Freneau: Our Sailor Poet." See also *The Freeman's Journal*, July 8, 1789; Freneau's copy of Robertson, *Elements of Navigation*; and "The Poetaster," in Freneau, *Poems of Philip Freneau Written Chiefly during the Late War*, pp. 38–41.

[23] Leary, "Freneau in Charleston," and *That Rascal Freneau*, p. 141; *The Freeman's Journal*, June 7, 1786.

> Who, pointing the finger, shall pensively shew,
> The lines that were written, alas! by Freneau.[24]

Perhaps the man who was now sailing the seas had not completely failed as a poet. The verdict could wait on the future. For the present, he was in a more remunerative business. Like his people before him, he was embarked on a promising venture in commerce. He might even succeed where all the others had failed. As the *Monmouth* breasted the waves, and the spume floated like a curtain before the wind, Captain Freneau was in high spirits.

[24] Freneau, *Poems* (Pattee), Vol. 1, p. xl; and *The Freeman's Journal,* June 21, 1786.

17. HONEYSUCKLE AND OTHER DELUSIONS

CAPTAIN PHILIP FRENEAU, as he soon was widely known, plied the waters of the Atlantic seaboard and the Caribbean Islands for four years from 1786 to 1790. After a fashion he made a living, though a precarious one since cargoes were light and sailings sporadic. The first one had been delayed until the cargo justified sailing at all. On the return to Charleston on February 6 there was a layover until March 7 before a shipload for New York became available. Impatient at the failure to get a commission in New York, the Captain hauled up anchor for Charleston again, stopping only at Middletown Point for a short visit with his mother and sisters at Mount Pleasant. When he sailed from Middletown Point on June 3 he still had no cargo, or little enough to make any note of it. Nor was business better in Charleston, where he arrived on June 28. The *Monmouth,* quite as discouraged as its captain, made a final voyage to New York, sailing on July 11. From the time it moored at dockside eight days later until May 1787 both ship and captain were without any business at all. He was little better off financially than before the partnership with Peter, but he did have ample time for his first love, to which, whatever else he might momentarily embrace, he always returned.[1]

His verses continued to appear in *The Columbian Herald* of Charleston, all of them signed by "K," and all of them concerned with

---

[1] Philip M. Marsh, "Philip Freneau: Our Sailor Poet," *American Neptune,* VI (April 1946), 115–120; Lewis Leary, "Philip Freneau in Charleston," *South Carolina Historical and Genealogical Magazine,* XLII, 3 (July 1941), 89–98; and Freneau's copy of Robertson, *Elements of Navigation,* in Freneau Collection (Rutgers).

matters alien to the political and personal controversies of the past. The new poems would offend nobody, while many pleased his readers with their good humor, kindly wit, and engaging aura of sadness. Freneau is more mellow in these poems, less bitter about the world. Perhap his new occupation, the salt of the air, the far-reaching roll of the sea, have made him more tolerant of men and their disquieting affairs. The brevity of life, the finality of death, the immensity of the forces of nature— they recalled to him the pitiful pride of man, victim of his own follies and futile hopes. Freneau, more disposed to take his recurrent troubles with stoical indifference, advises others to do the same. Nothing is worth the travail of a lifetime, and no one is happier than his "Newsmonger," who never makes the news but only dispenses it. Even so, he is no poorer than the richest when,

> At last, with death, he walks downstairs,
> And leaves the wide world to his heirs.[2]

He has nothing else to leave, but he has at least enjoyed some measure of freedom. The good things, the easy things, the fine things —are they also the necessary things, for which a man must exchange his liberty? In "The Prisoner" Freneau looks wryly at the poor man who has been imprisoned for debt. In prison a man may be happier than those who are forever scurrying about, endlessly engaged in making money and losing, in the process, the peace and tranquillity of those who are legally restrained from such trivial pursuits. The happiest of all, perhaps, is the old man portrayed by the poet in "The Last Adventure." For him, at any rate, the past is meaningless, the future irrelevant. Beyond all further fear and regret he may enjoy the present moment and thumb his nose at the problems of the world.[3]

Philip Freneau, not yet old, was not content with any such simple solution to his own problems. If there was no solution he could cease for a while to dwell on them and indulge the sunnier side of his nature. Other verses, in a lighter vein and with less concern for the serious aspects of life, interested the readers of The Columbian Herald. They

---

[2] The Freeman's Journal, Feberuary 2, 1787; and Freneau, The Poems of Philip Freneau (ed. F. L. Pattee), Vol. 2, p. 263. See also Marsh, "Freneau: Our Sailor Poet"; Leary, "Philip Freneau in Charleston"; and Freneau's copy of Robertson, Elements of Navigation.

[3] Freneau, Poems of Philip Freneau Written Chiefly during the Late War; "The Prisoner," in Freneau, The Miscellaneous Works of Philip Freneau, p. 72; and "The Last Adventure," in Lewis Leary, That Rascal Freneau, p. 141.

were eagerly read and quickly reprinted in other cities. Such poems as "The Drunken Soldier" and "The Roguish Shoemaker" appealed to many for whom the amusing quarrels of a coarse couple and the burlesque on Watt's "Indian Philosopher" afforded the cheapest entertainment available.[4]

It was cheap in more ways than one. It cost the readers little and the poet even less. He was too glib, too superficial, too flippant in these efforts to please others. He could do better, vastly better, than this, but who cared to read him when he did? "The Wild Honeysuckle," which appeared in *The Columbian Herald* on July 6, 1786, made scarcely a stir among those whom he most wanted to please—the literate, the cultured, those who might recognize its beauty, its integrity, its universality. "The Wild Honeysuckle" was one of the finest poems ever written in America, and Freneau would write a few more like it to place him in the first rank of American poets. Yet it was neither widely read nor often reprinted. Save for *The Pennsylvania Packet* and *The Freeman's Journal,* it was entirely forgotten until four years later, when *The Massachusetts Centinel* used it for a single issue. Not until 1814 was it noticed again, in the *New York Weekly Magazine,* but after that it found an honored place in all anthologies where the history of American literature was the concern of scholars and students alike.[5]

Infused with the deep compassion which he had for all men and the macabre mood of dissolution which was never far from his thoughts, the poem, in its symbolic treatment of the fragrant flowers that bloom for a little while and then wilt away, is a dirge for all men, for their lives, their hopes, their sad immutable destinies. Arrayed in beauty and nourished by "Soft, murmuring waters," the fragile, festive blossoms adorned like tiny bridesmaids in white and gold, are doomed to inevitable extinction.

> From morning suns and evening dews
> At first thy little being came:
> If nothing once, you nothing lose,
> For when you die you are the same;
> The space between, is but an hour,
> The frail duration of a flower.[6]

---

[4] Freneau, *Poems Written between the Years 1768 and 1794;* also see "Few Honest Cobblers" (originally called "The Roguish Shoemaker"), and "The Drunken Soldier," in *The Miscellaneous Works,* pp. 79–80, 154–155.

[5] Freneau, *Poems* (Pattee), Vol. 2, p. 306.

[6] *Ibid.*

Capable of work like this, the poet was too mercurial in temperament to dwell overlong on the chill summit of critical indifference. Ignored, he could not easily maintain a philosophic calm; attacked, he could not resist the impulse to throw a lance at the smug or the stupid who contemned him. Rarely free from controversy, Freneau was too thin-skinned to conduct his debates on the high plane of dignity and restraint. Critics were enemies of the poet, not of his poetry. They usually ignored him, when they did not attack him. They used swords when scalpels would do, and pikes when pens were needed. In Philadelphia they were even worse than in Charleston. For the Philadelphia brand he published in *The Freeman's Journal* of October 11, 1786, "A Severe Critic," a species of doggerel that merited much of the criticism that was heaped on it as well as on much of his other work for *The Freeman's Journal* during his enforced absence from the sea. What he received in cash for these pieces was not calculated to smooth the ruffled feathers of his pride either. Under the prod of penury he produced some poems that had little in common with either pride or poetry. The depth of his poverty was apparent in the details he wrote into "The Insolvent's Release, or Miseries of a County Jail," published in *The Freeman's Journal* of April 11, 1787. Only one who had known the inside of a jail as a debtor could write with such a degree of verisimilitude about

> ... the dreary dark abode
> Of poverty and solitude.

This time his tongue was not in his cheek, as when he wrote "The Prisoner." This time his readers were not amused.[7]

Freneau turned most of his experiences into verse, as a picture and commentary of his time rather than of himself. A depressing account of the debtor's lot was followed by a less lugubrious recital of his journey from Philadelphia to New York. It must have found more favor with readers, for Francis Bailey printed it in pamphlet form, introducing Robert Slender, the ostensible author of these humorous and penetrating observations to a wider public. Slender would be heard from again later, in more important revelations of the human comedy.[8]

One revelation, not yet made but only suggested, is soon prophesied

[7] *The Freeman's Journal*, April 11, 1787.

[8] Freneau, *A Journey from Philadelphia to New York;* "Robert Slender Letters," in *The Miscellaneous Works,* pp. 87, 352, 395.

for Freneau himself. Without any means of support, without any work in either Philadelphia or New York, he has spent some time at Mount Pleasant where he occasionally helps on the family farm. Though he is hardly adaptable to any heavy labor himself and little inclined to supervise the labor of others, yet he stays on as a pensioner of his mother's scant bounty. What keeps him there so long is revealed only by indirection in his "New Year's Verses." He has fallen in love again.[9]

While reticent on the subject of the gentler sex, Freneau has been far from oblivious to their charms. His declared reasons for avoiding any entanglements were only a part—a small part—of the truth. Perhaps it was true that

> Millions curse the day,
> When first in Hymen's silken bands
> The parson joined mistaken hands,
> And bade the bride obey.[10]

Were there more compelling, more personal, causes for being wary of the "silken bands?" Was the wanderlust so strong in him that he would not be tied to the stake of matrimony? Was he afraid of committing himself to anyone who would "obey"—and also command—him who could brook no command by anyone? If he was moved to caution by thoughts like these, another thought was more persuasive than all the rest. Marry? On what? With what? The gift of poverty, in its infinite and depressing variations, was a harsh one to offer a bride. It could also be a disastrous one, ruinous to any marriage, however desirable it might be.

In Monmouth there was one lady who apparently had displaced the memories of the dead Amanda. It is certain that Freneau entertained a lively interest for the daughter of Samuel Forman, a prominent and prosperous farmer of New Jersey and a close neighbor. In a day when girls were married off as early as possible, Eleanor Forman was still a spinster at twenty-four. The bloom of youth was like the frail duration of a flower—and it vanished like a vagrant dream. The impoverished poet, after the manner of his kind, was slight and already stooped; he was, moreover, considerably older than Eleanor Forman. But his deep-set, flashing grey eyes and his high forehead beneath luxuriant brown hair, combined with a certain grace of manner and a lofty bearing,

[9] Freneau, *The Miscellaneous Works*, pp. 393–395.
[10] *Ibid.*

meditative in repose "but lighting up with animation when speaking," imparted to his person a nobility that mantled his otherwise seedy appearance.[11] He was no dandy—far from it. He had none of the refinements of style, never wore anything but small clothes—the long hose, the buckled shoes, the cocked hat, the only ones he possessed. Untouched by any of the newer modes or flippancies of great cities like New York or Philadelphia, in addition to possessing nothing, he seemed to have no ambition to acquire anything.

Samuel Forman may have considered him a poor match for Eleanor —and Eleanor herself looked on him as anything but a cavalier. Yet he did impress them with his sincerity if not with his style. He was impractical, even improvident, but he was also personable, high-minded, cultured, and of good repute. His manners were not merely on the surface; they were also a spiritual essence of the man. He would not lift a finger to hurt anyone, but neither would he suffer an affront that hurt him. Freneau would not risk the affront of a refusal. In the spring of 1787 he had nothing more substantial than himself to offer, and this, it was possible, was not enough for Samuel Forman. Eleanor herself, either dutiful or indifferent, gave no sign. Philip, interested but impecunious, decided to move on. Another day he might return—and try again.

It was April and the air of Monmouth was bright with the promise of growing things and sunny days. The countryside blossomed in new garments of green, and all life was stirring again after the winter's hibernation. The poet, restless like all of nature, was thinking once more of the sea and his short-lived adventure with the *Monmouth*. There was nothing to retain him at home, and his keep was a burden to him if not to his mother. He decided to look for another ship, perhaps a luckier command than the one he had lost almost ten months before. He would leave behind him the personal problems which could not be solved in any event, as well as the persistent public problems which baffled his countrymen also.

It was not so strange that Freneau, politically conscious and socially curious, should remain aloof from events which were shaping in Philadelphia at the moment when he was seeking a new berth for himself. Hard pressed to earn a living, he was too absorbed in the crowding pressures of his own life to pay much heed to the pressures of others.

[11] M. S. Austin, *Philip Freneau*, pp. 147 ff. See also Hammell Notes, Mss.; S. S. Forman, *Narrative of a Journey Down the Ohio and Mississippi*, p. 28.

What could he do about his country's troubles, who had so many of his own? He had no remedy for the greed for gain, the lust for power, the bickerings between the states, the trade rivalries that exploded in the Mississippi question with the divisive force of dynamite and threatened the existence of the Union itself. If he knew about the rebellion of Daniel Shays and the disgruntled farmers of Massachusetts, or understood anything of the ugly sores that festered in America, he wrote no word to indicate that his antipathies against injustice were still as strong as ever. He had spoken out against imprisonment for debt, but what did he know of the hundreds of harassed souls who were jailed for trifling sums they could not pay, of homes foreclosed, of the heavy burdens of taxes placed upon the poor, of the old, ever-new cleavage between the "haves" and the "have-nots," however masked in colorful slogans of liberty and independence, illusions that were alien to the realities in the lives of the people. A new aristocracy of privilege was rising from the rubble of the old one, and Congress was helpless to construct a new Republic from the fragments of the old Colonies. If Congress was helpless, perhaps others could find some solution to the problems that threatened the peace and tranquillity of America.[12] It was imperative that they should be resolved. In the spring of 1787, when the world began to bloom again after a hard winter, the frozen, unyielding problems appeared likely to thaw with renewed hope when a convention of delegates from the states was called to consider them. Now, at last, they might bring order out of chaos, establish a strong central government, and provide the basic laws that would be binding on all the states equally.

The Constitutional Convention was called to meet on May 25. The eyes of the country, indeed, the eyes of the whole world, were on it. But not the eyes of Philip Freneau, who had just found a new job—perhaps a final answer to his long quest for a living. On May 20 the sloop *Industry*, loaded with a cargo of Jersey corn, had sailed into Charleston harbor under the command of the poet. It was more than a command— it was also a commission, for he was to sell the cargo as well as trans-

[12] On July 4, 1786, John Adams had written to James Warren that Americans had never been "spartans in their contempt of wealth," and he hoped they never would be (quoted in M. Jensen, *The New Nation*, p. 190). Gouverneur Morris also opposed any taxation of the wealthy; profit, he believed, was a fine thing (*ibid*, p. 183). See also Henry Christman, *Tin Horns and Calico*, pp. 26, 29; and Carl Carmer, *The Hudson*, Ch. 26. Oppressive and feudal practices were still rife in upper New York.

port it. The new venture was as profitless as the old, and was soon replaced by still another, when he sailed the sloop *Goodluck* from
Charleston to Philadelphia in the summer of 1787.[13]

Good luck! Was the name a happy augury for the future? He needed
a little of it desperately, now more than ever. He changed from one
vessel to another, from one city to another—from one failure to another. He was like a rolling stone, destined never to stop rolling. His
friends could not help—even friends began to mutter with ill-concealed impatience. And his enemies—his critics continued to growl at
him though he had long since ceased to bait them. They were acclaim-
ing another poet, one of the younger Connecticut conservatives, Joel
Barlow, whose "Vision of Columbus" they praised very highly while
his own "Pictures of Columbus," on a similar theme, was completely
ignored and forgotten. Even George Washington, from his retirement at Mount Vernon, deigned to notice Barlow's poem, to order
twenty copies of it, though he had never given any sign to the man who
was known as the poet of the American Revolution.[14]

Yet Freneau was not altogether neglected. A few of the cognoscenti
were not entirely ignorant of his work. They had no quarrel with the
poet's moral judgments, however inelegantly expressed, and they applauded his esthetic perceptions for the beauty of their form and substance. His poems were being published in the New York *Daily Advertiser*, the Charleston *Columbian Herald* and *The Connecticut Courant*. His work was appearing on the other side of the world too, in
the *European Magazine* and in the *London Morning Herald*. Equally
pleasant—and equally unremunerative—was the inclusion of his finer
verses in Noah Webster's *Reader*, while nearly each issue of Mathew
Carey's *American Museum*, a monthly published in Philadelphia,
printed some of his work. Not all of it was praiseworthy; nor did the
critic's growl change into a chant of praise.[15]

One of the poems, printed in the *American Museum* of November
1787, surely merited the acclaim which only posterity would give it.
The "Lines Occasioned by a Visit to an Old Burying Ground" had a

[13] Leary, *That Rascal Freneau*, pp. 152–153; Marsh, "Freneau: Our Sailor
Poet"; Leary, "Freneau in Charleston."

[14] Freneau, *Poems* (Pattee), Vol. 1, p. 89; C. B. Todd, *Life and Letters of
Joel Barlow*, pp. 53, 151.

[15] See Freneau's letters to Carey, in Lea and Febiger Collection. See also
Leary, *That Rascal Freneau*, pp. 150–151; and Freneau, *Poems of Freneau* (ed.
H. H. Clark).

sad beauty and stoical sentiment which was worthy of its subject—and
of its author. This was no simple satire or garrulous grumbling like so
much of his work; it displayed the humility of the true artist who is
concerned less with himelf than with his art. Freneau's understanding
of the red man, his concern and compassion for all men, are mirrored
in the limpid verses on the Indian brave, in death as in life prepared
for the immemorial duties of a child of nature.

> By midnight moons, o'er moistening dews,
>   In habit for the chase arrayed,
> The hunter still the deer pursues,
>   The hunter and the deer, a shade!
>
> And long shall timorous fancy see
>   The painted chief, and pointed spear,
> And reason's self shall bow the knee
>   To shadows and delusions here.[16]

Work like this merited some recognition. The edition of the poet's
first published volume of poems had not done too badly; perhaps another volume would be more successful now. Francis Bailey, a lover
of beauty as well as a businessman, had put aside the initial disappointment of his failure to obtain enough subscriptions for a second volume
of Freneau's poems. He was determined to try again. And while he
worked diligently and waited patiently for them, his friend, who had
neither the inclination nor the means for waiting, was back in Charleston again, stowing away a small cargo in the hold of the *Goodluck*.[17]

It was December, the year's end; and the end, too, of a year that had
brought no prospects brighter than any of the others. Would the new
year prove better? For one who already knew so much about the hopes
and delusions by which men were victimized, he was more sanguine
than usual. His new book was soon to be published—an event that
has stimulated many another author before the critics descended upon
him. Equally important for Freneau, he had given up the *Goodluck*
and become captain of a much finer vessel, the schooner *Columbia*.
There was no waiting now for a petty cargo. Adam Gilchrist, a Charleston merchant, was waiting to give him a large and profitable one.[18]

As Freneau prepared to sail for New York on February 26, 1788,

---

[16] Freneau, *Poems* (Pattee), Vol. 2, p. 369. Freneau understood the Indian
wisely if not too well.

[17] Leary, *That Rascal Freneau,* p. 382 n.

[18] Leary, "Freneau in Charleston"; Marsh, "Freneau: Our Sailor Poet."

the proposed Constitution of the United States finally became known to the people of America. The delegates to the Convention had labored for months in the sultry atmosphere of Philadelphia, but what they did had been kept a tight and guarded secret from the citizens who were to be bound by its provisions.[19]

Philip Freneau knew as little about the Constitution as the rest of his countrymen. Like them, he was about to learn more.

[19] C. Becker, *Our Great Experiment in Democracy, passim;* R. A. Billington, B. L. Lowenberg, and S. H. Brockunier, *The United States: American Democracy in World Perspective,* pp. 69–72. The transition from the Articles of Confederation to the provisions of the Constitution is given in full in Ch. 4 of *Select Readings in American Government,* by William B. Stubbs and C. B. Gosnell.

18. NEPTUNE AND CLIO

THE DEBATES of the delegates to the Constitutional Convention during the sweltering summer of 1787 had been held behind closed doors as the architects of a new government labored over the plans to perfect it. There were many differences of opinion among the leaders in the Convention, differences on the form and substance of the union that should replace the Confederation, with the strength and authority that it never possessed. Alexander Hamilton, George Mason, and James Madison held views that were often in conflict, and the conflict between them would have spread to the people themselves had they known what was involved in the words that were spoken, the ideas they promulgated, and the reasons advanced to support them. But the people did not know. No records were kept, no report was made, of the ideas proposed, or of the reasons which impelled the delegates finally to accept them. After four months of searching debate and revealing compromise, a Constitution was agreed on that bound the whole nation forever. Only later—much later—would the debates and compromises become known through the clear notes of James Madison and Robert Yates, and the fugitive memoranda and sketchy entries of the Official Journal of the Convention.[1]

Few men knew that Alexander Hamilton favored a monarchy, or that Madison, though he wanted a republic, was anxious to "protect the minority of the opulent against the majority," or that Elbridge Gerry of Massachusetts believed "the evils we experience flow from the excess of democracy." Hamilton and Gerry were close together in their

[1] L. M. Miner, *Our Rude Forefathers,* p. 203; Jacob Axelrad, *Patrick Henry: The Voice of Freedom,* pp. 243 ff.

views, but Hamilton was astute enough to understand that "Whatever may be my opinion, I would hold it, however, unwise to change that form of government." He meant the republican form, of which he was nevertheless skeptical and suspicious. "All governments divide themselves into the few and the many," he said. "The first are the rich and the well-born, the other the mass of the people. The voice of the people has been said to be the voice of God; and however generally this maxim has been quoted and believed, it is not true in fact."[2] Democracy was suspect; a republican form of government was possible without it. The Constitutional Convention, in any event, thought so. The struggle which had been waged for liberty was being repeated for democracy.

Philip Freneau, who had fought in the first, seemed to know nothing about the second. Composing his poems or sailing his ships, he gave no sign that he was interested in what was taking place in the suffocating atmosphere of Convention Hall. He had always been the champion of the little people, the common man, "the mass" of whom Hamilton was afraid, and about whom Madison, his old classmate, was not too confident either. The new Constitution would be a milestone or a millstone for the people of America. The issues, the problems, the philosophies, the results, of the Philadelphia labors were of as crucial importance to the poet as to the people—yet the poet, busy with other labors, appeared to ignore all that transpired at the Convention, apparently content with affairs quite alien to both freedom and democracy.

What he wrote now would offend no one. If it was a living he wanted, it seemed within his reach. As Captain Freneau he could sail a ship with the best of them—his record as a master was proof enough of this. And he could achieve a popularity of sorts for his writings in addition, if he wrote only what was pleasant and, above all, noncontroversial. For the time, at least, he was done with all controversy, even that which had absorbed the energies of the delegates in Philadelphia. They had fussed and fumed over the exhausting task of fashioning the basic law of the land, and composing the differences

---

[2] Max Farrand (ed.), *The Records of the Federal Convention of 1787.* See also George Washington, *Writings* (ed. Jared Sparks), August 1, 1786, Vol. 7, pp. 187–189. Washington had written to John Jay that some "respectable characters speak of a monarchical form of government without horror." In the Convention itself, Alexander Hamilton expressed his profound fear of democracy—*Works*, Vol. 1, p. 411. Goldwin Smith, in his edition of *The Federalist,* expands on Hamilton's views in this connection.

between the collective and individual rights of citizens and of states. Captain Freneau could have changed the results as little as some of the delegates themselves—as little, for example, as one of the most prominent among them, George Mason, who declared he would "sooner chop off his right hand than put it to the Constitution as it then stood." James Madison, Freneau's old friend, whom he had not seen since those distant days of Princeton, had tried to do more.[3]

Madison's was the guiding hand and head of the Convention. With greater vision than most of the others, he had put the case for the Constitution to his close political collaborator in Virginia, Thomas Jefferson.

It was generally agreed [he informed Jefferson] that the objects of the Union could not be secured by any system founded on the principle of a Confederation of States. A *voluntary* observance of the Federal Law by all the members could never be hoped for. A *compulsive* one could never be reduced to practice, and if it could, involved equal calamities to the innocent and the guilty, the necessity of a military force, both obnoxious and dangerous, and, in general, a scene resembling much more a civil war than the administration of a regular government. Hence was embraced the alternative of a government which, instead of operating on the States, should operate without their intervention on the individuals composing them.[4]

William Penn long before had recognized that "governments rather depend upon men than men upon governments." Perhaps Edmund Burke was close to the truth when he considered a constitution as a vestment that must be fitted to a body.[5]

The future would prove the wisdom of Madison's alternative. It was perhaps the only one that could have emerged from deliberations in which the radical leaders of the Revolution had no part. Jefferson was not there—he was in Paris. Samuel Adams was not there—he was in Boston. Patrick Henry was not there—he was in Virginia.

[3] Quoted from Irving Brant, *James Madison,* Vol. 3, *The Father of the Constitution, 1787–1800,* p. 142; also Farrand, *Records of the Convention,* Vol. 2, p. 479; and Miner, *Our Rude Forefathers,* p. 203. See Jackson Turner Main, *The Anti-Federalists: Critics of the Constitution, 1781–1788,* for an excellent review of all opposition. George Mason, like Patrick Henry, opposed ratification. His objections were given in full in *Pamphlets on the Constitution,* by P. L. Ford.

[4] Brant, *James Madison,* Vol. 3, Ch. 1.

[5] *The Federalists* (Smith), No. 10; and Allan Nevins, *The American States during and after the Revolution,* p. 662.

Thomas Paine was not there—he was in Europe. In the days ahead some of them would be heard from again. The cauldron of conflict would boil once more in America, and the men who were now busy with matters other than the Constitution would be deep in the bubbling waters before they cooled. If, in the fullness of time, they ever cooled.

Philip Freneau, far out at sea, for the first time in his life was not involved in any conflicts at all. As captain of the *Columbia* he was doing better than he had ever dared to hope. He was proud of this vessel, the best he had known, fast and commodious, with space for passengers as well as cargo. The runs between Charleston and New York, despite heavy seas in the early months of 1788, were pleasant and profitable; the hold of the *Columbia* was always full of all manner of merchandise—with indigo and tobacco, with tallow and wax, with hams and peanuts, with cider, rum, tea, glass, iron, and Windsor chairs. Soon, even better merchandise than this would fill his heart.[6]

As winter storms and heaving waters were calmed in the quiet weather of the spring, Freneau looked forward to something far more pleasant than any cargo. The second volume of his works was about to appear. At long last his friend Bailey announced its publication in Philadelphia. When it did appear, in May 1788, the author was pleased not alone with the work itself, but equally with the efforts of Francis Bailey and others to advance its sale. Robert Hodge, the New York bookseller, was pushing *The Miscellaneous Works of Philip Freneau* in attractive advertisements which proclaimed their high virtues and general excellence. The whole volume, Hodge promised, was "replete with the highest sentimental entertainment. Humor, wit, and satire flow in copious strains. It requires only to be read to be admired." Mathew Carey, alert and business-minded, saw a good opportunity to get rid of some copies of the first book with which he was saddled. He offered the earlier volume and the new one together at the bargain price of fifteen shillings.[7]

Like the first book, *The Miscellaneous Works* was only a partial success. The friends of whom Freneau had complained before were among the first to subscribe for the new volume. DeWitt Clinton of New York, Aedanus Burke and Charles Pinckney of Charleston—who

[6] *The Daily Advertiser,* March 24, March 29, 1788; Lewis Leary, *That Rascal Freneau,* pp. 153–154.

[7] Freneau, *The Miscellaneous Works of Philip Freneau; The Freeman's Journal,* April 24 to July 1, 1788; *The Daily Advertiser,* May 28 to July 12, 1788; Leary, *That Rascal Freneau,* p. 154.

were also close friends of Peter's—and David Rittenhouse of Philadelphia, bought copies, while Governor Moultrie of South Carolina, perhaps for Peter's sake more than for Philip's, ordered six of them especially printed for him on "fine" paper.[8]

The Works could offend scarcely anyone, for they contained almost none of the bitterness of controversy or political satire. The new volume represented only the poet's own choice of the poems and prose essays which he considered among his finest writings of the recent past. The "Pilgrim" pieces, now gathered into one sheaf which he called "The Philosopher of The Forest," together with a new series of papers written by a fictional weaver, "the late Robert Slender," were acute and searching appraisals of all sorts and conditions of men and affairs, shrewd probings of the springs of action, and gently ironical commentaries on the mores and morals of the times. Men of all classes and stations passed in review before their observant judge, nor did he forget the ladies, of whom he knew so little, yet pretended to know so much.[9]

His own experiences with Eleanor may have taught him a few things he did not know before. It seemed highly improbable that the rebel who never conceded anything without question, or yielded to anyone without debate, would ever adhere to the advice which he gave to those who sought a mate. "You must seem to give the preference to her judgment," he said, "in all matters that happen to be discussed." And he added: "Say nothing of your station unless you are a Governor of an island or happen to be some considerable officer of State," since "all women, we all know, are naturally fond of power." Was this a dig at Eleanor, who seemed so ready to rely on her father's judgment of the poet's worth? Had Philip known a similar rebuff at the hands of the governor of Bermuda, the father of Amanda? In any event: "Whatever she thinks it proper to assert, it is your business to defend and prove to be true. If she says black is white, it is not for men in your probationary situation to contradict her." To avoid embarrassing the lady, "Never mention the words petticoat, garters or shoes in her presence," and never, under any circumstances, refer to the "female anatomy." Freneau himself really believes in the questionably blessed state of matrimony, for "an old bachelor is, in most instances, wholly destitute of that benevolence, generosity, sympathy and ex-

---

[8] Freneau's copy, in the Freneau Collection (Rutgers), lists the subscribers.
[9] Freneau, The Miscellaneous Works.

pansion of soul, which we may constantly observe in married men."
A woman (or a man), like a poem (or an essay), could be a thing of
beauty. With Keats, Philip Freneau believed that "a thing of beauty is
a joy forever," and with Shelley he also sought "the spirit of beauty"
in human thought and form. Alas, too often that spirit was ephemeral,
or entirely missing from the scene surveyed by Robert Slender—or by
any philosopher who emerged from the forest.[10]

It is certain that Freneau's acerbic humor and blunted barbs are the
fruits of his own experiences in a life of struggle and penury. Such
poems as "Rules and Directions How to Avoid Creditors, Sheriffs,
Constables etc," "The Debtor," and "A Discourse upon the Law"
could only have been written by one whose knowledge was based on
much more than mere intuition or casual hearsay. "The Folly of
Writing Poetry" and "Advice to Authors," the first in verse, the second
in prose, contained the lessons he had learned, again and again, in his
own years of frustrated authorship. "Authors," he says, "(such I
mean as are not possessed of fortunes) are at present considered as the
dregs of the community: their prospects are truly humiliating." It
could not be otherwise in a country where "Fortune most commonly
bestows wealth upon fools and idiots." It is better to espouse beggary,
perhaps, because that, "with all its hideous apparatus of rags and
misery, becomes at once respectable if it exhibits the least independence
of spirit and a single spark of laudable ambition." These, no one could
doubt, were the nuclear substance of the restless soul that inhabited
the spare body of Philip Freneau.[11]

Authors were no exception to the prevailing rule of gross injustice
and questionable fame. It was a condition which was apparent in all
walks of life. The Revolution had thrown up not a few imposters,
whose rewards were golden though their deeds were rarely more than
tinsel. The contrast was too painful to accept with philosophic calm.
In a prose piece which he called "The Picture Gallery," Freneau, with
less humor than venom, attacked the "fatheaded animals that are also
putting in their claim for immorality." The canvases which lined the
wall of the gallery disclosed the smug, cunning features of too many
"who are remarkable for nothing but their wealth, their impudence,
or their meanness, and who, instead of having really contributed to the
establishment of the liberties of America, grew fat upon the miseries

---

[10] *Ibid.*, pp. 133–140.
[11] *Ibid.*, p. 42 n.

of the soldiery, and approved of the Revolution only as it promised to bring about a revolution in their own fortunes for the better." Swine were swine—it was nothing new that the pearls of the world were thrown to them. Must they also be pickled in pigment for the doubtful delectation of posterity?[12]

There was a humane philosophy in *The Miscellaneous Works* that examined man in all his sordid weakness and pathetic strength, in his rending reach for the stars and his debasement in the slime, in his futile fumblings for illusions and his tragic confrontation with reality. Freneau's scorn for the time-servers was tempered by his hope and belief in the future of America—America, which was the hope and conscience of an entire people. America had been born in high promise and baptized in great suffering. Would it forget the suffering and betray the promise?

In many conventions across the land the leaders of the people were laboring now for an answer to these questions. Before the summer of 1788 had cooled into autumn the answer would be given and the die would be cast for a long time to come, if not for the whole future of America. The poet, doubtful of the issue, left the answer to others as he plied the high seas for a living which was even more doubtful than this. Save for occasional verses of slight importance, and a few more relevant to his own affairs, he was completely taken up by this business of making a living. Madeira wine, New York rum, peach brandy made up the cargoes he carried in the *Columbia,* sometimes varied by more plebian merchandise like ham and herring, rice and indigo. Even a pair of "South American Ourang-Outangs" were among his live freight as he plowed the sea lanes between Charleston and New York, Baltimore and Wilmington, Yamacrow, Savannah, and Sunbury, Georgia.[13]

It was not all smooth sailing. A seaman expects rough seas and heavy weather. And stout ships will ride out any storm. It was fortunate that the *Columbia* was such a vessel. No longer a novice, Freneau had survived one hurricane in his early days at sea. No supercargo on a limping *Dromelly,* but a seasoned mariner in command of a fine schooner, he ran into a gale off Cape Henry on July 23, two days out of

---

[12] *Ibid.,* pp. 49–53.
[13] Leary, *That Rascal Freneau,* pp. 158–164; *The Daily Advertiser,* May 15, July 7, 1788.

New York. Deep in the water with a heavy load of iron, the *Columbia* was struck by the full fury of the storm and set on her beam ends; her mast toppled overside and the stern pointed to the darkened heavens as the cargo shifted dangerously in the hold, the decks were stripped of gear, and panic swept the heaving vessel fore and aft. "All my people," Freneau explained, "except one, an old man who stuck fast in one of the scuttles, were several times overboard." Two men, one of them a passenger, were lost, and the Captain himself "took refuge in the main weather shrouds." Saved from being "washed into the sea," he fell on the main deck, miraculously escaping the main mast, which was washed into the boiling waters of Cape Henry. As Freneau slid along the careening deck, he was struck on the head by the tiller and knocked unconscious for "nearly a quarter of an hour." When he came to, he found that the ship's hold was flooded by more than four feet of water, the pumps were useless, and only a single bucket was left with which to bail.[14]

It was providential that the *Columbia* did not founder or lose more men, in the desperate struggle with the hurricane through a terrible night. The harrowing experience was only slightly tempered by the free flow of grog to a crew that labored in a frenzy of effort with no "fire, no candles, our beds soaked with seawater, the cabin torn to pieces, a vast quantity of corn damaged and poisoning us to death." When they were towed into Hampton Roads and finally reached Norfolk on July 29, "the very dogs looked at us with an eye of commiseration—the Negroes pitied us." It took until late in September to recondition the vessel for use again.[15]

And again in mid-November the *Columbia* was battered by heavy seas on the voyage from Charleston to Baltimore, driven from her course, and so delayed in her passage that her master, now thoroughly discouraged by the misfortunes of this new command, doubted the wisdom of continuing it. He regretted that he had ever forsaken the simple, uneventful yet peaceful life of a poet for the turbulence of a mariner's career.

> Lost are my toils, my longing hopes are vain,
> Yet midst these ills permit me to complain,

[14] Quoted in Leary, *That Rascal Freneau,* pp. 158–159; see also Philip M. Marsh, "Philip Freneau: Our Sailor Poet," *American Neptune,* VI (April 1946), 115–120.
[15] Marsh, "Freneau: Our Sailor Poet."

> And half-regret, that finding fortune frail,
> I left the Muse to direct the sail.[16]

It was, however, only a half-regret, not a firm decision to retire from the sea. He wanted, above all things, to succeed at least in this new venture, to have something more than an empty promise and a doubtful future to offer to his lady back in Monmouth. He had not given up the hope to interest her, to persuade her, perhaps her father as well, who needed more persuasion than she. He still pursued her with letters that scanned and rhymed, with verses that were more earnest than passionate. At sea in more ways than one, he wished her to know that he had not forgotten her, that he always remembered her though

> From bar to bar, from Cape to Cape, I stray,
> From you still absent, still too far away.[17]

Eleanor, still a spinster, is not disinterested. She corresponds with the far from ancient mariner in similar vein, in letters that are also composed in iambic pentameter. While the metrical missiles continue the winter passes and the blessed spring approaches, in the year of 1789. As Freneau patiently waits for the thaw that will free his ship from the ice-floes, he does not neglect to let Eleanor know that he thinks of her all the time.

> I pass the lingering lazy hours
> Reflecting on the Spring—and you[18]

Who can tell the motives of the human mind, the reasons of the human heart? The suitor seems as placid as the approaching season, the lady as eager as the spent storm. If the poet dreams on the epistolary courtship at all, it is true that other thoughts also preempt his waking hours.

He derives great comfort from his reflections, not only of Eleanor and the spring, but equally of his prowess as a sailor. What poet, he asks, from Hesiod to Pindar, has ever been "*trusted* with the controul or possession" of a barque such as his? If the life of a sailor is a hard one, yet "the *sea* is the *best* school for philosophy (I mean the moral

---

[16] Freneau, "Polydore to Amanda," in *The Daily Advertiser*, February 10, 1791.

[17] *The Daily Advertiser*, April 15, 1789; see W. J. Mills, *Through the Gates of Old Romance*, pp. 123 ff., on the courtship of Freneau.

[18] *The Freeman's Journal*, January 29, 1789; Lewis Leary, "Philip Freneau and Monmouth County," in *Monmouth County Historical Association Bulletin*, Vol. I, No. 2 (July 1948), p. 74.

kind); in thirteen or fourteen years' acquaintance with that element, I am convinced that a man ought to imbibe more of your right *stoical* stuff, than could be gained in half a century on shore." He cannot forbear to inject a rather querulous note into this reflection. The sea like the land is the natural abode of poets and philosophers, but life on both is equally hazardous and ill-starred. On land as on sea the fortunes of men are precarious—for men of thought and men of feeling they are worse than for others. Alive, they are neglected; dead, they are forgotten. Freneau, it is certain, will never forget or neglect them. "Poets and Philosophers shall ever travel with me at a cheap rate indeed," because, if "the barque that bears them should make an eternal exit to the bottom of the ocean, the busy world, as things go, will regret the loss of most of them very little, perhaps not at all." The first sailor-poet of America, the first writer of its sea songs, the "inspired bard" of its naval service (who advocated sailor's relief for American seamen), loved the sea and the lonely souls who voyaged in ships or in fancy on the insensate waters of life. With him, all who wandered the far reaches of the world would always travel cheaply.[19]

While Freneau was fighting for survival at sea, other men, poets and philosophers in their own way, were fighting for survival on land. The struggle that was being waged in all the states for the ratification of the Constitution was in reality a stand for survival not only of men, but also of institutions—of the country itself, the United States of America. It was a long and often bitter contest, the opposing sides drawn up in full battle array. The questions debated in the Convention were debated once more in the thirteen states, and the answers proposed were scrutinized in each word and syllable. Every section of the covenant between the states was taken apart, examined, exposed to the white glare of publicity denied it when it was formulated and finally settled by the Convention. There had been little harmony inside the walls of the State House in Philadelphia, though the finished product was accepted even by those who questioned its entire validity. The elder statesman Benjamin Franklin, while he voted for its adoption, was not altogether pleased with the Constitution. In a letter to his friend Pierre Samuel Dupont de Nemours he ventured the opinion that "we must not expect that a new government may be formed, as a game of chess may be played by a skilful hand, without a fault." There

---

[19] *The Freeman's Journal*, July 8, 1789. See also Marsh, "Freneau: Our Sailor Poet"; Avis Lockwood, "Commonplace Book," Ms.

were too many players in this game, too many opposing views and clashing prejudices, too many conflicting interests, too many faults. The reasons advanced by the delegates for their pet theories were not always reasonable, but "the wisest must agree to some unreasonable things, that reasonable ones of more consequence may be obtained." The problem was essentially that of the precedence of the national government over the state governments. This was a prime objective of the Convention, but no less important was the precedence of liberty over power, the rights of man over the rights of property.[20]

The whole question of changing, of scrapping the Articles of Confederation altogether, was to be decided. The radicals outside the Convention—men like Patrick Henry—even the conservatives inside, were opposed to such a summary method of strengthening the national government. Rufus King, a successful merchant and an able orator, wanted the Articles unchanged while, at the same time, he insisted on a powerful central authority. Alexander Hamilton, who knew better, had no difficulty in persuading King as well as others of the incompatibility of the two viewpoints. Hamilton "revolutionized" the mind of Rufus King and other doubters, but the minds of men like Patrick Henry could not be changed by any arguments of Hamilton, or of Washington himself, who appealed to him directly for support of the Constitution. A year after the Convention had produced the finished instrument its acceptance by the states was still in gravest doubt. Jefferson remained unconvinced by the checks and balances of the Constitution. They appeared to check every liberty and balance every natural right. Once he had thought of the Convention as "an assembly of demigods." Now, he informed his friends Edward Carrington, John Adams, and James Madison, he was not so sure. Where, in the whole Constitution, were the guarantees of a free press, free speech, and the other civil liberties which were included in the Virginia Bill of Rights?[21] Sam Adams, the stormy petrel of Massachusetts, was similarly dissatisfied—though wavering. When he finally voted for ratification it was against his better judgment. "As I enter the building" (of the Massachusetts ratifying convention) he said, "I stumble on the threshold." He was not the only one.[22]

[20] Carl Van Doren, *The Great Rehearsal*, p. 9.

[21] Jefferson to John Adams, August 30, 1787, in Thomas Jefferson, *Writings* (ed. A. A. Lipscomb and A. E. Bergh), Vol. 1, p. 289; see also Van Doren, *The Great Rehearsal*, p. 15.

[22] Axelrad, *Patrick Henry*, pp. 247–248.

The threshold was finally crossed. The Contitution was ratified at last. And the amendments that guaranteed the personal liberties of the citizen, omitted or forgotten by the delegates to the Convention, later became a part of it. The logic of the Federalist essays of Madison, of Hamilton, of John Jay, together with the high prestige of George Washington, overcame the efforts of the opposition. The ship of state was provided with sufficient ballast to keep it steady through future storms, with helm and rudder to guide it safely past the shoals and shallows of political and social sandbars, and with ample strength to sail uncharted seas. Less than 10 percent of the white population of America had affirmed their belief in it; of nearly three million others, five-sixths had not even the right to affirm; lacking sufficient property they lacked also this. The great mass of the people for whom Philip Freneau had spoken over the years had no part in the crucial scene of the great American drama. Yet it was for them as for all the world the only hope for the future, and only the future would tell how well that hope would be realized.[23]

At the moment, it was as luminous as the evening star of the early springtime. George Washington, whose great courage and leadership had made it all possible, was himself at the helm, chosen first among his countrymen to guide the destinies of the new nation. On April 13, 1789, when Captain Freneau sailed into New York harbor, the *Columbia* was "dressed and decorated in the most superb manner," spic and span for the reception to President Washington the next day. The poet had a genuine respect for the man who had rescued liberty from the alien. He had given many proofs of his sentiments toward Washington, in poems celebrating the Commander-in-Chief's triumphs. He agreed with Count Moustier, the French minister, that "all is hushed in the trust of the people in the Savior of the Country."[24] The Master of the *Columbia* would have occasion to question that trust, while Washington, who had never taken any notice of the poet before, would one day notice him with a grimace, when the voice of the people became more audible and ominous in the growing conflict over domestic and foreign policies.

As yet all was quiet and harmonious. America, united and free, be-

[23] Main, *The Anti-Federalists*, p. 259; Farrand, *Records of the Convention*, Vol. 1, pp. xi, 9.

[24] S. E. Forman, "The Political Activities of Philip Freneau," *Johns Hopkins University Studies*, Vol. 20, Nos. 9–10 (1902), p. 27; *The Gazette of the United States*, April 25, 1789.

gan its difficult climb to greatness while Philip Freneau, certain at last that he could climb nowhere on the tossing waters of the sea, gave up the attempt entirely. On November 18, when he docked in Charleston, he knew that he would never again embark on a ship as a mariner. He would stay on for a short while in the South, writing regularly for *The City Gazette,* of which brother Peter was now a part owner, and sending an occasional piece to *The Daily Advertiser* of New York, where the seat of the Federal government had been established.[25]

The Massachusetts Centinel of January 27, 1790, carried a report by its editor, Benjamin Russell, of the poet's final divorce from the sea. Captain Freneau, he wrote, "from a long succession of calamities and misfortunes at sea, has determined once more to try the powers of his pen in his native city of New York." It was the wish of "every friend to genius and merit," Russell continued, " that the future success of this American bard—this genuine son of Neptune and Clio— whose writings in verse and prose have rendered such eminent service to his country, may be greater than he has hitherto experienced." Russel went so far as to call him the "Peter Pindar" of America, a tribute that placed him in the company of the ancient Greek poet, and of the modern English satirist John Wolcot, who used that pseudonym in his writings.[26]

Though his success, certainly, could not be much smaller, Freneau's reputation was greater than it had been for a long time. In Charleston his work for *The City Gazette* had a romantic aura which did not detract from the work itself and rather enhanced the interest in the poet too. A captain and a poet—this was an irresistible combination which spread his fame all along the Atlantic seaboard. Where he was little known, it was assumed that he was a "celebrated genius." In New York, where *The Miscellaneous Works* were still being advertised, many of his poems were reprinted in more papers than ever before. It was all very flattering—but was it success? Perhaps it was that also, since one event, more than any other, gave it the authentic stamp of approval. The poet was soon to marry. Samuel Forman had

[25] *The Daily Advertiser,* January 2, 1790; Marsh, "Freneau: Our Sailor Poet"; Lewis Leary, "Philip Freneau in Charleston," *South Carolina Historical and Genealogical Magazine,* XLII, 3 (July 1941), 89–98; E. S. Thomas, *Reminiscences of the Last Sixty-Five Years,* p. 76 and *passim.*

[26] *The Massachusetts Centinel,* January 27, 1790; also J. M. Lee, *History of American Journalism,* p. 92.

finally consented. Eleanor had given Philip a sign at last. The wanderer was coming home. The prodigal poet now *had* a home.[27]

Returning from Charleston on February 12, 1790, Freneau was no longer the master of the *Columbia,* but a paying passenger on the brig *Betsey.* As he passed the hills of Jersey, the springtime, not yet in the air, was already in his heart. After his long odyssey, he could take his ease, be married, and lead a sane and settled life with Eleanor. The future was bright with promise as he looked on the highlands behind which that future lay. Another Tannhäuser, he sang out his inmost soul:

> Proud heights: with pain so often seen,
> (With joy beheld once more),
> On your firm base I take my stand,
> Tenacious of the shore:
> Let those who pant for wealth or fame
> Pursue the watery road;—
> Soft sleep and ease, blest days and nights,
> And health, attend these favoring heights,
> Retirement's blest abode.[28]

Whatever the future might hold, retirement, soft sleep, ease, were to be no part of it. Neither Neptune nor Clio ever provided them for any of their disciples.

[27] *The Daily Advertiser,* December 21, 1789, January 9, 1790.

[28] Freneau, *The Poems of Philip Freneau* (ed. F. L. Pattee), Vol. 2, p. xlvii; see also Freneau's copy of Robertson, *Elements of Navigation,* in Freneau Collection (Rutgers); *The Massachusetts Centinel,* January 27, 1790.

19. SILKEN BANDS—AND OTHERS

No LONGER YOUNG, and fast approaching the indeterminate status of middle age, Philip Freneau was thirty-eight years old when Eleanor Forman made up her mind to marry him. Distance might have lent enchantment to his person and absence fired the sentiment she had for him. His epistolary poems helped a faltering cupid who was always stimulated by words more than by deeds. The groom looked no better for the battering of the wind and weather; indeed, he seemd more like a seaman than a poet. Of slightly more than middle height, he was thinner than before, his soft eyes were sunk deeper in their sockets, his face was tanned and taut from the sun and the sea.

His clothes, like those of a seaman, were shabby and unkempt, while his overcoat, when he appeared before the Forman family, was too disreputable even for a sailor. For a poet it was downright scandalous. The bride-to-be was clearly within her prescriptive rights to insist that her suitor obtain a new one. At twenty-eight and still attractive, Eleanor retained her romantic notions of matrimonial propriety. Gently urgent in her efforts to achieve some measure of sartorial sense in the man whom she was soon to join in holy wedlock, she did not find it an easy task to change the habits of a bachelor who had lived alone for nearly two decades. Philip offered no resistance to a new coat when Eleanor, with the help of a well-plied pair of scissors, slashed his old one beyond all further repair. Did he not once prescribe a similar capitulation for those who hoped to win a lady? If you want her then agree, or pretend to agree, to whatever she demands; a remedy simple enough to prescribe but far more difficult to swallow.[1]

[1] "Lines Addressed to Some Young Ladies," in *The Daily Advertiser,*

Freneau treated the whole episode as a merry prank, in which he joined with restrained gusto, to the extent of writing some double-edged lines about it for *The Daily Advertiser,* the oldest daily paper in the City of New York, published by Francis Childs and John Swaine at 190 Water Street, at the corner of King. It had a reputation for unbiased news service, and faithfully reported the proceedings of the Federal Congress as well as those of the various state legislatures. Always keenly alert to the interest of the people of America and of the City of New York itself, often it viewed with critical concern the measures debated in the national lawmaking body.[2]

New York, with a population of thirty-three thousand souls, was in a fair way of becoming the largest city of the country. The Federal Hall, remodeled by Major L'Enfant from the old city hall, was more imposing than most of the Dutch buildings with their lofty peaked roofs and gable ends or the English houses which had replaced many of the older ones. In a city where nearly all the buildings were of frame with brick fronts, Federal Hall seemed sturdier, more imposing, than all the rest, designed both for beauty and for durability, a modest monument to the power and dignity of the new government of the United States, and the pride of its capital, the great and growing city of New York.[3]

It was a bustling city, where business was daily increasing and where culture was not altogether neglected either. It boasted of only one theater, the John Street, but on these boards were presented the plays of Shakespeare and Goldsmith and Sheridan. Nor was music neglected. The Musical Society, from its office at 29 John Street, was active to foster and promote it among the people of New York. If they craved for lighter amusement, there were less taxing recreations like museums or animal shows or occasional sports events to enlist their interest and patronage. The poor could afford these entertain-

March 5, 1790; Lewis Leary, "Philip Freneau and Monmouth County," *Monmouth County Historical Association Bulletin,* Vol. 1, No. 2 (July 1948), p. 74.
[2] *The Daily Advertiser;* Philip M. Marsh, "Philip Freneau and His Circle," *The Pennsylvania Magazine of History and Biography,* LXIII, 2 (January 1939), 37–59; S. G. W. Benjamin, "Notable Editors, between 1776 and 1800," *Magazine of American History,* XVII (January–June 1887); C. S. Brigham, *History and Bibliography of American Newspapers.*
[3] Thomas E. V. Smith, *The City of New York in the Year of Washington's Inauguration,* pp. 20–23.

ments—or those which were still cheaper, the spectacles of color and gaiety among the fashionable who promenaded the walks and water front in their rich and attractive garments of silk and satin. *The Daily Advertiser* made equal and pointed reference to the people who wore silks and satins and those in Congress who seemed to be speaking only for them in the hot debate on the Funding Act, which had just been introduced by the Federalists. The Federalists appeared to be interested more in the welfare of the rich, the speculators, and the merchants, who would profit enormously by this new proposal, than in the needs of the mass of the people.[4]

It was not surprising, perhaps, that Childs and Swaine should have offered employment to the poet newly returned from the sea, since his sympathies for the little people, the small artisan, and the struggling farmer were common knowledge. *The Daily Advertiser* was as democratic in its principles as he was and the budding of such strange blooms on the tree of liberty caused it to examine the proposals of the Federalists with profound suspicion.[5]

The doors of the chambers of Congress were closed and well guarded against ordinary citizens, but *The Daily Advertiser* had gotten wind of the strange proceedings inside and was making some caustic comments about them. There were rumors, in addition, that Congress was considering removing the capital from New York to some city farther south, a calamity for the city's business and a body-blow to its pride and prestige. New York had spent a fortune on its Federal Hall; it had facilities to give people the news about their lawmakers and their peculiar laws; it was a city of wealth and power, not only because it was the capital of the country, but because of its thriving industry and commerce, the endless stream of shipping that filled its harbor, and the financial future that seemed so pre-eminently its own.[6]

Yet many voices were heard which questioned its desirability as a national capital. The question was already debated in Congress. There were those who wanted the seat of government removed to a city more closely identified with the Revolution—Philadelphia perhaps—a city also favored by southerners, who found in New York too hectic an

[4] *Ibid.*, pp. 96–98, 172–186; C. A. Beard's Introduction to William Maclay, *Journal*, pp. vi–vii.

[5] *The Daily Advertiser*, November 1790–December 1791; S. E. Forman, "The Political Activities of Philip Freneau," *Johns Hopkins University Studies*, Vol. 20, Nos. 9–10 (1902), pp. 1–105 *passim*.

[6] *The Daily Advertiser*, April 12, April 13, June 12, 1790.

atmosphere for the deliberations of a national body. The matter was still in the talking stage, with most of the newspapers opposed to a change, and only *The Gazette of the United States* at all uncertain about the wisdom of any change. Its editor, John Fenno, was marking time until the Federalist Party would make up its mind. As the Federalist wind blew, that way Fenno and his newspaper would blow also.[7]

Philip Freneau, at Mount Pleasant, was resting after his stormy years at sea, writing occasional pieces for *The Daily Advertiser*. While Eleanor was bustling about with plans for the marriage, he was acquainting himself more fully with the political affairs of his country, a necessary prelude to the job he had been offered with *The Daily Advertiser*. Early in March 1790 he became the editor and a regular contributor to the paper whose democratic policies were so like his own.[8] He wrote with complete approval of the French Revolution, still in its infancy, supporting, as did most Americans, the spread of liberty to the country which had so greatly helped to achieve it in the new world. What transpired in America itself was too uncertain in either direction or result to trouble him yet. There were premonitory signs, some of them disturbing, but in the spring of 1790 they had not reached the dignity of danger signals. Besides, the editor of *The Daily Advertiser* had a few problems of his own. He was looking for a home in New York, modest and within his means, to which he could bring the bride who would adorn it.

On April 15 Eleanor and Philip were married in Samuel Forman's house at Middletown Point by Hendrick Hendrickson, the justice of the peace.[9] The happy occasion was celebrated not only by the family in Monmouth, but by Peter in Charleston, whose love for Philip was in no wise diminished by their unsuccessful ventures into business. Peter, always more practical than the poet, was no rolling stone; and he knew how to gather the moss. Now perhaps his brother would settle down. There was nothing like a wife and family to steady a man. Peter himself had no need for such a counterweight. Not yet, anyway. He was busy with too many other projects to think of marriage—with real estate, with shipping, with newspaper publishing, with almost

---

[7] Susan Coolidge, *A Short History of Philadelphia,* p. 170.

[8] *The Daily Advertiser,* March 5, 1790, contained his first poetic contribution. See Marsh, "Freneau and His Circle"; also F. Hudson, *Journalism in the United States, passim.*

[9] Affidavit of Eleanor Forman Freneau, August 7, 1838, in General Administrative Services, Case #23069: Pension Records of Philip Freneau, Mss.

any business that promised a profit, and with an occasional turn in the slave trade. In addition to all these, Peter was something of a political figure in South Carolina. Among the influential men of Charleston he had many friends, some of whom knew about Philip, and more of them about his adventures with Neptune and Clio. To inform them of Philip's marriage Peter placed an appropriate announcement in *The City Gazette and Daily Advertiser* of Charleston. He knew nothing about the bride, but those who did know her thought she was an avid reader and lover of books, with "a sprightliness of disposition, elegance of manner, affability, excellent conversational powers, and a charming hostess."[10]

When Freneau and his wife moved into their new home in the East Ward of New York, they hired a free woman to help with the chores. Settled at last, Philip was too engrossed in the unaccustomed role of lover to give much time to the role of editor. He did punctuate his honeymoon with some necessary contributions to *The Daily Advertiser,* one of them inspired by an event that was almost as momentous as his marriage. Benjamin Franklin, a high peak among the lesser summits of the revolutionary upheaval, was dead, released at last from the sufferings of his last years. Franklin had given greatly to the cause of liberty, and almost his last words were of hope for the new revolution which was rending the feudal structure of France and blasting its aristocracy from their immemorial moorings of privilege and power. With many misgivings, he had voted for the Constitution of a new America, yet his prevision of its virtues was as profound as it was prophetic. Franklin had been a supreme defender of freedom, and a steadfast fighter for the rights of man. When Freneau received the news of Franklin's death, he was moved to compose a requiem for the fallen giant whose loss was not only America's, but the whole world's.

> When Monarchs tumble to the ground,
> Successors easily are found:
> But, matchless Franklin! What a few
> Can hope to rival such as you,
> Who seized from Kings their sceptred pride,
> And turned the lightning's darts aside.[11]

[10] M. S. Austin, *Philip Freneau,* pp. 148–149. See also "The Wife of Philip Freneau," *New York Evening Post,* May 6, 1893.

[11] *The Daily Advertiser,* April 28, 1790. Also Lewis Leary, *That Rascal Freneau,* p. 170; Carl Van Doren, *Benjamin Franklin,* p. 773.

It was the man of learning and of culture, the libertarian and the man of science, to whom Freneau paid "the tribute" of his tears. Franklin had gloried in the growth of man's power over nature, of man's understanding of nature herself. He had exulted in the promise of man's mastery of the skies—while warning the world of the implications of that miracle. Franklin's experiments with a new and fearful force were equally miraculous, though electricity was still to be harnessed to the needs of man. That was in the far-distant future, but even now, almost at the moment of Franklin's death, another marvel of the human intellect had been revealed to men. The era of steam-power was foretold by John Fitch, whose boat, with no help from the wind, was already navigating the distance between Burlington and Philadelphia at the phenomenal speed of eight miles an hour.[12]

Philadelphia—for one reason or another it was always in the news. The Quaker City had been the scene of many dramas, some comic, some tragic, all of them engrossing. As the birthplace of the Declaration of Independence and the Constitution of the United States it might merit the high honor, the supreme distinction, of being also the chief city of the government. The question recurred again and again on the floor of Congress, as the debates grew warmer and members pressed for a decision on the new capital.

The problem of a permanent home for the new nation was involved with still other problems. The North was opposed to any city in the South; the South, to any city in the North. The deadlock, to be resolved, must yield to a compromise that would compensate for the loss of the capital. Alexander Hamilton's Assumption Bill and the Funding Act offered the means for such a compromise, if an agreement could be reached between the opposing factions in Congress. The choice was a hard one for the leaders to make—but they made it. Sectional pride was paramount to fiscal theory when Thomas Jefferson and the Anti-Federalists voted for the Assumption Bill (to which was also tacked the Funding Act) in return for the new capital which was to be built on the banks of the Potomac. Until it was completed according to the plans of Major L'Enfant, who had done so well with New York's Federal Hall, the temporary seat of government would be moved to Philadelphia. After December 1790 it would quit New York forever.

---

[12] Fitch devised a propeller for boats, as yet too impractical for efficient use. One of his vessels, however, carried passengers for a short while in 1790 (John Geise, *Man and the Western World,* p. 800).

Philip Freneau, untouched by any feelings of sectional pride, was not too familiar with the reasons advanced for the acceptance of Hamilton's measures. Less concerned with the place where the laws were made than with the men who made them, he wondered about the political tug-of-war that was won and lost at the same time. Who had won? Who had lost? And what was really involved in all this sound and fury? What, exactly, did they signify?

Funding and assumption had the undeniable virtues of bolstering the national credit and strengthening the national government, matters of vast importance to the country, as men of influence and foresight, Federalists or otherwise, readily agreed. But what of the equally undeniable vice of enriching a horde of speculators both in and out of Congress, and burdening an entire people with the debts of those who failed to bear their own just burdens during the Revolution.[13] Such laws as these would help the Federalists to consolidate their power in the nation, a power that would inevitably be translated into still other laws, more drastic perhaps than these. They might control, even subvert, the rights of the states themselves, and of the people who thought, and still believed, they were sovereign masters in their own states. Jefferson, who had sensed the danger of a compromise once conceded, resolved there would be no other. All measures, all policies of the Federalists would henceforth be examined with minutest care for any encroachments on the welfare, the liberties, the revolutionary ideals of America; the democratic-republicans of Jefferson's Anti-Federalist Party would challenge any assaults on the natural rights of the men who had fought and suffered and died for them, rights which were seemingly threatened by a new aristocracy of wealth and power under the aegis of the Federalists and the leadership of Alexander Hamilton. Hamilton and Jefferson, soon to emerge as the chief protagonists of opposite and irreconcilable views of the national welfare, were to become almost mortal enemies. Like gladiators on the field, with none of the rules of knight errantry, they would do battle until one or the other was beaten. In the meantime, while the battle was being joined, the maneuvers of both sides were carried on in an atmosphere of almost complete secrecy.[14]

[13] Hamilton, personally, never profited from the Assumption Act, but his close friend and assistant in the Treasury, William Duer, prospered mightily—as Hamilton well knew—from the speculative orgy that followed.

[14] F. R. A. Chateaubriand, *Voyages en Amérique et en Italie*, p. 21; A. H. Wharton, *Social Life in the Early Republic*, pp. 16, 19, 20.

Neither Philip Freneau nor *The Daily Advertiser* knew any more than the people themselves of what was transpiring behind closed doors or in cabinet meetings. The doors, the meetings, were far away; no longer were gossip and the news within earshot as in New York, but in Philadelphia, ninety miles away. Miles away appeared also the government's concern for the common people, including the soldiers who had fought for freedom and were now the forgotten men of America. New measures were being debated in Congress that could benefit only the others, those of whom Freneau had once written in "The Picture Gallery," and more recently in quite another vein in *The Daily Advertiser.* This time he had included a picture of the soldiers, the heroes of liberty, whose portraits hung nowhere at all, whose very deeds were rapidly becoming nothing but a lost memory.

> Sold are those arms which once on Britons blaz'd,
> When flushed with conquest to the charge they came,
> That power repell'd and Freedom's fabrick rais'd,
> She leaves her soldier—Famine and a name.[15]

The editor of *The Daily Advertiser* was increasingly aware of the anomalies in the affairs of America. Slowly, he began to understand that something was surely wrong in a country where freedom was a watchword more than a watchtower. Freedom for whom, if not for the millions of the amorphous mass whose sacrifices made it possible? And what if their representatives, their government, made plans, passed laws, that were not for them but for their rulers? If this was democracy, then in what way did it differ from monarchy, from aristocracy, and how could it be made effective for the men and women who were presumed to possess certain inalienable rights, but apparently at the pleasure of those who still withheld them. Time would tell what only time could reveal, and until then Philip Freneau would contribute a piece about some things that might interest his readers—such things as would interest any reader not altogether bemused by the political vagaries of the moment.

Men were more than political pawns on the chessboard of liberty. They were human beings bedevilled by their needs and desires. They worked, they ate, they loved. These were good, these were natural employments of a man's life. They had their weaknesses too. They smoked—and they drank. Filling his allotted space in *The Daily Advertiser,* Freneau considered these weaknesses of men, even as he con-

---

[15] *The Daily Advertiser,* September 1, 1790.

sidered the weaknesses of government. About men he knew a good deal more. Tobacco "surely was designed to poison and destroy mankind." And wine? If that too was a weakness, then it also had its virtues. Freneau was afraid "of that man who was never known to transgress the demands of strict sobriety in drinking." Such a person was "cold and unfeeling," and "continually anxious to collect a hoard which it is most likely he will not long exist to enjoy. To be always serious is not true wisdom. Life should, in a certain degree, be chequered with folly."[16]

Freneau, ostensibly writing about the Indian Opay Mico, was also writing about himself. He harbored no anxiety to "collect a hoard," and he too was capable of a certain degree of folly. His greatest folly was a pervasive sense of seriousness, though he was not always solemn; like many who often smile, he could rarely laugh. For most people, laughter was frequently hysteria rather than catharsis. Since Freneau had settled down with Eleanor, his mood was perhaps a trifle more expansive, and he could counsel the need for fun in the exercise of wisdom. He was content in his new role of husband, and happy at the approaching birth of a child. The stability of his new condition did not, however, blind him to the benefits of occasionally transgressing "the bounds of strict sobriety." He had never transgressed in his own demands or desires, save in the demand for liberty and the desire for decency. The stimulants for these were plentiful and pressing. Perhaps equally pressing was the need for quite other stimulants.

Despite the Scotch inheritance on his mother's side, Freneau was almost as much French as American. Wine was as water to a Frenchman, and drink was a comfort no man should deny himself. Philip had written on the merits of drink a number of times. In an idle moment he had jotted down a bit of doggerel in his copy of *Miscellanies for Sentimentalists,* which was more than a passing whim:

> He that buys land buys many stones,
> He that buys beef buys many bones,
> He that buys eggs buys many shells,
> But he that buys good ale buys nothing else.[17]

His humorous verse, "The Jug of Rum," was more popular with his readers than "The Tea Drinker," in which, with tongue in cheek, he declared that the tepid brew

[16] *Ibid.,* July 31, 1790, February 5, 1791.
[17] *Miscellanies for Sentimentalists,* in Freneau Collection (Rutgers).

> Yields softer joys
> Provokes less noise
> And breeds no bad design.[18]

There was little in all this to whet the poetic appetite of others, and nothing to please his own palate, but there was a paucity of news from Philadelphia and *The Daily Advertiser* had to serve its readers. They were apparently losing interest in the paper, and Freneau, sensitive to the drop in circulation, was losing patience. The return in money from his multiple duties was meager enough for one who had a family to support, while the new book he contemplated was only a project for the future. There it would remain until enough subscribers were found willing to pay the seventy-five cents it would cost. There was no hope of help from that source, nor indeed from *The Daily Advertiser* itself. Since the removal of the government to Philadelphia, the paper had not prospered. Its revenue was inadequate to justify the services of an editor. And New York, bereft of its political eminence, had suffered commercially as well. There was no place in it for Philip Freneau. Poetry by itself was never a means of livelihood. Since he had edited a paper for others, perhaps he could edit one for himself. If there was no employment elsewhere, why couldn't he employ himself?

On February 5, 1791, a broadside appeared in which the world was apprised of a forthcoming weekly, *The Monmouth Gazette, or General Magazine of Information and Amusement*. It would be delivered each week by rider, and its columns would cover all foreign as well as domestic news, with important special features to fill eight pages, quarto, in every issue. The expenses of publisher and publication would be kept to a minimum, all printing done on Freneau's premises at Mount Pleasant. Only one thing was necessary for a start—money enough from subscribers to buy the type. Without type there could be no start. Waiting for these subscriptions to materialize, and for those others without which his third volume must remain a phantom, Philip and Eleanor together also waited for the baby, no phantom, momentarily expected. The baby, fortunately, needed no other subscribers.[19]

In Mount Pleasant, so remote from New York, Freneau was still pursued by other problems as pressing as his own. They concerned America, and though he was far from clear about many of them, their

---

[18] *The Daily Advertiser*, February 11, 1791.
[19] *The Monmouth Gazette* never materialized.

existence and the necessity for lifting the curtain which obscured them were never far from his thoughts. Whatever popularity—and criticism —he had achieved as a writer, was incidental to his only purpose in writing at all. He had rarely penned a poem, however bad or blessed with beauty, or an essay, however calm or impassioned, for the money it might bring him. It had brought him precious little in any event. His lighter pieces might win the plaudits of the crowd, but, like the events which induced them, they vanished and were forgotten. His serious work had brought him even less than this—it had brought him neither a living nor a laurel. Wanting approval, not insensitive to applause, he was singularly responsive to the critical praise he so seldom received, while scorning the kudos of the powerful who could easily break a man—or a poet. He had never written anything to curry favor with anyone. He was proud to proclaim of his work:

> While it walks the page, let no one say
> It flatter'd knaves, or help'd to puff the vain.[20]

Often the butt of censure, he had never willingly invited it. If he was abused, it was because he attacked the assumptions of a caste, the self-seeking philosophy which animated the possessors of wealth and inheritors of privilege. The Muse, whom he once had courted for herself alone, was often only a means to an end—the end of privilege, its conquest by the people who had won a revolution and were yearning to taste the fruits of their victory.

Political independence had been achieved, but not political maturity. The Revolution had stirred new thoughts not only in the conduct of government but also in the pursuit of culture. Almost single handed Freneau had won a measure of literary independence for his country, but American literature was still in its infancy. Writers, the poets especially, were still tied to the apron strings of the mother country. Popular poets like those of Hartford—they were known as the Connecticut Wits—were more interested in maintaining the status quo than in furthering the purposes of the Revolution. For them the Revolution was done, finished. Independence had been won from Britain; the old masters had been dispossessed; but masters were necessary. The wealthy and influential alone were capable of directing the destinies of the new republic.

John Trumbull, who believed in the sanctity of the rich and power-

[20] F. L. Pattee, "Philip Freneau," in *Chautauqua,* Vol. 31 (August 1900), pp. 467–475.

ful, was a good and faithful Federalist. Timothy Dwight, a godly man, considered democracy as synonymous with atheism; he attempted to prove his thesis in *The Triumph of Infidelity*. Lemuel Hopkins, an able physician as well as a poet, detested the democratic ideal, while David Humphreys, once an officer on Washington's staff, deplored the possible rule of the rabble. Hopkins and Humphreys, Trumbull and Joel Barlow had collaborated on *The Anarchiad*, an imposing series of poems, all of them integrated into one theme—Anarchy at the heart of Democracy.[21]

Barlow would later see another light and renounce his old allegiance to Federalist concepts of political power. By turns a preacher, a lawyer, a poet, and a land speculator, he was still as conservative as Dwight and Trumbull, as impeccably correct in his ideas and outlook as his classmate Noah Webster. His friends had no cause to doubt him, though the recently published "Vision of Columbus" may have given them some uneasy moments. He was probably safe enough, since Washington had subscribed for so many copies of the poem and had praised him to Lafayette as "one of those Bards who hold the key of the gates by which Patriots, Sages, and Heroes are admitted to immortality."[22] One day the Federalists would regret their misjudgment of this man, who became the friend of radicals like Thomas Paine and Joseph Priestley, and whose writings would include such cutting criticism of the foes of democracy as "The Conspiracy of Kings." When Barlow finally announced his credo as "the original, unalterable truth, that all men are equal in their rights," and added that this was "the foundations of everything," the Connecticut Wits would no longer doubt his apostasy.[23] Unlike their former friend, they would never betray their old beliefs, nor succumb to the blandishments of new ideas at home or abroad.

Freneau would never appease the men who believed that power belonged to the few. He would oppose any measure, any move, that might draw the curtain of silence around the efforts of the Federalists to perpetuate that power. A proposal to levy a tax on newspapers,

---

[21] V. L. Parrington, *Main Currents in American Thought: The Colonial Mind*, pp. 357 ff.; in *Letters of an American Farmer*, pp. 57–58, J. H. St. John Crèvecoeur had expressed views consonant with the beliefs of Philip Freneau.

[22] Leon Howard, *The Connecticut Wits*, p. 159.

[23] Parrington, *Main Currents in American Thought*, p. 385; see also R. A. Billington, B. L. Lowenberg, and S. H. Brockunier, *The United States: American Democracy in World Perspective*, pp. 93–94.

placing a premium on the people's sole source of information, wrung
from him a cry of protest seldom heard since the days of Peter Zenger:

> The well-born sort alone should read the news;
> No common herd should get behind the scene
> To view the movements of the State machine.[24]

Equality was the basis of democracy, not a levelling but a raising
of the rights and opportunities of all men. How was this possible
where the people were deprived of the knowledge of the words, the
actions, of their representatives? The doors of Congress were closed
against them, and now it was proposed to penalize the newspapers
which might inform them. What they learned was mostly hearsay,
embellished in the telling, some of it true, some of it distorted. Strange
stories circulated about the Congress, about the President himself,
stories which gathered force from repetition, which the people believed
because they seemed too fantastic for disbelief. The Executive Mansion
was the scene of the most sumptuous receptions, the finest fashions,
the greatest luxuries always associated in the public mind with royal
courts but never with republican government. The people did not
know that the President of the United States occupied an exalted position which demanded such trappings though he himself did not relish
them.[25] His lady was more partial to them than he. Martha Washington could become furious when her newly-painted walls were stained
by smudges from dirty hands—hands, she was certain, which belonged
to no one "but a filthy Democrat."[26]

And Congress? Rumor had it that the men who made the laws were
the first to profit from the laws they made. While they mouthed a
"rhetoric of patriotism and purity," they were busy justifying the defi-
nition of patriotism once made by the master of many definitions, Samuel Johnson. Patriotism was not the last refuge of scoundrels who
might qualify for Freneau's picture gallery, but the first. Of fourteen
senators who favored the Hamilton measures, ten were themselves
among the greatest beneficiaries, holders of securities bought from
soldiers in desperate need for almost nothing and guaranteed by the

[24] From lines "On the Proposed Taxation of Newspapers," *The Daily Advertiser,* February 18, 1791.

[25] Beard's Introduction to Maclay, *Journal,* pp. vii–lx. Jefferson also thought
that the country was on the road to monarchy—Thomas Jefferson, *Writings*
(ed. P. L. Ford), Vol. 1, p. 254.

[26] Jacob Axelrad, *Patrick Henry: The Voice of Freedom,* p. 264.

government to be worth their full face value. In the House of Representatives at least half the members were financially interested in the event. Almost every public transaction was controlled by sentiments of "the basest selfishness." While some were fighting this raid upon the treasury, the props of the republic appeared cursed with a horde of termites who were undermining its revolutionary strength and weakening its revolutionary ideals. To some observers it seemed as if the props would soon collapse altogether.[27]

Philip Freneau was not one of them. He was no Cassandra prophesying doom, though he deeply deplored the moral laxity in government. The trials and errors of a young country were part of its texture, into which was also woven the faith and courage of simple men, the hopes and aspirations of an entire people, the unselfish service of leaders animated by a high purpose, the blood and tears poured out for a lofty ideal. These were the everlasting and unimpeachable truths which the poet had written into his verse—and into his prose—throughout the critical years of the war. They were the ones he sought to emphasize even now, when their potency was less than reassuring. He was engaged on an ambitious work which he called "The Rising Empire." It was his purpose to portray the mettle of the people who had built America in the years of its greatest travail, and to honor each state of the union as it contributed to the consummation of liberty. The project was a bold and majestic conception, one never before attempted in the new world of letters, for which a number of stanzas were already composed and others in process of completion. The introduction to the entire work, prefaced in "A Philosophical Sketch of America" by *The Daily Advertiser* of March 13, 1790, revealed the scope of Freneau's grand design.[28]

Block by block, the gleaming mansion grew—"A Review of Rhode Island," "A Description of Connecticut," sections on Pennsylvania, on Massachusetts, on Maryland and Virginia. Then the series stopped. The mansion toppled. Perhaps the effort for so vast an edifice was beyond his powers. His energies were sapped by anxieties too great to withstand the burdens of creative work. He was forever moving backward while appearing to go forward. His third volume was quite evidently not wanted, and *The Monmouth Gazette*, not yet even launched,

---

[27] Maclay, *Journal,* pp. 179, 364; see also George Gibbs, *Memoirs of the Administration of Washington and John Adams,* Vol. 1, p. 62.

[28] *The Daily Advertiser*, March 13, 1790; Freneau, *The Poems of Philip Freneau* (ed. F. L. Pattee), Vol. 3, pp. 3–18.

seemed fated to remain unborn. Subscriptions were dishearteningly few, and though he still had the columns of *The Daily Advertiser* open to him for an occasional article on the ultimate triumph of the good and the true in government, the future had all the depressing aspects of a personal if not of a democratic failure. Nevertheless, it was pleasant to learn that Thomas Jefferson admired his work and especially liked his salute to Tom Paine's revolutionary labors. It was encouraging to know that the rights of man still held the allegiance of honest men and freedom was the first concern of honest leaders. If only the people were enlightened liberty would be safe. But how was that to be accomplished when there were too few schools to teach them, too few writers to instruct them, too few papers to speak for them?[29]

These were questions of more than passing interest. They were far from being merely rhetorical. In a state of public tension and private acrimony, when the sources of information were polluted by propaganda, questions like these were asked by all who were devoted to the democratic ideal and believed that it was in deadly peril. Liberty had been won, but could it not be lost again unless the people were informed of the need to guard it with the utmost vigilance? No one else could be trusted—all history was proof to the simple truth that no one else could be trusted to guard their freedom but the people themselves.

Philip Freneau, who knew the truth as few others of his time knew it, hoped to teach it also to the people. In the time of their greatest need, he was destined to become one of their greatest spokesmen.

[29] *The Daily Advertiser,* May 6, May 27, 1791; and Jefferson to Freneau, quoted in Leary, *That Rascal Freneau,* p. 186.

20. TRIUMVIRATE

MEN AFFECT THEIR TIMES and are affected by them. The play of personality on events is often as great as the events which play upon it. Action and interaction are ceaseless, and the sum of cause and effect is written in the pages of history—indeed, is the substance of history itself.

The countryside of Monmouth was clad in cold beauty during the winter months of 1790. Only seldom did the warmth of approaching spring presage another, more heartening kind of beauty. At Mount Pleasant the loveliness of Eleanor supported the dreams of a future which many disillusions had failed to dispel in the mind of the poet. That he retained those dreams, he himself had attested on the day of his marriage.

> The native of this happy spot
> No cares of vain ambition haunt;
> Pleas'd with the partner of his nest
> Life flows—and when the dream is out,
> The earth, that once supply'd each want,
> Receives him, fainting, to her breast.[1]

It was a stoical dream no doubt, leavened by humility, appropriate to the frozen season. All dreams, the good as well as the bad, must have an end. As the present moved into the past and the future loomed between them, Freneau was shaken from his brief indulgence in domestic ease. Not ambition but the need for money was the great shadow on his new happiness. Mount Pleasant and its spreading acres could offer

[1] "Kay-Grove," in *The Daily Advertiser*, April 15, 1791.

no solution to his problems, for his mother and his sisters lived on them, eking out only a poor living from the farm. For a while it seemed as if some solution to their need for cash might be found in the claims of Agnes to lands in the Ramapo tract, land bought long ago, in 1709, by André Fresneau and his partners. Encumbered with debts, it had finally been lost in the débâcle of the family fortunes. The claims of Freneau's mother were disallowed, and this solution, like all the others, yielded no answer to the pressing needs of Philip Freneau.[2]

Peter Freneau, concerned about his brother, must have learned of his difficulties. With a wife to support and a baby coming, Philip may have appealed to him for help. Perhaps Peter, who was doing so well in Charleston, could get for him the type he needed if his newspaper was ever to be started. Here was one solution to his problem more promising than any other he considered. But this one also came to nothing. Peter could not find the type. It would take time to locate what was necessary—if it was ever located at all. Then, suddenly, another solution appeared.

It appeared, first of all, to Peter, deep down in South Carolina, where he was known for his many enterprises, not least among them his quickened interest in politics. Already known as a staunch republican, Peter was a good friend and loyal supporter of Aedanus Burke, the sole republican Representative in a state that had chosen two Federalist Senators to the national capital. The ravelled fortunes of American politics, slowly unwinding in a semblance of party policies, had brought James Madison into the House of Representatives, where he was now the leader of the opposition to the powerful Federalist Party of Alexander Hamilton. Thus, the long and withered arm of coincidence was momentarily strengthened to prod Peter, to move Burke, to stir Madison, to help Freneau. As a close collaborator of Thomas Jefferson, the Secretary of State, Madison might recommend his old classmate to Jefferson for some place in the government, in which effort he would gladly be joined by another schoolmate of the poet's, Henry (Light Horse Harry) Lee, a Virginian like Jefferson and Madison. The gallant soldier of Paulus Hook and Eutaw Springs may have read his old comrade's poem on the battle of Eutaw Springs; like Jefferson, he may have admired the poet's work. Though he was no

----

[2] Lewis Leary, *That Rascal Freneau,* p. 187. This was the first of many erosions of the lands held by the Freneaus.

republican but a Federalist, Lee held none of the more extreme, conservative views of the leaders of his party. In any event he was happy
to join Madison in his recommendation to Jefferson. And here the
machinations of coincidence were no longer needed. The circumstances
of historical necessity took over the task of embracing the necessity of
Philip Freneau.[3]

James Madison had been elected to Congress over the opposition of
Patrick Henry, a foe of the Constitution which Madison, more than
any one else, had fashioned and created. Madison was in agreement
with Henry at least in this—both were opposed to the concept of a
central government with the compulsive powers advocated by the Federalists. Madison remained opposed as the concept was steadily translated into laws which impinged on the rights of the states, and thereby
threatened the rights of the people who were, in any analysis, the
quintessential substance of the states. In the battle against the Federalists and Alexander Hamilton, their leader, Madison was now the strong
right arm of Jefferson, who had come to regret his compromise with
Hamilton on the fiscal measures which were offensive to his sense of
justice. Moreover, Hamilton's imperious conduct of the office of Secretary of the Treasury was an affront to Jefferson's democratic instincts.
The forces of reaction in the Administration of President Washington
centered in the person, they revolved about the ambition, of this charming and sagacious young man, with whom, at every stage of debate,
Jefferson was in almost constant conflict. Hamilton's economic nationalism, his hostile attitude toward the French Revolution, which Jefferson had seen close at hand and with which he sympathized more deeply,
were opposed to the profoundest beliefs and most sacred sympathies of
the Secretary of State.[4]

Within the cabinet chamber, as well as outside, the struggle between these two was further embittered as the President of the United
States, needing them both and trusting them equally, tried with diminishing success to compose their differences and to soften their animosity.
Wanting peace above all things, Washington listened with sympathy

[3] Allan Nevins, *The American States during and after the Revolution*, p. 410;
Madison to Jefferson, May 1, 1791, in Irving Brant, *James Madison*, Vol. 3,
The Father of the Constitution, 1787–1800, p. 335.

[4] C. G. Bowers, *Jefferson and Hamilton, passim;* R. A. Billington, B. L.
Lowenberg, and S. H. Brockunier, *The United States: American Democracy in
World Perspective*, p. 78; Hamilton's "Financial Reports" were the basis of his
program as Secretary of the Treasury (William Maclay, *Journal*, p. 387).

to Jefferson, and mollified Hamilton with agreement. For Hamilton, the President was a fortress behind which he was safe from the logic and ideals of Jefferson. Washington's unalterable faith in the Constitution, and Hamilton's unshakeable belief in his own infallibility, made him invulnerable in the Federalist-controlled councils of state, where Hamilton usually won his way—and his laws—and Jefferson usually lost them both. With the approval of the President behind it, any law proposed by Hamilton was assured of passage. Senator Maclay of Pennsylvania, incensed and alarmed by what he considered a perversion of the democratic process, confided to his diary the fears he hesitated to voice in public. "If there is treason in the wish," he wrote, "I retract it, but would to God this same General Washington were in heaven. We would not then have him brought forward as the constant cover to every constitutional and irrepublican act."[5]

The political family which the President had acquired included John Adams, the Vice-President, and Henry Knox, his Secretary of War. Adams, little more than a figurehead in the constitutional capacity of President of the Senate, was assailed by some powerful misgivings on the excellence of democracy. Knox, more doubtful even than Adams about the rights of the people, had already complained to Washington of the widely held belief "That the property of the United States has been protected from the confiscations of Britain by the exertions of all and therefore ought to be the common property of all." This, Knox added, "was shocking to every man of principle and property in New England." Under the leadership of a conservative and brilliant man like Hamilton, views like these, which could undermine the strong foundations of America, must be ruthlessly exterminated, and the republicans, who gave them aid and comfort, must be beaten to the ground.[6]

For the republicans the policies of the Federalists were only planned maneuvers to entrench the rich and powerful at the expense of the poor and defenseless. They detested the logic as they abhorred the actions of those who derided democracy and lauded the rule of the

[5] Maclay, *Journal*, p. xl.

[6] Knox to Washington, October 23, 1786, quoted in V. L. Parrington, *Main Currents of American Thought: The Colonial Mind*, p. 277; also Noah Brooks, *Henry Knox*, pp. 194–195. Fisher Ames would agree, for to him democracy was "an illuminated hell"; see his "Dangers of American Liberty," in *Works*, Vol. 2, p. 382.

select. The assumption of state debts, the funding of all debts, the measure to establish a Bank of the United States—what end could they serve but to enrich a small minority and benefit no one else. If the people seemed complacent about them, it was because they knew only one side of the story, a rationalized version given to them in the distorted columns of a newspaper which was completely partisan. They were deprived of the truth, for what other paper of equal power and prestige was there to refute it? *The Gazette of the United States,* subsidized by Alexander Hamilton and his friends, had moved from New York to Philadelphia along with the government, and it was still published by John Fenno, who had finally discovered which way the wind blew.[7]

Madison and Jefferson—one in the Congress, the other in the Cabinet—also knew. So different in personal appearance, they resembled each other in their keen minds, their clear understanding and appraisal of Federalist goals and policy. Both of them were opposed to an all-powerful central government which was unresponsive to the will of the people by whom and for whom, the country had been wrested from autocracy. That new central government was itself autocratic and heavily weighted with conservative, indeed, reactionary, officials. Madison, once a foremost disciple of nationalism, in a sense was still so. But he was also a republican whose belief in a strong central power did not include such predatory measures as the Federalists were so busy advancing. In any fight on special privilege Madison was always dependable. Jefferson knew this and honored him with his confidence and friendship. No one, he said, was "a man of purer integrity, more dispassionate, disinterested, and devoted to genuine Republicanism; nor could I on the whole scope of America and Europe point out an abler head." Madison, the old classmate and confidant of Philip Freneau, felt somewhat the same about the poet of Monmouth.[8]

Freneau was unaware of all the links in the chain that led from Charleston to Philadelphia to Monmouth, but on February 28, 1791, he received a letter from the Secretary of State, whom he had never met, informing him that

The Clerkship for foreign languages in my office is vacant. The salary

[7] Alexander Hamilton, *Works,* Vol. 1, p. 411; Vol. 2, pp. 254–255; Vol. 9, p. 534.
[8] L. D. White, *The Jeffersonians,* p. 273.

indeed is very low, being but two hundred and fifty dollars a year; but also it gives so little to do as not to interfere with any other calling the person may chuse, which would not absent him from the seat of government. I was told a few days ago that it might perhaps be convenient to you to accept it—if so, it is at your service. It requires no other qualifications than a moderate knowledge of the French. Should anything better turn up within my department, that might suit you, I should be very happy to bestow it as well. Should you conclude to accept the present, you may consider it as engaged to you, only be so good as to drop me a line informing me of your resolution.[9]

Madison, it was evident, had not forgotten his old friend.

John Pintard, employed on *The Daily Advertiser* in New York, had also been a translator in the State Department when the capital was in that city. Unwilling to move to Philadelphia with nothing more to live on than the pittance which that employment afforded, Pintard had resigned. He and Freneau knew each other well; both had worked on the same paper, both were known as Anti-Federalists, the poet much more prominently identified as an old revolutionist who could write with a sharp pen. Pintard was a younger man, full of drive to get ahead in the world, with a good head for business as well as a love for the gentler things of life. The dusty cubicle of a petty clerk at a ridiculous salary in a distant city did not appeal to him at all.[10]

Neither did it appeal to his friend Philip Freneau, who was still seeking a solution to the problem of making a living in Mount Pleasant. Of course, he could handle the work of translation better than most. He had more than a "moderate knowledge" of French, his own language as much as English. There was no need for him to know any Latin and Greek, though some rare papers might require some knowledge of these languages. Latin and Greek were rarely used in the parlance of diplomacy. But a greater difficulty than this deterred him. He could not leave Eleanor for such miserable pay. What would he do with it? How could he support his wife, himself, the expected baby, in the Quaker City where he had once learned a little about Brotherly Love, and where it was now almost impossible to love anyone because

[9] Jefferson to Freneau, February 28, 1791, in Thomas Jefferson, *Writings* (ed. A. A. Lipscomb and A. E. Bergh), Vol. 8, p. 133.

[10] S. G. W. Benjamin, "Notable Editors, between 1776 and 1800," *Magazine of American History,* XVII (January–June 1887), 121; Philip M. Marsh, "Philip Freneau and His Circle," *The Pennsylvania Magazine of History and Biography,* LXIII (January 1939), 37–59.

of the enormous cost of everything. With the establishment of the new capital, the cost of living had sky-rocketed to high heaven.[11]

Finally, he had not ceased hoping for a newspaper, a paper of his own. *The Monmouth Gazette,* still in the blueprint stage, might become a reality very soon, before the winter was done and the spring, already in the air, had arrived. Peter had not given up his search for type, and Philip would think no more of moving. He paid no attention to Jefferson's offer. He even failed to reply to his letter.[12]

James Madison was not to be put off so easily. He wanted to help his old friend, whom he had not seen in all the years since Princeton. Like Freneau, he had been busy—and he was still busy, in ways different from the poet's, but in works that were essentially like his. Madison's efforts, too, were political, confined for the most part to political theory rather than action. Theory was important, but only if it was translated into action. A man like Freneau might arouse the people to thought and stir them to action. He had given ample proof in the past of his power to do this. Madison was resolved to try again to enlist him in the fight that was not his—and Jefferson's—alone, but Freneau's as well.

Could Freneau be persuaded? Why not? What future was there for him, for a newspaper, for anything at all in the tiny community of Monmouth? Why not publish his paper, if he was indeed anxious to publish a paper, in the city of Philadelphia, where he could reach a greater public, a public eager for news in the city of nearly fifty thousand souls? It was the capital of America, the one important place in the whole country for "a free newspaper, meant for general circulation," where it could "be some antidote to the doctrines and discourses circulated in favor of Monarch and Aristocracy." Freneau, according to Madison, was "a man of genius, of Republican principles." Who else but he so well understood, who else could so well expose, the spurious logic of the Federalists, their canny mouthpiece Alexander Hamilton, and their ventriloquent servant John Fenno?[13]

---

[11] Susan Coolidge, *A Short History of Philadelphia,* p. 170; George Morgan, *Philadelphia: The City of Firsts,* pp. 143 ff.

[12] In any event, there is no record of a reply from Freneau (Leary, *That Rascal Freneau,* p. 188).

[13] Madison to John Simons of Alexandria, August 1, 1791, in James Madison, *Writings,* Vol. 1, p. 535 (Copy in Dreer Collection, Historical Society of Pennsylvania; original in Haverford College of Alexandria). See also *Pennsylvania Cavalcade,* p. 155; Brant, *James Madison,* Vol. 3, p. 556.

It was a powerful argument that Madison presented to Freneau when he met him in New York. Yet Freneau was not convinced. He was unequal to the task of translator—and how could he accept money for something he knew so little about? Even his French was rusty after long disuse. Madison waived aside the objections. Despite his "delicacy," Freneau, he said, was "fully equal to the task." And he would prosper with his paper also. The family would find a stimulating challenge in the bustling city of Philadelphia. For the moment Madison appeared to have impressed his friend. On May 1 he informed Jefferson that Freneau "sets out for Philadelphia today or tomorrow, though it is not improbable that he may halt in New Jersey." Naturally. Then he continued: "The more I learn of his character, talents and principles, the more I should regret his burying himself in the obscurity he had chosen in New Jersey." It was an obscurity unthinkable for a man like Freneau; certainly "there is not to be found in the whole catalogue of American Printers a single name that can approach towards a rivalship."[14]

What was Madison thinking in thus emphasizing the journalistic virtues of Freneau? Was it that he, and certainly Jefferson, desperately wanted a newspaper—any newspaper—in the capital to combat the Federalist sheet published by Fenno? The hermit of Monmouth was surely the ideal man for such a paper, and since he was planning to publish one anyway, why not in Philadelphia. If the venture failed, the assured income from the government, small as it was, would still be an anchor to windward for the poet who needed one so badly. And if it was really more bait than anchor, it was in addition a promise of support in a struggle which thus far, as a writer and a poet, he had waged singlehanded—the struggle against the antidemocratic, antirepublican forces in the nation.

When Freneau did "halt in New Jersey" overlong, Jefferson wrote to Madison, on May 9, that the poet must have "changed his mind back again." "For which I am truly sorry," he added. He was, indeed. *The Pennsylvania Daily Advertiser,* published by Benjamin Franklin Bache, and *The Daily American Advertiser,* published by John Dunlap, were not unfriendly to his views. But they were no match for the aggressive Fenno and the brilliant Hamilton. Freneau, according to Madison, was not only the equal of these as a journalist—he was

---

[14] Madison to Jefferson, May 1, 1791, in James Madison Papers, Mss., XIV-8; Freneau, *The Poems of Philip Freneau* (ed. F. L. Pattee), Vol. 1, p. 1.

superior to both of them combined. Jefferson had come to believe it
too. He wrote as much to his son-in-law, Thomas Mann Randolph, on
May 15. "We have been trying," he said, "to get another *weekly* or
half-weekly set up . . . so that it might go through the States and
furnish a *Whig vehicle* of intelligence. We hoped at one time to have
persuaded Freneau to set up here, but failed." It was true. Freneau,
still hesitant, had finally decided to refuse Jefferson's offer of a government stipend for an essentially political purpose.[15]

Did Freneau refuse because of any ethical qualms at accepting a
public subsidy for a private purpose? If so, the moral problem was that
of Jefferson and Madison as much as his. A man, even an impractical
and impoverished idealist, may easily succumb to the bait of bread. But
Freneau did not succumb—nor was it entirely a question of ethics. He
had been frustrated so many times before in his undertakings that
Madison's warning about Monmouth was doubtless a valid one. The
prospects for success in the backwoods of New Jersey were no more
alluring because it was his home, among his neighbors, close to his
family. The publication of a newspaper anywhere, even in New York,
which he again considered briefly, was impossible without money, a
good deal of money. The lure of publishing a paper of his own was a
great one, but could he have that in Monmouth, even if Peter, still
searching, found the necessary type?

Perhaps there was a good future in a real newspaper, published in
a large city, backed by powerful friends, in a cause so close to his heart.
On the other hand, it was highly probable that the new venture proposed by Madison and Jefferson, should he embark on it, would subject him to slanders and insults by those powerful enough to destroy
him. He had been attacked so many times before—would he not be
pummelled many times again by such determined antagonists as the
Federalists? The bait held out to the poet was on a sharp hook which
would lacerate him unmercifully. He had never counted the pain
before, and he had never won any marked measure of esteem for all
his pain. He knew that he would stand alone—his friends would remain in shadow—a solitary and puny David, vilified as never before,
in journalistic combat with the Goliaths of Federalism who were
stoutly armored in the wealth, the power, and the public renown of
their leaders. The poison at the tip of their tongues, at the tip of their

[15] Jefferson to Thomas Mann Randolph, May 9, May 15, 1791, in Thomas
Jefferson, *Writings* (ed. P. L. Ford), Vol. 5, pp. 335–337. See also Leary, *That
Rascal Freneau*, pp. 188, 386.

pens, would be the bait itself, the pitiful pay of 250 dollars a year. They would say he wasn't the real master of the paper but its servant, the puppet not the speaker. That the voice that spoke, the hand that wrote, was not his but another's—Jefferson's—who had bribed and seduced him for ends that were not the government's but Jefferson's own, for his own ambitions and his own lust for power. It would be an intolerable situation for any sensitive and decent person. For Philip Freneau it posed a soul-searching dilemma.[16]

Like Jefferson he was a radical, a dissenter, for whom a dedicated cause was more than a mere struggle, an ideal more than a contest between right and wrong, between black and white. The dim greys of ethical concepts did not always provide acceptable answers nor clarify the blurred truths which were at issue. The problem of good and evil was also a problem of means and ends, for the means may infect the ends and cancel them out completely. Who could judge the moral basis for action when the basis was itself compounded of many morals to which precedent and prejudice had imparted the respectable patina of time and the holy sanctity of age? Whatever Philip Freneau might decide to do, he must resolve the dilemma of personal interest and public good with rationalizations acceptable at least to himself—if not altogether to James Madison and Thomas Jefferson. And his decision, as he revolved it in his mind, was influenced less by any involved system of thought than by his simple feelings of faith. All slanders and vilifications might come, but would liberty and democracy ever come to pass without them?

No squeamish conscience, no ethical debate, could provide a persuasive answer. Nor could Jefferson either, though he pleaded with Freneau in person to accept what he had already refused. Jefferson had traveled the long distance to New York to meet him at Mrs. Ellsworth's boarding house, where additional inducements failed to move the stubborn man.[17]

Deeply disappointed, Jefferson again wrote to Madison on July 21

---

[16] The entire problem of the ethical questions involved in the employment of Freneau is considered in Philip M. Marsh, "The Griswold Story of Freneau and Jefferson," *American Historical Review,* LI, 1 (October 1945), 68–73; and by S. E. Forman in "The Political Activities of Philip Freneau," *Johns Hopkins University Studies,* Vol. 20, Nos. 9–10 (1902), pp. 1–105 *passim.*

[17] Jefferson to President of U.S., September 9, 1792, in Jefferson, *Writings* (Ford), Vol. 6, p. 107.

about his latest failure. "I am sincerely sorry that Freneau has declined coming here," he informed him. "His own genius in the first place is so superior to that of his competitors." Why was this man so concerned about pulling up stakes in Monmouth, about making a living from his paper, about supporting Eleanor and the expected baby? "I should have given him the perusal of all my letters of foreign intelligence and all foreign newspapers; the publication of all proclamations and other public notices within my department, and the printing of the laws, which added to his salary would have been a considerable aid." Perhaps Madison, who knew him so much better, could still persuade his friend to accept the post. Perhaps.[18]

Madison tried again—and received a letter from Freneau promising "a decisive answer" in a few days. If he could get Francis Childs of *The Daily Advertiser* to finance the project and John Swaine, his partner, to print the paper in Philadelphia, he would accept the job as editor, with only one-third of the profits for his work—if there were profits, but with no responsibility for losses, if there were losses. Nothing was sure—nothing, that is, but the princely pay as translator, and a small newspaper as a weapon for democracy. The arrangement was completed. The parties agreed; and Freneau, yielding at last, gave Madison his "decisive answer."[19]

Querulous critics have raised heavy eyebrows at Freneau's acceptance of the juicier bait with which Jefferson had sweetened his hook. Let them talk and grimace—Hamilton and his friends were supporting the redoubtable Fenno and his complacent *Gazette*. They had abundant means to do so. Any government funds that fell into the coffers of Freneau's paper were legally expended for the purpose they were intended for. Freneau must render a service to the State Department which he was well qualified to perform. In addition, he must pay out of his own pocket for translations he could not himself make. Above all, he would wage the same war on the same principles he had fought from the remote days of Princeton. Let them slander him, let them crucify him; it was his duty to the common people, the confused and harassed little people of America, to teach them, to guide them, to arouse them

---

[18] *Ibid.,* and Forman, "The Political Activities," p. 31.

[19] Freneau to Madison, July 25, 1791, in Madison Papers, Mss., XIV–8; see also Freneau, *Poems* (Pattee), Vol. 1, p. lii; and Forman, "The Political Activities," p. 31.

in this new battle of an old and endless war, in which liberties already won were in danger of being lost again. In such a battle, Philip Freneau was prepared "to sacrifice other considerations" and fight once more.

On August 16, 1791, he received his official appointment from Thomas Jefferson.[20]

[20] August 16, 1791, Jefferson, *Writings* (Ford), Vol. 5, p. 336; Forman, "The Political Activities," p. 32.

21. *THE NATIONAL GAZETTE*

COMING EVENTS, so it is said, cast their shadows before them. It is not unusual for events, long finished, to project shadows after they have ceased to be. The light of a distant star, limitless in space, is visible though the time of its passage is infinite. The beam of a single sun may outlast the source from which it came. And words, like stars, still shed their light long after they have themselves passed into deep oblivion. For the spirit of man contains as many systems, and as spacious, as the universe it inhabits.

Philip Freneau, while preparing a prospectus for the new paper, stayed on in Mount Pleasant keeping watch with Eleanor for another birth than that of *The National Gazette: A Periodical Miscellany of News, Politics, History, and Polite Literature.* While notices of the projected journal appeared in *The Freeman's Journal* of Philadelphia, *The Daily Advertiser* of New York, and other papers across the country, he waited for his first-born to appear. On September 20 Eleanor gave birth to a daughter, Helena, and Philip, learning that John Swaine was ready for him in the Quaker City, left for the greatest adventure of his writing career. He had his baby—and now, unbelievably, he had his own paper.[1]

Freneau had used many pseudonyms in the past, according to the custom of the time. On occasion he would use them again—names like "Sinbat the Sailor," or just plain "Sinbat"—but only for his poems or tales of the sea which had no relation to the main purpose of the paper. Everything else that he wrote, whether political or not, would be shielded by no anonymity, masked by no subterfuge. His name

[1] Freneau Family Bible.

would appear at the masthead, and if there were brickbats, he would be a visible target for all attack. John Fenno, guarding the ramparts of *The Gazette of the United States*, would not hesitate to use them.

John Fenno, born in Boston and the son of a leather dresser and ale-house keeper, had been successively, but with no conspicuous success, an usher in Samuel Holdbrook's writing school, a secretary to General Artemus Ward, and a small businessman. Failing in business, he had turned to the printing trade in New York in 1789, establishing, with the help of Alexander Hamilton, *The Gazette of the United States,* which he moved to Philadelphia when his benefactor, as Secretary of the Treasury, accompanied the government to the new capital. It was Fenno's declared purpose to give a dignified, discreet account of the news in his tiny sheet of three columns, but the exigencies of partisan propaganda soon transformed the paper into a medium for the conservative policies of Hamilton and the Federalists. For this, Fenno was rewarded not only with most of the public printing, under the control of the Treasury Department, but with additional financial help from Hamilton himself as well as from his political friends.[2]

One of them, John Adams, the Vice-President of the United States, had already contributed to the paper, not indeed money, but some peculiar articles under the name of "Davila." John Adams, almost a legend of the Revolution, and a cousin of Sam Adams, the fiery old radical of Boston, had set forth his strange ideas of democracy, ideas which men of single mind and many memories could scarcely understand. "Take away thrones and crowns from among men," John Adams had written, "and there will soon be an end of all dominion and justice." True, he had once written to Sam Adams "that all good government is and must be Republican," but he also believed that "all men are bad by nature; they will not fail to show that natural depravity of heart whenever they have a fair opportunity." With relentless logic he had favored the rule of the elite and the wealthy, with certain brakes to balance their authority. In such wise, "The people of the United States may probably be induced to regard and obey the laws without requiring the experiment of courts and titles." Fearing all radical innovations, Adams was equally opposed to the unfettered aggression by the few and the unhampered power of the many. Not nearly as partisan as Hamilton, he was nevertheless a firm pillar of Washington's Administration and a stout supporter of the Federalist Party.

[2] Fenno Article in *The Dictionary of American Biography,* Vol. 6, p. 325.

With the help of John Fenno, that party would keep the republicans from undermining the government or weakening the Administration. They would see to it that the upstart from Monmouth and his puny paper were never a threat to their dominion.[3]

What about other threats, not yet considered because they were so remote from the printing shop of Philip Freneau? The French Revolution, sparked by centuries of tyranny and injustice and fired by the glory and success of the American Revolution, had cut down an ancient and seemingly invulnerable autocracy. Camille Desmoulins and the common people gathered in the Palais Royal had rejoiced over the victory of the rights of man—and feudalism had fallen with the Bastille. Now the Revolution was menaced by intervention and encirclement. England, against whom the American Revolution had so recently been fought, was the enemy of this new revolution also, which this time was not against her, though equally dangerous to her power. America owed so much—perhaps everything—to France (to her people more than to her rulers). To the French people, the conquest of a powerful political and commercial rival was of less interest than the destruction of tyranny. America could never forget its debt to France, but it was more and more confused by the conflicting propaganda which stirred the people to heated debate and threatened further dissension where so much already existed. To their own problems were added those of a war-torn Europe. For Federalists and Anti-Federalists alike there was a definite connection between the revolution that had begun in France and the one that was not yet quite finished in America. Democracy was on the march in France; its people were also battling for the rights of man. In both countries the march, the battle, were essentially the same.[4]

Old barriers to understanding and accommodation were raised still

---

[3] John Adams, *Works,* Vol. 6, pp. 483–484; also, Adams, "Defence of the Constitution," in *Works,* Vol. 6, pp. 9, 57, 97; R. A. Billington, B. L. Lowenberg, and S. H. Brockunier, *The United States: American Democracy in World Perspective,* p. 103. Parrington's views on Adams as a political thinker are perceptive and probing (V. L. Parrington, *Main Currents of American Thought: The Colonial Mind,* pp. 311–312). See also, *The Gazette of the United States,* March 1790; and S. E. Forman, "The Political Activities of Philip Freneau," *Johns Hopkins University Studies,* Vol. 20, Nos. 9–10 (1902), p. 37.

[4] F. R. A. Chateaubriand, *Voyage en Amérique et en Italie,* pp. 21–23, 94; A. H. Wharton, *Social Life in the Early Republic,* pp. 16–20; Leo Gershoy, *The French Revolution and Napoleon,* pp. 172 ff.

higher, as old clashes were exacerbated by new ones. John Quincy Adams, son of the Vice-President, was writing articles for *The Columbian Centinel* of Boston under the name of "Publicola" in which he argued against the right of a majority to change what they disliked in defiance of "the eternal and immutable laws of justice and of morality."[5] These "eternal laws" were now being abrogated in France, just as the Jeffersonian democrats, who opposed the measures of Hamilton, were clamoring to abrogate them in America. The "immutable laws of justice and morality" appeared to be the special provenance of the rulers in France and America alike. In America they were embedded in the measures clearly set forth by the Secretary of the Treasury in his "Financial Reports." Hamilton, slender as a rapier and equally incisive, went straight to the heart of his major problem, which was finance. Through money power the government could, and must, be made all-powerful, an injunction that a complacent and obedient Congress would follow to the letter. All debts would be paid at face value; all state debts would be assumed by the whole people; revenue would be obtained by a whisky tax and a tariff on imports; and finally, a national bank was to be chartered by the government. Hamilton's proposals were not compounded of justice and morality, yet they did possess some virtues of their own. They would restore the national credit, without which the young republic could scarcely prosper; they would bring in revenue sorely needed to give it strength and power; above all, they would make the central government the focus of the people's thought and allegiance, instead of dissipating their loyalty in fragments among the states. To build an effective union which was the master rather than the servant of the citizens, these measures were plausible instruments.[6] Wealthy speculators, who had obtained government scrip from starving veterans and impoverished citizens at eight or ten cents on the dollar, would garner profits that were not only unconscionable but fantastically immoral. The national bank—of no possible use to the millions who had nothing—would provide additional means through credit for those who already had so much. The assumption of state debts would only mean higher taxes for the people, the majority of whom were already burdened beyond endurance. The

      [5] *The Columbian Centinel*, articles by "Publicola," June 8 to July 27, 1791; also Parrington, *Main Currents of American Thought*, Vol. 1, p. 325; John Adams, *Works*, Vol. 1, pp. 70–71.

      [6] Billington, *et al.*, *The United States*, pp. 78 ff; Alexander Hamilton, *Works*, Vol. 2, pp. 254–255; William Maclay, *Journal*, pp. 179 ff.

citizens of a state with no debts whatever would be subject to the debts of states which had been profligate with their resources. In addition, the farmers, with no other method to transport their grain save in the form of whisky, would be further taxed on their thrift and industry. These were vices which could scarcely be transformed into virtues.[7]

That was not all. Some of these measures might fairly come within the terms of the Constitutional powers granted to the Congress. But where was the power for chartering a national bank? If, as Hamilton cogently argued, it fell within the principle of "implied powers," to be interpreted by means of a catch-all principle of "loose construction," then why not stretch that principle to any ends, extend its elastic qualities to circumscribe all possible limits? The Constitution would become nothing but a legal façade, behind which the monarchical, aristocratic, predatory interests could operate without the least embarrassment or scruple and with complete impunity, while the democratic liberties of the people, one by one, were inevitably and ruthlessly destroyed. In America the Revolution itself was in danger—even as it was in France.[8]

As Congress, as the people, debated the important issues, John Fenno spread them on his small sheet, *The Gazette of the United States.* On October 31, 1791, Philip Freneau's paper began to publicize them also. The first issue of *The National Gazette* had finally appeared, and its editor, the master of a journal now as once he had been master of a vessel, was in excellent spirits. He had never peered too closely into the future, and the future, while it often troubled him, was rarely more than a minatory finger, never a threatening, closed fist. With *The National Gazette* launched on the choppy waters of Philadelphia politics, the future seemed rosy enough, and if the waters were rough, they offered no immediate cause for concern to an old mariner who had known storms and hurricanes in his years of sailing. Eleanor and the baby, for the time being, were safe in Mount Pleasant, and he was free, free to fight if necessary, to enjoy himself if possible.

To some extent it seemed possible. Alone in the big city, Freneau was glad to meet the others, the men and women, who shared his views and respected his position. He had earned a modest fame during the Revolution, and *The National Gazette* was making him still

---

[7] *Ibid.;* George Gibbs, *Memoirs of the Administration of Washington and John Adams,* Vol. I, p. 62.

[8] Maclay, *Journal,* p. 151; Billington, *et al., The United States,* p. 77; Chateaubriand, *Voyage,* p. 94.

better known among the people his poetry would never reach. They found him attractive as a person, "Very gentlemanlike in his manners, and very entertaining in his conversation." It also appeared that he was "A great favorite with the ladies."[9] No longer shy of women, he was most attentive to the sex that was peculiarly susceptible to a ready tongue and a smooth pen. Writers, whether they waved their pens like wands or wielded them like weapons, held a certain fascination for the ladies. Poets, though they nodded like Homer or even if they snored, were creatures more divine than human.

It was possible that Philip, whose past experiences had afforded him few occasions to become "a great favorite with the ladies," had gained some proficiency in the gentle art of nibbling since his marriage to Eleanor. Before that no record save his own rare verses gave any intimation of sentiments that might make him a victim of feminine charm. His poem "To Lydia," published in 1788 and often reprinted, was the only one after the Amanda episode in which he had manifested the perturbations of love—for a Quaker lady who was evidently far beyond his reach. Lydia, like Shakespeare's dark lady of the sonnets, remains a mystery. The feelings of Freneau were discreetly exposed in the half-serious, half-playful musings of a rejected lover.[10]

> To what fond swain shall I resign
> The bosom that shall ne'er be mine;
> Those eyes, like diamonds, finely set
> In ivory—how shall I forget?
> Delighted with a face so fair,
> I half forgot my weight of care.[11]

We do not know whether the editor of *The National Gazette* was involved with any *one* lady however entertaining his conversation or attractive his manners. Despite these helpful attributes, he was no

[9] R. W. Griswold, "Philip Freneau: The Poet of the Revolution," *Graham's Magazine*, XLVII, 3 (September 1855), 197–199; see also Duc de la Rochefoucauld Liancourt, *Travels through the United States of North America*, Vol. II, p. 97.

[10] Avis Lockwood, "Commonplace Book," Ms.; "To Lydia" in Freneau, *Poems Written between the Years 1768 and 1794*. The description of Freneau in R. W. Griswold. *The Poets and Poetry of America*, pp. 31 ff. is the one given by L. Bailey in Freneau, *Poems Written and Published during the American Revolutionary War*.

[11] "To Lydia," in Freneau, *Poems Written between the Years 1786 and 1794*.

dashing figure. His slight stoop made him appear as a "small man," while his clothes, somewhat better for the ministrations of Eleanor, were never in the latest mode. Since his income was a small one, he lived on little, and he often paid out for foreign translations more than he received from the State Department in salary. His father-in-law gave him scarcely any help at all, because Samuel Forman, though once prosperous, had been despoiled by British and Tory raids on the Monmouth countryside. Samuel Forman, too old to rally from the wounds of outrageous fortune, was looking to his son Denise to recover what appeared irrevocably lost. Denise, together with "Black David," his nephew, had fought bravely in the Revolution. They were real heroes —even reckless devils, in war as in peace.[12]

Philip was not like these. In his own way he was a hero of sorts, but not to the ladies and gentlemen of Philadelphia. They aped the aristocrats of Europe in their manners as in their dress—often in their ideas as well. For them, a poor poet, the editor of a radical newspaper to boot, was of no consequence whatever. In a city of flashing figures, this one shone with only a pallid light.

Philadelphia, chosen as the interim capital of America for a period of ten years, was also the capital of wealth and fashion. Until the permanent seat of government was established according to the plans of Major L'Enfant in the "mud-hole" on the Potomac, it would grow in power and population as ever-increasing hordes flocked there for profit and pleasure, both of which appeared available in great abundance. One surprised observer confided to his receptive diary that he had never known a city with so many bastards, where women "become mothers for no reason except the pleasure they get out of it."[13] The Quaker City, no longer confining its love to brothers alone, was already the home of forty-five thousand assorted souls spreading beyond the strict confines of the Delaware and the Schuylkill. Soon profiteering in rent—the first scourge of prosperity—became so great that "some of the blessings anticipated from the removal of Congress to this city are already beginning to be apparent." Even on the outskirts rents increased from fourteen, sixteen, and eighteen pounds to twenty-five, twenty-eight, and thirty pounds a year, sums which were considered

[12] S. S. Forman, *Narrative of a Journey Down the Ohio and Mississippi,* pp. 10–11; M. S. Austin, *Philip Freneau,* p. 147; Freneau to Col. Jonathan Forman, June 8, 1793, in Freneau Collection (Rutgers).

[13] George Morgan, *Philadelphia: The City of Firsts,* p. 143.

"oppressive" by those who had to pay them or else sleep in the open.[14]

In the city itself the situation was worse, if possible. Tiny homes were built on narrow streets, as much alike as could be contrived, so that at night—even during the day—it took more than a keen eye and a strong scent to know one from the other. In spite of the cobblestones on the broader highways the roads were bad; while water was only obtained with the utmost difficulty from the few pumps that were available. Save for the stenches which blew across the plain from the waterfront, Philadelphia was a clean city, and a pleasant one in those fortunate parts where the monotony of its vast rectangular blocks was happily broken by ampler homes of the wealthy Quakers whose charming gardens and wide lawns were like oases of sudden beauty in the expanding desert of the commonplace. The "large, elegant building" of the Capitol, refurbished for the occasion of its newly acquired importance, and enlarged with new wings, gave to Independence Hall a luster and dignity that reflected the high eminence of Philadelphia as the first city in the United States of America. The President, as was fitting for the supreme leader in the land, occupied the mansion of his good friend Robert Morris, a fine, three-story brick house near Sixth and High, flanked by gardens on either side and only a few paces removed from the imposing Galloway mansion which was now occupied by Morris himself.[15]

For all classes the person of the President was a rich legend and a revered presence. Yet rumors of princely parties, lavish levees, and royal retinues which swirled and eddied about his Administration set some people to wondering whether Philadelphia was the capital of a republic or the adjunct of a monarchy. Chateaubriand, looking on with astonishment, thought that the elegant dress and equipage of the wealthy, the ostentation and airs of the powerful, were the same he had always known in Europe, where there were no republics and no presidents.[16] Washington himself, careful to observe the protocol of his position, was in reality bored by it. He would have preferred the solitude and simplicity of Mount Vernon, managing his large estates and those of Martha, varying his meticulous duties of overseer, bookkeeper, and farmer with an evening of good fellowship with a few

[14] Susan Coolidge, *A Short History of Philadelphia*, pp. 170–175; see also Griswold, *Poets and Poetry*, pp. 31 ff; Kenneth B. Umbreit, *Our Eleven Chief Justices*, p. 147. The Federal Census for 1790 gave the population as 44,996.
[15] Morgan, *Philadelphia*, p. 145; E. P. Oberholtzer, *Robert Morris*, p. 272.
[16] Chateaubriand, *Voyage*, p. 23.

close friends. The purple and panoply of his exalted office did not appeal to his more robust and earthy tastes.

His friend and close adviser, Robert Morris, who had earned several reputations, not the least flattering of which was as financier of the Revolution, was of a different mind. Possessed of great wealth and an even greater desire to parade it, he was now the Senator from Pennsylvania and a Federalist who loved the aristocratic refinements which his tastes demanded and his money provided. His "princely entertainments," mounted in an atmosphere of luxury and grandeur, were famous for their exotic foods and rare wines, their elegant and resplendent company. His speculations, fabulous and sometimes risky, would one day bring him to bankruptcy—and to imprisonment—but he was still beyond the pale of criticism, except by the "anarchists"— those despicable democrats who circulated the story of his fortune which, they said, was the fruit of his friendship with the government and those who controlled it. What other fruits there were, who gathered them, and what gifts were made to nourish their growth, could not be known. These remained in the private domain of the rich, who cultivated the powerful, and had their "entertainments" too, not as lavish as those of Morris, yet equally gaudy with alien finery and no less watchful for future favors. Abigail Adams, the attractive and observant wife of the Vice-President, was unhappy about the increasing demands on her time. "I should spend a very dissipated winter," she protested, "if I were to accept one-half the invitations I receive."[17]

Abigail was not like the women of fashion who did little more than build up the fences for their husbands. They vied with each other for attention not only in their parties, but also in their persons. Many of them built "magnificent structures" on their heads, ornate and fantastic beyond compare; their white and lovely bosoms were hardly concealed behind low bodices and fancy fabrics. They had their portraits done by Gilbert Stuart and John Trumbull and Willson Peale. Their "Dancing Assemblies" were the occasions for an ample display of wealth and beauty—and of wealth more than beauty. Their cream-colored coaches, their servants decked out in liveries of white cloth trimmed with scarlet or orange, their Paris gowns, their sparkling jewels, all the fripperies of a royal court, including the bowing and

[17] John Farris, *The Romance of Old Philadelphia*, p. 107 (see also Oberholtzer, *Robert Morris*, pp. 240, 270). Abigail Adams is quoted in Lewis Leary, *That Rascal Freneau*, p. 194.

scraping, the salutations of royal vintage—all these created an atmosphere strange indeed in a republic, offensive to republicans who were
outraged and affronted by a spectacle only seen in part, in part reported
to them with fabulous trimmings. Some of them saw, they heard, at
first hand, what the people rarely witnessed. What they saw, what they
heard, revolted them at the "royalty, nobility, and vile pageantry, by
which a few of the human race lord it over and tread on the necks of
their fellow mortals."[18] To the common people the pomp and pageantry
was nothing less than an extension of the government itself, and the
private proceedings were confused in their minds with those more public ones of the Federalists.

The city could boast of other, of better, things than these, things of
a spiritual and cultural nature, some of which contributed a bit of
pleasure even to the masses. They were not all interested, yet all were
proud of the Franklin Library with its growing list of volumes. They
could not all afford, but many could attend, the plays at the Southwark
Theatre, or the circus on High Street, the wax works of Bowen, and the
Museum of Peale. They did not read too much—many could not read
at all—and the field of letters was a barren one in Philadelphia. Still,
a young and promising author like Charles Brockden Brown, who was
imbued with strong ethical notions, would soon be writing the social
novels of the new nation. This Quaker lad, destined to become the
"Father of the American Novel," had been inspired by the teachings
of William Godwin and Mary Wollstonecraft; he had already given a
foretaste of his radical views in *The Rhapsodist,* whose revolutionary
overtones were later justified by his complete support of Jefferson's
policies. More profound than any writings of the day were the debates
of the American Philosophical Society, which gave to Philadelphia an
aura of learning it otherwise might have lacked. It was still only an aura,
a nimbus more colorful than substantial, as any keen-eyed observer
could detect. John Adams' daughter, visiting from Boston, believed
that the people back home were better educated than those of the
Quaker City.[19]

One of the members of the Philosophical Society was the Secretary
of State, Thomas Jefferson, whose education and intellect were beyond
question. Equally certain was his distaste for the opulence of the rich

---

[18] Maclay, *Journal,* p. 151; see also Coolidge, *History of Philadelphia,* p. 170.
[19] Agnes Repplier, *Philadelphia: The Place and the People,* pp. 285, 288–293.

and his sympathy for the poor. A rich man himself, as well as a learned one, Jefferson had little patience with the show of luxury and the spectacle of finery that pervaded the private and public life of Philadelphia. Tall, lean, sandy-haired, ruddy-faced, aristocratic and aloof, chilly and charming at the same time, he was almost ascetic in his tastes (despite a paradoxical love for exotic foods and rare wines), an epicure in his physical and in his spiritual preferences. Deeply troubled by the arrogance and presumptions of those who held the wealth and power of the country in their hands, what he had seen of the American and French Revolutions had given him insights into the life and hopes of the masses which he had once known only by hearsay. His own youth had been different from theirs. It had been made pleasant and gracious by wealth and refinement, by learning and beauty. He knew the work of the greatest minds of Europe, the spacious thoughts of the libertarians and philosophers of England and France. They had taught him a great deal about the burdens of injustice which the little people of the world were bearing. The physiocrats of France and the thinkers of England had suggested some of the ways for lightening those burdens. They too were concerned with the multiple facets of the human spirit. In addition he knew the law—he was once a practicing lawyer himself— a law written in the strange language of ancient precedent to curb that spirit, though it was the nature of man to brook no curb of his elemental and natural rights. Jefferson, a farmer among his many other professions, was partial to the tiller of the soil above any other class in the country; and as a man of culture he had a weakness for the educated and trained mind in government. But it was the spirit of man that interested him above all else, its freest flowering that was the sum of all things. Only in a democratic nation could it express itself fully, untrammelled by ancient privilege, inherited blood, or the power of wealth. He had put his ideas into one of the noblest papers ever penned by man, and it had been affirmed in the sacrifices of a whole people. And now?[20]

Jefferson was amazed and distressed by the mincing manners of the official "court" at Philadelphia. Even more, he was outraged at the laws proposed by his colleague Alexander Hamilton and passed by an acquiescent Congress, with but a few stout defenders of the faith—his faith and theirs—to oppose them. The manners, the luxuries, the laws,

---

[20] Dumas Malone, *Jefferson and the Rights of Man, passim.*

they were all of a pattern, and the pattern was strangely unlike that of any democracy he had ever dreamt of.

So it also appeared to his friend James Madison, a small, sedate man, reserved yet precise, shy but alert. Madison knew all about the wheels and cogs of the Federalist machine from the inside of Congress. As well as Jefferson, he knew whose hands moved them, whose mind powered them. He was not opposed to a strong Federal union—he was one of the great architects of its structure. Nor did he question the need for some proper limits on the power of majorities. There were men of integrity among the Federalists as well as in the camp of the opposition, and they honestly held the welfare and future of America as dearly as did the Jeffersonians. But Madison could not believe that to build a strong government it was necessary to enlist the baser passions and selfish ambitions of the men who possessed the ability to provide that strength. The people, the majority, must not be victimized by measures that appealed to the cupidity of the few and left the many to their own poor resources.[21]

If the President's prestige was behind the power of Hamilton and the Federalists, he was nevertheless not among those whom Madison and Jefferson considered as foes to democracy. Washington was only a foe to weakness, in the army or in the government, and for him no government could long survive unless it was strong. Conservative in his views, he wanted only to strengthen the nation and accepted the measures of his persuasive Secretary of the Treasury because he was convinced they would accomplish this purpose. If the rich and powerful were the chief beneficiaries of these measures, they were also the stout bulwarks, the guiding geniuses, of the country that was destined for a great future.[22]

These were also the views, these the substance of the articles, which appeared regularly in the columns of *The Gazette of the United States.* John Fenno published what the Federalists prescribed for him. Of the

[21] See Irving Brant, *James Madison,* Vol. 3, *The Father of the Constitution, 1787–1800,* and Madison, *Writings,* Vol. 2, p. 411, Vol. 3, and 4; also,*American Historical Review,* II, 1896–1897), 443–460, 675–687; *The Federalist* (ed. Jacob Cooke); and C. E. Merriam, *A History of American Political Theories,* pp. 100–122.

[22] Jefferson to Washington, September 9, 1791, in Thomas Jefferson, *Writings* (ed. A. A. Lipscomb and A. E. Bergh), Vol. 8, p. 405 ("Anas," Vol. 6, p. 231).

twelve newspapers in Philadelphia, only Fenno's had a circle of readers whose diameter reached beyond the limits of the Quaker City. Not even Bache's *Aurora,* republican and well-reputed, had achieved such an influence. More pacific than controversial, *The Aurora*'s appeal was limited, its circulation was local rather than general, its interest strictly confined to the more sedate among the liberal readers of Philadelphia.[23]

The National Gazette had larger aims. Freneau's purpose was to interest and attract readers in all parts of the nation. If it was to be a paper for the people, then *The National Gazette* must reach all the people, everywhere. They were the voice, the only real voice, of America, despite the doubts expressed by Hamilton about *vox populi*. If the people were informed and aroused they could be depended on to preserve the liberty which they had won on the field of battle and were in danger of losing on the field of politics. Liberty, unless nourished by democracy, would surely perish. For liberty to prevail, democracy must flourish throughout the land.

To ensure the widest possible circulation for his paper, Freneau's republican friends were actively soliciting subscriptions in many states. Henry Lee, more Federalist than republican, was helping in Richmond. It was natural for Jefferson, with the aid of Madison, to help in spreading the list of readers beyond the boundaries of Philadelphia, beyond the borders of Pennsylvania itself, into Virginia, into Massachusetts, into Georgia and Kentucky, further even than these if possible. The readers of *The National Gazette* were promised not only the news but "such political essays as have a tendency to promote the general interest of the Union." The editor, being also a poet, summarized his conduct of the journal in verse:

> Thus launched as we are in an ocean of news,
> In hopes that your pleasure our pains will repay,
> All honest endeavors the author will use
> To furnish a feast for the grave and the gay;
> At least he'll essay such a track to pursue,
> That the world shall approve—and his news shall be true.[24]

[23] P. L. Ford, "Freneau's *National Gazette*," *The Nation*, Vol. 60, No. 1547 (February 21, 1895), pp. 143–144; Leary, *That Rascal Freneau*, p. 167.

[24] *The National Gazette*, October 31, 1791; also Madison, *Writings*, Vol .6, p. 62.

The event would reveal how much the world would approve, and whether it approved at all. It might not even agree with the opinions expressed by Madison in his letters to Charles Simons of Alexandria and Mann Page of Fredericksburg that Freneau was "a man of genius and great integrity." His integrity, especially, would soon be attacked.[25]

[25] Madison to Jefferson, May 1, 1791, in Brant, *Madison,* Vol. 3, p. 335.

22. THE ISSUE OF DEMOCRACY

PHILIP FRENEAU, in the first months of his direction of *The National Gazette,* hewed close to the line promised in the first issue. Without comment he ran the complete "Report on Manufactures" prepared by Hamilton. The official bulletins of Congressional action were printed without editorial reflections. In his effort at strict impartiality in the news, he gave fair coverage to both sides of all questions, without indulging in any personal bias or criticism. The writings of others, the contributions of James Madison and Hugh Brackenridge, raised no dust in the columns of *The National Gazette,* for they were printed only in the interest of the "best hosts of public liberty and the strongest bulwarks of public safety"—the plain people, "who provided at once their own food and their own clothing." These contributions were not as yet openly connected with the conflict inside Congress or the Cabinet. Nor were the excerpts from Robespierre's speech to the National Assembly of France, and from Thomas Paine's "Thoughts on the Establishment of a Mint in the United States," which Freneau published as soon after they arrived as possible.[1] *The National Gazette* was no more than a mild irritant to John Fenno and his supporters. The real problems of America had not yet been touched on by Freneau.

His adversaries would hear of them soon enough, and they would learn, as Freneau learned, of the views of other men on problems simi-

[1] *The National Gazette,* various issues; the Brackenridge article in *The National Gazette,* February 2, 1792; the article from Thomas Paine, November 17, 1791; and one on Robespierre, December 19, 1791.

lar to these. Saint Simon, who had fought for America against the British at Yorktown, was making the point that a revolution is not only the end of an old order but also the beginning of a new one. Revolution was an endless process, while victory alone never solved the crucial problems which must be faced and solved before it was completed. "I felt," said Claude Henri, Baron de Saint Simon, "that the American Revolution marked the beginning of a new political era; that this Revolution would necessarily set in motion important progressive currents in our general civilization and that it would before long occasion great changes in the social order." To avoid, to prevent such changes was the prime object of the Federalists. To advance them was the aim of the republicans. Reduced to its simplest terms, that was the single, overriding issue between them.[2]

The issue was slowly, covertly, set forth in the pages of *The National Gazette*. Its editor was still writing his verses, some of them appearing over the pseudonym of "Sinbat the Sailor" or just "Sinbat." As the circulation of the paper steadily increased, its influence became more evident. By March 1792 readers were sending in letters which the editor was not displeased to print. While maintaining a pose of strict neutrality he provided ample space to every assault on the bills before Congress of which he disapproved. The excise laws, the funding system, the national bank—all were subjected to the closest scrutiny and attacked as plain abridgements of the country's liberties. The issue of March 1 contained the letter of a "Farmer," who complained that the "accumulation of that power which is conferred by wealth in the hands of a few is the perpetual source of oppression and neglect to the rest of mankind." Hamilton was pictured as the culprit who catered to the rich, and one writer, who signed himself "Brutus," proclaimed the iniquity of the funding system and the proposed plan for taxation. According to the writer, these were nothing less than conspiracies to perpetuate the power of the Federalists and their Secretary of the Treasury. "Brutus" hammered away on this theme from one issue to the next, deploring the low estate of decency in America. "Let the Secretary of the Treasury and his adherents beware," he cried out in a final blast.[3]

Slowly the Federalists began to take notice of *The National Gazette*.

[2] Frank E. Manuel, *The New World of Henri St. Simon*, p. 20 (see also p. 15); and P. L. Ford, "Freneau's *National Gazette*," *The Nation*, Vol. 60, No. 1547 (February 21, 1895), pp. 143–144.

[3] *The National Gazette*, March 1, March 19, 1792.

Tentatively they ridiculed its editor's poems. Gradually they sensed the purpose and direction of his policies. At last they recognized it for what it was—the product, according to John Fenno, of "mad dogs," "audacious scribblers," and "disordered imaginations."[4] The battle was joined, and it was a battle in which no quarter would be asked or given. Not two enemies were here warring for personal prestige or popular favor. Two theories of government, two philosophies of state, two ways of political, social, and economic life were fighting for the conscience of America. The struggle would have a profound effect on the time itself. The concepts which underlay the victories and the defeats, the words and the thoughts, would be important for a long time to come.

The opening guns in the new war were fired not in Philadelphia but in the home of the Connecticut Wits—in Hartford. The editor of *The American Mercury* fired a few salvos against the editor of *The National Gazette* who, like the Wits, was himself a poet. It was a good tactic in any battle to wound, perhaps mortally, the general of the army. If that general was a poet who bled easily the tactic might easily succeed. It was sure to draw blood. The blast of *The American Mercury* was aimed at

> Sinbat the author, captain, printer, tar,
> The newsboys' poet and the dog of war,
> The blackguard's pattern, and the great man's fool,
> The fawning parasite, and the minion's tool.[5]

There, in four lines, was the whole indictment against the editor of *The National Gazette*. He was a poor poet, a ventriloquist's dummy, a demagogue, and a parasite. Freneau, deeply hurt, answered in equally ill-tempered lines. If the enemy chose the weapons he would not fail to use them.[6]

All this was still a preliminary skirmish, with pot shots that drew some blood without inflicting any mortal wound. Neither side had fixed the range of fire on the issue itself. It came a bit closer, perhaps, when John Adams, the Vice-President of the United States, and a dependable member of the Administration, was declared unfit for office by "Valerius," who fired his shot in the columns of *The National*

---

[4] *The Gazette of the United States,* May 2, 1792.

[5] *The American Mercury,* March 12, 1792; and Lewis Leary, *That Rascal Freneau,* p. 200.

[6] *The National Gazette,* March 29, 1792.

Gazette on March 29. On April 2 James Madison, in an article entitled "The Union. Who are Its True Friends?" denied they were the speculators or the men who aped the manners of royalty. Both Hamilton's measures and the Federalist leaders who supported them seemed to favor the one and encourage the other. The true friends of the country would not tolerate either of them. Madison was severe but restrained. "Sidney," more outspoken than Madison, openly charged that Hamilton favored the wealthy at the expense of the poor, inasmuch as he proposed laws that were "injurious to the liberty and enslaving to the happiness of the people."[7]

The Federalists now clearly understood the policy of *The National Gazette*. Hamilton had made his own position clear enough before; he would leave no room for any doubt now. Democracy was a poison that would destroy the nation. "Every day proves to me more and more," he said, "this American world was not meant for me." The people? "Your people," he explained, "are a great beast."[8] Hamilton's friends were even more explicit. Fisher Ames, who had beaten Sam Adams in the campaign for Congress, thought the "country too big for Union, too sordid for patriotism, too democratic for liberty."[9] Jefferson considered Ames one of the "paper-men" in Congress, and he was accused of profiting from the funding system. Congress was full of such men. None was more definite in his opinions than Senator Cabot of Massachusetts. He was sure that "Democracy in its natural operation is the government of the worst." Its natural operation? There was little thought yet of universal suffrage.[10]

The operations on at least one sector of the battle front were made quite clear by John Fenno. The columns of *The Gazette of the United States* were filled with details of the social life of the capital reminiscent of the Court of St. James. The wives of the chosen were unfailingly referred to as "Ladies" and the men as "Most Honorable." Titles were absurd but their perfumed essence was generously sprayed

[7] *The National Gazette,* April 2, April 12, April 23, 1792. In the issue of March 29, 1792, Madison upheld "the rights of property" equally with "the property in rights" (S. K. Padover, [ed.], *The World of the Founding Fathers,* p. 269).

[8] S. E. Forman, "The Political Activities of Philip Freneau," *Johns Hopkins University Studies,* Vol. 20, Nos. 9–10 (1902), pp. 38–39; and Alexander Hamilton, *Works,* Vol. 7, pp. 229, 306.

[9] Article by Fisher Ames on Shay's Rebellion in *The Independent Chronicle* of Boston, October 12, 1786.

[10] Forman, "The Political Activities," pp. 40 ff.

on the leaders in government, finance, and commerce. Whatever they proposed in Congress, whatever Hamilton supported in the Cabinet, John Fenno also proposed and supported.[11]

Freneau, keen as a dog on the scent, began to attack what the Federalists wanted. He wrote no slander, he descended to no abuse. He had promised the truth—and the truth, according to Jefferson, was that "our Constitution was galloping fast into Monarchy."[12] In scathing satire and luminous logic Freneau derided and exposed what he considered dangerous to this country. Royalist mimicry would not pass unchallenged by him—with the solemnity of ridicule, he sought to kill it with laughter. Pretending to write the news of 1801, not of 1792, he informed his readers that "on Monday last arrived in this city in perfect health, his Most Serene Highness the Protector of the United States, who on Wednesday next will review the regular troops which compose the garrison." He continued: "Yesterday came on before the Circuit of the Protector, the trial of James Barefoot, laborer, for carelessly treading on the great toe of My Lord Ohio." Found guilty, "the court fined him only one hundred pounds or ordered him to be imprisoned for six months." The news is then amplified with items about "the levee of her Highness," the intrigues of "the Dutchess of Rye's footman," and some sly digs at the Treasury. The entire item closes with the unrelated and laconic statement: "A few copies of the act to restrain the freedom of press may be had at this office."[13]

Freneau was not, as he boasted, always impartial. Often he drew a caricature of the truth, but he rarely perverted it. When he fell into error, it was through inadvertence rather than malice that he sinned, though malice might cause him to exaggerate when the provocation was too great for calm judgment. He despised the arrogance and complacency of the Federalists and hated their presumptions as much as their policies. Piece by piece he unravelled the fabric of these; bit by bit he examined it.

[11] William Maclay, *Journal*, p. 31; various issues of *The Gazette of the United States* during March 1790; A. H. Wharton, *Social Life in the Early Republic*, p. 120; Susan Coolidge, *A Short History of Philadelphia*, p. 175; *The National Gazette*, December 12, 1792.

[12] Thomas Jefferson, *Writings* (ed. A. A. Lipscomb and A. E. Bergh), "Anas," Vol. 1, p. 353.

[13] Forman, "The Political Activities," p. 44. The Federalists, Fisher Ames among them, were increasingly incensed at *The National Gazette* and writers who, "like toads, have sucked poison from the earth" (Ames, *Works*, Vol. 1, p. 128).

Could the doctrine of "implied powers" be read into the "general welfare" clause of the Constitution? The policy of loose construction was a flaw that ruined the whole fabric. Only a strict interpretation of the Constitution could save it. If Hamilton was right, the "general welfare" clause could be invoked in any phase of government. If Congress had the undoubted and specifically prescribed power to "make all laws which shall be necessary and proper" to give effect to that elastic clause, then what became of all the other provisions of the Constitution? What about those provisions that concerned not only the government but the people themselves—the citizens and their civil liberties so belatedly appended as the Bill of Rights? Freneau struck out with all his force at the evident assumption that the Congress could pass restrictive laws in every sphere of life and liberty, not only to raise moneys—proper enough for the specific ends clearly set forth in the Constitution—but also to raise barriers of all kinds to the freedom of the people? Free speech, free press, even a man's religion could come under a sinister shadow, if money were needed to give it sanction—not the sanction of those who professed it, but of those who were hostile to it.[14]

What was the limit—or were there no limitations on Hamilton's doctrine? What of the states that make up the United States—what was *their* province, and what could *they* do without danger of nullification by Congress? The ultimate aim of reasoning such as this could only be the whittling away of the people's liberties and the certain growth of despotism—the same rule that was forced on man throughout the world, throughout all time, which Americans believed they had blown to bits with the guns of the Revolution.[15]

"Nothing but the perpetual jealousy of the governed," Freneau wrote in his paper, "has ever been found effectual against the machinations of ambition. When this jealousy does not exist in some reasonable degree the saddle is soon placed upon the backs of the people and occupied by a succession of tyrants." In a lighter vein he proceeded to suggest the best means of destroying representative government. Get rid of all constitutional shackles; confer titles; dwell on the dangers of the mob; continue and enlarge the public debt; establish a bank for the enrichment of the masters; provide a standing army; and enact any other laws the rich may need to preserve their power. All these

[14] Forman, "The Political Activities," p. 47; *The National Gazette*, May 31, 1792; H. C. Hockett, *Growth of the American People*, pp. 322 ff.
[15] *Ibid.*

measures were quite simple to accomplish, for all of them came under the "general welfare" clause. And who else would define it but those same men who were now using a perverse logic and a debased integrity to enlarge its clear intention? What, in all truth and soberness, *was* the condition of the general welfare now while the Federalists were so busy with their multiple interpretations of its meaning? There was "poverty in the country," "luxury in the Capitals," "corruption and usurpation in the national councils." If this was the present condition of the general welfare, how did the Federalists expect to improve it?[16]

Fenno did not attempt to reply to these questions. He preferred to attack instead those who asked them. He informed his readers that "the abusers of government" were "persons from other countries who having lately escaped from bondage, know not how to enjoy liberty."[17] The obvious insult to the large population of Irish, Scotch, and German immigrants in Philadelphia was hurled back at "John Adams' printer" and his "court gazette," while implications of the old method of divide and conquer were not lost on the democratic-republicans of the Anti-Federalist forces.

Freneau, no novice in the art of fencing, thrust his sword deep into the wounded sensibilities of the soldiers of the Revolution and the struggling artisans in many cities. "Hear! Hear! hear, and attend ye foreigners!" he trumpeted in *The National Gazette;* John Fenno swears "you *foreigners* are a set of rebellious dogs!" In the issue of July 18, 1792, he gave a more sober answer to the slanders on the "foreigners" who had come to America seeking a better way of life. In the poem "To Crispin O'Conner" he portrayed the lot of these refugees from Europe who had escaped from

> Nine pence a day, coarse fare, a bed of boards,
> The midnight loom, high rents, and excised beer;
> Slave to dull squires, King's brats, and huffish lords,
> (Thanks be to Heaven) not yet in fashion here!

The Revolution, despite its equalitarian professions, had failed to accomplish the acceptance of a democratic philosophy in government. That was still the phantom fruit of the Declaration, and of the Constitution—eternally within reach and eternally eluding the grasp of the people. Tantalus was not alone in his agony of frustration.[18]

---

[16] *Ibid.*
[17] *The National Gazette,* June 9, 1792.
[18] *Ibid.,* June 11, June 14, July 18, 1792.

The animus of Philip Freneau against the Federalists and their soothsayers was generated by his genuine fears for the cause of democracy. They were the fears of the republicans too, whose leaders had a deep antipathy for their political enemies. Jefferson, unwillingly impressed into service as Secretary of State though he had often expressed the wish to retire to private life, was temperamentally alien to the hurly-burly of partisan politics, its bad manners and worse ethics, its moral abandon and spiritual vacuum. He had retired once before when the burdens of Virginia warfare had proven too heavy for his studious and methodical habits. Relinquishing his duties as governor of the Old Dominion, he had hoped to be done forever with public office, yet he had gone to Paris as America's envoy in a time of crisis. Watching the violent upsurge of the people of France, he had rejoiced in this new revolution which promised freedom from despotism in the old world as it already seemed secure in the new. But was it secure? Now, he doubted it. There were signs that the old shackles were being forged again. The master craftsman was his Cabinet colleague, a younger man than he, handsome, vigorous, arrogant, ambitious, contemptuous of the people, and a firm believer in the superiority of the wealthy and well-born.[19]

Hamilton possessed a cold pride as well as a keen intellect, and his stubborn sense of power would brook no opposition. His integrity was compounded of these, and his honor was unsullied by any of them. To him, in turn, Jefferson was a man of "proud ambition and violent passions"; but, if so, these were in equal or greater measure the qualities of Hamilton himself. Perhaps Jefferson exaggerated the truth somewhat when he complained to Washington about the "corrupt squadron of the Treasury." But Madison, one time himself a Federalist, was equally suspicious of it—and of Hamilton. Nor was it the Treasury alone they suspected.[20] There were other squadrons too, ready and primed for antidemocratic measures, with other Federalists equally close to Washington at the very center of power to lead them. John Jay didn't believe that the people could be trusted to govern in an "equal, uniform and orderly manner," and his words had great weight with many citizens. John Jay was the Chief Justice of the Supreme Court, appointed by the President, more active as his close

[19] Hamilton, *Works*, Vol. 9, p. 519. The feud between Jefferson and Hamilton grew in intensity as *The National Gazette* continued its attacks on the policies of the Washington Administration.
[20] *Ibid.*, Vol. 9, p. 535.

adviser than as a judge of the highest tribunal. When Washington needed a special representative in England to settle the increasing difficulties arising from treaty infractions, John Jay would be chosen as the man most likely to settle them. John Jay *would* settle them, in a manner more agreeable to Lord Grenville than to the people of America. The other advisers of the President appeared no better. General Henry Knox, his Secretary of War, was obsessed by a fear of the radicals, and of all democrats, who were also radicals. Washington might scoff at the aristocratic, monarchic inclinations of some of his advisers. He was beyond any question opposed to them in the practice of government. But a republic was one thing, and a democracy was quite another. The Administration, while ready to accept the one, was opposed to the other. The spirit, if not the intent, of the Federalists appeared monarchical; the letter was republican—but the spirit was not democratic. *The Gazette of the United States,* which reflected as in a blurred mirror the entire Administration of George Washington, made that spirit quite manifest to the people of America.[21]

John Fenno's paper did not please everybody—not even all the Federalists. The editor's obvious fawning on Hamilton, whom he called "the highest jewel in Columbia's crown"; his diatribes against the "foreigners," which alienated many of their supporters; his stupid sallies against Philip Freneau, in which slander was masked by reason and logic diluted with vituperation, appealed to few men of intelligence and dignity, and offended not a few of the partisans of Federalist policy. It was a bit thick to accuse *The National Gazette* as the foe of order, virtue, and religion, to call its editor a "blackguard," a "crack-brain," and a "salamander." These attacks did no harm to *The National Gazette;* on the contrary, they popularized it as much as the articles of James Madison on "the monarchical spirit which characterized Fenno's paper," or Freneau's poems, essays, and editorials on the dangers of that spirit to the liberties of America. Madison contributed only occasionally to *The National Gazette,* and then only anonymously; Jefferson never at all save by indirection. And Fenno was not the real target for any of them.[22]

---

[21] George Gibbs, *Memoirs of the Administration of Washington and John Adams,* Vol. 1, pp. 390 ff; Kenneth B. Umbreit, *Our Eleven Chief Justices,* p. 146.

[22] Forman, "The Political Activities," p. 43. Madison contributed seventeen articles to *The National Gazette;* H. S. Randall, *The Life of Thomas Jefferson,* Vol. 2, p. 74.

To Freneau, Hamilton was the bête noire of Federalism, the menace above all others to democracy. To Jefferson, Hamilton was "a host within himself," and "really a colossus to the Anti-Republicans." The colossus, however, was vulnerable. The attacks upon him, with only the feckless Fenno to dispute them with spite and slander rather than with facts and reason, wounded him deeply in the one sentitive spot of his otherwise impenetrable armor. His pride was affronted. Freneau's paper, he declared, was "devoted to subversion of me and the measure in which I have an agency." But Freneau was not alone; behind Freneau was a power much greater than he. Who was it? Who was directing the attacks upon him with both safety and impunity? Could it be the man who had once complained about him to Washington, the man he saw every day at the Capitol, who eyed him with scarce-concealed distaste, and looked on him with ill-veiled hostility? Thomas Jefferson was the real power behind *The National Gazette,* the directing intelligence of the clerk who translated for the Secretary of State. The editor of *The National Gazette* was a puppet, controlled by strings pulled by the crafty democrat who fed his hireling out of the public treasury. No wonder the paper was against the Federalists and their policies. It was not surprising that *The National Gazette* only echoed the opinions of Jefferson and his fellow conspirators. Little wonder that it celebrated the French Revolution in a July 14 poem by its editor and showed its bias in favor of France and against England on every possible occasion. Jefferson was nothing but a politician seeking power, and Freneau's paper was only a propaganda sheet intended to destroy Jefferson's opponents and replace them with men who would inevitably destroy the government itself.[23]

Hamilton did nothing by halves. It was one thing to say that Freneau was the servant of Jefferson—it would be better to have the proof, if it could be gotten. He caused the coming of Freneau to Philadelphia to be investigated. The proof—the proof of the plan to subvert orderly government must be obtained, for his own sake, but even more for the sake of his party. The new national elections were due in the fall, and John Adams, Congress itself, were in jeopardy. Washington would doubtless survive—no one, certainly no democrat, could ever displace him. All the others, Hamilton himself, could be unhorsed unless the publisher of the subversive sheet was unmasked and the real culprits exposed.

[23] Forman, "The Political Activities," p. 49; Hamilton, *Works,* Vol. 9, p. 519; Vol. 10, p. 14.

On July 25, 1792, a notice appeared in *The Gazette of the United States,* signed with the initials "T.L.," but easily recognized as the writing of Hamilton. "The Editor of the National Gazette," the notice declared,

receives a salary from the government. Quere—whether this salary is paid him for *translations,* or for *publications,* the design of which is to vilify those to whom the voice of the people has committed the administration of our public affairs—to oppose the measures of government, and by false insinuations, to disturb the public peace? In common life it is thought ungrateful for a man to bite the hand that puts bread into his mouth; but if the man is hired to do it, the case is altered.[24]

Freneau, without the payment of any fee, published the identical notice in his own paper, and then proceeded to inquire whether he was not

more likely to act an honest and disinterested part toward the public than a vile sycophant who, obtaining emoluments from the government far more lucrative than the salary alluded to, finds his interest in attempting to poison the minds of the people by propagating and disseminating principles and sentiments utterly subversive of the true interests of the country and by flattering and recommending every measure of government, however pernicious and destructive its tendency might be to the great body of the people.[25]

It was a long and wordy indictment, yet clear enough for everybody to understand who was meant. John Fenno was the immediate target. The battle, however, was not solely between two papers, or two editors, or two leaders of opposed parties. It was a battle between two philosophies of government, in which the papers, the editors, the leaders, the people themselves, must take a part, for or against. It was a battle in which no holds would be barred, no quarter would be given, no weapon would be sheathed. In politics, as in love, everything goes.

Philip Freneau, with his own weapons of satirical verse and impassioned prose, was not always impartial, but he was always forthright and independent as the spokesman of the democrats. He was, beyond any question, his own spokesman as well. Let Hamilton and Fenno spew their slander—he was his own man, now as in all the long past of his country's travail. Honestly, passionately if not always

[24] *The Gazette of the United States,* July 25, 1792; Ms letters by Hamilton on Freneau, signed "An American," in Connecticut Historical Society.
[25] *The National Gazette,* July 29, 1792.

judiciously, he wrote for America and believed what he wrote. Only in a general way did he know of specific evils in remote parts of the country, even in remote parts of New York State, where a feudal system of land tenure had been fastened on the helpless tenant-farmers by patroon landlords with the help of the astute Alexander Hamilton, in bold defiance of the law against entail and primogeniture. The patroons were among the stoutest supporters of the Federalists who opposed the rising tide of democracy. When the issues of American politics were decided, Philip Freneau never doubted that the people would believe as he did.[26]

Issues, stemming one from the other, would be resolved sooner or later by the people. The ultimate issue of democracy itself would reach far beyond this struggle between the Federalists and the republicans; its meaning would grow and its limits expand with the country and the problems of an increasingly complex society. The concepts of government would enlarge as the control of power changed. In the decades and centuries stretching far into the future men would still be searching for solutions to their political and social problems, but whatever other problems might arise, the issue of democracy remained the most immediate of them all.

[26] Henry Christman, *Tin Horns and Calico,* pp. 26–29; Carl Carmer, *The Hudson,* Ch. 26, on "Federalism and the Hudson Valley."

23. OPEN UP THE DOORS!

PHILIP FRENEAU, in the early stages of the paper war between the factions, had assumed that his antogonist was John Fenno. The greater struggle between the parties and the policies of government included the lesser one between the editors of the two rival journals, each one concerned for the growth and influence of his own organ. A newspaper grew or stagnated according to the nourishment supplied by its own readers. Its policy, in turn, won or lost their support.

Fenno's paper was losing ground. It reached a small if influential circle of people who counted in elections, while over four hundred of its already depleted circulation were distributed free in a desperate effort to bolster up its apparently waning prestige. *The National Gazette,* on the other hand was expanding, spreading like a stream throughout the states of the Union, where its foreign as well as domestic news was eagerly read not only by the farmer, the tradesman, and the worker, but by intellectuals too. After six months, its circulation "exceeded beyond the editor's most saguine expectations," and it was "rising fast into reputation," as Henry Lee informed Madison. It soon became apparent to Freneau that the competition was less between two editors or two newspapers than between the principles for which they stood. Circulation, in such a case, though of the first importance, must flow from policy whatever the result.[1]

Hamilton, presumably the man behind the gun of the Fenno *Gazette,* was in reality the gun itself. Scarcely disguised by the signature

[1] Lee to Madison, February 6, 1792, in James Madison, *Writings,* Vol. 6, p. 84 n.; *The National Gazette,* May 7, 1792.

of "An American," the new series of articles which appeared in *The Gazette of the United States* was too sure in its aim, too penetrating in its effect, to be the work of the inept editor. Moreover, the new articles were no longer trained on Freneau—not, at least, on him alone, or chiefly—but on another, of whom Freneau was, according to the writer, only the "faithful and devoted servant." Whose servant? Hamilton had already received the proof he wanted. He could now reveal it in *The Gazette of the United States*. Jefferson, as he had guessed, was the master behind the dummy.[2]

Thomas Jefferson, in the words of "An American," had tried something "new in the history of political maneuvers in this country; *a newspaper instituted by a public officer* and the editor of it regularly pensioned with the public money." The "whole complexion of this paper exhibits a decisive internal evidence of the influence of that patronage." And more. Freneau knew but one language; how then could he be a "clerk for foreign languages in the Department of the United States for foreign affairs." If the Secretary of State wanted to fight the Administration's policies, he should resign his office; if he supported *The National Gazette,* dictated its views, and advanced his party's fortunes through its columns, there was but one course that "his own personal dignity and the principles of probity" demanded of him. Jefferson should resign![3]

The argument was a cogent one. There was a massive logic in it— perhaps even a kernel of the truth. But it was equally cogent and equally true that Fenno was also receiving moneys from the public treasury— much more, indeed, than Freneau. Fenno was official printer to the United States Senate; he received all the printing work of the United States Treasury; all printing contracts for the Bank of the United States were to be his. Together, all these amounted to nearly 2,500 dollars a year. "If two hundred and fifty dollars made Freneau a knave," one letter-writer asked, "what did twenty-five hundred dollars make John Fenno?" There was the further fact that Fenno, in frequent moments of financial distress, could call on his angel, Alexander Hamilton, for additional help. In a letter to Rufus King, Hamilton had requested that a thousand dollars be raised in New York immediately to aid the editor of *The Gazette of the United States,* promising in return "to raise another thousand at Philadelphia." Far

[2] Alexander Hamilton, *Works,* Vol. 9, p. 519; *The Gazette of the United States,* July 28, 1792.

[3] *The Gazette of the United States,* August 4, 1792.

from being free from sin himself, he was casting stones at others. He saw the mote in Jefferson's eye, while the beam in his own remained invisible. And always he was an active party in the fight of the two gazettes, writing and directing what was written in the paper supposedly edited by John Fenno.[4]

Jefferson had contributed nothing to *The National Gazette*. What appeared as the work of Philip Freneau *was* his work; the ideas expressed were his own ideas, though they were also Jefferson's. Others too wrote for the paper—Madison contributed seventeen articles during the life of *The National Gazette*. Freneau himself answered his detractors in the most effective manner possible. In an affidavit amply detailed and legally sworn to he stated

that no negociation was ever opened with him by Thomas Jefferson, Secretary of State, for the establishment or institution of *The National Gazette;* that the deponent's coming to the City of Philadelphia as the publisher of a newspaper, was at no time urged, advised, or influenced by the above officer, but that it was his own voluntary act; and that the said Gazette, nor the Editor thereof, was ever either directed, controuled, or attempted to be influenced in any manner, either by the Secretary of State, or any of his friends; nor was a line ever directly or indirectly written, dictated, or composed for it by that officer, but that the Editor consulted his own judgment alone in the conducting of it—free—unfettered—and uninfluenced.[5]

The affidavit, essentially true as to the facts, permitted some doubt as to their complete accuracy. Jefferson had not "negociated" with Freneau—but had not Madison and Lee done so for him? Jefferson had not urged Freneau to come to Philadelphia—perhaps not even when they met in New York—but had not his friends done so on his behalf as well as their own? It was indisputable that Freneau had come of his own volition after many hesitations and much self-searching; he, he alone, was responsible for the paper; and he was morally, spiritually, intellectually, and physically free, unfettered, and uninfluenced. His whole life, all his work, was of one piece; not a single act, a single word of his was ever the echo of another's, or uttered for any purpose save the purpose of liberty.

When he sent his affidavit to *The Gazette of the United States* on August 8, Hamilton quickly responded. "Facts," he said, "speak

[4] *The National Gazette*, August 15, 1792; S. E. Forman, "The Political Activities of Philip Freneau," *Johns Hopkins University Studies*, Vol. 20, Nos. 9–10 (1902), pp. 59–60.

[5] *The Gazette of the United States*, August 8, 1792.

louder than oaths." He had no trouble penetrating behind "the hackneyed tricks employed by the *purists* in politics, of every country and and age, to cheat the people into a belief in their superior sanctity, integrity, or virtue."[6] To expose these "tricks" further, he asked Elias Boudinot and Jonathan Dayton, both of them staunch Federalists and his good friends, for any information available concerning Madison's hand in the whole affair. If Jefferson was technically absolved, then it was only because James Madison, his alter ego in Congress, had made the moves which effectively screened his collaborator. It was important to show this, for "it will confound and put down a man who is continually machinating against public happiness."[7] The chief culprit, of course, was still Jefferson, the villain above all other villains, who not only disdained to answer him, but was not even in Philadelphia to confront him. Jefferson was in Monticello, at the moment deeply engrossed in matters more relaxing than politics—in some new designs for a better wheelbarrow and stonger mould-boards of greater plasticity.[8] Jefferson, Madison, and Freneau—the three-pronged fork of the democratic devil—had done their work well. The devil was slowly assuming the features of an innocent, indeed a highly attractive ornament, on the national scene. *The Boston Gazette* found no fault with Freneau even if *The Connecticut Courant* thought *The National Gazette* was a tool of "professed grumbletarians." When *The Independent Chronicle* of Boston supported *The National Gazette* because it *was* under Jefferson's eye, *The Columbian Centinel* gloated that here was the whole plot admitted. Only the plot was hardly a criminal conspiracy, though it would be better if the war was settled and peace again descended on the troubled waters of America. Only from one quarter was peace between the two antagonists suggested. President Washington, striving to be impartial, sought to end the war which could never be ended but by the decisive defeat of one side or the other.[9]

The real victim of this war was perhaps the President himself. Occupying the position of supreme power, he was also at the very

[6] *Ibid.,* August 11, 1792.

[7] Irving Brant, *James Madison,* Vol. 2, *The Nationalist, 1780–1787,* p. 361.

[8] Forman, "The Political Activities," pp. 55–58.

[9] Lewis Leary, *That Rascal Freneau,* pp. 213–214; Jefferson had no doubt that Fenno was making "way for a king, lords, and Commons" (Jefferson to William Short, July 28, 1791, in Thomas Jefferson, *Writings* [ed. P. L. Ford], Vol. 5, p. 361).

center of the cross fire, wounded equally by shots fired from both sides. He was as safe from any direct attack in his person as in his honor, and neither his power nor prestige was in the least jeopardized by the enmity between the two giants in his Cabinet. Respected by both of them, he had a high regard for each of them, for their personal probity and intellectual capacity. More stolid than they and rarely given to any sign of passionate feeling, he heard them out patiently and with close attention. The country was his trust, and like all the trusts ever reposed in him, he would honor it as he saw his duty, and fulfill it as he had the power and the strength to do so. He decided to sign the Hamilton measures despite Jefferson's opposition to them because the destiny of America lay in a strong union, and a strong union demanded measures such as these. To make America strong and invulnerable to any attack was his one aim and undeviating purpose. While disquieting shadows of far-off events already cast their gloom on American shores, no one threatened the peace from outside its borders. Inside the boundaries of the country the democrats alone were divisive and dangerous. That was why he was against them. The dangers from abroad were only inchoate ones; at home they seemed more imminent. They loomed large in the pages of *The National Gazette* and in the support of Jefferson to the views which those pages contained. They were disturbing the country, retarding its progress toward a great future, a future they all professed to advance and all were eager to serve.[10]

Writing to Jefferson from Mount Vernon, Washington appealed to him for a cessation of the war at home. He regretted "that while we are encompassed on all sides by avowed enemies and insidious friends, internal dissensions should be harrowing and tearing our vitals." *The National Gazette,* and Philip Freneau especially, were not helping to pacify the country. The President appeared to place particular emphasis on the role of the editor of *The National Gazette*. At the same time, he begged Hamilton to observe "charity in deciding on the opinions

[10] The paper war may be followed more closely in S. G. W. Benjamin, "Notable Editors between 1776 and 1800," *Magazine of American History,* XVII (January–June 1887), 1–28, 97–127; Philip M. Marsh, "Madison's Defence of Freneau," *William and Mary Quarterly,* third series, III, 2 (April 1946), 269–274; and Marsh, "Jefferson and Freneau," *American Scholar,* Vol. 16, No. 2 (April 1947), pp. 201–210; also Marsh, "The Griswold Story of Freneau and Jefferson," *American Historical Review,* LI, 1 (October 1945), 68–73; Leary, *That Rascal Freneau,* Ch. 8.

and actions of others." For himself, he had but one wish, that "balsam may be poured into *all* the wounds."[11] It was a noble wish, destined to be unfulfilled, for the opinions of men, honestly held and passionately pursued, can rarely yield to compromise in the sole interest of peace. Such a peace might only be the prelude to another war. All wounds may one day be healed but balsam alone will never heal them.

Believing as much, Jefferson answered the President in a full and revealing letter that left little doubt of his position. He readily admitted his interest in Freneau as a newspaperman as well as a translator in his department. The reputation of the poet, he began, was that of a "good Whig," a guarantee that "he would give free place to pieces written against the aristocratical and monarchical principles" of the Federalists. He had no intention of making "a convenient partizan" of Philip Freneau, but surely his own recommendations for appointment by Washington of such men as Rittenhouse and Barlow would negate any such assumption, and Washington could never doubt "that talents and science are sufficient motives with me in appointments." Moreover, "Freneau, as a man of genius," deserved any help he had given him. Jefferson had indeed furnished him with the Leyden Gazettes for such foreign news as Freneau cared to reprint, but he had never contributed to the paper himself, neither would he demean his office by writing anonymously anywhere. Nor did he, "by myself or any other, or indirectly, say a syllable nor attempt any kind of influence" on the control of *The National Gazette* by Freneau. Jefferson did not mention what may have been an indirect if unimportant influence in the form of an essay he had sent to Freneau for use in his paper. The essay was written by another—by Mr. Nenno—not by Jefferson; yet the implied approval of Jefferson in sending it to Freneau did not make it any more acceptable to the editor of *The National Gazette*. Freneau had refused to print it because it was "generally superficial and tedious."[12]

Concluding his answer to Washington, Jefferson clearly stated his position on *The National Gazette*. "As to the merits or demerits" of the paper, he said, "they certainly concern me not." Freneau "and Fenno are rivals for the public favor. The one courts them by flattery, the other by censure, and I believe it will be admitted that the one has

[11] Washington to Jefferson, August 23, 1792, in George Washington, *Writings* (ed. W. C. Ford), Vol. 12, pp. 171–176.
[12] Thomas Jefferson, *Writings* (ed. A. A. Lipscomb and A. E. Bergh), Vol. 6, pp. 105–109; Forman, "The Political Activities," p. 62.

been as servile as the other severe. No government ought to be without censors, and where the press is free, no one ever will." Freneau's business was to see to it that the press was free, and he would never fail in his role of censor.[13]

The peace hoped for by Washington was a chimera doomed from the beginning. Neither Freneau nor Jefferson was disposed to yield in any degree to the wish of the President. And Hamilton, replying to Washington, stubbornly maintained that he was "unable to recede *for the present.*"[14] If he wavered at all, the democrats would never waver, never recede, for the present or in the future. Freneau's attacks in *The National Gazette* would continue, more virulent and incisive than ever before, while he sounded the alarm for eternal vigilance in a time of continuing crisis.

> Columbia!—watch each stretch of power,
> Nor sleep too soundly at the midnight hour,
> By flattery won, and lulled by soothing strains,
> Silenus took his nap,—and waked in chains.[15]

To better watch each stretch of power Freneau now demanded an end of the closed sessions by the Senate. Motions to open its doors were made only to be defeated "in defiance of every principle which gives security to free men." This secrecy of the law makers was a monstrous perversion of the people's rights "to know the individual conduct of [their] legislators." How, Freneau asked, were freemen "to know the just from the unjust steward when they are covered with the mantle of concealment?" Secrecy, he thundered, "is necessary to design and a masque to treachery; honesty shrinks not from the public eye." Is the Senate aping the privileges of the British House of Lords? "Remember," he admonishes his readers, "that you are still freemen; let it be impressed on your minds that you depend not upon your representatives but that they depend on you, and let this truth be ever present to you, that secrecy in your representatives is a worm that will prey and fatten upon the vitals of your liberty." Open up the doors and let the people hear you![16] It was the life-long task of Philip Freneau to force open any public door shut fast against the people. The

---

[13] Jefferson, *Writings* (Lipscomb and Bergh), Vol. 6, pp. 105-109. See also Forman, "The Political Activities," pp. 69-72.

[14] Hamilton, *Works,* Vol. 6, p. 30.

[15] Freneau, *The Poems of Philip Freneau* (ed. F. L. Pattee), Vol. 3, p. 170.

[16] Forman, "The Political Activities," pp. 63-64.

doors of Congress were finally opened—but still others remained closed. Those of the Church, perhaps the stoutest of them all, also needed to be pried open, so the minds of men would not be shut to truths which otherwise they might not learn.

Freneau was a godly man; but he was also a devout follower of the Huguenot tradition of religious freedom. He was a Deist whose simple piety was not complicated by supernatural beliefs or dogmatic formulas. His allegiance was to man—God needed no help—for man was the sole source of all good and evil. The spiritual life of man should not be entrusted to a professional churchman who so often seemed more concerned with the flesh than with souls. "There is not a sight in all the walks of men," Freneau said, "That gives me half the disgust as that of a Christian Clergyman rolling in his coach, swelling with pride and impertinence, associating only with princes, nobles and the wealthy men of the land." He was no scoffer at the true faith of humility, and no one who followed in the footsteps of the lowly Nazarene ever was the object of his scorn. The ancient partnership between the powerful and the priestly was a barricade which he wanted to break down so men could see what transpired behind it. "If they give us their Bishops," he wrote, "they'll give us their law." The spiritual and material well-being of man was sacrificed by those who were preoccupied with power in any form, religious or political, and the exploitation of the weak by the strong extended to all domains of human concern.[17]

> Left to himself, wherever man is found,
> In peace he aims to walk life's little round;
> In peace to sail, in peace to till the soil,
> Nor force false grandeur from a brother's toil.

A man may become as Prometheus himself if only he remains unshackled by the fetters of state and church, of politics and religion.

> . . . leave the mind unchain'd and free,
> And what they ought, mankind will be;
> No hypocrite, no lurking friend,
> No artist to some evil end,

[17] Freneau, *Poems of Freneau* (ed. H. H. Clark), p. xxxiv. See also H. M. Morais, *Deism in Eighteenth Century America, passim.* N. H. Adkins, *Philip Freneau and the Cosmic Enigma,* is a perceptive treatment of the entire problem of Freneau's position on Deity.

> But good and great, benign and just,
> As God and nature made them first.[18]

These were the echoes from Rousseau and Voltaire and Thomas
Paine; they were Philip Freneau's beliefs as well in the ultimate triumph of the human intellect, free and generous for the world's salvation. It was his view of man in his relation to God and Nature, serving
as a balance wheel to the pessimism of the orthodox in any field of
thought, rebelling at constraints and disciplines incompatible with free
spirits and proper only to a race of helots. He attacked no man's religious beliefs, though his own studies in theology had revealed nothing
to strengthen those beliefs which he questioned. Not men's beliefs,
but the institutional doors which were closed against full understanding and free inquiry were the objects of his attack, and the men who
guarded those doors and sealed up the cracks they developed in any
field of human interest were the objects of his scorn. It was not true,
as his enemies averred, that he "vilified" the clergy or "ridiculed"
religion in the columns of his paper. He was opposed to "The holy
man by Bishops holy made," as he had written long ago in the "Jamaica
Funeral." Holy men were not made so easily. No one rode to heaven
on the coattails of the pious.

> What if this heart no narrow notions bind,
> Its pure good will extends to all mankind—
> Suppose I ask no portion from your feast
> Nor ride to heaven behind *your* parish priest.[19]

Freneau refused to be silent on any question that affected the liberty
of America, and the principles of democracy included the freedom to
discuss religion as well as politics. What, indeed, was the essential
difference between them? Equally they affected the welfare of all men
and therefore were properly discussed and debated in the columns of
The National Gazette and *The Gazette of the United States*, with re-
prints carried in other papers throughout the country. *The National
Gazette* was fast gaining new readers in places where no other source
of news was available. At home and abroad its editorials were molding
public opinion—Jean de Ternant, Minister of France to the United

---

[18] "The Alien," in Freneau, *Poems* (Clark), p. 119. See also *ibid.*, p. xl;
Leary, *That Rascal Freneau*, pp. 216–217.

[19] "To an Angry Zealot," in Freneau, *Poems* (Clark), p. 119. See also *ibid.*,
p. xxxix; *The National Gazette,* September 19, 1792. Freneau's opinion of
organized religion had not changed since the days of his theological studies.

States, not only kept his chief in Paris, M. Bonne-Carrére, informed of the news contained in its columns and the opinions reflected in its editorials, but he sent him the paper itself for further elucidation and enlightenment. In the South the cause of Jefferson was considerably strengthened by the paper, while in New England, which had so often sneered at its editor, it was now being read with a greater degree of respect if not of sympathy. It was even "getting into Massachusetts under the patronage of Hancock and Sam Adams," no small feat in the stronghold of Yankee rectitude.[20]

John Adams, re-elected with Washington to the highest offices in the land, was justly dismayed by the deep inroads into the vote he had received because of Freneau's paper. Washington's popularity remained undiminished. He had never been attacked by *The National Gazette*. But Adams, frequently assailed for his views, had suffered heavily in the new election. The first time, he had been an almost unanimous choice for second place. Now, five states had crossed over to the Jeffersonian camp. To the ever-faithful and distressed Abigail, John had explained his fall from grace by the fact that "there is no other newspaper circulated in the back country of the southern states than Freneau's *National Gazette,* which is employed with great industry to poison the minds of the people."[21]

Was Freneau really poisoning the minds of the people? *The Independent Chronicle* of Adams' home town was not alone in thinking so. Others thought so too—and John Fenno, believing or disbelieving, took up the cry of John Adams and amplified it in crescendos of ever-mounting fury.[22] Unruffled, even amused, by the loud barking of his enemies, Freneau, descending to his rival's level, replied in kind.

> Hark ye, my dogs—I have not learned to yelp,
> Nor spend my breath on every lousy whelp—

And he added a word of caution:

[20] Ternant to Bonne-Carrére, August 4, 1792, in "Correspondance des Ministres Français aux Etats-Unis, 1791–1797," *Annual Report of American Historical Association, 1903,* Vol. 2. See also Lee to Madison, February 6, 1792, in Madison, *Writings,* Vol. 6, p. 84; Jefferson to Thomas Mann Randolph, November 16, 1792, in Jefferson, *Writings* (Ford), Vol. 6, p. 134.

[21] John Adams, *Letters Addressed to His Wife,* Vol. 2, p. 119.

[22] Leary, *That Rascal Freneau,* p. 219; and Jefferson to Randolph, November 16, 1792, in Jefferson, *Writings* (Ford), Vol. 6, p. 134.

> Learn this,
> (Tis not amiss)
> For men
> To keep a *pen*
> For dogs—a cane.[23]

Freneau never had occasion to use a cane, though Bache, detesting the Federalists and Fenno as much as did Freneau, was moved to use one on the editor of *The Gazette of the United States*.[24] Violent only with his pen, Freneau struck only with words. As the year 1792 hurried to a close he was about to strike harder than ever before.

[23] *The National Gazette*, August 29, 1792.
[24] *The Dictionary of American Biography*, Vol. 6, p. 235; Bernard Fay, "Benjamin F. Bache: Democratic Leader of the 18th Century," *American Antiquarian Society*, 40 (1931), 295.

24. OLD FRIENDS AND NEW FOES

BENJAMIN RUSH, the eminent physician and patriot of Philadelphia, had once said of the struggle between the Colonies and Great Britain, that "the American war is over, but that is far from being the case of the American Revolution."[1] The events of 1791 and 1792 seemed to bear him out. A foreign enemy had been subdued, but the enemy within, according to the Anti-Federalists, was still in the saddle, still to be vanquished. The enemy was not only inimical to the liberty for which so much blood had been spilled, but also to the concepts on which America had been reared and by which it was fostered. Those concepts had come from abroad, many of them from England itself, from John Locke and his *Two Treatises on Government,* which had inspired Jefferson and his radical friends. Libertarian ideas had also stemmed from France, from Voltaire and Rousseau, from Diderot and Condorcet and D'Alembert, leading thinkers of the Enlightenment and the Age of Reason. It was France that had provided the material help as well, and mingled its blood with that of Americans to defeat the tyranny of an alien power. It had sent its ships, its soldiers, the flower of its manhood, and leaders like Lafayette and Rochambeau, Destouches and De Grasse, to ensure a victory for America. Louis XVI had not been moved by a love of freedom to extend the hand of friendship to the rebels, but by his fear of England's imperial power, yet Frenchmen were truly fired by the

[1] R. A. Billington, B. L. Lowenberg, and S. H. Brockunier, *The United States: American Democracy in World Perspective,* p. 102; also Leo Gershoy, *The French Revolution and Napoleon,* p. 62, and *passim.*

struggle for freedom across the sea.[2] That struggle, once another's, was now their own.

In 1789 it had flared into the open. The spark of revolution, barely extinguished in America, had fired the feudal tyrannies of France. France had revolted. Under the triune standard of Liberty, Fraternity, and Equality, an ancient autocracy was destroyed, while other autocracies, fearful for their own safety, began to encircle the French people, in a vast effort to restore the old privileges and put to rout the usurpers. A few timeservers, in that as in all revolutions, were ready to serve their purpose and to profit by the success of the counterrevolution. In an access of fear and passion, the revolutionists of France were turning on former comrades suspected of treachery, exorcising the terror in their own souls by a greater terror suddenly blown to fantastic and hideous dimensions. Men of good will, staunch friends of the French Revolution, were being alienated everywhere by the senseless bloodletting of the Jacobins. The enlightenment of the eighteenth century had collapsed at the foot of the guillotine, and the Age of Reason was drowned in the blood of innocent men. Liberty, a bloom of fragrance and beauty, had decayed into a noisome weed which befouled the clean air of Fraternity and poisoned the soothing balm of Equality.[3]

In America the Federalists were similarly alienated. Here was the proof of what Hamilton feared in a democracy. The people were beasts, they could not be trusted, they must be restrained. John Adams, with his simple philosophy of a strong restraint on the masses, recalled what he had once written to his cousin Sam Adams when the Massachusetts radical maintained that liberty was deep-grained in the soul of man. "So it is," replied John, "according to La Fontaine, in that of a wolf."[4] The Jacobins—all of them—were obviously wolves who would rend the garment of liberty and stain it with the blood of martyrs. Even Thomas Paine—surely no Federalist—whose *Rights of Man* had been composed as an answer to Edmund Burke's "Reflections on the Revolution," was opposed to the Terror as an instrument of justice. He had escaped from England to avoid arrest for supporting those rights and was imprisoned in France and threatened

[2] S. Bonsal, *When the French Were Here, passim.*

[3] *Ibid.*; Gershoy, *The French Revolution*, Ch. 3; John Geise, *Man and the Western World*, pp. 679–680.

[4] S. E. Forman, "The Political Activities of Philip Freneau," *Johns Hopkins University Studies*, Vol. 20, Nos. 9–10 (1902), p. 38.

with the guillotine when he deplored the excesses of the French Revolution.[5]

Others deplored them too, with anger but without hatred, with anguish but with understanding. For them the Terror was only a natural result of revolution beset by enemies, the product of hope betrayed by ambition and the human spirit frustrated by self-seeking. To overcome tyranny men are driven to be tyrannical; suspicion breeds violence; and danger is the midwife of unreason. If the common people of the world would be the masters of their fate, their errors, their cruelties, their tragic gropings toward the light were evils which men must suffer in the struggle for freedom. The radical democrats believed all this, and a few conservatives who had been of quite another mind had come to believe it too.

Joel Barlow, one of the Connecticut Wits, had changed his mind about the masses. He was now in France, where his "Advice to the Privileged Orders," recently published, had explained and supported the rights of man. "Only admit," Barlow had written, "the original, unalterable truth, that men are equal in their rights, and the foundation of everything is laid." The French Revolution, he declared, "is to be decided by men who reason better without books, than we do with all the books in the world."[6] France would honor him for views like this and make him a citizen in 1793, but America, its vision blurred by the red fog of Paris, was in no mood for words like these. The Federalists, among whom the fear of a similar incitement in America was a real one, suspected that the democrats might tolerate if not welcome a similar avalanche of hatred and cruelty if it would serve to win their ends.

What else could one expect if Jefferson, even Jefferson, defended the butchery in France? On January 3, 1793, he wrote to William Short, the American Minister to Holland: "The tone of your letters had for some time given me pain, on account of the extreme warmth with which they censured the proceedings of the Jacobins of France." He had no censure for the Jacobins. "A few of their cordial friends met at their hands the fate of enemies. But time and truth will embalm their memories, while their posterity will be enjoying that very liberty for which they would never have hesitated to offer up their lives. The liberty of the whole earth was depending on the issue of the contest,

---

[5] Paine's *Age of Reason* was written during his imprisonment. See C. D. Hazen, *Contemporary Opinion of the French Revolution, passim.*

[6] *The National Gazette,* August 4, 1792.

and was ever such a prize won with so little innocent blood?" Since
the question was entirely rhetorical he continued: "My own affections
have been deeply wounded by some of the martyrs to this cause, but
rather than that it should have failed, I would have seen half the earth
desolated; were there but an Adam and Eve left in every country, and
left free, it would be better than it is now."[7]

To Freneau as to Jefferson, the hostility of the Federalists to the
democratic process at home was of a piece with their hostility to the
French Revolution abroad. In both cases counterrevolution was the
impetus for their hostility; fear and hatred of the masses, the rules for
conduct. In the mounting tension between France and England, and
the growing threat of war between them, the Federalists were on the
side of England, their former enemy, and against France, their former
friend.

The columns of *The National Gazette* supported the new conflict,
which did not replace the old one but served to emphasize it. Under the
circumstances it was not surprising that Hamilton should hate the
French Revolution, but why did he deny America's debt to France for
its help to his own country?[8] Did John Adams, the Vice-President,
really believe that "Dragon's teeth have been sown in France and come
up Monsters?"[9] *The National Gazette* printed an open letter from
Thomas Paine to the people of France to show what democrats thought
of their struggle,[10] while Freneau included a number of excerpts from
Barlow's "Advice to the Privileged Orders" to give a somewhat different picture of the "dragon's teeth" that were being sowed and the
"monsters" that were coming up.[11] He pointed out the indelicacy of
the United States Senate in retaining on its walls the portraits of
Louis XVI and Marie Antoinette, and the affront it offered to the
American people.[12] To those who condemned the Jacobins, he replied

[7] Jefferson to Short, January 3, 1793, in Thomas Jefferson, *Writings* (ed.
P. L. Ford), Vol. 6, pp. 153–157. Also, Jefferson to Short, January 8, 1825, in
which he wrote that on his return to America in 1790 "I was astonished to find
a general prevalence of monarchical" ideas (*Writings* [ed. A. A. Lipscomb,
and A. E. Bergh], Vol. 16, p. 92).

[8] Alexander Hamilton, *Works,* Vol. 5, p. 207; Vol. 6, p. 274.

[9] John Adams to Abigail, January 14, 1793, in John Adams, *Letters Addressed to His Wife,* Vol. 2, pp. 119–120.

[10] See Paine's, *The Rights of Man,* in *The National Gazette,* February 2,
1793.

[11] *The National Gazette,* August 4, 1792.

[12] *Ibid.,* December 22, 1792.

with ringing praise for the cause of liberty and with abiding confidence in the essential outcome of the Revolution, whose goal, he maintained, was also ours.

> On the same grounds our fortunes rest,
> And flourish, or must fail.[13]

The affairs of France and America were confused and embittered even more when James Madison, on the floor of the House, asked some pointed questions about the money that was due to France. Why wasn't it paid? What was the condition of the Treasury anyway? Madison demanded that Hamilton render a complete and simple report that the people could understand. Still the gadfly, he raised more questions about Hamilton's figures, and about their veracity.[14] Analyzing the report finally submitted by the Treasurer, *The National Gazette* found it remiss in vital details, and revealed that Congress, though it apparently accepted the figures of Hamilton, did so by a vote of his own party henchmen. Freneau, hammering away at the political morals and social ethics of the Federalists, missed no opportunity to expose them to the ridicule and contempt of his readers; while Fenno, answering in kind, was supported in his rebuttals by *The Connecticut Courant, The Columbian Centinel,* and *The American Mercury,* which pictured Freneau as

> Sinbat, the smutty link-boy of the muse,
> Who blacks himself to clean his master's shoes—
> Sinbat, who sells his dirty soul for pay,
> Then tries in vain to swear the bribe away.[15]

To this low ebb in national politics had the country fallen. Washed on the scummy shores of power, the wreckage of reputations floated in deep pools of partisanship, while the people looked on, amused and bewildered in turn, sometimes listless when not altogether bored by the new battle of words, sometimes as impassioned as the protagonists themselves. Both sides wondered at the issue of events, the Federalists confident the people would maintain them in office, the republicans waiting for the turn of the tide that would cleanse the waters of the elements that endangered the health and freedom of America.

[13] *Ibid.,* December 19, 1792.
[14] United States Congress, *Annals of Congress,* Vol. 3, pp. 753, 757, 840.
[15] *The American Mercury,* February 4, 1793, quoted by Lewis Leary, *That Rascal Freneau,* pp. 226–227.

As yet the Federalists were impregnable. The measures they proposed were passed by their majorities in Congress, their strength seemingly enhanced by the bloody events which cast a somber shadow on the French Revolution. Louis XVI, whose help had saved America in her time of desperate need, had been beheaded by the beastly rabble of France. Others, neither kings nor tyrants, would be destroyed as he was—including even those who had once been leaders of the Revolution itself. The republican sun was streaked with bands of blood and darkened by scudding clouds of fear and suspicion. The old world, struggling out of the chaos of endless despotism, seemed doomed by frothing madmen to a new chaos of Godless insurrection. The republicans of the new world had condoned, indeed encouraged, what sane men denounced and reasonable men deplored. What was sane? What was reasonable? What help or sympathy could honest men, firm in the faith of freedom, give to those who tore down the slender pillars of freedom in the name, in the high and holy name of freedom?[16]

The answers, sought by many decent Americans in both political camps, must wait on a change in the climate of opinion, on the clearing of the clouds of prejudice, on a turning of the tide of political fortunes. Those fortunes still favored the Federalists, while the work of Freneau, of Madison, of Jefferson, of all those who cried up the cause of the people in France as in America, was powerless to topple them. France, bleeding badly from many wounds self-inflicted, was to be left to her fate, defenseless before the naked swords of a host of enemies, the greatest of whom was the same scarcely chastened Britain of George III, so recently the foe of America.

The British aristocrats, still smarting from the lash of one revolution, were in no mood to temporize with another. They saw eye to eye with the monarchs of Europe on the need to destroy the sans-culottes of Paris and to extirpate, for once and for all, the idea of democratic freedom in the old world. When the Duke of Brunswick was ready to offer his battalions of Austrians, Prussians, Hessians, and émigrés for a march on Paris and a joint encirclement of the French people, it seemed plain to the friends of France that the Revolution was all but doomed. And the American people, confused and bewildered by the swift turn of events long before the formal declaration of war by France on England early in 1793, again felt the tug of old loyalties and

[16] Gershoy, *The French Revolution,* pp. 238 ff.

the revulsion of old antipathies. Many who had doubted before doubted no longer. The darker side of the French struggle was forgotten, and they recalled their own revolution in a new setting, with new actors but with the same enemies as before. England was the ancient foe of freedom, while France was still the lone friend of liberty. Now who would save France? Not the Federalists, surely; as American patriots they had fought against England. As patriots still, they would now support England against France. That was the new challenge to the democratic ideals of the Anti-Federalist forces of Thomas Jefferson.[17]

The republicans, aware of the new danger to democratic principles, accepted the Federalist challenge. For them England was still the enemy, France was still the friend. The treaty of reciprocal aid between America and France must be strictly observed. American ports must remain open to French ships in the war with Britain; they must be closed to all the enemies of France. When Hamilton maintained, with a certain legalistic logic, that the treaty was with a government now defunct, Jefferson replied that a change in government did not vitiate a treaty with its people. Yet a strict observance of that treaty might lead to war—another war with Britain—and how could America, with no ships to oppose British naval strength, undertake such a risk? The matter required the most careful consideration before such a danger was incurred. There was perhaps less danger in receiving the Minister of the French Republic, M. Edmund Genêt, an active and ardent agent of the Revolution, who was already in America and would soon present his credentials to the President.[18]

Washington was in a quandary. Always he was between two fires, exposed to each of them, anxious to placate, hoping to mediate, seeking to unite where there was nothing but division. As the responsible head of the government he feared embroilment in a quarrel in which his country was scarcely concerned and for which it was ill-prepared. Internal hostilities were not yet resolved before these new ones from abroad had begun to plague him. Genêt had brought into the Port of

---

[17] G. M. Trevelyan, *History of England*, pp. 563–565, *passim;* Burke's *Reflections* and Paine's *Rights of Man* represented the opposing philosophies of the Federalist and Republican parties in America. See Hamilton, *Works*, Vol. 6, p. 371, and Jefferson, *Writings* (Lipscomb and Bergh), April 18, 1793, and Jefferson's accompanying Opinion, all in Vol. 1, pp. 349–351.

[18] Jefferson to Madison, April 28, 1793, in Jefferson, *Writings* (Ford), Vol. 4, p. 232; Hamilton, *Works*, Vol. 6, p. 371.

Charleston two captured British vessels and was, in addition, bustling about to outfit a number of privateers for raids on British shipping. As if that was not enough, Americans would man them and American guns would arm them. Genêt, young, charming, and energetic, was acting with all the assurance of a welcome emissary to a friendly ally. Once a correspondent of La Rochefoucauld and Condorcet, he was a man of culture with a background of radical activities among the Girondists, who had appointed him as the first American Minister from the French Republic. Only the year before he had been expelled from Russia by Catharine the Great, who found him too revolutionary for her tastes. The Jacobins, seizing power in France, soon considered him not revolutionary enough.[19]

On his journey from Charleston to Philadelphia, Genêt was winning the hearts of all the people who saw him, who heard him, who accepted his mission as if it was their own. The President, to avoid any entanglement with Britain, must act quickly. Genêt must be curbed; his ardor must be cooled. The time to placate, to mediate, was gone. There was only one course which he believed open to him—neutrality. Even Jefferson agreed on the need for a neutral stand; as Secretary of State he couched in words that softened its impact if not its effect the Presidential policy.[20]

On April 22, 1793, Washington issued his proclamation forbidding any privateering by American citizens and any conduct that was in violation of a strict neutrality. It was, perhaps, a cautionary measure, as statesmanlike as it was necessary. To the republicans (sometimes also known as democratic-republicans and increasingly dignified by the title of Republicans), who persisted in recalling the American Revolution, the Presidential paper was considerably less than that. Freneau, in *The National Gazette* of April 27, 1793, declared his continued faith in the French government and solicited cash contributions for the Patriotic French Society of Philadelphia, organized to help the Revolution, with which to purchase food for France.[21]

Was this a breach of neutrality? While the government was considering an answer, the citizens of Philadelphia were preparing a grand welcome for Genêt, whose ship *L'Embuscade,* gaily bedecked

---

[19] Forman, "The Political Activities," pp. 66–67; Leary, *That Rascal Freneau,* p. 230.

[20] *The National Gazette,* May 18, 1793; *The Gazette of the United States,* April 24, 1793.

[21] *The National Gazette,* April 27, 1793.

with liberty caps and the colors of the French Revolution, appeared in the roadstead of the Delaware River. A crowd of three thousand people, wild with enthusiasm for the genial Genêt, lustily cheered his vessel strung with banners which proclaimed "We are armed for the Defense of the Rights of Man," and "Enemies of Equality, Reform and Tremble," sentiments similar to those of the Declaration of Independence. Writing of the reception to Genêt, Freneau rejoiced at the wonderful welcome to the "defenders of the rights of man and real friends to America in the dark days of war and desolation." If this too was a breach of neutrality let those who thought so make the most of it.[22]

But what could they do if the people also hastened to express their sympathies for France? Liberty poles appeared in public places. French foods were served everywhere, while French bread was eaten with as much pride as gusto. More important, Jacobin clubs and democratic societies began to spring up in many cities as rallying points and meeting places for the friends of the Revolution. Intensive propaganda campaigns were instituted to persuade the hesitant or doubtful of the righteousness of the French cause. Fisher Ames was not too far wrong when he said: "Jacobin Emissaries are sent to every class of men, and even to every individual man, that can be gained. Every threshing floor, every husking, every party at work on a house frame or raising a building—the very funerals are infected with brawlers or whisperers against government."[23]

Edmund Genêt, the darling of the democratic-republicans, had done his job well. He had won not only the esteem of the common people but also the good will of many intellectual leaders in Philadelphia. Men like Dr. David Rittenhouse, the president of the Philosophical Society, and Thomas McKean, the chief justice of Pennsylvania, led a committee of welcome for him at the City Tavern. He was feted by democratic societies where "Citizen Philip Freneau" was asked to translate into English a French ode composed by Citizen Pichon especially for the occasion. It was a less thrilling work than the "Marseillaise" or the "Carmagnole," but that was only because the music was missing. Music was supplied when the French revolutionary anthem saluted the suave and indefatigable M. Genêt. For the

[22] *Ibid.*, May 4, May 18, 1793; Forman, "The Political Activities," p. 60.
[23] Fisher Ames, *Works,* Vol. 2, p. 115; see also J. A. Krout and D. R. Fox, *The Completion of Independence,* p. 159; Freneau, *Poems of Freneau* (ed. H. H. Clark), p. xxxi and *passim.*

moment his mission had been accomplished. Washington, correct in all his international obligations, had received him as Minister Plenipotentiary from the Republic of France.[24]

Philip Freneau, however, was not content. All this was not enough, if Washington's Proclamation of Neutrality was strictly enforced. The government of the United States had recognized the new Republic, but would it implement its recognition with help more substantial than pious platitudes? The editor of *The National Gazette* expected something in addition to a meaningless gesture in which the form but not the substance of recognition was accorded. The embattled forces of France needed help not huzzas, nourishment not neutrality. The people of America had clearly indicated their feelings for France; it was the part of their President to heed their wishes and comply with their demands. If Washington was not properly informed of them, it was his duty to find out. Or was he "so much buoyed up by official importance as to think it beneath his dignity to mix occasionally with the people?" Freneau refused to believe it. "Sir," he pleaded with the President, "let not, I beseech you, the opiate of sycophancy, administered by interested and designing men, lull you into a fatal lethargy at this awful moment. Consider that a first Magistrate in every country is no other than a public servant whose conduct is to be governed by the will of the people."[25]

To apprise him of that will, letters began to appear in *The National Gazette* warning the President against a policy of neutrality, and appealing to him not to "view the state of the public mind through a fallacious medium." One persistent writer, who signed himself "Veritas," cautioned Washington not to mistake "the buzz of the aristocratic few and their contemptible minions of speculators, tories, and British emissaries" for "the exalted and generous voice of the American people." The President must never forget that *"Principles and not men* ought ever to be the objects of *republican* attachment." *The National Gazette*, each issue of which was being sent by the Minister of France to his government, was now urging its readers to ignore the Proclamation of Neutrality, while subtly inciting the people to continue their generous support of France.[26]

[24] *The National Gazette*, May 22, 1793; Leary, *That Rascal Freneau*, p. 232.
[25] *The National Gazette*, June 5, 1793.
[26] *Ibid.*, June 1, June 5, June 8, June 12, 1793; "Correspondance des Ministres Français aux Etats-Unis, 1791–1797," *Annual Report of American Historical Association, 1903*, Vol. 2.

Jefferson, though he approved the principle of neutrality, was out of sympathy with its rigorous enforcement. As a member of the government, he could scarcely condone the conduct of Philip Freneau, especially so since the arrogance of the French Minister was becoming almost insupportable. Yet the provocations for Freneau's attacks on the Administration were great.

When of two nations [Jefferson said], the one has engaged herself in a ruinous war for us, has spent her blood and money for us, has opened her bosom to us in peace and has received us on a footing almost with her own citizens, while the other has moved heaven and earth and hell to exterminate us in war, has insulted us in all her councils, in peace shut her doors to us in every port . . . to place these two nations on an equal footing is to give a great deal more to one than to the other.

And he concluded:

To say in excuse, that gratitude is never to enter into the notions of national conduct is to revive a principle which has been buried for centuries, with its kindred principles of the lawfulness of assassinations, perjury, and poison.[27]

The freckle-faced, sandy-haired, angular figure of the Secretary of State refused to bend before the concerted blasts of the enemy.

The oldest member of Washington's Cabinet, Jefferson was also the most combative, the least susceptible of all to a policy of compromise or diplomatic double-talk. Stubborn in his belief in elementary justice, he refused to accept an easy expediency in its place. With such a man one could argue if not agree; one could respect if not persuade. In any event, Washington needed him, if only because his was the one voice that varied the monotony of uniform agreement among all the others in his Cabinet.

Philip Freneau was something else again. He was no Jefferson, surely; he showed none of the restraint, the dignity, the responsibility of the Secretary of State. Without any power of office, he was also without the discipline which any office imposed. His hands were not tied nor his lips sealed by any allegiance other than the command of his own free conscience or the obligation of his own free press. It was nothing to him if those in power frothed with impotent anger. They could not stop him. Let them say that his villainous articles, his

[27] April 28, 1793, Jefferson, *Writings* (Ford), Vol. 6, pp. 219–231.

presumptuous demands, his gratuitous insults, the scabrous letters which he published—all levelled at the government which kept him on the public payroll—were an unforgivable breach of the common laws of decency. The editor of *The National Gazette* was unmoved. They had slandered him before and he had not submitted. He had no intention of submitting now.

On May 23 Washington proposed to his Secretary of State that he "should interpose in some way with Freneau; perhaps withdraw his appointment of transclerk to his office." Jefferson, no less stubborn than Freneau, refused to fire him. Freneau's paper, he told the President, "has saved our Constitution, which was galloping fast into Monarchy, and has been checked by no means so powerfully as by that paper." He did not tell Washington what else he thought—for his manners were far better than those of Freneau. The President, he thought, was "not sensible of the designs of the party, has not with his usual good sense and sang froid, looked on the efforts and effects of this free press."[28] Certainly the President's sangfroid deserted him at the next cabinet meeting, where he renewed his attack on "that rascal Freneau," who persisted in sending him "three copies (not one) of his paper every day as if he thought he would become the distributor of them." Clearly, such conduct was "nothing but an impudent design to insult him."[29]

Whatever the designs of Philip Freneau, the wish to insult the President surely was not one of them. He had extolled his courage and honor on more than one occasion. He never doubted his true, inward integrity. Yet he also believed him to be the victim of unscrupulous men who would not hesitate to use him for their own selfish ends. To frustrate these men he had published the series of "Probationary Odes," written not by himself as everyone believed, but by St. George Tucker of Virginia. Without mincing words, and naming names, they struck out at Hamilton and John Adams as the men chiefly responsible for official enmity to France, for measures that were harmful to

[28] Jefferson, *Writings* (Ford), Vol. I, p. 231. The same volume, p. 254 contains the reference to Washington's about "that rascal Freneau." Volume I, pp. 231, 254, also contains the "Anas," which are notes by Jefferson relating to his official life and duties. They were meant, in each case, to be private. See also F. W. Hirst, *Life and Letters of Thomas Jefferson,* pp. 265–270.

[29] George Washington, *Writings* (ed. J. C. Fitzpatrick), Vol. 12, p. 312; Forman, "The Political Activities," p. 69.

America, and for laws that derogated the rights of the people themselves.[30]

Freneau's own ideas, more reasonably stated, were contained in his
poem, read at a dinner honoring Genêt at Oeller's Hotel on Chestnut
Street. "God Save the Rights of Man" voiced the aspirations of France
and of freemen throughout the world. Popularized later when it was
sung by Republicans everywhere to the familiar tune adopted for the
National Hymn, it proclaimed:

> Let us with France agree,
> And bid the world be free,
>   While tyrants fall—
> Let the rude savage host
> Of their vast numbers boast
> Freedom's tremendous host
>   Laughs at them all.
>
>   . . .
>
> If e'er her Cause should fail,
> Ambitious fiends assail,
>   Slaves to a throne—
> May no proud despot taunt
> Should he her standard plant
> Freedom shall never want
>   Her Washington.[31]

Here was no insult by the man whom the President had privately
called a rascal. For Freneau as for the people of America, the Father of
his Country was still beyond the pale of censure if not of criticism.
If Freneau continued to send his paper to Washington, not one but
three at a time, it was a species of pressure to offset the tremendous
pressure of others. This was no personal feud with the Federalists.
This was a struggle for principle, the same principle that had been at
stake in the American Revolution. Liberty and Democracy were the
issues now as they had been then, and neutrality was but another
weapon against them, brandished this time by friends instead of foes.
Despite the provocations of England as well as of France, France was

[30] *The National Gazette,* June 1, 1793, and following issues, all supposedly
by Jonathan Pindar; Leary, *That Rascal Freneau,* p. 235.

[31] "God Save the Rights of Man" (later published as "Hymn to Liberty"),
in *The Jersey Chronicle,* July 11, 1795. See also Leary, *That Rascal Freneau,*
p. 234.

the only victim of neutrality, and England the country which all but ignored it.

The pressures to maintain it were continuous, indeed increasing, as Hamilton, under the pseudonym of "Pacificus," upheld the principle of neutrality with renewed vigor in many articles published in *The Gazette of the United States,* and Madison, writing as "Helvetius," answered him in the same paper. Hamilton and Madison argued their cases well in *The Gazette of the United States,* employing all the arts of debate to win support for their respective views. But more than reason and logic or law and justice were used as instruments of persuasion in the competing gazettes of Philadelphia. Abuse and slander were also enlisted in the fight. Washington, wondering at the passions aroused in men of high intelligence and sober minds, turned to Henry Lee for some crumb of comfort. How, he asked, would it all end? "Common decency" was outraged, he said, and his opinion was shared by Federalists throughout the country, who looked on *The National Gazette* and its editor as agents of a scarcely concealed conspiracy to defame the President—the one man whom neither had ever personally attacked or ever intended to malign.[32]

Freneau's insistent and raucous defense of the French, his continued support of Edmund Genêt were added thorns in the side of his enemies. Even Jefferson was becoming annoyed with the Minister from France, who was taking a high-handed view of his importance. Ignoring the neutrality of America, he had brought a captured English merchantman to Philadelphia, where he hired an American crew to sail her as a privateer. Ordered to stop these flagrant breaches of Washington's proclamation, he arrogantly threatened to "appeal to the people" of America over the President's head. Finally, he sent the vessel out anyway, not only an act of defiance of Washington himself, but an insult to the entire government as well. Jefferson could see that—he wrote Madison as much. And Madison, thoroughly infuriated, informed James Monroe that not only was Genêt's conduct that of a madman, but "he is abandoned even by his votaries of Philadelphia." What was far worse, Genêt had "ruined the republican interest in that place."[33]

[32] *The Gazette of the United States,* June 29 to July 20, 1793; also August 24 to September 18, 1793; Washington to Lee, July 21, 1793 (marked "Private"), in Washington, *Writings* (Fitzpatrick), Vol. 33, p. 24.

[33] Jefferson to Madison, August 25, 1793, in Jefferson, *Writings* (Lipscomb

One place in Philadelphia where Genêt's conduct had not ruined the republican interest was the office of *The National Gazette*. So often criticized as the mouthpiece of Jefferson, Freneau did not agree with him on the business of Edmund Genêt. Celebrating the achievements of his ship *L'Embuscade,* he refused to temper his admiration for the rampant representative from France. "Why," he asked, "all this outcry against" Genêt? "The Minister of France, I hope, will act with firmness and with spirit. The people are his friends, or rather the friends of France, and he will have nothing to apprehend, for as yet the people are sovereign in the United States." And he concluded: "If one of the leading features of our government is pusillanimity, when the British lion shows his teeth, let France and her Minister act as becomes the dignity and justice of their cause and the honor and faith of Nations."[34]

Freneau's voice found few echoes in any of the halls of state or national government. Now not only Jefferson but many others among the Republican leaders believed that Genêt must be curbed, while not a few of the readers of *The National Gazette* were also convinced that Freneau's support of a man who flouted the government's authority was worse than the neutrality law itself. Perhaps Freneau was not altogether wrong in believing that law to be only another door shut upon decency and honor when it should have been opened wide by generosity and gratitude. But Washington was justified in asking for the recall of Genêt, who impudently went beyond all bounds to embarrass and embroil America in domestic as well as in foreign troubles. He was even involved in a plot to take Louisiana, and in a scheme to seize Florida, from Spain. It was important that his official status and the immunity which it gave him should be revoked without any further delay.

The enemies of France, needing no further proof of the debasement of its Revolution, received it nevertheless. The Girondists had been deprived of power, and now the bloody Jacobins were in full control,

---

and Bergh), Vol. 9, pp. 211; also Jefferson to Madison, September 1, 1793, in *ibid.* Vol. 9, pp. 212–215; and Jefferson to Madison, August 7, 1793, in Jefferson, *Writings* (Ford), Vol. 6, pp. 338–339. Madison was at last disillusioned with Genêt (Madison to Monroe, September 15, 1793, in Irving Brant, *James Madison,* Vol. 3, *Father of the Constitution, 1787–1800,* p. 384). Finally, he wrote that Genêt was acting like "a madman" (Madison to Monroe, September 15, 1793, in Madison, *Writings,* Vol. 6, pp. 197–198.

[34] *The National Gazette,* August 17, 1793; Forman, "The Political Activities," pp. 68–70.

while the guillotine was busy as never before. Genêt himself, appointed by the Gironde, was liable to be cut down if he returned to
France. But Genêt, no fool, refused to return. With more caution and
less bravura than he had ever shown before, he decided to remain in
America, to become a citizen of the country, and to marry the daughter
of Governor Clinton. Though Freneau doubted the revolutionary virtues of Citizen Genêt at last, the virtue of the French Revolution and
the injustice of the neutrality policy of Washington were beyond all
doubt. If the readers of *The National Gazette* did not entirely agree
with him or with the policy of his paper, it was only because their
minds had been poisoned by *The Gazette of the United States* and the
fulminations of the Federalists. He had done his best to prepare the
people for the turning of the tide of democracy, and if they were not
yet prepared, if the time was not yet ripe for a change, he was willing
to wait—and to work—for the day of days.

Not unexpectedly, the circulation of *The National Gazette* fell off
alarmingly. Its influence, once so strong, had begun to weaken. Other
papers, *The Boston Gazette, The Independent Chronicle,* still friendly
to France, held fast their small circle of the faithful, but in Philadelphia, the capital of America and the stronghold of the Federalist
party, the voice of democracy was weakened almost to a whisper. Only
the stubborn will of Philip Freneau kept it from sinking into silence
altogether.[35]

And soon not even he would be able to prevent it from expiring.
What the Federalists had tried so diligently to accomplish, another
enemy, more virulent than they, would bring to pass. They had failed,
but the yellow fever, raging throughout the city of Philadelphia,
would surely succeed. Where so many died, *The National Gazette*
must also perish.

[35] D. A. Goddard, *Newspapers and Newspaper Writers in New England,*
passim.

25. FEVER AND FAILURE

EPIDEMICS were not new in America. They had decimated vast numbers of human beings in the brief history of the new world, their causes as little known as the means to prevent them. No adequate knowledge of the principles of hygiene existed, and there was little scientific learning to cope with a scourge that killed quickly and with tragic abandon. Once started, the plague must run its course, leaving only desolation in its wake, a ghostly reminder of the utter defenselessness of man.

In Philadelphia during the awful summer of 1793, a few wise men were ready to believe that he was not altogether without defense. For Philadelphia was the great—indeed the greatest—city of America in many respects; in this respect above all others, that its hospitals, medical equipment, and doctors were the best in the country. The first medical school in America was established there, and among its staff were the foremost physicians and scientists of the day, not the least of whom was the patriot of the Revolution and experimenter in medicine, Dr. Benjamin Rush. Yet they were powerless to solve the increasingly complex problems of sewage disposal, pure water, and uncontaminated food. There was no scavenger system, no bureau for cleaning the streets of refuse, no official group charged with the duty of guarding the health of the people. Garbage and filth cluttered the gutters, streets, and wharves of the Quaker City; stenches from the tanneries and starch factories mingled with the noisome odors of the public privies; water was befouled and food was exposed in the hot sun to swarms of insects that defied the best efforts of the street commissioners to prevent the "noxious effluvia of the atmosphere." The poor had no choice but to remain in that atmosphere, while those who could afford to do so, decamped to the green fields and cool hills along the Schuylkill, to their country homes where the stenches did not reach them or the refuse of the city offend them.[1]

No more had left during this hot month of July than in any summer before. By August it appeared that many more were leaving than was usual in the dog days of a sultry climate. The rumor of an epidemic spread slowly at first, when only a few cases of scarlet fever, cholera morbus, and malaria were reported. People will cling to their homes on the slopes of Vesuvius, on the hills of Aetna, though they erupt a little or even a great deal, if they rock in convulsions or run with molten lava. As the rumor of epidemic gained momentum and old diseases were augmented by a new one, stranger and more terrifying, ruthless and more destructive than any yet known to the distracted victims, rumor was converted to fact, and fact became—panic! Yellow fever, a swift and implacable killer of men, was loose among them. Philadelphia was a charnel house of the dead and the dying. Terror stalked the streets, looting had begun, the almshouse—a hospital for the poor—was filled to capacity and turning away the stricken and the helpless. Mayor Matthew Clarkson was urging the College of Physicians to formulate some drastic rules for avoiding infection.[2]

One rule—the best of all—was flight. Escape from the scorching streets, from the narrow, stinking alleys, from the broad boulevards where the enemy could also strike, was the one real hope for safety. The pestilence was no respecter of persons, and the rich as well as the poor were vulnerable before its fetid breath. Eighteen thousand, almost half the population of Philadelphia, did escape, on foot, by coach, in any way possible, often without food and rarely with more than a bagful of their worldly goods. Tents were pitched along the Schuylkill, where many slept; others slept beneath the stars unless more fortunate citizens offered a few of them the shelter of their homes in the country. Most of them, the great throngs who had no tents or homes to sleep in and could not afford to hire them, pleaded for help but pleaded in vain. They were shut out by exorbitant rentals or by fear of contamination.[3]

The great migration from Philadelphia became a frantic search by the wanderers for a home, any home, in the nighttime of their despair. Many of them perished not from fever but from want, not swiftly

[1] *Pennsylvania Cavalcade,* pp. 154–155.
[2] *Ibid.*
[3] *Ibid.*

but slowly, from hunger and exposure, from panic and fear. Men became beasts, forsaking, denying even their own. A touch of the hand, a breath on the lips, a glance of the eye, if they seemed the least bit strange or distempered, were signals for a merciless avoidance and inhuman refusal. "Many people," Dr. Benjamin Rush informed his wife, "thrust their parents into the streets as soon as they complained of a headache." Dr. Rush knew the full measure of the tragedy but was helpless to soften its impact. He tried everything—a gentle emetic, blisters on the limbs, head, and neck, blankets dipped in warm vinegar to wrap around the body, cold water by the bucketful to throw on the prostrate victims, endless bleeding and purging. All of them failed—and most of the afflicted died.[4]

Nor was the suffering that of the victims alone—all were caught in this trap of terror that stopped the hearts and choked the cries of men. The officials of the city were gone; the lawmakers had fled; all business had ceased; prices were fantastic; but the people, the poor who stayed and those who fled, were the greatest victims of all. Their rotting bodies lay everywhere; corpses were looted; burials were few; and only Negroes could be induced to touch the dead for interment. For some people it was a time of affluence greater than any they had known in the past. The coffin-makers thrived in a city where nearly five thousand souls succumbed to the scourge.[5]

The unfortunate city of Philadelphia had its heroes as well as its harlots, the men who refused to flee but stayed to succor. Doctors like Benjamin Rush and Jean Devéze, who knew little about yellow fever but a great deal about the Hippocratic oath, remained to salvage what they could of the human rubble left by the hurricane of death. A few ministers of the Gospel stayed on to comfort their afflicted flocks; and there were some businessmen for whom business was a giving as well as a taking process. Stephen Girard and Israel Israel, more concerned with people than with profits, were swept by a flood-tide of compassion to put away trade to deal with suffering. And the merchant Caleb Lownes, forsaking the market-place, held the macabre bastion of Bush Hill Hospital for the sick and the dying, aided by black men who were as generous and brave as some of their brothers were greedy and skulking. For all of them the courage of despair was the only hope of

4 *Ibid.*, p. 160; Benjamin Rush, *An Account of the Bilious Remitting Yellow Fever*, pp. 193, 195, 203.

5 *Pennsylvania Cavalcade*, p. 161; John Davis, *Travels of Four Years and a Half in the U.S.*, p. 147.

salvation, and the cause of salvation was the ineffable one of life itself.[6]

When Mayor Clarkson called a meeting of public-spirited citizens to help in this cause only a few, only these few, came to help him. There was no longer any panic, only a dumb resignation that neither gave nor any longer asked for help. Death was too visible, too common, to inspire pity. Even "the loss of relations and friends" wrung no tears; the "common signs of grief" were gone. Grief was a luxury which there was little energy to enjoy, though a few luxuries still remained for some. Leaders of government, men in high places, could flee to safety and enjoy them. Washington, properly enough, had left the capital for Mount Vernon, while Jefferson, shortly to resign anyway, was home in Monticello. Knox had fled; and Hamilton, touched by a bit of fever, had followed him. As the days dragged their ghastly course through July and August and into September; as cool days and clear autumnal nights swept away the last specters of the plague from the exhausted city, a day of "general humiliation, thanksgiving and prayer" was ordained by the governor of Pennsylvania. The fever was over. The panic was gone. The City of Brotherly Love settled down once more to its accustomed ways.[7]

Philip Freneau had not left the city at all. Eleanor and the child, who had been with him in Philadelphia, were back in Mount Pleasant. Struggling to keep his paper afloat in a sea raging with suffering and cluttered with death, he continued his defense of the French Revolution as if nothing had happened. There were few in Philadelphia to read what he had to say, or to read anything, but there were other cities where the plague was known only by hearsay, and where the enemies of democracy were as active as ever. Though *The National Gazette* was sinking, indeed, like so many of the people of Philadelphia, appeared to be dying, it was still alive while most of the other newspapers of the city had already given up the ghost. *The Pennsylvania Packet* had quit on September 11; Dunlap's *Daily American Advertiser* followed suit on September 14; Bache, not easily discouraged, had closed down *The General Advertiser*. And John Fenno, even Fenno, had stopped publication of *The Gazette of the United States*, on September 18, leaving only *The Federal Gazette* and Freneau's own paper in the field—a sere and fallow field indeed.[8]

It was no quixotic defiance of danger that held Freneau to his post,

[6] J. H. Powell, *Bring Out Your Dead,* pp. 281–282, and Introduction.
[7] *Pennsylvania Cavalcade,* p. 161.
[8] Powell, *Bring Out Your Dead,* p. 141.

nor a hope for increased circulation in a city shorn of almost all competitors. No captain deserted his command in a time of danger—there was both pride and a sense of responsibility in Freneau's determination to stay on to the end, whatever that end might be. Missing no single issue, he continued to publish the paper as a public and a private duty, attempting to soften the tragedy of the plague wih an occasional bit of humor, a rollicking satire on the shepherds who had flocks, or a piece stuffed with puns as a pastry with raisins. He tried to temper the horrors of those who remained in the stricken city, of those who could still see through tears that blinded so many eyes. There were, apparently, not many of them left in Philadelphia; too few, indeed, to keep *The National Gazette* and its master afloat any longer.[9]

Try as he would, the paper could not survive. There was too much trouble collecting fees due from distant subscribers. Delivery outside of the city was precarious and always uncertain. Childs and Swaine were losing money too rapidly and refusing to take any further risks. Not only the readers, even the printers, had been alienated by Freneau's loyalty to Genêt. They saw nothing but bankruptcy ahead. And the editor could do nothing, financially, to help them. His work as translator for the State Department had proven only a loss to him. At his own expense he had hired others to translate papers from Holland and Germany and Russia, "at an exorbitant rate of charge." When it became inevitable that the paper must be an additional drain on his meager resources, he decided to quit. On October 1, 1793, he resigned as clerk in the office of the Secretary of State. On October 27 he was also finished with *The National Gazette*.[10]

Perhaps he could resume its publication at some later date, if he raised the money to do so. "Some new and elegant" type, acquired for the old paper, would do just as well for a new one. The hope was never realized. The precious type would be used—but not for *The National Gazette*. His work would go on; he would publish other papers. His life had been given to the fight for democracy and that fight would end

[9] *Ibid.*, p. 239.

[10] *The National Gazette,* September 11, 1793, October 2, 1793; Lewis Leary, *That Rascal Freneau,* p. 244, cites *The City Gazette* of Charleston, January 5, 1801; R. W. Griswold, *The Poets and Poetry of America,* p. 50, states that Freneau admitted to Dr. Francis that Jefferson did supply many articles against Washington's Administration to *The National Gazette.* See also, Phillip Marsh, "Madison's Defense of Freneau," *William and Mary Quarterly,* third series, III, 2 (April 1946), 269–274; and Marsh, *Monroe's Defense of Jefferson and Freneau.*

only with his death. His struggle seemed like a losing one and the tide was far from turning, yet men were more keenly aware of the issues of the time, though they still felt powerless to resolve them.

To achieve a greater revulsion against the policies of the Federalists would require some events more dramatic, some threats to men's liberties more pressing, than any so far experienced. Convinced that they would come, Freneau never wavered in his faith that his own labors, which rarely faltered, would be proven not to have been in vain. If he had accomplished so little with his political or literary works, he had dallied with no compromise nor bowed to any expediency. Through every misfortune he had remained

> Hostile to garter, ribband, crown and star,
> Still on the people's, still on Freedom's side,
> With full determin'd aim, to battle every claim,
> Of well-born wights, that aim to mount and ride.[11]

This was no idle boast, no prideful pose. It was true—the only truth he could carry back with him to Mount Pleasant. The idea of liberty and the ideal of democracy were in the nature of moral laws and categorical imperatives which must never yield to any expediency or to any pressure of time and circumstance. If, in a world of practical men, they seemed more like a poet's illusions than the substance of truth, then Philip Freneau, leaving Philadelphia, had few others besides them.

Of more private illusions, as he considered his situation on the long ride home, he had none at all. Nor was the back-breaking, comfortless stage, with its three hard benches on which nine passengers were crowded together, a contrivance calculated to induce any. By the time it reached Frankfort, six miles away, he could scarcely get off to restore the circulation in his numbed legs while the four horses were watered at the trough. The travellers needed something stronger than water to brace them against the crippling ride to Bristol, the interminable wait for the ferry across the Delaware to Burlington, and the equally trying if more interesting jog-trot through the delightful countryside to Trenton, frequently broken by "some stretches of poor and barren soil." As the stage hurried through fields of wheat and flax on the road to Princeton, the hilly country of Freneau's golden years loomed before them, and Princeton itself, a pleasant memory of bucolic peace and quiet walks lined with green catalpas which gave such lovely shade in hot and sultry weather. And now the climb begins, when driver and

---

[11] Freneau, *Poems of Freneau* (ed. H. H. Clark), p. xxvii.

passengers must get off and walk—a blessed relief for some, for others a trial even worse than the cold, cutting wind that blows through a vehicle curtained only on the side but open to all the elements in front. There might be a change to another stage, perhaps an overnight layover at some inn where a bed would be shared with another. For those bound for New York, the journey is far from finished; it will go on and on, seemingly forever, to Brunswick by way of Rock Hill, across the Raritan by barge (if the tide is high) and on to Woodbridge and Rahway and Elizabethtown and Newark and Bergen and Paulus Hook, at long last the final, precarious crossing of the Hudson, sometimes in fifteen minutes and sometimes in all of two hours.[12] Philip Freneau did not regret that his own travels were less extensive than this, which might consume as much as a day and a half more.

At Mount Pleasant again, he was faced with problems he had rarely considered in the time of the plague in Philadelphia. He was of no value whatever on the farm where his mother, with constant supervision, still managed to live with his sister Mary. Margaret, the younger girl, was married to John Hunn and no longer dependent on her for support, but in her place there was Eleanor, who was soon expecting another baby.[13] What could he contribute to the household besides his presence, and an occasional poem that earned as little as he did? There was little nourishment in his fine collection of books, nor much pleasure either in reading them when there was more urgent work to do, the kind of work he could do only with pen on paper, not with a spade in the ground. It was more than a matter of making a living; he must feel some importance as a cog, if only that and nothing more, in the vast wheel that moved the world, the world he lived in and loved so well, the world of America, in whose soil he had labored so long for a harvest of universal freedom. He had never appealed to others for help as he now appealed to James Madison, not for himself, but for another. His old friend Francis Bailey had suffered severe financial reverses during the epidemic in Philadelphia. Unless he received the printing of the House of Representatives, he could not survive after a lifetime of honest and useful labor. Madison, an influential leader in the House, might be able to get this patronage for Bailey. Freneau asked him to try. For himself he needed little, and what he did need was providentially as close to his hand as it was to his heart. He would

---

[12] M. L. E. Moreau de Saint Méry, *American Journey*, pp. 96–97, 100, 109, 118–119.

[13] Hammell Notes, Mss., p. 3.

start another paper with the "new and elegant" type he had bought for *The National Gazette*. Now he could use it for a newssheet printed in Mount Pleasant.[14]

The old project of publishing a journal in Monmouth, given up at the behest of Madison and Jefferson, came alive again. For two hectic years Freneau had labored on *The National Gazette* and he had made it the greatest—certainly the most widely known—of all newspapers in the United States. He had instructed the people, the government itself, on the democratic issues of the day, and had suffered the vilest attacks on his honor and probity for his pains. "Free of all ambitious displays" in his person or his politics, he was no man's man, and if the seed he sowed had fallen on barren ground, he had tended his garden with the utmost care, and cultivated the soil for a few of the flowers of liberty.[15] In this as in his other enterprises he had possibly failed, if failure or success was measured by his personal fortunes. But he had never made these the sole criterion of any undertaking, seeking in his literary as in political works to express only his profoundest beliefs. His verse often, too often, fell to the level of mere propaganda and pamphleteering; frequently it failed to achieve the high stature of poetry. The failure of the times to foster and encourage the expression of spiritual insights was as much to blame as the conflict in which the flights of fancy were less useful than earth-bound necessities to his country's survival. Released from these he was capable of writing some of the loveliest of America's early poems, richly evocative of the native scene and its life, its hopes, its aspirations, and its achievements. Freedom—and the struggle to maintain and enlarge it—was his single theme in all the infinite variations of his work.[16]

His prose, unequalled in early American literature for its salty satire and gentle humor, its devastating irony and homely logic, was often cheapened like his doggerel by passion and invective, sometimes by meanness and exaggeration. He used the tools of his enemies and employed their means for ends that were different from theirs. He willingly paid the price for those ends, believing that the ends of liberty and democracy were worth whatever they cost. *The National Gazette*

[14] Freneau to Madison, April 6, 1795, in Freneau Collection (Rutgers).

[15] E. A. Duyckinck, "Memoir," in Freneau's *Poems Relating to the American Revolution*, p. lxiv.

[16] H. H. Clark, "What Made Freneau the Father of American Poetry?" *Studies in Philology*, xxvi, 1 (January 1929), 1–22; and Freneau, *The Miscellaneous Works of Philip Freneau*.

had failed—but did the ideas which he had fostered also fail? The Federalists appeared impregnable, the tide had not yet turned—but was it really so? The battle was over, but the war would go on. For the moment, Freneau could turn to other things.[17]

He was building a small printing house near his home, and ordering some engravings in New York for his new paper. He was looking for subscribers—at least five hundred of them—to sign up for it, each at one dollar and fifty cents a year. If he got them, as he announced on July 4, 1794, the new weekly would appear in October, with foreign as well as domestic news, all "impartial and judiciously compiled" by himself. He already had a name for it. *The Monmouth Gazette and East Jersey Intelligencer*, except for subscribers, was ready to be launched. And the subscribers never materialized. Before it was born the paper had died.[18]

If one project failed, Freneau could try another. The smell, the smudge of printer's ink were more than the marks of a trade, and type was more than metal. They were not only a living—if that—but far more a way of life. He could not publish a paper, but he could print something else, something that was more in demand by the people of Monmouth. He might make enough money on *The Monmouth Almanac* to start a newspaper without any subscribers at all. Certainly he should earn enough to support his family while he set type and printed another book of his poems.

Using his "new and elegant type," Freneau printed a compendium of knowledge filled with a miscellany of information about the zodiac, the moon and stars, the weather, the use of oxen on farms, and the methods for preserving peach trees against the ubiquitous worm. Almanacs were nothing new in America. Frequently, they were the only source of information, both practical and legendary, in small communities where no other was available. In many homes across the country they were second in importance only to the Bible. In Monmouth, an almanac supplied a real need. For those who were interested, Freneau listed the sessions of the New Jersey Supreme Court and the meetings of the Quakers. He lifted material from other almanacs, added a little of his own, and aimed to give it all a seasoning of humor

[17] *Ibid.;* Freneau, *The Prose of Philip Freneau* (ed. Philip M. Marsh).
[18] Broadsides, July 4, 1794, copies in Monmouth County Historical Society; S. W. Patterson, *The Spirit of the American Revolution as Revealed in the Poetry of the Period,* p. 218.

rarely found anywhere else.[19] It sold even better than he had hoped;
more important, it allowed him the leisure to begin the almost hercu-
lean task of putting into type the 450 pages of his new collection of
poems, most of them old ones rewritten and carefully polished, some
of them never before in print. Completed in April 1795 the volume
was destined, for all the labor that went into it, to have only a modest
success.[20]

But it was not for such enterprises that he had acquired his type and
built his little workshop. He still nourished the persistent ambition to
print a newspaper. If only a few subscribers could be encouraged to
sign up, he might be able to publish it with the help of a few odd jobs
in printing, and the sale of some books otherwise unobtainable in
Monmouth. Thus far, the only book that lovers of literature could buy
in Freneau's shop was the fat and dumpy volume of his own poems
recently printed. Plenty of these were available. Now they would find
other works too, but most of all they would find the new paper which
made its first appearance on May 2, 1795. It was called *The Jersey
Chronicle.*"[21]

Its readers became speedily aware that Freneau was still the unre-
generate radical, the fighter for democracy in a continuing contest
between the Federalists and the Republicans. The quiet, secluded hills
and valleys of Monmouth barely had heard the echoes of the political
tumult which the yellow fever had muffled but not entirely dissipated.
In the City of Brotherly Love the alarms and excursions had resumed
once more with greater animosity than ever. An uprising had occurred
as ominous as the rebellion of Daniel Shays and his disgruntled farmers
in Massachusetts. Not in Massachusetts, but in Pennsylvania, a new
rebellion by farmers had challenged the authority of the Administration to enforce a tax on whisky. Washington, on September 25, 1794,
had informed Burges Ball that the insurrection in the western counties
"may be considered as the first ripe fruit of the democratic societies,"[22]
a fruit that must be cut down with troops—with fifteen thousand of
them—a most peculiar use of such great power for a crop like this.

---

[19] Leary, *That Rascal Freneau*, pp. 249–250.

[20] Freneau, *Poems Written between the Years 1768 and 1794.*

[21] *The Jersey Chronicle*, May 2, 1795.

[22] Washington to Ball, September 25, 1794, George Washington, *Writings*
(ed. J. C. Fitzpatrick), Vol. 33, p. 505. See also George Gibbs, *Memoirs of the
Administration of Washington and John Adams, passim;* and N. Schachner,
Alexander Hamilton, p. 338.

Hamilton, charged with the duty of putting down the rebellion, had sent Henry Lee to do a job which must be done quickly to be effective. The farmers of Pennsylvania proved more docile than those of Massachusetts—and their leaders were more fortunate, too. Freneau's classmate Hugh Brackenridge was lucky to escape from tangling with the troops of Hamilton, or he might never have worked on his novel, *Modern Chivalry*, the long-projected satire on America and some of its less lovely aspects. Fortunately the temerity of Hugh Brackenridge cost him only the good opinion of Hamilton, who called him "the worst of all scoundrels,"[23] but then the Federalists had called Freneau even worse things than that without ever silencing him.[24]

And he was not silenced now either. In the very first issue of *The Jersey Chronicle* he was appealing to his readers to emancipate "themselves from those shackles of despotism" which had "rendered the rights of the many subservient to the interests of the few." He promised to keep them informed of what transpired "in the present history and politics of the world" as well as enlighten them on the condition of liberty in America.[25] He kept his word.

The news of Europe and America was printed for the readers of *The Jersey Chronicle* as quickly as he could learn it from newspapers published in larger cities, since there was no other source of information in the backwoods of Monmouth. From papers closer to the fountain of knowledge, he reprinted what knowledge they contained of the struggle between the Republicans and the Federalists. The Philadelphia *Aurora*, the New York *Argus, Journal,* and *Patriotic Register,* the Boston *Independent Chronicle,* the Maryland *Journal,* the Charleston *City Gazette,* the Albany *Register,* and the *New Jersey State Gazette*—all were carefully combed for any items that might be helpful in understanding that struggle, with special reference to and a marked bias for the policies and principles of the democratic partisans in America. In addition he made his own observations and comments on the news, all of them written as simply as possible for home consumption and all carefully calculated to make *The Jersey Chronicle* a stout organ of Republican opinion—an extension of *The National Gazette* rather than a substitute for the defunct paper.[26]

[23] C. M. Newlin, on *Modern Chivalry,* in *Life and Writings of Hugh H. Brackenridge.*
[24] *Ibid.;* see also George Washington, *Letters and Addresses,* p. 364.
[25] *The Jersey Chronicle,* May 2, 1795.
[26] *Ibid.;* Leary, *That Rascal Freneau,* p. 254.

"It will scarcely be expected," Freneau informed Madison, "that in a crude barbarous part of the country I should calculate it for the polite taste of Philadelphia." His own taste, he continued, was for the simple life of Mount Pleasant, where he expected "to pass the remainder of my days on a couple of hundred acres of an old sandy patrimony." Between the farm and the paper, he might perhaps support himself and his family—and a visit from Madison and his recently acquired bride, "should you ever take an excursion to these parts of Jersey," would be most welcome. Madison, once rumored in love with Freneau's own sister Mary, had married the young and charming widow Dolly Payne Todd instead. They never found the time or occasion for the visit to Mount Pleasant, for Madison was too busy in Congress, always fighting the old battle of the Republicans, while his friend Freneau was equally busy with the same fight in the columns of *The Jersey Chronicle.*[27]

Freneau was probably too critical of the "barbarous" country of Monmouth, yet demands for the books he sold at his shop singularly justified his skepticism. The tastes of the people who patronized him ran to such volumes as *The Strangers' Assistant, and Schoolboy's Instructor,* a textbook on arithmetic, and *The Cavern of Death: A Moral Tale,* or Richard Brother's *A Revealed Knowledge of the Prophecies of the Times.* He sold them Hugh Blair's *Sermons* and Soame Jenyn's *Free Inquiry into the Nature and Origin of Evil,* while Cornaro's *Treatise on the Benefits of a Sober Life* was doubtless an effective antidote to another book which he featured at the store—the *Poems* of Philip Freneau himself. The other volumes which he displayed were more suited to the "polite taste" of Philadelphia than Mount Pleasant, but a customer might still ask for a copy of Johnson's *Rasselas,* or Cowper's *Poems* or Goldsmith's *Essays.* Whatever was sold helped him a little in the publication of his paper, which, together with some sporadic attempts at farm work, kept him busier than he had ever been before.[28]

The living from them all was a poor one, but he was not unhappy on that account. Eleanor had given birth to another girl, named Agnes after his mother, and a peace such as he had rarely known pervaded

[27] Freneau to Madison, May 20, 1795, in James Madison Papers, Mss., XVIII–51; also Freneau, *The Poems of Philip Freneau* (ed. F. L. Pattee), Vol. I, pp. lxiv–lxv; Leary, *That Rascal Freneau,* p. 410.

[28] Francis Bailey, Day Book, Ms., p. 14; *The Jersey Chronicle,* September 12, 1795.

the modest, locust-lined estate at Mount Pleasant.[29] Eleanor seemed
more content than she had ever been in the hostile atmosphere of
Philadelphia, while her husband, no longer a pariah in "polite" society,
was slowly achieving a local eminence untarnished by slander and vilification. His poem, "God Save the Rights of Man," sung at Middletown Point on the Fourth of July, almost made him a hero among the
hardy folk of Monmouth. Soon he was the honored Secretary of a
Committee chosen by the townships of Middletown and Freehold to
prepare resolutions to Congress against the new treaty negotiations
pending between England and America.[30]

Philip Freneau was making his mark at last. The prophet was not
without honor in his own land. His acres were "sandy," and so indeed
were his fortunes, but now they had the glint of gold in them.

[29] Freneau Family Bible; Agnes was born June 22, 1794.
[30] *The Jersey Chronicle*, July 11, August 22, 1795.

26. TREATIES AND TRAITORS

THE PROPOSED TREATY between the former enemies was a subject on which Freneau had some definite if hostile opinions. Through the columns of his eight-page *Chronicle,* his readers received a fair appraisal of its terms, not all of them revealed to his subscribers for not all of them had yet been revealed to the country. Most of them were carefully guarded from the people. What Freneau knew he published, including the arguments of its friends as well as its foes. John Jay, the Chief Justice of the Supreme Court, sent by Washington to negotiate for America, had a most difficult task, faced with but few alternatives to the acceptance of a treaty imposed by a government possessing a navy powerful enough to enforce its demands.[1]

It was also true, perhaps, that John Jay, able and well-intentioned as he was, had a "weak spot" that made him vulnerable to the blandishments of Grenville, the British Foreign Minister with whom he was closeted so much and so often in London. Grenville had carefully studied a secret report on Jay prepared for him by the British Minister in America. The Chief Justice, the report stated, could "bear opposition to what he advocates provided regard is shown to his ability." It clearly summarized his character with the observation that "almost every man has a weak spot and Mr. Jay's weak spot is Mr. Jay." He was flattered and feted while the conversations dragged on interminably until the treaty was finally drawn and agreed to. As the debate and some of its strange conclusions were carried across the sea, the strength and weakness of each side were seized on by Federalists or Republi-

[1] Kenneth B. Umbreit, *Our Eleven Chief Justices,* pp. 46 ff.

cans according to their interests, while Philip Freneau, turning from the distasteful "grubbing" on the farm and the often equally distasteful customers in the shop, wrote a scathing criticism of the treaty terms in *The Jersey Chronicle*.[2]

Britain, in violation of her former treaty obligations with America, had failed to remove all her garrisons in the northwest posts. She had justified her failure by a dereliction on the part of America to enforce the payment of debts due to English creditors. Now that England and France were at war, American shipping, despite American neutrality, was being attacked by Great Britain, which did not consider her spoilations, her impressment of American seamen, as in any respect illegal. The rules of international law, fixed in the treaty of 1778 between France and America, were at the mercy of England, and America was bereft of any means to enforce them if the new treaty brought back by John Jay from England was sustained. All questions, including that of impressment, would then be decided by a mixed court of claims, thus effectively cloaking what was obviously unlawful in a mantle of false legality so transparent as more than ever to increase the contemptuous consideration of any solemn American obligation to France. France, already at war with most of Europe, would literally be maneuvered into a state of war with America.[3]

In America the Republicans bitterly fought against this perversion of justice as well as of law. They called for the rejection of the Jay Treaty as forcefully as the Federalists pressed for its ratification. In his attacks upon it, Freneau was supported by Jefferson and Madison, who once more took up the cudgels they had never really put down. The old struggle between the Administration and the democratic-republicans, interrupted by the plague, was renewed with all its venom and rancor, while Hamilton, speaking strongly for the treaty, was stoned by a hostile crowd and Jay, more fortunate than he, was only hung in effigy. Looking on and rightly appraising the turmoil in America, was the French Minister Fauchet, whose lengthy reports to his government kept it fully informed of the crisis in the new world. Fauchet's countryman, M. Moreau de Saint Méry, who had helped to take the Bastille, and was now himself a refugee from the guillotine, noted a few disturbing aspects of life in America, where the vaunted liberty he had sought was sometimes far from manifest in many parts of the country,

[2] *Ibid.*, and *The Jersey Chronicle*, May 2, 1795.

[3] *Ibid.*; R. A. Billington, B. L. Lowenberg, and S. H. Brockunier, *The United States: American Democracy in World Perspective*, pp. 86–89.

even in such places as New York, where he witnessed the shackling of Negro children and the whipping of slave boys for the most petty of "crimes." There were many iniquities in America, but the greatest one of all, not alone for Frenchmen, but for Americans—for Philip Freneau especially—was the Jay Treaty.[4]

American commerce had suffered badly from the depredations of England, yet the treaty carried a reward instead of a penalty for these depredations, Freneau said. This he added, "is quite a phenomenon in national affairs." It was the very height of iniquity that "America licks the hand just raised to shed her blood." Such conduct enjoined on his countrymen the solemn obligation to "examine and judge for yourselves. Remember that national rights, once abandoned, are not easily regained, that national interests once surrendered are not easily retrieved. Let not the sovereign people of the United States be converted into a nation of dupes for the aggrandizment of individuals, or of the British Empire."[5] Freneau was referring particularly to the provisions of the treaty on the payment of debts due her nationals.

The question he raised would be broached again by Patrick Henry when actions at law were begun to recover debts incurred by patriots during the Revolution. As Patrick Henry would be defeated by the Supreme Court later in his opposition to payments exacted by Loyalists who had battened on the needs of America, so Freneau was destined to wage a losing battle now, though he made it quite plain that the Jay Treaty was an instrument, a weapon, with which England could nullify its defeat in the new world while restoring "monocratic" rule and despotism in the old. The long article "On Monarchy" made it crystal clear to Freneau's public what he meant by monocratic rule in America. It was the sum of all the antidemocratic policies of the Federalists, which must be strenuously resisted at the peril of losing whatever freedom had already been won. The lessons of the past, the portents for the future, were set down so that no man could mistake them.[6]

---

[4] *The Jersey Chronicle,* May 9, May 16, 1795; M. L. E. Moreau de St. Méry, *American Journey,* pp. xv, 156. In the issue of May 16, 1795, Freneau gives a report from the Proceedings of the National Convention of France and the Committee of Public Safety.

[5] *The Jersey Chronicle,* May 2, 1795.

[6] *Ibid.,* May 9, May 16, May 23, May 30, 1795; also issues of June 13, June 20, 1795. See Julian P. Boyd, *Number 7: Alexander Hamilton's Secret Attempt to Control American Foreign Policy.* In this work, Boyd clearly shows that Hamilton was tireless in his efforts (his secret efforts) to have his own policies prevail. Freneau's charges were amply justified long after the event.

Whatever the reasons, valid or otherwise, for Federalist acceptance of the treaty, Freneau dwelt on their monarchical inspiration and tendency, repeating with infinite variations the recurrent theme of despotism inherent in all Federalist measures. "Freemen of America," he cried, "you have purchased your liberty at the expense of blood; guard it with increasing vigilance!" The issue on June 6, 1795, carried a logical, if occasionally warped, analysis "On Despotic Form of Government," as well as the first of a series of articles which he called "Political Extracts," interpreting "The Aristocratic Form of Government." In the issue of June 20 these were followed by an essay on "The Democratical and Mixed Forms of Government." They were all of one piece, educational and hortatory by turn, always emphasizing the iniquity of government by one or by a few and the virtues of a democratic order in which the people were the sole masters of their destinies.[7]

Whether or not Freneau persuaded all his readers of the strict sobriety of his opinions, those who lived in Monmouth were surely persuaded. They had never forgotten the cruelties they had suffered at the hands of the redcoats and their brutal mercenaries. They agreed with his sober criticisms and intemperate attacks on the British with equal relish, and accepted the passionate revelations of their poet about the treaty that practically made America an ally of a former enemy and an enemy of a former ally. To simple men of good will and honest instincts it was all wrong, almost indecent—how wrong, how indecent it really was they did not know, nor could their poet tell them, for the full terms of the treaty were not released until July 11 and July 18, when the complete text was printed in *The Jersey Chronicle.* Then Freneau in high anger demanded: "Was ever a nation treated with such indignity? Were we worse off as English colonies?"[8]

The answers were not slow in coming. A petition and remonstrance by the citizens of New Jersey was sent to Washington, followed by a resolution prepared under the guidance of Colonel Asher Holmes, with whom Freneau had served in the Revolution. Readily passed at a meeting of citizens at Middletown Point, it was loudly acclaimed at a protest rally in the home of Major Thomas Hunn at Mount Pleasant.[9]

Also, J. G. Wilson, *The Memorial History of the City of New York,* Vol. 3, pp. 125–126.

[7] *The Jersey Chronicle,* June 6, June 20, 1795.

[8] *Ibid.,* July 11, July 18, August 22, 1795.

[9] *Ibid.,* August 8, September 5, 1795.

Other parts of the country were not silent either. From a Philadelphia town meeting came still other resolutions against the treaty while Boston, Fredericksburg, Portsmouth, and Charleston seethed with opposition. *The Jersey Chronicle* noted them all, feeding fuel to the fire with incendiary articles by "Valerius," lifted from the Philadelphia *Aurora,* which went beyond the attacks of Freneau himself to more specific assaults on the honor and integrity of the President of the United States.[10]

Valerius informed the citizens that Washington's "voice may have been heard when it called to virtue and glory, but it will be lost when it shall speak the language of lawless ambition." It *was* lost, in the same writer's opinion, when the Senate ratified the treaty and Washington signed it. "Heaven," Valerius warned Washington, "is not more distant from Hell, than the opinions and feelings of my fellow citizens are from yours." If this was not enough, Freneau printed still another letter, this time from "Political Watchman," whose attack on the President was even more vitriolic than that of Valerius. Nor did he refuse to run a final blast by Valerius himself, who cautioned the President that "the hour in which [public men] neglect the voice of the people, is the date of their infamy."[11]

The loudest cry of infamy came from the most unlikely source of all—from Thomas Paine, the patriot pamphleteer of the American Revolution. The cry of denunciation came from overseas, hurled across the Atlantic because Washington had failed to intervene for Paine's release from a French prison. Washington had done nothing to help the man who had so passionately appealed for the country's support of its distracted leader. James Monroe, appointed by Washington as Minister to France, alone had befriended the author of *The Crisis* and *Common Sense* in a time which also tried men's souls. Paine's aggrievement at the President's ingratitude was further sharpened, his sense of outrage was further increased, by Washington's acceptance of the Jay Treaty. Mincing no words, he sent him one of the most scathing letters ever received by the harassed father of his country. "As to you, Sir," it read, "*treacherous in private friendship* and *a hypocrite in public life,* the world will be puzzled to decide whether you are an *apostate* or an *imposter,* whether you *abandoned good principle* or whether *you ever had any.*" It was natural for the victim of all these

[10] *Ibid.,* September 8 to December 5, 1795; Lewis Leary, *That Rascal Freneau,* p. 259.

[11] *The Jersey Chronicle,* September 19, October 3, October 10, 1795.

attacks to exclaim that they were "in such exaggerated and indecent terms as could scarcely be applied to a Nero, a notorious defaulter, or even to a common pickpocket."[12] Glory is not of this life, but the next.

Philip Freneau, attempting to maintain some semblance of dignity and balance in the discussion of the treaty, hoped to present the issues in as objective a manner as possible. Reprinting an article from *The American Mercury* which supported and defended the treaty, he had no desire to go too far in the direction of fairness. The private thoughts of the President were as hidden from him as from any other citizen. What they might reveal of the man's inner spirit in a time of crisis was a secret closely guarded from even the most intimate advisers. Was it any clearer because Freneau gave space to letters from "Portius" and "A Calm Observer" which questioned the virtues of the "blue ribbon and eagle" presented by the Society of the Cincinnati to the President? There was no stigma attached to the award by the Society, a hereditary military organization founded by officers of the Revolution to which none but they and their descendants were admitted. The decoration was "emblematic of the Union of America and France," but what had happened to that union in the face of Washington's proclamation of neutrality? And what would happen now with his acceptance of John Jay's Treaty?[13]

As the controversy over the treaty and the President raged anew in the columns of *The Chronicle,* space was not denied to Hamilton's successor in the Treasury, Oliver Wolcott, a Connecticut Federalist and a staunch conservative, nor were the answers of the questionably "Calm Observer" refused a prominent place to refute him. If these seemed a bit too tender of official sensibilities, *The Chronicle* hastened to print still other answers by that ever persistent gadfly of the Administration, "Valerius," inflammatory and unrestrained pieces of propaganda in which the Federalists were damned as conspiratorial enemies of the people and the Republicans lauded as the only true friends of the country. Both sides were given space to say their say, to defend the President or to condemn him. The ultimate verdict was left to the readers of the paper.[14]

---

[12] James Parton, *Life of Thomas Jefferson,* p. 522. See also Washington to Jefferson, July 6, 1796, in George Washington, *Writings* (ed. J. C. Fitzpatrick), Vol. 25, p. 118; C. A. and M. R. Beard, *The Rise of American Civilization,* Vol. I, p. 371.

[13] *The Jersey Chronicle,* August 15, October 17, November 7, 1795.
[14] *Ibid.*

Not many of the readers were unbiased—but neither were those of the Federalist press. Opinions varied with the social and economic prejudices of each side. In Connecticut, where the Federalists were strongly entrenched, Timothy Dwight, the president of Yale, wanted to know "Whether our sons [shall] become the disciples of Voltaire and the dragons of Marat, or our daughters the concubines of the Illuminati?"[15] The Illuminati, of course, were the atheists and anarchists in the ranks of the Republicans, and the democrats as much the devil's disciples as they were. Voltaire's. A New England divine made it clear that papers like Freneau's were the real dangers to America. "The Editors, patrons and abettors of these vehicles of slander ought to be considered and treated as enemies to their country." And he added: "Of all traitors they are the most aggravatedly criminal; of all villains they are the most infamous and detestable."[16]

Noah Webster, a man of learning and once also a man of the people, wrote in *The Connecticut Courant* that "a Republican is among the last kinds of government I would choose. I would infinitely prefer a limited monarchy, for I would sooner be subject to the caprice of one man, than to the ignorance and passion of the multitude." His paper, *The New York Minerva*, established with the help of Hamilton and Rufus King, had essayed a fair-minded review of both sides until he quit the field of journalism altogether to devote himself to his great work on the dictionary. He would change his mind again.[17]

The passions engendered by the Jay Treaty flamed with the same intensity as ever, though the fuel supplied by either side was not always limited to the treaty itself. The whole question of basic principles was involved in this as in all conflicts between the conservatives and the radicals. The treaty was but another proof of the deep and abiding cleavage between the parties. It made little difference that Hamilton himself also thought the treaty "Execrable," and Jay "an old woman for making it." Like all the other Federalists, Hamilton was a faithful partisan, strong for its ratification and tireless in his efforts to keep in power the party that accepted it.[18]

[15] Beard, *Rise of American Civilization*, Vol. 1, p. 336.
[16] V. Stauffer, *New England and the Bavarian Illuminati*, pp. 10 ff.
[17] H. R. Warfel, *Noah Webster: Schoolmaster to America*, pp. 148, 237–238.
[18] R. Gilder, *The Battery*, pp. 119 ff; *The Jersey Chronicle*, May 2, 1795; Parton, *Life of Thomas Jefferson*, p. 517; C. A. Beard, *Economic Origins of Jeffersonian Democracy*, pp. 255 ff; and Alexander Hamilton, *Works*, Vol. 4, p. 171.

Freneau, who had lost so many other fights, lost this one too. But he was still the publisher of a paper; and a paper, to survive, may lose its fights but not its readers. To hold them; to give them something more than a weekly rehash of lost causes, he had begun a series of philosophical essays reminiscent of his old "Pilgrim" papers, in which the sage who meditated on the ways of man and the world was no longer a cultured traveler seeking the solitude of a cave for his soul's sake, but a redskin with as much spirit as soul, Tomo Cheeki. This colorful character is a fine specimen of the Natural Man, simple and untutored, with a genial contempt for the civilization of the White Man, its spurious codes, its mean morals, its petty politics, its questionable culture, its cruelty, egotism, lust, vanity, and greed. Tomo Cheeki is the greatest skeptic in early American letters, and his creator has missed no irony, urbane or brutal, in holding the mirror up to nature—the nature of man in particular. Freneau, despairing of present prospects for the regeneration of man, is in rapport with the skeptics of all time, the Voltaires, the Montaignes, the Swifts, the Popes, who were his mentors and whom he resembles in his antipathies as much as his sympathies. From them, as from his own experiences, he has learned a skepticism that is alternately bitter and benign, scathing and generous, hurtful and healing. With Tomo Cheeki he comes to the ineluctable conclusion that makes all things clear in an opaque mass of contrarieties. "I take the whole of this stupendous system to be a great machine, answering some prodigious purpose, of which the white men, any more than ourselves, have not the least idea."[19]

If the Tomo Cheeki essays were not entirely the product of Freneau's own mind, the readers of *The Jersey Chronicle* were none the less anxious to get them as sweeteners of the weekly dose of acrimony between the Federalists and the Republicans. The homely style, the humorous insights, the pervasive tone of sincere groping in a world baffled and befogged by politics, religion, and science—these essays appealed to many in Monmouth and far beyond its borders. The main stream of the editor's thought was not neglected either. The unending theme, sometimes subdued but never forgotten, was still the villainy of the Federalists, the continuing conflict between them and the radical democrats whom they stigmatized as Jacobins, "as disorganizers— aliens by birth—enemies to America in principle—Genêt's mob—

[19] *The Jersey Chronicle,* May 23 to October 3, 1795; see also H. H. Clark, "The Literary Influences of Philip Freneau," *Studies in Philology,* XXII, 1 (January 1925), 24–28.

institutors of Democratic clubs where darkness and drink make them shameless." The slander on the common people was played up at every turn, and the appeal to liberalism was featured in every issue. "The political ship," Freneau warned his readers, "is indeed leaky, from rottenness in some of her planks, or the weakness of her timbers."[20]

The editor of *The Jersey Chronicle* might have added that not only was the political ship leaky, but his own as well. His enemies had spared no pains to prove its rottenness, not knowing that it was sinking fast for lack of any financial pumps. Soon they would rejoice to see it vanish altogether. Subscribers had failed to come up to Freneau's hopes or expectations; the venture, after a year of hard labor, was foundering. Like all his other efforts, this one too was doomed to survive but a little while since he had no money with which to nourish it.

Yet his hopes were imperishable. This time, he thought, he might do better in a big city, in New York itself, if he could only get the backing of a few men whose beliefs and sympathies were like his own. There was nothing else for him to do but publish a paper. He could not endure the drudgery of a farm or the fallow life of a bookseller whose toil was usually quite as fruitless. Monmouth had proven "sandy soil" indeed. Perhaps New York would yield a better harvest, though his notices in *The Jersey Chronicle* of the impending publication of the *Register of the Times* in New York City brought him few subscriptions and a scant showing of interest from both potential readers and actual friends. DeWitt Clinton, who considered Freneau's plans for the new publication with cool reserve, was altogether doubtful of its success. The idea was dropped.[21]

DeWitt Clinton, once secretary to his uncle George, for many years the governor of New York, was an Anti-Federalist in a good position to advise Philip Freneau. He knew the city very well indeed—far better than most citizens. From his youth he had been close to the machinery of state and city governments; and he was, moreover, one of the wheels that moved them. Not yet thirty, his knowledge of politics was an intimate one, based on his own experience as well as that of his uncle. Both uncle and nephew would be eclipsed by a Federalist victory in New York before the year 1795 was finished, but De-

---

[20] *The Jersey Chronicle*, March 19, April 30, 1796.

[21] The last issue of *The Chronicle* was that of April 30, 1796; *The Register*, never appeared. See Leary, *That Rascal Freneau*, p. 269, and *The Jersey Chronicle*, April 23, April 30, 1796.

Witt would survive the set-back, for him only a temporary one. His future, slightly delayed, would be as brilliant as his uncle's past. He could bide his time—while missing no occasion to advance the fortunes of the democrats. It was the reason he was glad to help the poet of Monmouth, though he disapproved his initial project.[22]

DeWitt Clinton proposed another one. Freneau, with high ideals but little money, would do better to associate himself with a man already established and experienced in the newspaper business, a man like Thomas Greenleaf, the publisher of *The New York Journal* and *The Argus,* both well-known, as Freneau hastened to inform Madison, "for a steady attachment to Republican principles." The negotiations, however, disclosed that money even more than principles was needed for any partnership with Greenleaf. A loan of nearly a hundred pounds was necessary if Freneau was to join him in the new project. It seemed certain that all petty details—including a loan of the money—were almost completed, and Madison had learned from his friend that the "Spirit of the National Gazette" would animate the new paper. This time Freneau was confident of success, since he hoped "to make all the friends here that I decently can among men of eminence and ability." Madison too would help, at least to the extent of contributing a note to Chancellor Robert R. Livingston of New York telling him of his "interest in the success" of Freneau's "laudable pursuits." More than that, Madison asked Livingston's "favorable attention" to "the particular undertaking he has in hand."[23]

Freneau apparently had it less in hand than in prospect. The men of "eminence and ability" to whom he appealed were cool to any project by one who had failed in so many others and whose "literary talents and steady application to the true principles of liberty"—as Madison phrased it—were too incendiary for comfort and too radical for respectability. He was a chronic fault-finder who wrote endlessly of the people's rights and too little about their obligations. Most of the eminent men in the city had their own rights, which might easily clash with those of the people of New York. The loan could not be raised, nor the enthusiasm necessary to start a paper without it. As the months

[22] M. J. R. Lamb, *History of the City of New York,* Vol. 2, pp. 487–488, 553 ff. Lamb says: "What Franklin in his generation did for Philadelphia, Clinton, half a century later, accomplished for New York" (p. 553).

[23] Freneau to Madison, December 1, 1796, in James Madison Papers, Mss., XIX–101; also L. M. Miner, *Our Rude Forefathers,* p. 257 n.; E. P. Link, *Democratic Republican Societies, 1790–1800,* p. 84; Livingston Papers, Mss.

of 1796 sped by in a futile round of letter-writing, interviews, and distracting details, it became increasingly apparent that all Freneau's hopes and efforts would come to nothing. Nothing, that is, but a meeting with one man who *was* interested in publishing a paper as much as he was himself.[24]

Alexander Menut, a printer recently come from Canada and now a United States citizen, agreed to set the "elegant type" salvaged from previous failures, while Freneau wrote and edited the material itself. As equal partners, with a minimum of expense, they might succeed in a venture which offered them the work they loved, and who could tell, perhaps a living as well. The year 1796 drew to a close as the partners were busy with their plans for *The Time-Piece*, to be published soon in the modest printing shop at 123 Fly-Market, in the City of New York, where rooms were also being prepared for the editor and his family.[25]

The announcement of the birth of the new paper promised its first issue for March 13, 1797, nine days after the inauguration of John Adams as President of the United States.

[24] Timothy Dwight regarded Freneau as a "mere incendiary, or rather, as a despicable tool of bigger incendiaries"; George Gibbs, *Memoirs of the Administration of Washington and John Adams*, Vol. 1, p. 107; C. G. Bowers, *Jefferson and Hamilton*, pp. 145–147; Hamilton, *Works*, Vol. 7, p. 132.

[25] *The Time-Piece*, March 13, 1797; also *ibid.*, April 3, 1797; *Longworth's American Almanac*, 1797, p. 183.

27. *THE TIME-PIECE*

POLITICS, reputed to make strange bedfellows, was to vindicate its reputation in the year 1797. In retrospect the stormy career of Washington as a soldier and statesman was a time of peace and goodwill by comparison. As commander-in-chief he had chosen his own bedfellows; Congress, at any rate, was too weak to hamper him with anything more than inaction. As President he was still the master, choosing his own aides and keeping them until they had almost mutually extinguished each other, while Congress, no longer inactive, stoutly supported him in all his demands. The threat of mutiny was often in the air, but it had rarely been more than a threat, for he never lacked an adequate majority to quell it. The crew of the ship of state might sometimes grumble; a few might even denounce him; but at the end as at the beginning his command was intact. The ship, listing badly, had weathered every storm.

One man, the Vice-President, saw eye to eye with the master on all his policies. John Adams was a Federalist, a conservative, occasionally wavering and indecisive, yet always amenable to the strange course followed by the Administration. The short, stocky man from Massachusetts had made few enemies, for he had had few opportunities to cross anyone and none to oppose them. The Vice-President of the United States was of little consequence so long as the President was alive. The Constitution placed him on the dais of the Senate, a manikin who rarely used his head and never his voice save in the event of a tie vote. In the United States Senate that was an exceedingly unusual occurrence. Among the Founding Fathers there were few whose abilities or inclinations fitted them for such a passive role as Vice-President, and John Adams was a man of consequence, a sincere, well-meaning, and honest man of real ability, an honored name in the history of the American Revolution. He was no passionate partisan of Alexander Hamilton; nor was he unfriendly to Thomas Jefferson, despite his dislike of the French Revolution and his real sympathies for Great Britain.[1] Like others of his party he looked with grave suspicion and growing disapproval on the antics of the young military engineer Napoleon, a corporal bubbling over with vast plans for the conquest of Europe, who had already shown his unique and sanguinary talents by crushing a large force of French insurgents with a much smaller one of the Directory's soldiers. The triune truths of Liberty, Fraternity, and Equality were being subverted to new goals of invasion, plunder, and "la Gloire," a peculiar brand of glory that was eating like a canker into the ailing body of France. The old terror had died with Robespierre; a new one, greater and bloodier than that, now menaced a continent instead of a people.

In America the war between France and England had created problems which affected the great and the small, the rich and the poor, the conservatives and the radicals. The country was torn between those who would divorce the old bedfellows of France and those who refused to lie with the new ones of England. Washington, equally uneasy with any of them and often with all of them, waited eagerly for the end of his term. It would close before the problems were solved or the struggle for their solution was ended. In 1796 he relinquished all further hope of solving them. He had little hope left for anything else but to retire from all public duties to the peace and quiet of his estates at Mount Vernon. He had earned no less in the service of his country.

In his Farewell Address, issued to the people of America in September, the President counseled them to beware of any problems that were not domestic but foreign, cautioning them against enemies both at home and abroad. In simple though eloquent words he pleaded for a united nation free from sectional rivalries and "permanent alliances with any portion of the foreign world." It was a noble leave-taking by one who had strived to be above party and had given of himself without stint or profit for the greatness of America. His old friend and fellow soldier, Henry Lee, later put into words what many Americans

---

[1] V. L. Parrington, *Main Currents of American Thought: The Colonial Mind,* pp. 307 ff.

felt now in the hour of parting. Washington, said Lee, "was first in war, first in peace, and first in the hearts of his countrymen." It was essentially true, and Washington's message of farewell reflected the truth of his own feelings after many years of sacrifices for the cause of liberty.[2]

The Republicans professed to think otherwise. For them, the message was less noble than partisan. It was nothing more than a thinly veiled attack on them and on their principles, sweetened with honeyed sentiments to beguile a people who were about to vote for his successor. That vote, more than anything else, would determine what the people really thought of Washington's policies, if not of his person. To the Republicans, the farewell message was a challenge which they accepted as the opening shot in the new campaign, in their own campaign to annul those policies, to revoke the measures enacted by the Congress in conformity with them, to turn the tide which would sweep the Federalists from power and replace them with democrats— a term that expressed their ideals far better than any used before. The acknowledged leader of all democrats, Thomas Jefferson, would lead the new fight as their candidate for President of the United States.[3]

To oppose him with one of Washington's exalted stature was impossible. The choice of John Adams by the Federalists was a necessity based on expediency. Adams would inherit the prestige if not the reputation of his predecessor. Hamilton doubted this, but Hamilton had been much closer to Washington than he could ever be to Adams. John Adams, in the opinion of Alexander Hamilton, was not dependable or consistent in his loyalties. Too often he faltered. Frequently he vacillated. As President of the Senate he had made some rulings which were not, to say the least, the acts of a truly partisan nature. He usually voted as Washington may have expected—or wanted—him to vote, not as Hamilton wished. In addition, he was too seclusive, too aloof in his friendships. Rarely combative, neither was he warm and confiding. Ambitious for honors, he was too rigid to pursue them in the company of those who were also ambitious. One honor really absorbed all his ambitions—he wanted to be President, not of the Senate but of the United States itself. This was his due, the one goal he yearned to

---

[2] "Farewell Address," George Washington, *Writings* (ed. J. C. Fitzpatrick), Vol. 35, pp. 156–157. Also *Farewell Address* (ed. V. H. Paltsits).

[3] R. A. Billington, B. L. Lowenberg, and S. H. Brockunier, *The United States: American Democracy in World Perspective*, pp. 79–81.

achieve before he died, the crowning glory of a career which so far had achieved only a few minor kudos. "There is only the breath of one mortal between me and it," Adams had once confided to his friend James Lowell.[4] Now that breath was gone. Washington was no longer an impediment. As the shadow of the President receded from the field of contenders, his own image emerged clearer in the sunlight, no longer hidden by the reputation of another. Henceforth, he would be no rubber stamp, no mere cipher, no innocuous figurehead in the Senate where he seldom had a vote and never had a voice. Now he could even drop the ridiculous sword that always dangled at his side; a weapon, so said the *Aurora,* that he wore to appear heroic, though he presented only a "sesquipedality of belly." Lacking the power, he craved a little of its adornment.[5]

John Adams feared the rule of the masses, but he was no less opposed to the rule of a few, and he had no love for monarchy. Hamilton was never quite certain what he did love, but he was afraid that Adams changed his mind too often for comfort—for the comfort of Hamilton in any event—and that he had too high a regard for the enemy, especially the enemies of Hamilton, Madison and Jefferson not the least among them. Hamilton preferred a more trustworthy ally for the highest post in the nation, someone like Thomas Pinckney of South Carolina, a stalwart tried and tested. Let Adams run with Pinckney on the Federalist ticket— Hamilton would see to it that Pinckney got the highest electoral vote, and Adams only the vote below him. Pinckney would then be President, Adams could go back to the Senate again, as harmless as before, with his sword and all. Hamilton would remain the king behind the throne, and Adams would still be without any power to thwart him.[6]

This was the plan that Hamilton perfected and carefully pursued. If Adams was in the dark about it, so was Hamilton in the dark about the temper of the people. Adams was known, far more widely known, than his man Pinckney from South Carolina. There were also sectional

---

[4] John Adams to Lowell, September 1, 1789, in John Adams, *Works,* Vol. 8, p. 494.

[5] G. M. Stephenson, *American History to 1865,* pp. 184–185; *The Aurora,* November 4, 1796.

[6] The clash between Adams and Hamilton had its basis in their economic, as well as in their political, philosophies; see Parrington, *Main Currents of American Thought,* pp. 318–320, and C. A. Beard, *Economic Origins of Jeffersonian Democracy,* p. 317.

considerations which could affect the result, of which Hamilton was equally in the dark. For the South was not without a leader of its own whom it might prefer over Pinckney, the straight-line Federalist. Thomas Jefferson, the democrat, was a man who held some strong notions of states rights as against tight centralized controls; and he was closer to the people too. He was not yet close enough, perhaps, for any decisive victory, but Hamilton could scarcely believe that he had moved so near, so dangerously near to the moment of supreme power. The Secretary of the Treasury had forgotten about the constant drumming on the people's sensibilities by the bandleader of the democratic triumvirate.

The work of Philip Freneau not only had seriously damaged the Federalists, but John Adams himself had suffered from Freneau's frequent allusions to the fat man who, he said, despised the "lower order vote." Years of democratic propaganda had not been altogether in vain, and the electoral vote proved it. Adams was indeed elected as President, but only by three votes, and Jefferson, who lost the Presidency by those same three votes, became the Vice-President instead. The Anti-Federalists, perilously close to occupying the whole bed, were already sharing it with their enemies. Pinckney was out—and so was Hamilton. He would retain his power with the party—but scarcely any at all with the new President of the United States.[7]

The surprise election of Thomas Jefferson gave an added impetus to the new publication of Philip Freneau. The paper, which he called *The Time-Piece and Literary Companion,* now had an additional reason for its existence. The Anti-Federalists had no present power, but they had the promise, perhaps the certainty, of power to come. Jefferson cared little enough for the office that took him once again from his study at Monticello and from the solitude which his retiring nature needed. The new honor was meaningless in everything save the hope it held for the future. It was a straw in the wind—and the wind might one day blow more strongly, strong enough possibly to blast the Federalists out of office entirely. There was no longer a *National Gazette* in Philadelphia to keep watch on the weather vane of public opinion, but Benjamin Bache was still publishing *The Aurora* to carry on the vigil. And Freneau, who had given effective service in New Jersey with *The Chronicle,* was now in New York with *The Time-*

---

[7] Urich Tracy to Oliver Wolcott, January 7, 1797, in George Gibbs, *Memoirs of the Administration of Washington and John Adams,* Vol. I, p. 415.

Piece. The wind might change. The tide could turn. The ship of state might yet make a safe and speedy run to shelter in democratic waters. All Anti-Federalists were preparing for the turn.

In New York the Republican forces were in need of help. The wealth of the few was in sharp contrast to the condition of the masses, and their political power was as marked as their financial strength. This was most apparent in the fashionable sections of the city around Wall and Pine Streets and from Hanover Square to John Street. Near the bay the turrets of the houses rose "like a new creation from the sea." Not all were as pretentious as that of Mr. Delafield, who was rumored to have made his fortune from government securities bought for almost nothing and sold at par thanks to Hamilton's fiscal measures, but Yankee shrewdness and energy had paid off equally well for those who brought a thriving industry to the city. The merchants, purveyors of the people's food, the builders, the cotton and textile manufacturers, had made New York the Liverpool of America. These enterprising gentlemen were more than just exploiters of labor or crafty jobbers who controlled the necessities of life. They might even be the best patrons of the Tontine Tavern and Coffee-House where the stock exchange was housed in the large public room. Many of them, at least, were no lily-fingered, soft-palmed gentry who traded solely on the labor of others; they labored themselves. Their day usually began with a breakfast at eight, after which they checked their accounts until ten and then worked alongside their men in the shops or on the wharves till four in the afternoon. More often than not the manufacturer was at his plant in Hell Gate or in Brooklyn across the river, busy as the hired help at the business of weaving fustians and calicoes, nankeens and dimities, on machines of wood and steel and brass, made in New York itself from models brought over from England and Scotland. As the profits rolled in from the endless wars in Europe, the owners grew strong and powerful, while the prices of their goods and services mounted to heights beyond any ever known even in Philadelphia. New York was the most expensive, as it was already the largest, city in all the country.[8]

And no wonder. To New York came immigrants from abroad to

[8] John Davis, *Travels of Four Years and a Half in the U.S.*, pp. 162, 165; Henry Wansey, *The Journal of an Excursion to the United States of America in the Summer of 1794*, p. 73; Duc de la Rochefoucauld Liancourt, *Travels through the United States of North America*, pp. 227–231; John Bernard, *Retrospections of America, 1797–1811*, p. 52.

make their fortunes in the New World—a polyglot mass of people from England and France, from Italy and Ireland, from Germany and Scotland, who had given a year's income in exchange for their passage across. People also poured into New York from other states, from Kentucky and Vermont and the Carolinas, to sample the wonders of the big city by the Hudson, and to get hold of some of the wealth that abounded there. A new city was rising beside the old one on the banks of the tranquil and lovely river which wound its way serenely for many miles beyond the limit of any habitation. Within that limit, fine, spacious homes were rising, more modern and exclusive than the yellow brick houses of the old Dutch nabobs. These had a forbidding ostentatiousness of their own, with their peaked roofs, and their barred doors and windows, and their high garden walls, capped by broken glass set in mortar to keep out the *hoi polloi*. The Dutch didn't care much for the newly rich, and they seldom mixed with the crowd of lesser citizens who sunned themselves on the Battery walks or watched the porpoises "roll and tumble" in the waters that flowed to the sea. More fortunate people who lived at places like Mrs. Loring's near the Battery could enjoy such pleasures too without mingling with the crowd. In addition, they could see the ships that came into port or sailed away, for their view was unimpeded as far out as Long Island, as far as Governor's Island or even Staten Island, many miles across the harbor. More affluent citizens, seeking both diversion and nourishment in the continental manner, might find them in the Vauxhall Gardens, out in the open country, where food and music were dispensed to those who ventured so far on upper Broadway. Still others could find both refreshment and exercise at the elegantly appointed Belvidere, overlooking the eastward river, two miles out of the city, where a lovely view of the bay added zest to a leisurely stroll on its circular gallery.[9]

Most of the men, the women, the children, who labored for a living, were content to walk abroad for a sight of the sea or a breath of bracing air when the day's work was done or the Sabbath gave them a respite from work. They lived in narrow, crooked streets which were

[9] Bernard, *Retrospections of America*, pp. 50–52; Liancourt, *Travels*, pp. 227–228; Wansey, *Journal*, pp. 76, 83–84; *The Diary*, March 7, May 7, May 11, November 12, 1797; R. Gilder, *The Battery*, pp. 127–146; J. G. Wilson, *The Memorial History of the City of New York*, Vol. 1, p. 146; Vol. 2, p. 165; Vol. 3, pp. 136, 304; W. T. Bonner, *New York*, pp. 201, 268.

no more than footpaths, with only the common pump to supply water for all. If illness struck, there was a hospital, and if poverty, a poor-house, while the calloused hand of charity was held out to those who had no other hand to help them. Their children could be apprenticed to some trade until they were of age, and thus they were assured of board and lodging—perhaps even a little of learning—until they were twenty-one. They received no money. The women might earn as much as two dollars a day, and the men somewhat more, to meet the high cost of living and enjoy some of the modest pleasures afforded by Baker's Museum on the Battery, or the musical clocks on Water Street, or an African lion at the Fly-Market, or a real elephant on Front Street. The menagerie on Pearl Street was free, but this was a tame pastime compared to the bear-baiting farther out of the city. The best of all was the circus on Greenwich Street, where a thrilling show was always assured. Such amusements cost money and were only for gala occasions. On special holidays, the people were likely to indulge themselves for a performance at the John Street Theater.[10]

Men are nourished by more than bread, and the amusements of New York did not altogether supply the spiritual pabulum which they also needed. That was a scarce commodity in the year 1797, to be found mostly in the books men read. The poorer folk read no books, or much of anything else. The newspapers provided the only reading they were likely to get. There were twenty newspapers in the city when Freneau began to publish his *Time-Piece,* but few libraries of any importance. The Society Library, like the Literary Coffee House, was not for the common man; nor was it likely that he would patronize the library of Mr. Caritat on Pearl Street, a "charming" rendezvous for the ladies who wanted books like *Female Frivolity,* or *Posthumous Daughter,* or *Devil in Love.* If anybody was interested in something like "political, moral, or other interesting matters," including "useful as well as ornamental knowledge," and craved "Literary Amusement" at the same time, they could get *The Time-Piece,* which promised all this and a lot more. Any budding poet, moreover, who sought a vehicle for his own master-pieces, would find Freneau, its editor and publisher, ready to make "every endeavor" to encourage him so as "to promote the rising genius and literary ability of this country and of the flourishing Capital of

---

[10] Gilder, *The Battery,* pp. 123–124; *The Diary,* January 12, January 17, March 6, May 11, 1797.

New York in particular." Cultural capital is what Freneau meant, as others meant commercial or financial capital of America.[11]

Publishers are not the only ones who must bear the cross of another's ambition. Editors, and those who protect them from the avalanche of manuscripts, have also known the trials of Tantalus wallowing in a sea of words to reach the fruit of genius which always seems to elude them. Freneau had invited contributions to *The Time-Piece* for the double purpose of enlisting readers and giving them, together with the news, a literary outlet and interest. The readers, many of them watching only for their own offspring, did help the circulation, but the literary tone of *The Time-Piece* was rarely enhanced by the poems which appeared in its columns. The ladies especially had discovered the opportunity to indulge their egos with an assortment of verse on love and freedom, on war and peace, on all manner of sentimental involvements that were more lugubrious than literary. The little printing shop at Fly-Market was besieged by women who had not even any literary pretensions, but sought out the editor for help of a more mundane nature.[12]

Deborah Gannet, the only woman who had volunteered as a common soldier in the American Revolution, and had dressed and fought like one under the name of Robert Shurtleff, was seeking a pension from the government. She was destitute, and clearly entitled to the pittance which she could persuade nobody else to obtain for her; Freneau prepared her petition and publicized her case in his newspaper. She got her pension, an achievement more agreeable to the editor of *The Time-Piece* than many literary efforts of other lady supplicants.[13]

Always ready to help another, he was no longer willing to pamper those who sought, not his help, but his approval. Their poetic effusions were beyond all help. It seemed the better part of wisdom to discourage any further contributions, and finally to discontinue them altogether in *The Time-Piece*. As a result many disgruntled readers stopped their subscriptions, while Freneau tried to recoup his loses by getting others. He offered one free subscription to anybody obtaining fifteen

[11] Wansey, *Journal*, p. 74; Davis, *Travels*, p. 204; *The Time-Piece*, March 13, 1797.

[12] Hammell Notes, Mss.

[13] J. A. Vinton, *Life of Deborah Sampson, passim;* Hammell Notes, Mss., p. 11; Freneau's plea to Congress for a pension for Deborah Gannet, *The Time-Piece*, December 4, 1797. The lady's name changed on her marriage. Freneau, *The Poems of Philip Freneau* (ed. F. L. Pattee), Vol. 1, p. 182 n.

paid ones. Henceforth, he promised, the poems, like the prose pieces, would be on the high plane outlined in his Poetical Address in the first issue. Whatever the fate of *The Time-Piece,* it would adhere to its policy of literary as well as political integrity, for it had no meaning, no excuse for being, unless the tastes of the people were guarded even as he intended to guard and preserve their liberty and the purity of their democracy. The theme was the same as of old, freedom, and the endless, timeless struggle of man to achieve it—his fumbling and his failure, his folly and his faith, his defeat and ultimate victory.

> 'Tis time a new system of things was embrac'd,
> To encircle a world that has long been debas'd—
> As Here, with our Freedom, that system began,
> Here, at least keep it pure—
> For the Honor of Man.[14]

To keep it pure Freneau still tried to give his readers all sides of a question. If he printed the speech of the Vice-President, he also ran that of the President, though he had little faith in the words of John Adams. The new Administration, he believed, like the old one was a menace to democracy and a friend of monarchy. His readers were kept informed of the war on the other side of the Atlantic, and lest they forgot their own debt to France, he printed some chapters of his translation from the *Travels* of the Abbé Robin. To maintain the high literary tone he had promised he published humorous sketches by Oliver Goldsmith and satirical ones by Jonathan Swift. The news from Charleston, Boston, and Philadelphia was loaded with the philosophy of Tomo Cheeki, while a translation from Lucian or an anecdote by Samuel Johnson appeared together with poems written by himself years before or new ones composed for some special purpose or occasion. All of them supplied a certain momentary as well as long-range interest to *The Time-Piece,* conforming more to its literary pretensions than the somber and stupid lines of lady poets who had sought immortality in its pages. A few of them were great admirers of the editor's own poetry—and wrote to tell him so in flattering letters. They were also a nuisance, though not the most baffling to contend with.[15]

---

[14] *The Time-Piece,* March 13, 1797.

[15] *Ibid.,* March 15, 1797–March 17, 1797; Hammell Notes, Mss.; Freneau's views were greatly influenced by "the God-like Addison," and *The Spectator,* and by the classical writers of antiquity. See Moses Coit Tyler, *The Literary History of the American Revolution,* Vol. 1, pp. 274 ff.

One difficulty, more sinister than the rest, was the ever-recurring problem of the paper's finances. *The Time-Piece* was always in financial difficulties. The ladies had deserted it; the free subscription offer had brought in few paid ones. Scarcely three months after the first issue a real danger loomed that the last would soon be announced. On September 13 Freneau warned that "pecuniary engagements" by readers had failed, and that they "must be immediately answered," or the paper would be forced to discontinue—a disaster of more than ordinary dimensions for the man who had moved his family to New York and lacked any other means to support them.[16]

More than this, however, it would mean the finish of a new vehicle for his democratic and Anti-Federalist views, needed more than ever now in the parlous state of the Union. The country was once more in crisis. Despite the admonitions of Washington, the foreign entanglements of America were more acute than ever. France, only suspicious of American friendship in Washington's Administration, was convinced of American hostility in the Cabinet of John Adams. It refused to receive the American Minister who had replaced young James Monroe. Monroe, a protégé of Jefferson, was the man who had freed Thomas Paine and sheltered him in his home when no one else in Washington's Administration had raised a hand to help him. Sent to Paris in the first place to mollify Jefferson as well as the French people themselves, he quickly made it apparent that a Republican Minister of a Federalist government was more than a political anomaly; he was a bad blunder and a political danger to its conservative policies as well. Monroe was withdrawn in August 1796. He was not good enough for the Americans—but Charles Cotesworth Pinckney was not good enough for the French. The refusal of the French Directory to receive him was obviously an insult to the United States, and John Adams, the new President, was acutely sensitive to any insult. This one could be avenged, easily enough, by a complete severance of diplomatic relations as was advocated by the Federalists—but such an action might lead to war. Adams, loving peace, did not want war. Perhaps some compromise might be found, some accommodation reached, between France and America, in which peace would be preserved and honor maintained.[17]

[16] *The Time-Piece*, September 13, 1797.
[17] Stephenson, *American History to 1865*, p. 186; *The Time-Piece*, May 29, 1797; Arthur Styron, *Last of the Cocked Hats: James Monroe and the Virginia Dynasty*, pp. 63 ff.

President Adams decided to send a commission to France, a commission of three that would meet with the French Foreign Minister, the machiavellian Talleyrand, to seek a *modus vivendi* between the two countries. If this maneuver failed, America, taking time by the forelock, would prepare for war—if war was indeed inevitable. It did not seem so to Adams even when Talleyrand demanded what was virtually a bribe of 250,000 dollars before he would see the American plenipotentiaries at all. Congress, examining the XYZ papers dealing with the whole episode, waited for the President to take the final step. And Philip Freneau, still holding onto *The Time-Piece* against all financial and political odds, used its pages as sounding boards for clarion calls against that or any step which might lead to open conflict between the two former comrades-in-arms.[18]

It was no easy task to prevent conflict. The arguments of the Federalists had a peculiar potency in the light of French diplomacy. Americans were peace-loving people, averse to saber-rattling yet quick to resent an insult, and they gagged at blackmail. However wrong-headed and politically inspired Federalist tenderness for Britain, Republican sympathy for France appeared like a naked acceptance of dishonor without any pretense of democratic integrity. The Genêt episode had been difficult enough to support and defend, and only the providential issue of the Jay Treaty had softened the tempers of many whose allegiance was democratic. The contemptuous—and contemptible—conduct of the French was playing right into the hands of the conservatives. It was conduct hard to explain and impossible to forgive. Republicans as well as Federalists were now loud in their denunciations, and both were passionately proclaiming: "Millions for defense, not a cent for tribute.[19]

The country was aroused. The people seemed ready to rise. The army, the navy, were on the alert. George Washington, in retirement at Mount Vernon, was waiting for orders to lead them again as the commander-in-chief. War was imminent.

[18] Billington, *et al., The United States,* pp. 86–87; *The Time-Piece,* May 11, 1797, and Gibbs, *Memoirs of the Administration,* Vol. 2, pp. 6 ff.

[19] Robert G. Harper, in a toast given at a dinner in Philadelphia, June 18, 1798, quoted in *The Daily American Advertiser,* June 20, 1798.

28. MEN AND PORCUPINES

PHILIP FRENEAU, hanging on to peace like a dog to a bone, used his small influence in *The Time-Piece* with a show of power he was far from possessing. War? It must not be! He repeated the injunction endlessly; in spite of the Talleyrands and all the other unscrupulous leaders of a confused and distressed people, war would be a crime against both nations, a crime that history would record as unjustified and unforgivable though American ships were ravaged, American property stolen, American citizens insulted, American rights trampled. Extortion, slander, intrigue, lawlessness—all were recorded in the indictment against France, but were they not recorded also in the indictment against England? Who but the British had fought Americans—who but the French had saved them? This was for Freneau an irrefutable truth which he repeated ceaselessly so the people would never forget it. At first cautiously, then more boldly, he struck out at the warmongers. War—he asked—what for?

> From Britain's yoke so lately freed,
> Wouldst thou, new legions basely lead,
> To crush that power, whose valour gain'd
> And once her sinking cause sustain'd.
> From each true heart be banished far
> The thought of so profane a war—
> A curse would on her arms attend
> And with that war your honors end.[1]

[1] *The Time-Piece*, March 29, 1797; and "To the Americans," in Freneau, *The Poems of Philip Freneau* (ed. F. L. Pattee), Vol. 1, pp. 185–187.

The deepening shadow of a war psychology was spreading over the whole country as new indignities, new infractions, new insults were added to the old ones. Neutrality was treated with a cavalier disdain, and law with a consummate contempt. No one, though he were a patriot instead of a partisan, could excuse such conduct as this.

Freneau excused it. His hatred of the Federalists and their sticky sentiments for British accommodation and their enmity toward the French was second only to his hatred of war itself, war for principles which appeared to him altogether commercial and for purposes that were entirely material. The few alone would profit from such a conflict, while the many gave their blood to enthrone ingratitude and debase the spirit of brotherhood. For him, the proposed war was part of a plan to defeat the democratic strivings of the common man in America and throughout the world. The French Revolution had been sidetracked by the same forces which conceived that plan and were now engaged in executing it at home and abroad, while French imperialism was the perfect instrument for their purpose. The French people, who had given so generously of their blood and treasure to thwart it in America, were suffering from their own exploiters as well as from those in other countries. Must America too join the bestial hordes of destruction? American ships were already fighting the French without any declaration of war. There still could be peace. War could still be averted. A new effort must be made, another envoy must be sent to France for the sake of peace.

James Monroe, whom the French trusted, had been withdrawn as Minister because the Federalists suspected his friendship for their Revolution. A scion of the Virginia Tidewater aristocracy, Monroe had fought under Washington in the battle of Monmouth while still in his teens. Later, he became a follower of Jefferson, sharing with him the agrarian philosophy of democracy based on a small-farmer economy rather than the emergent capitalist ideal of industrial expansion. Opposed to the Constitution, he finally had accepted it as the cornerstone of a fortress in which the liberties of the people might be secured against all future assault. A protégé of Jefferson's, he was also a disciple who worshipped the master. Tall, ungainly, with little imagination and a plodding intellect, Monroe wholly accepted the libertarian views of the democrats and supported them with vigor and conviction. Like Freneau, he understood the Federalist's plan for circumventing them and he too suspected their anguished outcries against the French excesses as a means of destroying the democratic societies at home and the democratic spirit everywhere. "The fact is," he said "that such societies cannot exist in an enlightened society *unless there is some cause for them."* With the signing of the Jay Treaty the cause had become increasingly clear, for the pact with Britain had dragged "our national honor in the dust; we have been kicked, cuffed, and plundered all over the ocean; our reputation for faith scouted; our government and people branded as cowards."[2]

In a well-reasoned if not entirely objective paper Monroe set forth his "View of the Conduct of the Executive in the Foreign Affairs of the United States," and while a good part of it was an echo of democratic criticism widely disseminated by Philip Freneau, it was none the less an able summary of events and a fair interpretation of Federalist policy. What exactly *was* Federalist policy? Was it peace or war, now that Pinckney had been spurned by France as a substitute for James Monroe, and Adams' three commissioners were not only spurned but insulted with a demand for blackmail as well?[3]

Hamilton, for one, believed in war. His courage, never in any doubt, was as quixotic as his judgment was questionable—it had been questioned many times before and would be again. His adulterous affair with Mrs. Reynolds, his repeated payments of blackmail, were known to a few of his enemies, but neither political nor party considerations would have ever induced them to divulge secrets such as these. When the details of the scandal became known, it was not his enemies, the democrats, who made them public property, though Hamilton, quick to take umbrage at all rumors whether they were true or false, suspected them all. Monroe himself was one of those he suspected. But he could not be sure. Proud, impatient, often unreasonable, Hamilton could also be just. He refused Monroe's offer of satisfaction when Aaron Burr, who had been a candidate with Jefferson on the Anti-Federalist ticket and was now the New York leader of the democrats, undertook arrangements for a duel. These two—Hamilton and Burr—would later fight their own duel with tragic results now happily avoided. Hamilton had a greater quarrel to settle first—a duel of vaster proportions and greater importance to the pride of a country than that of a person. He wanted a war with France. If this was Federalist policy, then Adams, never dependable, as Hamilton always be-

[2] Arthur Styron, *The Last of the Cocked Hats: James Monroe and the Virginia Dynasty,* p. 163. See also E. P. Link, *Democratic Republican Societies, 1790–1800,* pp. 16, 17, 58 ff.

[3] Styron, *Last of the Cocked Hats,* p. 164; *The Time-Piece,* March 27, 1797.

lieved, was not yet ready to declare it. In the dark days of 1797 the President was still seeking for a way to peace rather than to war.[4]

Philip Freneau, aware of the powerful currents that were moving the country one way or another, trimmed his own sails accordingly. It would be unwise to alienate the people whose sympathies were with John Adams in his efforts to maintain the peace when the clamor for war was loud and raucous. *The Time-Piece,* tempered to the wind of public sentiment, was not relinquishing its fight against the Federalists; yet it was more circumspect in its attacks on leaders whom Freneau once had pilloried. The right and the wrong were confused, and honest men were loath to disparage the intent of those whose views veered with the wind of circumstance. Whatever winds might blow, men like Freneau never wavered in their loyalty to democracy. The arrows of the enemy might find their mark as often as possible, and the vices of the people be proven against them time and time again. Men were wicked for reasons other than wickedness, and they were often victimized by themselves as well as by others. Even so it was better to live on one's feet, if only for a moment, than die on one's knees, though one was allowed a lifetime to do so. Freedom was eternally the prize however the struggle was fought, and democracy the only weapon to achieve it, however blunted its edge or debased its metal or perverted its uses.

No longer the young and impetuous poet of the Revolution, Freneau was not even the heady antagonist of the days of *The National Gazette.* In those days he had used the weapon of satire to demolish the opposition. Satire, a literary scalpel used under the anaesthetic of humor, had served his purposes well, though the scalpel was often blunted and the humor frequently more wry than funny. At forty-five, with the tide of Federalism almost at the flood, the publisher of *The Time-Piece* was in danger of foundering on financial shoals and there was little to uplift his flagging spirits. Forever on the brink of bankruptcy, *The Time-Piece* was almost over the brink after six months of slow starvation.

Alexander Menut had decided to withdraw before it perished

---

[4] See C. G. Bowers, *Jefferson and Hamilton,* for an excellent discussion of Hamilton's position. The political struggle was, of course, reflected in the columns of *The Time-Piece* and *The Gazette of the United States.* See also Jefferson to Mazzei, August 3, 1797, on "the apostates whose heads were shorn by the harlot England," quoted in Irving Brant, *James Madison,* Vol. 3, *The Father of the Constitution, 1787–1800,* p. 453.

altogether, and Freneau, casting about for a new partner to save it, found one in Matthew L. Davis, a young man of twenty-four whose republicanism was as pure as his own and whose spirit and energy were fresh and eager for the fight. Davis, in addition, operated a printer's shop at 26 Moore Street, where *The Time-Piece*, thus rejuvenated, hopefully gained a new lease on life. Freneau, reanimated and optimistic once more, promised to pay all the old creditors—and promptly began to acquire new ones. He renewed his pledge to bring "home those great truths to every one's reflection that most nearly concern the rights and liberties of man," and to continue to publish the news that is "a record of the history" of the times, not omitting "those hints and sketches of information, those lights and disquisitions, at the views of which tyrants tremble," and invaders of the rights of man "sink back into annihilation and insignificance."[5]

Like the old *Time-Piece*, the new one was filled with Francophile material, with poems and prose pieces by the editor himself, heavily seasoned by propaganda bits of others which left no doubt as to its unalterable position against war or any gesture of friendship for Britain. Unrelentingly it hammered at the whole Federalist Party and welcomed all outside help to place the party's leaders in the most unfavorable light possible. Washington, the grand old man of the Federalists, was not spared even in retirement. His large estate served by a host of slaves was the special object of criticism by Edward Rushton, while his tenderness for the conservative elements of the government, his lack of leadership in the treatment of France, were proven out of the mouth of his old comrade Thomas Jefferson. In a confidential letter to his friend Philip Mazzei the year before, Jefferson had revealed his inmost feelings, feelings that were now made known to all the world in the reprint published by Freneau in *The Time-Piece*. The censure of old leaders was brought up to date with censure by new ones in speeches by Albert Gallatin, the latest leader of the democrats in Congress.[6]

Gallatin was a man whose speeches were lucid and logical beyond those of most of the other members, Republican or Federalist. When

---

[5] *The Time-Piece*, September 13, 1797. The new *Time-Piece* began with the issue of September 15, 1797.

[6] *Ibid.*, April 24, May 5, May 8, 1797; and Jefferson to Mazzei, April 24, 1796, in Thomas Jefferson, *Writings* (ed. P. L. Ford), Vol. 7, pp. 72–78. See also Frank Smith, "Philip Freneau and The Time-Piece and Literary Companion," *American Literature*, IV, 3 (November 1932), 270–287.

he spoke, the House listened to him with respect if not always with agreement, despite the slurs that were whispered about his foreign accent and strange mannerisms. The Swiss immigrant with the keen mind and commanding presence was still a young man under forty, and already behind him was a colorful career as a teacher of French at Harvard and a teacher of liberty everywhere. This was not surprising, perhaps, for a lad who lived in the same city with Jean Jacques Rousseau and had often listened to Voltaire at his home in Ferney. Gallatin had come to America to "drink in a love of independence in the freest country of the universe." In the eyes of many others besides Jefferson, he was a true citizen of the world as well as of his adopted country. His speeches were always printed in *The Time-Piece* so that the country might learn, in simple figures and with proven facts, what portended in peace—and in war.[7]

With men like Albert Gallatin in Congress to give the people a clear picture of the meaning of war, Freneau was emboldened to give them an added incitement to peace. The issue of September 18, 1797 struck a note of defiance, missing or somewhat muffled before. There must be no war, by action of the government or by default of the people. The real enemy of America was not abroad—he was right here at home. And at home was the first line of defense.

> Keep bright the flame which every bosom fir'd,
> When Hessian hirelings from these lands retir'd—[8]

Did the Federalists train their guns on Freneau and threaten him with dire retribution? Did Noah Webster accuse him of spattering *The Time-Piece* with "filth like the *National Gazette* formerly?" Webster was only echoing the friends who had subsidized his sheet, *The New York Minerva,* when he compared Freneau to a dog who "returns to his vomit, and the sow that was washed, to her wallowing in the mire."[9] The taunts and slanders meant nothing to the publisher of *The Time-Piece.* He was immune to the poisoned barbs of his enemies. He had been the object of these all his life. They wounded him, but not so deeply as to deflect him from his course. Besides, he now had the sympathy and support of many others who were victims of the same attacks.

They were members of the Society of Saint Tammany or Columbian

---

[7] J. A. Stevens, *Albert Gallatin,* p. 10.
[8] *The Time-Piece,* September 18, 1797.
[9] *The Minerva,* September 21, 1797.

Order, a New York organization which had been started in 1789 "to preserve the just balance of power." Now it was active to preserve the democratic rights of the people. Named after the legendary Tamanend, Indian Chief of the Delaware Nation, the Society of Saint Tammany, in contrast to the conservative Society of the Cincinnati, was infused with the radical spirit of the Jeffersonians and believed in the democratic policies of the Anti-Federalists. It was natural for its members to support the French Revolution, as its first Sagamore—or leader— John Pintard, Freneau's predecessor in the State Department, supported it. The Society was in the vanguard of the opposition to all the "enemies of liberty," whom it threatened with physical assault if they did not cease their vilification of "our brethren from France." When the members of Saint Tammany toasted "Citizen" Jefferson, they vowed "at the risk of life and liberty to support their equal rights in opposition to Ambition and Tyranny, Sophistry and Deception, Bribery and Corruption." In 1797, when Philip Freneau became a member of the Society, the fortunes of the democrats were at such low ebb that an organized brotherhood of men dedicated to democracy was urgently needed to support and defend its tenets. It was needed, moreover, to arouse the American people to the imminent danger of Federalist embroilment in a war with France.[10]

Freneau and his new partner Davis were active in a twofold way. In addition to doggedly maintaining the publication of *The Time-Piece* at almost unbelievable sacrifice, they gave their time and energy to spread the precepts of the Society throughout the city. Though often nebulous, these were never really in doubt, while the work of Saint Tammany, at least for the democrats, was always above suspicion. This was not true of some of its leaders, who were not always above reproach. Aaron Burr, the real if not the nominal chief of the Society, was one such.[11]

Aaron Burr, once a schoolmate of Philip Freneau and James Madison at Princeton, was a powerful figure in the political arena of New York. An astute lawyer as well as a keen politician, he was the great rival of Alexander Hamilton in both of these fields. The two men had more than stubborn wills and great ambitions to fire their rivalry and

[10] Gustavus Myers, *The History of Tammany Hall*, pp. 1, 2, 9–10, and E. P. Kilroe, *Saint Tammany and the Origin of the Society of Tammany or Columbian Order in the City of New York*, pp. 135–136.

[11] *Ibid.*; also Aaron Burr, *Memoirs*, Vol. 1, pp. 406, 407, 408; and N. Schachner, *Alexander Hamilton*, p. 357.

enflame their conflict. Their temperaments, their personalities were
involved as well. Hamilton was usually forthright and unequivocal in
his views, while Burr was essentially devious and ambiguous. No
democrat could ever have any doubt as to the position of Hamilton,
but many Federalists were inclined to think of Burr as sometimes
amenable to the blandishments of power. A few believed he might
even be a good risk for them. Hamilton considered him a bad risk from
any point of view at all, and when he ran with Jefferson on the Anti-
Federalist ticket in 1796, Hamilton was happy to see him trail behind
Jefferson. Jefferson, in the opinion of Hamilton, was a man whom one
could at least respect, but Aaron Burr he despised as a vulgar oppor-
tunist and self-seeker. "There is no circumstance," he wrote to Oliver
Wolcott, "which has given me so much pain as the idea that Mr. Burr
might be elected to the Presidency."[12] The struggle for New York was
usually more than a contest for the pivotal state and its largest city.
And now the nation itself was at stake in the political battle that was
about to be waged.[13]

   This battle was further enlivened by still another warrior who was
neither a lawyer nor a politician. He possessed the aggressive qualities
of both and a few that were as foreign to them as he himself was foreign to the country of his new activities. An able gentleman of good
mind and confused emotions, William Cobbett was no American but
an immigrant from England, to which he had never renounced his allegiance since coming to America in 1792. Like many others, Cobbett
had sought freedom for his tenuous beliefs which his own country had
made it difficult for him to express. Supporting himself as a teacher of
English to French *émigrés* from Santo Domingo, he soon looked
around for fatter fields to cultivate. Most promising of all was the
struggle between the Federalists and the Republicans. Too late to join
the outcry against Genêt, he found another victim on whom to vent his
conservative spleen—no Frenchman at all, not even an American, but
a fellow Englishman who was a peculiar species of democrat—British,
and at the same time American. Cobbett himself was also British—but
he was no American.[14]

   Dr. Joseph Priestley was a mild-mannered man of sixty who had

   [12] Hamilton to Wolcott, December 1800, in Broadus Mitchell, *Heritage from
Hamilton*, p. 140.
   [13] Schachner, *Alexander Hamilton*, p. 358.
   [14] M. Bowen, *Peter Porcupine*, pp. 72 ff; see also G. H. Payne, *History of
Journalism in the United States, passim.*

come to America in 1794 after fleeing from England to escape the persecutions of its provincial gentry. A nonconformist in religion, he was also a dissenter in politics. Because he was too outspoken in his sympathies for the French radicals, his home at Fairhill in Birmingham had been sacked, his books burned, and what was worse still, his chemical apparatus entirely destroyed. A chemist and the discoverer of oxygen, Dr. Priestley was always searching for the secrets of nature, secrets which eluded him in all his studies as a minister of the Gospel. The burning at Birmingham was not his first experience with violence. In 1783, when he was pastor of the Mill Hill Chapel in Leeds, it was not the mob but the common hangman of Dordrecht who had burned one of his books as offensive to the Dutch Calvinists there. Dr. Priestley had antagonized his countrymen for reasons even worse than this, if possible. He had passionately supported the struggle of the Americans in their war with his own country, writing numerous political tracts to prove the justice of their cause. When he arrived in Philadelphia his reception clearly showed that he was welcome to the City of Brotherly Love as a man of great learning, high ideals, and democratic sympathies.[15]

Some people did not agree. William Cobbett, enraged by the encomiums heaped on a man whom he considered as a renegade and even a traitor to their common country, at once prepared a pamphlet attacking not only Priestley but all that he stood for. Here was a fat field that might yield a rich harvest. A master of invective, given to hyperbole and careless of the facts, William Cobbett assumed the mantle of a great champion of the Federalists, a new Goliath who would quickly polish off with his special brand of vitriol such puny Davids of democracy as Priestley. Hamilton, quick to recognize the man's real abilities, so attractively illustrated in his pamphlet *A Bone to Gnaw for the Democrats*, urged Cobbett to start a newspaper, a medium which offered much greater scope for his talents than any ephemeral writings. The tiny *Weekly Political Register,* which soon appeared in Philadelphia, contained prickly articles by a man who properly masqueraded under the pseudonym of "Porcupine," and bristled with the sharpest of poison quills. Whatever was tainted with democratic belief was fatal —whatever was perfumed with Federalist policy was good, and right,

---

[15] Bowen, *Peter Porcupine,* pp. 65 ff; see also Joseph Priestly, *Memoirs,* and Edward Smith, *William Cobbett,* pp. 110–113. The memoirs of Priestley leave no doubt as to his love of freedom and justice.

and just. Here, for the conservatives, was more than a Goliath; here was a Daniel come to judgment. Let the democrats beware![16]

Brandishing his pen with rare abandon, Cobbett needed a lot more room than the narrow columns of *The Register* for his inexhaustible energies. In March 1797 the room was found. The new paper, also published in Philadelphia and called *Porcupine's Gazette*, was large enough to contain all the abuse and scurrility of which its editor was the indisputable master. Dr. Priestley, having unhappily already come to his notice, was the first victim of his attacks.[17] As others followed, it became apparent that this Englishman was not content with spewing his venom only on his countrymen. His main business was not with foreigners at all but with native Americans. He, an alien, was to pour his filth on those who harbored the least hatred of Britain, or the least love for France; on the press that echoed their sentiments; and on all who gave them any comfort or support. Violent in his language, he was also lively and colorful in its use, holding the interest of a reader even as he deeply offended his sense of fairness and decency. The Anti-Federalist newspapers were his greatest hate. After a bout with Bache and the Philadelphia *Aurora,* he turned his attention to Hamilton's own bailiwick. *The Time-Piece* now became the prime target of his gargantuan wrath. From Philadelphia, and across the ninety miles of intervening space, the Porcupine propelled the missiles that pierced the tender flesh of Philip Freneau.

On September 8, 1797, *The Porcupine's Gazette* began the assault. Starting with a summary of Freneau's life as a journalist, it first considered his conduct of the "Jacobin Gazette in Philadelphia," which "expired with the office of his patron," and then proceeded to regale its readers with an account of Freneau's career in New Jersey, "where he endeavoured to barter his *patriotism* for bread," with little success however, since Jerseymen, "with their unusual justice and good sense refused to a literary vagabond what they never refuse to unmerited distress." Thereafter, it appeared, the hard-pressed and impoverished poet "took shelter in New York, and once more set his press and his types to grinding sedition." Concluding, Corbett added: "He is hard at work at it," which should surprise no one, for what was this fellow Freneau but "a tool, a toad-eater, a lick-spittle etc., etc." Here was yellow journalism at its worst—flagrant and unabashed. William Cobbett,

---

[16] Smith, *William Cobbett*, pp. 133–134.
[17] *Porcupine's Gazette,* March 4, 1797.

hitting hard and without scruple, had descended to the meanest gutter of politics in a cause which, as an alien, he could not even call his own.

Cobbett may have been animated by concern for his native land, now facing the Grande Armée of Napoleon, the terror of all Europe. Italy, Austria, Germany, Egypt would soon be under the heels of the Corsican's legions. But in what way was Cobbett any different from Genêt —and Genêt had been silenced as an interloper? If neutrality was a valid policy for Americans, what of those aliens who ignored its spirit in their unprincipled attacks on everyone, on all Americans who professed any sympathy for France or any hostility toward England?[18]

The nation, already divided in its political and social views, could be still further confused by the half-truths, the whole lies, of such scandalmongering as Cobbett indulged in without responsibility to anyone for his words. In the name of free speech and a free press, he operated within the pale of the law—unless a libel could be found against him—but he was perverting the issues and falsifying the facts; insult and slander, the language of the guttersnipe, were his weapons when they suited his purpose. He could be suave and sensible, simple and sometimes also appealing, if the occasion required it; but too often his words were fraught with gross innuendo, and too frequently they savored of crass insensibility. A knight of the Federalist host, he was without fear though not without favor, a knight neither shining nor puissant, but always flaunting and usually inept. When Cobbett complained that "he was plagued" with Freneau and his paper, the editor of *The Time-Piece* informed his readers that there were other plagues, worse ones, perhaps, than those the Porcupine spoke of. The recurring yellow fever was one of them, but far more virulent than that were the infections which honest people could neither evade nor escape, whatever precautions they might take to avoid them.

> But still there remain
> Two vipers, that's plain.
>
> . . .
>
> Old Porcupine preaching,
> And Fenno beseeching
> Some dung-cart to wheel him away.[19]

Fenno was still on the job, but neither he nor his party could quite approve the language or tactics of their new spokesman. John Adams,

18 *Ibid.*, September 30, 1797; also June 7, and June 12, 1798.
19 *The Time-Piece*, September 13, 1797.

the President, found them repulsive to his refined sense of fairness, while Abigail, though she thought that Cobbett could "write very handsomely," was offended because "he can descend and be as low and vulgar as a fish woman."[20] Cobbett was not only vilifying the writers and the press of the opposition; he had launched on a campaign of slander against the greatest, most beloved doctor of his time, a man of the highest reputation as a patriot as well. Benjamin Rush, undeniably, was a prominent democrat; but he was also a signer of the Declaration of Independence. Those who could not agree with him politically still held him in greatest respect. Not a few felt a deep reverence for Dr. Benjamin Rush, recalling his refusal to escape the miasmas of Philadelphia in the raging epidemic of 1793. When it recurred in 1797, he remained at his post, helping, saving, comforting the stricken and the dying. He might be wrong in his theory about the causes for the plague and ignorant of the remedies to assuage its terror. The state of medicine was at fault, not the learning or the integrity of the man, nor his immense devotion to duty. Hippocrates never was honored more by any disciple.[21]

In 1797 as in 1793 Dr. Rush was still sure of his theories on the yellow fever. Its cause lay in the "miasmata" of the Quaker City itself, not in the swamps of the distant West Indies as many believed; its prevention could only be effected by proper sanitation and not by quarantine, as his opponents maintained. The cure, if there *was* a cure, might be found in bleeding, and in purging with calomel and jalap. Unfortunately his patients died with disconcerting regularity in spite of all he could do for them, and no one was more disconcerted than the doctor who prescribed the remedies. But no other remedies were known to science. The medical profession had not yet emerged from the dark shadows of trial and error.[22]

Fenno, knowing nothing of the matter, attacked the ability of Benjamin Rush as a doctor; while Cobbett, who knew even less if possible, saw in his failures an excellent opportunity to destroy not only his reputation as a physician but his fame as a democrat also. Cobbett went to work with a will to accomplish both these ends at the same time. While Dr. Rush argued in strictly scientific terms, backed by such proof

[20] Abigail Adams to John Adams, March 13, 1798, in Abigail Adams, *New Letters of Abigail Adams,* p. 144.

[21] Payne, *History of Journalism,* p. 169; Benjamin Rush, *An Account of the Bilious Remitting Yellow Fever,* pp. 12–22.

[22] *Ibid.*

as he possessed, the theoretical if not the practical value of his pre-
scriptions, Cobbett, with sham objectivity, reviled and ridiculed the
man who had no other means to defend himself but these—and perhaps one other. He could sue his assailant for libel. A jury of his peers
could then determine the facts which would effectively silence him.

A jury did promptly find the facts in the case of Rush against Cobbett, and with them also found a verdict in the sum of five thousand
dollars against the Porcupine which he must pay on penalty of forfeit-
ure. But William Cobbett was not so easily silenced. Fleeing from Philadelphia to New York he might avoid all penalties. In addition, he
could with the greatest impunity continue his attacks on Dr. Rush.
Indomitable and persevering, Cobbett may have been convinced of the
justice of his position. After all, the remedies of Dr. Rush were almost
as lethal as the plague itself. Sanitation alone was *not* a preventive.
Bloodletting and purging were *not* cures. Neither Rush nor anybody
else knew that the mosquito *Aëdes aegypti* was the carrier of the fever,
and the findings of a jury could never be proven either true or false
until nearly a century later. Whatever science might say, nobody knew
the truth about the killer that returned again and again, with no other
defense against its murderous onslaught but endless—and altogether
fruitless—bloodlettting and purging, varied by continuous cold vinegar
baths and hot compresses, futile, all futile walls of sand to stem the
recurring flood of death and destruction.[23]

In opposing the romantic illusions of science with the tragic reality
of its impotence, the courage of Cobbett was beyond question, however
doubtful the purity of his motives. His courage and *élan* were parts of
his nature that compelled a certain admiration, and there were other
sides, not yet revealed, that would one day command respect as well.
In a few years he would shake the dust of America from his feet and
return to the homeland he had never really left. Rid of the Federalist
harness and moved by causes far more grateful to his sense of decency,
he would discover other outlets for his indisputable talents and bound-
less energy and a wider field for his fertile mind and courage. From a
foremost preceptor of jingo journalism and scurrilous debate he would
develop into an effective champion of the poor and helpless of Britain,
a political economist and agrarian expert, a man of the highest principles, always ready to pay the penalties imposed by courts and juries

---

[23] Rush, *Account of the Yellow Fever,* pp. 193–195, 203; Bowen, *Peter
Porcupine,* pp. 71 ff; Benjamin Rush, *Autobiography,* pp. 97–100.

in fines and imprisonment for his defense of the underdog. But all that was long after he fled to New York to escape the penalty of his present principles.[24]

As yet, these were only a noisome stench to democrats everywhere, as virulent as the plague which he had used indifferently for good and evil purposes. According to Philip Freneau, Cobbett was worse than the plague. That, he believed, did have some obvious virtues. It carried off many innocent victims but it also struck at a few who were not so innocent. His old enemy, John Fenno, the editor of *The Gazette of the United States* and Cobbett's partner in vilification, was dead, taken by the pest that spared no one. Men like Fenno, like Cobbett, like others among the enemies of democracy, were vile encumbrances on the earth, parasites as deadly as any that afflicted the soul and spirit of man.

> Perhaps below this turf in silence rests
> Those, who when living were of men the pests,
> Patrons of titles, ribbons, crowns and crests.
> What though made sacred by a parson's whine,
> Why sorrowing on these *tombs* should I recline,
> Sheltering some Fenno or some Porcupine.

Such men always had the ear of power. They helped to fasten on the people an oligarchy of wealth, though it was also true that not all democrats were poor or virtuous nor all Federalists rich and grasping. Both camps sheltered many men who were neither black nor white, but only grey. Impatiently, they watched for the main chance to change their color, and not a few remained colorless without it.[25]

There were many facets to the struggle between the democrats and the Federalists, but one was clearer than all the rest in the present contest for war or peace. Federalism was the commercial and financial ally of Britain, and it was prepared to become its military ally as well. Jefferson understood the Federalist aim which he summed up for his friend Mazzei as a combination of "British merchants and American trading on British capital."[26] The expenditures in preparation for a war on France were rising to fantastic heights, using money desperately

[24] The apparent transformation of Cobbett from a conservative, even a reactionary, extremist, into a liberal, indeed a radical disciple of the humanistic virtues, is perceptively treated by Edward Smith in his volume on Cobbett.

[25] *The Time-Piece*, September 15, 1797. See also *ibid.*, September 13, 1799.

[26] Jefferson to Mazzei, April 24, 1796, in Jefferson, *Writings* (ed. Ford), Vol. 7, pp. 72–78.

needed for the public welfare instead. The poor, the small farmer, the worker, the artisan, and craftsman were being burdened by ever-increasing taxes while the rich, the stockjobbers, the financial and industrial nabobs were growing more arrogant and powerful under the beneficent ministrations of Federalist philosophy. John Adams had already stated the simple truth when he explained to James Warren that Americans had never been "Spartans in their contempt of wealth." Adams hoped that they never would be, as otherwise the people might become only "lazy drones." Gouverneur Morris, certainly no Spartan or drone, agreed. Moreover, like most of the Federalist leaders, he believed that the taxing or control of wealth was bad for the country. Profit and monopoly—free enterprise unlimited—these constituted the greatest good for America, if not for Americans.[27]

Everybody, said Freneau, was "upon the watch to take advantage in business and trade." The country under the influence of the Federalists had become a "chinese kennel of sharpers." Never before in history, so it seemed to Freneau, had material aggrandisement and self-seeking "gained so much on any people, in the same short space of time, as upon the Americans." The universal prayer seemed to be:

> O Satan! I thy aid implore,
> That thou wouldst yet increase my store,
> For much does always covet more.[28]

Congress, controlled by the Federalists, was doing its part to conform to their policies. It was building frigates for the protection of the shipping of the mercantile class. It was voting more money for warships like the *Constellation*, the *Constitution*, and the *United States*. The national debt was being burdened by costs from which the people would derive nothing but suffering and dishonor. Albert Gallatin would make his futile objections in Congress as Thomas Greenleaf made them in *The New York Journal* and Philip Freneau in *The Time-Piece*. The Federalists still had their way. The democrats had no recourse but to bide their time. They must wait for the tide to turn—if it ever turned at all.[29]

Waiting with the rest, Philip Freneau pursued his unalterable course of attacking with bland ridicule or angry passion the leaders of the opposition. In a series of satires which he called "odes," he considered

[27] C. A. Beard, *Economic Origins of Jeffersonian Democracy,* pp. 353–358.
[28] *The Time-Piece,* September 29, 1797.
[29] *New York Journal,* September 29, 1797.

the current events, using them as pretexts to lampoon the men who approved them, to prick their pride or pierce the armor of their complacent conscience. He followed the odes with a number of prose pieces whose protagonist, Hezekiah Salem, a Connecticut preacher and a fount of sodden wisdom, was already defrocked by those who were much wiser than he. Amusingly oracular, Hezekiah indulged in obese declarations on the thinnest of subjects, as in issue after issue of *The Time-Piece* Freneau impaled the enemy on the pointed barbs of wit and humor, gleeful when he drew some blood, and often despondent because he did not also draw some subscribers.[30]

The Time-Piece had come to such a pass that he felt "my attempt to establish a newspaper in New York was the wrongest step I could possibly have taken." His voice—like Gallatin's in Congress—was scarcely heard above the din of indignation which became more strident as French attacks on American shipping increased in number. It made little difference that France felt justified in her questionable treatment of American commerce by Federalist tenderness for British power and Federalist sympathy for British trade. French feeling was at a dangerous level, while the political climate of America, of New York itself, was more conducive to the failure than the success of any newspaper as partisan and militant as *The Time-Piece*. If the editor wasn't a little more circumspect in his writings, his creditors might become a bit more pressing. They could clamp down on him altogether. They might even send him to a debtor's prison. Less in fear than in sorrow at the dejecting prospect, the harassed democrat composed his allegory "On a Fly Fluttering around a Candle," which summarized his own repeated failures and thwarted ambitions, his real or threatened destruction by public indifference or hostility. It was man's fate—to be recorded endlessly in the sorry annals of the race as Freneau recorded it now.

> Thus man, like thee, ambitious still
> Some dangerous course to run,
> Aspires to drive with fancied skill,
> The Chariot of the Sun,
> And while to mount the seat he tries
> Like Phaeton, he falls and dies.[31]

He had tried with more than fancied skill to keep *The Time-Piece*

[30] *The Time-Piece,* October 31, November 10, November 13, November 17, December 18, and December 22, 1797.
[31] *Ibid.,* December 8, 1797.

afloat. Perhaps another would succeed where he had failed. Like a dog he had hung onto a picked bone, and the bone *was* picked, the marrow itself was gone out of it. By the end of 1797 the forces of reaction were stronger than ever; his own prospects were worse than any he had ever known before. Eleanor and the two children were back again in Mount Pleasant where, at any rate, they had a place to live. Eleanor expected another, still another baby, soon, and Philip could be of little help to her, or to his partner Davis either. Davis could carry on with *The Time-Piece* alone while he, its editor now in name only, visited with his brother Peter in Charleston for a respite from politics and printing, from debts and demagogues, from babies and other burdens. On January 3, 1798, he left New York on the sloop *Caty,* bound for lotus land and a little peace.[32]

Charleston was a city of gracious living, fine gardens, and imposing mansions, where slaves and blooded horses were the more obvious signs of social worth and dynastic pride. The lovely, polished surface of Charleston did not mirror the cruelty practiced on the black man, whose master could still believe himself "humane" while he advertised for a runaway slave easily recognized "by the incisions of the whip on his back." Nor did it disclose the discipline of the Sugar House, where the uniform price for punishment of recalcitrant Negroes was one shilling for twelve lashes laid across the shoulders by an agent for the master—or the mistress.[33]

Peter hated the cruelty and bondage of chattel slavery as much as Philip. He was a democrat also, and his papers, *The City Gazette* and later *The Carolina Gazette,* waged the same fight against the Federalists that Philip had waged. He too had opposed Jay's Treaty, which, he said, "had placed America in a humiliating situation." His papers were vehicles of Republican sentiment in the South, and his loyalty to Jefferson and the democratic ideal was steadfast and dependable. A fine linguist, an intense idealist, Peter was also a simple, unpretentious person, affable, generous, and forever on the verge of either affluence or bankruptcy. Over six feet tall, his spare figure was known to all of Charleston, while even those whom he opposed considered him a kindly, honest man—a real man of the people, a genuine commoner. Between him and Philip there always had existed a comradeship of mutual love and understanding, and at Peter's home Philip would

[32] Freneau's copy of Robertson, *Elements of Navigation,* in Freneau Collection (Rutgers).

[33] John Davis, *Travels of Four Years and a Half in the U.S.,* pp. 98–117.

never fail to find rest and relaxation he never knew in New York, perhaps not even in Mount Pleasant.[34] It was in Peter's home that he learned of the new baby, named Catherine, who was born to Eleanor on February 25.[35] Because of the baby; because of the greater need to provide for the family augmented while its breadwinner was basking in the sun of the southland, Philip at once engaged passage home. By March 14, after a short visit to Monmouth, he was back in New York again, busy with a new project for a book on which he had worked for a long time. *The Interesting Travels of John Ledyard,* a biography of the explorer and intrepid adventurer who had rounded Cape Horn with Captain Cook, was to be published as soon as enough subscriptions for it were obtained. John Ledyard's journals and letters had been confided to the care of Philip Freneau by Dr. Isaac Ledyard, brother-in-law to Eleanor's sister Catherine. But he as well as Philip might have saved themselves the trouble—the subscriptions, like so many others the poet had sought, never materialized.[36]

Only one matter, long held in abeyance, at last came to pass. On March 21, 1798, the name of Philip Freneau disappeared from *The Time-Piece.* Matthew Davis, deep-sunk in the venture, would continue it alone.

[34] R. B. Davis and M. B. Siegler, "Peter Freneau," *Journal of Southern History,* XIII, 3 (August 1947), 395–405; also Ms. letter, "Freneau to Read," July 30, 1795, and E. S. Thomas, *Reminiscences of the Last Sixty-Five Years,* pp. 75–80.

[35] Freneau Family Bible.

[36] Freneau sailed from Charleston, March 7, 1797 (Freneau's copy of Robertson, *Elements of Navigation*); Lewis Leary, *That Rascal Freneau,* p. 398, says that the materials to which Freneau had access were later used in part by Jared Sparks in his life of John Ledyard.

29. THE REIGN OF TERROR

THE WRITINGS of Philip Freneau in *The Time-Piece* had left their mark. As the responsible editor, through numerous articles—his own as well as those by others—he had kept its readers in many states abreast of events at home and informed on developments abroad. At the same time the drum-stick propaganda of the newspaper had served to keep the flagging spirits of the democrats from succumbing to the pressures of political conflict and the mounting tension between France and America, or their depleted courage from collapsing under combined French and American belligerency. All hope for the ultimate triumph of their cause had appeared more remote than ever in spite of Freneau's insistent harping on the demand for peace and his infinite variations on the theme of democracy. The dignity and equality of all men, so feebly assured by two revolutions, would be destroyed altogether in a war that none but the Federalists wanted, from which none but they could profit. To inform—sometimes to incite—the people had been Freneau's aim; a knowledge of the dangers that beset them was the sole surety for their political patrimony.

The people needed to be informed. The times were dark with sinister portents and the crucial moment for action was drawing ever closer. War with France was a matter of weeks, even days, away. According to reports credited by many, a French invasion was not impossible. Congress was already debating the impending crisis and considering adequate measures to meet it. The dangers, it was said, threatened not only from across the sea—they were closer at home, in the persons of dangerous democrats who were the avowed friends of France. The Federalists of Massachusetts and Connecticut were especially concerned about them. Fisher Ames had begged his friend, President John Adams, not to "be discouraged in your endeavors to keep this generation of vipers from ruining us."[1] At the same time he urged the Secretary of the Treasury "to arm and prepare force and revenue" for the purpose of defense. War, Fisher Ames maintained, was the only answer to the enemies of America. "Cowardice will cry peace; it has been the popular cry," he continued, and the "government is paralyzed by faction."[2] His own faction was not silent either. In Boston Dr. Tappan and Father Thayer, Chief Justice Dana himself, were preaching hatred for France and its American friends, all of them a present—and a pressing—danger to the peace and tranquillity of the United States. The liberty the democrats so glibly ranted about was nothing more than license. Democracy, "like death, is only the dismal passport to a more dismal hereafter."[3]

In Connecticut, the stronghold of Federalist reaction, a democrat was considered to be morally deficient and was a political leper. The voices of preacher and politician were raised against everyone who was friendly or neutral toward the France of Talleyrand and Napoleon. The XYZ scandal was bad enough in all conscience. The repeated raids on American shipping, the losses to American business, the persistent threat to American safety from French émigrés like Volney and Connecticut rabble-rousers like Abraham Bishop—all these showed the need for attention, immediate and drastic attention, from the government to all the enemies of the country. Dr. Timothy Dwight of Yale echoed the warning and demanded action in no uncertain terms.[4]

In Philadelphia, the august seat of government, all demands sounded through Cabinet rooms and Congressional halls alike; they were heard in streets and barrooms where once democrats had been popular. Now they were threatened with assault. A new species of patriot made the expression of unpopular opinion an occasion for argument not limited to words alone. These men knew what they wanted—they wanted war! Violence and terror stalked the City of Brotherly Love,

[1] John Adams to Fisher Ames, March 24, 1797, quoted in George Gibbs, *Memoirs of the Administration of Washington and John Adams,* Vol. 1, pp. 472–477.

[2] John Adams to Wolcott, April 24, 1797 in *ibid.,* Vol. 2, p. 41.

[3] Ames to Christopher Gore, in Fisher Ames, *Works,* Vol. 1, p. 324.

[4] C. G. Bowers, *Jefferson and Hamilton,* p. 145.

searching out the advocates of peace and all those who voiced any radical views.

The President, wanting no war, was still uncertain of what he did want. Beset by many problems which he found difficult to resolve, he discovered little sympathy or understanding within his own Cabinet. A deep suspicion of his advisers further clouded his indecision, and the man he had defeated for the Presidency by only three votes was suspect above all the others. To his friend Cunningham he confided that Thomas Jefferson, though he pretended a spurious friendship for his chief, at the same time remained unmoved by villainous attacks upon him by Philip Freneau and others of the democratic press. Unsure of his friends, uncertain of his policy, jealous of his power, and fearful for his prestige, John Adams continued to temporize on the question of war while tolerating the disturbances repeatedly staged by the new patriots of Philadelphia. In his home town of Quincy, where he could have the peace that no one questioned and no one disturbed, the atmosphere, both political and domestic, was far more tranquil. As often as possible he went there with his beloved Abigail, for, as he said, he could transact the Nation's business in Quincy as well as in the capital.[5]

In the early days of May 1798 some of that business could be transacted nowhere else but in Philadelphia. The President must review a parade of patriots, twelve hundred of them, as they stepped along to the stirring tunes of martial music. It was a demonstration of loyalty that gladdened the heart of the rotund little man who watched from his window, dressed out in full military regalia as befit the commander-in-chief of all the armed forces of America, his sword hung smartly at his side, a proud and arresting figure whose eloquence soon inspired the crowd, as it also inspired the Porcupine and the enemies of France throughout the Union.[6]

The speech of the President was acceptable to them all, though far from acceptable to the democrats. James Madison called it "the most abominable and degrading that could fall from the lips of the first magistrate of an independent people, and particularly from a Revolutionary patriot."[7] The lusty lads who had been inspired by the words

---

[5] Gibbs, Memoirs of the Administration, Vol. 1, p. 472; L. D. White, The Federalists, p. 241.

[6] Bowers, Jefferson and Hamilton, p. 366; The Porcupine's Gazette, May 7, 1798.

[7] Madison to Jefferson, May 20, 1798, in James Madison, Writings, Vol. 6, p. 320.

of their chief had refreshed themselves at the taverns, then proceeded to invade the home of Benjamin Bache, publisher of *The Aurora,* celebrating the holiday further by terrorizing all the known or suspected democrats in the City of Brotherly Love. The patriots had their reasons, as provocative as the words of their President. Rumors were circulating in Philadelphia that the radicals were preparing to free all slaves in a huge conspiracy of revolt and riot, rape and robbery. The city itself was to be burned to the ground. Democrats, capable of any treason, would seek the help not only of slaves, but also of foreign saboteurs and spies, of Irish agitators and French sappers, of all the enemies of England and aliens everywhere who were only waiting for a sign to assault the city and capture the country itself. The proof of the great conspiracy was clear—it was already at hand.[8]

From his pulpit at North Church in Boston, the Reverend Jedediah Morse offered it to his countrymen. The father of the future inventor of the telegraph, himself a man of no mean ability, saw all too plainly the "awful events" precipitated on American soil by the illuminati of Europe. Author of America's first geography, a good Federalist as well as a learned and persuasive speaker, the Reverend Mr. Morse was as devout as he was learned; all democrats were atheists to him, or else Deists, which was much the same thing to a learned man. All of them were ungodly, just plain demagogues whose baleful influence was an infection like swift poison. What further proof was necessary to convince America that men like these were willing tools for French intrigues to overthrow the civil authority and the religious institutions of the country, debauch freedom with irreverence and destroy it with license? Those who heard the Reverend Jedediah Morse were impressed by his proof.[9]

Still others heard proof of another kind, by another preacher. Elihu Palmer was no longer a minister of the true gospel, but he preached a type of word that New York heard with a certain respect and even admiration. Palmer was a democrat—why else would Philip Freneau join with others in a petition to have him speak at the City Hall? A man like Elihu Palmer must be heard, for unlike the Reverend Mr. Morse, he had given up the security of the Church to denounce the clergy and laity alike, indeed all men who opposed the revolution at

[8] Bowers, *Jefferson and Hamilton,* pp. 366–368; *The Time-Piece,* May 14, 1798; and *Porcupine's Gazette,* June 1, 1798.

[9] J. Morse, *A Sermon Preached at Charleston, November 29, 1798;* also V. Stauffer, *New England and the Bavarian Illuminati,* pp. 10, 34.

home or abroad. Did the clergy speak glibly of God as their partner in this fight against Man? Palmer would quote from Thomas Paine's "Age of Reason" to refute them. Like Paine, he too had given a great deal—more perhaps than the men who spoke so confidently about God—for the cause of freedom. In this fight between democrats and Federalists Palmer had lost all he had ever possessed—he was now a pauper, and it was not easy to be a pauper when one had also lost his wife and his sight in the plague of 1793. For Palmer, the French Revolution was not the same as for men like John Trumbull—"a frenzy which made the very streets of Paris flow with blood." On the contrary, it was a blessing "to afflicted humanity," to whom it had given "the consoling hope of suffering alleviated or wholly destroyed." Who knew about suffering more than he did? To a Deist, God was no stern judge or jealous autocrat, the ancient Yahweh whose only rule of justice was an eye for an eye and a tooth for a tooth. He was the benevolent author of the universe, enthroned in the heart of man, not found in revealed religion alone—or at all. Jedediah Morse might convince the followers of Oliver Wolcott and Timothy Pickering, pillars of Federalist society, but Elihu Palmer spoke the language of Thomas Jefferson—and Philip Freneau. The truth was that neither side needed further conviction; and all Federalists were not devout nor all democrats Deists. Each party was already convinced of its own purity; each side was sure of the other's sinfulness.[10]

John Adams, to cleanse the country of all sin, called for a day of prayer and fasting. And since the pulpits of Philadelphia were filled by Federalists, the day of prayer became also a day of denunciation of democrats. On the same day, too, before or after the fasting, a second assault was made on the home of Bache, with an added insult to his grandfather, Benjamin Franklin, whose statue was smeared with filth. If this was not enough, *The Porcupine's Gazette* announced on June 1, that "when the occasion requires, the Yankees will show themselves as ready at stringing up as in stringing onions." In New York, where the citizens were not much calmer, Joseph Hopkinson, a Federalist who had endeared himself to the Administration with his song "Hail Columbia" (happy land), suggested that the "whole city [should]

[10] *The Time-Piece,* July 24, July 26, and September 8, 1797; and Adrienne Koch, *Republican Religion,* pp. xiii–xv, 53–57. Palmer's "Enquiry Relative to the Political Improvement of the Human Species," was recognized as a noble statement of the democratic faith. See J. W. Francis, *Old New York;* and N. F. Adkins, *Philip Freneau and the Cosmic Enigma.*

undergo the Turkish ceremony of the bastinadoes." He wanted the strong-arm lads to "rouse the lazy drones with a whip," the drones, of course, those democrats who refused to go to war against France.[11] If Hopkinson and his friends wanted war, the Society of Saint Tammany replied, "May the old Tories, and all who wish to engage the United States in a war with any nation, realize the felicity they anticipate by being placed in the front of the first battle." A suggestion worthy of the mischievous Aristophanes or his conniving creature Lysistrata.[12]

Philip Freneau, without a paper in which to voice his views, was not for that reason entirely silent. *The Time-Piece,* with Davis at the helm, was steering a middle course that affronted no one and pleased nobody. Albert Gallatin had written to his sister-in-law Maria Nicholson complaining about him. "I do not admire much the manner in which the new Editor of the Time Piece conducts his paper," he said, a criticism he never voiced when it was under Freneau's direction.[13] Nor had he any fault to find with his writings in another journal, *The New York Argus.* In the issue of June 15, 1798, Freneau had cried out against war and had pleaded for an enduring peace.

> Americans! would you conspire
> To extinguish this increasing fire?
> Would you, so late from fetters freed,
> Join party in so base a deed?
>
> . . .
>
> Oh, No! but should all shame forsake,
> And gratitude her exit make,
> Could you, as thousands say you can,
> Desert the common cause of man?

Without waiting for an answer, he supplied it himself in the next day's *Argus.* "The Republic and Liberty" gave to the people of America a song set to the music of "Anacreon in Heaven," music which later was adopted for their national anthem.

[11] *The Porcupine's Gazette,* June 1, 1798.

[12] Bernard Fay, "Benjamin F. Bache: Democratic Leader of the 18th Century," *American Antiquarian Society,* Vol. 40 (1931), pp. 277–304; and *Porcupine's Gazette,* June 1, 1798; *The Time-Piece,* May 14, 1798; Bowers, *Jefferson and Hamilton,* pp. 368 ff; Philip Marsh, "Philip Freneau and Francis Hopkinson," in *Proceedings of New Jersey Historical Society,* LXIII, 3 (July 1945), 141–149.

[13] Gallatin to Nicholson, July 10, 1798, in Henry Adams, *Life of Albert Gallatin,* p. 196.

> Americans! rouse at the rumours of war,
> Which now are distracting the hearts of the nation.
> A flame blowing up a race you abhor—
> That aided so lately old England's invasion,
>   When with heart and with hand,
>   And a murdering band
> Of vagrants, she plunder'd and ravag'd our land.
> In Liberty's cause we are ever array'd,
> But yield not her substance to feast on her shade.

In poem after poem Freneau waged his own war against war. War —What for? He asked the question again and again, and as often answered with lines of high beauty and deep sentiment, with words of reason as well as with words of passion. A poet and polemicist, he had forsaken satire and humor for the serious business of peace. There was no room for satire in the state of national hysteria, and only occasionally was there need for the felicitous phrase. Revolutions and upheavals, attempting to shake loose the masters as well as the slaves, often succeeded in dislodging only the freemen of a country. Spiritual symbiosis was a rare phenomenon, impeded in its accomplishment of any certainty in truth by the fumblings of humility. The footstools and the footpads of the race remained impregnable, and—so it seemed— the friends of liberty, like Sisyphus, labored in vain against the gravitational pull of an indifferent fate. Philip Freneau refused to concede any such defeat for man, or any such victory for his enemies. His enemies? They were also the enemies of democracy, men like William Cobbett, who wanted to "destroy, banish or proscribe every man of democratic principles in the United States."[14]

Congress was moving swiftly to the brink of war with more ships, more armament, more taxes to pay for them, even a tax on slaves. Southerners objected that New England's losses on the sea, in ships and in commerce, could not be recouped by war against those who had rescued a prostrate South from British cruelty. In addition, taxes on slaves were an intolerable burden on an economy based on slavery. New England had no slaves, or too few to be affected by such a tax; and the trade of the South was not victimized by French assaults on the commerce of New England. These were perhaps partisan answers; but the South could vote, and when it voted the Federalists would have an answer that was powerful as well as partisan to all the injuries inflicted on democrats by an arrogant war party. As the Federalists be-

[14] New York *Argus,* June 25, 1798.

came more aggressive in their challenge to France, so the vigilance of
the democrats become more alert. As the danger of war became more
imminent, so the urgency of peace became more pressing. Freneau, in
the vanguard of opposition, demanded a united front against all hate-
mongers.

> Americans! will you controul such views!
> Speak—for you must—you have no time to lose.[15]

It was the literal truth; there was little time to lose. On June 21
Adams declared that no other minister would be sent to France without
guarantees of an honorable reception, virtually a severance of diplomatic relations between the two countries. As the tension rose to fever
pitch in both camps, the factions in the country prepared for any
emergency. Reason alone did not emerge. Former friends became
enemies; those who had once been enemies were ready for strange alliances. The question of war or peace was splitting the ranks of both
sides wide open, while even among Republicans themselves the problem of national honor confused many men of peace and good will. The
fever of war gripped the entire nation.

Then came the fever of another plague. In 1798 a recurrence of the
yellow fever brought new panic to inflame the old one. To the miasma
of intrigue, slander, and impending catastrophe was added the stench
of death and disease from the epidemic that swept men still farther
from their moorings. To sweep them away altogether, persistent rumors of invasion were carried across the country by the fetid wind of
fear.[16]

Not all men were infected. A few were optimistic. Jefferson, for one,
believed that the "fever" of war would not last. The plague of disease
would run its course—and the plague of war would never strike. The
new taxes, he thought, would cool the ardor of the warmongers. The
men of peace would yet prevail. Where men were free to speak their
mind reason must surely triumph over error.[17]

Jefferson was too sanguine. Reason rarely prevails over passion;
power never suffers what it can destroy. As Federalist attacks increased, democratic insults against its leaders became more virulent,
and as the specter of the French terror still haunted the minds of con-

[15] *Ibid.,* July 7, 1798.
[16] Fenno and Bache died in this year of the plague, both of them in the
month of September 1798. Fay, "Benjamin F. Bache," p. 295.
[17] F. W. Hirst, *Life and Letters of Thomas Jefferson,* p. 351.

servatives, the fear of a war haunted the minds of the radicals. So long as words were a solvent of both fears and specters, the danger of violence was submerged or diminished, and the freedom to speak one's mind reduced the hazards of the threat of war. It was a freedom permitted—nay guaranteed—by the greatest of all the laws of the land. The Bill of Rights, imbedded in the Constitution as the soul in the body, clearly, unequivocally, simply, said so.

Now, another bill, containing other laws, was discussed in Congress. It cast a gray shadow on the right to free speech, but did not blot it out entirely. It only proposed a change, a small change, an apparently innocuous one, in the laws of citizenship. It proposed that the foreign-born, men like Albert Gallatin, who spoke so much of peace, could be deported to their native land. This powerful leader of the Congressional minority had once before lost his seat because of his alien status and might lose it again as one of the big fish in the fine-spun net of the Alien Law. Others too would be caught—aliens like Constantin Volney, once the close friend of the unspeakable Robespierre and now the equally close confidant of such rabble-rousing democrats as Thomas Jefferson. Volney, the eminent historian, whose perceptive and prescient volumes included *Les Ruines,* a scholarly study of revaluations, was more inimical to America than a man like Cobbett and should be sent back where he came from. And what about Priestley? The quiet, inoffensive Dr. Priestley, an "infidel" as well as an Englishman, had no place in a God-fearing country either. America was better off without such riff-raff in its midst to speak the language of nonconformity and dissent.[18]

Philip Freneau was wise to warn his countrymen against such laws as this: "Speak—for you must—you have no time to lose." Soon it would be too late, for the opening of one door would also open many others. First the aliens—then the native Americans would feel the lash of the law. They could never be deported—but there were other punishments to fit the crime of subversion. If free speech was outlawed what else would be spared?[19]

In the babble of voices that argued about it and about it, the need for clarity was the greatest need of all. In the confusion of factions, the people, only the people, could speak with authority. But they had failed to heed the warning of Freneau and now it was too late. Before

[18] *Ibid.,* p. 330; United States Congress, *Annals of Congress,* Vol. 6, pp. 363 ff; and J. A. Stevens, *Albert Gallatin,* p. 10.
[19] New York *Argus,* July 7, 1798.

they could speak, the Federalist majority among their Representatives in Congress had spoken instead. Urged on by the President of the United States, they passed the laws meant to seal the lips of citizen and alien alike. John Adams, hoping to silence his enemies, real or suspected; hoping also to destroy their party, had demanded laws which would halt the opposition and reduce its members to impotence. In June the Alien Act was passed—in July, the Sedition Laws.[20]

For the first time—but not for the last in American history—to utter the truth according to one's conscience was a high crime and misdemeanor. The statute law of the Bill of Rights, and the common law of John Peter Zenger, were set aside as if blood and treasure had never been expended to insure them. The First Amendment to the Constitution had been nullified and Freneau's warning had not been heeded. The people had failed to speak. John Adams and the Congress of the United States had spoken before them. Next time they might speak first.[21]

John Quincy Adams, the son of the President, considered the Sedition Act as "an ineffectual attempt to extinguish the fire of defamation." On the contrary, he added, "it operated like oil upon the flames."[22] The son, more astute than the father and far less impervious to democratic doctrine, was concerned for the good name of the President who was the victim of increased and envenomed democratic attacks. It was true that some of them were only the mouthings of demagogues, but the President never feared the slanders of men like these. Washington had survived worse ones. Many Republicans had openly sympathized with Adam's sincere efforts to avoid a war. He was as popular with the people as he had ever been if only because of his insistence on France's recognition of the honor and dignity of America. John Adams had some better friends among those who were not of his own party than he had inside his own Cabinet. Yet he struck out blindly against all Anti-Federalists, friend and foe alike, in an access of partisan folly and ambitious maneuver.[23]

[20] The Alien Act was passed in June 1798, the Sedition Act in July 1798; *The Time-Piece,* July 13, 1798.

[21] G. H. Payne, *History of Journalism in the United States,* pp. 177–180; R. A. Billington, B. L. Lowenberg, and S. H. Brockunier, *The United States: American Democracy in World Perspective,* pp. 87–89.

[22] New York *Argus,* July 7, 1798, "On the Causes of Political Degeneracy."

[23] *State Trials of the U.S. during the Administration of Washington and Adams* (ed. F. Wharton), pp. 658–681; and John Quincy Adams, *The Diary of John Quincy Adams,* pp. 468–469. John Adams had expressed his views on

More than defamation, the coming elections had inspired the new laws. They were meant to stifle free speech, muzzle the democratic press, imprison the truth, and deport the men who spoke it. Controversy would be suspended, the democrats would be routed, and the Federalists would ride to victory over the inert bodies and abandoned field of the opposition. The spirit of America would be tamed, radical slogans abolished, the ideals for which a revolution had been fought wiped out in a universal chorus of reaction. The President himself, aloof from all contamination, would remain above the battle, involved in no personal attempts to use the laws against the enemy. There would be no need for him to do so. The Secretary of State, the Federal Judges, the District Attorneys, the multiple machinery of government would operate in closest harmony for the strict and speedy enforcement of the new laws.[24]

The hounds of the government were soon in full cry. The scent of suspicion attached to all men who questioned the virtues of Federalism or its leaders, while an accusation alone was enough to place a democrat at once in jeopardy. The finger of suspicion pointed at any of the opposition press was sufficient to bring it within the scrutiny of the law. Noah Webster, in *The Commercial Advertiser* of June 11, accused John Daly Burk, the new editor of *The Time-Piece*, of possessing "tenfold" the malignity of Philip Freneau. The law would reckon with Burk, and with William Duane, editor of the Philadelphia *Aurora*, who was in a position to do as much harm as anybody. Indeed, Burk was soon indicted for libel against the President, and no one knew on whom the axe would fall next.[25]

Freneau did not remain silent. In *The Time-Piece* itself, he fought both the prosecution of Burk and the laws under which it was instituted. Was this America, he asked, where oppression had once been buried, and now reared its evil head again? He replied in cautious strophes that touched the conscience of all lovers of liberty who had

---

free speech long before (see John Adams, *Works*, Vol. 1, p. 587). Hamilton had even less faith in government by the people (see Alexander Hamilton, *Works*, Vol. 5, p. 441; Vol. 6, p. 54; and Vol. 8, p. 260). "The people," he said, "are a great beast," quoted in Henry Adams, *History of the United States during the First Administration of Jefferson* (ed. H. Agar), Vol. 1, p. 85.

[24] H. C. Lodge, *Studies in History*, pp. 160–164.

[25] Lewis Leary, *That Rascal Freneau*, p. 305; and *The Time-Piece*, June 13, 1798. Also F. M. Anderson, "The Enforcement of the Alien and Sedition Laws," *Annual Report of the American Historical Association*, pp. 116 ff.

allowed such sacrilege—without too closely touching the sensibilities of the law itself. As he had once held aloof from the army for fear of being "knocked on the head" by foreign enemies, so he was wary now of being imprisoned by domestic oppressors. He had never forgotten his experiences in a British prison ship. Perhaps he felt now as he felt so long ago in another crisis:

> Steep me, steep me some poppies deep
> In Beechen bowl, to bring on sleep.[26]

But forgetfulness was impossible when more powerful men than he, men of means and distinction, men of influence and position, were being arrested and jailed and persecuted. He had neither the means nor the power to defend himself. The courage to stand alone was tempered by a pervasive doubt that the people for whom he had always spoken were really concerned. The example of John Burk was not a reassuring one, and the people chosen for the juries who sat in judgment upon him and others seemed concerned only to convict. It had not always been so in America. In another, in an earlier, time the writers and newspapers had received more considerate treatment at the hands of juries. Long before there had been any Bill of Rights at all, a jury had released Peter Zenger and thrown out a charge of libel on the government. It was established then that a free press was free at least to speak the truth. Many decades later it appeared that there was no such freedom.[27]

Freneau, while he had no paper of his own, might have used the columns of Duane's *Aurora* or Greenleaf's *Argus* had he chosen to invite the hosts of hatred and vengeance. However, although he did not remain altogether quiet, his contributions were couched in language that saved him from the wrath—the legal wrath—of the Federalists and their picked juries. Sharp and incisive as his words were, they skirted the edge of utmost danger, as he shrank from the full force of Federalist fury. Courage was not a conspicuous attribute of maturity. John Randolph of Roanoke called the storm of legal outrage a new "Reign of Terror," a description richly earned before the administration of John Adams was finished with all the prosecutions under the Alien and Sedition Acts.[28]

[26] *The Time-Piece,* July 13, July 16, 1798; Leary, *That Rascal Freneau,* p. 43.

[27] In 1735 John Peter Zenger, editor of the *New York Weekly Journal,* was imprisoned, tried, and acquitted of libel by a jury.

[28] Hirst, *Life and Letters of Jefferson,* p. 349.

Nothing was left of Freneau's dream of democracy. Like his other illusions, that too was gone. What remained was his old revulsion against violence, his renewed discouragement at his country's plight, his everlasting despondency over his own plight as well. There was no place for him anywhere, unless, perhaps, he could find some respite in the "beechen bowl," some surcease from private and public realities in the lotuslike solitudes of Mount Pleasant. In the year 1798, while the plagues of fever and persecution were rampant in America, in Monmouth they were scarcely known at all.

With impartial vigor and lethal purpose the yellow fever attacked all its victims, while political crimes were assessed only against the enemies of John Adams and his Federalist friends. John Fenno was already dead—now Benjamin Bache was also stricken. Thomas Greenleaf succumbed in New York, where fourteen hundred others, of both parties, perished by the end of October. The war which threatened would never kill as many—indeed, it would kill none at all, for it would never come to pass. But the laws it had spawned would wound many who opposed it. John Burk, to escape any further wounding with arrest and imprisonment, had disappeared entirely, while William Duane, the new editor of *Aurora,* was in greatest jeopardy of serious injury. John Adams had expressed himself as "very willing to try" the strength of the new laws on Duane because his "matchless effrontery" was intolerable to him personally.[29] No less intolerable was it to the host of Adams' followers in Philadelphia. Not only was Duane indicted—he was set upon and badly beaten as well.

In other cities, too, the mills of justice ground fast and ground exceedingly large. Thomas Adams, editor of *The Boston Independent Chronicle,* and David Frothingham, of *The New York Argus,* were arrested and charged with writing "libels" on the Administration of the President. Matthew Lyon, Congressman from Vermont, was tried and sentenced to four months imprisonment in addition to a fine of 1,000 dollars for attacks he had made on the Administration *before* the enactment of the Alien and Sedition Laws. Lyon had accused the President of an "unbounded thirst for ridiculous pomp, foolish adulation, and selfish avarice." The democrats could do nothing about his prison term,

[29] Bowers, *Jefferson and Hamilton,* p. 374. See also Payne, *History of Journalism,* pp. 181–182; Adams to Pickering, July 27, 1799, in John Adams, *Works,* Vol. 9, p. 5. Also, *The Aurora,* May 20, 1799. Duane's trial for libel, in *State Trials of the U.S.,* p. 345, and Anderson, "Enforcement of the Alien and Sedition Laws," p. 116.

but with the help of Jefferson, Madison, Gallatin, and John Taylor of Caroline, they paid the fine of the hapless legislator.[30]

And still the mills ground on. The Reverend John C. Ogden, an inoffensive clergyman of advanced views, was mobbed by soldiers at Litchfield, Connecticut, because he was "a damn democrat," and Charles Holt of New London was jailed by Judge Bushrod Washington for his acerbic criticisms in *The New London Bee.* Edward Livingston, elected to speak for the people, was threatened with violence because he argued against the offensive laws on the floor of Congress, while the Vice-President of the United States, Jefferson himself, was spied on, insulted, and repeatedly threatened with bodily assault. Gangs of bullyboys roamed the streets in cities of the North and South armed with swords and pistols, uprooting liberty poles, destroying printing plants, forcing the discharge of all democrats from their places of employment, terrifying citizens who questioned the laws, and cowing into silence those who murmured the least dissent. Brutality became the sole arbiter of justice, and justice itself was clothed in the garment of brutality. Judge Chase, brutal beyond all his brethren, was doing his utmost "to teach the difference between liberty and licentiousness of the press." With great alacrity and abandon, he went around his circuit from one court to another, from the North to the South, to practice his special brand of judicial terrorism.[31]

In all walks of life men were silenced by threats of legal or other violence, while effective boycotts were steadily enforced on the known or suspected culprits of democratic beliefs. Dr. Thomas Cooper of Philadelphia, daring to criticize John Adams in *The Sunbury and Northumberland Gazette,* was tried, found guilty, and sentenced to serve six months in prison in addition to paying a heavy fine. James Callender, a rabid and often irresponsible Anti-Federalist, none too accurate in his charges against the President, was treated in kind by a picked jury from which democrats were carefully excluded. To ensure his conviction, Judge Chase permitted only biased and prejudicial testimony against him and clamped the lid down still tighter on an assured verdict with stump speeches from the bench. Lynch law was as rampant

[30] *State Trials of the U.S.,* pp. 658 ff; Bowers, *Jefferson and Hamilton,* pp. 374, 386, 388 ff, and 393 ff.

[31] Bowers, *Jefferson and Hamilton,* pp. 366–368, 389–398, 404. Hamilton, who was no advocate of the Alien and Sedition Laws, had accused J. Chase of being a scoundrel and profiteer himself (Hamilton, *Works,* Vol. 1, pp. 562, 567, 580).

as the yellow fever. A time of terror had come, in the halls of justice as in the homes of citizens, when no man was safe from official vengeance and a new concept of freedom included the ancient warning of lese majesty. Now, a man could be fined for wishing that a wad from the cannon fired in salute to the President might catch him in the broadest part of his breeches.[32]

It was not surprising, perhaps, that a Republican like John Taylor of Caroline could seriously propose a dissolution of the Union which sanctioned and permitted outrages such as these. John Taylor was no irresponsible demagogue. He was one of the ablest thinkers and finest intellects of the opposition. His breadth of knowledge and his depth of understanding had contributed greatly to clarify Republican doctrine. He had served in the Senate and was a southern leader whose democratic principles encompassed a profound belief in states' rights. If the state was nothing but a cog in the wheel of government then government, which was made up only of the states, was a wheel on which they would be broken. The Alien and Sedition Laws, their stupid and vengeful enforcement against all the safeguards of the Constitution, the gross perversion of the Constitution itself as well as the Bill of Rights, all these were but added proofs of the dangers to democracy and added warnings of the awesome threats of tyranny.[33]

The Republicans were not alone in voicing these sentiments. A good Federalist like Thomas Marshall objected to the Alien and Sedition Laws because, though he believed in a "well-regulated democracy," he could never countenance regulations such as these. Alexander Hamilton—even Hamilton—who had always doubted the virtues of democracy, also doubted the virtues of laws like these. The people might be beasts, but what about the rulers? "Let us not," he warned, "establish a tyranny. Energy is a very different thing from violence."[34]

In all human history, tyranny had never triumphed without violence.

---

[32] Payne, *History of Journalism*, p. 182; G. M. Stephenson, *American History to 1865*, pp. 189 ff; *State Trials of the U.S.*, re "Fries," pp. 610, 648; re "Callender," *ibid.*, p. 688.

[33] C. A. Beard, *Economic Origins of Jeffersonian Democracy*, p. 356; A. E. Smith, *James Madison: The Builder*, p. 184.

[34] Hamilton to Wolcott, June 29, 1798, quoted in Gibbs, *Memoirs of the Administration*, p. 68. Hamilton, nevertheless, was not opposed to the Alien and Sedition Laws (see Hamilton to Pickering, June 7, 1798, Alexander Hamilton, *Works*, Vol. 10, pp. 292–294). See also James M. Smith, "Alexander Hamilton: The Alien and Sedition Libels," *The Review of Politics*, XVI, 3 (July 1954), 305–333.

And it was extremely doubtful that it could ever be abolished peacefully. That, in any event, was the nuclear thought, however carefully concealed in the cocoon of language, of the resolutions which were now prepared by Thomas Jefferson and James Madison. The Virginia Resolutions, drawn by Madison, deplored, with "deep regret," the spirit "manifested by the Federal government to enlarge its powers by forced construction of the Constitutional charter which defines them." Passed by the Virginia Legislature in December 1798, the resolutions denounced the Alien and Sedition Laws as obvious violations of the Constitution and appealed to the rest of the country for help in opposing them. The Jefferson resolutions, passed by the Kentucky Legislature a few weeks earlier and later enlarged, flatly asserted that each state was the sole judge of any federal constitutional usurpations. They went even further than the Madison resolves. The Sedition Act, they declared, was unconstitutional and "altogether void and of no effect," and added: "nullification by those sovereign [states] of all unauthorized acts done under the color" of the Constitution "is the rightful remedy." If an increasingly powerful central government attempted to frustrate the democratic impulses of the people, then the people, who were sovereign in the states which composed the government, had the right, indeed they had the duty, to defend themselves. John Taylor of Caroline had spoken of secession. Madison and Jefferson now spoke of nullification. What weapon would come next from the arsenal of democracy? Were weapons like these the best ones available to democrats to save their cause? Only the people themselves could save it, not by withdrawing from the fight and leaving the field to the enemy but by standing their ground and defeating him. The time for a decisive battle was near.[35]

Philip Freneau, in his ancestral refuge at Mount Pleasant, had not given up his fight against the Federalists. He could never change his mind about them, and his opinions were the same now as when he had called his countrymen

> To arms, to arms, and let the trusty sword,
> Decide who best deserves the hangman's cord.[36]

---

[35] Stephenson, *American History to 1865*, p. 190; see also F. M. Anderson, "Contemporary Opinion of the Virginia and Kentucky Resolutions." *American Historical Review*, V, 1 (October 1899), 45–63, and 2 (January 1900), 225–252.

[36] Leary, *That Rascal Freneau*, p. 59.

He relished neither the sword nor the cord, save as convenient rhymes, nor was he sorry to cheat the voracious enemy of another victim. The Federalists would have been happy to get their hands on him—but who would support his family if they did? Many of the Republican leaders were in a strong position to oppose the Alien and Sedition Laws. The burden of want was not added to all the others which they bore. He had this one too, rarely relieved, and now more than ever a weight beyond his strength to endure.

Like so many others, the poet was property poor. The estate left by his father was no small one, but heavy debts had reduced it considerably, while returns from the rest of it were never sufficient for his modest mode of living. He had already sold some tracts for sorely needed cash. Now he deeded another one of fifty-five acres to John S. Hunn, the husband of his sister Margaret, for 150 pounds,[37] little enough for his own needs and his creditors' demands, yet more money than he had possessed in a long time. In any case, it freed him from the hovering shadow of destitution and the pervading gloom of futility. His old mood of urbane and ironical good humor returned, and with it, like the sun's rays splashing through scattered clouds, his satirical sense of the absurdity of current events.

In *The Aurora* of March 25, 1799, there appeared an essay signed by "A Monarchist." Written by Freneau in a serio-comic vein, it supported the Federalists and attacked the democrats. How wrong it was, the writer, with tongue in cheek, maintained, to think that "princes or presidents ought always to act fairly, openly, or ingenuously." Rulers were their own judges and could not be held accountable by any other. Some of the greatest thinkers knew this—men like Plutarch, Tacitus, Pliny, and Plato. What was all the bother about the Alien and Sedition Acts? What was wrong with them? What was wrong with taxes? No prince or president could be abused with impunity, neither could they rule without sufficient funds. Here was logic both simple and irrefutable. The foibles and follies of lesser men were no measure for the conduct of the great, and the conduct of rulers was above the censure of the people. *Quod erat demonstrandum.*[38]

The whole essay might have been written by some Machiavelli in collaboration with a jesting Pilate, or by some Voltaire cultivating

[37] Monmouth County Deeds and Mortgages, Mss., March 23, 1797, L. 336, R. 448.

[38] Slender letter #1, in Freneau, *Letters on Various Interesting and Important Subjects.*

his garden with a spade that was shaped like a pen. There was nothing in it for which Freneau could be hauled into court, unless, indeed, the courts possessed a sense of humor which was itself outlawed by the Alien and Sedition Acts. As if in proof of this, Freneau continued his devious attacks on them in a series of letters to *Aurora* fashioned after his old essays on Tomo Cheeki, and signed by Robert Slender, the same stocking weaver who had once taken "A Journey from Philadelphia to New York" back in 1787. Freneau had buried Robert Slender some years earlier, but resuscitated him for purposes less didactic and more penetrating than before. Robert Slender, as simple as ever, was an older if not a wiser man—his years in heaven or on earth had taught him little about the vagaries of men and the law. He wanted to learn —and so he wrote his letters, begging for information from "A Monarchist" whose laudations of the Alien and Sedition Acts had puzzled him so greatly. In the manner of a shadow duel, but with bare swords, these two lunged and retreated, thrust and parried, fought and bled.[39]

In these papers Philip Freneau voices his deepest antipathies to all conservative measures of the Federalist government from the very beginning of their power, and to the reactionary policies of the Adams Administration in particular. Bitter and facetious by turns at its strongarm methods of insuring its perpetuation in office, he is also scornful of employers who "plainly tell all their labourers and tradesmen, if they do not vote as they order them, they shall not be employed by them another day." More playfully, Robert Slender speaks of "liberty and all such nonsense," preferring safety to the loss of his life—or his limb. He still hopes for an alliance with Mother England, and is fearful of France, which "will make a perfect Bedlam of all America." Liberty is taken too seriously by the people, for "we have too much *freedom*, our chief magistrate has too *little* power." It is much better "not on any account [to] have anything to do with State affairs, but mind your own proper business and get money as fast as possible." A representative government, he concludes, "is the *highest note in the gamut of nonsense*."[40]

Robert Slender, who calls himself "one of the swinish multitude," inasmuch as he is not of the well-placed and high-born, can make no

[39] The "Robert Slender Letters," written by "O.S.M." (One of the Swinish Multitude), which appeared in *The Aurora* from March 29 to May 20, 1799, were published in Freneau, *Letters on Various Interesting and Important Subjects*.

[40] I have pieced together various excerpts from the Letters #4 to #14.

sense out of the Alien and Sedition Laws—and what he does not understand is assuredly good. Who is he to question the motives of the powerful, or the means which they employ to achieve their ends? The means are bribery and imprisonment, spying, violence, the secret service, and diplomatic shenanigans, but "the end justifies the means." How one gets to a place is less important than where one is going. What was the goal of the good Federalists? Naturally it was to eliminate the wicked democrats, all of them "sinners and rebellious. Mark that—they speak against authority and revile Kings, which you know are God's ordinance." "The only friend of good government and good order [is] a federalist, *not* a democrat who claims that governments originate in the people and make rulers who are responsible to them for their conduct." In short, "Democrats are disorganizers and Jacobins." Their press is even worse. It would be best, according to Slender, to "bake a democratical printer in a *well-heated oven,* and for such a *length of time,* that for the future he should never give them a single moment's uneasiness."[41]

Freneau understood as well as any Federalist that the greatest danger to usurped power was a free press. If that were destroyed, the reign of terror would not have been in vain and the new elections would be safe for the authors of the infamous Alien and Sedition Laws. Above all, John Adams' ambitions for a second term would be gratified.

Robert Slender wrote his penetrating pieces of pseudo-logic and contrived reason to titillate the reason and logic of literate voters. Perhaps Adams could be defeated by laughter and ridicule. Others used different methods. All were determined that the time was ripe for a thorough housecleaning in American politics. The event was in the hands of God—and the people.

[41] Also from Letters #16 to #18. See Philip M. Marsh, "From Ezekiah Salem to Robert Slender" in *Modern Language Notes,* LXI, 7 (November 1946), 447–451, for a resemblance between Peter Zenger and Philip Freneau.

30. THE TURNING OF THE TIDE

IRONY IS A WEAPON which becomes blunted with use, and satire, which amuses while it causes one to think, may end only in amusing. There is a time when cap and bells must be cast aside so that it may be more than a stimulant to laughter. Humor was a solvent but not a savior. The serious business of government needed more than the benign banter of a Robert Slender, while laughing at usurpers of the law neither changed the law itself nor injured those who enforced it. If America was to be saved from evil laws and lawmakers alike, there was a better way, neither satirical nor violent, the way so plainly set forth in the Constitution of the United States. The nullification resolutions of Virginia and Kentucky could not be taken seriously—for if they were, then the Constitution would come to mean nothing at all. If the Federalists used methods of suppression which the democrats decried as illegal, then of what moral—or legal —value was the highly irregular and escapist solution, also illegal, threatened by the democrats themselves? If the Congress arrogated to itself the power to act in a manner clearly unconstitutional, no state— without a civil war—could claim the equally unconstitutional right to nullify the acts of its elected representatives. Unless, indeed, the Constitution itself was nullified and America once more broken into the old fragments of a Confederation. Tyranny was bad. Was anarchy better? No patriot could believe, no American could want, a solution as catastrophic as that.[1]

Thomas Jefferson and James Madison, despite their brave resolu-

---

[1] G. M. Stephenon, *American History to 1865*, p. 190; R. A. Billington, B. L. Lowenberg, and S. H. Brockunier, *The United States: American Democracy in World Perspective*, p. 88.

tions, did not want or believe it either. Philip Freneau, casting off his cap and bells, refused to consider even the possibility of secession suggested by John Taylor of Caroline. There was a better way than this to remedy the great malaise of the country. Said Freneau: "the invaluable right of election is still ours. Let us but use this right well—let us be diligent to canvas the character of these men that are candidates," and "who are known to have advocated the British Treaty, Alien and Sedition Bills, stamp act, standing army etc." "It is a duty which every man owes to God, his country and himself, to inform himself of the character of every candidate," and "if he be the poor man's friend, and ever ready to curb the rich," then "let us support him, for such a man is undoubtedly a treasure."[2]

The way to change the laws was to change the lawmakers. The time was drawing near when America could and indeed must make that change, which men must make solely on the basis of the country's welfare without self-seeking or self-interest. An honest man could do no less. A patriot could do no more. "Shew me a man" Freneau added, "who would vote against his judgment lest he should hurt his interest, and I'll shew you a traitor, who, were it in his power, would sell his country—only make it for his interest." Freneau was partisan, but only to the country itself. Without violence, without secession, without nullification, the liberty of America could be saved in the coming elections by its literate and intelligent voters. Robert Slender did not altogether cease his satirical probings of Federalist sores. Like his more serious work, the satires were effective to point up the perversions of power in the Adams Administration, while steadily hammering at the weakness of John Adams himself in the four years of his office. Like Simple Simon and other puppets whose strings Freneau had manipulated, Robert Slender enlightened as well as amused the readers of his letters, clearly posing the problems of the day while suggesting their solutions. The problems remained—their solutions were almost ready at hand.[3]

To his own problems Freneau had less glib answers. Improvident and impractical as ever, he watched the money he had realized on the sale of his property to Hunn fast melting away. The Slender articles for *Aurora* could have brought him little cash, and the "sandy patrimony," also melting away, yielded scarcely more. The farm did furnish

[2] "Robert Slender Letters," #20, in Freneau, *Letters on Various Interesting and Important Subjects.*

[3] *Ibid.,* #21.

the family's food, but the chores to produce it were not for him. More important than any chore was the persistent need for an income, any income that was dependable, as his articles and his farm surely were not. Philip's thoughts turned once more to his brother Peter; Peter—perhaps Peter's friends—might find a vessel for him to sail again. On May 26, 1799, he booked passage on the schooner *Rambler,* bound for Georgetown, South Carolina, on his way to Charleston. Except for Peter he had no one to turn to.[4]

In the hot and sluggish city of Charleston, Philip was content to loaf a while until a vessel should be found for him. But Peter could not loaf. He was always busy, always industrious, especially now that he owned *The City Gazette and Daily Advertiser,* which was full of democratic reasons for throwing out Federalist officials. Peter was also one of the printers of the Acts of Congress, and he often turned a profitable deal as real estate and merchandise broker as well. No one questioned his business ability or his democratic beliefs, nor his friendship with some eminent Federalists who respected his integrity though they disagreed with his politics. Unlike Philip, Peter never wrote about them in anything but calm, impersonal language that was controversial without being offensive. Men like Charles Cotesworth Pinckney and Governor Edward Rutledge, leading Federalists in Charleston, were never angered by Peter's opposition. Besides, it seemed harmless enough. They were so powerful and Peter so weak. With all his industry and friends, his multiple irons in various fires, he was never very far from the verge of bankruptcy. Like his brother at least in this, Peter managed to hold off complete collapse while he pursued his democratic course in conservative Charleston, busy, industrious, sometimes rewarded for his industry, with few enemies anywhere, even in the camp of the enemy. He was a businessman whose business seldom clashed with that of others.[5]

Philip, after the manner of poets, had clashed with everybody; in a time of crisis it was the business of poetry to do so. America was a succession of crises, and the poets had described them, given them meaning, revealed their comic and tragic aspects, their moments of ugly despair no less than their moments of hope and beauty. The

[4] Freneau's copy of Robertson, *Elements of Navigation,* in Freneau Collection (Rutgers).

[5] W. L. King, *The Newspaper Press in Charleston, South Carolina,* pp. 38–39. See also Lewis Leary, "Philip Freneau in Charleston," *South Carolina Historical and Genealogical Magazine,* XLII, 3 (July 1941), 89–98.

writers pictured their times and the thoughts that inspired them; they encompassed the trials and the errors, the virtues and vices, of a common humanity struggling blindly and often quixotically, heroic and vicious by turn and sometimes both at once, recording the story of man not only for the moment but for all moments in the long travail of history. For history was the record of the crises in human affairs, and writers alone could make that record, in story or song or symbol known to them but understood also by others as proof that man persists beyond all his crises and can still surmount them. If a poet can bring no other balm than this, he may at least offer the one weak certainty that man himself endures, not always the victim of an inscrutable fate, not forever the pawn of universal chaos. Confused with passion and beset by doubt, life persisted and hope remained, never tranquil and never fulfilled.

Philip Freneau was himself possessed of all these doubts and passions. Priding himself on being a poet, he did not always recollect his feelings in tranquillity. Capable of lofty lines and purity of thought, he lived in times which were often inimical to sustained effort on a high plane. Freedom and democracy were their own justification without the studied embellishments of art. There was no need always to paint the lily.

The times were no more propitious now for poesy than they had ever been. America was slowly acquiring an indigenous culture, one that had no surface or hidden roots which sucked their nourishment from an alien soil. Freneau never had ceased to demand a new orientation in literature, completely American and entirely native to its soil and climate. At the turn of the century there were stirrings of such a culture, but the days of its flowering were still in the future. In literature, with few exceptions, the spade was in the earth of America, but the seed was barely planted. Writers were too busy with more practical affairs to probe more deeply or soar too high. The personal, political, and immediate problems of recurring crises were too pressing in a time when literature was a luxury and liberty a necessity.

In the preface to the published Slender letters Freneau rededicated himself to the necessity rather than the luxury—to the "Freemen, the lovers of Liberty, the Asserters, Maintainers and Supporters of Independence throughout the United States." To these and to these alone he gave "Not my works only, but my life also, and all that I have, and God knows that's not much." No mere dissenter, he was also an "Asserter," and though he often asserted what was questionable, or in questionable taste, he rarely deviated from the path he had chosen as a youth and stubbornly plodded to the end of his days. Beyond a momentary hurt, it bothered him little that he was abused and hounded by those who hated and feared his power with the pen. Timothy Dwight, safe from censure in his fortress of culture and respectability, might call him an incendiary, but a pen that flared like a torch shed a light as well as a spark. Dwight was right. Philip Freneau *was* an incendiary—as Patrick Henry and Sam Adams and Thomas Paine, as Thomas Jefferson and James Madison, were incendiaries. Some of these, like so many others who once had fanned the flames of revolution, were now more reasonable, but he was not reasonable. If he had shown less zeal as a radical, some of his friends believed, he might have been more successful as a writer. Once it was his ambition to achieve fame as a great poet, but time had ravelled his hopes, and the laurels of the Muse, together with more substantial rewards of worldly success, had not seduced him. Content to be the conscience of those whom Hamilton had called the "people of no importance," he remained, as he signed himself in the published volume of the Slender papers, "just one of the Swinish Multitude," the plain, humble, average, common men of America, whose patrimony was freedom and whose timeless struggle was to maintain it. To excite their imagination, to stimulate their thought, to fire their energies, to awaken them from their torpor, was the task he had chosen and relentlessly pursued, often stooping to accomplish it, rarely rising above the means which he used to further its aims. The means were not always happy ones, but neither was the enemy overscrupulous in the methods it employed in the bitter and endless battle.[6]

The balance in the struggle for supremacy, which way it dipped and how it rose, would soon be decided by the people themselves. That decision, untiringly pressed by Freneau and the leaders of the democrats, was given further impetus by the Federalists as the day of decision drew closer. Not only the Alien and Sedition Acts—their own acts, in secret conclave and in party councils, would hasten the hour of their disaster and an end to their power.

John Adams, as he was frequently reminded, was President by the slim margin of only three votes. Alexander Hamilton, though he was no President, nor indeed any official at all, was still the colossus of the

[6] Freneau's Introduction to *Letters on Various Interesting and Important Subjects*; and H. H. Clark, "What Made Freneau the Father of American Poetry?" *Studies in Philology*, XXVI, 1 (January 1929), 1–22.

Federalist Party. Between him and Adams a feud of growing intensity, nourished by motives that were personal as well as political, was not abated but increased by the stringencies of the Alien and Sedition Acts, while the government's vacilations throughout the negotiations with France served still further to alienate Hamilton from the man whom he considered little more than an ambitious weakling. Hamilton believed in war as the great arbiter between the two countries, but if war should come, who was to lead the armies of America? For Adams, the only possible choice for leadership on the field was the old man of Mount Vernon. For Hamilton, such a choice was a measure of clear desperation. Washington was too tired, too exhausted, too ill, for such exacting and strenuous duty. Only one man in all America was worthy, by experience and aptitude, to replace him, only one person could adequately assume the mantle of George Washington—Hamilton himself. Who else had fought by the old man's side during the entire Revolution; who but he had counseled him in critical moments when few others were as deep in his confidence? Hamilton's had been the prevailing word for the great show of force which had brought the Whisky Rebellion to a swift and successful conclusion. He would do no less in any contest between France and America.[7]

Hamilton was not alone in his high opinion of his own capacities. Within the Cabinet, among the President's closest advisers, there were not a few who agreed with him. For them, Hamilton was the power behind the throne, the invisible power of the throne itself, and Adams a weak shadow they would willingly have erased altogether. Where the President had expected loyalty, he had been undermined with indifference and betrayal; seeking friends, he had found only enemies. As the time to choose his successor drew near, it was evident that those whom he trusted in the inner councils of the party were placing their confidence in Hamilton, not in him. Far from considering him an ornament of Federalism, the leaders looked on him as an encumbrance rather than a help for the future success of the Federalist Party. Hamilton had never considered John Adams an ornament,

[7] Arthur Styron, *The Last of the Cocked Hats: James Monroe and the Virginia Dynasty,* pp. 217 ff. Clinton Rossiter, *Alexander Hamilton and the Constitution,* p. 23, quoted J. Q. Adams to the effect that Hamilton had a "natural temper aspiring to military renown." See also John Adams to M. O. Warren, September 20, 1807, in Page Smith, *John Adams,* Vol. 2, p. 1068. Adams was well aware that Hamilton was opposed to him.

though he often shone in the reflected glory of his predecessor. Now, even that luster was tarnished—and the glory was gone.[8]

The old man of Mount Vernon, first and finest gem in the whole crown of Federalism, was lost forever, snatched away by a perverse fate in a time of its greatest need, from those who tried to illumine their own shadows by the bright refulgence of the man who was no more. Washington was dead, and all things conspired to hasten the end of those who had used his name and his fame for ends of their own. At last—at last—the tide might turn, despite the efforts of the Porcupine to blame the death of the revered leader on the democrats—on Dr. Rush in particular, for the futile methods of bleeding and purging used to save him. Such measures had killed Washington just as surely as they had killed so many others during the great plague. The Porcupine's last and greatest effort to help the Federalists would prove as fruitless as the propaganda to retain their power. The Federalists would need better arguments than this to persuade the people of the villainy of the democrats. And the democrats would not delay to inform America of the villainies of the Federalist Party, of its Hamiltons as well as its Adamses, since the first day they were ever entrusted with power.

Jefferson, as Vice-President, was in a paradoxical position. As the leader of the opposition, he had the duty to lead it in the campaign against the Federalists; as a high government official, as the man next in rank to the President himself, he could not openly attack the government and his closest colleague. The dignity of his office precluded such demeaning conduct. Whatever he did, he must work behind the scenes, safe from prying eyes or critical comment. He must corral the forces of democracy in America, provide them with the ideological ammunition for the great (perhaps the final) conflict between the Federalist and Anti-Federalist parties, and lay plans for the most effective use of the democratic dogmas.

Jefferson had set forth his ideas in a letter to the Massachusetts democrat, Elbridge Gerry, one of the three envoys to Talleyrand, whose report on the lessening tension between France and America was not publicized by the Federalists for political reasons. He also wrote to Edmund Pendleton, the Virginia leader, urging him, in spite

[8] Alexander Hamilton, *Works,* Vol. 8, pp. 309–364; also Page Smith, in *John Adams,* who clearly indicates that the enmity between Adams and Hamilton was close to a climax.

of his advanced years, to enter the fight against Adams. Pendleton, a powerful political figure, was an old hand at party maneuvers. At the same time, he appealed to Aaron Burr, the New York sachem of the Tammany Society, to set up the necessary political fences in the key city. Finally, he sent word to James Monroe, his protégé and agent in the field, admonishing him not to "let my name be connected in the business." Thorough and methodical in all things, Jefferson kept a close watch on the changing tide of public opinion. He computed the Republican vote in all the states, and found, as he informed Monroe, that "the whole issue was still in doubt." To reduce the element of doubt, he made use of the often irresponsible firebrand Callender to stir up Republican sentiment in Virginia, himself providing the pamphlets and propaganda on the huge increase in the national budget for the war that never happened.[9]

The war scare had fizzled; there would be no war. John Adams, anxious to avoid one if it were at all possible to do so, had succeeded in averting the conflict. His negotiators, working diligently in Paris for many months, at last won a Treaty of Peace from Napoleon on September 30, 1800, in which all quarrels between the two countries were amicably resolved and settled. The bitterness which these quarrels had engendered still remained. As the national election of 1800 drew closer, it increased, and the Republicans saw to it that the martial measures of the Federalists to embroil the country and imprison the peace-makers were not easily forgotten. One man, no democrat at all, indeed, a foremost enemy of democracy, contributed perhaps the greatest measure of help to defeat the Federalists in the unique and fabulous campaign of 1800.

Alexander Hamilton had not forgotten his feud with John Adams. Though Washington had died; though no one but Hamilton—he himself believed it—was able to replace the lost leader as commander-in-chief of the army, the President had turned a deaf ear to his ambitions. Hamilton would see to it that the President's ambitions were equally thwarted. If he could prevent it John Adams would never again be President of the United States. To prevent it Hamilton was moving

    [9] Thomas Jefferson, *Writings* (ed. A. A. Lipscomb and A. E. Bergh): Jefferson to Gerry, January 26, 1799, Vol. 10, pp. 77–78; Jefferson to Pendleton, January 29, 1799, Vol. 10, p. 87; Jefferson to Burr, February 11, 1799, Vol. 10, p. 87; Jefferson to Monroe, January 12, 1800, Vol. 10, p. 136; and G. Chinard, *Thomas Jefferson: The Apostle of Americanism*, pp. 354, 360.

his political friends about like pawns in a monstrous chess game, to
checkmate the man who had already been chosen by his party as its
candidate for a second term. Hamilton had no greater love for Jefferson, his old and relentless enemy, who was the choice of the democratic-republicans. He would work no less diligently for the defeat of
Jefferson than for that of Adams. In the most critical political struggle
ever waged in the new world, Hamilton, the foe of all democrats and
the colossus of all Federalism, would finish as the unwilling friend of
one and the unwitting enemy of the other. The Federalist Party, like
Carthage, would be destroyed.[10]

In such a struggle, Philip Freneau would give what he had always
given and contribute what he had never failed to contribute. Relegated
by circumstances more pecuniary than political to the side lines, he was
not, therefore, reduced to silence. If the enemy had ever doubted that
he could be calm as well as incendiary, impartial as well as controversial, generous as well as just, he now gave them the final proof. It was
not really proof of anything, perhaps, but the sorrow of one man at
the loss of another whom he considered to be great and honest, above
all a Man. Freneau, still waiting for a ship in Charleston, had just
heard of Washington's death. His poems on the passing of the patriot
who had called him a "rascal" were sincere tributes to a leader in the
fight for freedom, the first one of all in the terrible trials of the American Revolution. The poet had not stinted his praise of him before—
now he wrote:

> Ah, gone! and none your place supply,
>   Nor will your equal soon appear;
> But that great name can only die
>   When memory dwells no longer here,
>   When man and all his systems must
>   Dissolve, like you, and turn to dust.

As a last farewell he wrote:

> O Washington! thy honored dust
> To parent nature we entrust;
> Convinced that your exalted mind
> Still lives, but soars beyond mankind,

---

[10] Chinard, *Thomas Jefferson,* p. 362. In the end, it was clear, Hamilton's
"only client" was "the whole country" (Broadus Mitchell, *Alexander Hamilton,* Vol. I, p. xii).

> Still acts in virtue's sacred cause,
> Nor asks from man his vain applause.[11]

And when the Federalists attempted to use the fame of Washington as a cloak for their own political purposes, Freneau, outraged by the sacrilege, responded with his old venom and bitterness:

> He was no god, ye flattering knaves,
> He own'd no world, he ruled no waves,
> But—and exalt it, if you can,
> He was the upright, Honest Man.[12]

It was the caliber of a man, any man, which the poet reviled or revered, whether of his party or another. When Governor Edward Rutledge of South Carolina, also a Federalist, died on January 23, 1800, Freneau, who knew him well and admired him greatly, penned a eulogy for a signer of the Declaration of Independence who was, despite his conservative views, a fine patriot and an honorable gentleman. To the first injunction of calm reason—Know Thyself!—a man of quality must add a second, equally important: Rule Thyself! With these two guides, no man was ever wholly lost.[13]

There were not too many of that kind in the world, as Freneau knew from his own experiences. Many patriots were not honorable—and many who were too sensitive about their honor were not gentlemen. Their own interests were first among all others. Power, position, money, were the stars by which they were guided, and their hearts, their minds, moved only as those stars moved. No one could forget it, least of all one so frequently beset by financial troubles. Freneau still had them. He had returned to New York from Charleston empty-handed, without funds and without work, to be met by creditors who demanded, then threatened, finally carried out the threat, to sue him. Only the loan of a hundred dollars from Seth Paine, Peter's partner, sent posthaste to Monmouth, saved him from a debtor's jail. The threat appeared again from other quarters. He was "under a pressure of difficulties, chiefly arising from an ill-grounded confidence I had in designing or malicious individuals . . . in a land inhabited by sharpers

---

[11] Freneau, *The Poems of Philip Freneau* (ed. F. L. Pattee), Vol. 3, p. 233; Leary, "Philip Freneau in Charleston." These poems appeared in *The City Gazette,* January 10, and January 15, 1799.

[12] Freneau, *Poems* (Pattee), Vol. 2, p. 235.

[13] Lewis Leary, *That Rascal Freneau,* p. 314.

and ruffians."[14] They were not scarce in the autumn of 1800, as the political campaign grew warmer, as the day of days drew nearer, and Philip Freneau, never ceasing to work for a democratic victory, looked on, like Banquo's ghost, at the image of his own defeat. Whatever the outcome of the campaign, he himself was in greatest jeopardy unless he could "get charge of a vessel in some southern trade where there may be a chance of making something." Waiting, always hoping for that bright chance, he wrote his pieces for *Aurora,* letters that lashed at patriots who were not gentlemen, at the godly who threw religion into the arena of politics, at the speculators, the ballet-box stuffers, at the goblins of doom and the preachers of hate who foresaw chaos and secession if the Federalists lost. They even prophesied civil war if the democrats won. If they won![15]

A Republican victory? In the face of all the slanders leveled against Jefferson, which Jefferson refused to dignify by any answer, was it possible? Here was the Reverend Cotton Mather Smith openly accusing him of "having robbed a widow and fatherless children of an estate of which he was executor." Jefferson, it was also charged, was an atheist (all Deists were atheists) and the friend of atheists, of men like Volney and Priestley. For the first time—but not the last—the question of a man's religion became a major issue in American politics. The clergy were active as never before in a field foreign to their faith; they were moving heaven—and earth—to defeat the Republicans. Dr. Abercrombie of Philadelphia was warning Congress against the election of an atheist, while *The Hartford Courant* of July 25, 1800, quoted Dr. J. B. Smith of Virginia as the source of an attack on Jefferson, with implications which even his worst enemies would hesitate to use. Passing by a dilapidated church Jefferson was reported to have observed that "It was good enough for Him who was born in a manger." The Reverend David Osgood believed that the people, the common people, ought not to meddle in politics at all. If any minister of the gospel thought otherwise, Reverend Osgood was of the opinion that he should be deprived of the right to say so in any pulpit. Because he did not agree, Reverend Ebenezer Bradford of Massachusetts *was* deprived of his pulpit. Intolerance flourished like a weed. A spark of gossip kindled a blaze of slander.[16]

[14] Freneau to Paine, August 12, 1800, Mss.

[15] *The Aurora,* September 10, October 9, 1800, also October 2, and November 18, 1800.

[16] Chinard, *Thomas Jefferson,* pp. 363–365, 474–475; see also *The Aurora,*

As the battle for power spread to all the corners of the country, the democrats—Jefferson himself—were not idle either. In the state of New York the contending forces were especially active, since New York, doubtful and wavering, was a pivotal state. The struggle for control of its legislature was a bitter one. On the legislature depended the political complexion of presidential electors in a race that might be close, too close, for any decisive choice. Hamilton, pre-eminent among Federalist leaders in New York, was acutely aware of the danger of a possible stalemate in the electoral college. And he was obsessed by still another problem. Feverishly active against the Republicans, he was no less hostile to John Adams and worked behind the scenes for the election of Thomas Pinckney, Adams' running mate on the national ticket. In the camp of the Federalists the confusion of the campaign was confounded by these machinations of its colossus, whose personal antipathies could only serve to strengthen the opposition. By dividing the Federalists the strange antics of Alexander Hamilton would inevitably hand the victory to the democrats.[17]

The laws for the election of a President and Vice-President were confusing; electors chosen not by the people but by the legislatures of the states made the decision on the winning candidates. Two men were placed on each ballot, the candidate receiving the highest vote on either ticket becoming the President—the one below him being relegated to the innocuous office of Vice-President of the United States. In the last national election Hamilton had hoped that Adams would be defeated for the first office. Surprisingly, he had won by the substantial margin of three votes, while Jefferson—not Thomas Pinckney, who ran with Adams on the Federalist ticket—was elected Vice-President. This time, Hamilton was resolved, that would not happen again. New York, more doubtful than ever, was the one state that could clinch the defeat of John Adams.[18]

August 5, September 10, October 9, 1800; C. G. Bowers, *Jefferson and Hamilton,* pp. 473 ff.

[17] In the four years of his tenure, John Adams said, Hamilton had been "commander-in-chief of the House of Representatives, of the Senate, of the heads of departments, of General Washington, and last, and least, if you will, of the President of the U.S." (John Adams, *Works,* Vol. 9, p. 435; Vol. 10, pp. 127, 155, 162. See Rossiter, *Alexander Hamilton,* pp. 30 ff; *The Federalist* (ed. H. C. Lodge), p. 278; and William Maclay, *Journal,* pp. 202, 203, 282–283, 376; and Mitchell, *Alexander Hamilton,* Vol. 2, pp. 435, 469, 511–512, 525–526.

[18] N. Schachner, *Alexander Hamilton,* pp. 392–394.

There was, however, one hurdle that might be insurmountable. It appeared in the person of Aaron Burr, who was not only the foremost democrat in New York but the second man on the Republican ticket with Thomas Jefferson. Burr wanted, more than anything else in the world, to be the first—the first in the final vote for President. An ambitious politician, tirelessly at work welding a personal following among the enemies of Hamilton as well as the democrats of New York, he was less attractive than the Federalist leader though equally as ruthless. No novice in the business of politics, he was using the enormous strength of the Society of Saint Tammany for his own ends while playing off one faction of the Federalists against the other. Not all of them saw eye to eye with Hamilton in his questionable maneuvers to sacrifice the party's choice for President, and Aaron Burr, never squeamish about the weapons he used against an enemy, reaped the full value of electoral confusion and took full advantage of any weakness in factional or individual maneuvers. He saw many of them—not only in the Federalist Party, but in Alexander Hamilton himself. Without fear, perhaps without reproach, he lunged at every vulnerable spot in the armor of each of them. Only figuratively did he draw blood, though later he would draw that too. To Hamilton he was now as "unprincipled and dangerous a man as any country can boast—as true a Cataline as ever met in midnight conclave."[19]

And John Adams? Adams was not much better. He was—so Hamilton said—guilty of "disgusting egotism, distempered jealousy, and ungovernable indiscretion." Adams might have thrown the same words back at Hamilton, if he had known about them; but he knew nothing of this malodorous description of himself by the leader of the Federalists.[20]

The New York elections of April and May in 1800 resulted in the first resounding defeat for Hamilton. Aaron Burr had managed supremely well. The electoral vote of New York was assured to the Republicans. But what of the other states? New England held fast for the Federalists; the South and West were divided. When the electors met in each state on December 4, 1800, and the toll was taken on December 13, it became apparent that the split in the Federalist camp

[19] *Ibid.*, p. 399. Burr, a moderate, was an aristocrat by temperament, socially acceptable in places that counted in New York. He was ambivalent in his political affections (*ibid.*, pp. 396–397); see Bowers, *Jefferson and Hamilton,* p. 147; and Aaron Burr, *Memoirs,* Vol. 1, pp. 331 ff.

[20] Schachner, *Alexander Hamilton,* pp. 396 ff.

had cost them an electoral victory. Whoever won, John Adams had already lost. But who had won? Jefferson and Burr were tied in the electoral vote. Who was President, who was Vice-President?[21]

The question was one for the Federalists in the House of Representatives to decide. From them must come the votes to break the deadlock. No one doubted, among the Federalists any more than among the Republicans, that Jefferson was the choice of the democrats for first place in spite of the efforts of the New York leader to prevent that choice. The party and the people were for him—whatever the electors may have done to stymie or frustrate their wishes. But the Federalists in the House, like the electors, also preferred Aaron Burr to Thomas Jefferson. He was safer than Jefferson, and less, far less, radical than his wing of wild-eyed democrats. As the ballots were slowly counted, one after the other—twelve on the first day alone—it appeared that the House of Representatives, which voted by states, and had the task of breaking the deadlock, would never agree on a candidate. Each side refused to budge while deals were made and consultations continued for five days more. If a compromise was achieved, it was increasingly likely that the man nobody really wanted, Aaron Burr, would be the victor, not Thomas Jefferson. Hamilton, carefully watching, busily directing the drama hidden from the public view, was alert to its possible denouement. Having won his fight against Adams he was faced with a defeat by Burr. Whatever else happened now, this was something he had scarcely foreseen and must at all events forestall. Jefferson, even Jefferson, was preferable to the detestable Cataline, the "unprincipled and dangerous man" who wanted to be President.[22]

And Hamilton, the greatest foe of Jefferson, pleaded for the defeat of Burr. "For heaven's sake," he begged his friends, "let not the federal party be responsible for the election of this man." To Oliver Wolcott, the Secretary of the Treasury, he wrote: "There is no doubt but that, upon every virtuous and prudent calculation, Jefferson is to be preferred. He is by far not so dangerous a man, and he has pretensions to character. As to Burr, there is nothing in his favor."[23]

Some Federalists were still voting for Burr, while others had already switched; no state majority was sure for either candidate. Still working feverishly to swing a majority for Jefferson, Hamilton moved

[21] Chinard, *Thomas Jefferson*, p. 368.
[22] Schachner, *Alexander Hamilton*, pp. 397–399.
[23] *Ibid.*, p. 401; see also Stephenson, *American History to 1865*, p. 193.

closer to the Jefferson camp, moved further from his earlier goals. Now, only a few votes stood between stalemate and defeat—then defeat was turned into victory when Delaware withdrew its support from Burr and gave it to Jefferson. Jefferson was the new President of the United States. Hamilton could not keep Burr from second place—but that was of no importance whatever. James A. Bayard, the Delaware member, said that Jefferson had promised to leave undisturbed some of the financial and military laws already on the books in return for his support. Perhaps the efforts of Hamilton, generous to a foe whom he greatly respected, had won the day. In the conflict of motives and the cross currents of personalities, one fact emerged with luminous clarity—the tide had turned at last; the people had captured their government, democracy had won its greatest victory. War had been averted and peace assured. The Bill of Rights was secure. Now men could turn their energies to life, liberty, and the pursuit of happiness.[24]

Deeply wounded by his defeat, Adams was haunted by the question "what shall I do with myself?" Was he to work his land and "exchange honest virtue and honor for manure?" Were there no longer any "Americans in America?" In time his many wounds would heal; the bitterness would blanch with age. Even Jefferson "eaten to a honeycomb by ambition, yet weak, confused, uninformed, and ignorant" would one day be restored to his old place of respect and affection in the heart of John Adams. Abigail had never lost her "friendship for that gentleman." They might even regret the tragic death of that "Creole bastard" Hamilton.[25]

Philip Freneau they did not forgive to the day they died.

[24] Bayard had the deciding vote in the election of Jefferson. Hamilton to Bayard, January 16, 1801, in Hamilton, *Works,* Vol. 10, p. 415; Schachner, *Alexander Hamilton,* p. 402. On the other hand, see Jefferson to Monroe, February 15, 1801, in Jefferson, *Writings* (Lipscomb and Bergh), Vol. 10, p. 201, in which Jefferson refuses to take the Presidency "with my hands tied."

[25] The despondency of Adams went far deeper than he would publicly admit. Adams to C. Tufts, December 26, 1800, in Page Smith, *John Adams,* Vol. 2, pp. 1055, 1071; Adams to Stoddert, March 10, 1801, in John Adams, *Works,* Vol. 9, pp. 582–583; Adams to Uriah Forrest, June 20, 1797, and Abigail to John Adams, November 18, 1796, in Page Smith, *John Adams,* Vol. 2, pp. 833, 1043, 1053.

31. POETS ARE PAUPERS

A NEW ERA would now replace the old one of turbulence and reaction. The prophecies of men like Fisher Ames would be proven false; America was not "too big for union, too sordid for patriotism, too democratic for liberty." George Cabot would also be proven wrong in saying that "democracy [is] the government of the worst." The people were no beasts, as Hamilton had once declared, nor democrats vermin, as Fenno had once proclaimed. Strong again after a wasting illness of counterrevolution, America would survive in fact as it had already survived in theory. Political parties might now formulate their conflicting philosophies of government while clashing interests could chart the future course of the country, a course now set with triumphant democrats in the lead toward the spiritual and material enhancement of the many rather than the few, the good of all rather than the profit of some. It was a task to which the more than five million souls in America must be dedicated in this year of 1800, as men like Jefferson and Madison—and Philip Freneau —had dedicated themselves.[1]

John Adams, with the ever-faithful Abigail at his side, was soon on his way to the new and dismal capital at Federal City—less a city than a hamlet—on the muddy banks of the Potomac. The new seat of government, moved from Philadelphia after its ten-year tenure, presented a depressing change from the opulent comfort and refinement of the Quaker City; and it was doubly so for the man who had been defeated by his friends as well as his foes. His cup of bitterness was full enough without the democratic slurs on his personal as well as

[1] Henry Adams, *History of the United States during the First Administration of Jefferson* (ed. H. Agar), Vol. I, p. 44.

political defeat, nor could he escape the jibes of the Republican press
—of papers like *The Aurora,* which rubbed the salt of despair deep
into his wounded pride. "What," it jeered, "no parade to salute him?"
There was indeed no parade to greet him, no guns to salute him, as he
rode the weary miles away from lost ambitions.[2]

John Adams had done what he could for the Republic he had
helped to establish. No one could point a finger of accusation against
his honor or integrity, and if he had made mistakes they were those
which he had made honestly and in good faith. Who could have done
more than he? Whose courage and candor had been greater than his
from the very beginning? In the days of the Boston Massacre, in an
atmosphere of seething hostility, he had defended an Englishman, an
enemy of his own people, because the law must be maintained equal
for friend and enemy alike. He was bitter now, and he had reason to
be bitter, but the hurt would vanish, the wound would heal. In 1804,
when Jefferson was again the candidate of the Republican Party, John
Adams, a Republican elector of Massachusetts this time, would cast his
vote for the great leader of democracy.[3]

As he retired from the field to finish his term of office, many were
convinced that in John Adams there was no feeling at all for democracy. It was true that in the moment of his defeat, before the reins
of power could be taken from his hands, he had made some appointments, especially to the judiciary, for which he was reviled. Against
the manifest wishes of the people who had just voted them out of
office, he had appointed Federalists to lifetime jobs. In love, in war, in
politics, there were no standards of ethics. To the vanquished belonged
the spoils.

The sniping by the enemy was vicious—but what about his friends?
Adams knew that many within his party had worked against him,
though he did not know the full extent of betrayal by members of his
own Cabinet. One thing he was certain of: his downfall was the result
of attacks on him by the democratic press—by the writings of Philip
Freneau above all the others.

In a letter to Benjamin Stoddert of March 31, 1801, he put the
name of the Monmouth poet first on his list of those who had encompassed his defeat. Abigail had already informed her son John Quincy

---

[2] *The Aurora,* June 7, 1800. See also note 25, Ch. 30.

[3] *The Adams-Jefferson Letters* (ed. Lester J. Cappon); these clearly prove
the high respect, even the affection, that each had for the other to the very end.

Adams that though Jefferson was a "man of strict honor and rare integrity," his conduct was not above reproach. "The most reprehensible part of his conduct," she added, "was countenancing that Frenner [Freneau] when he was continually libelling the government." The Freneaus, the foreigners of America, had ruined the country. From the depths of his humiliation, Adams querulously complained to Stoddert: "We have no Americans in America." The old stock was corrupted by alien blood, a belief held by others besides Joseph Dennie, the most clever of all the Federalist writers, who mourned that under a monarchy things might have been different. "What," he wanted to know, "can men of liberality and letters expect?" The rabble-rousers had won, and America, America had lost. There were no more Americans in America. The labors for liberty were wasted, license not liberty was the watchword of the new era.[4]

The work of Philip Freneau seemed finished. The election had climaxed the career of Jefferson, while for him it appeared also in the nature of an anticlimax. The future might hold great promise of things to come for others; for him it held little more hope than the past—or the present. The prospect for making a living was as remote as ever. He had no money, and his "sandy patrimony" was slowly but inexorably being washed away by powerful currents of necessity. He wrote his occasional pieces for *Aurora,* dug an occasional spade into the recalcitrant soil of Mount Pleasant, and contemplated, with more concern than pleasure, the near advent of another—still another—baby.[5]

Peter, who had been active in the political struggle in the state of South Carolina, was more confident of the future though his present condition was far from prosperous. He was more concerned about his brother's affairs, of which he was kept fully informed. From a letter

[4] Adams to Stoddert, March 31, 1801, in John Adams, *Works,* Vol. 8, p. 514; Abigail to J. Q. Adams, February 1797, in J. Whitney, *Abigail Adams,* p. 265; Adams later said, "The causes of my retirement are to be found in the writings of Freneau" (Adams to Jones, March 11, 1809, in John Adams, *Works,* Vol. 8, p. 414); and he wrote to Jefferson, "Shall I remind you of Philip Freneau?" (Adams to Jefferson, June 30, 1813, in *Adams-Jefferson Letters* [Cappon], Vol. 2, p. 346). Also see *The Aurora,* July 30, 1799; W. G. Bleyer, *Main Currents in the History of American Journalism,* p. 126; and M. Curti, *The Growth of American Thought,* pp. 193–194.

[5] Agnes Kearney to Peter Johnson, Quit Claim Deed, November 17, 1801, Monmouth County Historical Association, Mss.; and Freneau to Paine, August 12, 1800, Ms.

which Philip had written him on March 1, he learned of "new cares and vexations coming on" to afflict the poet of Monmouth. For the moment all Peter could do was send his brother the sum of five hundred dollars with which to put his farm, and his home, in some sort of order. He had spent so much time on politics that his multiple business ventures were in a somewhat precarious condition. If he wasn't careful he could fall into bankruptcy himself.[6]

The outlook for Philip was no better. Not only must he provide for his own family, but for his mother as well. Agnes Kearney was staying in New York with her married daughter Margaret, but her support was his obligation, not his sister's. In addition, his elder daughter, Helena, was away at school in New York, and little Agnes, almost of school age now, must soon be sent there too. Debts—always there were debts—must be paid, creditors must be placated, and lawsuits avoided. They could only lead to a debtor's prison. The stoop of the poet was more pronounced than ever before. He seemed shorter, slighter, than he really was. The dark, melancholy eyes were sunken deeper in their sockets. His hair, still thick about the high forehead, was iron-gray. For lack of something more modern, he wore the same small-clothes and the old cocked hat, old in time and fashion, which he never changed whatever the changes that transpired about him. Nearly fifty, he was as far from any goal as he was at five. A brave new world appeared close at hand, but not for him.[7]

Was it close for anyone? Would the political change bring also a social, an economic change, a future in which the everlasting search for security would be lifted from the backs of men? The system was wrong in more ways than one. In one way, in one spot of the world, it was freer than anywhere else—but in America too, as everywhere on the habitable globe, men were the victims of injustice, inequity, and exploitation. Philip Freneau, a philosopher of the forest, not of an emerging industrial economy, was groping toward an understanding of problems like these. As yet he could only understand the results—not the causes—of his, and all men's, burdens.

[6] Philip Freneau to Peter Freneau, March 1, 1801, in Freneau Collection (Rutgers). Peter was active as manager of Jefferson's campaign in South Carolina.

[7] John W. Francis, quoted in E. A. and G. L. Duyckinck, *Cyclopoedia of American Literature*, Vol. 1, p. 333; Philip to Peter Freneau, March 1, 1801, in Freneau Collection (Rutgers). The child, Margaret, was born June 10, 1801 (Freneau Family Bible).

> How can we call that system just,
> Which makes the few the high, the first,
> The lords of all that's good;
> While millions, robb'd of all that's dear,
> In silence drop the ceaseless tear,
> And leeches suck their blood.[8]

It was not good poetry—it was not even altogether true. In a time of increasing industrialization, when the agrarian economy of America was perceptibly changing to one of laissez-faire capitalism, it seemed true enough. The Revolution, which had promised only political freedom, had held out the hope of social and economic amelioration. The victory of the democrats, which assured political freedom, had brought that hope closer to the heart of America. Would it become a reality as well?

The Muse, like everything else, had failed the poet of Monmouth. He was not only a poor poet; he was, indeed, almost a pauper. His was the cry of one simple, suffering soul to all who labored without incentive, created without reward, and lived—as they died—without joy in the present or hope in the future. It had always been so; and it might always continue to be, unless America showed the way to ampler justice in the days ahead. The real problem of the time lay in the answer to the question: "What was the way?" Philip Freneau believed it was to be found in the ever-expanding practice of democracy. His question about the "System" implied the answer, yet the answer itself implied many other questions.

Thomas Jefferson, the President of the United States, in his inaugural address, attempted to apply his keen mind and generous sentiments to these questions. He could not be sure of the answers either, any more than other men. Perhaps it was the task of all men to supply them, the vanquished as well as the victors, or if not able to supply them, then to make the effort without fear or favor to help in their solution. "If there be any among us," Jefferson said, "who wish to dissolve this union, or change its republican form, let them stand undisturbed, as monuments of the safety with which error of opinion may be tolerated where reason is left free to combat it." There was no high road to justice in a democratic country. There was only the rough and muddy

---

[8] "On False Systems of Government and the Generally Debased Condition of Mankind," Freneau, *Poems Written and Published during the American Revolutionary War,,* Vol. I, pp. 253–256; also, "Reflections on the General Conditions of Mankind," in *ibid.*

road of idealism, along which men of good will and honest purpose must plod and stumble to the goal of the common good. For such a journey democracy was necessary, it was imperative, so all could walk the path to glory—or Golgotha. Jefferson pledged himself and his Administration to "A wise and frugal government which shall restrain men from injuring one another, which shall leave them otherwise free to regulate their own pursuits of industry and improvement, and shall not take from the mouth of labor the bread it has earned. This is the sum of good government, and this is necessary to close the circle of our felicities."[9]

As Jefferson spoke these words of hope and wisdom in Washington, the man who had contributed to the occasion of his speech was absorbed in the more restricted circle of his own felicities. Without enthusiasm or application, he was cultivating his farm at Mount Pleasant, "doomed to end my life among the enlightened, disinterested, and philosophical folks of Monmouth."[10] Jefferson, his Secretary of State Madison—these old friends had great and momentous problems to consider, but for him there was only the simple yet infinitely complicated problem of making a living from the sandy soil of his patrimony. There were some slaves to help him, those he had inherited with the land itself—he never bought, never sold one, himself. They must do most of the work; for the routine of the farm, its heavy duties and monotonous labors, was beyond his strength or inclination. It was pleasant enough to feed the cackling chickens, to care for "all dumb animals," but to kill one of them for dinner was something he refused to do. He still paled at the sight of blood.

Nor did he relish the routine of public office. He was not invited to take any post in the national government, but it was suggested that he could become a candidate for the New Jersey State Legislature. His experiences as postal clerk and as translator in the State Department had been far from satisfying or remunerative. To become a lawmaker "was better than being sent to jail for editing newspapers," but he refused "to meddle with the public or their business."[11] The amorphous people had not been kind to him before. When, at long last, he was offered a place in the Administration of President Jefferson, he refused that too. He had suffered too much from the slanders of the Federal-

[9] Thomas Jefferson, First Inaugural, March 4, 1801, *Writings* (ed. P. L. Ford), Vol. 8, pp. 1–6.

[10] Freneau to Seth Paine, June 26, 1801, Ms.

[11] Hammell Notes, Mss.

ists when he had received only a pittance of 250 dollars a year from the national treasury. He would not expose himself again. Besides, he had never, not once, received any personal acknowledgment from Jefferson for the work he had done to help hoist him to the highest office in the land. When he was informed that the President had asked to see him, he replied: "Tell Jefferson that he knows where Philip Freneau lives, and if he has important business with him, let him come to Philip Freneau's house and transact it." Jefferson had done that before, in the old days when he badly needed him as an editor in Philadelphia.[12] The entire episode, unsubstantiated by any records, is apocryphal and legendary. It may also be true. True or not, fact or fable, Jefferson had other matters far more pressing than the problem of Freneau. Not he, but others, would worry about the penniless poet.[13]

Eleanor was one of them. Her husband, inept at farming, seemed equally so at anything else that might earn him a living. She was not only worried, she was also annoyed with the man who was writing, always writing, though not always for publication. She complained to her brother that "Mr. F and the children [the children too] are always scribbling and never fail to spoil both pen and ink." It was a bad enough example to set the children; for their father it seemed downright malingering. Eleanor had once loved to scribble a bit herself, but that was a long, long time ago. If she took a pen in hand now, it was not to write a poetic epistle to a suitor, but to air her concern for a husband.[14]

Others were also concerned. Aedenus Burke, who had once written to Madison about the financial plight of their mutual friend, wrote him again now. "I am sorry to have to say," he informed the new Secretary of State, "that Freneau is still in embarrased circumstances. He is an honest man, and an undeviating Republican, yet utterly incapable of soliciting for himself."[15] What reply Madison made to Burke is not known; neither is it known what response he made to the letters of Pierce Butler, a maverick Federalist of South Carolina who as Senator had opposed the treaty of John Jay. On June 3, 1801, Butler wrote to Madison about "any little place in the Post Office" for the poet who was "in indigent circumstances." Again, on July 3, he pressed for an answer: "Pray has anything been done for poor Freneau? I feel solicitous to see him out of the reach of want. I am pursuaded you have not

---

[12] M. S. Austin, *Philip Freneau*, p. 173.
[13] Hammell Notes, Mss.
[14] Eleanor to S. Forman, February 28, 1803, in Samuel Forman Papers, Mss.
[15] Burke to Madison, June 5, 1801, in James Madison Papers, XXII–89, Mss.

less friendly feeling towards him."[16] Nothing, apparently, occurred either to expose the friendly feelings of Madison or to lighten the financial burdens of his old classmate. It is only known that the poet-farmer continued to "spoil both pen and ink" with nothing to show for his pains but an occasional piece in *The New York Weekly Museum* or a translation of Ovid, while he waited, still waited, for something to turn up more nourishing than these. If nothing turned up soon, he wrote Peter, he would quit Monmouth and "embark on some new expedition or plan before long." Increasingly desperate, he would go "wherever or to whatever the devil shall see fit to drive me."[17]

The devil was not one but many conflicts, in his home and in himself. The frustrated pride of a man as breadwinner; the wanderlust of his forebears, needing only the purge of circumstance to seek a solution in places far removed from the scene of his troubles; the annoyance of Eleanor, who had no confidence in his work on the farm and little more in his ceaseless scratches on paper—all were conjoined in his feelings of futility and his resolve to escape all conflicts by running off to something that had the promise, at least the illusion of a promise, of an ampler life and a better living. "While I live I must be active," he wrote to Seth Paine. "A sedentary dull life has a strange effect on me. I must be in motion to be happy."[18]

Motion is not conducive to creation, nor action to thought. Freneau had often taken refuge in motion, and often mistaken action for thought; his essentially introspective nature was inadequate to meet the multiple demands upon it. The contemplative, quiescent mood was rarely a ruling factor in his life, for other moods crowded the scholar, the teacher, the poet, the thinker, the observer, and the critic with their insistence and compulsions. Easily inflammable, he caught fire quickly, and was almost consumed while quenching the flames. Among the ashes were the ruins of some of the dreams he once had known at Princeton, not modest, unassuming dreams, which had to do with such gossamer stuff as poetry and liberty and the future of a new and lovely country inhabited by builders who loved peace as well as justice.

Yet the dreams persisted. In good times or in bad they had sustained the navigator, the farmer, the revolutionist—and the poet. Adept in the vulgar art of cheap invective and raw doggerel, he could turn as easily to finer forms of versification, though now he seldom

[16] Butler to Madison, July 3, 1801, in *ibid.*, XXII-5.
[17] Philip to Peter Freneau, March 1, 1801, in Freneau Collection (Rutgers).
[18] Freneau to Paine, August 12, 1800, Ms.

soared on the wings of poesy. The old hopes of achieving the highest flights of lyrical expression were often dispossessed by urgent and recurring needs, needs of the moment, of many moments, which all but exhausted the creative spirit. The "dull and sedentary" processes of thought yielded to more immediate and mundane pressure. When he wrote his verse or prose in a more durable medium he rarely won the plaudits or understanding of more than a few, and among those few little else besides the flattering but futile tribute of a borrowed line for which, however, they forgot to give him any credit. His books had sold in modest numbers; he had been copied by many papers; he had been included in a few anthologies—all without the least profit to himself. Always driven by the devil of necessity, when he ignored the devil he was accused, and not alone by his wife, of spoiling the pen and the ink which were the body and the blood of his deepest affections. In Monmouth, among his own "disinterested and enlightened folks" his best work found few readers and little response. "There is no taste for anything good or philosophical in this place" he bitterly complained. "The vilest trash has here a currency above all the eloquence of Plato." Freneau was not Plato, nor could he always rise above the penalties in neglect and poverty exacted from his sensitive and passionate soul.[19]

A man like any other, he possesed the ambivalent features common to all men. Courage and cowardice, pride and prejudice, the frailty of a flower and the strength of steel—by turn mean and noble, God and man. Leonardo da Vinci, seeking a model for Jesus in his painting of The Last Supper, chose the same peasant as a model for Judas. A man has many causes, meets many challenges in a lifetime, and Freneau had accepted the challenge of poetry before all the rest. The causes for which he had fought were seemingly won; poetry, for which he lacked the strength to fight, was seemingly lost. It had long since ceased to be the only way of life. It was just one of the ways of living.

He must search once more for another way. And now, as so many times in the past, Peter obtained for him the means to pursue it. The *John*, a schooner in which Peter had just acquired an interest, offered the poet another chance to escape from the stringencies of both poverty and poetry to the high seas which he loved so well. On November 13, 1802, Philip assumed command as its master. Two weeks later, with a full cargo of salt, he turned the helm of the *John* southward to Fred-

[19] *Ibid.*

ericksburg. On rough seas and in busy ports there was all the motion he craved after the doldrums of Monmouth, though little more money than before. Another cargo, this time of wheat, scarcely paid the expenses of a voyage; while a shipload of stone and earthenware and "red streak New Jersey cyder, apples in barrels, and butter in firkins" was sold at a net loss. The loss was large enough to induce Peter to sell the vessel almost immediately.[20]

It was not the end, however of Peter's efforts for Philip, nor of Philip's quest for action. Soon after the sale of the schooner, Peter acquired the *Washington*, a brig fitted out for the run to Madeira, one of the lovely islands of Philip's old dreams, in the wine trade.[21] During the four months of the voyage, the waitover and the return, the cares of family, fortune, and future were completely lifted from his shoulders in one of the pleasantest interludes of his entire life. A later voyage was not so pleasant. Caught in a "hurricane of wind all the way," the brig provided more motion than even he could relish. Tossed about by surging waters harnessed to mighty winds, the vessel lurched with a fine fury that defied the puny powers of the Captain to assuage it. When it was over, Freneau was aware as never before of the conflict between human hope and man's fate.

> How feeble are the strongest hands,
> How weak all human efforts prove!
> He who obeys, and who commands
> Must wait a mandate from above.[22]

Man was helpless in the struggle with life. He might soften its harshness, brighten its bleakness, outwit for a while its venom. By reason, with humility, a man could circumvent many assaults on his weak nature and forever-exposed nakedness. But only for a while. In the end, he must succumb. In the end, there was only annihilation, extinction, the ineluctable submersion beneath the waters of oblivion. The theme was not a new one for Freneau. As he grew older, he tried to elude it, or forget it in the embrace of motion, of action. It is in the nature of man to avoid oblivion, and nature's huge jest to thwart him. The skeptic no less than the romantic accepts the illusion of even a brief permanence

[20] Freneau's copy of Robertson, *Elements of Navigation,* in Freneau Collection (Rutgers).

[21] *Ibid.*

[22] Freneau, "A Midnight Storm in the Gulph Stream," in *The True American,* September 21, 1822.

when life appears to be something more than "the frail duration of a flower." The illusion is also perishable, sustained by the memory of some fleeting loveliness, some vanished fragrance but a moment beyond its own demise.

During his stay in Madeira Freneau contemplated the virtual destruction of Funchal by floods from tropical rains, in which many hundreds of people were drowned and whole sections of the city were swept into the sea. He was reminded of the tale of "Noah's deluge come again," a tale that was old and tragic as the history of man, of man's fate in a world he never made but seeks, ever hopefully, to make over. Freneau had also tried, sometimes with bricks, sometimes with brickbats. He had used both, for both were needed in the world he lived in, the world he loved most when he cried out most against it. The tenacity of man, his spiritual greatness and moral grandeur, the power of reason to temper the fury of passion, these were still promises of the future as they had been the salvation of the past despite the selfishness, the greed and cruelty, the lust for power that baited the traps and lured the strong as well as the weak, the gentle as well as the ruthless, and snared the best together with the worst of men. In the poems which he wrote in 1804 during his voyages on the *Washington,* Freneau set forth in simple terms the shifting moods of man's experience, his protective colorations of love and hate, ever hopeful that love would prevail over hate—and life over death.[23]

In "On the Peak of Teneriffe" he reviews the volcanic action that buried the smiling hillsides in an eruption of hot ashes, yet rejoices that in the womb of time all is healed, all is born again.

> These, barren once, neglected, dead,
> Are now with groves and pastures spread.

The countryside will bloom again, and other men will live again, until time prepares its next tragic stroke. The principle of life will outwit the destructive genius of Nature, while Nature itself forever thumbs its nose at all the living.[24]

When his mood was unequal to a calm appraisal, Freneau could outwit the ravages of time or the boredom of inaction with the means that men have often used to win a moment of respite. His Gallic

---

[23] "Stanzas Written at the Island of Madeira," in Freneau, *A Collection of Poems on American Affairs,* Vol. I, pp. 171–176.

[24] "On the Peak of Teneriffe," in *ibid.,* Vol. I, pp. 261–262, and in Freneau, *The Poems of Philip Freneau* (ed. F. L. Pattee), Vol. 3, p. 261.

heritage, his years at sea, the ancestral business of wine-handling, had made the juice of the grape as obvious as it was a pleasant elixir to quicken the pulse and lift the spirits. It induced a sense of well-being not otherwise easily achieved. More than once Freneau had written of the virtues of drink, and often he had practiced those virtues himself. Few could picture as he did the bounty of Bacchus unless he had known and enjoyed it at first hand. In Madeira, which he called the "favorite isle" of the god, it was known and enjoyed better than anywhere else.[25]

This was the last time Freneau would visit the abode of Bacchus. Indeed, the voyage home was the last he was to make as master of the *Washington.* Not he but Captain Edward Slocum would sail the brig to Malaga and other ports for Peter. For Philip, the sea as a career had all but finished. There would be a few more commissions, which he would fill for others but not for Peter. Perhaps it was Bacchus who made the final decision for both of them. It is not known why Freneau relinquished his command—or whether it was taken from him. Peter did employ his brother as his agent in the purchase of some lands in Kentucky, but never again as master of his ship. Peter, though he never failed his brother, may have found him failing in return.[26]

With this last means for making a livelihood gone like all the rest, the poet, with little left to hope for, returned home. Nothing awaited him there either, only Eleanor and the children, which was a good deal for one who so often had wandered away in search of security that forever escaped him. When a man has passed the half century of his life, he may still yearn for the open road—or the open sea—yet rest content with the small security of a roof and a hearth, the little comforts of a home that is anchored to what is left of a sandy patrimony.

If Philip Freneau decided there was no future for him, he did not for that reason cease to hope for it. On the title page of his well-worn copy of Robertson's *Navigation,* the constant companion of all his voyages, he wrote the words that men in all times, in all conditions, have used to conjure good from evil. *"Il faut bien l'espérer, car sans cette consolation il n'y aurait qu'à mourir."* The one treasure that remained in Pandora's box was also his, and hope was one of the few illusions that still survived in a world of crass realities. Some of his

[25] "A Bachanalian Dialogue," in Freneau, *A Collection,* I, 169–170, and *Poems* (Pattee), Vol. 3, p. 257.

[26] Lewis Leary, *That Rascal Freneau,* p. 323; Philip M. Marsh, "Philip Freneau: Our Sailor Poet," *American Neptune,* VI (April 1946), 115–120.

friends were safe in high places; some were secure in niches carved by stronger hands than his. He had no place, no niche. For him, there was nothing but a vagrant hope that one day—one day—he might still find a shelter, however modest, but good enough for one whose youth was far behind, and one for whom the future, shrouded in fear and uncertainty, loomed darkly with approaching old age.[27]

It loomed for others, too, forbidding, not with old age, but with old hatreds. The festering enmity between Alexander Hamilton and Aaron Burr had burst the bounds of polite endurance. Almost at the moment of Freneau's return to New Jersey, Hamilton lay mortally wounded on its soil, felled by a bullet from Aaron Burr's pistol. On July 12, 1804, the day after he was shot, Hamilton was dead, the victim of a duel which he felt would be fatal, yet was honor bound to fight with a man he despised more than any other. Burr had never forgiven Hamilton for his part in the election of Jefferson, and Hamilton's letters to Rutledge and others, denouncing Burr and disparaging his character, had brought a challenge which the giant of the Federalists could not refuse. A great man does not run from a little one. Now the great man was dead, destroyed in a single moment by the Vice-President of the United States.[28]

This was a deed no one, neither enemy nor friend, could condone. The quick death of Hamilton was the slow death of Burr. His political career was at an end, to be finished off finally by his secret scheming with General James Wilkinson, once a patriot and now a mercenary and self-seeking character who betrayed their secret. Aaron Burr had made his last bid for power to replace the power he had lost with a bullet. He would be acquitted of treason but not of opportunism, of ambition, of strange and vulgar maneuvers against his country. His reputation was ruined, his fortune was lost, and nothing remained of the old Revolutionary hero, the brilliant politican, the powerful leader of the democratic forces of New York.[29] Only his daughter was left to

[27] Freneau's copy of Robertson, *Elements of Navigation;* and M. S. Austin, *Philip Freneau,* p. 191.

[28] Hamilton to Bayard, January 16, 1801, in Alexander Hamilton, *Works,* Vol. 10, p. 415, in which Hamilton expressed his opinion that Burr's "peculiar notions will easily give way to his interest." Also Clinton Rossiter, *Alexander Hamilton and the Constitution,* p. 115; Rossiter thinks Burr was both a scoundrel and a sharpshooter. Gallatin was enormously relieved at the defeat of Burr, Gallatin to his wife, February 17, 1801, in Albert Gallatin Papers, Mss.

[29] A full report of his trial in Congress is contained in United States Congress, *Annals of Congress,* 9 Cong., 2 Sess., pp. 1008–1019, and 10 Cong., 1

him, his beloved Theodosia, the one person on whom he had lavished the greatest resources of his heart and mind. Soon she too would be taken from him. When he sought refuge in France from the anger and contempt of his own people, Theodosia stayed behind. When at long last he tried to see her again, the tragic fates which still pursued him demanded one final retribution. Theodosia, hurrying to meet her father at a neutral rendezvous, never reached it. Her ship foundered in a raging sea. She and the ship were lost forever. And few were left to mourn her besides the stricken man who had waited in vain. Fewer still were left to sorrow for the man himself. Only Philip Freneau, Aaron Burr's old schoolmate at Princeton, remembered the disconsolate soul whom fortune had dealt the unkindest cut of all—the loss of a talented and deeply loved daughter. The one remaining star in his crumbling firmament had been blotted out in a whelming surge of tragedy. He gave his old comrade what small crumb of comfort was possible—and this was the due of any man, of all men who lived and suffered and must one day die.

> Oh, shed no more tears of sad regret;
> The hymns of joy, the lofty verse prepare—
> Her briny doom, the ingulphing wave forget,
> For Theodosia is the Morning Star.[30]

Freneau did not voice any opinions on the feud between Hamilton and Burr. There was no place or purpose to express them. He was outside the field of politics, nor was he needed any longer to play a part in them. If it seemed to him a strange reversal of policy for Jefferson to join with England—even with England—against France in an effort to annex the vast territory of Louisiana, he did not say so. The purchase of the fabulous domain from Napoleon was a better expedient but that was not an act of constitutional rectitude either. Jefferson, as the responsible head of government, was apparently learning that the old democratic slogans against Hamilton and the Federalists were not always apt for the pressing problems of government. The greater use of executive power was not bad in itself, but only bad if it

---

Sess., pp. 385–778. Also see Henry Adams, *History of the United States* (Agar), Vol. 2, p. 395.

[30] Freneau, *Poems* (Pattee), Vol. 3, p. 312; Theodosia was lost on the steamer *Patriot*, out of Georgetown on the Carolina Coast. S. H. Wandell and Meade Minnigerode, "Theodosia Burr," *Saturday Evening Post*, September 6, 1924.

was unleavened by republican ideals. A President must wield whatever power was necessary for the good of the country, eschewing a too rigid control by the legislative branch and without too dogmatic an adherence to the Constitution.[31] A leader must lead, if also follow, the people. It would not be long before Jefferson, forgetting that the dead colossus of the Federalists had expressed some strikingly similar views, himself maintained: "A strict observance of the written laws is doubtless *one* of the high duties of good citizen, but it is not the highest. The laws of necessity, of self-preservation, of saving our country when in danger, are the higher obligation."[32] A strict constructionist like Jefferson was not unaware of the anomaly inherent in the new democratic logic, but it was as easy for him as it had been for others to invoke the general welfare clause for whatever must be done in the interests of the American people. Their interests, Jefferson was convinced, demanded the extension of America's borders to the limits of the continent on the south, perhaps even on the north, and the cleansing of the land all alien powers within those borders. He had visions of enlargement that would "cover the whole Northern, if not the Southern continent," he wrote Monroe. Louisiana was only the beginning—the Floridas might come next. One way or another, Spain must be compelled to disgorge. "If we push them strongly with one hand, holding out a price in the other, we shall certainly obtain the Floridas, and all in good time," the President had confidentially informed John Breckinridge, his Attorney General. Breckinridge, of great help in the purchase of Louisiana, had been equally keen to consummate another for Florida.[33] The voice of secession, muted at

---

[31] Long before, on February 23, 1791, Hamilton had said: "The powers contained in a Constitution of government ought to be construed liberally in advancement of the common good" (in "Opinion on the Const. of the Bank of the U.S." in Alexander Hamilton, *Papers,* Vol. 8, pp. 63–134). See also Hamilton to Washington, in Hamilton, *Works,* Vol. 8, p. 135.

[32] Jefferson to Dupont de Nemours, February 1, 1807, in Thomas Jefferson, *Writings* (eds., A. A. Lipscomb and A. E. Bergh), Vol. 10, pp. 347–352. Jefferson further considers the question of construction in Jefferson to William H. Cabell, August 11, 1807, in *ibid.,* Vol. 11, p. 318. See also L. D. White, *The Jeffersonians,* pp. 6 ff, 34–35.

[33] Jefferson, once a "strict constructionist," and a foe of "implied powers," made the Louisiana Purchase, which was a constitutional flouting of the first, and a constitutional recognition of the second. Nor was this the first time—or the last—that Jefferson was compelled by circumstances to trim his political sails to the winds of reality, as in his cavalier treatment of civil liberties (see Leonard W. Levy, *Jefferson and Civil Liberties: The Darker Side, passim*).

the Hartford Convention, was heard again. The South, not altogether immune from the fever of dissent, recovered quickly, and all sporadic fevers were soon cooled. For the time being they subsided—until the body of America was assailed once more, with greater virulence than ever, in the days of irrepressible conflict for power. That conflict was still far in the future; the power that threatened a conflict now was quite different from that which the Federalists had lost and the Jeffersonians had won. It was no longer the Federalists who were the enemies, but others, the ancient foes of all democrats—the British.

England was conducting her war against France with increasing vigor, and in this war America, at peace with both, was again the victim of British outrage. American citizens were being seized by English raiders on the high seas for service in the British Navy. Impressment by Britain was perhaps justified in the case of her own nationals who had deserted for better pay and safer berths on American ships of commerce. But Americans were also taken; in any event the boarding of American vessels was an unconscionable practice, contrary to international law, and a contemptuous infringement by the rulers of the sea on the sovereignty of a free people.[34]

The battle of Trafalgar in 1805 had decided the question of mastery on the seas. England was the master, in no mood to be thwarted by neutral America, or by any seamen, its own or another's, who sought the shelter of American ships. Britain had the power to stop a traffic that swelled the profits of New England merchants while endangering its own struggle with a ruthless enemy. It would not be stayed by threats, nor stopped by declarations, even by declarations of war. While Federalists like Timothy Pickering and Harrison Gray Otis opposed any measures that might lead to war, Republicans like William Lowndes of South Carolina and Felix Grundy of Tennessee cried out for action, for any action, including war, to stop the impressment of American seamen. In 1807, it appeared that no other recourse but war was possible when the English cruiser *Leopard* closed in on the American frigate *Chesapeake* and forcibly removed four sailors, deserters from the British Navy. The President wanted to avoid a bloody contest. He knew, if some of his colleagues did not know, that America was too weak to withstand the might of the British Navy. It was better, perhaps, to place an embargo on shipping. It would delay, if

[34] R. A. Billington, B. L. Lowenberg, and S. H. Brockunier, *The United States: American Democracy in World Perspective,* pp. 114–116.

not altogether remove, the threat of conflict. Only the future would tell for how long. The Federalist John Adams had averted war— could the Republican Thomas Jefferson do less?[35]

The new alarms had reached the shores of New Jersey and echoed in the backwoods of Monmouth County. At Mount Pleasant, Philip Freneau, though he heard them, was preoccupied with alarms that touched him more closely. Composing his occasional verses, he was also contributing some new letters to *The Aurora* under the pseudonyms of Jonathan and Polly Bunker as well as Tomo Cheeki, letters that were concerned with political troubles of Pennsylvania in which William Duane, the editor of *The Aurora,* was interested.[36] None— state or national—were as obdurate as his own concerns. As usual, they had to do with money. As usual, too, they were solved, but for the moment, by the simple expedient of selling more and more land of his fast diminishing patrimony. He had just mortgaged one piece of land for three hundred dollars; he was about to sell another. Slowly, relentlessly, the soil and the sand of his estate was being washed away.[37]

He could do nothing to prevent it. Eleanor was desperately trying to work the farm herself, while he, as he wrote to Jefferson, could only indulge in "the old habits of scribbling verses."[38]

For the country, if not for him, greater follies were brewing.

---

[35] G. M. Stephenson, *American History to 1865,* pp. 212 ff; Billington, *et al., The United States,* p. 116; and Madison to Monroe, quoted in C. G. Bowers, *Jefferson in Power,* p. 430.

[36] *The Aurora,* August 30, September 29, and October 5, 1804; and Leary, *That Rascal Freneau,* p. 400 n.

[37] Monmouth County Deeds and Mortgages, Mss., E.27, E.509, H, 331, Y.317, Y.520, Y.583. See also Leary, *That Rascal Freneau,* pp. 364, 407 n.

[38] S. E. Forman, "The Political Activities of Philip Freneau," *Johns Hopkins University Studies,* Vol. 20, Nos. 9–10 (1902), pp. 88, 95; The letter to Jefferson was in reality a résumé of his travels; of his circumstances there is but a hint, and no plea for help. There is no evidence of any reply from Jefferson. Freneau's letter was sent in 1815. See also Freneau, *Poems of Freneau* (ed. H. H. Clark), p. xxiv.

32. MAN SHALL BE FREE

DARK CLOUDS, heavy with portent, scudded across the skies of American politics. The Non-Importation Act of 1806, followed by the Embargo Act of 1807, were futile attempts to dispel them. Jefferson was not unmoved by the British outrages, but he knew the paucity of American power to prevent them. He had written to William Short, former Minister to Holland, an old friend and political adviser, that "If we can delay but a few years the necessity of vindicating the laws of nature on the ocean, we shall be the more sure of doing it with effect. The day is within my time as well as yours, when we may say by what laws other nations shall treat us on the sea. And," he concluded, "we shall say it."[1]

The debates on the British impressments became warmer as their effect on American commerce grew worse. John Quincy Adams, whose voice was being heard as his father's lapsed into silence, considered the British outrages as "on a par with murder," though Senator Timothy Pickering, leader of the Essex Junto, declared that England "had done no essential injury" to American trade. The New England press and clergy echoed his views, and William Cullen Bryant, a child prodigy of thirteen, repeated in verse what all the others said in prose about the Embargo Act.

> Curse of our Nation, source of countless woes,
> From whose dark womb unreckoned misery flows.[2]

[1] F. F. Beirne, *The War of 1812*, p. 21. Also Jefferson to Short, October 3, 1801, in Thomas Jefferson, *Writings* (ed. A. A. Lipscomb and A. E. Bergh), Vol. 10, p. 288.

[2] Beirne, *The War of 1812*, pp. 21 ff, 42.

The effects of impressment and embargo were barely felt in Mount Pleasant. The even temper of the people was scarcely ruffled by alarms from the outside, and Philip Freneau, having quit "the bustle and distraction of active life," was undisturbed in his desultory chores on the farm or the continuous "scribbling" at his desk. Eleanor had found little to commend in his work, but the world of letters was more aware of his writing than he had ever thought possible. In a time of recurring British dangers, the greatest enemy of Britain was not forgotten. Nor his reputation as a poet either. For the first time since he had published anything at all, the critical attention which his work over many years merited was provided in a series of articles in the Philadelphia *Port-Folio*. A review, running to four articles in as many issues, appeared in October and November 1807, appraising his poetry as comparable to the best ever written about the sea, and his Indian pieces as superior interpretations of the red-man's character. Some of his work, the critic declared, might be compared with that of Cowper and Jonathan Swift, though his language and politics were too often outside the pale of poetic form or feeling. Yet, "of the *poetry* of this versatile bard we must say that, by the impartial, it will be at length considered and entitled to no ordinary place in a judicious estimate of American genius." From a Federalist like Joseph Dennie this was no mean praise.[3]

In addition, his stirring poem on the martyrs who had perished in British prison ships was published in *The New York Public Advertiser* on the occasion of their decent interment with appropriate honors after many years of neglect. This was followed by excerpts from "The British Prison Ship," an "elegant poem" based on the prose account of his own experiences as a prisoner.[4] His modest fame, rejuvenated by poems like these, was further enhanced by a new volume of his later work, written and perfected in the solitude of Mount Pleasant. Free from the press of politics or party interest, Freneau had varied his sporadic labors on the farm with the more exacting ones of "scribbling." While others recalled the contributions he had made to his country's freedom, he was writing a tribute to the one man he honored above most others. His "Lines Addressed to Mr. Jefferson" on his approaching retirement from office was a sincere and deeply moving poem on the "patriot and sage" who,

[3] *The Port-Folio,* October 31, 1807.
[4] The New York *Public Advertiser,* May 19, May 26, 1808.

> When to the helm of State your country call'd
> No danger aw'd you and no fear appall'd.

In the midst of all alarms and threats of war, despite all criticisms of his policies, the truth about Thomas Jefferson was as clear as the noonday sun. The past had proved it; the future would not disturb it. The greatest democrat of his or any time, was, according to Philip Freneau

> Safe in the realms of immortality.[5]

For himself he harbored no such hope as this. His little fame, made more manifest by the kind reception of his latest volume, was lighted from time to time by republications of old poems and press printings of new ones. They brought him scarcely any money, but neither did his infrequent voyages, strange interludes for an exhausted landlubber. The last one of all, in July 1809, on the Schooner *Polly* bound for Savannah, was the final fling for "Captain Freneau." His days of seamanship were over. He would never take a vessel to sea again.[6]

Fame, as he had discovered long ago, was a poor substitute for immediate necessities. He could not help himself, but there were others whom he might help because he had a little fame. When the widow of the son of Francis Bailey, his old friend and publisher, in desperate straits herself, appealed to him for help with a new edition of his work in two volumes, he agreed to edit, supervise, and finance its publication for her sole benefit. It was a considerable undertaking from which he would receive no single cent for himself. It was even doubtful whether Lydia Bailey would get anything from a project begun with Freneau's usual business optimism and entire lack of funds. These must come from subscriptions, and where would he obtain them for the widow when he had so often failed to get them for himself?

To ensure the success of this one venture at least, Freneau had tried to interest James Madison, the newly elected President of the United States. "Perhaps," he wrote Madison on April 8, 1809, "some of your particular friends in Virginia may be induced to subscribe their names." The quick response of the President was heartening. Not only did he subscribe for ten sets of the projected work, but sent the money in

---

[5] Freneau, *The poems of Philip Freneau* (ed. F. L. Pattee), Vol. 3, p. 294.
[6] Lewis Leary, "Philip Freneau and Monmouth County," *Monmouth County Historical Association Bulletin*, Vol. 1, No. 2 (July 1948), pp. 59–81; also Philip M. Marsh, "Philip Freneau: Our Sailor Poet," *American Neptune*, VI (April 1946), 37–59.

advance to pay for them. He also suggested that a number of Freneau's prose pieces be included, to which, however, the poet was averse, fearing "that anything I have written in that way is so inferior to the poetry that the contrast will be injurious to the credit of the publication."[7] Jefferson, to whom Freneau also wrote on May 27, 1809, wanted two sets, adding, "Under the shade of a tree one of your volumes will be a pleasant pocket companion." He replied less pleasantly to the Bailey widow when, in an access of pressure salesmanship, she sent him ten sets instead of two. The other eight he promptly returned to her with a curt note resenting her presumption.[8]

The two volumes of *Poems Written and Published during the American Revolutionary War* were indeed pleasant pocket companions. More than that, they were surprisingly more profitable to Mrs. Bailey than any volume had ever been to him. Of all the editions of the poet's work these were the most meticulously edited. Many of the poems were polished and rewritten; others were changed only in part; included with them were his old translations from the classical poets as well as new ones from Ovid's "Tristia" and the "De Rerum Natura" of Lucretius. Appropriate footnotes were supplied, and some of his more recent poems were added which showed the poet's old, yet ever-recurring preoccupation with the tragic sense of life, the transient condition of man, and his concern with the problems of man's fate in a hostile world. Dedicated "to his Countrymen, the real *Patriotic Americans, the Revolutionary Republicans,*" the books were quickly taken by those whose sentiments they echoed more clearly than any other. With pardonable pride, Freneau informed Madison that there was a "popular frenzy" for them.[9]

Frenzied, too, was the critical praise which they received from the Republican press. *The Pennsylvania Democrat* confidently asserted: "That Mr. Freneau ought to stand in the first rank of the Columbian poets no person qualified to judge will dispute." And it continued: "It may truly be said that he contributed more towards the success of

[7] Freneau to Madison, April 8, 1809, in James Madison Papers, Mss. XXX-VII–73. See also Freneau, *Poems* (Pattee), Vol. 1, p. lxxxiii; and Lewis Leary, *That Rascal Freneau,* p. 410.

[8] Freneau to Jefferson, May 27, 1809, in Thomas Jefferson Papers, Mss., Ser. 2, XXXIV, 13. See also M. S. Austin, *Philip Freneau,* pp. 197–198; and Leary, *That Rascal Freneau,* p. 410.

[9] Madison's copies of these volumes are to be found in James Madison Papers, Mss. See also Lydia Bailey, "Waste Book," Ms.

the Revolution by his pen than did a great majority of those who commanded in the field of battle." In short, the poet was "entitled to the respect and applause of every American as a man, as a poet, and as a patriot." In conclusion, "his works ought to be universally read by Americans, and every true born son of Columbia ought to feel proud that his country has given birth to Philip Freneau."[10]

The Federalists were less laudatory. They admitted that his work was "good for the time and circumstances under which it was written." It was even "tolerably good for American poetry." But it was too much to expect "that the pampered taste of our literary epicures should indulge in a coarse and unsavory, though perhaps a wholesome, morsel."[11] Both praise and criticism were equally deserved and equally true. Freneau had achieved some work that touched the topmost crest of beauty. He had also written a great deal that was "coarse and unsavory." Whatever its deficiency as poetry, it was frequently wholesome in its purpose and effect. Not always chaste, his poems were often virtuous.

In a day when moral values were confused by political exigencies and artistic integrity suborned by political necessity, cultural and aesthetic standards were rarely high and seldom maintained. Poets were less concerned with phonic quality, high imagery, or fine form, with rhyme, rhythm, and meter, than with the substance of the message they conveyed. Freneau, peculiarly susceptible to the pressures of his time, was the first, if not indeed the foremost interpreter of the tempo and the temper of revolutionary resurgence in America. For him it was synonymous with all the spiritual values of the people, values in which materialism had little if any place at all. When America became more conscious of its destiny as a moral and political power, it would also understand that the greatness of a country resides in the physical well-being of its people no less than in its professed ideals. By that time, other poets would sing her greatness, but they were as yet unborn, or scarcely out of their swaddling-clothes. Longfellow and Lowell, Poe and Holmes, Bryant and Whittier, Emerson and Whitman would examine and interpret their own times; they would praise or denounce what they discovered, to be praised or denounced in turn for their discoveries. Each in his own way would be, like Philip Freneau, a "useful Poet" if also, indeed, a greater one.

[10] Leary, *That Rascal Freneau*, p. 329.
[11] *Ibid.*

Of his own stature this man had little notion or concern. He had received so many harsh words for his writings, so few kind ones, and none had mattered much in the acute business of his life. His pride was brief and variable, for pride was but a momentary respite from pain, an evanescent comfort in a time of despair, a cooling hand for a fever that remained long after the heat had vanished. All pride fled the instant some creature need pursued it. There was an example, if it were needed, in the tragedy of Thomas Paine. Sunk in poverty, all but forgotten by the country he had served so well, Paine was dead in New York. Freneau's sorrow for the patriot who passed from the scene on June 8, 1809, was tinged with contempt for the democrats themselves who were oblivious to his needs when he lived, and forgetful of his labors when he died. It was Freneau who reminded his own people, the same people who fought the good fight Tom Paine had fought, of the great loss they had suffered.

> In vain the democratic host
>   His equal would attain;
> For years to come they will not boast
>   A second Thomas Paine.[12]

The democratic hosts were too busy with the living to honor the dead. There were too many problems that demanded their attention. The new President of the United States, the third Virginian to win the highest office, was anxiously scanning the horizon for signs of the impending storm from which Jefferson had happily escaped. Back home in his beloved Monticello, Jefferson was occupied with his thousands of acres and hundreds of slaves, his flour mill and workshops, his astonishing machines for spinning and weaving the wool from his flocks of sheep. "Never did a prisoner released from his chains feel such relief as I feel on shaking off the shackles of power," he wrote his friend Dupont de Nemours in Paris.[13] James Madison was now bound by the same shackles.

The Embargo Act had been replaced by the Non-Intercourse Law, which prohibited commerce with both France and England, while attempting to mollify the Northern interests by permitting trade with other countries. Followed by still other laws, each in turn accompanied

---

[12] "Stanzas on the Decease of Thomas Paine," in Freneau, *A Collection of Poems on American Affairs*, Vol. 2, pp. 28–29. Also C. F. Heartman, *Unpublished Freneauana*, pp. 13–14.

[13] F. W. Hirst, *Life and Letters of Thomas Jefferson*, pp. 446–447.

by mercantile maneuvers to circumvent them, they were all equally
flouted by both Britain and France. Caught in the vortex of commercial
and political manipulations, America was soon beset by new threats of
disaster. Storm clouds gathered and grew darker in the skies. It was
evident that the thundercap of war would strike at any moment.[14]

Madison, a better lawmaker than a peacemaker, strove valiantly
to avert a war which few of his countrymen wanted. Many of them
were opposed to the measures that had reduced American exports to a
fifth of their normal size. Increased in value from 19 million dollars in
1791 to 94 million in 1802, by 1807 they had reached the phenomenal
figure of over 108 million dollars. As the old world bled from its many
wounds American commerce and industry had supplied the rich trans-
fusions. Now the shipping interests of New York and New England
were themselves anaemic, while the agriculture of the South and West
faced ruin as the overseas' market was tightly closed against them.
Jefferson had tried to avoid encroachments which caused the imposition of such drastic measures, but British outrages had forced his
hands. Not only had the *Chesapeake* been fired on, but other attacks
also were common, and still the assaults on American vessels continued. Six thousand separate instances of impressment were recorded.
Neither Jefferson nor Madison could stem the flood of outrage and
hatred that swept the country in a great demand for reprisals. The
effort to clear the seas of American shipping, to avoid the ultimate
reprisal of war, was a palliative that hurt even more. Injustice was
bad; the loss of profits was worse. And many who lost them were
prepared to suffer one without the other.[15]

When Napoleon promised to respect American rights—a promise
he did not keep—and England continued to ignore them, the thunder
of martial music crackled and rumbled more ominously in America.
It flared with forked lightning, when it was learned that British agents
in Canada were stirring up the Indian tribes of the Northwest under
Tecumseh against isolated settlers who were powerless to defend
themselves. These outrages against Americans on land as well as on

[14] R. A. Billington, B. L. Lowenberg, and S. H. Brockunier, *The United
States: American Democracy in World Perspective*, p. 118.

[15] A. Nevins and H. S. Commager, *The Pocket History of the U.S.*, pp. 164–
165; G. Chinard, *Thomas Jefferson: The Apostle of Americanism*, pp. 459–
460, and Henry Adams, *History of the United States during the First Administration of Jefferson*, (ed. H. Agar), Vol. 1, p. 178; H. U. Faulkner, *American
Political and Social History*, p. 115.

the sea could be stopped only by a war. War might serve a twofold, perhaps a threefold purpose. Canada, vast and tempting, would be taken from the British, its broad acres opened up to new settlers who were moving west. At the same time, Britain's ally Spain would be heaved from the mainland and Florida, at the southern edge of America, at length released from alien control. England, of course, would be given a lesson she would never forget. American business and American pride would become as sacred as American power. The reasons for war seemed unanswerable.[16]

Yet they were answered. New England and New York, despite the damage to their commerce, were still opposed to any armed conflict. They had other ways of avoiding ruin. A war with a sea power like Britain would mean an irretrievable loss to their blooming industry and commerce. Besides, reason might yet prevail. Britain even seemed ready for reason, as her revocation of the Orders-in-Council indicated. Would the attacks on American shipping, the impressment of American seamen, indeed stop? The people doubted it; Congress refused to wait and see. The War Hawks in Congress, young, gallant, eager for spoils, and jealous for the honor of their country, demanded war. The thunderbolt fell. On June 17, 1812, it struck America by decree of the House of Representatives, 79 to 49, and of the Senate 19 to 13.[17]

President Madison, unable to avoid the storm and confused by alarms and cries from warmongers and peacemongers alike, nevertheless saw clearly enough that this was an adventure for which the country was ill-prepared. War was a gamble of the utmost danger, though Jefferson himself, on retiring from office, had assured him that war "may become a less losing business than unresisting depredations." For Madison, however, it was a business that was daily, hourly, becoming "more than ever puzzling." Powerful factions were for and against it. His own advisers were uncertain about it. The greatest fire-eaters were among the young, eloquent, even brilliant, War Hawks, new and aspiring leaders from the West and the South, men like Henry Clay and John C. Calhoun, who rallied the doubters and the timid behind them. Madison's own Secretary of State, James Monroe, prepared the resolution that was pushed through Congress. The deed was done. War was declared against Britain.[18]

[16] Billington, et al., The United States, p. 119; Arthur Styron, The Last of the Cocked Hats: James Monroe and the Virginia Dynasty, passim.

[17] G. M. Stephenson, American History to 1865, pp. 215–217.

[18] A. E. Smith, James Madison: The Builder, p. 302; American Historical

Less a leader than a follower, rarely sure of his own position in the welter of controversy that boiled within his own party, Madison had left to Congress the decision on war or peace—and now the decision was made for him. The mess of uncertainties which he inherited from Jefferson's Administration was now resolved in his own, and nothing remained but for him to pursue a war of which the only sure result was his own re-election for another term. Within a few months after the declaration of war, Madison won a second term by a safe margin of his countrymen's votes. They approved what he himself had scarcely wanted.

Watching these martial maneuvers of his old friends from the peaceful environs of Mount Pleasant, Philip Freneau was engaged in a war of quiet desperation all his own, the old one of money. Debts were piling up again. His aged mother, no longer living with the Hunns, was back with him in Monmouth. His daughters, the older ones, at any rate, wanted feminine refinements that would help them toward marriage. Among other things, they needed dowries which he could never give them. Where was the money to come from? His sandy patrimony would not last forever. Already he was negotiating for a loan—still another mortgage—on a tract of fifty-three acres. Some lands he had sold outright; others must soon be sold. Pecuniary pressures never ceased to bear down upon him with relentless insistence.[19]

For a little while he might escape them, not by running off to sea again, but by crossing the small stretch of water which separated New Jersey from New York. New York was close enough for frequent and pleasant journeys after seclusion in the Jersey backwoods. In the company of Agnes, his favorite daughter, the only one of his children who liked to scribble verses, he felt at perfect ease. With her, more than with Eleanor, he could converse on an intimate basis, about matters that concerned him the most—poetry, and the new war that distressed him so greatly. Eleanor was too much taken up with household chores and the farm to be more than a silent critic of her feckless husband. Moreover, she was getting hard of hearing, and what she heard from him was never too helpful in easing the burdens she must bear with almost no help at all from him. If it were not for her, the farm would have gone the way of most of the other lands. Eleanor was holding the

Review, XIII (1907–1908), 309–310; and Hirst, *Life and Letters of Jefferson,* p. 450.
[19] Monmouth County Deeds and Mortgages, Mss., E.341, X.251.

place together, even if the poet managed to get away from it whenever he could.[20]

He preferred a few hours of amiable talk with friends like DeWitt Clinton and Cadwallader Colden, fountains of information from whom he obtained the latest news of the war and the latest ideas of old friends who were in the seats of power. What he learned only added to his distress; the war was going badly, as badly as the first war with Britain had once gone. Who would help America now, as France had helped her then? The future was black indeed, his country's no less than his own.[21] His future seemed utterly hopeless when he received word of a loss more immediate than the possible loss of the war.

Peter, his ever-faithful brother Peter, was dead. The only solace, the one man to whom he could always turn in time of need, was gone. The generous and gracious gentleman who was respected by his political foes as much as by his friends, had died suddenly on November 9, 1813, at the age of fifty-six, leaving behind him a destitute widow, a host of creditors, and a sheriff who descended on "his house before the remains were carried out of it." Philip, bearing so many other burdens on his bent shoulders, carried this one too. He could offer nothing to the bereaved widow but to share her sorrow. In the privacy of the Family Bible he would pour out his own deep sense of loss, as once he had confided the loss of his father to other pages. One thing more he did, having little else but words to give—he wrote the simple sentiment for the tombstone of his beloved Peter, buried in the Huguenot Cemetery of Charleston. Words, always words—for the dead as for the living, for those who were already free as for those who must forever guard their freedom.[22]

In the war against Britain, Freneau had slowly come to an acceptance of the conflict. Listening to his friends as they denounced or supported the struggle that was inexcusable yet perhaps unavoidable, he wavered a while before his repugnance to bloodshed was subdued. As the climate of public opinion changed with the news of added outrage, and the temper of the people veered with the wind of victory or defeat,

[20] Austin, *Philip Freneau*, p. 227; E. Ellis, *History of Monmouth County*, p. 846.

[21] Philip M. Marsh, "Philip Freneau and His Circle," *The Pennsylvania Magazine of History and Biography* LXIII, 2 (January 1939), 37–59; and A. E. and G. L. Duyckinck, *Cyclopoedia of American Literature*, p. 347.

[22] Peter died November 9, 1813 (Freneau Family Bible); E. S. Thomas, *Reminiscences of the Last Sixty-Five Years*, p. 82.

Freneau became again the champion of democracy and the defender of liberty in the ancient battle between freedom and autocracy. In poem after poem he sought to incite his countrymen to greater hatred of Britain and to more determined efforts to defeat her.

> Must our freedom, our labors, our commerce, our all,
> Be tamely surrender'd, to tyrants convey'd;
> Must the flag of the country disgracefully fall,
> To be torn by the dogs of the slaughtering trade?

He asked the questions—and, as before, he answered them too.

> To reason with tyrants is surely absurd,
> To argue with them is to preach to the deaf;
> They argue alone by the length of the sword,
> Their honor the same as the word of a thief.[23]

The theme was ever the same. Freedom was threatened by the enemy who had threatened it before, and America must beat him down again or submit to a new tyranny as vicious as the old one. Liberty was one of the supreme goals of man. For Freneau it never ceased to be the only goal.

He wrote poems for the new war as he did for the old one, and revamped many of his old poems for use in this one. Nothing now seemed of more importance to him, for America, according to all reports received in Monmouth or New York, was being beaten in one sector after another. The campaign against Canada appeared doomed to ignoble failure. Detroit had fallen in August without a single shot fired in its defense, and the old Revolutionary hero, William Hull, had been powerless to prevent the fall against the combined forces of the British and their Indian allies under the wily Tecumseh. New York militiamen had refused to fight beyond their own state borders, and both New York and Massachusetts had failed to furnish men or supplies for the push against Canada. Sabotage and incompetence spelled the inglorious end of the whole Canadian campaign, while unpreparedness in men and matériel had hastened the débâcle. Officers were too old, too sunken "into either sloth, ignorance, or habits of intemperate drinking," to show the way to victory, while younger men were both "coarse and ignorant." Even the more educated among them were "swaggerers, dependents, decayed gentlemen," not fit to lead anyone to anything but disaster. They were no match for the British veterans of

[23] Freneau, *Poems* (Pattee), Vol. 3, p. 291.

the European wars who were recently released for combat in America after the defeat of Napoleon at Leipzig.[24]

When they appeared on the Chesapeake their advance toward Washington was hardly impeded by General William H. Winder at Bladensburg. The Americans retreated with such haste as to open the way wide to the capital itself. It was threatened—it was overrun. But not before the President had happily escaped to the Virginia woods as the torch was put to the White House in retaliation for the burning of the Parliament building in York (now Toronto) by the Americans. Little was saved from the flames besides the unfinished portrait of the first President by Gilbert Stuart. At the last moment, the efficient and doughty Dolly Madison had snatched it from its frame together with a few of her personal belongings which she also managed to save.[25] The poems of Philip Freneau, in the new edition of his works, were not saved. With much more of greater value, perhaps, they perished in the flames. Dolly may have heard the story about her husband's romantic interest in Freneau's sister. Despite a warm invitation, Madison had never brought his bride to Mount Pleasant. As for the poems—there were many of those, by Freneau and by others. There had been only one Washington. America could have used another.

The reverses on land were in great measure offset by some victories at sea. Freneau, in articles appearing in *The Aurora,* had urged a strong navy to cope with British sea power, and it was on the sea, after the disheartening defeats on land, that new hope and new courage were offered the American people. On Lake Champlain British ships were defeated by Commodore Lewis MacDonough. Captain Oliver Hazard Perry vanquished a British squadron on Lake Erie, compelling the evacuation of Detroit and ensuring the victory of William Henry Harrison in the battle of the Thames. At Baltimore, the attack on Fort McHenry, though it gave little profit to either side, produced the national anthem—which it inspired in young Francis Scott Key. American seamen and American ships were no match for the "Mistress of the Seas," yet in close and desperate encounters it was the Americans who usually won. The *Wasp* defeated the *Frolic*; the *United States* defeated the *Macedonian*; the *Constitution,* a strange apparition such as had

---

[24] Nevins and Commager, *The Pocket History,* pp. 166–167. See also Beirne, *The War of 1812,* Ch. 10.

[25] Beirne, *The War of 1812,* p. 285.

rarely been seen on any water, ironclad and pugnacious as a bull-dog, easily defeated the *Guerriere*.[26]

Freneau, busily turning out words to bolster the morale of American soldiers, was no less actively engaged in composing others to celebrate the victories at sea. Few other poets knew the sea as he knew it, or loved it as he did. As in the days of the Revolution, each victory, each defeat, called for a poem in which he rejoiced with his countrymen or sorrowed with them, as the fortunes of war rose or receded. Only occasionally did any of them touch the hem of beauty but they never failed to move the men who lived through each hard-fought and bloody encounter.

The war seemed no brighter in 1814 than in 1812 despite the victories at sea. The British were still pushing on; their strength was still a fearsome force. The fruits of victory, like those of defeat, were bitter ones for the American people whose land was not yet free of the invader and whose commerce was still tied up by his powerful navy. In October 1814 the British, apparently impregnable in New Orleans, seemed safe from dislodgment behind the massed Wellington veterans of General Edward Packenham. As long as they stayed there, the menace to America was both real and frightening. Unless they were routed and beaten neither the land nor the sea was safe. But only a miracle could accomplish such an event. A miracle had happened at Yorktown; perhaps another would occur at New Orleans. America was a land of miracles.

Andrew Jackson, an old hand at fighting against great odds, had already proven himself at Horseshoe Bend, where he had defeated the Creek Nation on March 27, 1814. His reprisals on Indians who had massacred defenseless Americans at Fort Mims in the Mississippi Territory required the ingenuity of a tactician and the courage of a leader whose qualities had infected his men with an abiding faith in victory. Qualities like these had won him a commission as major general in command of the District of New Orleans when a faith such as this was sorely needed to offset the military might of Britain so firmly entrenched in the town of New Orleans near the mouth of the Mississippi. The lean, lank Scotch-Irishman, once a lawyer and judge in Tennessee and now a canny fighter facing Packenham, waited with

[26] Billington, *et al., The United States,* pp. 121–122; *The Aurora,* December 22, December 25, 1812. Also Freneau, *Poems* (Pattee), Vol. 3, pp. 310 ff; and Freneau, *A Collection,* II, 39–40, 40–42, 51–52.

forensic patience and judicial calm until the British should make the first step. When they did, after many delays, he was ready for them. The British were routed. Packenham was killed. On January 8, 1815, the victory for America was complete. The war was over. It had, indeed, been over for some time, though Jackson and the people did not know it. The Treaty of Ghent, signed on Christmas Eve, 1814, had already brought to a close the war that was still being fought by "Old Hickory" at New Orleans.[27]

It had been fought elsewhere in America too and not alone against England. The Federalists had opposed it with more than words. Openly and actively they had given aid and comfort to the enemy. They had even sent food and clothing to the British armies in Canada. Massachusetts, under the leadership of Josiah Quincy, supported the cause of Britain, while young Daniel Webster, ambitious, eloquent, and persuasive, had harassed the Administration on the floor of Congress with barbed resolutions against France. Rumors of secession were heard in public places, as the Massachusetts Legislature sent out a call for the Hartford Convention, at which delegates from the Bay State, from Connecticut, and from Rhode Island prepared to take measures inimical to the welfare of their country. Ready to consider a plea by *The Boston Centinel* for "deliverance" at their hands, New England Federalists like Timothy Pickering were prepared for extreme measures against the national government, measures not soon forgotten by the people who were hard-pressed on all sides by invaders from abroad and by sappers from within. The war, so miraculously ended at New Orleans, had happily put a period to the dangers that threatened America; the greatest one of all, the break-up of the Union, was happily averted. There had been many losses and few gains in this war, but it had revealed the strength of America as well as its great weakness. Self-interest was still the first enemy of the public good, while the country's gains and losses, often indistinguishable and sometimes the same, were the stuff of both its greatness and its weakness. Twice divided by conflict, it had twice been saved by the will of its people to follow in the way of freedom and justice, however great the forces that were arrayed against it.[28]

[27] Beirne, *The War of 1812*, pp. 353–373; Billington, *et al.*, *The United States*, pp. 122–125.

[28] A. E. Smith, *James Madison*, pp. 313 ff; Henry Adams, *The War of 1812*, pp. 275–280.

To the strength of that will Philip Freneau was a witness, and he recorded it now as he had done so many times before. He set down the events of the war as they transpired, not always with objective candor, frequently with more propaganda than poetry, yet never with less truth than error. In satires like "The Terrific Torpedoes," in scorching criticisms like "Political Sermons," in stirring battle calls like "The Volunteer's March," in bitter diatribes like "The British Invasion," and in angry lashing like "The English Devastations," his point, well or badly expressed, and his purpose, beautifully or indifferently achieved, was the denunciation of "the slaves of a King," conscripted from "England's dregs or Scotland's scum," and the triumph of liberty and democracy in spite of them all. Throughout the entire struggle he "scribbled" the verses that laid bare the heart of the man who wrote them as much as the heart of America. As in his older pieces, there was never a note of doubt as to the justice of his country's cause or the infamy of the enemy's conduct. In the poetic dialogue between "Goth and Vandal," his undiminished hatred of Britain is couched in revolting pictures of its latest depredations in America.[29]

It was not Freneau's intention to weigh and assess the praise and the blame. In the face of force, reason was unreasonable. Philosophy never averted disaster, nor was violence the only handmaiden of justice. But neither was oppression an arbiter of the right. Truth might also be spoken from a gun, and blood had often washed out a lie. Poems—such poems as Freneau wrote—spoke the truth, the truth that was for him clear beyond all other truths. Freedom for America was one truth that must never be silenced, and no one more nobly expressed this truth than Philip Freneau:

> By oppression's woes and pains—
> By our sons in servile chains,
> We will bleed in all our veins,
> But they shall be—shall be free.[30]

The people who did the fighting and the dying read his lines, sang them, and were moved by them as they had been moved during the difficult days of the Revolution. The new poems plumbed the depths of feeling, the deep sources where the love of liberty lingers in the soul of man however it is masked by strange compulsions. It was true at Lexington and Concord, at Lake Erie and Lake Champlain, at Valley

[29] Freneau, *Poems* (Pattee), Vol. 3, pp. 297, 302, 321, 330, 331, 343.
[30] *Ibid.*, p. 338.

Forge and Yorktown, Washington and New Orleans—all of them variations on the same theme, often played and endlessly repeated, old and ever new in the history of America, everlasting in the history of Man.

The history of Man! The poet knew it well. War, violence, desolation—these were the substance of that history, softened by interludes of a sweet tranquillity. It was true of man himself, as of all nature. In his lovelier poems Freneau treated of the mysteries of Nature, of man as a part of Nature, with the sad beauty and calm acceptance of tragic inevitability. In one of these, written when the war was ended and the peace was signed, he compares the silent stream of "The Brook of the Valley" with the moments of release from conflict, its tumbling rapids with the tumult of war.[31]

The rapids and the shoals, the ebb and the flow, of blood as of water, were the same. Beneath the surface, however calm it seemed, the forces of Nature forever played havoc with all the aspects of life. There was no more respite in a time of peace than in a time of war, and man was still the victim of violence, though it was clothed in the habit of righteousness.

At sixty-three, Freneau was bereft of all illusions, but not of all faith. The picture of mankind, contrived of many pictures, was not too flattering, yet one aspect, one feature, brightened and suffused it with a light that was imperishable. Dignity if not beauty, charm if not sweetness, strength if not power, gleamed in that light, in the striving, soaring spirit of man—to be free.

In the evening of his life, as in its rosy dawn, Philip Freneau, believing little more, believed in this above all things. Though he bleed from all his veins, man "shall be—shall be free."

[31] *Ibid.*, p. 376.

33. REAP THE HARVEST

THE COUNTRY, finished again with the problems of war, settled down to the problems of peace, the same—though now intensified—as they had been before. Problems of trade and commerce, of sectionalism and nationalism, of domestic and foreign policies, required immediate attention and solution. The ideal of liberty which had animated the country in two wars must be justified in the life of the people—by political equality and economic opportunity. They were the twin goals of democracy and the twin demands of Philip Freneau in all his preachments on freedom. In the past they had been all but ignored. And in the future?

The future seemed promising enough. The embargo and the war had cut off the importation of manufactured goods from Europe, compelling a measure of self-sufficiency scarcely known in America before. Slowly its industries blossomed in homes and in shops, as America, in ever-increasing abundance, began to produce its own textiles, its own paper, its own iron, leather, and woodenware. From New York, Pennsylvania, and New Jersey came the coal, iron, and limestone for smelting. From the Gulf of Mexico to Virginia, cotton was grown and processed in huge quantities by Eli Whitney's cotton gin for the busy textile mills of New England. Jackson's victory at New Orleans had opened wide the valley of the Mississippi, and corn and wheat bloomed there in vast profusion for the nourishment of a whole people. America was growing fast in the material things of life; how well would it grow in the gentler, more spiritual, aspects? Hopes were high; the future seemed assured; an aura of good-will and unity pervaded the country. Freedom was secure and the democracy Philip Freneau had prophesied appeared in a fair way toward realization.[1]

[1] R. A. Billington, B. L. Lowenberg, and S. H. Brockunier, *The United*

The miracle of New Orleans had happened—and the man who had brought it about was not Jackson, or Madison, whose term as President was now expiring. More than any other, the victory belonged to James Monroe, Secretary of State and Secretary of War at one and the same time—the time of the greatest crisis for America. It was to James Monroe that a grateful people turned for continued leadership when a new President was elected. The "Era of Good-Feelings" bubbled and flowed over as the old protégé of Thomas Jefferson and the old benefactor of Thomas Paine, James Monroe, the democrat tried and true, became the fourth of the Virginia dynasty to assume the supreme honors—and the heavy duties—of President of the United States.[2]

The honors were great indeed. The broad-shouldered, angular man with the gray-blue eyes and deeply lined face had craved them more than anything else he had ever wanted in his life. Monroe looked a little like Washington, thought a great deal like Jefferson, and had served his country well on many occasions, in many offices; he would serve it well in the office which was his dearest ambition. To allay, if possible, the sectional suspicions of New England, he appointed John Quincy Adams as his Secretary of State. The son of the old Federalist was hardly a democrat himself, but he might be useful to bind many wounds left by the war, and by the Hartford Convention. John Quincy Adams, while watching the peace at home, did not neglect the possible recurrence of trouble from abroad. To prevent any future foreign encroachments, he prepared a new instrument of policy which the President promulgated as his own. Known to history as the Monroe Doctrine, it warned Europe against any imperialist adventures or attempts at colonization on the American continents. The democratic institutions of America were made invulnerable against all infections from abroad.[3]

For the time, at any rate, they seemed safe enough. The foes of democracy had been beaten down, yet one of them, perhaps the greatest of all, still remained. Domestic rather than foreign, slavery was the most persistent enemy of true tranquillity in America, always threatening and forever unappeasable. Visible to all men, to foreigners

---

States: American Democracy in World Perspective, pp. 331 ff; E. C Kirkland, *A History of American Economic Life, passim.*

[2] W. P. Cresson, *James Monroe,* pp. 273–282; Billington, *et al., The United States,* p. 139.

[3] John Geise, *Man and the Western World,* pp. 977–979; Billington, *et al., The United States,* pp. 142–144.

as well as Americans, it was a running sore on the body of a whole people. M. de Montulé, travelling up the Mississippi from New Orleans, was saddened by the anomaly of black bondage in a land where "one enters, lives, and travels without any passport."[4] America was a country with two souls, each in conflict with the other. No passports were needed to travel its entire length, but it was not free in its entire body. Spiritually as well as politically it was out of joint. The Missouri Compromise of 1820 would attempt some kind of balance between the North and the South, between an economy based on free labor and one based on slave labor. But no compromise could subsist for long. The great expansion westward, the vast growth of industry and agriculture, the political power necessary to control the economy of the country through its multiplying states and conflicting laws—they would all prove that no compromise could ever be found to heal the open wound of America. John Quincy Adams, clear-minded above most men, prophesied the ultimate failure of all compromise. "'The present question,'" he noted in his diary, is a mere preamble—a title page to a great tragic volume." Other pages must still be written before that volume was completed.[5]

Philip Freneau, writing as usual his own pages, was busy on another volume of his poems. Not too confident of their merit, he confided his doubts to James Madison, as always receptive to his friend's misgivings. Mr. Longworth, the New York bookseller, he wrote Madison on January 12, 1815, had "prevailed" on him to publish the poems, though "after the age of fifty the vanity of authorship ought to cease." It was a vanity to which the poet of Monmouth succumbed as often as anybody who ever dipped a pen in ink. But what could Madison, who had a few doubts of his own, advise him? Freneau had asked him for nothing, not even for a subscription, and what reply the little, harassed man whose term was drawing to a close sent him, is unknown. Madison wrote letters sparingly to everyone but Jefferson, but it is probable that he subscribed for the new book, since his single copy of Freneau's previous edition had been destroyed by the fire in the White House— and he did want his old friend's poems in his library. In any event, on March 3 he received another letter from Freneau expressing regret for the delay in sending two duodecimo volumes of *A Collection of*

---

[4] E. de Montulé, *Voyage en Amérique*, pp. 18 ff.

[5] John Quincy Adams, *The Diary of John Quincy Adams*, pp. 360, 364–391, 401; for Billington's treatment of the Missouri Compromise of 1820, see Billington, *et al., The United States*, pp. 141, 208–209.

Poems on American Affairs just published, "bound in an elegant manner," together with a set of the edition of 1809 to replace the books lost in the "flames of Goths and Barbarians." Other flames, not those of the "Goths and Barbarians," later destroyed the Madison letters and much more besides in a great fire at Mount Pleasant.[6]

On May 10, when Freneau finally dispatched the books to Madison, they were sent "as a mark of my attention, respect, and esteem, in regard to your private as well as public character." He refused any payment for them. What Madison thought of the poems we do not know. The author himself believed that they were "mere trifles." His modesty was not altogether justified, nor perhaps fully intended. Like his previous publications, these small volumes contained some lyrical verses of a high order that were printed and reprinted in *The New Brunswick Fredonian, The New York Columbian, The Newark Centinel of Freedom, The Trenton True American,* and the Philadelphia *Aurora.* Critics like Gulian C. Verplanck compared the work to that of the famous English balladist Dibdin, at the same time pointing out the defects in the poet's style and diction. Yet he conceded that Freneau's "martial and political ballads have an arch simplicity in their manner that renders them very poignant and striking."[7] John Davis, an English reviewer, found some "grain in the bushel of chaff," while Dr. Samuel Miller, judging the literary status of America, assayed the poems as "honourable to themselves and their country . . . noticed with respect by foreign as well as domestic critics."[8]

There was a good deal of chaff in these books, but not a little good, nourishing grain also. The lilting lines of "The Volunteer's March," though they owed a good deal to Robert Burns in both style and substance, were fully worthy of the Bruce and Bannockburn.

> Lay the proud invaders low;
> Tyrants fall in every foe,
> Liberty's in every blow,
> Forward! let us do or die.[9]

Songs like those of Robert Burns have been preserved and treasured for their universal and timeless appeal. The songs of Philip Freneau,

---

[6] Freneau, *The Poems of Philip Freneau* (ed. F. L. Pattee), Vol. 1, p. lxxxvii.
[7] Lewis Leary, *That Rascal Freneau,* p. 340.
[8] John Davis, *Travels of Four Years and a Half in the U.S.,* p. 156; Samuel Miller, *A Brief Retrospect of the Eighteenth Century.* Vol. 2, pp. 230–233.
[9] Freneau, *A Collection of Poems on American Affairs,* Vol. 2, pp. 43–44.

carried on the lips and in the hearts of an age that had passed, once had
served some special purpose—and were then forgotten. Never concerned with the mere vicissitudes of romance in love or in war, they
were written to elicit response far removed from the gentler emotions.
In a period of perpetual crisis their appeal was to action, not to medi-
tation, to hatred as much as to love. Unlike the songs of other, older
lands, they evoked no ancient memories of a country or a race and
preserved no ancient experience of one or of many. The inspiration for
his song was immediate, its relevancy was intended for the time, not
for all time. A poem like the "Hymn to Liberty," written to stimulate
the flagging revolutionary ardors of America at the moment of Edmund
Genêt's decline in national esteem, was all but forgotten with Genêt's
complete eclipse. Yet it deserved much better than this.

> God save the Rights of Man!
> Give us a heart to scan
>   Blessings so dear;
> Let them be spread around
> Wherever man is found,
> And with the welcome sound
>   Ravish the ear.[10]

Wherever men met together, in camp or in tavern, on the march or
in the field, the songs of Philip Freneau were heard. The simple folk,
like the common soldiers, understood their stirring message, and because they *had* a message they spluttered like a spent candle when the
need for a message was done. In his own Monmouth, where songs like
"The Voice of America," "To the Soldiers of America," and ballads
like "The Navy" were popular with all the patrons of Major Thomas
Hunn's tavern at Mount Pleasant and Denise Forman's inn at Middletown, they were finished when the wars were over and the candle
burned out.[11]

With the signing of the Treaty of Ghent, the message and the songs
were forgotten; they were topical, and the topics which had induced
them were crowded out by others more relevant to the day. It was the
same fate that met Freneau's new editions too. Though Longworth
had confidently assured him that the "town would have them," so few

---

[10] "Hymn to Liberty," in *The Jersey Chronicle*, July 11, 1795.
[11] *The True American*, June 29, July 12, and November 23, 1812. See also
Lewis Leary, "Philip Freneau and Monmouth County," *Monmouth County
Historical Association Bulletin*, Vol. 1, No. 2 (July 1948), pp. 76–77.

copies were sold even in the City of New York, where they might have been successful, that the unhappy author lamented the books had "fallen deadborn from the Press." Writing to Dr. John Wakefield Francis, an eminent physician and scholar of New York, one of the cultured circle who had encouraged their publication, the poet bitterly recounted the reasons for the literary fiasco on which he had lost the heavy sum of "almost two hundred dollars." Forgetting that he himself had held no high opinion of the quality of his writing, Freneau ascribed its failure to the cultural heathens of the city. "As I take it," he told Dr. Francis, "the genius of the City of New York is so entirely commercial, that I suspect it swallows up all ideas of poetry, or refuses any attention to poetical productions, further than what is calculated for the fly-market stalls." What else could one expect "Where all the ideas of people seem to be devoted to Commerce, Speculation's Bank Shares," and similar ingredients of the flesh-pots.[12] It would have been better, he complained to Madison, if he had never left the "Solitude and the wild scenes of nature in New Jersey for the ever execrated streets and company" of New York.[13] His Monmouth neighbors always showed him a great deal more kindness. The politics he had espoused, the poems he had written, were never a cause for enmity and rarely resulted in unfriendliness; his politics were not always unacceptable, nor was his religion—what the Monmouth faithful thought his lack of religion—offensive. In a community of free spirits and unselfish friends, he again informed Dr. Francis, he would never be victimized by the "enmity of some, the politics of others, and the general inattention of all." Who could wonder that he was "disgusted" with authorship? It was not the first time—nor the last—that he firmly resolved to forever abjure the "vanity of authorship."[14]

Literature was a snare and a delusion. More dependable was the land still remaining from his sandy patrimony. Everybody preferred property to poetry. Buyers of this commodity were never concerned with a man's politics or religion. They would scarcely turn down a cheap acre because its owner was a democrat or his interpretation of

[12] Freneau to Francis, May 15, 1815, in C. F. Heartman, *Unpublished Freneauana,* pp. 12–17.

[13] Freneau to Madison, March 3, 1815, in Freneau, *Poems* (Pattee), Vol. 1, p. lxxxviii.

[14] Freneau to Francis, in Heartman, *Unpublished Freneauana,* pp. 12–17; and Freneau to Madison, January 12, 1815, in M. S. Austin, *Philip Freneau,* pp. 204–205.

the Bible unacceptible to sensitive souls. Piece by piece the land was being cut up, sold, or mortgaged, while the poems remained unsold. Two acres, five acres, fifty-three acres, one tract, then another, year after year, almost month after month—four tracts in 1815 alone—his inheritance was whittled away. Other acres, other tracts, would follow after these, until the flesh, and the bones, and the marrow in the bones of his patrimony were quite consumed. Like his poems, the property would remain only as a memory. They would be recalled, one as much as the other, only in the faded volumes of forgotten lore, in yellowed parchments of metes and bounds, all transient and elusive as life itself, as fleeting as all fame and fortune.[15]

As a father he was, perhaps, more fortunate. Four fine daughters were at home, all that remained to comfort the old man who was now as disgusted with authorship as Eleanor had been disgusted long ago. The two elder girls, Agnes and Helena, were soon to be married, a destiny denied to the younger girls Catharine and Margaret. For Freneau himself, the problem of marriage had long since lost all interest. His early fears of entrapment had been dissolved, but he had not been too happy through the years with Eleanor. The years had only strengthened his early belief that

> A man's best fortune or his worst's a wife,
> A steady friendship or continual strife.

He was singularly reticent about his private life, and it is not possible with certainty to assert that he spoke of his own life wih Eleanor in the half-serious, half-jesting verses of "The Neglected Husband." Perhaps he also felt like a neglected father when Helena became the wife of John Hammell on December 16, 1816, and Agnes, closest to him of all his children, was married to Edward Leadbeater, a New York merchant, on December 25 of the same year.[16]

Now, when he went to New York, he went alone. He went there to walk the "execrated streets" and exchange the "solitude and the wild scenes of nature in New Jersey" for the men who knew and understood him, the company of a few friends whom he trusted, and who honored him in turn with their confidence and respect, as others once

[15] Monmouth County Deeds and Mortgages, Mss., E.341, E.509, L.2, L.412, X.251, R.341, Y.317, Y.520, Y.583; Leary, *That Rascal Freneau*, p. 407 n. Leary, "Freneau and Monmouth County," has complete notes on the Freneau properties (p. 81 n.).

[16] *The True American*, December 23, 1816.

had honored him. They were gone now; still alive, they were removed not only by distance, but by time and station as well. The two men with whom he had had so much in common were as alien to him as if they had never existed. Jefferson and Madison, at Monticello and Montpellier, lived a life he had never known, in a world that he never knew, on high Olympus where they were destined to abide. He had been their write-hand, a collaborator in establishing the democratic creed of America, and together they had plowed a path of reason with the light of freedom.[17]

Washington and Hamilton had been men of action, while Jefferson and Madison were men of thought. The feeling without which the people could never be stirred to either thought or action was supplied by men like Patrick Henry and Thomas Paine, by men like Sam Adams and Philip Freneau, each in his own way a poet who moved men to thought and action—and to sacrifice. They moved mountains of apathy to achieve a Revolution. They differed in their means, they diverged in their methods, yet their ends were the same—a land where freedom was the highest good and a people who would guard it above all other treasures. In the time of its greatest perils, in the days of its greatest crises, the goal was never forgotten by the thinkers who furnished the plans, or by the builders who labored to erect the structure, or by the poets who inspired them all when the spirit flagged. Men think with their hearts and move with their souls; their emotions made the idea of liberty viable in America, and the ideal of democracy, though it often faltered, an eternal one in the United States. Philip Freneau had always sought to harness the ideas and ideals of his countrymen for purposes like these. Like Pascal, he too could say that "The heart has reasons the mind does not know," for the heart is the unique province of poets, which men of thought and men of action know less intimately —or not at all.

Because he was so utterly unlike Jefferson and Madison, Freneau had lost them. Less resilient then they, he had refused to deviate from the path which for him was also a strait and narrow one. When Jefferson was ready to drop Genêt, Freneau still continued to champion the firebrand of France, because the French people, after the Terror as before, after as before Napoleon, remained the victims of self-seeking and ambitious men, the pawns of power that frustrated both

---

[17] J. W. Francis, *Old New York, passim.*

liberty and democracy. Without any responsibility for official policy, Freneau also lacked the political acumen to understand any need for compromise. The victory of the Jeffersonians had accomplished little more than a shift of governmental authority from the mercantile North to the agrarian South, while Federalist policies, without which that authority might be jeopardized, were substantially retained.[18]

The Genêt troubles were long past, but others still disturbed a political innocent like Philip Freneau. The Alien and Sedition laws had wrought havoc with free speech and a free press. They were unspeakably wrong under Federalist control, and Jefferson had righted the wrongs they inflicted as soon as he won the power to do so. But the Republicans had not been without sin either. In Pennsylvania John Ward Fenno, the son of Freneau's old enemy, had been fined 2,500 dollars for a libel on a Republican, a sum far in excess of the worst Federalist exactions. Moreover, Jefferson, as he informed Governor McKean of Pennsylvaia, had been quite willing to allow a "few prosecutions of the most prominent offenders [against] the integrity of the presses." One day Jefferson, in an aberrant mood, would even doubt the value of a press for anything else but advertisements.[19]

Again, there was the baffling problem of a loose construction of the Constitution, formerly advocated by the Federalists alone, but now proposed by the Republicans as well. Madison, though he had fought the first Bank of the United States as unconstitutional, signed the bill which chartered the second one. It was doubtless as necessary a step in the growing political and economic structure of America as Jefferson's choler was pardonable in the face of unrelieved slander and chicane. Conditions change and with them the definitions of right and wrong, of good and evil—even the interpretations of constitutions and the democratic process which they advance or retard. Freneau hardly changed at all. His ideas of democracy were simple—and elemental. Democracy was the handmaiden of liberty. Liberty was the supreme

---

[18] Clinton Rossiter, *Alexander Hamilton and the Constitution,* pp. 238–239.

[19] Leonard W. Levy, *Jefferson and Civil Liberties: The Darker Side,* pp. 18, 44, 56. This volume has already been commented upon. See Jefferson to McKean, February 6, 1803, in Thomas Jefferson, *Writings* (ed. P. L. Ford), Vol. 8, p. 218; and Jefferson to James Brown, October 27, 1808, in Thomas Jefferson, *Writings* (ed. A. A. Lipscomb and A. E. Bergh), Vol. 12, pp. 182–185, in which Jefferson expresses his belief in "the universal resource" of "a dictator or martial law." Also see W. G. Bleyer, *Main Currents in the History of American Journalism,* p. 126.

possession of the people. Political equality and economic opportunity gave it both meaning and substance, while the sacred fire of individual worth and human dignity was forever fanned by the poets of America.[20]

Jefferson, dignified and austere in his bearing, cool and correct in his manner, an aristocrat in his tastes and training, was a democrat more by intellectual persuasion than by spiritual sympathy. His concept of equality did not include the masses who toiled for a living. For him the ideal society was one controlled by the tillers of the soil who also had a stake in the soil they tilled. He lived on beyond the time of a strict agrarian economy, and witnessed the slow transformation of America into an industrial country. He saw only the dawn—and he died before the sun had fully risen. Madison, like Jefferson, was alien to the life Freneau had known, at home or at sea, in the taverns or in the printing office. The solitude of the study was the natural haven for both of them, while for the poet it was the sea as much as the study, a ship equally with a shop.[21]

Jefferson had not deserted the man whose service he once had sought. He had never really been attached to the "genius" of whom he had said that he saved the Constitution "which was fast galloping into Monarchy." The Secretary of State rarely had condescended to notice the humble clerk in the State Department, and his aesthetic sensibilities were often offended by the strong language the poet had used against their common enemy. The well-groomed Jefferson had never cared much for the slovenly attire of the man whose appearance, so he said, "belied his genius." Not once had the Republican leader publicly defended the poet against the villainous attacks on him during the hectic days of 1792—it was his protégé James Monroe who undertook this belated task at the behest of Madison. Madison, more generous than Jefferson, had praised the poet's "accurate and refined taste in the English language" as well as "his morals without blemish," but even Madison, save for a few kind words, had never made any gesture of real friendship or true understanding.[22]

---

[20] Rossiter, *Alexander Hamilton,* pp. 239 ff.

[21] C. G. Bowers, *Jefferson in Power,* pp. 483 ff.

[22] Philip M. Marsh, *Monroe's Defense of Jefferson and Freneau;* "Madison's Defense of Freneau," *William and Mary Quarterly,* third series, III, 2 (April 1946), 269–274; and "Philip Freneau and James Madison," *Proceedings of New Jersey Historical Society,* LXV, 4 (October 1947), 189–194. Monroe,

When the fruit of their collective labors were ready for the harvest, it was Jefferson and Madison who garnered the fruit while Freneau never savored even the taste of it. He remained, as he always had been, one of the people—"one of the swinish multitude"—who reached for fruit that forever eluded his grasp.

---

rather than Madison, came to Freneau's defense, with adequate gusto (see articles in John Dunlap's *Daily American Advertiser,* from September 22 to October 20, 1792; also James Monroe, *Writings,* Vol. 1, pp. 240–245.

34. WAY OF ALL FLESH

JEFFERSON AND MADISON were now scarcely more than memories, far beyond Freneau's reach for any warmth or comfort, but friends like Dr. John Wakefield Francis, a learned historian as well as an able physician, always made him welcome when he came to New York. Dr. Francis found the poet with the persistent stoop and thinning gray hair a repository of "rich funds of antiquarian lore" and "highly cultivated in classical knowledge, abounding in anecdotes of the revolutionary crisis." The old man was flattered to learn from Dr. Francis that the eminent Scotch reviewer Francis Jeffrey thought so well of his work "that the time would arrive when his poetry, like that of Hudibras, would command a commentator like Gray." That time might never be, but the regard of Dr. Francis himself, a distinguished member of the New York Academy of Medicine, was sufficient unto the time. So too was the friendship of Dr. Francis' colleague in medicine and antiquarian research Dr. David Hosack, a founder of both the Historical Society and the Academy of Fine Arts, who had been present as attending surgeon at the duel between Burr and Hamilton.[1]

On his visits to New York Freneau might spend some time with DeWitt Clinton, and discuss with him the fabulous canal Clinton was building between the Hudson River and the Great Lakes. He would also meet for an exchange of thoughts with Bishop Samuel Provoost, a devout and erudite cleric who had once shouldered a musket for his country. The Bishop was a fine scholar and a gentle soul, and Clinton a distinguished statesman as well as a student of the natural sciences.[2]

[1] Freneau, *The Poems of Philip Freneau* (ed. F. L. Pattee), Vol. 1, p. xciii; see also Philip Hone, *Diary*, Vol. 2, p. 210.

[2] Francis Fresneau had married into the Provoost family years before; he had

New York was rich in such intellects. In Monmouth one learned nothing of the new cultural currents that flowed so swiftly in the big city, and Freneau was eager to drink at the fountains of friends like these. All he wanted from life was an hour of friendliness and companionable talk into which no conflict of political or social interests could ever obtrude. Fools he could never suffer gladly.

Dr. Francis sometimes thought of other things not entirely germane to high intellectual interests. They were unspoken yet no less evident on all these occasions. The poor appearance of the poet, his conspicuous lack of money, often moved Dr. Francis to make him some small loans. Freneau could not have come to New York without them. Once he would have been too proud to accept such help, save to satisfy a creditor who was pushing him too close to a debtor's cell. If he had once refused as a species of charity Jefferson's offer of a post in his government, Freneau was a bit wiser now. "Interest has never been my ruling motive," he informed Clinton, who offered to help him, "but with years and experience it appears to me to be an ingredient in composing our little heap of life that should by no means be neglected." Self-interest had never helped him to compose his "little heap of life," and now there was scarcely any time for that.[3]

His friend John Pintard, whom he had replaced as translator in Jefferson's office, had been far more successful in utilizing that ingredient. Pintard had become a wealthy and influential citizen, and a lover of literature and the classics. Equally eminent as a scholar and a merchant, he had done well to leave all radical vagaries to impractical poets and reach out for the greater rewards of business. Nearly ruined in the days of Hamilton's assumption measures, he was prosperous now, a shrewd and careful operator, who had learned the lesson of profits quickly made—and quickly lost. Somewhat chastened, Pintard had continued his quest for wealth, at the same time modestly pursuing the same democratic ideals as the poet of Monmouth. Freneau had pursued nothing else, while his friend, who had never changed his mind about the Federalists, continued to profit by their example. Pintard had accomplished even more than wealth. To ensure the purity of democratic professions and the growth of Republican power, he

---

taken to wife Helena, daughter of David Provoost, a prosperous merchant of New York. The canal was finished in 1825. See A. E. and G. I. Duyckinck, *Cyclopoedia of American Literature*, Vol. I, p. 333.

[3] Freneau to Clinton, November 8, 1796, DeWitt Clinton Papers, Mss.

had organized the "American Museum," an institution as unique
as it was interesting, "for the express purpose of collecting and preserving everything relating to the natural or political history of
America," to the end that Saint Tammany was justified as "a political
institution founded on a strong republican basis whose democratic
principles will serve in some measure to correct the aristocracy of our
city." John Pintard was indeed a rare man with whom Freneau could
spend some pleasant hours, and the two old friends had many memories in common, memories to which most of the younger men were
strangers.[4]

Freneau's friends, even those who did not agree with his political
and social views, admired the old poet whose "pen was more acri-
monious than his heart." They liked him for "his private worth and
his courteous manner," his complete lack "of all ambitious display."
Those who succeeded in spite of their radical views—perhaps because
of them—considered him a victim of his "indiscreet zeal as an advocate of the radical doctrines of the day." Such ideas were no more
popular in these times, when the winds of all doctrine were tempered
to the shorn lambs of business. The lambs were growing fat again,
and warm against the wind, as America manured the pastures and
sheltered the flock from adverse weather. All good citizens were concerned with this. And the better citizens were concerned with art
and science, with culture and beauty, as well.[5]

Whatever there was of beauty and learning in the City of New
York absorbed the interest of Philip Freneau. The Academy of Fine
Arts with its wide display of portraits by Stuart and Peale was a
reminder of other days, of other times and other men. He also had
been somebody then, but his was not among the portraits on the walls.
Perhaps it was his own fault that he was not there, for he had rebuffed
every effort to put his features on canvas, resisting the invitation of

---

[4] E. P. Kilroe, *Saint Tammany and the Origin of the Society of Tammany
or Columbian Order of the City of New York*, pp. 135–136; *Appleton's Encyclopedia of American Biography*, Vol. 5, p. 28; Gustavus Myers, *The History
of Tammany Hall, passim*. Freneau was a member of the Tammany Society
(Society of Saint Tammany, Constitution and Roll of Members of the Tammany Society or Columbian Order, 1789–1816, Mss., Member No. 503). He
was also a member of the "N.Y. Society for Promoting the Abolition of Slavery" (E. P. Link, *Democratic Republican Societies, 1790–1800*, p. 154).

[5] Dr. Francis, in Freneau, *Poems* (Pattee), Vol. I, p. xciv; and Duyckinck,
Cyclopoedia, Vol. I, p. 333; C. F. Heartman, *Unpublished Freneauana*, pp.
12–17.

"a body of gentlemen" who had commissioned Rembrandt Peale to paint him. His objections were not the same as those he had expressed in "The Gallery," though they were not too dissimilar. Another time, when he had detected a surreptitious attempt to draw him at a dinner given by Dr. Hosack, he protested vehemently that it was an infringement on his right to privacy. The attempt of J. W. Jarvis, the well-known artist, to catch his features for posterity, had failed, not because of Freneau's objections to the artist himself. Jarvis had been a kind and generous host to the penniless Thomas Paine, and he had sheltered the impoverished patriot in his own home for over five months. In a life devoted to painting, the artist had made but one piece of sculpture —that of the author of *The Crisis* and *The Rights of Man.* If any artist appealed to the radical democratic beliefs of Freneau, it would be Jarvis.[6]

Not Jarvis, nor any artist, was the object of his aversion. Neither was it false modesty on his part, any more than his life-long adherence to small clothes and a contempt for all fashion. If others affected long trousers, which were now the vogue, he refused to change. They were doubtless more comfortable as well as more fashionable than breeches, and his old spindly legs would be better hidden, right down to the ankles. Yet a true disciple of Nature never indulged in artifice like this, or in any other "counterfeit presentment." To preserve in pigment what was destined to dissolution for the sake of a spurious immortality was the greatest of all affectations. Men survived in their works, not in their looks. To the end of his life Freneau held fast to his resolution against any portraits, which were defilements of the spirit and a corruption of the soul. One likeness of him was later drawn—not from the man living but from the memory of one already dead. Declared a satisfactory likeness by members of his family, it is the only one which exists (see frontispiece). At the heart of his democratic ideal, the nucleus of a rampant individualist remained secure. And the friends who welcomed him, honored him because it was so. The visits of Philip Freneau were as stimulating to them as they were to him.[7]

In Monmouth there was little enough to engage his mind. With Agnes, his favorite daughter, gone to a home of her own, there were

<hr/>

[6] Edwin Salter and G. C. Beckman, *Old Times in Old Monmouth,* pp. 110–111; H. E. Dickson, *John Wesley Jarvis,* p. 102.

[7] Duyckinck, *Cyclopoedia,* Vol. 1, p. 333; article by Marianne Harris, in *The Monmouth Inquirer,* July 31, 1884; Freneau, *Poems* (Pattee), Vol. 1, p. xciii.

precious few occasions when the boredom of his life at home was refreshed by outside interests. The placid surface of Mount Pleasant was rarely ruffled by anyone but Eleanor, who was often exacting and nudging in a quiet and unobtrusive manner. She had become "very deaf" and carried her cross with few audible complaints; the soft impeachments of her husband's endless scribbling and inept chores continued. Without any profit to himself, his efforts had never brought any comfort to her either. He was useless on the farm and his poetry appeared equally ineffective. Her brother Denise, to whom she had once complained about Philip—Denise was quite different. He had wasted none of his precious time on matters that were really none of his business. Denise *had* a business, and he had prospered while her feckless huband was forever on the verge of pauperism. Her patience was exhausted, the more so since he scarcely bothered to answer her save with a silence that was more eloquent than words—words, in any event, that she could hardly hear anyway. What was even worse, perhaps, was his complete indifference to her religious faith. He had almost none of his own. Eleanor was deeply devoted to the Episcopal Church, and Philip was devoted to no church at all, or to any faith except his faith in freedom.[8]

In New York there were friendly, sympathetic voices, learned and understanding voices. At the home of Dr. Francis on Bond Street, Freneau would not only listen; he could also speak. There was more than the news of the day to occupy the company that met there. There were memories of another time too, the exciting memories of a poet of the American Revolution. Dr. Francis was not one to think of Freneau's work as wasted; he had read the old man's poetry long before he had ever met him and his devotion to literature was as deep as his interest in medicine. He had a few memories of his own that he liked to share with his friend. Dr. Francis liked to recall that his classmate, Washington Irving, a bright new luminary on the literary horizon, had once delighted the young fry with his lusty rendition of the songs and ballads of Philip Freneau. Washington Irving had become less enamored of the poet of Monmouth since then; he had even called him a "barking cur" because of his radical views, views with which the famous author of the *Knickerbocker History of New York* did not agree. Nor would Dr. Francis ever agree with such a characterization

[8] Eleanor to Denise Forman, February 28, 1803, in Samuel Forman Papers, Mss. Also, "The Wife of Philip Freneau," *New York Evening Post,* May 6, 1893.

of the man he admired not only as a poet but also as an idealist of the
highest principles. The old man was "highly cultivated," he possessed
great "charm," and his face, according to Dr. Francis, was always
"lightened with intelligence."[9]

Those who had no occasion to know the poet except by his outer
appearance may have doubted these qualities in the eccentric gentleman
who looked more like a farmer than a poet and less like a farmer than
a seedy old loafer. The charm and cultivation, the lightened intelligence, could easily be missed beneath the lackluster surface of sartorial
indifference. Like a candle without a wick, he seemed beyond the
power of illumination. Decidedly stooped now, and painfully thin,
only his "firm step" belied the years that had passed over him. He
was still "a great walker," and on his visits to New York he must
have enjoyed the new beauty of the Battery, freshly restored after the
destruction of the war years. Castle Clinton was not yet refurbished as
Castle Garden, but when that too was accomplished, he could try his
thin legs on the circular promenade overlooking the waters of the
upper bay. The old mariner might indulge the memories of those
distant days, so far away and long ago, when he was the master of
sailing vessels like those that came in on the wind and the tide to moor
at the wharves of the Battery. There were so many ships that M.
de Montulé, arriving in New York from the water side, was impressed
by the "forest of masts" which he saw there.[10]

Freneau was too old now for more than a weak nostalgia for ships
that sailed the seas, but he was not too old to take a turn on the wave-
washed wall from which the rolling hills of New Jersey were plainly
visible. The hills he knew so well had lost none of their old allure for
him, even when he left them for a short spell with his friends in New
York and a pleasant interlude of loafing on the streets that teemed with
busy life. Yet he always returned again to the home in Monmouth,

[9] "Memoir of Dr. Francis," by H. T. Tuckerman, in J. W. Francis, Old
New York, pp. xlv ff, and Ch. VI; also Freneau, Poems (Pattee), Vol. 1, pp.
xciv ff; Edward Wagenknecht, Washington Irving, p. 107; Lewis Leary, "The
Time-Piece," in Princeton University Library Chronicle, Vol. 2, No. 2 (February 1941), pp. 65-74.

[10] Freneau, Poems of Freneau (ed. H. H. Clark), p. xxv; Freneau, Poems
(Pattee), Vol. 1, p. xciii; M. S. Austin, Philip Freneau, p. 208; R. Gilder, The
Battery, pp. 141-146; Henry Wansey, The Journal of an Excursion to the
United States of America in the Summer of 1794, pp. 76-85; E. de Moutulé,
Voyage en Amérique, p. 18.

and to the hills of Jersey, now as always beckoning to the wanderer
from afar.

> These hills the pride of all the coast,
> To mighty distance seen,
> With aspect bold and rugged brow,
> That shade the neighboring main:
> These heights, for solitude design'd,
> This rude, resounding shore—
> These vales impervious to the wind,
> Tall oaks, that to the tempest bend,
> Half Druid, I adore.

Happy to be off for a change of scene, he was glad to return home
again, where there was work to be done—the kind of work which
Eleanor silently observed with little enthusiasm, and which he quietly
pursued with little profit. In his age, as in his youth, it was still the
only work for him.[11]

On March 3, 1815, Freneau had written to Madison about his
project for "Eight hundred lines in heroic measure" on "the grand
subject of the Repulse of the British Army at New Orleans." A few
lines, tentative rather than finished, were already written on the flyleaf of his copy of Rousseau. Though he doubted his power to complete
it, he wrote not eight hundred lines, but nearly twice that number,
certain that the epic, with a number of shorter poems, would be published by Mr. David Longworth, the same bookseller who had burned
his fingers with a previous publication. Dr. Francis was more confident than Madison of the success of the new venture, and he was
as optimistic as Freneau himself that Longworth would publish it.
The new volume was never published—nor the poem done "in heroic
measure" either. The shorter pieces were printed in *The Weekly
Museum,* but they were of little importance. The epic on the battle
of New Orleans never appeared anywhere. It disappeared completely,
perhaps in the flames that later destroyed the poet's home. He was not,
for that reason, too greatly distressed. After so many disappointments
he was not too easily dejected. He was only ironically hopeful:

> Life is a probation, human life a task,
> A task of toil, but with it we should bear—

[11] Freneau made frequent trips to New York (Freneau to Francis, May 14,
1822, in Heartman, *Unpublished Freneauana,* pp. 20–21). Also see Freneau's
"Stanzas Written on the Hills of Neversink," in *The Freedman's Journal,* February 2, 1791.

> When this world's winter and its storms are past,
> Spring, in its beauty, will no doubt appear.[12]

Despite the access of age and the inevitability of death which would cancel out all disappointments, Freneau meditated on the spring which "will no doubt appear." No doubt? In a poetic mood, that was permissible. In the sober search for truth there was room for considerable doubt. As he searched he revealed it in an article in *The Weekly Museum*. Science was noncommittal about the certainties of religion. God created the world, set the sun in its place, and the seasons followed as the cycles of life. Studying the sun-spots, Freneau was convinced that these "exhalations from the globular surface of the sun" might one day "gain such an ascendancy as to obscure or incrust the whole solar orb." Planets would perish "and all that exist theron." They, "like the systems of government contrived by men," contained "the seeds of their own dissolution." Would anything at all survive? What about spring "in its beauty," which "will no doubt appear?" With few other beliefs, Freneau held fast to this one. There was no survival but in intellect, and its beauty was the substance of whatever rejuvenation the spring portended. The credible evidence permitted no other conclusion, if, indeed, it permitted this one. "Intellect alone, that emanation from Deity, is secure," he believed. "Mind, we have powerful reason to conclude, will survive when matter is no more."[13]

The philosophy of Deism, which spanned the centuries of rationalism from Descartes to Thoreau, from Spinoza to Emerson, was comforting to the skeptic whose quest for certainty had yielded so little in a long lifetime of searching. Like the later transcendentalism of Emerson, with its basic belief in the oversoul, the Deism of Freneau, with its emphasis on the overintellect, held fast to the hope of spiritual immortality, the survival of what was best in man, in his thought and feeling, through all the aeons of time. The emanation which Freneau ascribed to Deity was the substance of his own faith in the truth as he had gleaned it from his own life and the life of the race—the persistent, dogged, everlasting quest for freedom in which the heart and the mind of man were eternally engaged. Comic and tragic by turn, the quest never ceased. That was the essence of his religion, in this was

[12] Freneau to Francis, May 14, 1822, in Heartman, *Unpublished Freneauana*, pp. 20–21; "Stanzas on an Ancient Burying Ground in Maryland," in Freneau, *Poems* (Pattee), Vol. 1, p. lxxxviii; and Lewis Leary, *That Rascal Freneau*, p. 343.

[13] *The New York Weekly Museum*, September 7, 1816, signed, "P.F."

the truth about immortality and the promise of the spring that shall follow the winter, in time and in eternity. It was a spiritual certainty which a man approaching the end needed as a solace for despair, the only flower, beyond the frail duration of a life, that might bloom and bloom forever. No crisis, catastrophe, or cataclysm could destroy it. It contained the truth, the whole truth, about God—and it was indestructible.[14]

Philip Freneau, no stranger to a few other truths equally persuasive, came to know them more intimately as the years sped by. The death of his mother at ninety-one, the passing of his friends and intimates— this was the way of all flesh. The death of one's intellect, the destruction of the mind's progeny—that was an affront to Deity itself. In the old Bible where the births and deaths of his loved ones were recorded, Freneau also made another entry; the death of his home at Mount Pleasant, on October 18, 1818, "precisely one year after my mother's death," when a fire swept through the old homestead of Locust Grove, was a tragedy from which he scarcely rallied. Built by his father among the tall locusts on a rise overlooking the wide-spreading acres, the house, like many of the acres themselves, was now destroyed. Tract after tract of the lovely woodland had already been taken from him; now his home was a pile of ashes, mingled with the dust of many poems "some of my [best] which had never been published." The epic of Jackson's victory, the letters treasured through the years as durable links with the past, with the dead or still living—all, all had been consumed by the ravenous flames.[15]

As Eleanor and the two girls, with Philip slowly following after them, moved into a "partly furnished" house nearby, he gave thought only for a moment to the ashes which he left behind. He was more saddened by the loss of his poems—of the one on New Orleans in particular, of which he had written to Madison: "If there be anything in inspiration, it will be needful for such a theme." The inspiration, the theme, the poem, the feeling and reason that had fashioned it, all were now in ruins, forever demolished like the prospect of rebuilding this home, or any home, in the years that yet remained to him.[16]

14 Like Jefferson and many of the Founding Fathers, Freneau was a Deist. See N. F. Adkins, *Philip Freneau and the Cosmic Enigma, passim.*

15 Freneau Family Bible; R. W. Griswold, *Curiosities of American Literature,* p. 25.

16 Freneau to Madison, May 10, 1815, in James Madison Papers, Mss. LIX–

Little was left of a long life of labor; but still more labor was left. Other poems would be written to replace those which had been lost. As long as he could write, nothing else mattered. The "emanation of Deity," weakened but intact, was indestructible. "Burnt out," some small bit of life remained.

---

51. Also W. J. Mills, *Historic Houses of New Jersey,* p. 172; Freneau to Cary, October 26, 1818, in Lea and Febiger Collection.

35. THE OLD—AND THE NEW

FAME AND FAILURE have much in common. Fame, distilled, may yield nothing but a sediment of failure; analyzed, failure could reveal only the essence of fame. Often, their taste upon the tongue is equally bitter.

Philip Freneau had known them both. A new poem, a new book, a new house, they were all phantoms which men pursued, to find at last only their reflections among the debris of a lifetime. No man wholly fails, as no one altogether succeeds, as a poet or a peasant. Like all men who refused to compromise, Freneau looked too closely at the facts, and was confused by their reflections which blurred the facts themselves. He had never quite learned the lesson of alternatives as the law of life.

Freneau was less of a failure than his critics—or he himself—believed. He had lost his way as a poet. Seeking the pathways to liberty, he had wandered into byways that were not always poetic. Impatient of fancy when the fact loomed before him, he did not always find the exacting Muse a sure guide in a time of perpetual crisis. A lover of the classics, Freneau was familiar with the precept of Aristotle that the poet is he who understands and expresses the age he lives in with aesthetic rectitude. But Aristotle also stressed another precept—equally important in the raw state of American culture—that the poet's duty was to instruct as well as elevate the simple, unlettered folk of a new land. Without instruction, men might see but they would not understand; they might feel but they might not also think. Freneau wanted them to understand what they saw; he wanted them to feel—but also to think. When he tried to ignite his countrymen into action, aesthetics were less important than revolution; plain, even vulgar, speech was more important than all the fancy flights of poesy. He stirred the people, with fact more than fancy, with propaganda rather than poetry. He turned from his greatest love to another, more imperious and compulsive; and having forfeited his Eurydice, he remained, like Orpheus, faithful to the end. He never quite found his way again as a poet—as a man he never lost it.

The road from Princeton had been a long one, with many trials and turnings. From the time he had first transcribed Pope's adaptation of Horace, it was a road he had charted for himself, seeking fulfillment and the praise of men along the way. With some premonition of the future he had underscored the words of warning by Pope himself, that "the natural consequence of praise is envy and calumny." At sixteen, in the "Prophet Jonah," he already had noted his disbelief in the durability of praise or of fame.[1]

One thing, perhaps, was durable, or as durable as man himself. Tentatively treating it in "Columbus to Ferdinand," Freneau expanded the theme in "The Pyramids of Egypt," and proclaimed it with utmost confidence in "The Rising Glory of America," all while he was still a student at Princeton. The theme was one which he never forgot, nor permitted anyone else to forget. The central pillar of all his thought, it was the nucleus of all his labors.

> Of liberty and life, sweet liberty!
> Without whose aid the noblest genius dies.[2]

Freneau was no genius, and he had his many moments that were less than noble. Yet in poetry or prose, in songs and ballads, in lines of surpassing loveliness as well as in lines of cheap doggerel and venomous propaganda, he pronounced the poverty of life without liberty. With infinite variations, the theme was always the same. Alternating the playful with the perverse, the trifling with the truculent, the carping with the critical, he passed through all the mazes of doubt and disillusion and stumbled on all impediments of pride and prejudice, pursuing the path he had chosen from the beginning. Wherever it led him, the path he unfailingly sought was the way to freedom.

---

[1] Freneau, *Poems of Freneau* (ed. H. H. Clark), pp. 193–202; also E. G. Ainsworth, Jr., "An American Translator of Ariosto: Philip Freneau," *American Literature*, IV, 4 (January 1933), 393–395; H. H. Clark, "The Literary Influences of Philip Freneau," *Studies in Philology*, XXII, 1 (January 1925), 1–33.

[2] "The Rising Glory of America," in Freneau, *Poems* (Clark), pp. 3–17.

This was his supreme task. For its accomplishment he conceived the need to exalt the spiritual as well as the political life of America. Before him, the beauty of the new world, its flora and fauna, its natural and human resources, were scarcely noticed in the cultural life of its people. No one had observed as keenly or used as freely the allurements of native hills and valleys, of domestic scenes and homely concerns. As much as anyone he had learned and loved the culture that came from abroad, from England in particular, but few others had pleaded as he did for a new orientation of learning, for a culture rooted in the land he lived in, which should be nourished by the genius of its own writers, living their own lives instead of lives long turned to dust. Not only must there be an end to political ties—the cultural umbilical cords must be severed as well. His voice, if often strident, stirred others to reappraise the old and embrace the new. The past had its uses. The future lay in America, not in England.

> Can we never be thought
> To have learning or grace
> Unless it be brought
> From that damnable place?[3]

It was a necessary challenge to writers who, when they did not follow in the footsteps of foreign guides, were immersed in matters for which there were no guides at all. For the most part they were not concerned with this world but with the world beyond. Their fancies roamed the heavens far more than the earth. Freneau was more interested in the world he lived in, in the special corner of it that had few traditions of its own and a wide expanse of opportunity for establishing them. America, a whole new world emerging from the chrysalis of the old, the traditional, the narrow and despotic, was great enough to test the genius and evoke the "learning or grace" of its children. Into his poems of America Freneau put what he saw, what he felt, what he understood of his country, its golden no less than its tinsel wealth— the Indian, as noble savage or ignoble man of nature; the slave, a victim above all others of man's inhumanity to man; the physical, material largesse of America; the spiritual efflorescence of its people; the beauty and the travail of both man and nature; the large sacrifice and the weak indulgence of men grappling for a living; the lofty patriot and the selfish seeker equally caught in the toils of a hard life. These

---

[3] Freneau, *Poems Written and Published during the American Revolutionary War*; Freneau, *The Poems of Philip Freneau* (ed. F. L. Pattee), Vol. i, p. cxi.

were the many motifs of his theme, the strands he wove into the fabric of his work, the variations he played in the soft or raucous music of liberty.[4]

The Revolution was more than a political and military struggle. It was a single skirmish in an endless series of struggles for social and economic justice. Independence was not alone freedom from foreign dominion; no less was it freedom from domestic aristocracies of blood or of wealth. Democracy in the life as well as the laws of a people was a revolutionary goal that transcended all others, for without it independence and freedom were as trees without roots and branches without leaves; they could bear no fruit or only such as was stunted and bitter to the taste. To make democracy a growing, flowering force in America, Freneau had supported or attacked the elements that nourished or destroyed it, using such weapons as he possessed, with such knowledge as he had. Some of his knowledge was inchoate and elemental, intuitive and emotional. The rights of man, not clearly defined, took precedence over the rights of property, only too well defined and always more exacting. Too intense for balanced judgment, he often lost his balance. Too partisan for purity, he was often prejudiced. When he tried to be impartial, he only succeeded in being controversial. Gifted in the use of a saber, he also became adept at brandishing the broadsword. Though he understood the use of the scalpel, there were few occasions for the exercise of finesse.[5]

With Thucydides he believed that in a time of revolution, boldness and energy were to be preferred over any other quality; and he supplied the words which moved others to use them effectively. In his world there was little room for ivory towers or sequestered thought, yet he loved these too. As far back as 1773 he had expressed his views on man's fate, here, as well as hereafter. Familiar with the *Meditations and Contemplations* of James Hervey and the works of other divines, he could quote at will from the Bible. His "House of Night" was a highly original transcription of the words of Scripture. If divinity was a source of power—of the power of the mind above all else—and

---

[4] Pattee's three volumes of Freneau's poems have been frequently referred to above for the poet's many variations on the single theme of liberty and democracy.

[5] H. H. Clark, "What Made Freneau the Father of American Poetry?" *Studies in Philology*, XXVI, 1 (January 1929), 1–22; and Clark, "What Made Freneau the Father of American Prose?" *Transactions of the Wisconsin Academy of Sciences, Arts, and Letters*, XXV (1930), 39–50.

immortality was manifest only in the survival of thought, then Man and God were one. A true religion would make them equally the object of worship and adoration. And in such a worship, the tolerance of political or social inequities was a contempt of deity and a crime against Man. In his poem "On the Abuse of Human Power" Freneau deplores the perversion of all power, however derived, for ends like these. The true stature of Man can be revealed only in the ripening of his intellect, and the innocence of his instincts.[6]

It was no saccharine romanticism that he preached, any more than a stark classicism. Realist as well as romantic, Freneau was a link in American literature between the Colonial enslavement to European thought and the emerging native school of romantic naturalists. In his poems on the Indian as in those on the sea—as in his writings on man himself in all the vicissitudes of circumstance and environment— he was the naturalist more than the romantic, the realist more than the classicist. His was the beginning of a new note and a new method in the treatment of purely American subjects. His portraits of the Indian were more authentic than any others in literature before the work of Cooper. And his seascapes pictured the heaving domain of wind and water with all its grandeur, mystery, and terror, long before they were portrayed by any writer in America—or in England.[7]

Not in these but in his satires, he was influenced by the work of others. Charles Churchill, an English foe of all oppression, having revived political satire in the manner of Dryden and Pope, had sug- gested the form which Freneau then flavored with a purely American idiom. Endlessly revising, he was scrupulous in his efforts to make the final product worthy of his first love, though another had all but dis- placed it. In his ephemeral pieces, even in the doggerel that was more fleeting than those, he tried to adhere to the facts, however weighted they were with vituperation or contumely. He rarely stooped to conquer by falsehood. Charles Adams might have believed otherwise, just as his brother John Quincy and his mother Abigail—indeed as his father,

---

[6] J. F. Jameson, *The American Revolution Considered as a Social Movement,* pp. 17–18. "The Pyramids of Egypt" is reminiscent of Hervey's volume issued by Rivington in New York, in 1774 (Lewis Leary, *That Rascal Freneau,* p. 52; and Freneau, *Poems* [Clark], p. 168).

[7] Freneau's Indian poems (see "The Indian Burying Ground," and "On the Civilization of the Western Aboriginal Country," in Freneau *Poems* [Pattee]) were perhaps too optimistic about the "natural man." He was as romantic as Fenimore Cooper later proved to be. Freneau's sea poems were also infused with pardonable poetic license.

more than they—believed. Few others, even among their own people,
also believed it. Washington had once called him a rascal, not for what
he had said but what he stood for. That, he had made plain enough in
all he had ever written. The trails he blazed in prose and in poetry
were new ones in American literature, followed by greater writers than
he, though his footprints remained untouched by time.[8] In the new
world his trails were needed through thick woods of political and
social injustice; the only compass by which he found—or lost—his
way was his deep sense of duty, his dedicated purpose, despite all
obstacles. As always, he hoped to be of that choice company who

> Above all praise pre-eminence they claim
> Nor leave a sting behind—remorse and shame.[9]

And now, in the winter of a long life, he was still at work, clearing
the same trails, pulling out the weeds which obscured them, planting
new seeds to adorn them. He was contemplating another edition.
Poems were being written, revised, line by line, almost word by word,
while others, old ones saved from the fire, or from the files of *The
True American,* were added to the new ones. The new edition, "correct
and elegant," would include his choicest work from all previous volumes now out of print, as he wrote Dr. Francis on May 14, 1822. The
new volume would be "more complete, interesting and extensive than
any of the former." The new venture was more than a desire for a last
flicker from the candle of fame. It might succeed financially too. Dr.
Francis may have thought so, since he offered to help in its publication.
But few others beside him were willing to see it through. It seemed
certain, as Freneau himself declared in "The City Poet," that a book of
verses could not yet earn a loaf of bread in America. "The sheriff," he
said "only deals in prose." And not in his prose either.[10]

He should know; for on October 14, 1823, Richard Lloyd, the
sheriff of Monmouth County, attached a piece of his remaining land on

---

[8] J. M. Beatty, Jr., "Churchill and Freneau," *American Literature,* II, 2
(May 1930) 127–128; John Quincy Adams, *Writings,* Vol. 1, p. 149. I have
quoted earlier from the writings of John Adams and the letters of Abigail
Adams to show what they felt about Freneau and his work in *The National
Gazette.*

[9] "Winter," Ms. See also Freneau, *Poems* (Pattee), Vol. 3, pp. 78–79;
Freneau, *Poems* (Clark), p. xxvii.

[10] Freneau to Francis, May 14, 1822, in C. F. Heartman, *Unpublished Freneauana,* pp. 20–21; Leary *That Rascal Freneau,* p. 350; "The City Poet," in
The True American, October 16, 1821.

a writ from the Court of Chancery of New Jersey. There was little left to take from him, nor the prospect of anything more, when the proposed edition, not even "deadborn," was never born at all.[11] It was not surprising, perhaps, that prospective readers were hard to find. The old poet might hold them for a moment with some new verses of current interest, lines like those on the great canal or on the theater that had replaced the Park, recently destroyed by fire. His "Recollections of Past Times and Events" would recall to an older generation some memories of the Boston Tea Party, the old, old story of liberty poles, the tragic, thrilling days of the American Revolution. A new generation wanted something new. The editor of *The New York Statesman,* was still pleased with the old man's work, and generously lauded the Revolutionary poems "That often nerved the arm" of the soldier. He even hoped that the "venerable author" would "be blest with frequent visitations of the Muse." The visitations were frequent enough and their results appeared in *The True American* of Trenton as well as *The Fredonian* of New Brunswick. Reprinted in other papers too, they brought in a pittance for the poet's present needs and no subscriptions at all for his new book.[12]

Others were now writing, breaking new paths from old trails, more rewarding ones than the old. Other men, with a message not unlike his own, possessed a deeper insight into modern problems. Less concerned with events of the day, they treated of the timeless, ageless events of which the experience of man is composed and transmuted into the life of a people. Some of these writers were not even Americans, but Americans read them because they felt a kinship in time and eternity with what was written. Byron and Thomas Moore, Campbell and Wordsworth—these men were writing poems that could be read with a relish far beyond the moment of their creation. They possessed an excellence that transcended the fleeting moment and a meaning more profound than that of any mundane occurrence. Freneau had not been able to stem the tide of "learning and grace" that flowed in from abroad. There was increasing evidence, indeed, that he had not altogether failed—yet a new novel by Walter Scott could "set the city [of New York] in an uproar," and "the publishers at Philadelphia,

---

[11] Lewis Leary, "Philip Freneau and Monmouth County," *Monmouth County Historical Association Bulletin,* Vol. 1, No. 2 (July 1948), p. 81. See also Appendix to this volume.

[12] *The New York Statesman,* June 12, 1822.

New York and Boston, by the ears." An old poet and his new editions were lost to readers and publishers alike.[13]

Besides, some American writers were better risks by far. One of the younger luminaries, William Cullen Bryant, impressed the critics with his "Thanatopsis," a poem on death which probed more deeply than Freneau's "House of Night" the ultimate destiny of man. Fitz-Greene Halleck, who admired many of Freneau's "long remembered lines," was now himself admired for the collected edition of his poems. Prose writers were also finding their way in the thorny field of letters. Washington Irving, who had married the daughter of Freneau's old enemy, John Fenno, was already well-known as a writer of delicate humor and sunny fantasy. The honors and acclaim of two continents made it certain that Irving would have no trouble finding a publisher, while James Fenimore Cooper, hailed as the American counterpart of Walter Scott, was winning an enviable place in public esteem with his muscular romances about natives like Natty Bummpo. Cooper knew the sea too, better perhaps than he knew the forest, and a ship as well as a scalp. These men, like Freneau, wrote of the majesty of American woodlands, of American life with its trials and its triumphs, the promise that always outshone its fulfillment. Irving was often busy with the foreign scene as well, while Bryant, always interested in domestic matters, soon added fuel to the fires Freneau had tended so diligently in the past. As editor of *The Evening Post* Bryant could soon carry on the fight which Freneau had waged in the columns of *The National Gazette, The Freemen's Journal,* and *The Time-Piece.* And as Freneau had once supported Jefferson, so Bryant supported a new champion of the people.[14]

Andrew Jackson, the hero of New Orleans, was a tall, thin man, spare of everything but a certain gruff affection for the common people, erect as a Carolina pine and as full of its acrid juices, his jutting jaw not belying an iron will that was not easily deflected from its course. That course had led him from the Hermitage, his home in Tennessee, almost—but not quite—to the highest office of the land. As he had won a battle against Britain at New Orleans, so he was resolved to win another one against Federalism, which threatened Amer-

---

[13] W. E. Leonard, *Byron and Byronism in America,* pp. 20–25.

[14] N. F. Adkins, *Fitz-Greene Halleck,* pp. 87, 179; Allan Nevins, *The Evening Post,* pp. 122–137; Van Wyck Brooks, *The World of Washington Irving,* pp. 254 ff, 275 ff.

ica with a return to power. The National Republicans, as the Federalist forces now called themselves, thwarted the democratic legions of Andrew Jackson and elected their own candidate, John Quincy Adams, instead. Their victory had been accomplished through an electoral legerdemain made possible by constitutional quibbles which placed the final choice with the House of Representatives. One day the constitution would be changed to avoid another such injustice; the people themselves would avoid it the next time Jackson ran for the same office. John Quincy Adams, like his father before him, would never serve a second term. After four years of power, both he and his National Republican Party were swept from office by an aroused electorate that wanted more, not less, democracy in government. The triumph of the leader from Tennessee was the triumph of the common people of America.[15]

Andrew Jackson, the new President of the United States, was not as gently reared nor as well-mannered as the men who had once led the nation along the road of an exalted destiny. The destiny of America was now conceived as the welfare of all its citizens, the poorest and the meanest no less than the wealthy and the well-born. Not only Jackson but other leaders too would teach a larger concept of freedom and lead the way to a greater enjoyment of its benefits. The awakening of America became manifest in literature as well as in politics, while the exploration of new, of higher, values would enlist such romantic craftsmen as John Greenleaf Whittier and Henry Wadsworth Longfellow. Poets like these would soon take their places among the leaders —and the teachers—of the nation, as new champions of democracy, with voices more melodious but with messages fully as strident as those of the poor poet of Monmouth. His voice was almost mute now, rarely reaching beyond an occasional column in *The True American, The New Statesman,* or the small and struggling *Fredonian.*[16]

What he wrote, until he ceased to write at all, was little changed from all that he had already written. The theme was the same; the varia-

[15] A. M. Schlesinger, Jr., *The Age of Jackson,* pp. 6–7, 32–33; Brooks, *Washington Irving,* pp. 399 ff; Gustavus Myers, *The History of American Idealism,* pp. 72–75, quoting from the *Providence Phoenix,* September 5, 1829; R. A. Billington, B. L. Lowenberg, and S. H. Brockunier, *The United States: American Democracy in World Perspective,* Ch. IX.

[16] Brooks, *Washington Irving,* pp. 260 ff; J. D. Hart, *The Popular Book, passim;* Robert E. Spiller, *et al.* (eds.), *Literary History of the United States, 3rd Series,* Vol. 1, pp. 424 ff, and Vol. 2, Ch. 35. See also Rica Brenner, *Twelve American Poets before 1900.*

tions scarcely differed. He voiced the old criticisms of the spurious; he indulged the same hopes for what he conceived as the eternal verities. The truths about man and his works were not susceptible to change by the accidents of time and circumstance. No veneer, however polished, could hide the nature of Nature itself; the simplicity of truth would outlast all error and the exactions of truth would outlast all fraud. Thoughts like these, recurrent as the years, found their way into the poems which Freneau continued to write as he grew old, and older still, from 1816 to 1827.

In a series of poems which he entitled "Elijah, the New England Emigrant," he enlarged on the simple virtues that were needful above all others in the new America, alternating between the playful and humorous and the solemn and satiric; adding still other verses "On the Civilization of the Western Aboriginal Country" where such virtues must prevail. Only by precept and example could men be persuaded to do the right. By force no one was persuaded; and conformity was no sign of conviction. In his "Salutary Maxims" he pleaded for a greater tolerance of new thought, warning especially against the coercion of ideas, however well-meant they might be.

> Would you peace and safety find,
> To live in quiet with mankind,
> Do not quarrel with their notions;
> Let each have his own devotions.[17]

The mellow admonition was unlike the old cry of fierce partisanship, and its permissive quality a long turn from the peremptory passions of another time. Old certainties were diluted by new doubts, the idea of freedom was expanded to include ideas that were once suspect. At seventy-five Philip Freneau was unsure of what was right, what was just. Of old, his own simplicity had made all things simple; now, at the edge of extinction, nothing was clear save the growing complexity of the country that was flexing its muscles and slowly finding its immense strength. America was coming of age.

New voices reached out from cities North and South, competing for attention with poetry that was far different in theme or treatment from anything Freneau could offer. No present crisis had conceived them, no future crisis would destroy them. The baffling genius of Edgar

[17] *The New York Weekly Museum,* October 5, 1816. See also *The True American,* July 20, October 13, November 3, December 1, and December 15, 1821.

Allan Poe, the engaging charm of Edward Coote Pinkney, the appealing verses of Lydia Sigourney, "sweet singer of Hartford"—these were the new singers who disturbed no one, uplifted everyone, and possessed a soothing, almost mystical power grateful to an age of material resurgence. Other voices were also heard, not in poetry but in prose, voices like that of William Gilmore Simms, once a lawyer and now a writer, who had turned from fact to fiction, from reality to illusion, and acquired in the process a host of readers who found in his novels the romantic release so often absent in their own lives. More concerned with realism than Simms, another writer of fiction, Timothy Flint, devoted his novels to the pioneers of the Ohio Valley, to their fantastic struggles with a hostile environment. Among them, such writers spanned the whole gamut of the American dream; they appealed to a wider public than poetry—even the finest poetry—could ever win. Freneau was all but forgotten; but even Bryant, the first edition of whose poems included examples of his best work—"Thanatopsis" and "To a Waterfowl"—sold so poorly that after five years the profits from publication were less than fifteen dollars. Freneau, as Mathew Carey, his publisher, learned too late, did even worse. It took nine years to dispose of an edition of one thousand copies. In this case there was no profit whatever. The Muse, so often an exacting mistress for a poet, to a publisher was little more than a faithless hussy. The taste of the people was improving, but the arbiters of taste were few and rarely heeded.[18]

In the field of polite letters, the guardian of good taste was *The North American Review,* though only the charmed circle of the learned was likely to profit from its perceptive articles. In an era of industrial expansion the common people were busy cultivating more practical arts than literature, leaving to the poets, novelists, artists, and scientists the more leisurely task of searching for higher standards in America. Naturalists like John J. Audubon and Constantine Rafinesque, scientists like J. D. Dana and Benjamin Silliman, inventors like Cyrus H. McCormick were contributing to a knowledge that might one day raise those standards. The knowledge they accumulated should be more than the private preserve of a few; it should be accessible to all, according to James Smithson, an Englishman, who left his fortune to the

[18] Brooks, *Washington Irving,* pp. 275–287; V. L. Parrington, *Main Currents of American Thought: The Colonial Mind,* pp. 123 ff; R. E. Riegel, *Young America, 1830–1840,* pp. 400–404.

people of America "for the increase and diffusion of knowledge among men." It was a magnificent gesture of friendship for a country that had few provisions for the diffusion of knowledge among the poor. They were already demanding that the concept of freedom include the freedom of education. Workers, learning slowly, were proclaiming "that until the means of equal instruction shall be equally secured to all, liberty is but an unmeaning word, and equality an empty shadow."[19]

Philip Freneau could contemplate with some measure of satisfaction the slow lifting of the shadow from the face of America. He had always demanded a better, simpler life for the masses, and this they could achieve only through a deeper understanding of the world they lived in. Education was the answer to many problems of democracy; through education men would learn how to maintain and enhance the blessings of liberty. In New York, in New England, in the North, and in the South, a few first steps toward a free education for all had been taken. The higher learning was to some extent provided in many states to a select few. Academies were multiplying—institutes of art, science, and music—where the roots and branches of a native culture were lovingly tended and encouraged as Philip Freneau had pleaded so long that they might be. Newspapers, which for him were the best means of spreading the gospel of democracy, increased as printing was simplified from type to plate. In 1800 there were but two hundred of them in all the nation; by 1830 their number had grown to a fantastic thousand or more, which carried the whole world to the doorsteps of simple, common men from one end of America to the other. Not all of them practice what Freneau had preached, nor did they all provide the learning he had brought to the common folk from his first days at Princeton to the very present in countless poems and essays. The sense of urgency had passed, perhaps, and the recurring crises of other years as well, when he had been lashed by the whip of circumstance.[20]

Like many others before him, he had failed more often than not to withstand the lash of circumstance, but if so, unlike Candide, he had

<hr/>

[19] *North American Review*, May 1817 and July 1818. The Smithsonian Institution, founded by an English chemist, James Smithson, was approved by Act of Congress on August 10, 1846. See *Dictionary of National Biography,* XVIII, 580, and *Encyclopoedia Britannica* (11th ed.), XXV, 273–275.

[20] Brooks, *Washington Irving,* pp. 287 ff; C. R. Fish, *The Rise of the Common Man,* pp. 212–217, 239–242; A. M. Schlesinger, *New Viewpoints in American History,* pp. 58–64; F. J. Turner, *The Frontier in American History,* pp. 199–227.

discovered some solace in what he had always professed to disbelieve.
Men might fail but God,

> Who life through all creation spread,
> Nor left the meanest atom dead,[21]

never failed. In spite of everything life persists; and even the atom
may hold in its nucleus an abundant energy of beauty and of truth. In
the end, he believed,

> . . . conscious goodness soars above the clod,
> And life, well spent, secures the path to God.[22]

There was some proof that the world was moving on and upward.
Freneau's old dreams might yet come true. Even now, an American
utopia was making at New Harmony, Indiana. New promises were
emerging in the poet's homeland, and the sun was rising in the political
heavens too. In the surge of the great democratic victory of 1828, the
highest hopes of the people might find new refreshment. If any of
them came true, the labors of Philip Freneau would be justified.

The evidence for too great an optimism was far from clear. Illusions
persisted and the truth itself was not always to be trusted, as Freneau
had so many times averred—nowhere more strongly than in "The
Brook of the Valley."

> All pacific as you seem;
> Such a gay elysian stream;
> Were you always thus at rest
> How the valley would be blest.
>
> Emblem thou of restless man;
> What a sketch of nature's plan!
> Now at peace, and now at war,
> Now you murmur, now you roar;
>
> Muddy now, and limpid next,
> Now with icy shackles vext—
> What a likeness here we find!
> What a picture of mankind![23]

[21] "Reflections on the Constitution and Frame of Nature," in Freneau,
Poems (Clark), p. 414.

[22] "Philosophical Fortitude," in *The Fredonian*, July 18, 1822; N. E. Adkins,
Philip Freneau and the Cosmic Enigma, p. 77.

[23] "On the Universality and Other Attributes of the God of Nature," in
Freneau, *Poems* (Clark), p. 422.

But faith in the perfectability of man had never quite deserted the old man whose entire life had been built upon that foundation despite his many disillusionments. In his last years his faith sustained him that in this, the best of all possible worlds, kindness and compassion, above all love, would prevail through the intercession of the God of Nature.

> All that he did he first approved,
> He all things into *being* loved.[24]

Freneau was at the sunset, almost at the twilight, of his life. The world itself often appeared to him to be hovering in the shadows of the twilight—but America was at a new and lovely dawn. The old quibbles about freedom and democracy were finished. The double-talk of Federalists, of Republicans, of Democratic-Republicans, of National Republicans, all this was done. America was in the hands of the common man at last.

The world must now reckon with the people. The trimmers, the traders, the self-seekers, the enemies of democracy everywhere should take heed. "The game is over," the poet admonished them, "you must pay respect and honour to America."[25]

[24] "Brook of the Valley," in *ibid.*, p. 417.

[25] Philip Freneau wrote these words on the half title page of the volume of *Poems Written between the Years 1768 and 1794* which he presented to Philip Leadbeater Freneau. This young man, the son of Freneau's daughter Agnes Leadbeater, was adopted by Freneau. He changed his name from Philip Freneau Leadbeater to Philip Leadbeater Freneau. He died in 1880, and his copy of *Poems* is now in the Freneau Collection (Princeton) (Leary, *That Rascal Freneau*, pp. 147–148). Freneau often made notes and comments on the flyleaves and other pages of his books, a custom which he began in his youth and continued almost to the end of his life.

36. THE BOOK IS FINISHED

A FEW YEARS still remained to the old man of Monmouth. He wrote only a little more, dredging his memories of things past for the few remaining nuggets among them.[1] As his visits to New York were reduced in length and number, his walks about his native and familiar countryside increased. He was the same great walker as of old, though his pace was slower, and his thin frame stooped more often with fatigue like a pine with the wind. He missed the company of his friends in the city, especially the "jolly and learned Dr. Francis"—a description which Philip Hone, the recent mayor of New York, confided to his diary, but equally acceptable to the poet who treasured his friendship.[2] The long journey to see him and the others had become more exhausting with the passage of time, and now, increasingly, he was seen trudging slowly along the road to Freehold, two miles distant, his thin shanks, a bit bow-legged, as usual tightly enclosed in cheap cotton hose and his bony feet as always encased in old buckled shoes. He had no errands in town, but then neither did he have any on the hilltops that he climbed, ever so haltingly, to look out over the lovely landscape visible for miles to the naked eye.[3]

With the help of the newly installed telescope on Pine Hill, the highest point in all Monmouth, he could survey the fields and farm-lands which lay like an open book before him, and on crystalline days of an early fall, there, on the far horizon, he even discerned the dim

[1] Freneau, *The Last Poems of Philip Freneau.*

[2] Philip Hone, *Diary*, Vol. 2, p. 210. For conditions in New York see Axel Leonhard Klinckowström, *Baron Klinckowström's America, 1818–1820*, p. 14.

[3] W. S. Horner, *This Old Monmouth of Ours*, pp. 166 ff.

outlines of Princeton College, where first he dreamt of fame and first knew the fellowship of men who would one day achieve it. How far away, how long ago, they all seemed now. The past was irrevocable, forever gone, and the future—the future he had once foretold in "The Rising Glory of America"—was looming also on the horizon. The country was expanding—as he had prophesied it would—

> . . . from th' Atlantic to Pacific shores.

Through the wilderness of virgin forests, over mountains reaching to the open sky, across swift-flowing waters and treacherous shoals, the pioneers would push and force a pathway with

> . . . unnumbered boats and merchandise and men.[4]

From the Northwest Territory and the fertile lands of the Mississippi, from vast domains north of the Ohio and west of the Great Lakes, new states were already blossoming—Ohio and Michigan, Illinois and Indiana and Wisconsin. Others were blooming from the seeds of the Louisiana Purchase—Missouri and Arkansas and Iowa, the Dakotas and Nebraska, Oklahoma and Kansas, Louisiana, a state in its own right. Men were migrating, singly, in families, in companies, and in hordes, by covered wagon and by barge, on horseback and on foot, loaded with all their worldly (and spiritual) goods, and all their heavenly hopes, moving north and west over Indian trails and by portage paths, across inland rivers, through Cumberland Gap, over the great Kanawha, along La Belle Riviere, the beautiful Ohio, which opened up its arms to them like a passionate lover, strong and eager to sport with them for a full thousand miles of travail.[5]

It was all as he had foreseen it. They came from Virginia by Braddock's Road, and from Philadelphia by Forbe's Road. They passed through New York by the Genesee Road, meeting at Redstone on the Monongahela, at Kittanning on the Allegheny, and at Pittsburgh near the forks. Some travelled by steamboat, while many braved the tumbling waters in pirogues and batteaux, in keelboats and arks, hacking their route overland from Pittsburgh to Steubenville, from Zanesville to Columbus, or from the south across Kentucky, all of them bearing

---

[4] "Ode Written on a Remote Perspective View of Princeton College, etc.," in *The Fredonian,* October 31, 1822; R. Kirk, "Freneau's View of Princeton," *The Rutgers' University Library Journal,* III, 1 (December 1939), 20. See also Lewis Leary, *That Rascal Freneau,* p. 101.

[5] H. U. Faulkner, *American Political and Social History,* pp. 231 ff.

their precious freight of civilization to the outposts of America, to the Northwest and the Southwest, to a wild and glorious country, waiting only to be tamed and loved and cherished. A great hunger for the land impelled men farther and farther from the known, the accustomed life of the East, from the cities where life was hard for those who could not bear confinement in dark factories or coax a living from recalcitrant soil. They were moving, always moving, "from th' Atlantic to Pacific shores."[6]

As much as the hunger for land, more compelling than the distaste for industry, for reasons that were perhaps far less tangible but equally alluring, they swarmed from the cities. They had lived too long in an aura of independence; they had hoped too much to achieve it for themselves as well as for their country. The Revolution, though distant in time, was close enough in memory, but the fruits of liberty were still beyond their grasp. They might yet win some of these fruits for themselves and for those who followed them in this fantastic trek into the unknown. Death and disease, famine and thirst, heartbreak and failure would attend their great adventure, yet the spirit that had won two wars against overwhelming odds would win this one too. Years would pass before the dreams of a better democracy were realized in territories where laws were lacking and the knowledge of justice must grow from seeds not yet planted in the ground. Tragic disillusions would stay the march of progress, but the march would persist as it persisted even now, when it seemed as if all America was "breaking up" in the great exodus to the promised land. The call of the West to the American spirit of independence was powerful and irresistible. And Americans answered the call, as others would answer it also, when steel rails were placed upon the earth and canals weaved their way through it to bind the nation closer together. The rainbow, many-colored and seductive, led them to the far future of a prosperous country as Philip Freneau had foreseen and foretold.[7]

Not only Americans, but people from other lands would wend their

[6] "Ode Written on a Remote Perspective View of Princeton College, etc.," in *The Fredonian*, October 31, 1822; Kirk, "Freneau's View of Princeton," p. 20; Leary, *That Rascal Freneau*, p. 101.

[7] *Ibid.*, and R. A. Billington, B. L. Lowenberg, and S. H. Brockunier, *The United States: American Democracy in World Perspective*, pp. 130–135; E. C. Kirkland, *A History of American Economic Life*, pp. 57–61, 130, 174, 176, 218–219.

way also to the end of that rainbow—immigrants from Ireland and Britain, from Germany and Sweden, who would seek in America, in the virgin lands of the frontier that were rich with hope and full of promise, another citadel of liberty and democracy. Like Goethe, they too saluted the new world, and in their hearts as on their lips they believed: *"Amerika, du hast es besser."* The old, decrepit bastions of privilege and injustice were still standing in Europe; in America it would be better. The turmoil of the old world was behind them, and they, like the men who escaped the turmoil of America, were ready for any danger, any hardship, any trial, to savor at last the heady wine of equality, and breathe full-lunged the blessed air of democracy. For such men Freneau had a message.

> If honor's ardor in the bosom glows,
> Nor selfish motives on yourselves impose,
> Go, and convince the natives of the West
> That Christian morals are the first and best.[8]

The message was a timely one for all who suffered the wind and weather to penetrate the wilderness. In the new lands they would need something more than labor and courage and wisdom to build a better life for themselves. For survival they must observe the morals of a brotherhood of man, an ethic and conduct without which the savage would destroy them and all their dreams, according to the law of the jungle.

A small sign of such an ethic was evident in the cities they left behind them. The victors of 1828, the people who had chosen Jackson for their President, were democrats in a way that Jefferson and Madison had not imagined as adequate for a democracy. They were neither gentlemen of learning nor of property—few of them were *aristoi*, whom Jefferson once had considered the natural rulers of America. Their manners, like those of Jackson himself, left much to be desired. Like him, they could chew tobacco and spit the juice with rare precision. They had a vast contempt for mere wealth or station, and believed more in man than in manners. The age of Jackson was their age too, for did he not proclaim that "There is no man however low or

[8] Freneau, *Last Poems*, p. 71; see also Van Wyck Brooks, *The World of Washington Irving*, p. 399. On the Jacksonian era of Democratic reform, see A. M. Schlesinger, Jr., *The Age of Jackson;* Billington, *et al.*, *The United States*, pp. 178 ff.

however high he may be born," who could not aspire to the highest offices in the land?[9] Equality now had a new meaning, one that gave an added meaning to liberty itself. There was a high and hopeful note in American life, yet its tone was not always clear nor its call altogether pure. Often it sounded with a resonance more of brass than of bronze. Strangers noticed its cacophonous clamor and were critical of its offensive irritations.

Frances Trollope heard it in her travels through the states. The short, plump, ruddy-faced lady who had come to America to recoup her fortunes was sorely distressed by the manners of Americans while aware of the hustle of enterprise to which those manners were somehow related. Her friend Fanny Wright found many things to criticize, not least among them the bondage of the black man in a country which boasted so much about freedom. Another foreign observer was more optimistic. Alexis de Tocqueville, studying the new democracy with deep tolerance and profound understanding, was impressed by "the general equality of conditions" and applauded the extended practice of self-government. Not the rich and well-born, the powerful planters and the great merchants, but the poor and humble were the wielders of power in America—and also, perhaps, the cause of many of its failures. The complexion of American society was colored by the inexorable changes in the social and economic life of America. Jefferson had been forced to compromise with many of the ideas—if not the ideals —of the Federalists. Madison, Monroe too, had done the same. Politics were forced into the Procrustean bed of economics. Morals metamorphosed—but they retained the nucleus of "honor's ardor," or they perished. And all else with them. Nothing was permanent in the life of a man or a country. Compromise was the condition of survival. The Founding Fathers had learned that this was so, and the greatest of them all, Jefferson himself, understood its inevitability. "We are all Federalists and all Republicans," he had declared.[10]

The old order was passing. The agrarian economy, despite the thriving plantations of the South and the opening up of new lands in

---

[9] Gustavus Myers, *History of American Idealism*, pp. 74–75, quoting from the *Providence Phoenix*, September 5, 1829; Frances Trollope, *Domestic Manners of the Americans*, pp. xx, xxxix, 16–30, 275.

[10] First Inaugural, March 4, 1801, in Thomas Jefferson, *Writings* (ed. P. L. Ford), Vol. 8, p. 3. See also Allan Nevins, *The Evening Post*, p. 216; Alexis de Tocqueville, *Democracy in America*, pp. 14, 180–202; Harriet Martineau, *Society in American, passim.*

the West, was falling under the ever-lengthening shadow of industrial capitalism. There were few beggars, a small unemployed class, and no large body of paupers in America before this. Under the law of 1820, not many were able to afford even the easy terms for the purchase of new lands; there were some, at least, who could buy the required minimum of eighty acres which that law prescribed, and the speculators rather than the people were the real beneficiaries of the government's largesse. The craftsman, never affluent, who received more pride than profit from his handiwork, was doomed to penury as the increase of machine production and a competitive market relentlessly deprived him of a living. The pressures of industrial and financial power were growing steadily more burdensome, while in the open spaces of America the same pressures became more urgent as that same power reached out to encompass and control even the produce of the soil. In the cities a feeble attempt to cope with new and bewildering conflicts was made by the first workingmen's party organized in 1828 by the Mechanic's Union of Trade Associations, but the efforts of confused and simple men to achieve political influence and avert industrial domination could never impede the stride of the seven-league boots of business.[11]

The spirit of independence, strong on the land, was not altogether subdued in the cities either. Liberty was something more than political freedom; men were learning that it also meant economic freedom. Exploitation on the land or in the factory might perhaps be controlled. The power of finance could be reduced if not entirely eliminated. Democracy could be implemented by a few practical ideals to bring it closer to the needs of the common man.

The victory of Andrew Jackson augured well for ideals like these, as his disciples flocked to Washington to witness the triumph of their hero who believed that "A moneyed aristocracy [was] dangerous to the liberties of the country."[12] The mass of people who worshiped him also believed it. They might disturb the serenity of Justice Story of the Supreme Court who feared the impending "reign of King Mob,"[13]

[11] Schlesinger, Jr., *The Age of Jackson*, pp. 32–33.

[12] *Ibid.*, pp. 6 ff. See also Billington, *et al., The United States*, pp. 155–165. Late in his life, Madison wrote that "our country, if it does justice to itself, will be the Officina Libertatis [the workshop of liberty] to the civilized world" (see "The Idea of America," by Adrienne Koch, in the *Yale Review*, XLI, 2 [December 1951], 222–232). This thought was basic to all Freneau's writings.

[13] Schlesinger, Jr., *The Age of Jackson*, p. 6.

but the Supreme Court itself was the greatest bulwark against that mob. Daniel Webster and Henry Clay, with ambitions of their own to rise to rulership of the country, looked with grave misgivings on the uncouth hordes who acted as if *they* were the new rulers of America, while John Randolph of Roanoke considered them as the poorest material for any kind of rule. "Where," he sadly inquired, "could we find leaders of a revolution now?"[14] He did not understand that *this* was the new revolution, enlarging the first one against Britain, expanding the second one against the Federalists. There would be still others, beyond the understanding of men perhaps more ambitious than Clay and Webster and Randolph.

A new one was already hatching. John C. Calhoun, the Vice-President of the United States, was threatening the most disruptive tactics of all against the new ideals of the Jackson Administration. Fearing that the measures of the new democracy would jeopardize the slave economy of his beloved southland, Calhoun was ready to impose on America his own ideal of nullification—if necessary, even of secession. Small conspiracies were fomenting, destined to grow, in time and dimension, into full-blown revolts against the growing idea—and ideal —of democracy. The road to freedom was beset by many hurdles, troubled by many obstacles, and the goal was not the same for all men. Liberty was a virtue—but democracy could be a vice. Equality was a catch-word, good for one revolution, but finally the bane of all revolutions. The poor, the enslaved, were the handiwork of God, who might have other notions of equality. And democracy was surely not practiced in heaven.[15]

Such thoughts, if they circulated in the mind of Philip Freneau, were scarcely clarified on his long walks over the rolling countryside of Monmouth. Neither, indeed, were they quite germane to the problems that never ceased to vex him as they vexed also his countrymen. For them, as for himself, he offered a word of wisdom if not of solace. Americans, despite everything, must remain

Patriots still, though cursed with poverty.[16]

Only so, with the general welfare as a guide, would America justify the hopes of men everywhere. Freneau had no other solution to the troubles of his country. In trial and error it might one day ascend to

[14] *Ibid.,* p. 7.
[15] Billington, *et al., The United States,* pp. 163–164.
[16] "Stanzas Written on a Military Ground," in Freneau, *Last Poems,* p. 8.

the high plateau of a true democracy, with the patriots—of whatever class—to lead the way. This was the meaning of a people's, of a man's, life, if it had a meaning. Beyond it, no one could say, for no one knew.

> The fools on life, the wise, on death depend,
> Waiting, with sweet reverse, their toils to end;
> Quit the vain scene, where few have found or know
> The first grand purpose—*why we live below*.[17]

It was a question which he underscored, the most futile question of all, the only one remaining to a man who was nearly done with all the others.

He was close to the end of his labors. He had outlived most of his friends, and his enemies, too. Of America's giants, John Adams and Thomas Jefferson were gone, one outliving the other by only a few moments in 1826. Freneau had nothing to say of Adams' death, but of Jefferson he had said that

> . . . he merits all
> The fame, that men immortal call,
> The public grief, a nation's tears—[18]

As the dusk deepened his humility expanded. In the approaching hour of dissolution he was agreeable to wait for the appointed hour, free from all further contention.

> My little is enough for me,
> Content with mediocrity.[19]

Such humility was more than a metaphysical concept borrowed from the Greek poet Bion or derived from his reading in Lucretius.

He had been reduced to labors not common to poets in that time, not usual for old men in any time. The neighbors may have cast a furtive eye at the ancient relic who worked on the public roads in payment of his taxes. These were few, fortunately, since so little was left of his sandy patrimony. There were other demands upon him more pressing than the taxes, and to meet them in a most inadequate way, he must earn what he could as an itinerant tinker or odd-job man for his neighbors in Monmouth. Had not his ancestors, the Huguenot

[17] From "Philosophical Fortitude," in *ibid.,* pp. 65–66.
[18] "Lines on a Transient View of Monticello," in *ibid.,* p. 99.
[19] "Fragment of Bion," in *ibid.,* pp. 103, 107. Dr. Francis said of Freneau, "He was free of all ambitious display; his habitual expression was pensive," in E. A. and G. L. Duyckinck, *Cyclopoedia of American Literature,* Vol. 1, p. 333.

refugees in London, been "poor weavers" who had followed their fortunes to America, only to find them—in bankruptcy? No wonder that the gray-haired poet, who rarely looked like one even in his better days, was now considered a feckless eccentric without a penny in his pocket and only some useless ideas in his head. Some people would greet him with an air of ill-concealed superiority, others with a hearty condescension.[20]

Only the older men of Monmouth remembered the tenacious fighter for freedom, the writer of the poems of the Revolution, and of its songs and ballads. The young bloods were more concerned with the future than the past and knew little or nothing about the shabby road mender and beggarly tinker who seemed also to find the time and the energy for the long walks to Freehold, two miles away. It was truly strange that so old a man would venture on the open road, but stranger still perhaps that he never missed a visit to the town library and the country store for a bit of small talk with some ancient cronies. These interludes, less strange than necessary for one who savored life as he waited for its "sweet reverse," were never complete without a stop, however brief, at the inn for a stimulating glass or two before beginning the long trek home. Sometimes the stop was not so brief, when, his tongue loosened and his memories refreshed, he regaled the old-timers with remembrances of times past, or "descanted on Italian poetry and the piscatory eclogues of Sannazarius." At such times all "traces of care" vanished from the deeply-lined face, and for a moment the weight of eighty years was lifted from the bent back of Philip Freneau.[21]

His neighbors, the younger men especially, were not pleased by these antics of an octogenarian. Steady, substantial citizens like Captain Haddock Whitlock and Asbury Fountain "had no very high opinion to express of him as a man." They were doubtless informed of the loss of his land, bit by bit, under the relentless pressure of mortgage foreclosures and forced sales. They knew all about the lawsuits

[20] Middletown Township, Town Book, Records from 1699 to November 15, 1823, Mss., March 16, 1822; Leary, *That Rascal Freneau*, p. 362; Horner, *This Old Monmouth of Ours*, pp. 166 ff; Lewis Leary, "Philip Freneau and Monmouth County," *Monmouth County Historical Association Bulletin*, Vol. 1, No. 2 (July 1948), p. 63 n.

[21] J. W. Francis, *Old New York*, p. xlv; see also Horner, *This Old Monmouth of Ours*, p. 166. Freneau owned a share in the Freehold Library Company: receipt of September 30, 1830, in Freneau Collection (Rutgers).

brought against him by still other neighbors, by thrifty and honored men like John Van Pelt and Samuel Ellison, by Joseph Hendrickson and Daniel Ellis against the improvident old man for trifling sums which he could not pay, and only paid in part when the constable was hard upon his heels. These men knew almost nothing about him as a poet—and poetry was but meager nourishment for stalwart, honest men whose parched souls thirsted after the good, the quenching things of life. The failure of a man like Philip Freneau, who possessed none of man's goods and was skeptical of God's, was no surprise to the Whitlocks and the Fountains who labored with equal energy in the vineyard of the Lord as in their own. Mr. Fountain, diligent beyond most men, was destined to become one of the prominent pillars of Monmouth society—two of them indeed—the president of the Farmers and Merchants Bank of Middletown Point as well as president of the Monmouth County Bible Society. Such exemplars of the good life were surely more inspiring than the old reprobate, a poet and a pauper, who carried his conscience like a cross—to the tavern not to Golgotha.[22]

If further proof of his failure was needed, he hastened to supply it when his harassed family was compelled to move once more, this time to an old, abandoned farm-house owned by Denise, the alert and practical brother of the long-suffering Eleanor. At least they had a roof over their heads, while Samuel, another brother, deeded her still another piece of property left by their father. This, too, soon went the way of all property, of all the poet's patrimony. There were too many mouths to feed. The Hammells now also lived with the Freneaus, and the grandchildren had come as often as the seasons. Sarah, the baby, was born in the old house soon after they moved in.[23]

Others died there, or in homes of their own, while Philip, surviving them all, carefully noted the events in his Bible. Edward Leadbeater, his son-in-law, was dead; Margaret Hunn, his youngest sister, and John, her husband, were gone; Mary Freneau, the oldest sister, had passed on. The day, the year, of their passing was recorded. And time was pressing on him too. Soon, the record would be completed, the book would be finished.

[22] Horner, *This Old Monmouth of Ours,* p. 166; see also F. Ellis, *History of Monmouth County,* pp. 363, 839–346.

[23] Philip M. Marsh and M. Ellis, "Freneau's Last Home," *Proceedings of New Jersey Historical Society,* XVII, 2 (April 1939), 108–111; see also Freneau Family Bible. Sarah was born in Freehold, October 26, 1826.

He had no strength left for mending the roadways. A man of eighty did not wander about searching for odd jobs at tinkering. Even the writing of a poem was a chore he seldom accomplished. The last one of all that he wrote, the poem he called "Winter," might have furnished Captain Whitlock and Mr. Fountain the final testimony of his total depravity:

> Happy with wine we may indulge an hour;
> The noblest beverage of the mildest power.
> Happy, with Love, to solace every care,
> Happy with sense and wit an hour to share;
> These to the mind a thousand pleasures bring
> And give to winter's frosts the smiles of spring,
> Above all praise pre-eminence they claim
> Nor leave a sting behind—remorse and shame.[24]

In the winter of his discontent he had recourse to few others besides Bacchus, the god of his fathers, for what else was left to an exhausted body and a depressed spirit that could contend no more? In all the corridors of time such sentiments as these echoed in many lonely or forsaken souls, of poets no less than of ordinary men.[25]

Freneau's abundant reading of the past, his deep delving into the enigmas of the future, had yielded only this—life was the greatest enigma of all and if it had a meaning each one must seek it out for himself. The vision of mortality would blur that meaning like a breath upon a window pane, yet man's fate and man's hope, however pathetic or even tragic, would put off the ultimate surrender of his courage and his conscience. The eternal longing for some meaning beyond illusion and some life beyond breath, would persist as an emanation of the spirit long after it had ceased to be. And it was Freneau's belief, always ripening in the cocoon of his skepticism, that all men harbored their inmost dreams, their nuclear visions, and the true freedom of thought and action in their desperate need for immortality.

Freneau had nothing more to say to those who scoffed or sneered, or slandered him. Indifferent to their disapproval he trudged the long road to the village, even now, even in the winter, when the frost was already in the air and on the ground. The tavern was surely more cheerful than the hearthstone, and a bibulous comrade more friendly than the silence of Eleanor or the noise of the children. Did his

---

[24] Freneau, "Winter," Ms.
[25] See Charles Pierre Baudelaire, *Les Fleurs du Mal,* xciv, xcv.

neighbors consider him a stubborn, defiant old fool, absurd, even grotesque, in his outmoded, tight-fitting breeches and comic cocked hat? Obviously he was lacking in any good sense to court disaster on a cold winter's day. And for what? He spent so much of his time—the little time that was left to him—at the inn, mulling over the dead past and drinking more than was good for him. When the weather was not too bad, the ancient relic would walk abroad, walk alone, though sometimes his steps were unsteady. But sometimes the wind blew up sharp and biting, or the snow fell, soft and melting. Let them talk and censure him. He was immune to his neighbor's opinions. He had no shame, no remorse, for anything in his whole, long life.

A little shame he did have when he was compelled to apply for a pension before the Judges of the Inferior Court of Common Pleas on August 1, 1832. At the end of his life he had also reached the end of all his resources. There were no remaining tracts to sell, no roads to mend, no odd jobs to do, no poems to write. Nothing was left but the doubtful promise of a grateful government to all who had fought its battle for liberty. The old suppliant for this final charity, still vaguely remembered as the poet of the American Revolution, had received nothing for his services but the bullet he still carried in his body, the sole souvenir of a lifetime of labor for freedom and democracy.[26]

The records of his military service, so long after the event, were difficult to find, and the affidavits of surviving friends were scarcely sufficient to start the cumbersome machinery of justice to hunt them out. Slowly, too slowly for his immense need, the wheels began to turn, the wheels that must grind out the paltry sum of thirty-five dollars *a year* for one man's service to his country. And when it reached him at last, he was no longer there to receive it. His widow and the children who survived him would receive it instead, to brighten the "destitute circumstances" of their remaining years.[27]

Philip Freneau received nothing. Waiting from midsummer to midwinter, he turned for comfort to the one place where he always seemed to find it, at the village library where he was still a member, and in the tavern where he was still welcome. "The noblest beverage," he had written in his final poem, could "solace every care" and bring "to winter's frosts the smiles of spring." Good talk, and good drink—

[26] Freneau's application, affidavits, *etc.,* General Administration Services, Case #23069: Pension Records of Philip Freneau, Mss.

[27] The pension, in the sum of $35.00 a year, was finally paid under the Act of February 2, 1848, Certificate 2880.

these were always on tap at the tavern, though a man might tarry too long in such a place.

> Yes, there are joys that may all storm defy,
> The chill of nature, and a frozen sky.[28]

The beguiling warmth of an open fire, the close companionship of other men, old and lonely as he was, shut out the darkening winter day and the heavy shadows of his shame. Here was peace, the peace that only age conferred, and that made indolence a virtue. One could forget—or ignore—the time that also passed, while the fading sun sank lower in the heavens and the last rays of light reached almost to the horizon.

It was the close of such a day, almost the shortest day of the year, December 18, 1832. The time had come to bestir himself, for there were long, dark, frosty miles to cover before he would reach his home. And there was still one stop to make, a brief stop, for the usual exchange of greetings with his friends of the country store, Davis and Lippincott.

At long last he begins his journey in the gathering dusk to the farm-house, which now seems so far, far away.[29] The sun has already set. The dark deepens. The wind blows gently, slowly gathering strength as it veers to the north. The vagrant rays of extinguished light are gone as the snow begins to fall, silently at first, more noisily in a little while. The wind rises, it whips and eddies about the old man's feet as he plods on steadily, doggedly, following the roadway he has walked so many times before and knows so well. He is not sure this time as the snow falls faster, thickens, and the wind blows harder, colder. The barren fields, the stubby stalks, the ice-encrusted roads, all are hidden from his sight. He is confused, he is weary, stumbling now, unsteady, frozen, lost. A field, a roadway, a mud-filled bog—they are all the same to him, all white and clean, soft, alluring as clean linen to a tired and weary body. It is not home—but now there is no other home for him.[30]

[28] Freneau, "Winter," Ms., second and third verses.

[29] *New Jersey State Gazette,* December 19, 1832; *The Monmouth Democrat,* August 1, 1935, account by D. V. Perrine.

[30] The blizzard occurred during the evening and night of December 18, 1832. See *The Monmouth Inquirer,* December 16, 1880, account by John Connolly; also E. F. De Lancey, "Philip Freneau: The Huguenot Patriot," *Proceedings of the Huguenot Society of America,* II, 2 (1891). Perhaps the best summation of the poet's life was that of Moses Coit Tyler, who wrote that he "was

If he cried for help, no one could hear him. If he needed shelter, where had he ever found it before? He wanted only to rest, to lie down, to sleep. He needed nothing more than this, to be lulled to everlasting peace by the raging wind and the blinding blizzard.

Not until the next morning did they find him. And when they buried him near the homestead at Mount Pleasant, no son of his was there to make any record of the event. The entry in the family Bible by his daughter prosaically informed posterity that the poet was buried on the 21st of December 1832 "by his own particular request in the Locust Grove very near his beloved mother."[31]

His book of plagues and vexations was finally finished.

---

the satirical gladiator on behalf of the Revolution" (Tyler, *The Literary History of the American Revolution,* Vol. 1, p. 172).

[31] Freneau Family Bible. The grave is on U.S. 9, at the southern end of the community once called Middletown Point and now known as Freneau. Eleanor, also buried there, died on September 1, 1851.

APPENDIX A

Records of Deeds and Mortgages in
Hall of Records, Monmouth County, Freehold, New Jersey

Agnes Kerney, Philip Freneau and Eleanor his ux : Deed dated 8–1–1815
to   : Rec. 8–10–1815
Samuel Ellison   : Book Y Page 317

CONVEYS

7 Acres Easterly side of Highway from Monmouth County
House to Middletown

- - - - - - - -

Same Grantors : Deed date 8–1–1815
to   : Rec. 1–23–1816
Titus Schanck : Book Y Page 520

CONVEYS

6 Acres Freehold Twp.

Same Grantors   : Deed date 8–1–15
to   : Rec. 3–12–1816
Hendrick Van Brunt Schenck : Book Y Page 583

CONVEYS

12.93 Acres Freehold Twp.

- - - - - - - -

Same Grantors : Deed dated 5–14–1812
to   : Rec. 6–4–1814
Samuel Ellison : Book X Page 251

CONVEYS

2.28 Acres Freehold Twp.

Same Grantors   : Deed dated 8–1–15
to   : Rec. 5–25–1826
Hartshorne Van Mater : Book L2 Pg. 412

CONVEYS

1.62 Acres Freehold Twp.

- - - - - - - -

John Neaper   : Letters of Atty
        to   : Dated 1–16–1775
Agnes Kearny[1]   : Rec. 9–25–1808
Witness by Philip Freneau : Bk R Page 451

Philip Freneau   : Mtg. dated 8–29–05
        to   : Rec. 8–26–07
Thomas Gardner   : Bk E Pg. 27
                  : Amt. $300.

C O V E R S

Middletown Twp. Property

- - - - - - - -

Philip Freneau : Mtg. dated 8–28–1815
        to   : 9–1–1815
James Kearny   : Book E Page 509
               : Amt. $150.

C O V E R S

32½ Acres Middletown Twp.

- - - - - - - -

Agnes Kerney,   : Mtg. dated 3–22–1813
Philip & Eleanor Freneau   : Rec. 3–24–1813
        to   : Book E Page 341
William Crawford   : Amt. $200.

C O V E R S

55 Acres Freehold Twp.

- - - - - - - -

In addition to the above, the records of the Court of Chancery of the State of New Jersey indicate that a writ dated October 7, 1823 was issued to Richard Lloyd, sheriff of Monmouth County, for the sale of all lands, the property of Philip Freneau to be sold to pay a mortgage given April 29, 1805. Manuscript Monmouth County Deeds, H2, 331.[2] See also Manuscript indenture, dated November 22, 1830 (New Jersey Historical Society) and Manuscript Monmouth County Deeds, T2, 11 and 46; also A3, 438.

---

[1] The different spellings of the name of Agnes Kerney (Kearney) are in the original.

[2] Lewis Leary, *That Rascal Freneau*, p. 407 n.

APPENDIX B
Legal Dockets of Actions for Debts

John P. Vanpelt
against
Philip Freneau
&
Agnes Kearney
May 13th 1812
$35 ″ 65

In Debt

Summons Returnable the 21st the Constable made Return Served the Plaintive filed a note In Demand the Defendant appeared by Philip Freneau & after Calculatin the Note I Gave Judgment in favour of Plaintive for thirty five Dollar & sixty five Cents Debt with fifty three Cents Cost my Cost Paid

> Cornelius P. Vanderhoef
> 1818–1826 Legal Docket of Cornelius P.
> Vanderhoef, page 145

Bowne & Wright
vs
Philip Freneau
August 1813
Granted Execution
October 30th 1813
Delivered Pllff
$38.90

In Debt

Summons Returnable the 28th Const made return Served Plaintiff filed his demand I adjourned until Saturday the 4th Sept. Defendant appeared & agreed to adjourn till Monday 6th Defendant did not appear Judgment by default for thirty eight dollars & ninety cents Debt with fifty three cents cost

> Cornelius P. Vanderhoef
> 1818–1826 Legal Docket of Cornelius P.
> Vanderhoef, Page 193

Joshua Wilson
Assigne of
Samuel Ellison
vs
Philip Freneau

In Debt

Summons Issued September 11th 1819 for $25 Deliverable the 18 at House of Peter Johnstons Nicolious M. Disbrow Constable Made Return Served by Coppey Lest with the Defendants wife Sept 11th 1819 September the 17th 1819 the Plaintiff filed His note of hand the Defendant appeared and Said the note was Just and Confessed Judgment For Twelve Dollars & Seventy four Cents with the 73 Cents Cost John P. Vanpelt Justice Novem-

ber the 3th 1819 Executed granted & Deliver
ed to Plaintiff
Return this Execution with Plaintiff's Receipt
Recvd my Cost from M. N. Disbrow Constable
1818–1826 Legal Docket of John VanPelt.
page 64

Joseph Hendrickson &   In Debt
Daniel M. Ellis   Summons Issued September 2th 1818 for Nine
vs   Dollars and sixty one Cents Returnable at the
Philip Freneau   House of Peter Johnstons the 12 at 2 oClock
P.M. Nicolious M. Disbrow Const. Made Re-
Paid To me Jn P. Van-   turn served the 3 Day of September by reading
pelt Recvd My full De-   to Defendants Sept. 12 The plaintiff appeared
mand of this Judgment   Produced his Books of Account Defendant
$9.72 January the 21   Did not appear after Examining the Same I
Recd The Judgment &   gave Judgment agnt Defendant for $9.61
Constables Cost of the   Cents Debt 73 Cents Cost
above for Hendrickson
& Ellis   John P. Vanpelt Justice
Jos Hendrickson   1818–1826 Legal Docket of John Van Pelt.
Page 22

BIBLIOGRAPHY

Published Sources

Books and Articles

Abbott, W. C. *New York in the American Revolution*. New York: Charles Scribner's Sons, 1929.

Adams, Abigail. *New Letters of Abigail Adams* (ed. S. Mitchell). Boston: Houghton Mifflin Company, 1947.

Adams, C. F. SEE Adams, John; Adams, John and Abigail.

Adams, Henry. *History of the United States of America during the First Administration of Jefferson*. 9 vols. New York: Charles Scribner's Sons, 1931.

———. *History of the United States during the First Administration of Jefferson* (ed. H. Agar). 2 vols. Boston: Houghton Mifflin Company, 1947.

———. *Life of Albert Gallatin*. New York: Peter Smith, 1943.

———. *The War of 1812*. Washington, D.C.: Infantry Journal, 1944.

Adams, John. *Diary and Autobiography* (ed. L. H. Butterfield). 4 vols. Cambridge, Massachusetts: Belknap-Harvard Press, 1961.

———. *Letters Addressed to His Wife* (ed. C. F. Adams). 2 vols. Boston: Little, Brown & Company, 1861.

———. *Works* (ed. C. F. Adams). 10 vols. Boston: Little, Brown & Company, 1854.

Adams, John and Abigail. *Familiar Letters* (ed. C. F. Adams). Boston: Houghton Mifflin Company, 1875.

Adams, John Quincy. *The Diary of John Quincy Adams* (ed. Allan Nevins). New York: Longmans, Green & Company, Inc., 1928.

———. *Writings* (ed. W. C. Ford). 7 vols. New York: The Macmillan Company, 1913.

Adams Family Correspondence (ed. L. H. Butterfield). Cambridge, Massachusetts: Belknap-Harvard Press, 1963.

Adams-Jefferson Letters, The. (ed. J. Lester Cappon). 2 vols. Chapel Hill: University of North Carolina Press, 1959.

Adkins, N. F. *Fitz-Greene Halleck*. New Haven, Connecticut: Yale University Press, 1930.

———. *Philip Freneau and the Cosmic Enigma*. New York: New York University Press, 1949.

Agar, H. *The Price of Union*. Boston: Houghton Mifflin Company, 1950.

———. SEE ALSO Adams, Henry.

Agnew, David C. A. *Protestant Exiles from France in the Reign of Louis XIV*. London: privately printed, 1886.

Ainsworth, E. G., Jr. "An American Translator of Ariosto: Philip Freneau," *American Literature*, IV, 4 (January 1933), 393–395.

Alden, John R. *The American Revolution: 1775–1783*. New York: Harper & Brothers, 1954.

Allen, G. W. *American Prosody*. New York: American Book Company, 1935.

Ames, Fisher. *Works* (ed. Seth Ames). 2 vols. Boston: Little, Brown & Company, 1854.

Ames, Seth. SEE Ames, Fisher.

Anderson, F. M. "Contemporary Opinion of the Virginia and Kentucky Resolutions," *American Historical Review*, V, 1 (October 1899), 45–63, and 2 (January 1900), 225–252.

————. "The Enforcement of the Alien and Sedition Laws," *Annual Report of the American Historical Association, 1912*, pp. 115–126. Washington, D.C.: American Historical Association, 1912.

Appleton's Encyclopedia of American Biography (ed. J. G. Wilson and John Fiske). 10 vols. New York: D. Appleton & Company, Inc., 1898–1924.

Austin, M. S. *Philip Freneau*. New York: A. Wessel & Company, 1901.

Axelrad, Jacob. *Patrick Henry: The Voice of Freedom*. New York: Random House, Inc., 1947.

Beam, Jacob N. *The American Whig Society of Princeton University*. Princeton, New Jersey: Published by the Society, 1933.

Beard, C. A. *The American Party Battle*. New York: The Macmillan Company, 1928.

————. *Economic Origins of Jeffersonian Democracy*. New York: The Macmillan Company, 1949.

Beard, C. A. and M. R. *The Rise of American Civilization*. 2 vols. New York: The Macmillan Company, 1927.

Beatty, J. M., Jr. "Churchill and Freneau," *American Literature*, II, 2 (May 1930), 121–130.

Becker, C. *Our Great Experiment in Democracy*. New York: Harper & Brothers, 1924.

Beirne, F. F. *The War of 1812*. New York: E. P. Dutton & Co., Ltd., 1949.

Beloff, Max. *Thomas Jefferson and American Democracy*. London: Hodder & Stoughton, Ltd., 1948.

Benjamin, S. G. W. "Notable Editors between 1776 and 1800," *Magazine of American History*, XVII (January–June 1887), 1–28 and 97–127.

Bergh, A. E. SEE Jefferson, Thomas.

Bernard, John. *Retrospections of America, 1797–1811*. New York: Harper & Brothers, 1887.

Bill, Alfred H. *New Jersey and the American Revolution.* Vol. 11 of the *New Jersey Historical Series.* Princeton, New Jersey: D. Van Nostrand Company, Inc., 1964.

Billington, R. A. *Westward Expansion.* New York: The Macmillan Company, 1949.

Billington, R. A., B. L. Lowenberg, and S. H. Brockunier. *The United States: American Democracy in World Perspective.* New York: Rinehart & Company, Inc., 1947.

Binkley, Wilfred E. *American Political Parties.* New York: Alfred A. Knopf, Inc., 1949.

Bleyer, W. G. *Main Currents in the History of American Journalism.* Boston and New York: Houghton Mifflin Company, 1927.

Bonner, W. T. *New York.* New York: R. L. Polk Co., 1924.

Bonsal, S. *When the French Were Here.* New York: Doubleday, Doran & Company, Inc., 1945.

Boswell, James. *Life of Samuel Johnson.* New York: Modern Library, Inc., 1952.

Bowen, M. *Peter Porcupine.* New York: Longmans, Green & Co., Inc., 1935.

Bowers, C. G. *Jefferson and Hamilton.* Boston and New York: Houghton Mifflin Company, 1925.

————. *Jefferson in Power.* Boston: Houghton Mifflin Company, 1936.

Boyd, Julian P. *Number 7: Alexander Hamilton's Secret Attempt to Control American Foreign Policy.* Princeton, New Jersey: Princeton University Press, 1964.

Boyd, Thomas. *Light-Horse Harry Lee.* New York: Charles Scribner's Sons, 1931.

Boyer, J. T. SEE Priestly, Joseph.

Brackenridge, Hugh H. *Modern Chivalry.* New York: American Book Company, 1937.

Bradsher, E. L. *Matthew Cary.* New York: Columbia University Press, 1912.

Brant, Irving. *James Madison.* 6 vols. Indianapolis and New York: The Bobbs-Merrill Company, Inc., 1941–1954. These volumes bear individual titles as follows: 1, *The Virginia Revolutionist*; 2, *The Nationalist, 1780–1787*; 3, *Father of the Constitution, 1787–1800*; 4, *Secretary of State, 1800–1809*; 5, *The President, 1809–1812*; 6, *Commander in Chief, 1812–1836.*

Brenner, Rica. *Twelve American Poets before 1900.* New York: Harcourt, Brace and Company, Inc., 1933.

Bridenbaugh, C. and J. *Rebels and Gentlemen.* New York: Reynal & Hitchcock, Inc., 1942.

Brigham, Clarence S. *An Account of American Almanacs.* Worcester, Massachusetts: American Antiquarian Society, 1925.

————. "Additions and Corrections to the *History and Bibliography of American Newspapers, 1690–1820,*" *American Antiquarian Society,* Vol. 71–72 (April 19, 1961 and October 18, 1962), pp. 15–62.

————. *History and Bibliography of American Newspapers.* Worcester, Massachusetts: American Antiquarian Society, 1947.

————. *Journals and Journeymen.* Philadelphia: University of Pennsylvania Press, 1950.

Brooks, Noah. *Henry Knox.* New York and Boston: Putnam's Sons, 1900.

Brooks, Van Wyck. *The World of Washington Irving.* New York: E. P. Dutton & Co., Inc., 1944.

Brown, H. G. and M. O. *A Directory of the Book Arts and Book Trade in Philadelphia to 1820.* New York: New York Public Library, 1950.

Buley, R. C. *The Old Northwest.* Indianapolis: Indiana Historical Society, 1950.

Burnett, E. C. (ed.). *Letters of Members of the Continental Congress.* 2 vols. Washington, D.C.: Carnegie Institute of Washington, 1921.

Burr, Aaron. *Memoirs* (Ed. M. L. Davis). 2 vols. New York: Harper & Brothers, 1837.

Burrill, James, Jr. *Poems of J. L. Arnold.* Providence, Rhode Island: Carter & Wilkinson, 1797.

Butterfield, L. H. SEE Adams, John; *Adams-Family Correspondence.*

Cady, E. H. *The Gentlemen in America.* Syracuse, New York: Syracuse University Press, 1949.

Cahn, Edmund. *The Great Rights.* New York: Macmillan Company, 1961.

Calverton, V. F. "Philip Freneau," *Modern Monthly,* Vol. VII (October 1933).

Cambridge History of American Literature. New York: G. P. Putnam's Sons, 1917.

Cameron, H. C. *History of the American Whig Society.* Princeton, New Jersey: Steele and Smith, 1871.

Cappon, Lester Jr. SEE *Adams-Jefferson Letters, The.*

Carman, H. J. *Social and Economic History of the United States.* New York: D. C. Heath and Company, 1934.

Carmer, Carl. *The Hudson.* New York: Farrar & Rinehart, Inc., 1939.

Chafee, Z., Jr. *Free Speech in the United States.* Cambridge, Massachusetts: Harvard University Press, 1941.

Channing, Edward. *A History of the United States.* New York: The Macmillan Company, 1924.

Chastellux, Marquis de. *Travels in North America.* London: G. G. J. and J. Robinson, 1787.

Chateaubriand, F. R. A. *Voyage en Amérique et en Italie.* Paris: Lavocat Libraire, 1827.

Chenery, William L. *Freedom of the Press.* New York: Harcourt, Brace and Company, Inc., 1955.

Chinard, G. *Honest John Adams.* Boston: Little, Brown & Company, 1933.

————. *Thomas Jefferson: The Apostle of Americanism.* Boston: Little, Brown & Company, 1929.

Christman, Henry. *Tin Horns and Calico.* New York: Collier Books, 1961.

Clark, G. L. *A History of Connecticut.* New York: G. P. Putnam's Sons, 1914.

Clark, H. H. "The Literary Influences of Philip Freneau," *Studies in Philology* XXII, 1 (January 1925) 1–33.

————. "What Made Freneau the Father of American Poetry?" *Studies in Philology,* XXVI, 1 (January 1929), 1–22.

————. "What Made Freneau the Father of American Prose?" *Transactions of the Wisconsin Academy of Sciences, Arts, and Letters,* XXV (1930), 39–50.

————. SEE ALSO Freneau, Philip.

Coit, M. L. *John C. Calhoun.* Boston: Houghton Mifflin Company, 1950.

Cooke, Jacob. SEE *Federalist, The.*

Coolidge, Susan. *A Short History of Philadelphia.* Boston: Robert Brothers, 1889.

Corner, G. W. SEE Rush, Benjamin.

"Correspondence des Ministres Français aux Etats-Units, 1791–1797" (ed. F. J. Turner), *Annual Report of American Historical Association, 1903,* Vol. 2. Washington, D.C.: American Historical Association, 1904.

Cowie, A. *The Rise of the American Novel.* New York: American Book Company, 1948.

Cresson, W. P. *James Monroe.* Chapel Hill: University of North Carolina Press, 1946.

Crèvecoeur, J. H. St. John. *Letters from an American Farmer.* New York: Fox, Duffield & Co., 1904.

Cunningham, Noble, E., Jr. *The Republicans in Power: Party Operations, 1801–1809.* Chapel Hill: University of North Carolina Press, 1963.

Curti, M. *The Growth of American Thought.* New York: Harper & Brothers, 1943.

Davidson, P. *Propaganda and the American Revolution.* Chapel Hill: University of North Carolina Press, 1941.

Davis, John. *Travels of Four Years and a Half in the U.S.* New York: Henry Holt and Company, Inc., 1909.

Davis, M. L. SEE Burr, Aaron.

Davis, R. B., and M. B. Siegler. "Peter Freneau," *Journal of Southern History,* XIII, 3 (August 1947), 395–405.

Deane, Silas. *Papers, 1774–1790: Collection of the New York Historical Society, 1887–1809.* 5 vols. (XIX–XXIII). New York: Printed for the Society 1890.

Decree in the Case of Solomon de Midina etc. against Rene Het etc. New York: William Bradford, 1728.

De Lancey, E. F. "Philip Freneau: The Huguenot Patriot," *Proceeedings of the Huguenot Society of America*, II, 2 (1891), 1–21.

Dickson, H. E. *John Wesley Jarvis*. New York: New York Historical Society, 1949.

Dictionary of American Biography. 22 vols. New York: Charles Scribner's Sons, n.d.

Dictionary of National Biography (ed. Sir Leslie Stephen and Sir Sidney Lee). London: Oxford University Press, 1917.

Diebels, M. C. *Peter Markoe*. Washington, D.C.: The Catholic University of America Press, 1944.

Donovan, Frank, *The Jefferson Papers*. New York: Dodd, Mead & Company, Inc., 1963.

Dorson, R. M. (ed.). *American Rebels*. New York: Pantheon Books, Inc., 1953.

Douglass, E. P. *Rebels and Democrats*. Chapel Hill: University of North Carolina Press, 1955.

Duyckinck, E. A. and G. L. *Cyclopoedia of American Literature*. Philadelphia: W. Rutter & Company, 1877.

Edwards, Bryan. *The History, Civil and Commercial, of the British West Indies*. London: n.p., 1798.

Ellis, F. *History of Monmouth County*. Philadelphia: R. T. Peck & Co., 1885.

Farrand, Max (ed.) *The Records of the Federal Convention of 1787*. 4 vols. New Haven, Connecticut: Yale University Press, 1937.

Farris, John. *The Romance of Old Philadelphia*. Philadelphia: J. B. Lippincott Company, 1918.

Fauchet, Joseph. "Memoire sur les Etats-Unis d'Amérique," *Annual Report of American Historical Association, 1936*, Vol 1. Washington, D.C.: American Historical Association, 1936.

Faulkner, H. U. *American Political and Social History*. New York: F. S. Crofts & Co., 1948.

Fay, Bernard. "Benjamin F. Bache: Democratic Leader of the 18th Century," *American Antiquarian Society*, 40 (1931), 277–304.

Federalist, The (ed. Jacob Cooke). Middletown, Connecticut: Wesleyan University Press, 1961.

Federalist, The (ed. H. C. Lodge). New York: G. P. Putman's Sons, 1891.

Federalist, The (ed. Goldwin Smith). New York: The Colonial Press, 1961.

Federalist Papers. New York: New American Library, 1961.

Fish, C. R. *The Rise of the Common Man*. New York: The Macmillan Company, 1927.

Fiske, John. *The Critical Period of American History*. Boston and New York: Houghton Mifflin Company, 1898.

Fithian, P. V. *Journal and Letters*. Princeton, New Jersey: The University Press, 1900.

Fitzpatrick, J. C. SEE Washington, George.

Flexner, J. T. *The Traitor and the Spy*. New York: Harcourt, Brace and Company, Inc., 1953.

Ford, P. L. "Freneau's *National Gazette*," *The Nation*, Vol. 60, No. 1547 (February 21, 1895), pp. 143–144.

———. *Pamphlets on the Constitution*. Brooklyn: n.p., 1880.

———. SEE ALSO Jefferson, Thomas.

Ford, W. C. SEE Adams, John Quincy; Washington, George.

Forman, S. E. "The Political Activities of Philip Freneau," *Johns Hopkins University Studies*, Vol. 20, Nos. 9–10 (1902), pp. 1–105.

Forman, S. S. *Narrative of a Journey Down the Ohio and Mississippi*. Cincinnati: Robert Clarke & Co., 1888.

Foster, A. J. *Jeffersonian America*. San Marino, California: The Huntington Library, 1954.

———. SEE ALSO Tinkcom, H. M.

France, Ambassadors of. SEE "Correspondance des Ministres François aux Etats-Unis, 1791–1797."

Francis, J. W. *Old New York*. New York: W. J. Widdleton, 1866.

French, Allen. *The First Year of the American Revolution*. Boston: Houghton Mifflin, 1934.

Freeman, Douglas Southall. *George Washington*. 7 vols. New York: Charles Scribner's Sons, 1948–1957.

Freneau, Philip. *The American Village* (which also contains the poem "The Miserable Life of a Pedagogue"). New York: S. Inslee and A. Car, 1772. Copy in the Library of Congress.

———. *A Collection of Poems on American Affairs*. 2 vols. New York: David Longworth, 1815.

———. *A Freneau Sampler* (ed. Philip M. Marsh). New York: The Scarecrow Press, 1963.

———. *General Gage's Confession*. New York: H. Gaine, 1775.

———. *A Journey from Philadelphia to New York*. Philadelphia: Francis Bailey, 1787.

———. *The Last Poems of Philip Freneau* (ed. Lewis Leary). New Brunswick, New Jersey: Rutgers University Press, 1945.

———. *Letters on Various Interesting and Important Subjects*. Philadelphia: D. Hogan, 1799.

———. *The Miscellaneous Works of Philip Freneau*. Philadelphia: Printed by Francis Bailey, 1788.

———. *Poem of Freneau* (ed. H. H. Clark). New York: Harcourt, Brace and Company, Inc., 1929.

———. *The Poems of Philip Freneau* (ed. F. L. Pattee). 3 vols. Princeton, New Jersey: Princeton University Press, 1902.

————. *Poems of Philip Freneau Written Chiefly during the Late War.* Philadelphia: Francis Bailey, 1786.

————. *Poems Relating to the American Revolution, with a Memoir by E. A. Duyckinck.* New York: W. J. Widdleton, 1865.

————. *Poems Written and Published during the American Revolutionary War.* 2 vols. Philadelphia: Lydia R. Bailey, 1809.

————. *Poems Written between the Years 1768 and 1794.* Mt. Pleasant, New Jersey: Printed by the Author, 1795.

————. *The Prose of Philip Freneau* (ed. Philip M. Marsh). New Brunswick, New Jersey: The Scarecrow Press, 1955.

————. *Some Account of the Capture of the Ship "Aurora."* New York: M. F. Mansfield & A. Wessels, 1899.

————. *A Voyage to Boston.* New York: John Anderson, 1775.

————. SEE ALSO Heartman, C. F.; Robin, Abbé, C. C.

Geise, John, *Man and the Western World.* New York: Harcourt, Brace and Company, Inc., 1940.

Gershoy, Leo. *The French Revolution and Napoleon.* New York: F. S. Crofts & Co., 1947.

Gibbs, George. *Memoirs of the Administration of Washington and John Adams.* 2 vols. New York: Printed by Subscription, 1846.

Gilder, R. *The Battery.* Boston: Houghton Mifflin Company, 1936.

Goddard, D. A. *Newspapers and Newspaper Writers in New England.* Boston: A. Williams & Co., 1880.

Greene, E. B. *The Revolutionary Generation.* New York: The Macmillan Company, 1943.

Greene, Nathanael. "General Greene's Report of the Battle of Eutaw Springs," *The Magazine of History, with Notes and Queries,* Extra No. 139 (1928), 11 pages at end.

Griswold, R. W. *Curiosities of American Literature.* New York: n.p., 1859. (Reprint from *Southern Review,* January 1853).

————. "Philip Freneau: The Poet of the Revolution," *Graham's Magazine,* XLVII, 3 (September 1855), 193–201.

————. *The Poets and Poetry of America.* Philadelphia: Perry and McMillan, 1856.

Grundy, J. C. "Philip Freneau: Jersey Patriot and Poet of the Revolution," *Proceedings of the New Jersey Historical Society,* new series, XIV, 4 (October 1929), 481–488.

Hageman, J. F. *History of Princeton and its Institutions.* 2 vols. Philadelphia: J. B. Lippincott Company, 1879.

Haines, Irvine. "Peggy Shippen,' *New York Times,* January, 31, 1932.

Hall, William. *Philip Freneau.* Vol. 18 of *New York Genealogical and Biographical Record.* New York: New York Genealogical and Biographical Record, 1887.

Hamilton, A. M. *The Intimate Life of Alexander Hamilton.* New York: Charles Scribner's Sons, 1910.

Hamilton, Alexander. *Papers* (ed. Harold C. Syrett). 9 vols. (to date). New York: Columbia University Press, 1965.

————. *Works* (ed. H. C. Lodge). 12 vols. New York: G. P. Putnam's sons, 1903.

Hamilton, S. M. SEE Monroe, James.

Hart, J. D. *The Popular Book.* New York: Oxford University Press, 1950.

Hazen, C. D. *Contemporary Opinion of the French Revolution.* Baltimore: Johns Hopkins Press, 1897.

Heartman, C. F. *Unpublished Freneauana.* New York: Hartman, 1918.

Hirst, F. W. *Life and Letters of Thomas Jefferson.* New York: The Macmillan Company, 1926.

Hockett, H. C. *Growth of the American People.* New York: The Macmillan Company, 1940.

Hone, Philip, *Diary.* 2 vols. New York: Dodd, Mead & Company, Inc., 1889.

Horner, W. S. *This Old Monmouth of Ours.* Freehold, New Jersey: Moreau Bros., 1932.

Howard, Leon. *The Connecticut Wits.* Chicago: University of Chicago Press, 1943.

Hudson, F. *Journalism in the United States.* New York: Harper & Brothers, 1873.

Hughes, Rupert. *George Washington.* 3 vols. New York: William Morrow & Company, Inc., 1927.

Hunt, Gaillard. "Office Seeking during Jefferson's Administration," *American Historical Review,* III, 2 (January 1898), 270–291.

————. SEE ALSO Madison, James.

Hustvedt, S. B. "Phillipic Freneau," *American Speech,* IV, 1 (October 1929), 1–18.

Hutchinson, William T. SEE Madison, James.

Irving, Washington. *Life of George Washington.* New York: G. P. Putnam's Sons, 1859.

Jameson, J. F. *The American Revolution Considered as a Social Movement.* Princeton, New Jersey: Princeton University Press, 1940.

Jarvis, J. A. *Brief History of the Virgin Islands.* St. Thomas, Virgin Islands: n.p., 1938.

Jefferson, Thomas. *Notes on Virginia* (ed. P. L. Ford). Brooklyn, New York: Historical Printing Co., 1894.

————. *A Summary View of the Rights of British America.* Reprint from *Writings* (ed. P. L. Ford), I, 421–467. New York: G. P. Putnam's Sons, 1892–1899.

―――. *Writings* (ed. P. L. Ford). 10 vols. New York: G. P. Putnam's Sons, 1892–1899.

―――. *Writings* (ed. A. A. Lipscomb and A. E. Bergh). Monticello Memorial Edition. 20 vols. Washington, D.C.; Published by order of Congress, 1903.

―――. SEE ALSO *Adams-Jefferson Letters, The;* Rosenberger, F. C.

Jensen, M. *The New Nation.* New York: Alfred A. Knopf, Inc., 1950.

Johnston, H. H. *The Negro in the New World.* London: Methuen & Co., Ltd., 1910.

Kilroe, E. P. *Saint Tammany and the Origin of the Society of Tammany or Columbian Order in the City of New York.* New York: n.p., 1903.

King, W. L. *The Newspaper Press of Charleston, South Carolina.* Charleston, South Carolina: Lucas & Richardson, 1882.

Kirk, R. "Freneau's View of Princeton," *The Rutgers University Library Journal,* III, 1 (December 1939), 20–25.

Kirkland, E. C. *A History of American Economic Life.* New York: F. S. Crofts & Co., 1932.

Klinckowström, Axel Leonard, *Baron Klinckowström's America, 1818—1820* (ed. F. D. Scott). Evanston, Illinois: Northwestern University Press, 1955.

Koch, Adrienne. "The Idea of America," *Yale Review,* XLI, 2 (December 1951), 222–233.

―――. *Jefferson and Madison: The Great Collaboration.* New York: Alfred A. Knopf, Inc., 1950.

―――. *Republican Religion.* New York: Henry Holt and Company, Inc., 1933.

Koehler, Albert F. *The Huguenots or Early French in New Jersey.* Princeton, New Jersey: The Huguenot Society of New Jersey, 1955.

Krout, J. A., and D. R. Fox. *The Completion of Independence.* New York: The Macmillan Company, 1944.

Ladd, Joseph B. *The Prospects of America: The Literary Remains of J. B. Ladd.* New York: H. C. Sleight, 1832.

Lamb, M. J. R. *History of the City of New York.* 3 vols. New York: A. S. Barnes and Company, 1877.

Leary, Lewis. "The First Biography of Philip Freneau," *Proceedings of New Jersey Historical Society,* XLV, 3 (July 1947).

―――. "The Log of the Rebecca," *The Rutgers University Library Journal,* V, 2 (June 1942), 65–70.

―――. "Phaeton in Philadelphia," *Pennsylvania Magazine of History and Biography,* Vol. 67 (January 1943), pp. 49–60.

―――. "Philip Freneau and Monmouth County,' *Monmouth County Historical Association Bulletin,* Vol. 1, No. 2 (July 1948), pp. 59–81.

―――. "Philip Freneau in Charleston," *South Carolina Historical and Genealogical Magazine,* XLII, 3 (July 1941), 89-98.

————. "Philip Freneau's Captain Hanson," *American Notes and Queries,* II, 4 (July 1942), 51-53.

————. "Philip Freneau's Father," *The Rutgers University Library Journal,* II (June 1939), 46-52.

————. *That Rascal Freneau.* New Brunswick, New Jersey: Rutgers University Press, 1941.

————. "The Time Piece," *Princeton University Library Chronicle,* Vol. 2, No. 2 (February 1941), pp. 65-74.

————. SEE ALSO Freneau, Philip.

Lee, J. M. *History of American Journalism.* Boston: Houghton Mifflin Company, 1923.

Leonard, W. E. *Byron and Byronism in America.* Boston: The Nichols Press, 1905.

Levy, Leonard W. *Jefferson and Civil Liberties: The Darker Side.* Cambridge, Massachusetts: Belknap-Harvard University Press, 1963.

Liancourt, Duc de la Rochefoucauld. *Travels through the United States of North America.* 2 vols. London: R. Phillips, 1799.

Link, E. P. *Democratic Republican Societies, 1790–1800.* New York: Columbia University Press, 1942.

Lippincott, H. M. *Philadelphia.* Philadelphia: Macrae, Smith Co., 1926.

Lipscomb, A. A. SEE Jefferson, Thomas.

Lodge, H. C. *Studies in History.* Boston: Houghton Mifflin Company, 1884.

————. SEE ALSO Hamilton, Alexander.

Longworth's American Almanack. New York: T. and J. Swords, 1797.

Maclay, William. *Journal.* New York: Albert and Charles Boni, Inc., 1927.

MacLean, John. *History of the College of New Jersey.* 2 vols. Philadelphia: J. B. Lippincott Company, 1877.

Madison, James. *Letters and Writings.* Philadelphia: J. B. Lippincott Company, 1865.

————. *Papers* (ed. William T. Hutchinson and W. M. B. Rachal). 3 vols. Chicago: University of Chicago Press, 1962–1963.

————. *Writings* (ed. Gaillard Hunt). 9 vols. New York: G. P. Putnam's Sons, 1900–1910.

Main, Jackson Turner. *The Anti-Federalists: Critics of the Constitution, 1781–1788.* Chapel Hill: University of North Carolina Press, 1961.

Malone, Dumas. *Jefferson, The Virginian,* Vol. 1, of *Jefferson and His Time.* Boston: Little, Brown & Company, 1951.

————. *Jefferson and the Rights of Man,* Vol. 2 of *Jefferson and His Time.* Boston: Little, Brown & Company, 1951.

————. *Jefferson and the Ordeal of Liberty,* Vol. 3 of *Jefferson and His Time.* Boston: Little, Brown & Company, 1962.

Manuel, Frank E. *The New World of Henri St. Simon.* Cambridge, Massachusetts: Harvard University Press, 1956.

Marble, A. R. "Philip Freneau: America's First Poet," *New England Magazine*, first series, XXIX (September 1903–March 1904). Reprinted in *Heralds of American Literature*. Chicago: n.p., 1907.

Marsden, Peter. *An Account of the Island of Jamaica*. Newcastle, Jamaica: n.p., 1788.

Marsh, Philip M. "Freneau and Jefferson: The Poet-Editor Speaks for Himself," *American Literature*, Vol. 8, No. 2 (May 1936).

———. "From Ezekiah Salem to Robert Slender," *Modern Language Notes*, LXI, 7 (November 1946).

———. "The Griswold Story of Freneau and Jefferson," *American Historical Review*, LI, 1 (October 1945), 68–73.

———. "Jefferson and Freneau," *American Scholar*, Vol. 16, No. 2 (April 1947), pp. 201–210.

———. "Madison's Defense of Freneau," Institute of Early American History and Culture, in *William and Mary Quarterly*, third series, III, 2 (April 1946), 269–274.

———. *Monroe's Defense of Jefferson and Freneau*. Oxford, Ohio: privately printed, 1948.

———. "'Philip Freneau and Francis Hopkinson," *Proceedings of New Jersey Historical Society*, LXIII, 3 (July 1945), 141–149.

———. "Philip Freneau and His Circle," *The Pennsylvania Magazine of History and Biography*, LXIII, 2 (January 1939), 37–59.

———. "'Philip Freneau and James Madison," *Proceedings of New Jersey Historical Society*, LXV, 4 (October 1947), 189–194.

———. "'Philip Freneau: Our Sailor Poet," *American Neptune*, VI (April 1946), 115–120.

———. "Philip Freneau's Ms of the Spy," *The Rutgers University Library Journal*, IX, 1 (December 1945), 23–27.

———. "Philip Freneau's Personal File of *The Freemen's Journal*," *Proceedings of New Jersey Historical Society*, LVII, 3 (July 1939), 163–170.

———. SEE ALSO Freneau, Philip.

Marsh, Philip M., and M. Ellis. "Broadside of Freneau's British Prison Ship," *American Literature*, X, 4 (January 1939), 476–480.

———. "Freneau's Last Home," *Proceedings of New Jersey Historical Society*, XVII, 2 (April 1939), 108–113.

Martineau, Harriet. *Society in America*. London: Saunders and Otley, 1837.

Matawan, 1686–1936. Keyport, New Jersey: Federal Writers Project, 1936.

Maury, Ann. *Memoirs of a Huguenot Family*. New York: G. P. Putnam's Sons, 1853.

McCormick, Richard P. *New Jersey from Colony to State, 1609–1789*. Vol. I of the *New Jersey Historical Series*. Princeton, New Jersey: D. Van Nostrand Company, Inc., 1964.

McDonald, Forrest. *We the People: The Economic Origins of the Constitution*. Chicago: University of Chicago Press, 1958.

Merriam, C. E. *A History of American Political Theories*. New York: The Macmillan Company, 1906.

Midina et al. vs. Het et al. SEE *Decree in the Case of Solomon de Midina etc. against Rene Het, etc.*

Miller, Ann. "Checklist of Freneau Material in the Monmouth Historical Association, Freehold, N. J.," *Monmouth County Historical Association Bulletin*, (July 1948), pp. 49–57.

Miller, John C. *Crisis in Freedom: The Alien and Sedition Acts*. Boston: Little, Brown & Company, 1951.

Miller, Samuel. *A Brief Retrospect of the Eighteenth Century*. 2 vols. New York: T. and J. Swords, 1803.

Mills, W. J. *Glimpses of Colonial Life and Society at Princeton College, 1766–1773*. Philadelphia: J. B. Lippincott Company, 1903.

———. *Historic Houses of New Jersey*. Philadelphia: J. B. Lippincott Company, 1902.

———. *Through the Gates of Old Romance*. Philadelphia: J. B. Lippincott Company, 1903.

Miner, L. M. *Our Rude Forefathers*. Cedar Rapids, Iowa: The Torch Press, 1937.

Minnigerode, Meade. SEE Wandell, S. H.

Mitchell, Broadus, *Alexander Hamilton,* 2 vols. New York: The Macmillan Company, 1957–1962.

———. *Heritage from Hamilton*. New York: Columbia University Press, 1957.

Mitchell, S. SEE Adams, Abigail.

Monroe, James. *Writings* (ed. S. M. Hamilton). 7 vols. New York: G. P. Putnam's Sons, 1898–1903.

Montulé, E. de. *Voyage en Amérique*. Paris: Chez Delaunay, 1821.

Morais, H. M. *Deism in Eighteenth Century America*. New York: Columbia University Press, 1934.

More, Paul E. *Shelburne Essays*. New York: G. P. Putnam's Sons, 1908.

Moreau de Saint Méry, M. L. E. *American Journey* (translated, K. and A. M. Roberts). New York: Doubleday & Company, Inc., 1947.

Morgan, George. *Philadelphia: The City of Firsts*. Philadelphia: The Historical Publ. Society, 1926.

Morse, J. *A Sermon Preached at Charlestown, November 29, 1798*. Boston: Samuel Hale, 1798.

Mott, Frank L. *A History of American Journalism*. New York: The Macmillan Company, 1962.

———. *A History of American Magazines*. Cambridge, Massachusetts: Harvard University Press, 1939.

Murray, James. *Letters from America, 1773–1780* (ed. E. Robson). New York: Barnes & Noble, Inc., 1951.

Myers, Gustavus. *The History of American Idealism.* New York: Boni & Liveright, 1925.

———. *The History of Tammany Hall.* New York: Boni & Liveright, 1917.

Nevins, Allan. *The American States during and after the Revolution.* New York: The Macmillan Company, 1927.

———. *The Evening Post.* New York: Boni & Liveright, 1922.

———. (ed.). *America through British Eyes.* New York: Oxford University Press, 1948.

———. SEE ALSO Adams, John Quincy.

Nevins, A., and H. S. Commager. *The Pocket History of the U.S.* Boston: Printed by Pocket Books by permission and copyright of Little, Brown & Company, 1942.

New Jersey, State of. *Marriage Records, 1665–1800.* 1st Series, Vol. XXII. Trenton, New Jersey: John L. Murphy Publ. Co., n.d.

———. *Official Register of the Officers and Men of New Jersey in the Revolutionary War.* Trenton, New Jersey: Nicholson & Co., 1872.

———. *Archives.* 2nd Series, Vol. II, New Jersey: n.p., n.d.

Newlin, C. M. *Life and Writings of Hugh H. Brackenridge.* Princeton, New Jersey: Princeton University Press, 1932.

Newton, A. *Wordsworth in Early American Criticism.* Chicago: University of Chicago Press, 1928.

New York City. *Minutes of the Common Council of the City of New York, 1675–1776.* New York: Dodd, Mead & Company, Inc., 1905.

Oberholtzer, E. P. *Philadelphia: A History of the City and Its People.* Philadelphia: S. J. Clarke Publishing Company, 1912.

———. *Robert Morris.* New York: The Macmillan Company, 1903.

Onderdonk, J. L. *History of American Verse.* Chicago: A. C. McClurg & Co., 1901.

Padover, S. K. (ed.) *The World of the Founding Fathers.* New York: Thos. Yoseloff, 1960.

Paltsits, V. H. *A Bibliography of the Works of Philip Freneau.* New York: Dodd, Mead & Company, Inc., 1903.

———. SEE ALSO Washington, George.

Parker, William B. SEE Washington, George.

Parrington, V. L. *Main Currents in American Thought: The Colonial Mind.* New York: Harcourt, Brace and Company, Inc., 1927.

Parton, James. *Life of Thomas Jefferson.* Boston: Houghton Mifflin Company, 1887.

Pattee, F. L. "Philip Freneau," *Chautauqua,* Vol. 31 (August 1900), pp. 467–475. Cleveland: The Chautauqua Press, 1900.

———. "Philip Freneau as a Postal Clerk," *American Literature,* IV, 1 (March 1932), 61–62.

————. *Side-Lights on American Literature*. New York: The Century Press, 1922.

————. SEE ALSO Freneau, Philip.

Patterson, S. W. *The Spirit of the American Revolution as Revealed in the Poetry of the Period*. Boston: R. G. Badger, 1915.

Payne, G. H. *History of Journalism in the United States*. New York: D. Appleton & Company, Inc., 1924.

Peattie, D. C. *Green Laurels*. New York: Garden City Publishing Company, Inc., 1938.

Peden, William. "Jefferson, Freneau and the Poems of 1809," *The New Colophon*, Vol. 1, Pt. 4 (October 1948), pp. 394–400.

Pennsylvania Cavalcade. Philadelphia: University of Pennsylvania Press for Pennsylvania Federation of Historical Societies, 1942.

Peterson, Merrill D. *The Jefferson Image in the American Mind*. New York: Oxford University Press, 1960.

Powell, J. H. *Bring Out Your Dead*. Philadelphia: University of Pennsylvania Press, 1949.

Preston, John H. *Revolution—1776*. New York: Harcourt, Brace and Company, Inc., 1933.

Price, W. J. "Genesis of the Fourth Estate in Philadelphia," *American Historical Magazine*, IV (September 1909), 672–676.

Priestley, Joseph. *Memoirs* (ed. J. T. Boyer). New York: Taplinger, 1964.

Quarles, Benjamin. *The Negro in the American Revolution*. Chapel Hill: University of North Carolina Press, 1961.

Rachal, W. M. B. SEE Madison, James.

Randall, H. S. *The Life of Thomas Jefferson*. 3 vols. New York: Derby and Jackson, 1858.

Repplier, Agnes. *Philadelphia: The Place and the People*. New York: The Macmillan Company, 1898.

Riegel, R. E. *Young America, 1830–1840*. Norman: University of Oklahoma Press, 1949.

Robin, Abbé C. C. *New Travels through North America, Translated by Philip Freneau*. Philadelphia: Robert Bell, 1793.

Robson, E. SEE Murray, James.

Roche, O. I. A. *The Days of the Upright: A History of the Huguenots*. New York: Clarkson N. Potter, 1965.

Rosenberger, F. C. (ed.). *Jefferson Reader*. New York: E. P. Dutton & Co., Inc., 1953.

Rossiter, Clinton. *Alexander Hamilton and the Constitution*. New York: Harcourt, Brace and World, Inc., 1964.

Rush, Benjamin. *An Account of the Bilious Remitting Yellow Fever*. Philadelphia: T. Dobson, 1794.

————. *Autobiography* (ed. G. W. Corner). Princeton, New Jersey: Princeton University Press, 1948.

St. Croix Packet Companies. Copenhagen: n.p., 1780. Records of the Danish government.

Salter, Edwin, and G. C. Beckman. *Old Times in Old Monmouth.* Freehold, New Jersey: J. S. Yard, 1887.

Savelle, Max. "Nationalism and Other Loyalties in the American Revolution," *American Historical Review,* LXVII, 4 (July 1962), 901–923.

———. *Seeds of Liberty.* New York: Alfred A. Knopf, Inc., 1948.

Schachner, N. *Alexander Hamilton.* New York: D. Appleton-Century Company, Inc., 1946.

Schlesinger, A. M. *New Viewpoints in American History.* New York: The Macmillan Company, 1928.

Schlesinger, A. M., Jr. *The Age of Jackson.* Boston: Little, Brown & Company, 1946.

Scott, F. D. SEE Klinckowström, Axel Leonhard.

Smith, A. E. *James Madison: The Builder.* New York: Wilson-Erickson, 1937.

Smith, Edward. *William Cobbett.* London: Sampson, Low, 1879.

Smith, Frank. "Philip Freneau and The Time Piece and Literary Companion," *American Literature,* IV, 3 (November 1932), 270–287.

Smith, Goldwin. SEE *Federalist, The.*

Smith, H. N. *Virgin Land.* Cambridge, Massachusetts: Harvard University Press, 1950.

Smith, James M. "Alexander Hamilton: The Alien and Sedition Libels," *The Review of Politics,* XVI, 3 (July 1954), 305–333.

———. *Freedom's Fetters: The Alien and Sedition Laws and American Civil Liberties.* Ithaca, New York: Cornell University Press, 1956.

Smith, Page. *John Adams.* 2 vols. New York: Doubleday & Company, Inc., 1962.

Smith, Thomas E. V. *The City of New York in the Year of Washington's Inauguration.* New York: Anson, D. F. Randolph & Company, 1889.

Sparks, Jared. *Correspondence of the American Revolution.* New York: Little, Brown & Company, 1853.

———. SEE ALSO Washington, George.

Spiller, Robert E., *et al.* (eds.). *Literary History of the United States, 3rd Series.* 3 vols. New York: The Macmillan Company, 1962.

State Trials of the U.S. during the Administration of Washington and Adams (ed. F. Wharton). Philadelphia: Carey & Hart, 1849.

Stauffer, V. *New England and the Bavarian Illuminati,* Vol. LXXXII of *Studies in History, Economics, and Public Law.* New York: Columbia University Press, 1919.

Stephenson, G. M. *American History to 1865.* New York: Harper & Brothers, 1940.

Stevens, J. A. *Albert Gallatin.* Boston: Houghton Mifflin Company, 1900.

Stubbs, William B., and C. B. Gosnell. *Select Readings in American Government*. New York: Charles Scribner's Sons, 1948.

Styron, Arthur. *The Last of the Cocked Hats: James Monroe and the Virginia Dynasty*. Norman: University of Oklahoma Press, 1945.

Syrett, Harold C. SEE Hamilton, Alexander.

Thomas, E. S. *Reminiscences of the Last Sixty-Five Years*. Hartford, Connecticut: n.p., 1840.

Thomas, Owen P., Jr., "Philip Freneau: A Bibliography," *Proceeedings of New Jersey Historical Society*, LXXV, 3 (July 1957), 197–205.

Tinkcom, H. M. (ed.). "Sir Augustus in Pennsylvania: The Travels and Observations of A. J. Foster in Early 19th Century Pennslyvania," *The Pennsylvania Magazine of History and Biography*, LXXV, 1–4 (October 1951), 369–399.

Tocqueville, Alexis de. *Democracy in America*. New York: The Colonial Press, 1899.

Todd, C. B. *Life and Letters of Joel Barlow*. New York: G. P. Putnam's Sons, 1886.

Trevelyan, G. M. *History of England*. New York: Longmans, Green & Co., Inc., 1926.

Trollope, Frances. *Domestic Manners of the Americans*. New York: Alfred A. Knopf, Inc., 1949.

Tucker, Glenn. *Poltroons and Patriots: A Popular Account of the War of 1812*. Indianapolis and New York: The Bobbs-Merrill Company, Inc., 1954.

Tuckerman, H. T. *An Historical Sketch of the Life of Silas Talbot*. New York: G. and R. Waite, 1803.

Turner, F. J. *The Frontier in American History*. New York: Henry Holt and Company, Inc., 1928.

———. SEE ALSO "Correspondance des Ministres Français aux Etats-Unis, 1791–1797."

Tyler, Moses Coit. *The Literary History of the American Revolution*. 2 vols. New York: Barnes & Noble, Inc., 1941.

Ulmann, Albert. *A Landmark History of New York*. New York: A. Appleton-Century Company, Inc., 1939.

Umbreit, Kenneth B. *Our Eleven Chief Justices*. New York: Harper & Brothers, 1938.

United States Congress. *Annals of Congress* (ed. Gales and Seaton). 42 vols., 1st to 18th Congress, from March 3, 1789 to May 27, 1824. Washington, D.C.: 1834–1856.

Van Doren, Carl. *Benjamin Franklin*. New York: The Viking Press, Inc., 1945.

———. *The Great Rehearsal*. New York: The Viking Press, Inc., 1948.

———. *The Secret History of the American Revolution*. New York: The Viking Press, Inc., 1941.

Van Tyne, C. H. *The Causes of the War of Independence.* Boston and New York: Houghton Mifflin Company, 1929.

———. *The Loyalists in the American Revolution.* New York: The Macmillan Company, 1902.

———. *The War of Independence.* Boston and New York: Houghton Mifflin Company, 1929.

Viles, Jonas. SEE Washington, George.

Vinton, J. A. *Life of Deborah Sampson.* Boston: J. K. Wiggin and W. P. Lunt, 1896.

Wagenknecht, Edward. *Washington Irving.* New York: Oxford University Press, 1962.

Wallace, George R. *Princeton Sketches: The Story of Nassau Hall.* New York: G. P. Putnam's Sons, 1893.

Wandell, S. H., and Meade Minnigerode. "Theodosia Burr," *Saturday Evening Post,* September 6, 1924.

Wansey, Henry. *The Journal of an Excursion to the United States of America in the Summer of 1794.* London: J. Easton, 1796.

Warfel, H. R. *Charles Brockden Brown.* Gainesville: University of Florida Press, 1949.

———. *Noah Webster: Schoolmaster to America.* New York: The Macmillan Company, 1936.

Warner, G. J. *Means for the Preservation of Public Liberty.* New York: Thomas Greeenleaf, 1797.

Washington, George. *Farewell Address* (ed. Victor Hugo Paltsits). New York: The New York Public Library, 1935.

———. *Letters and Addresses* (ed. William B. Parker and Jonas Viles). New York: Unit Book Publishing Company, 1908.

———. *Writings* (ed. J. C. Fitzpatrick). 39 vols. Washington, D.C.: U.S. Government Printing Office, 1940.

———. *Writings* (ed. W. C. Ford). 14 vols. New York: G. P. Putnam's Sons, 1889–1893.

———. *Writings* (ed. Jared Sparks). 12 vols. New York: Harper & Brothers, 1847.

Wecter, Dixon. *The Hero in America: A Chronicle of Hero-Worship.* New York: Charles Scribner's Sons, 1941.

Wertenbaker, T. J. *Father Knickerbocker Rebels.* New York: Charles Scribner's Sons, 1948.

———. *Princeton, 1746–1896.* Princeton, New Jersey: Princeton University Press, 1946.

Wharton, A. H. *Social Life in the Early Republic.* Philadelphia: J. B. Lippincott Company, 1902.

White, L. D. *The Federalists.* New York: The Macmillan Company, 1948.

———. *The Jeffersonians.* New York: The Macmillan Company, 1951.

Whitney, J. *Abigail Adams.* Boston: Little, Brown & Company, 1947.

"Wife of Philip Freneau, The," *New York Evening Post,* May 6, 1893.

Williams, J. R. *Bermudiana.* New York: Rinehart & Company, Inc., 1936.

Williams, S. T. *The Life of Washington Irving.* New York: Oxford University Press, 1935.

Wilson, J. G. *The Memorial History of the City of New York.* 4 vols. New York: New York History Company, 1892.

Wilson, William E. *The Angel and the Serpent: The Story of New Harmony.* Bloomington: Indiana University Press, 1964.

Wiltse, C. M. *John C. Calhoun: Nullifier.* Indianapolis: The Bobbs-Merrill Company, Inc., 1947.

Witherspoon, John. *Works.* 3 vols. Philadelphia: William T. Woodward, 1802.

Wood, W. B. *Personal Recollections of the Stage.* Philadelphia: H. C. Baird, 1855.

Woodward, W. E. *The Way Our People Lived.* New York: E. P. Dutton & Co., Inc., 1946.

Wright, B. F., Jr. *A Source Book of American Political Theory.* New York: The Macmillan Company, 1929.

Newspapers

Included in the list of newspapers given below are those in which many of Freneau's poems were originally printed or later reprinted, often with changes in words, lines, and even titles. It is certain that in his published volumes, Freneau included the version which he considered most acceptable, and the details of these volumes will be found in the published bibliography by Victor Hugo Paltsits. The dates and details of the poems themselves are given in the three volumes of the collected poems edited by Fred L. Pattee, and more comprehensively in the extended bibliography by Professor Lewis Leary in *That Rascal Freneau.* As to the location of the newspapers, I know of no better guide than the two volume bibliography of Clarence S. Brigham and his more recent "Additions and Corrections to the *History and Bibliography of American Newspapers, 1690–1820.*"

GENERAL LIST

Albany Register (Albany, New York)
American Mercury, The (Hartford, Connecticut)
American Museum (Philadelphia)
Argus (New York)
Aurora, The (Philadelphia)
Boston Gazette, The (Boston)
City Gazette, The (Charleston, South Carolina)
Columbian Centinel, The (Boston, Massachusetts)
Columbian Herald, The (Charleston, South Carolina)

Connecticut Courant, The (Hartford, Connecticut)
Daily Advertiser, The (New York)
Daily American Advertiser, The (Philadelphia)
Diary, The (New York)
Evening Post (New York)
Fredonian, The (New Brunswick, New Jersey)
Freeman's Journal, The (Philadelphia)
Gazette of the United States, The (Philadelphia)
General Advertiser, The (Philadelphia)
Greenleaf's New Argus & Daily Advertiser (New York)
Independent Chronicle, The (Boston)
Independent Gazeteer (Philadelphia)
Jersey Chronicle, The (Monmouth, New Jersey)
Maryland Journal, The (Baltimore)
Massachusetts Centinel, The (Boston)
Massachusetts Federalist, The (Boston)
Minerva and Evening Mercantile Advertiser, The (New York)
Monmouth Democrat, The (Monmouth, New Jersey)
Monmouth Inquirer, The (Monmouth, New Jersey)
National Gazette, The (Philadelphia)
New Jersey State Gazette (New Jersey)
New York Daily Gazette, The (New York)
New York Journal (New York)
New York Mirror, The (New York)
New York Statesman, The (New York)
New York Weekly Museum, The (New York)
Patriotic Register, The (New York)
Pennsylvania Daily Advertiser, The (Philadelphia)
Pennsylvaia Gazette, The (Philadelphia)
Pennsylvania Packet, The (Philadelphia)
Porcupine's Gazette and General Advertiser (Philadelphia)
Port-Folio, The (Philadelphia)
Public Advertiser, The (New York)
Rivington's Royal Gazette (New York)
Time-Piece and Literary Companion, The (New York)
True American, The (Trenton, New Jersey)
United States Magazine, The, Vol. 1, 1779 (Philadelphia)

NEWSPAPERS PUBLISHED BY FRENEAU HIMSELF

1781–1784 *The Freeman's Journal,* New Jersey Historical Society.
1790–1791 *The Daily Advertiser,* New York Historical Society.
1791–1793 *The National Gazette,* New York Historical Society
1795–1796 *The Jersey Chronicle,* New York Historical Society.
1797–1798 *The Time-Piece,* New York Historical Society.

Various issues are missing from the above files of Freneau's Papers. Copies may be found in the New York Public Library, the Philadelphia Public Library, and elsewhere, and for these see also the Brigham volumes.

Manuscripts, Typescripts, and Miscellaneous Collections

Alexander, James. Papers. Box III, New York Historical Society, New York City.

Anderson, Alexander. Diary for 1794. Columbia University Library. New York City.

Bailey, Francis. Day Book. Historical Society of Pennsylvania, Philadelphia.

Bailey, Lydia. "Waste Book." Historical Society of Pennsylvania, Philadelphia.

Bible. Freneau Family Bible. I have examined the photostats, owned by Professor Lewis Leary of Columbia University, of the pages bearing the holograph records made by members of the Freneau family, the details of which are given in the text and notes.

Bradford, William. Papers. Historical Society of Pennsylvania, Philadelphia.

Brig Brittania Papers. New York Public Library, New York City.

Clinton, DeWitt. Papers. I-35, Columbia University Library, New York City.

Danish Government. Virgin Islands Records. National Archives, Washington, D.C.

Duyckinck Collection. New York Public Library, New York City.

Forman, Samuel. Papers. New York Historical Society, New York City. Contains a letter from Eleanor Freneau to Samuel Forman, February 28, 1803.

Freneau, Peter, to Jacob Read, July 30, 1795. Morgan Library, New York City.

Freneau, Philip. Freneau's Notebook. Historical Society of Pennsylvania, Philadelphia.

————. Letters to Seth Paine. Library of Congress, Washington, D.C.

————. *Miscellaneous Works* (1788) and *Poems Written between 1768 and 1794,* containing holograph revisions by the author, Monmouth County Historical Association, Freehold, New Jersey.

————. "Winter," in Manuscript Division, New York Public Library, a separate file of the first 32 lines; the last 4 lines are attached opposite p. 330 of Vol. II, part 2, of the large edition of Freneau's *Poems Relating to the American Revolution* (1865).

Freneau, Philip and Peter. Letters. Historical Society of Pennsylvania, Philadelphia.

Freneauana. American Philosophical Society, Philadelphia.

Freneau Collection. Rutgers University Library, New Brunswick, New Jersey. Manuscript materials in this collection include the following:

Pierre Freneau's Letter Book; Freneau's Note Book; Freneau's Log Book; Freneau's Theology Note Book; Freneau's "Some Account of the Capture of the Ship Aurora"; and Freneau's "'The Spy." The collection also includes books on which Freneau had made holograph annotations: *The Spectator;* Pope's *Works;* Robertsons' *Elements of Navigation;* Freneau's *Miscellaneous Works;* Beccaria, *Essay on Crime and Punishment;* and *Miscellanies for Sentimentalists.*

Freneau Collection. Princeton University Library, Princeton, New Jersey.

Fresneau, André. Will of André Fresneau. 1893, XXVI, New York Historical Society Collections, New York City.

Fresneau, Pierre. Executor of Francis Fresneau. 1897, XXX, New York Historical Society Collections, New York City.

————. Will of Pierre Fresneau. K 161, Secretary of State, Trenton, New Jersey.

Gallatin, Albert. Papers. New York Historical Society, New York City

General Administration Services. Case #23069: Pension Records of Philip Freneau. National Archives, Washington, D.C.

Hamilton, Alexander. Letters to *Gazette of the United States,* in reference to Philip Freneau and the *National Gazette.* Connecticut Historical Society, Hartford, Connecticut.

Hammell Notes. Monmouth County Historical Association, Freehold, New Jersey.

Holmes, Asher. Papers. Monmouth County Historical Association, Freehold, New Jersey.

Huguenot Society of America Collection. Register of Births, Marriages and Deaths of the Eglise Française à la New York. Ed. A. V. Wittmeyer. Church of St. Esprit, New York City.

Jefferson, Thomas. Papers. Library of Congress, Manuscript Division, Washington, D.C.

Latting, John J. Collection of Freneau Papers. New York Genealogical and Biographical Society, New York City.

Lea and Febiger Collection. Historical Society of Pennsylvania, Philadelphia.

Livingston Papers. Bancroft Collection, New York Public Library, New York City.

Lockwood, Avis. "Commonplace Books." New York Public Library, Manuscript Division, New York City.

Madison, James. Papers. Library of Congress, Manuscript Division, Washington, D.C. The publication of the Madison Papers by the University of Chicago Press is far from being complete. Only three volumes have been issued to date. See section on Books and Articles.

Middletown Township. Town Book, Records from 1699 to November 1823. Monmouth County Historical Association, Freehold, New Jersey.

Monmouth County Deeds and Mortgages. Monmouth County Court House, Freehold, New Jersey (see Appendix).

Monroe, James. Collection. New York Public Library, New York.

New York City. Roll of Freemen. 1885, XVIII. New York Historical Society Colllections, New York City. The Roll of Freemen includes the name of Andrew Fresneau.

Old Tennent Church Records. Monmouth County Historical Association, Freehold, New Jersey.

Pickering, Timothy. Papers. XXII–196, Massachusetts Historical Society Collection, Boston.

Rhea and Wickoff. Manuscript Ledger. Monmouth County Historical Association, Freehold, New Jersey.

"Satires against the Tories' and "Father Bombo's Pilgrimage." Historical Society of Pennsylvania, Philadelphia.

Tammany, Society of Saint. Constitution and Roll of Members of the Tammany Society or Columbian Order, 1789–1816. New York Public Library, New York City.

Vanderhoef, Cornelius P. Legal Dockets. Monmouth County Historical Association, Freehold, New Jersey (see Appendix).

Van Pelt, John. Legal Dockets. Monmouth County Historical Association, Freehold, New Jersey (see Appendix).

INDEX

Abercrombie, Dr.: 345

Adams, Abigail: 244, 309, 318, 349, 350; on Philadelphia, 217; on Freneau, 351–352, 408

Adams, Charles: 408

Adams, John: 73, 218, 232, 366, 367; on Navigation Laws, 55; on First Congress, 74; and U.S. Constitution, 178; as Vice President, 200, 244; and *Gazette of the United States*, 210; concept of democracy of, 210; and Federalist controversy, 225–226, 244, 287, 289, 317, 318, 320; on *National Gazette*, 244, 257–258; on French Revolution, 247, 249, 287; as President, 285, 286–290, 296–297, 350; character of, 286–287, 288–289, 351; and Hamilton, 287, 288, 289, 339–341, 342–343, 346, 347, 349; and Jefferson, 287, 289, 318, 349, 351, 352; on Napoleon, 287; as candidate for President, 288, 334, 339–341, 342–343, 346, 348, 349; and Madison, 289, 318; and Freneau, 290, 295, 318, 333, 336, 349, 351–352, 408; and relations with France, 296, 300–301, 317, 318, 323, 324, 340, 342; on Cobbett, 308; on the American character, 164 n., 312; and Alien and Sedition Laws, 324, 327, 328, 329, 334; death of, 425

Adams, John Quincy: 351; and French Revolution, 212; on Sedition Act, 325; on British conflict, 367; as Secretary of State, 384; and Monroe Doctrine, 384; prophesies Civil War, 385; and France, 408; as President, 412

Adams, Samuel: 49, 55, 210, 226, 247, 339, 390; and Boston Massacre, 29; British attempt to capture, 56; and U.S. Constitution, 170, 178; and *National Gazette*, 244

Adams, Thomas: 328

Addison, Joseph: 5, 24

"Advice to Authors," by Freneau: 173

"Advice to the Privileged Orders," by Barlow: 248, 249

Albany Register: 272

Alien Law: 324–330, 339, 340, 391

Allen, Ethan: 57

America: Freneau's dedication to, 19, 28, 67–68; Freneau's predictions about, 31, 37–39, 44, 63–64, 150, 371, 405–406, 419–420; as theme of Freneau's writing, 38, 42–43, 44, 50–51, 61, 67–68, 128, 149–150, 192, 338, 381, 406; bonds of, with England, 55–56, 58; character of, 164 n., 297, 312; support of French Revolution by, 251–252; as subject for literature, 411; expansion across, 419–420. See also United States

—, Bank of. See Bank of North America

"American Independence," by Freneau: 95, 142

"American Liberty," by Freneau: 62

American Mercury, The: 225, 250, 280

American Museum: 165

American Museum: 396

American Philosophical Society: 218, 254

American Querist, The, by Cooper: 69

"American Village, The," by Freneau: 42

Ames, Fisher: 150, 226, 254, 317, 350

Anarchiad, The: 193

Anderson, John: 62

André, Major: and Peggy Shippen, 101; and Arnold's betrayal, 102, 113, 114

Annapolis, Maryland: 45, 46, 100, 141

Anne, Queen: 5

Anti-Constitutionalists: 141

Anti-Federalist Party: and Assumption Bill, 187–188; and Federalist controversy, 198–201, 229–234, 246, 290–291, 325; in New York, 283; and 1796 election, 290; and *Time-Piece*, 290; and Society of Saint Tammany, 304; and Burr, 305; and 1800 election, 341. See also democratic-republicans; radicals; Republicans

Argus, The: 272, 284, 321, 327, 328

"Aristocratic Form of Government, The," by Freneau: 278

Arnold, Benedict: at Ticonderoga, 57; at Saratoga, 88; as military governor at Philadelphia, 100–101, 102; marriage